John Logie Baird
a life

Portrait of John Logie Baird © Lucy McKie

John Logie Baird
a life

ANTONY KAMM AND MALCOLM BAIRD

National Museums of Scotland Publishing

Published by NMS Publishing Limited
National Museums of Scotland
Chambers Street
Edinburgh EH1 1JF

British Library Cataloguing in Publication Data
A catalogue record of this book
is available from the British Library.

ISBN 1 901663 76 0

Typographical layout by NMS Publishing Limited.
Cover design by Cara Shanley.
Diagrams by Robert Britton.
Printed by Bell and Bain Ltd, Glasgow.

Contents

List of Plates

List of Text Figures

Acknowledgments

Our approach to the task of writing this new biography of John Logie Baird has been to re-examine existing sources, obtain and consider fresh information, and draw conclusions from the evidence.

Specific contributions to the research for this book are, wherever possible, acknowledged in the reference notes, in which the curious reader will also find additional data, often of an idiosyncratic nature. The narrative would, however, have been infinitely less comprehensive without the ready help of several people to whom we, and Baird studies, owe particular thanks. In order of seniority of age, Paul Reveley, Baird's personal technical assistant from 1933 to 1938, has on many occasions meticulously provided descriptive material which supplements and enhances the nine-page memoir of his work with Baird, written in 1995. Ray Herbert, another who features in this narrative, has patiently responded to numerous technical and historical questions, and has spontaneously made available copies of rare documents and press articles from his personal archive. Lord Reith's daughter and son-in-law, Marista and Murray Leishman, have given, besides much encouragement to the project, priceless insights into Reith's character. Baird's daughter, Diana Richardson, supplied a memoir of her early life between 1932 and 1946 which is a unique source of family detail, willingly answered probing questions, and provided comments on the later chapters of the book. Peter Waddell has been a continuous and enthusiastic source of information and provider of documents from his own research into the subject.

No praise can be too high for Jacqueline Kavanagh, Written Archivist, BBC Archives Centre, and her research colleagues, for indicating material which might be of value, making available individual documents and files, providing photocopies, and answering questions. Special thanks are due too to Peter Sindell, for giving us access to documents from the papers of Major A G Church which throw light on hitherto unknown aspects of the story, to Victoria Williams, Curator, Hastings Museum, for speedily providing copies of newly acquired documents and photographs, and to Michael Bennett-Levy,

Early Technology, for making available to us documents from his collection.

That we have been able to illuminate so many of the more unusual aspects of the life of Baird and those associated with him has been largely due to original research which has generously been undertaken on our behalf by such as Roger Bristow (Hastings Reference Library), Bob Cowan, Sarah Dodgson (Librarian, the Athenaeum Club), Adrian Hills, Sophie Houlton (Archivist, Hastings Museum), Ian Love, Susan Knowles (BBC Written Archives Centre), Melanie Machin (Tunbridge Wells Reference Library), Robert Simpson (Pc297, Central Scotland Police, Motorcycle Section), Richard Smout (County Archivist, Isle of Wight), T A Stankus (Royal Signals Museum).

We are equally grateful to all those other individuals who have given us their time, professional expertise, and the benefit of their personal knowledge by responding to questions, and in other ways: A S Adams (Reader Services Librarian, Honourable Society of the Middle Temple), Peter Asplin (Glasgow University Library), Geoff Bailey (Falkirk Museums), Bruce Baillie (Archivist, Dollar Academy), Iain Baird, Nina Ball, Graham Beastall, Neil Bettridge (Derbyshire Records Office), Douglas Brown, Ian Brown (Historical Radar Archive), Professor Russell Burns, Hazel Carstairs, Iain Carstairs, S M Caws (County Reference Librarian, Isle of Wight), Honor Clerk (Curator, 20th Century Collection, National Portrait Gallery), Clare Colvin (Archivist, Royal Television Society), Steve Cooney, Charles Cormick (Company Secretary, Rank Group), John Crompton (National Museums of Scotland), Richard Dean, Susan Dillon (formerly Mrs Jack Buchanan), Trevor Enefer (Crystal Palace Foundation), Marian Fallon (BBC Written Archives Centre), Norman Flett, Ian Goode (Ministry of Defence), Nicola Gray (Archivist, RSA), Laura Hamilton (Curator, Collins Gallery, University of Strathclyde), Eleanor Harris (Helensburgh Library), John Hart, Winifride Hart, Professor Simon Haykin (Department of Electrical Engineering, McMaster University), Andrew Henderson (Editor, *405 Alive*), Michael Holroyd, Frank Imrie, Brandon Inglis, Nick Jackson, Derry Jeffares, Coral Johnston (née Seeman), Richard Kamm, Sir John Keegan, Jan Leman, Haven Lutaaya (BBC Written Archives Centre), James G Lyon, Ian McGregor (Meteorological Office), Isobel Mackay, Rod Mackenzie (Argyll and Sutherland Highlanders Museum), Rusty MacLean (Archivist, Rugby School), Dennis McMullan, Alex Magoun (Director, David Sarnoff Memorial Library, Princeton), Anthony Marangos, Sir Michael Marshall, Alan Montgomery, Keith Moore (Senior Librarian and Archivist, Institution of Mechanical Engineers), Iona Muncaster, Hew Naylor, Edith Philip (Scottish National War Museum), Adam Robertson, Trevor Royle, Jack Sanderson (Museums Manager, Falkirk), Susan Scott (Archivist, Savoy Hotel), Angela Seenan (University of Strathclyde Archives), Julie Snelling (BBC Written Archives Centre), Leslie Steeples (Buxton Museum), Colin Taylor, Gilbert

Tomes, Harry Traynor, John Trenouth (Senior Curator, National Museum of Film, Photography and Television), P J Varney (Secretary, Caledonian Club), Helena Walker (née Grinyer), John Walker (Falkirk Historical Society), Keith Wallis, Peter Wallis, Ros Westwood (Buxton Museum), Richard West. It is to be regretted that two or three people declined to give answers to questions which might have filled gaps in the narrative, but we have respected their right to silence on these matters.

Practical assistance has also been received from Companies House, Dundee Local Studies Library, Edinburgh Central Library, Falkirk Reference Library, General Register Office for Scotland, Glasgow City Archives, Institution of Electrical Engineers, McMaster University, Ministry of Defence (Defence Records 2b), Mitchell Library (Glasgow), National Archives of Canada, National Archives of Scotland, National Library of Scotland, Office of National Statistics, Portsmouth District Land Registry, Probate Registry, Public Record Office, Radio Society of Great Britain, Stirling University Library, Strathclyde University Archives, Vintage Motorcycle Club.

Our thanks are due to the following for permission to quote extracts from copyright material: British Broadcasting Corporation, documents and letters in BBC Written Archives Centre, Caversham Park, including the personal diaries of Lord Reith; Royal Television Society, *Television* and J D Percy's memorial paper 1950; Rank Group, documents and letters written in the course of business by directors and staff of the former Baird companies; Marista Leishman, Lord Reith's *Into the Wind* and her own article about him; Nick Jackson; Sir Michael Marshall; Iona Muncaster and the estate of the late Donald Gilbert; the trustees of the estate of the late Eustace Robb; Times Newspapers; *Nature*; *Falkirk Herald*; Crystal Palace Foundation. The copyright in all documents and letters written by John Logie Baird in a private capacity belongs to the Baird family. Every attempt has been made to trace and obtain permission from other copyright holders. Where this has not proved possible, omissions can be rectified in subsequent editions of this book.

We are grateful to those who have supplied prints of photographs and allowed us to reproduce them; their names are indicated in the captions. Unacknowledged photographs are from the Baird family archive.

To publish a book of this extent and nature calls for the exercise of special skills, as well as a great deal of faith. We owe particular thanks to Lesley Taylor (NMS Publishing Limited), to her predecessor Helen Kemp, under whose auspices this book was originally commissioned, and to Iseabail Macleod (general editor), Ann Vinnicombe (editor), Cara Shanley (cover design), Richard Britton (diagrams), and Claire Carruthers (marketing).

Antony Kamm acknowledges the generosity of the Authors' Foundation in granting him an award in respect of the writing of this book.

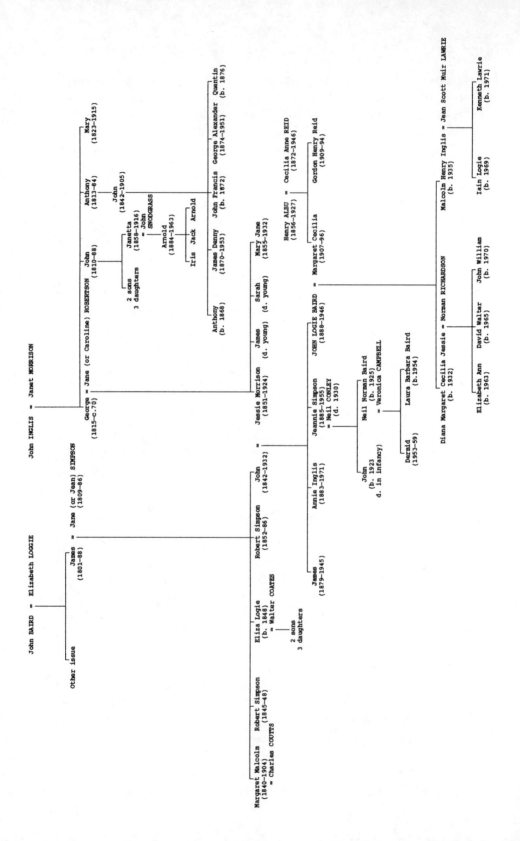

1
Helensburgh Days
1888–1919

When John Logie Baird was born on 13 August 1888 at 'The Lodge', West Argyle Street, Helensburgh, homes in Scotland were lit by candles, or by gas or paraffin lamps. Though the telephone (a Scottish invention) had been in limited use for business purposes for several years, wireless telegraphy had not been invented. Baird first saw a motor car when he was eight. Yet at the age of thirteen, this son of the manse, without any formal scientific education, had discovered for himself how to take photographs by remote control, constructed a private telephone exchange, and installed power-generated electric light in his parents' house. He began experimenting with television when he was about fourteen, and there is a distinct possibility that he envisaged a complete working system while he was still a student at technical college.

Baird, John to his relatives and close friends, JLB to his staff, and Logie to his wife (who, like Gwendolyn in Oscar Wilde's *The Importance of Being Earnest*, could not abide the name John)[1] was the fourth child of Rev. John Baird and his wife Jessie. The minister's paternal grandfather (also called John) was originally a carter to the Carron ironworks in Falkirk. On the death of his father he took on the farm, Sunnybrae, in the Camelon district of Falkirk, which had been in the family since 1754. In 1825 John Baird's son James, a blacksmith at the Greenhead Foundry in Glasgow, took over the farm, and fourteen years later married the daughter of a Falkirk builder. Sunnybrae remained in the family until 1905.*

Rev. John Baird was born in 1842, and had a brilliant academic career at Falkirk Grammar School before entering the University of Glasgow. He was the first member of his family to go to university. The typical Scottish lad o pairts, he lived in a humble rented room in Glasgow during term time, and spent the university vacations helping on the family farm. He

---

* Baird family papers and related items

took his MA degree in 1863, and graduated as Bachelor of Divinity in 1867. Soon afterwards he was called to the newly-formed West Parish of the coastal town of Helensburgh, which needed a young and energetic minister to build up the congregation – the church was later known as St Bride's. Helensburgh was then a dynamic community which had expanded rapidly since the railway connection to Glasgow, 23 miles to the east, opened in 1857.

Jessie Baird's paternal grandfather was an innkeeper and carting contractor in Anderston, Glasgow. Her father, George Inglis, had been a coppersmith's apprentice, but is described on Jessie's death certificate as an artist. George married a flighty wife, who duly ran off with someone else, leaving him to bring up their surviving children. Sarah fell off a breakwater in Southampton, where they were living, and drowned. When her father died of pneumonia, Jessie was taken into the family of her wealthy uncle John, and her sister Mary Jane into that of his brother Anthony; the two brothers were the founders of the Glasgow marine engineering and shipbuilding company A & J Inglis. Jessie met her future husband when she and her adoptive family were staying in Helensburgh for the summer season. They became engaged in 1876 and after a dignified two-year interval were married in 1878; he was then thirty-six and she was twenty-seven. The ceremony took place at John Inglis's posh residence, 23 Park Circus, Glasgow.

In 1881 Mr Baird bought the stone-built, single-storey house called 'The Lodge' for £1100, with the help of his wife's dowry. It had originally been built for a local woman whose ambition was to have the largest dining-room in Helensburgh. That accomplished, she died. The garden was large, with a croquet lawn. Here the children and their friends played, and ten-year-old Baird's two lop-eared rabbits ran wild for a time after escaping from their pen. When the family outgrew the house, Mr Baird added a second storey, in which the main room became his study. Communication between the two floors was by speaking-tube; those down below wishing to speak to the one above blew up the tube, sounding off a whistle stuck into its top end. The device was still in place and in working order when the house passed out of the Baird family in 1971.

Over the years Mr Baird became the typical Victorian paterfamilias, and his features disappeared into a large black beard. Though he was a figure of awe to his parishioners and children alike, he was nevertheless open-minded in his theological convictions and had a broad sense of humour. To a theological student who claimed the literal truth of the story of Jonah and the whale, he commented, 'Aye, Willie, you and the whale rival each other in swallowing capacity.' He disapproved of marriages of necessity, which were common enough at that time. When the groom had the nerve to point out that he was late in arriving to conduct the ceremony, the minister replied, after looking the bride up and down, 'Aye, about six months late, I'll be thinking!'

Mr Baird was a kindly, upright man, with an unfortunate, caustic manner which sometimes had repercussions within the family. He expected his older son, James, to follow his academic example. This did not happen, and there were major disagreements which eventually led to James emigrating. When Mr Baird proposed to his younger son that he might consider the ministry as a career, the young Baird, with teenage bravado, suggested that he could not be a sufficiently good hypocrite. Mr Baird's sense of humour prevailed: 'I think you might have managed that all right,' he remarked.

Jessie Baird was a woman devoted to the care of others, and especially to her fourth child, who was often ill. With only one servant in the house, she did all the shopping and prepared breakfast, lunch, high tea, and supper for the family. Her husband maintained that in the short Scottish days of winter, the best time to be out and about walking and making parochial visits was between 11am and mid-afternoon. So he would arrive back expecting lunch at 3pm. This meant that there had to be two sittings not only of lunch, one for the rest of the family and one for Mr Baird, but also of supper, for which he did not feel himself ready at the time when the others needed to eat.

When Jessie was not managing the affairs of the household, she was visiting the sick and the poor of the locality. Through accompanying his mother on these visits, Baird came to understand early on the effects of poverty and despair on decent, respectable people. It was a genteel poverty compared to what he was later to see in the Glasgow slums, but it affected him just as much. These experiences instilled in him a lifelong adherence to socialism. Though he never engaged in organised political activity, he liked, even during his brief period of affluence in his forties, to sport a cloth cap. It was perhaps as a mark of his upbringing that throughout his life he maintained a pure, precise Scottish accent. He spoke with a voice which was in the tenor range.

Baird was an imaginative and impressionable child, in whom the dominant atmosphere at home of the church, and particularly the austerity of the Sabbath, imbued a fear not only of God but also of a host of evil beings, in ghostly spirit or human form, surrounding him and waiting for an opportunity to exact retribution. A portrait in 1889 pictures him as a fat, bouncing baby with a full complement of fair curls.* He had a serious illness when he was two, involving also a stoppage of the bowels; for the rest of his life he was chronically susceptible to any infections that were going around, particularly colds and flu. By his own account, his early formal education was a disaster.[2] The proprietor of his first school, Ardenlee, went bankrupt; at his second, Miss Johnson's Preparatory School, he felt terrorised. Larchfield, to which he went at the age of eleven, as his elder brother James had done, was a local independent school run on English public school lines. In common with many other institutions of its kind, there was no science taught and only rudimentary mathematics. Latin and Greek and sport were paramount, and after each daily session of games there was a statutory cold shower, which for Baird meant a succession of chills, weeks off school, and low marks in every subject except drawing.

Though Baird's school career was undistinguished, his extra-curricular activities at this time were to shape his life. He was a voracious reader of anything and everything. His ill health gave him ample opportunity to read, and his father's study contained a wealth of classic authors such as Shakespeare, Voltaire, and Tolstoy. Probably with the help of his father, he obtained enough German to read Goethe's *Faust* in the original. His mother bought him books by the popular authors of the day, in particular W W Jacobs, Jerome K Jerome, and H G Wells.

Wells wrote fine stories of science and invention, featuring astonishing discoveries such as the art of invisibility, space travel, or the drug which could speed up human thought and reflexes. His heroes are often ordinary human beings, perhaps a trifle eccentric, who take a step beyond the conventional academic bounds of known science. Baird first came across Wells's stories when he was eight; they transported him out of the damp, cloistered Helensburgh manse into a world in which anything was possible. He may well have read *The Sleeper Wakes* when it was published in 1899 – it directly anticipates television and its effect on the viewer.

At the same time Baird was keeping up with current scientific discoveries. It was an era of great confidence and interest in scientific progress. Among his old books is a small volume given to him by his mother for Christmas 1904, *Electricians and Their Marvels* by William Jerrold. It includes accounts of the history and development of the telephone, electric traction and lighting, and telegraphy, with people such as Thomas Edison and Alexander Graham Bell presented as heroic figures. Though it is unlikely that there was anything in it which he had not already worked out for himself, it may well have helped to direct his talents towards his lifelong absorption in television.

When he was twelve Baird bought, with his own savings, his first proper camera, an instrument whose elaborate technical specifications he was able to quote ever afterwards. He added to it a remote-control device of his own construction to enable him to take pictures of himself. Because he was also, in spite of an inherent shyness, a natural leader, he was an obvious choice to be president of a group of school friends who established a photographic society, which doubled up as the Argyle Street cricket club. According to his own account, the society was dissolved after it had taken some rather shameful revenge on the tulips, pigeons, and person of a Mr Forbes. This Forbes had objected to his son being taught to climb a lamppost by one of the society's members, who was motivating his pupil by applying a rubber strap to his bottom. The boy with the strap was Jack Buchanan, known as Chump,[3] who subsequently became internationally known as an actor and theatrical impresario. He was a lifelong friend and supporter of Baird, as was Gavin Fullarton Robertson, usually called Guy, which in Scotland is the pet name for Gavin. Both were some two years younger than Baird, having been born in 1890. Robertson, who with his sister Iris was brought up by an aunt,[4] was for his dark good looks later nicknamed Mephistopheles, or Mephy for short. Another member of the gang was Godfrey Harris, with whom in 1900 Baird conducted his first recorded scientific experiment.

The Wright brothers and other pioneers were working towards the first powered and controlled flight; H G Wells had written vividly about the challenge of flying. Inspired by the possibilities, and having studied the available literature, Baird and Harris built a glider, which looked like two box-kites joined together by a middle section. They hoisted their contraption onto the flat roof of 'The Lodge'. Baird sat in it, just to try out the controls, for he had no intention of being the one to do the flying. Harris, who had other ideas, suddenly gave a heave, and launched the shrieking pilot into the air. The machine broke in two, and deposited Baird on the lawn, fortunately without breaking any bones.[5] As a result of that experience, though, he never went in an aeroplane again.

Baird now found another outlet for his imagination, which had a signal effect on his ultimate career. From the simple do-it-yourself telephone of thread and cocoa tins described in what he later referred to as 'The Boys' Book of Stories and Pastimes', he progressed, via the more elaborate model with wire and pillboxes, to making the real thing. He installed an exchange in his room (operated from a stout wooden box rather bigger than a shoe-box), with wires running overhead to the homes of four school friends. One stormy night, the local cabby, high up on his box above West Argyle Street, failed to see one of the lines, and was lifted out of his seat and deposited in the gutter. Shaking with rage, he knocked up the local manager of the National Telephone Company, which was the official operator of the rudimental service in Helensburgh at that time, and threatened him with the law for allowing his cable to hang down over the road. The line was traced to its source, and the pirate exchange was closed down; by then, though, its originator was busy on another home improvement plan.

Though Glasgow Corporation had been able to supply electricity since 1891, there were still at this time fewer than three thousand domestic consumers in the city,[6] and electricity had not arrived in Helensburgh. Baird bought a second-hand oil engine and made a small dynamo which charged up a series of accumulators, consisting of lead plates wrapped in flannel and packed into jam jars filled with sulphuric acid. With this, he lit the house by low-power bulbs – he also contracted lead poisoning and carried a scar on one finger for the rest of his life. The system worked well as long as it was supervised. One night, when Baird was absorbed in other things, his father fell down the unlit stairs from his study to the ground floor, and gas lighting was resumed. The Bairds' was the first house in Helensburgh to be lit by electricity: it was one of the last to have electric light officially installed, in the late 1930s.

Baird's next recorded experiment,[7] in 1903,[8] was in the field of what had now begun to be known as television. The term was first used by the Russian scientist Constantin Perskyi in 1900 to describe the process of transmitting images at the precise moment at which they are picked up.[9] Perskyi's theory was based on the magnetic properties of selenium, an element which conducts electricity in proportion to the intensity of light which it receives.

Our intrepid young inventor reckoned that if sound waves could be converted into waves of a different kind and sent over wires, then why not also light waves? He obtained an illustrated fifty-eight-page paperback book in German by Ernst Ruhmer, *Das Selen und sein Bedeuten für die Electrotechnik*, published in 1902, describing experiments in which letters or figures were transmitted by opening and closing shutters connected to twelve selenium cells fixed to the wall. The first thing to do was to make a selenium cell, which Baird tried on the kitchen range by wrapping wire round a piece of porcelain, heating it up, and then rubbing the device with a stick of selenium. This resulted in burnt fingers and an appalling smell, but he did learn that the current from a selenium cell is so minute that it would have to be amplified by some means; he tried different methods but could achieve nothing sufficiently sensitive. As he himself later acknowledged,[10] he would never have produced his first television pictures without the amplification made possible by Ambrose Fleming's valve, patented in Britain in 1905, and Lee De Forest's improvement on it, his control grid, patented in the USA in 1908. These became commonly available after World War I.

In his teens Baird became an accomplished painter of still life, an ability possibly inherited from his artist grandfather, George Inglis; his studies reveal a particular fascination with the effects of light. He was also a stylish writer who later contributed sketches, pastiches, and parodies to his college magazine. At the age of thirteen he used regularly to beat his eighteen-year-old sister Annie at chess, to her chagrin, as she notes in her diary.

Annie's diaries* record some of the minutiae of middle-class life at the time: croquet on the lawn, boating, skating, reading, going into town, attending a subscription concert ('a little classical for my uneducated ear') and, with her younger brother, a lecture on South Africa 'illustrated by a magic lantern and a cinematograph'. There were also visits to pay, often accompanied by her first-cousin Jeanie Coates, who was a year younger than she was. Out walking one day, she encounters her younger sister Jeannie, known as Tottie, returning from 'posting letters for the servant, who gives her a half-penny for every five she posts'. In 1902 Annie and Tottie call on their aunt (Mary) Jane and their great-aunt Mary in Glasgow, where they have 'roast beef, cabbage, apricot tart and fruit, not a bad dinner at all'. The Inglises, however, with the exception of these two aunts, 'seem to be a nasty lot, thinking a lot of themselves and very little of their fellow-creatures'. Some twenty-five years later, however, when Baird was desperately seeking investors to back the development of his invention, the Inglis cousins (John Inglis's grandsons) responded handsomely.

It was a time of comings and goings at 'The Lodge'. In 1899 James, just twenty, had run away to join the army, but returned in dissatisfaction three months later. In 1902 he was off again, with parental sanction, and enlisted in the Argyll and Sutherland Highlanders en route for South Africa. The Boer War ended in May of that year, and shortly after that he was back home again. He went to New Zealand in 1903, returned home three years later, and almost immediately departed to work the silver mines in New South Wales, Australia, where he finally settled. Annie left home to train as a nurse, and Jeannie went to Glasgow University, where she obtained a MA degree in 1908.

There had been movement among Baird's friends, too. Buchanan had gone to Glasgow Academy. In October 1904, when he was fourteen, Mephy was sent to board at Dollar Academy as a paying pupil, presumably for his education to receive some fine tuning. The attempt was a failure. He boarded at McNabb House, and was put in Class II (Boys). In 1905 he was promoted into Class III, but had to repeat the year in 1906. His record is marked 'not promoted' after two years in the class; he seems to have left the school at this point.[11]

Once parental thoughts of Baird becoming a minister were abandoned, it was inevitable that his own choice would be to study electrical engineering.

In 1906, immediately from school, he enrolled at the Glasgow and West of Scotland College of Technology, known locally as the Tec. This highly regarded institution trained most of Scotland's engineers for the ship-building and engineering industries or in the service of the British Empire. King George V, on a tour of India, was so impressed by the fact that nearly all the railway bridges had been designed by graduates of the Tec, that in 1912 it was dubbed the Royal Technical College. In 1964 the college evolved into the University of Strathclyde.

Baird studied mathematics, electrical engineering, and motive-power engineering. It took him eight years to graduate; he finally gained an associateship of the college with the Diploma in Electrical Engineering in 1914. He enjoyed his first year, during which there was much to learn, but found the rest of the work boring, and commuting between Helensburgh and Glasgow in draughty railway carriages played havoc with his health.

From 1909, as part of the course, he was apprenticed to various engineering firms, and lived in squalid digs. He spent nine months as an engineer with Halley's Industrial Motors in Yoker, six months in the drawing office of the Argyll Motor Company in Alexandria, Dunbartonshire, and eighteen months as a draughtsman in Brash & Russell's electrical works in Glasgow. The sheer drudgery of chipping individual and identical grooves in castings at Halley's in winter conditions from 6am to 5.30pm and often later, and the general tedium, affected him as deeply as did the conditions in which many of his workmates were forced to labour for the lowest of wages, and left him with a contempt for authority but a profound respect for hard work.

While Baird was living at 'The Lodge' he was under strict parental supervision, and though he enjoyed his leisure pursuits there was one thing lacking.[12]

> In Helensburgh, in my circumstances, it was difficult to speak with a young lady, and as to a love affair, well that was completely out of the question. This did not greatly worry me. Self-denial, for a time, I could put up with. All would be well when I went into digs and got away from supervision and threw off the yoke. I thought that when I left home I would throw off all restraint and become a soul untrammelled. 'Then would I quench my glowing passions in a sensual sea, nor in the shallows dabble.'[13] I was to find, however, that I was not of the stuff of which Don Juans are built; I tried hard, but circumstances and temperament were hopelessly against me. I had been told by other students that it was easy: you simply walked out in the evening and, when you saw a young lady who appealed to you, you simply walked beside her for a few paces,

remarked 'Good evening', and the rest followed. I tried it and, in a state of complete nervousness, bungled it hopelessly and got the snub I deserved, returning home in a state of nervous collapse. My dreams of Don Juan and sensual seas showed no hope of realization. Strumpets were thoroughly repulsive. The idea disgusted me. Finally, in desperation, I took out the landlady's niece, a gaunt raw-boned creature. I was determined to have an affair at all costs. In a quiet spot I endeavoured to embrace this gaunt trollop. A drop of mucous hung from the end of her long nose. She laughed harshly, showing a row of decayed teeth, and grunted, 'Hands off the beef,' digging her bony elbow into me.

Even this grotesque travesty of womanhood would have nothing to do with me! My technique was as hopeless as my opportunities were confined. Later I became more adroit, but it forms a sorry tale. Any cheap little counter-jumper could tell a better story. Futile and frustrated opportunity passed me by.

This period of Baird's life was also one of metaphysical, philosophical, and religious introspection, with Godfrey Harris acting as a sympathetic sounding board. After fearing divine retribution in his early years, Baird, most probably influenced by the writings of H G Wells, was now beginning to question religious tenets. On occasions he would even try to convert to his brand of religious doubt the young clergymen who came to his father's door when serving as supply assistants. It was symptomatic of Baird's rather harsh sense of humour that he should later claim deliberately to have extended his college career as long as his father was paying, in order to pursue his personal interests. He never revealed the full extent of these interests, but subsequent evidence suggests that from 1912 he was experimenting with television in his own time, away from the college.

The central component of his idea for a complete television system was a perforated disc of the kind invented in 1884 by the German Paul Nipkow, though Nipkow never put it into operation.[14] Its purpose, an extension of the technique described in Ruhmer's book, was to scan an image by means of twenty-four holes arranged round the disc's outer rim in the form of a spiral, so as to break up the picture into transmittable elements. The disc revolved very fast, and, as it did so, each narrow vertical strip of the image was successively scanned by a moving hole, allowing light through to the cell and producing a rapidly fluctuating, but weak, electrical signal. Baird's original discs were made of plywood or cardboard, and there are descriptions relating to this period of lodging rooms filled with rudimentary equipment obtained for a few shillings, and tales of chipped washbasins, external aerials coming adrift in the wind, explosions, and inevitably irate landladies.[15] He did not, however, have anywhere in Glasgow to set up the motors and other apparatus he would have required, and he had not yet succeeded in making a selenium photo-cell of sufficient sensitivity, though he may well have sketched out his system on paper. Thus no firm results seem to have been achieved, but the ground had been laid for later work.

For the only time in Baird's adult life, he was during his college days preoccupied with other things than television and earning money. Not that he could always keep off the latter topic.

How to Make Money

Some geniuses put whisky and water, with a little cinnamon and sugar, into medicine bottles, label it 'Swamp Root Tonic Laxative – a Pure Vegetable Extract', and sell it at a shilling a bottle. They make millions.

Other geniuses make pills with liquorice powder and bread paste, label them 'Dod's Backache Kidney Pills – Every Picture Tells a Story', and sell at one shilling per box. They make millions.

Other geniuses put salt water into bottles and label it 'Fruit Salts – a Healthy Mind in a Healthy Body'. They make millions.

Other geniuses make 'Home-Made Strawberry Jam' with wood chips, turnips, and molasses. They make millions.

Thousands upon thousands of d—d fools drudge all their lives in drawing offices. They make from 25s to £3.10s per week.

What then shall we do to be saved? If we had capital we might mix candle grease with soft soap, put it into packets, and sell it as 'Clenso – put it in the bath with the clothes, and they clean themselves; no rubbing required; Clenso draws out the dirt.' But we have no capital. If, however, you are handsome, have a pleasant manner, and an entrance into good society, you might marry an heiress; but competition is keen, and the clergy carry off most of the prizes.

There is another way of making money. Get a piece of plate glass from the glazier, 4in. by 4in., or thereby, a quarter of a pound of plaster of Paris from the chemist, and a new half-crown from Aunt Jane. Place the half-crown on the glass, mix the plaster of Paris with about a pint of pure water, place a large match-box, with the bottom removed, over the coin, and pour the mixture into the receptacle thus formed. While the mould is hardening, get the Encyclopaedia Britannica and read the article on coining. You will find that it is felony, and punishable with seven years confinement. If you decide, however, to proceed, you will get full particulars under 'Moulding' (medal duplicating).

All the above methods have, you will see, some disadvantage. They are either already overcrowded or require special talents. We have, however, evolved a simple, original, and effective means of money making. No special talents are required, and only a few minutes of your spare time once a month. Full particulars will be forwarded on receipt of your name and address and a postal order to cover postage and clerical expenses. Do it now.[16]

H_2O

H_2O was the name under which Baird contributed eighteen articles and stories to the college magazine between 1909 and 1914. 'How to Make Money', with its echoes of Stephen Leacock and of H G Wells's scientific romance about a patent medicine, *Tono-Bungay* (1908), illustrates with remarkable accuracy avenues which he would explore during the next ten years. *Zerubabel and the Mirror Galvanometer*,[17] on the other hand, is a scientific parody in the language of the Bible. Further Wellsian parallels, with the story 'Filmer', inform 'Desire',[18] which has as its climax the suicide of a character named Gavin Fullarton Robertson. Twenty-eight years later, there would be a ghastly sequel in real life. Clearly Baird's contemporaries appreciated his writing talents. The editor of the journal singles out H_2O as a 'literary genius' in a New Year editorial in 1913.[19]

Other leisure pursuits centred on a succession of curious automobiles.

I remember seeing a motor car for the first time. I must have been about eight years old. It was a strange affair, with immense wooden wheels. Ten years later I bought a second-hand motor cycle, with a tiny engine under the seat. It had been, in its day, the last word in cycles, and was called a 'Kellycomb Antoinette'; it cost me five pounds. After a little while I sold it, and became the possessor of a nondescript tri-car, a perfect scrap heap on wheels, which was known locally as 'young Baird's reaper and binder', from the appalling noise it made.[20]

This was one of at least three tri-cars, also known as forecars, which he owned over the next few years. They were not unlike a motorised tricycle, but with the pair of wheels above which the passenger sat, braving the elements, at the front. Baird managed to coax one of these machines up the formidable hill, 'Rest and be Thankful', which was regularly used for hill-climb trials, but later he crashed and wrecked it by Loch Lomond.[21]

With his final examinations looming, Baird wrote out of the blue to an old college friend, Gavin Hamilton, asking for advice. Hamilton had graduated in 1912, and was now working in Edinburgh. Hamilton replied in pencil, having that morning burned his right hand severely at work. Apparently he had started the big booster first thing in the morning without noticing that the starter had been left full up all night. His advice was:

(1) Exclude the fair sex absolutely and completely from your mind for the next 6 months.

(2) If you have a girl explain to her what you are about and that you can only meet her once a week 8 till 10 on Friday evenings. She has not to flirt with other boys in your absence.

(3) You must work every evening, including Sats and Sundays.

(4) Pay *particular* attention to your home exercises, especially in Elect. and Mechanics.

(5) You must work out every possible problem you can lay your hands on. I cannot lay enough stress on this as I consider it really the most particular. When you come to an exam it is not really writing questions that you get but problems. Mechanics is the subject I mostly refer to and unless you can work out problems and have all the formula memorised you are usually no use. I would strongly advise you to take out the books on Structures and Hydraulics and work all the examples you possibly can from them. I think I would have every Hydraulics book in the place home with me.

(6) Keep sweet to the Profs.[22]

Baird presumably at this time would have had no problems with numbers (1) or (2), but he seems to have taken notice of the other precepts, and graduated on 1 October 1914. Then, the twenty-five-year-old graduate, with further financial support from his patient father, and the reluctant acquiescence of his mother, enrolled at Glasgow University to take a short course leading to the degree of BSc, which his studies at college qualified him to do. He appears to have done the minimum amount of work but to have taken maximum advantage of the active social life of the university.[23]

The continuation of World War I, which had broken out in the summer of 1914, and clearly would not be over by Christmas as some optimists had predicted, put paid to his degree. A Hartley, who was introduced by Mephy to Baird in 1916 and subsequently worked for him as a part-time accountant, recalled in 1958 that at the beginning of hostilities Baird and Mephy joined up, he thought with the Glasgow Yeomanry, a territorial outfit, but were both invalided out and discharged. According to Dollar Academy records, Gavin Fullarton Robertson was a trooper in the Queen's Own Royal Glasgow Yeomanry in 1914,[24] and later served as a second lieutenant in the 10th Battalion, Argyll and Sutherland Highlanders.[25]

Whether Baird was briefly a territorial or not, he answered an advertisement, and was taken on as an assistant mains engineer in the Clyde Valley Electrical Power Company, to supervise the repair of all electricity breakdowns in the area of Rutherglen. He had a telephone by his bed so that he could be called if the failure was during the night. He recollected standing all night in the rain and cold, watching gangers digging holes in the road to find faulty cables, trying to break up fights between drunks among his crew, and placating labourers who wanted to knock off at 4am.[26] Colds and flu laid him low more frequently than ever. He could not qualify for an increase in his thirty shillings a week salary or for promotion, as he discovered when he accidentally intercepted an internal memorandum, because he was always off sick.

On 25 February 1916, under the Military Service Act 1916, which introduced conscription, Baird reported to the Army recruitment office in Dumbarton, where, having been enrolled, he opted to be transferred to the Army Reserve.* This meant that he and the group to which he had been assigned would receive fourteen days' notice to report for service. On 17 April he attended a medical examination at the Recruiting Medical Board in Glasgow. After his chest had been examined and the doctor had shrewdly and correctly diagnosed that he spent much of each winter *hors de combat*, he was declared 'unfit for any service' on the grounds of conjunctivitis, defective vision, and flat feet.*

He went before a further medical board in Stirling on 20 December 1916, and was now deemed 'fit for service at home only, in labour units or on command garrison or regimental outdoor employments'.* On 22 June 1917, however, giving his address as 2 Millar Terrace, Rutherglen, Baird was classified as being in a protected occupation and was given a war service badge to wear (number X69381).*

There is something sardonic about his reference in his memoir to the job at the power station as his 'war work'.[27] It could not have helped that his sister Annie, who had joined Queen Alexandra's Imperial Military Nursing Service, was serving if not actually at the front, at least just behind the front line. After doing duties on military trains taking wounded from the casualty clearing station to the base hospital, she worked in one of the clearing stations itself. These were horrific places. Annie became an assistant matron (the equivalent to an army colonel). She was twice mentioned in dispatches,[28] and was awarded six medals. One of these, the Royal Red Cross, was given to her in person at Buckingham Palace; she was summoned by telegram to attend on 23 January 1918.* Though she lived until 1971, she never talked about her experiences, even to her own family.

Baird stuck it out at the power station for three years, frequently on the lookout for ways of supplementing his earnings. Marketing a cure for piles, invented by one of his colleagues, got no further than the testing stage – he recorded that he could not sit down for several days.[29] More spectacularly, he used the firm's facilities in an attempt to manufacture diamonds, which in nature are made by carbon being subjected to extreme pressure and temperature. He passed wires from the power-station grid bars through a switch to a carbon rod, which he embedded in concrete in a heavy iron pot. His idea, probably inspired by H G Wells's short story, 'The Diamond Maker', was to create the effect of nature by passing a gigantic electrical charge through the rod. He waited until the middle of the night, and then threw the switch. The effects were frightening. There was a heavy thud, then a cloud of smoke from the pot. The machines flashed right round their commutators, all the belts of the steam-driven generators came off, and the mains power supply crashed. Baird had anticipated this, and soon got things going again. At about 1am the chief engineer came cycling up to see why the power had gone off. He did not seem to be able to find anything wrong, and cycled off home again. Suspicions had been roused, however, and Baird's days with Clyde Valley were now numbered.[30]

By contrast, his next ploy was surprisingly successful. Cold feet, from which he suffered, are usually caused by damp. He used to alleviate his own problems by wrapping his feet in newspaper or absorbent toilet paper before putting on his socks. His commercial application of the principle was to buy six dozen pairs of inexpensive short socks, sprinkle them inside with borax powder, which, in addition to its antiseptic properties, absorbs water, and sell them as the 'Baird Undersock', for wear inside one's normal hose. ('In summer the socks may be worn alone, and worn thus keep the feet wonderfully cool and fresh in the hottest weather.') Though the borax would be largely washed out when the undersocks went into the tub ('The socks should be allowed to dry every night. When they become soiled they may be washed in the usual way'), the enterprise, after a slow start, prospered through imaginative marketing techniques. He began business on 1 May 1917. From a one-room office in 196 St Vincent Street, he had sales representatives, who worked on commission, covering Scotland and parts of England as far as London. Sandwich boards were a common enough sight on the streets then, but Baird hit on the idea of employing women to carry his advertisements. He obtained free publicity through press photographs of his female advertising team, in coats and hats, with their sandwich boards. These appeared as news items in newspapers and illustrated journals, with captions such as, 'First sandwich women in Glasgow; new occupation for ladies.'

In February 1918 he advertised an 'Improved Pattern. Medicated: Soft: Absorbent' at 1s.6d. per pair or eight shillings for half-a-dozen pairs, above a 'quote' from a '2nd Lt G. H.', serving in France: 'They are the very things required out here. Woollen socks get sticky and clammy and we can't get them washed. The Undersocks keep the feet and the ordinary socks fresh for weeks.' It is not known whether this, and other similar puffs, were genuine or were invented by Baird himself.[31]

Baird's profits enabled him to give his notice to Clyde Valley, just before he was due to be sacked for moonlighting. He was now on his own. He created a demand for undersocks in the major departmental stores in Glasgow by sending in his friends in relays, with money provided by him, to buy up all the stock. Substantial orders resulted, and the smaller drapers' stores followed suit. He added sidelines such as boot polish, solid scent, and other commodities. Tin was very scarce, and boot polish was being sold in folded paper, but round cardboard pill boxes could still be obtained. Baird bought up polish in bulk and employed young women to fill up the pill boxes with it. Always on the lookout for ways of expanding his operation, in July 1918 he answered an advertisement for freelance representatives to sell the Reliance Lubricating Oil Company's oils and greases. The company rebuffed his application, claiming 'you appear to have an established business of your own'.*

A Hartley, whom Baird employed as a part-time accountant, recalled in 1958:

> It was evident to anyone who knew Mr Baird that his mind was often on other things. He seemed partly or wholly oblivious to what was going on around him. He wore a light-brown suit, a brown crotal coat, and a brown hat. All blended with his sandy coloured hair and fair countenance. The assistant who kept his books got to know how to bring him down to earth. Mr Baird would arrive at the office with a week's growth on his chin and his thoughts away in the clouds. The assistant would address him thus: 'Now, Mr Baird, before we put pen to paper you are going down with me to Bamber's for a shave and a hair cut.' Without saying a word he would follow the assistant to Bamber's. The operation would bring him down to earth again.[32]

On 9 September 1918, quoting his home address as 17 Blairbeth Road, Burnside, Baird applied for the registration of the Baird Undersock Company.[33] A thriving and expanding business seemed on the cards, when a spring cold turned to flu, and he was laid up for six weeks. For someone who operated as a one-man show, this was a major setback.

It was during the undersock period that he met, in a library, the woman who was to play a considerable part in his emotional life. 'Alice' (as we will call her, for reasons which will become apparent in chapter 2) was about the same age as he was,[34] and therefore of the generation of young women whose chances of marriage had virtually been destroyed by the war. There could be no question at the moment, however, of marrying Baird: his health was too bad and his business prospects were now dubious.

World War I ended in November 1918. Of the original Argyle Street gang, Jack Buchanan, after a brief and unhappy spell in the family auctioneering business, had gone on the music-hall circuit in 1911 as 'Chump Buchanan, patter comedian'.[35] Rejected as unfit for active service, he had during the war years begun to establish himself as a revue artist, and actor in straight and musical comedy. He later became also a successful theatrical producer. The amiable but indecisive Mephy, who can safely be described as one of life's low fliers, had inherited £3000 from his aunt, which gave him enough to live on while making up his mind what to do, an almost permanent preoccupation. He had been active in amateur theatre productions in his youth, and for a time he thought of going on the professional stage, but he did not make the grade. Then for a time he was secretary and general factotum on an estate near Ludlow to a wealthy Belgian who was rumoured to be a count and an illegitimate descendant of a member of the Belgian royal family.[4] Godfrey Harris, having taken a university degree in science, had gone to the USA and found work as a service engineer with the Pitometer Company, based in New York.

Buchanan had married an actress vocalist in 1915, thus making him liable to a fine of thirty shillings:

> We the undersigned do hereby agree that in the event of marriage of one previous to the marriage of the others he shall pay the sum of ten shillings to the remaining signatories. Signed this 22 day of April 1911 at the Lodge Helensburgh: John Logie Baird, John B[uchanan], G H Harris, G F Robertson.*

The marriage was subsequently dissolved.

On 4 June 1919 Baird obtained a driving licence.* Two weeks later he acquired second-hand from his cousin, William Smith Inglis,[36] a four-year-old, powerful American Excelsior motorbicycle with sidecar.[37]

On 13 September he was issued with a passport.* It was from Harris, who had been to the Caribbean, that Baird had got the idea that the climate of Trinidad might cure his chest, and that there he might also find means to improve his financial position. Certainly Harris's report of the business possibilities were enhanced by the guide books' descriptions of Trinidad as an island paradise. Baird closed down his business, noting that in the previous twelve months it had brought him in £1600, considerably more than he would have earned with Clyde Valley in twelve years.[38] He sold the motorbicycle, which he had had for just four months.[37] He packed three trunks with samples of cotton goods, safety pins, and other commodities which he reckoned would appeal to the natives, and booked a passage in a cargo ship, to keep as much as possible of his capital intact. He also had in his luggage scientific books and journals to keep him up to date with activity in the fields of electricity, sound, and light, and with any developments in television. At some point he obtained the first book incorporating a history of television, *Handbuch der Phototelegraphie und Telautographie*, by the Germans Arthur Korn and Bruno Glatzel, which had been published in 1911.

Baird sailed on 19 November 1919. He was freer of restraints than he had ever been. He had a certain amount of money, with which he hoped to build a prosperous business. He was confident that the warm climate would restore him to health. Away from the pressures of post-war Britain, he would have the opportunity to reflect on his consuming preoccupation with transmitting images by wire or radio waves. And 'Alice' was waiting for him, back in Glasgow.

2
Entrepreneur with Problems: Trinidad and London
1919-1923

The venture began rather unpromisingly. The crossing took three weeks, the vessel heaved, and Baird, not for the last time in his life, was subjected to a certain amount of scepticism as to the wisdom of his course of action. A Venezuelan fellow-passenger pointed out that his merchandise was unsaleable, and the ship's captain added that, because of the booze and the incidence of venereal disease, virile young men only lasted about a year in the West Indies.[1]

Port of Spain was hot, sticky, and packed with people of numerous races. The room in the inaptly named Ice House Hotel, which Harris had booked for him, was carpetless and also comfortless, as Baird found when he spent the best part of his first week flat out on the bare bed with a virulent dose of dysentery. He was assured that most Europeans contracted it sooner or later: it was just that he had lost no time. As soon as he could, he moved to Columbia House, a boarding house run by a kindly soul called Mrs Brisbane. His fellow guests were three bank clerks, one of whom had venereal disease, a young commercial traveller sent out to Trinidad by his family to cure his dipsomania, and an English governess who had lost her job and been stranded without the means to get home.

Baird shared a room with the alcoholic, who, though obviously anxious to share his professional expertise to the extent of making a list of potential buyers and offering himself to take round some of the samples, was not as encouraging about the outcome as Baird would have liked. For three weeks Baird tramped the choking streets of Port of Spain in the damp heat. He secured just one order, for 5lb safety pins. Then he went down with a fever.

He was in bed for a week, during which his inventive mind came up with a fresh scheme for making money. The island teemed with citrus fruit, guavas, and mangoes, and produced huge quantities of sugar. Why not make bulk supplies of jam and mango chutney, and package them for sale in a form in which they would not go mouldy? He studied cookery books, scaling up the recipes to mass-market proportions. He bought himself a Ford Runabout car, registration number P 1255, and was issued with a local driving licence on 19 February 1920 – within a month he had been fined $10 for 'failing to slow down and blow horn approaching a cross street'.* He toured the region by car, and selected Bourg Mulatresse (Mulatto Town), which was in the fruit growing area of the Santa Cruz valley, as his centre of operations.

He rented a room in a wooden bungalow owned by a plantation overseer; it was beside a river and surrounded by giant bamboos. Here he set up his jam factory in a series of lean-to, brushwood huts, assisted by his two senior employees, Ram Roop, a Trinidadian of Indian origin, and Tony, a beefy but simple individual of mixed race. From a scrap merchant in Port of Spain he obtained a superannuated copper wash tub, capacity one hundredweight. They built a brick fireplace with a chimney, filled the tub with sugar and chopped-up fruit, and lit the fire underneath. The atmosphere got so hot that Baird stripped down to his shorts. The sugar melted, and he and Ram Roop stirred the seething mixture vigorously with large wooden paddles. Clouds of sticky, sweet vapour floated out into the surrounding jungle, meeting clouds of flying insects of different species intent on discovering the source. Thousands of them perished in the viscous steam and dropped into the pot.

Baird's bedroom swarmed with mosquitoes and vast cockroaches. One night a colony of enormous ants invaded the factory area and made off with fifty kilograms of sugar. He went down with fever again, this time worse than before. The insects and his health put paid to the enterprise. In June 1920, Baird returned to Port of Spain with such of his produce as was eatable, having in the meantime, extraordinarily, appeared to have managed also to conduct some scientific experiments, probably with light beams.[2]

He set himself up in business as John L Baird and Co (with a cable address of 'DRIAB – Port of Spain'). It is possible to piece together some of his activities from entries in a petty cash book,* and in a notebook in which he jotted down names, addresses, calculations, things to remember to do, drafts of documents, and ideas for making money.* In spite of the efforts of two assistants, Arthur and Anthony, whom he paid $4 a week each (often in advance) plus commission, there seems to have been little market for his produce; it is not recorded whether this was anything to do with the admixture of insects. The pair did succeed, however, in unloading about 30lb safety pins. There was also someone referred to simply as 'boy', who was paid $3 a week to do odd jobs.

At the same time Baird was experimenting with various methods of preserving the local produce, with a view to setting up a company in Trinidad, with a branch office in London, to utilise the supply of 'mangoes, guavas and several varieties of citrous fruit which are at present thrown away'. It was to be established with a capital of $50,000, or so Baird intended, and he solicited local support for his scheme.

In September, still a sick man, he decided to cut his losses and return home, taking with him, in a series of casks and cans, what he could salvage of his produce: fruit pulp, marmalade, chutney, guava, mango, tamarind, and toffee. He had already in March 1920 despatched ten thirty-gallon casks of lime juice to the Glasgow-based export/import business of W & R P Moir.*

He would have a companion on the voyage. Robert Pound (Baird calls him Harold Pound in his memoir) was a genial British coconut merchant whom he met in Port of Spain. For a time they shared a bungalow. The drink flowed, and one night Baird returned to find Pound, whisky in hand, his eyes glazed, staring at what appeared to be a monstrous grasshopper on the table. Baird was able to explain that the creature was real, not a drunken hallucination, and together they managed to catch it in a wastepaper basket. It turned out to be a giant locust. They kept it for amusement in a bird cage, and fed it on grass and whisky and soda, which it appeared to enjoy, perhaps too much, for it died of the shakes.

Having corresponded with Godfrey Harris in New York about credit arrangements with banks for shipping his produce,* Baird, with Pound in tow, sailed on 6 October 1920 for London, via French Antilles, in SS *Stuyvesant*. He had been in Trinidad for ten months. He had lost three-quarters of his capital. His health was worse than when he arrived. Indeed, it was much worse. Whether he realised it or not, he had contracted malaria, which plagued him for the rest of his life, weakening a system which was already vulnerable to illness.

And 'Alice' had not waited for him. While he was away, she had married someone else!

It has been assumed that Baird only found out about this on his return to Britain. A snapshot and a slip of paper which recently came to light in his effects now suggest otherwise.* The photo is of a cheerful 'Alice' sitting on the slope of a sweeping meadow between two men, supporting her elbows on their knees. The younger one, who looks about twenty, may be her brother. The other, in his early forties, with a pipe in his mouth, is referred to on the back as 'Sid', with the inscription, 'taken Easter 1920' (see plate 9). Someone obviously sent it to Baird. The upright piece of paper, 18cm by 10.5cm, has simply the inscription, in Baird's handwriting,

Alice
Where
art
Thou ?

and at the bottom the date, '19.6.20'.

'Alice where art thou' was originally a poem by Alfred Bunn (1796–1860), London theatrical manager and librettist. It was first published as a song in 1861, with music by Joseph Ascher and words by Wellington Guernsey, and was still enormously popular in the 1920s. Since Baird was tone deaf,[3] it must have been the lyrics rather than the tune which made such an impact on him. Sure enough, they include,

> One year past this even
> And thou wert by my side,
> Vowing to love me, Alice,
> What e'er might betide.

'One year past' would take us back to June 1919, the very month in which Baird acquired his motorbicycle with sidecar. It is difficult to avoid the conclusion that his 'Alice' married Sid on 19 June 1920, which was a Saturday, and that this was Baird's anguished reaction. There was clearly nothing he could do about it now, especially from Trinidad, so he carried on with his foundering programme.

Baird spent his first fortnight back in Britain with his sister Annie, who was working as a district nurse in Deptford after her notable service during the war. Baird's shivering was so bad that at night he pulled the carpet over himself on top of the bedclothes. Probably as a joke, he asked Annie whether he should try television again or invent something useful, such as a permanently sharp razor. She thought there would be more money in the razor, and she may have been right. He did at some point construct a glass safety-razor which would not tarnish, with a glass blade that would not need to be sharpened. He cut himself so badly with it that the idea was abandoned.

From Annie's, he moved into London itself, to a boarding house identified in the *Post Office London Directory* as being at 19 Endsleigh Street, Bloomsbury, and owned by Miss Caroline Borthwick – in his memoir Baird calls her Selina. Mephy, in the course of one of his frequent periods of unemployment, had a bed in a disused wash house at the back. At least Mephy had hot and cold running water. Baird's room, one of the cheapest in the house, was a bare, carpetless attic with a tiny barred window with broken panes. For this, with a meagre breakfast and a disgusting evening meal, and lunch thrown in on Sundays, he paid twenty-five shillings a week. He moved out after about a month or so; on 10 January 1921 he wrote to Godfrey Harris in New York, 'I am in London, but write to The Lodge as I may change my lodgings.'* It is likely that this was when he went to lodge with Mr and Mrs Charles Impett at 57 Ellerby Street, Fulham, where he had meals with the family.[4] Mephy was now back in Helensburgh 'in a state of fed up ness and not over well'.

Harris had written to Baird about the possibility of his going to Trinidad to start up again the very business at which Baird had failed, with Baird handling sales at the London end. Baird was surprisingly upbeat about the idea, suggesting that Harris spend two months experimenting with 900kg oranges and 60kg sugar. Indeed, during the first half of 1921, there are frequent references in Baird's notebook to a correspondence with Harris, and to efforts to establish a West Indian business. Advertisements were drafted, variations on the same theme: 'Partner wanted willing to reside W. Indies capital £1000' (for *The Times*), 'Partnership desired, preferably produce, in established business by W. Indian merchant' (for the *Daily Telegraph*).

Nothing came of the idea, however. The next time we hear of Harris, he had sunk his savings into a few acres of land in the Louisiana wilds, built himself a shack, purchased some goats and hens, and planted vegetables. Here he lived a life of self-sufficiency while meditating on free will and immortality. He finally blew himself up while trying to dynamite a tree root out of the way to make more space for his livestock.[5]

The notebook offers a tantalising glimpse of Baird's frenzied efforts during the first half of 1921 to establish a viable business. Through the estate agents Rodgers, Chapman and Thomas he rented premises at 131 Lupus Street in Pimlico, which had probably been unoccupied ('Who pays for removal of boarding?'). His initial priority was to sell his Trinidadian produce. He tried first the provision merchants in Mark Lane and Mincing Lane in the City. In his memoir he makes a joke of it: 'Nobody wanted mango chutney and nobody appeared to want the guava jelly; the quality was not up to standard. Finally, in desperation, I sold the whole stock to a sausage maker to mix up with the other material which went into his sausages. He gave me £15 for the lot.'[6] This may have been true of part of his produce, but there were other kinds of chutney, and marmalade, and tamarind, which formed part of his stock-in-trade.

He was also dealing, or investigating the prospects of dealing, in a bewildering variety of commodities. These included government and army surplus stores, and bulk lots of chocolate, cigarettes (in cases of 2500 packets of ten), caramels (five tons), fresh and crystallised fruit of different kinds, honey, lime juice, and marmalade. He was prepared to import from abroad what he could not get at the right price locally. There is mention of aluminium teaspoons and forks, 10,000 razor blades, scissors, paper toilet-seat covers (which he was planning to manufacture) and toilet rolls, tin strainers, sieves, fish lifters, cake containers, thimbles, and jackknives. Not having his own distribution facilities, he used Carter Paterson, or Herbert and Co in the Hop Exchange in Southwark, for bulk consignments. Numerous names and addresses are recorded of business contacts of different kinds. He was also meeting Pound, whose home was in the village of Redenham, near Andover, Hampshire, on a regular basis.

On Saturday, 12 March 1921, Baird packs a bag. He includes a black suit and 'papers', but decides against his bowler hat and spats. He arranges for his letters to be forwarded from the office and has the bag sent to St Pancras Station. The next page in the notebook is headed with the date 7 April.

Though St Pancras was the London terminus of the Midland line, trains also ran from there to Glasgow, slower but cheaper than on the west coast route from Euston. This would have been his first visit home since he returned from Trinidad. It was also his opportunity to have things out with 'Alice' and, as it turned out, her husband too. The extraordinary upshot was that a sharing arrangement was agreed. For the next ten years 'Alice' flitted between them, staying with Baird for several weeks or months at a time.[7] There is no doubt that she was still in love with him, and he with her. Her decision to accept a firm offer of marriage and security, rather than hope that Baird might miraculously recover his health and his prosperity, is understandable. She would now have been in her thirties, and was effectively on the shelf because of the casualties in World War I. It is possible that her marriage was on both sides one of convenience. (It is known to the Baird family that she did not want children, whereas Baird did.[8] This may have been a further factor in her decision to jilt him.)

London activity resumes on 7 April. Baird was now into medicinal products and naphthalene, and had ideas for manufacturing fibre mats and dealing in cement. It was also probably at this time that he applied his imagination, with a further glance at the patent medicines which featured in 'How to Make Money' and in H G Wells's *Tono-Bungay*, to a cosmetic product to be called Baird's Osmotic Astringent:

> This most remarkable discovery, not to be compared with so-called skin foods, enables the wrinkles and crows' feet, the lines and sagging folds about the mouth, all of which are caused by relaxed tissue, to be removed in the most novel and remarkable way. The treatment consists in

applying two lotions, the first opens the pores and renders the skin receptive to the action of the second, which is applied immediately afterwards and exercises a powerful bracing tonic and contractile effect on the subcutaneous tissue.

The discovery has only very recently been put before the public but we have already received many appreciative letters. From one of these we give the following extracts: Dear Sirs, Please send me your full size packet of Baird's Osmotic Astringent. I have now tried your sample packet and may say that I am amazed by the results.[9]

The lotions were in the form of two powders, one yellow and one white, which were to be dissolved in water and 'applied every third night before retiring'. The user is warned that the solutions do not keep and should be thrown out after being applied. There is no evidence that Baird's Osmotic Astringent was ever put on the market, which is probably a good thing. Baird was, as we have seen, not averse to making extravagant or even fallacious claims for his early wares; when he came to television, however, this was not something it was in his nature to do.

These were hard times. There is a series of notes headed G. P. (General Programme). Item 1 comprises the texts of small ads offering to share or dispose of his office accommodation, and seeking employment. Of the latter, 'West India Merchant unable to continue his business owing to trade depression, desires position, has good connexions abroad' appeared with a box number in *The Times* for 13 April 1921. Item 2 is, 'Buy scales put chocolates and dates and B[ritish] P[harmacopia] in window'. Underneath is simply, 'Sell artificial flowers'. He soldiered on, however, and did branch out into selling artificial flowers – the names and addresses of seven artificial flower makers appear at this point in the notebook. He also now insures himself against 'partial incapacitation'. This, as it turned out, was a very wise decision, though one that is surprising in the light of his general improvidence even when he was in funds.

It was not all gloom and hard effort. He was regularly in touch with Jack Buchanan. The Impett daughter has recalled Baird hiring a dress suit to meet Buchanan on stage after a performance.[4] This must have been in May. The show, a burlesque entitled *Faust on Toast*, at the Gaiety Theatre, having been taken off for 'reconstruction' in its second week, folded at the end of the month, having had only thirty-four performances in all.[10] It may be sheer coincidence, but thirty-two years later, in one of his most successful screen appearances, in *The Band Wagon* (1953), Buchanan played a bigshot artistic director who proclaims that a minor Broadway show is a modernistic Faust and insists on hiring for it a prima ballerina, played by Cyd Charisse. (Buchanan had better fortune later in 1921, in a revue at the Prince of Wales Theatre, called *A to Z*, in which his co-star was Gertrude Lawrence, making her first appearance in a lead part. It was a smash hit!)[11]

In July Baird makes a note of the two hottest shows in town, *Bull-Dog Drummond* by 'Sapper' starring Gerald du Maurier, and *Paddy the Next Best Thing*, from Gertrude Page's best-selling novel, with Peggy O'Neil in the lead. And he is having dancing lessons! He is also making a list of available 'apartments', noting those which offer facilities for tennis. These entries can only refer to the first visit of 'Alice' to him. She could hardly be accommodated in lodgings in which he ate with the family.

Early in August he reminds himself to collect his sports coat from the cleaners, make out a balance sheet of the state of his business, and notify 'Moir, Baird, Robertson, etc. of new address'. The balance sheet is not healthy: 'Debtors and bank balance £90: creditors £117.16.7, rent £57.10.0, gas £1.6.0.'

According to Baird's memoir, Pound 'introduced me to his uncle, [who] owned a little horticultural business which included a small shop and large storage accommodation. He wanted to get rid of it and, finally I bought it from him for, I think it was £100 cash. ... The place was most unhealthy, the office being under a railway bridge and the walls running with damp.'[12] He does not name the business, but it was none other than William Herbert and Co (officially described in the *Post Office London Directory* as 'Garden Requisite Stores'), 28 Southwark Street, whose storage and and distribution facilities in the Hop Exchange at the same address Baird had used before. And 28 Southwark Street was right under the main line between Cannon Street and Waterloo stations! An entry in the notebook suggests that in fact he and Pound may have paid £300 between them for the business, with a half-share of all profits to each of them, and a salary of £3.10s. a week to Baird. Conveniently, the London warehouse of W & R P Moir, with whom Baird was still dealing on his own account, was in the same block. Their account to him at the end of the year showed that they had now sold all the lime juice he had sent from Trinidad. They had also disposed of three further puncheons (extra large casks) of lime juice and two barrels of ginger which he had obtained elsewhere – at a net profit to him of £2.4s.11d.*

It was shortly after this that the breakthrough occurred to which he refers in his memoir. 'I heard that Australian honey could be bought at a very low price as considerable quantities of it were lying in the docks and the owners were anxious to clear at almost any price. I took a gamble and bought two tons.'[13] The gamble paid off. Among a number of advertisements which his advertising agent Flowerdew placed was this, in the Poultry and Provisions column of *The Times* of 17 September: 'Honey 6d per lb. Finest Australian 60lb tins carriage paid 200 miles 30s. Herbert and Co. 28 Southwark St, London. Established 50 years.' Baird now did some further calculations:

9 lb Honey @ 6 [pence]	= 4/6
tin	= 6 [pence]
box	= 6 [pence]
post	= 1/6

He concluded, 'advertise at 8/6'.

In the end he settled for 7s.6d., and in the issue of 24 September offered, 'Honey, pure, fine 60lb tins 30s, 9lb tin 7s6d, sample free all carriage paid. Herbert and Co, 28 Southwark Street, established 50 years. Phone HOP 1089.' If anyone queried whether Baird had been in business for fifty years, no doubt he intended to say that this applied to Herbert and Co.

Whatever the actual quality of the product, orders poured in, and the same advertisement appeared regularly each Saturday throughout the rest of the year. He was also advertising in the *Daily Mail, Sunday Times*, and *Daily Chronicle*, as well as in other journals, and experimenting with different kinds of packaging, such as thirty-six four-ounce pots in one box.

In *The Times* on 31 December 1921, a 'sample' now cost 4d., and the goods on offer included 'Chocolates, finest assorted, nine 1lb boxes 22s6d'. On 4 February 1922 appeared, 'HONEY, Superior Choice 60lb tin 40s; 9lb tin 8s6d; sample 4d'. It was the last such advertisement.

This may well have been the point at which he was struck down with yet another devilish cold, and could not leave his bed. A friend of Pound, recently arrived from Trinidad, offered to buy a share in his half of the business, and to look after it while Baird was ill. The illness set in, and on medical advice Baird went for an extended stay to Buxton spa in Derbyshire.[14] His partner now bought him out, for £100 in cash and £200 worth of shares in an oil company, which proved to have no value whatsoever. According to Baird's wife, the experience instilled in him a lifelong distrust of the stock market, which inhibited profitable investment of his personal savings.[15] This is borne out by the fact that the 'schedule of securities' held by Baird's bank in May 1936 lists, apart from shares in Baird Television Ltd, only a holding of 500 units in National Savings Certificates, at a time when he had £14,000 in his bank deposit account.*

Fortunately the insurance policy which he had taken out the previous year paid £6 a week for the whole of the time he was out of circulation and covered the bills for board and treatment. Wherever he went for his treatment, the rest and the cure certainly seem to have done him good, to judge from his healthy appearance in a wedding photograph of his sister Jeannie to Rev. Neil Conley on 6 June 1922 (see plate 6).

Apart from this family event, for the next period of Baird's life, until October 1922, we only have his own account in the personal memoir he composed twenty years later.[16] With little more than £100 in his pocket, and no business, he took lodgings in Notting Hill Gate (7 Pembridge Crescent) and looked around for opportunities. Through an advertisement in the *Grocer* offering cheap soap in bulk, he met a Mr Young, who advised him not to buy it, but put him onto something better. Baird took a one-room office at 16 Water Lane, Great Tower Street, appointed Young as sales manager, ordered a ton of 'twin-tablet, double-wrapped pale yellow soap', and advertised for representatives to sell his 'attractive sideline' on commission. A somewhat decrepit sales force was sent out on the road with samples of 'Baird's Speedy Cleaner'. Business boomed. Baird rented the basement of a dilapidated house in Southwark, on the other side of the River Thames, as a warehouse, and put Young in charge of it. Young insisted on having a boy to do the shifting and packing. An advertisement for 'Strong boy wanted to help in warehouse' produced an alarming response. Water Lane was blocked by the throng of applicants who, after the first in the queue had in self-defence been taken on, for days afterwards took to menacing the office and its incumbents.

The secret of Baird's Speedy Cleaner was its price; Baird scoured the markets for the cheapest products, and even imported supplies from France and Belgium. Quality was not a consideration. One customer complained that the soap was 'water held together by caustic soda', but then what could he expect for at eighteen shillings a hundredweight? And as Baird himself pointed out to another disgruntled customer who appeared in the office carrying the stark evidence of her dissatisfaction, it was meant for floors and ships' decks, not for washing her baby's bottom!

On 20 October 1922, John L Baird and Company, Soap Merchants, was registered as a limited company, with a nominal capital of 2000 shares of £1 each. The purpose of the new company was

> To carry on the business of manufacturers of and dealers in soap, oils and oleaginous and saponaceous substances, toilet requisites, chemicals, drugs and chemists' sundries, furniture and household goods and effects, pianos, gramophones and other musical instruments, hardware, electrical, gas and photographic apparatus, fittings and accessories, lenses, glasses and other optical goods, boots and shoes, and wearing apparel of

all kinds, and all other goods, articles, wares and merchandise of every kind or description.

The two directors, Baird and Samuel Joseph De Biere, described as a retired civil servant, took up one share each.[17]

On 3 November Baird sold the goodwill and stock of John L Baird and Company, and also of the Cromwell Trading Company, a mail order business, to the new company in return for 500 shares in the business, plus £250 in cash 'if and when application is received for a further one thousand shares in the company and payment in full made for same'. He was also appointed general manager at a salary of £4 a week.[17]

On 11 December the appointments of two additional directors were recorded: the ever-helpful Robert Pound (described as coconut merchant) and Edward Rumney, an accountant. Shortly afterwards, Thomas Brinkley, another coconut merchant, joined the board. Between them the five directors now owned all 2000 shares: Pound and Brinkley 250 each, and the others 500 each. Rumney became company secretary.[17]

One fateful day in January 1923, Young reported that Baird's Speedy Cleaner was being undercut by a new product, Hutchinson's Rapid Washer, selling at sixteen shillings a hundredweight. Hutchinson was Captain Oliver George Hutchinson, already known to Baird from their apprentice days with the Argyll Motor Company.[18]

The captain had in the meantime not had a very good war. According to documents found in the Public Record Office, Hutchinson enlisted in World War I in a cycling regiment, but was bitten in the neck by a scorpion in Italy, after which he joined the tank corps. At Cambrai in November 1917, the first time that this new weapon was unleashed, Hutchinson's tank broke down. While he was trying to get out of it, a wounded German officer shot him in the knee. There followed a number of formal requests to him to report back from sick leave, which he seems to have ignored, to the extent that at one point the Irish Garda were asked to intervene. To be discharged 'honourably' from the army in 1919 must therefore have been rather a relief to him.[19]

Baird renewed the acquaintance, and suggested they discuss joining forces in the soap business. They met that night at the Café Royal in Piccadilly and settled the details of a merger over numerous cognacs. Baird started to feel ill as Hutchinson saw him off at Leicester Square Underground Station to return to the converted conservatory that was his bedroom in the cheap residential hotel into which he had now moved. The next morning he had a violent cold and a high temperature. Hutchinson, who came bearing a bottle of eau-de-Cologne, was so alarmed that he called in a doctor.

The condition deteriorated. It would seem that Baird was moved from his hotel to his sister Annie's flat at 26c Breakspears Road, Brockley Rise, which is given in the company records as his address on 2 February 1923.[17] She was now working at the Great Ormond Street Hospital for Children in Bloomsbury.

The decision that Baird should leave London altogether for somewhere more healthy was made not so much on medical advice as on his doctor's express instructions. On 14 March Rumney acknowledged Baird's resignation as a director and the manager of the company 'on account of ill health'.* Baird's shares were bought by Lionel De Biere (probably a son of Samuel), who took his place on the board. On 13 April the company moved its offices to 1-4 Cromwell Buildings, Red Cross Street, Southwark, and then on 11 December, presumably at the instigation of Pound, to 28 Southwark Street, the premises of William Herbert and Co. It was further relocated, on 29 April 1924, to 26 Guildford Street, SE1.[17]

Whether the company did any business after Baird's resignation is unlikely. On 7 December 1925, Rumney replied from his home in Cheshire to an enquiry from the Registrar that 'business is now practically non-existent' and asked for the company to be struck off the register. In response to a further communication, he revealed that the assets of the company comprised 'two chairs and two wooden benches for which I have had the offer of 2/- for the lot'; apart from thirty shillings in cash, the capital 'has gone, £1500 trading loss, £500 purchase price to vendor'.[17]

John L Baird and Company, the first of several limited companies to bear his name, was finally dissolved on 9 March 1928.[17]

3
The Beginning of Television: Hastings and Other Places
1923–1924

'When I arrived in Hastings in 1923, I came in search of health after a serious illness, and thought I should never be fit and well again; the doctor who sent me thought the same, but in a very short time the exhilarating atmosphere of Hastings made me a changed man.'[1] So Baird said himself, in a brief speech on 7 November 1929 after the unveiling of a plaque commemorating his experiments in the town.

According to his memoir, he arrived 'coughing, choking and spluttering, and so thin as to be almost transparent'.[2] Hastings may have been chosen because Mephy was living there at the time. Mephy met him at the station, and took him to the house where he had rooms. Untimely illness had now cost Baird three thriving businesses. The good news was that, as a result, true television was about to be born, in the surroundings not of a corporation-financed laboratory, but of a bedroom in a seaside house which took in lodgers.

'Alice' arrived from Glasgow to nurse him and be with him. Baird's wife is quite unequivocal about this,[3] as she is about the fact that 'Alice' was 'with John in the early days of television'.[4] From now on, television was Baird's life.

The race was on to produce a genuine television transmission of instantaneous, recognisable, moving images in natural shades of light and dark. In 1911, the Scottish scientist Alan Archibald Campbell Swinton had given an address to the Röntgen Society of London, of which he was president. In the course of his paper, he reviewed the various proposals for television that had been aired previously and suggested a fully-electronic working system which depended on transmission and reception by means of cathode-ray tubes.[5] Though, according to Baird, the system was perfectly workable,[6] to Campbell Swinton himself it was only an idea.[7] In 1914 Georges Rignoux, a Frenchman, claimed that he had succeeded in transmitting outlines of letters and other objects, and accounts of his experiments appeared in French and American scientific journals.[8] In the USA, Charles Francis Jenkins, who had the backing of the General Electric and the Westinghouse companies, was in 1922 researching into phototelegraphy and television using mechanical techniques.[9] Westinghouse had also, in 1920, hired the services of the Russian immigrant, Vladimir K Zworykin, who had studied under Boris Rosing, an early proponent of cathode-ray television.[10] In Britain, Edmund Fournier d'Albe was working on a system of telegraphic transmission of pictures and images, which he patented in January 1924.[11]

Baird had none of the advantages of these. He had to find or make his own equipment, and build up his operating system from scratch. He was also often a sick man. He possessed, however, a determination born of necessity (he had to invent in order to live) and a crusading nature. He was an individualist, but he employed the qualities of leadership, which he had first demonstrated as a schoolboy, to organise into his scheme the technical dexterity and knowledge of other enthusiasts who contributed their skills to the cause, almost all, if not all of whom did so voluntarily. For all his untidy appearance and erratic habits, his indecisiveness in the face of authority, and his outward vagueness about detail, Baird had a certain charisma which is reflected in the devotion of staff and close friends. He persevered with his mechanical system not only because he did not have the resources to buy more expensive equipment, but also because he believed that it could produce pictures at least as good as the electronic cathode-ray method. And, with his methods, he got there first.[12]

In his memoir, Baird says that the inspiration to pick up the threads of his earlier experiments with television came to him while taking an invigorating walk in the spring sunshine along the clifftops to the east of Hastings in the direction of Fairlight.

> I thought out a complete system. ... Over the raisin pudding I broke the news to Mephy.
> 'Well, sir, you will be pleased to hear that I have invented a means of seeing by wireless.' 'Oh,' said Mephy, 'I hope that doesn't mean you are going to become one of those wireless nitwits. Far better to keep to soap. You can't afford to play about you know.'[13]

Nevertheless Baird and Mephy set to and constructed in Baird's bedroom an embryo working system out of tin, cardboard, darning needles, cotton reels, a powerful electric lamp, a bull's-eye lens from the local cycle shop, and an electric fan motor. They cut out shapes and drilled holes with a pair of scissors, and stuck the thing together with glue and sealing wax. To this contraption they added in due course an array of batteries, connected by clips, wireless valves from a government surplus store, transformers, neon lamps, and a selenium cell, and, hey presto, the shadow of a small cardboard cross was transmitted a distance of two feet.

On 27 June 1923, Baird advertised in *The Times*, with a box number, 'Seeing by wireless. Inventor of apparatus wishes to hear from someone who will assist (not financially) in making working models.' This modest appeal caught the eye of William James Baird Odhams – there was no family connection between them, nor does the name Baird appear elsewhere in the Odhams genealogical tree. Odhams replied the same day.[14] Now in his sixty-fifth year, Odhams was the autocratic chairman of Odhams Press and, by a further coincidence, the uncle of Muriel Odhams, who in 1921 had married John Reith. Reith had overlapped with Baird between 1906 and 1908 at the college of technology in Glasgow, and was now general manager of the newly established British Broadcasting Company.

According to Odhams, on 14 July Baird rang him from Hastings to ask for an interview, which was fixed for 16 July; as a result of this Odhams was offered a seven-day option on a twenty per cent interest in the Baird television invention in return for £100. Odhams immediately set up another meeting, on 18 July, at which Captain Albert G D West was also present.[14] West, twenty-five years old, had served as a wireless officer in World War I, then had a brilliant academic career at Cambridge, and subsequently spent a year as a research student at the prestigious Cavendish Laboratory in Cambridge. The previous month he had joined the British Broadcasting Company as assistant chief engineer and chief research engineer under Peter P Eckersley (now thirty-one), who had come from the Marconi company at the beginning of the year to be chief engineer. To judge from his personal diaries, Reith got on well with his uncle-by-marriage. It is thus likely that Odhams consulted him about a suitable wireless expert, Reith passed on the request to his chief engineer, and Eckersley nominated his newest recruit.

At the meeting there was much technical talk between Baird and West. A few days later Baird turned up again, explaining that he was held up by the lack of certain components. Odhams recalled: 'These by courtesy of Mr West, I was able to obtain viz: three D. E. R. valves, three L. S. 5 power valves, two R. 1 intervalve transformers, one 3-valve note amplifier.' West had enclosed a note with the parts: 'I hope this will be sufficient for Mr Baird's requirements, but if he requires any more I hope you will ring me up and I might be able to send round this afternoon further apparatus.'[14] There is an irony in the fact that Baird may have been using the British Broadcasting Company's electrical equipment in his early experiments.

There was now a delay; Baird had succumbed to flu. When he had recovered and reported that the apparatus was working, West went to Hastings to inspect it. Almost forty years later, Eckersley recalled the occasion:

> I have a vivid recollection of Capt. A G D West coming into my office, bright eyed, with an account of a demonstration he had seen, in which the shadows of solid objects were transmitted from a sender to a receiver. Moving shadows, be it understood! The inventor was one John Logie Baird. ... The apparatus was, of course, rather crude, but surely presaging fantastic possibilities. Should not the British Broadcasting Company take an interest? The inventor was obviously in need of funds and, perhaps, of advice.
>
> West was assured of the BBC's interest, but, to his disappointment, not of its active participation. By its constitution the Company could not even seem to foster a development that would, if successful, benefit private enterprise.[15]

Odhams recalled that West 'reported to me that undoubtedly the claims made for Television were scientifically sound but that it would be a considerable time before they would be likely to become commercially available'. He concluded that he could not avail himself of Baird's 'handsome offer [of a partnership] ... because, having already put in over fifty years of strenuous work, I felt it would be unwise of me to embark on what would evidently be a long-drawn-out period of further anxious toil'.[16] Baird, though, still remembered him with affection: 'Mr Odhams was very charming, gave me tea and entertained me with a respect and consideration which were balm to the soul of a struggling inventor accustomed to being regarded as a dangerous crank.'[17]

In the event, Odhams put in a further ten years of strenuous work, retiring at the end of 1933, coincidentally the year in which West joined the board of Baird Television Ltd as technical director.

On 26 July 1923, Baird filed an application for a patent for 'A System of Transmitting Views, Portraits and Scenes by Telegraph or Wireless Telegraphy',[18] followed by two further applications under the same general heading on 29 December.[19] The July application described a viewing screen of small lamps arranged in rows, precisely the method he employed for his notable large-screen presentation at the London Coliseum seven years later. A screen of 'minute electric lamps ... mounted in a picture frame' occurs in an article about Baird's system in *Chambers's Journal* in November 1923,[20] which also refers to the prospect of sitting at home and watching 'the finish

JOHN LOGIE BAIRD: A LIFE

of the Derby'. This piece was good publicity, and prophetic, but does not seem to have brought in any much-needed cash.

In January 1924 it would appear that Baird was still experimenting with shadows of the cross, between a transmitter and a receiver which were mechanically connected, though the cardboard cross was later replaced by a metal Maltese cross. On 14 January 1924, to attract funds, he organised a demonstration of his apparatus at 21 Linton Crescent, where he was lodging, to journalists from the *Hastings & St Leonards Observer*[21] and the national *Daily News*.[22] A separate interview seems to have been given to each reporter, accompanied by a certain amount of technical obfuscation, to judge from the reports they printed. According to Baird's memoir, the piece in the *Daily News* caught the eye of one of his father's former congregation. Mr Baird responded with a donation of £50, which enabled Baird to move his place of work from Linton Crescent to the upper floor of 8 Queen's Arcade, a covered pedestrian precinct later known as Queen's Avenue. The back room which was his laboratory was above an artificial flower shop, a coincidence which he no doubt appreciated.

That is one version of events between March 1923 and January 1924. In order to understand how and why it comes about that there are other versions, it is necessary to delve further into the mind and circumstances of John Logie Baird and his dedicated but protective, bordering on secretive, attitude to his work. He was brilliant at inventing machines, but less skilled at doing the detailed construction work, for which he needed the assistance of others. Perhaps this was one reason why, having designed a machine which he knew would work, he was then able readily to envisage other applications of that particular invention, rather than be bogged down with the problems of actually making it do what he wanted. And because he could not afford anything but the most basic components, he had to devise the simplest means of resolving technical difficulties.

Baird was not a professional scientist; for a start he had no doctorate, and his associateship of the Royal Technical College was recognised as equivalent to a university degree only in engineering circles. He had to provide his own equipment and finance his own research; a lot of his time was spent begging for parts or cash. It was probably also his innate Scottishness that dictated that he play things close to his chest, though it would have been professional suicide if any of his technical secrets leaked out or if a press demonstration failed. He committed little to paper. Letters were often written in pencil on odd scraps of paper; diagrams were sketched on the backs of used envelopes, or scrawled on the walls of his workshop or on restaurant tablecloths. He could draw, but he was not a draughtsman. In the early years of television he had volunteer helpers working not only individually on different components for his inventions, but also in different locations. He avoided being photographed with an up-to-date machine; most photographs show the working parts covered, or boxed in with plywood, or are poses with obsolete apparatus, or even with equipment that could not possibly have worked. So neurotic was he about the possibility of industrial sabotage that he would remove key parts of a piece of apparatus and take them away for the night.[23] His public announcements and press demonstrations never reflected the apex of his current research, but rather a point which he had reached several stages before. Whereas many applications for patents are concerned with theoretical processes, Baird invariably tested an operation under laboratory conditions before submitting it for consideration. At hardly any time between 1923 and 1929, when he was conducting all his preliminary experiments, did he have a permanent home address. He was almost continually moving from one set of lodgings to another.

When Baird did come to compose a personal memoir, in 1941, it was originally undertaken to fill in time at a health farm while he was drastically reducing his weight after a heart attack, and dictated to a shorthand typist. While full of graphic observations and amusing anecdotes, it is short on dates, inaccurate about names, and vague about timing; selective events are telescoped or recounted in the wrong order. Because of World War II, people had other things to think about, and it is possible that Baird intended at the time to hold back from publication until he had the opportunity to render a more accurate account of what, for better or for worse, had become the Baird legend. Nor of course could he mention in his memoir any developments which were on the government secret list.[24] The apparatus publicly demonstrated in January 1924 could well have been put together by Baird and Mephy at home. So much so that Baird felt he had to apologise for it to the *Daily News* reporter: 'It's very crude!'[22] On the face of it, he had not progressed very quickly or very far since his first successful effort the previous year. That is what he wanted people to believe. It does not take into account systems that he had been developing and experiments he had been conducting not only in Hastings, but in other locations in the south of England and also in Scotland.

Members of the Hastings, St Leonards & District Radio Society, formed in 1924, had been helping Baird almost from the start. It has been suggested that they outnumbered the entire staff of the first Baird television company.[25] The chance to assist in the development of a new, and largely untried, branch of radio technology was a welcome extension to their interests. The individual contributions of this largely unseen band of technical helpers were never publicly acknowledged in Baird's lifetime. He did, however, after the unveiling of the plaque at Queen's Arcade on 7 November 1929, refer to 'the cordial assistance of a number of Hastings residents, some of whom are present now'.[1] The record was finally put straight in 1976, the fiftieth anniversary of the first public demonstration of true television, by a member of this select team, Victor Mills.[26]

The twenty-two-year-old Mills, who had been reported in the local press as having built a sophisticated radio set, was recruited in December 1923 or early January 1924. It was snowing, and Baird, wearing a dirty old raincoat, called at the house where Mills was living with his parents, and explained that the background noise from his selenium cell was interfering with the vision signal.[27] Mills, who ran a radio shop in the town, looked at the problem and suggested a solution, which involved reducing the size of the cell and rearranging the optics. He also lent Baird a powerful amplifier. This was part of the equipment used in the January 1924 demonstration; without it, the demonstration would have had to have been delayed.[28]

Norman Loxdale was still at school at the time. He was advised to seek Baird's advice after making a one-valve radio set which he could not get to work. He called on Baird, who showed him how to make a grid leak with a piece of chewed string, and then how to measure the resistance and replace the string with a resistance made out of a piece of bakelite, marked between two points in pencil. To Loxdale's amazement, the set now worked.[29] He also recalled, sixty years later, making to Baird's specifications a Nipkow disc with two spirals of holes covered respectively with orange-red and blue-green filters. It was capable of scanning for colour and stereoscopic television trans-mission at a time when officially Baird had not demonstrated that he could achieve any picture at all.[30] Other local voluntary helpers included Vincent Edwards, an electrical engineer with the Tramways Department, and Boyd Alexander, who supplied the electric motors to drive the discs. A coffin board from Burton's the undertakers is said to have served as a base for the main apparatus. Holes were gouged out of plywood discs with a trepan made by Loxdale's science master at Rye College Grammar School.[29]

The most notable helper of all, and the most modest, was James Denton, whose wife ran a boarding house in Hastings at this time.[31] Denton was from 1898 for over forty years a part-time lecturer in physics at the Morley College, Bedford College, and the Working Men's College, where in 1913 one of the first wireless transmitting stations was installed under his supervision. During World War I, and also World War II, he conducted research for the govern-ment through his own experimental station, DXV. He was a founder member of the Faraday Society and was in 1927 the first honorary secretary of the Television Society. As J Darbyshire Monteath he contributed numerous articles on technical subjects to the journal *Television*, which began publication in 1928. Denton was the technical expert who undertook the responsibility for setting up and fine tuning the equipment for Baird's public demonstrations; he also contributed to the preparations for the first transatlantic transmission. He was never officially employed by any of the Baird companies, though it is understood that he received some form of financial recognition, perhaps out of Baird's own pocket.[32] Denton was to be associated with Baird's work until his death in 1945, just before Baird himself died.

Baird, with an imaginative leap of mind of which H G Wells would heartily have approved, had already been thinking of other uses for his invention. Norman Loxdale is reported as having recounted later how he and three other Boy Scouts were conscripted by Baird on a bitterly cold, clear evening in the winter of 1923/4 to push a trek cart up the road and pathway to the top of West Hill in Hastings (today there is a lift). There, a device was unwrapped, which Baird pointed out to sea, up to the sky, and towards neighbouring East Hill, examining the results on a screen.[33] At the end of an article, 'An Account of Some Experiments in Television', in the *Wireless World and Radio Review* in 1924,[34] Baird wrote, 'It is possible that at some future date, means may be discovered of sending out energy from point A, bringing it to bear on an object at a distant point B, and causing the object to radiate from its surface energy which, penetrating intermediate obstacles, can be brought to focus at A, rendering it visible.' One may be fairly certain that he had already discovered the means.

On 21 December 1926, Baird filed an application for a patent on a form of television in which the object was viewed not by light but by very short radio waves produced by a spark gap transmitter.[35] The radio image reflected from the object was scanned by a rotating, spirally-perforated disc, as in his normal television system. The scanned signals were picked up by a radio detector such as a crystal and cat's whisker, and then amplified and sent to a receiver screen, on which the image was reproduced.

This particular system of Baird's has been compared to radar, which stands for ra(dio) d(etecting) a(nd) r(anging), but strictly speaking it was rather a method of radio imaging. Although his invention did not provide the range of the object, as in the case of conventional radar, it performed one of the functions of an imaging radar system known as H2S, which was developed during World War II as a navigational aid for aircraft.

In parallel with Baird's work in the 1920s, Professor Edward Appleton at King's College, London, was using radio waves to study a layer of ionised gases 200km above the earth's surface, known as the ionosphere, which was capable of reflecting radio waves. It was the ionosphere reflection which made it possible for Marconi to send the world's first transatlantic radio signals in 1901, and Baird himself used the same means to send television signals to New York in 1928.

The workshop at 8 Queen's Arcade was Baird's second experimental laboratory in Hastings. In 1923 he had rented a work place near the station, which he was forced to give up when the premises were required for a shop.[21]

It may have been the lack of a workshop that drove or encouraged him, at the beginning of August, to embark on a curious odyssey whose itinerary is described in the local paper of his home town. 'Recently Mr Baird was in Helensburgh on a visit to his home, and in conjunction with Mr Yeudall of Messrs Yeudall & Sprott, carried out several experiments in connection with his invention. Ill-health and a lack of material, however, drove him south, and he has since been in Folkestone, Tunbridge Wells and London.'[36]

The business of Yeudall & Sprott was electrical engineering, and Mr Yeudall was the Bairds' next-door neighbour on Argyle Street. The experiments may have been conducted on the firm's premises, though Mrs Elizabeth Honeyman later recalled Baird at this time using as a workshop a wash house behind a house at the corner of Colquhoun Street and West Clyde Street, where she used to spend her days off.[37]

The allusion to London may refer to a brief visit to stay with his sister Annie in her flat. Baird then took lodgings in West Terrace, Folkestone. His landlady was less indulgent than had been the case in Hastings, and he was evicted for using his bedroom as a laboratory. He now found accommodation in the building of an electrical contractor, T C Gilbert & Co, who also gave him space in their workshop and provided him with electrical equipment. He remained in Folkestone several weeks. During this time he was in contact with someone in Tunbridge Wells who was experimenting with a light cell, the most crucial element in Baird's television system.[38]

He then transferred himself and his apparatus to Tunbridge Wells itself, where he had board and accommodation at 40 Upper Grosvenor Road, a boarding house owned by Mrs Emily Grinyer.[39] There is no record of his having a car at this time, which he could hardly have afforded anyway. His equipment would probably have been packed in boxes, to accompany him in the luggage van of the train, or be sent separately by carrier. It is possible that he used for this purpose a van belonging to Herbert and Co, whose distribution facilities he had employed before he took over the business.

There are several reasons why Tunbridge Wells may have attracted him at this time, including the presence of the person working with light cells. It was a spa, offering the same kind of therapeutic facilities that had apparently proved efficacious at Buxton.[40] The period coincided with a visit by 'Alice'. It was easier for her to stay in a place where they were both unknown. Even so, they appear to have acted with the greatest discretion, to the extent probably of having separate rooms.

Broomhill, an extensive house and estate near Tunbridge Wells, was the home of Sir David Salomons. A pioneer of the motor car, he was also the first director of the City of London Electric Lighting Corporation and treasurer and vice-president of the Institution of Electrical Engineers. He lectured extensively on electricity, optics, and photography, and added a workshop wing to his house, with fully-equipped laboratories which were from time to time used by some of the leading scientists of the day. These included Ambrose Fleming, inventor of the thermionic valve which had first made Baird's early experiments with television possible, and who later became one of Baird's most influential supporters and a personal friend. Sir David was at this time seventy-two, and died in 1925, but he was still keeping an eye on the very latest scientific developments. In a little, privately-published book, he wrote, 'Since electric waves can be Broadcasted, it is "on the cards" that light waves can so be done, since both are the same, differing only in length. Then Television will be an accomplished fact.'[41] It would seem possible that the person in the locality experimenting with light cells was doing so in the Broomhill laboratories.

Baird made a considerable impression on the family in Upper Grosvenor Road, and Mrs Grinyer afterwards confessed that she felt sorry for him because he was so short of money. Her daughter Helena, who was ten years old at the time, still remembered many years later that he affected the eccentric inventor, going around in his dressing-gown and wearing socks without slippers – he said they were long-life socks and he was seeing how long they lasted. It was also convenient if he wanted to take a nap during the day. At night the sounds of a typewriter came from his room.

The highlight of Baird's stay was his asking Helena and her younger brother to bring their friends along to the back garden of the house the next morning, when they would have

> A nice surprise, which we certainly did when we discovered that it was one of the first pictures of TV. It was taken aboard ship in the Channel, and we were taken down into the galley and could see the chefs moving about and preparing the meal all dressed in white overalls and tall white hats – the faces of the chefs were not at all clear, but John was highly

delighted and he was explaining that we would all be able to have entertainment in our own homes eventually.[42]

Before one dismisses this as fantasy, two things should be taken into account. In her eighty-eighth year, Helena described the event in exactly the same terms, with precisely the same detail, as her husband had done on her behalf fifteen years earlier, when she also referred to the receiver as a 'box-like contraption, with a screen, and mounted on a pedestal framework'.[39] Her description of an 'upright picture in a frame'[42] matches the apparatus described in *Chambers's Journal*.[20] While Baird's party trick could not have involved a live television transmission, it is technically feasible that, with the equipment he is known to have had with him, he could have transmitted even at this time a piece of cine film.

During the 1920s Baird had a further, more regular base of operations in the historic Scottish town of Falkirk. The link was John Thomas Hart, who was born in 1896. His father, a police officer, drowned while trying to save a woman who was attempting suicide. During World War I, Hart was a signaller in the Argyll and Sutherland Highlanders, whose main recruitment area included Falkirk. He was on active service for four years, and was mentioned in dispatches. In 1920 he married an eighteen-year-old local girl, Jean Dickson, who converted to Roman Catholicism to be his wife.[43] The Hart family believes that it was at her instigation that John Hart gave up being a foundry worker to open a bicycle and radio business. He built and sold radio receivers and was experimenting with radio transmission and reception before there were any official radio stations. Jean helped him by serving in the shop; she also learned about the components of a radio and was able to wire up two- and three-valve sets.[44] Latterly, the business became a partnership between them, with Hart supplying the technical and sales expertise, and his wife the impetus and organising ability, including the dressing of the windows. It was just the right place and time for a man with an interest in radio development to open such a business. Falkirk had a resident population only half that of Hastings, but the Falkirk & District Radio Society had its first meeting on 22 February 1922, over two years before the establishment of an equivalent club in Hastings.

It is not known how and where Baird and Hart first met. It may well have been at a meeting of radio specialists in England. The relationship between them was both a personal and a business one. They were both Lowland Scots. Hart was a man of progressive ideas with a particular interest in the latest technologies, a fixation with radio development, and a penchant for electrical gadgets and optical devices. He was a trained signals engineer if not also a trained radio engineer, neither of which Baird was. It may not be insignificant that on 11 May 1927, Baird applied for a patent for a secret radio signalling system.[45] Hart had workshop facilities, radio equipment and components, and, as a purveyor of bicycles, an endless supply of cycle-lamp lenses, a staple of the early Baird machines. These particular lenses, about 5cm diameter, were fitted to carbide bicycle lamps, which were very popular also among coal miners, who used them to light their way to and from their shifts in the local collieries.[46] Hart was a generous person, who gave Baird some financial assistance.[47] He was also socially minded. He forged links with the Italian community in Falkirk, and in the early 1930s sent his three eldest children to learn Italian in Stirling on Sundays.[48]

Baird, in the interests of security, liked to keep his experimental work compartmentalised. Falkirk was a suitable distance away from his various centres of operation in southeast England. It was a place with family associations and was within easy reach of his parents' home at Helensburgh.

Fifty years later Falkirk residents recalled the man with the striking blue eyes who was often in the shop when they came to have their accumulators charged or to buy radio parts.[49] That it was a relaxed relationship is attested by the fact that Hart called him Logie, using that name presumably to avoid confusion with his own. Baird was a stickler for etiquette, and almost invariably referred to his business associates as 'Mr'.

The Harts had six children. The eldest, Honor, born in 1921, remembers her father taking her to the shop in the Pleasance, to help out Jean when there were two further children to cope with, and seeing Baird there. Hart made her a crystal set with earphones, and said that one day, if 'it' worked, she would not only hear but also see what was happening. By 'it' she understood the project on which he and Baird were working.[50] Opinions are divided as to whether or not Baird held any public demonstrations of his invention in Falkirk. If he did, then the first of these, in the Carron Church Hall in 1923, seems to have been a failure.[51]

We have now, by a more roundabout route, arrived back at events in Hastings in January 1924, to which Baird had returned from Tunbridge Wells at the end of the previous year. He and Mephy were ensconced in 21 Linton Crescent, with the apparatus set up in one of the living-rooms. They were likely to have been paying guests rather than boarders. The house was owned by Charles S Wheatley, who occupied it with his wife Alice and their three grown-up children, Cyril, Gwendolen, and Winifred. Cyril was an inventor, too. In 1927, from 21 Linton Crescent, he filed a patent,[52] through the same patent agent employed by Baird, for a 'Direction- or Position-finding and Recording Apparatus', with subsequent applications specifying improvements to it. These particularly appertained to equipment for controlling the direction of an unmanned aircraft by wireless, something which had been forecast by Dr W H Eccles, president of the Radio Society of Great Britain, in an interview in November 1924.[53]

To the Wheatley family, it must have been much the same as having two small boys running their clockwork trains through the house.

Charles Wheatley had purchased the property from John Vint on 11 May 1922,[54] but it would seem from the electoral roll that the family did not move in until later that year – no-one from that address is listed for autumn 1922, but both Cyril and his parents appear in spring 1923. It has been assumed that it was to 21 Linton Crescent that Mephy took Baird when the latter arrived in Hastings in March 1923, and that it was there that Baird conducted his initial experiments in his bedroom. This begs certain questions. How was it that Mephy was installed at the Wheatleys' so soon after they moved in? Why did Baird need a workshop in the summer of 1923, when later the same year he was able to use a living-room in number 21? Why did he embark on his extensive round trip in the late summer and autumn of 1923, taking his apparatus with him?

There is one scenario which fits the existing evidence and answers these questions. When he arrived in Hastings, Baird moved into a house (not 21 Linton Crescent) in which Mephy had a bedsitting-room, or possibly a bed-room and a sitting-room, which was utilised as an extra bedroom. When Baird's apparatus grew too large for his bedroom, he rented the workshop. When the workshop was no longer available, he set off on his tour, with his kit, having no longer a base in Hastings in which to work. In the meantime, Mephy found this ideal billet for them both: a scientific family, with space in the house for a laboratory for Baird.

The text of Baird's memoir confuses the issue, since he refers to returning from Fairlight to Mephy and raisin pudding at 'Walton Crescent', with no number.[13] As there was no Walton Crescent then in Hastings, this could be a mistyping, or a misreading of a shorthand outline, for Linton Crescent, or else a lapse of memory – throughout the memoir Baird is very vague about addresses. On the other hand, it could equally well be another of the twenty-four substantial Victorian houses in Linton Crescent to which he is referring. According to the street directories, no house in Linton Crescent was registered as a boarding house at this time, but this does not mean than one or more of the owners or occupiers did not have a lodger or lodgers (as did the Wheatleys).

In the absence of any firm evidence as to where Baird spent the months March to August 1923, the balance of probability is that it was in some lodgings other than 21 Linton Crescent, and that he first moved into number 21 in December 1923.

The apparatus which Baird demonstrated in January 1924 had incorporated a significant development designed to compensate for the slow response of the selenium cell to the effect of light. In conjunction with the transmission disc, which rotated at two hundred revolutions per minute, was a serrated disc, revolving ten times as fast in the opposite direction, and acting as a light chopper. This converted the light signal image into a series of pulses to which the cell responded more readily; the rapidly alternating signal was also easier to amplify.[55] With his makeshift equipment Baird was on the way to resolving the selenium problem which had been exercising physicists since shortly after the turn of the century.

The light chopper was a feature of the apparatus which had accompanied Baird on his travels, though it is not mentioned in the November 1923 article in *Chambers's Journal*,[20] nor in Baird's first patent,[18] which the article closely reflects. The image, about two inches square and with a bright light behind it, is focussed through a lens on to the outer part of a disc, about twenty inches in diameter, perforated by a series of pinholes arranged round the edge in one spiral turn. As the disc revolves, the holes break up the image into successive vertical strips, one strip for each hole. This is the process known as scanning. The light from the scanned image then falls on a light-sensitive cell. The varying current produced from the cell is amplified and passed on to a copper brush at the end of an arm which is synchronised with the transmitting disc. The brush passes over a series of contacts, each connected to a miniature lamp bulb which reflects that part of the image which has been scanned by the corresponding hole in the transmitting disc. The number of holes in the transmitting disc governs the number of vertical strips which comprise the final picture. Holes of both 1/32 and 1/18 of an inch in diameter are referred to in the patent.

While the column in the *Daily News*[22] was excellent publicity, it made no mention of money, which had been the object of the exercise. The *Helensburgh and Gareloch Times*, which picked up the story from the *Daily News*, stated that Baird was held up for the sum of £1000 to £1500, which would enable him to build a fully-working system. The *Hastings & St Leonards Observer* made a point of the money aspect.[21] So did Mephy, in letters he now addressed to the press. And on 30 January, Jessie Baird was writing to her daughter Jeannie, 'John is still working at "television". He wants a company or a rich partner, as it is not quite finished yet, or ready to make a profit.'*

A curious little news story also appeared (on 26 February, with a

Helensburgh by-line): 'A great stream of people have been visiting the house in Hastings since the news of his invention first became public. Among the visitors was a representative from the War Office and Mr Wm Le Queux, the well-known novelist, who is also a radio expert.' It ended with the refrain that had become standard: 'The inventor has recently been laid aside with an attack of influenza, and his work has been interrupted.'

William Le Queux's interests, which also included espionage, Egyptology, the occult, medieval manuscripts, monastic seals, and murder, were almost as extensive as his literary output – he is credited with over 130 novels and biographical studies. He was a frequent visitor to the laboratory in the Arcade in Hastings, where he appears to have been living in 1924. He was the first president of the Hastings, St Leonards & District Radio Society, to which Baird gave the inaugural lecture on 28 April 1924. Le Queux was good at attracting publicity, but unwilling to help financially, claiming that his money was tied up in Switzerland,[56] a pretext which may not have been as ingenuous as it sounds, as he is recorded as having been a resident of Switzerland at this time.[57] He wrote several press articles about Baird and encouraged him in other ways. He died in Belgium in 1927 at the age of sixty-three.

On 26 March 1923, Campbell Swinton read a paper to the Radio Society of Great Britain on 'The Possibilities of Television with Wire and Wireless', in which he developed his theory of analysing the image by means of a controlled cathode beam, influenced by magnetic fields. It was reprinted, with an account of the subsequent discussion, in the *Wireless World and Radio Review* in the issues of 9, 16 and 23 April. In the course of the discussion, Ll B Atkinson suggested, 'I do not believe there is any sufficient call for seeing by electricity to lead anybody or any corporation to lay out the large sum of money which is necessary.' Campbell Swinton, in his summing up, stated, 'I entirely agree with Mr Atkinson that the real difficulty is that it is probably scarcely worth anybody's while to pursue it. That is what I have felt all along myself. ... If you could only get one of the big research laboratories like that of the GEC or of the Western Electric – one of those people who have large skilled staffs and any amount of money to engage on the business – I believe they would solve a thing like this in six months and make a reasonable job of it.'[58]

At this time the General Electric and Western Electric companies in the USA were still experimenting with versions of the mechanical system. At some point between the middle of 1924 and the end of 1925 (there is no record of the exact date), Zworykin demonstrated a full electronic television system to his masters at the giant Westinghouse company, but the results were so poor that he was effectively told to transfer his energies to something more useful.[59] Whether or not Baird knew about the situation in America, he had no permanent staff, only minimal facilities, and no money. Campbell Swinton's conclusion effectively confirmed that Baird was on the right lines with his mechanical system. Indeed, Baird said as much in his article in the *Wireless World and Radio Review*.[34]

In an article in the *Radio Times* (25 April) Le Queux wrote that Baird had now separated the transmitter and receiver of his system, 'and has successfully transmitted images between two totally disconnected machines, synchronism being accomplished with perfect accuracy by comparatively simple and inexpensive apparatus'.[60] This is the first recorded instance of Baird transmitting moving shadows between two separate machines synchronised by an electrical current from a motor. Meanwhile, it had been reported in *Radio News* and *Popular Radio* in the USA that Jenkins had achieved similar results with a 'crude and cumbersome' mechanical system in December 1923.[61]

In a subsequent article, 'The New Spy Menace to Britain', Le Queux referred to Baird's apparatus as having been seen 'by the experts of the War Office' and to an apparent attempt by a 'German correspondent' to obtain details of it.[62] It may well be that it was Le Queux who opened Baird's eyes to the potential uses of his apparatus for signalling, though if what Helena Walker heard as a child from his room in Tunbridge Wells really was the sound of a typewriter, it is possible that he had already worked this out for himself. Certainly, except for one instance in 1941,[63] there is no evidence of his ever using a typewriter to produce personal letters or other documents, which he invariably wrote by hand. Paul Reveley, who worked alongside him from February 1932 to November 1938, cannot recall his using one,[64] nor was there ever one in the Baird home.

That there really was government interest in Baird's invention at a very early stage in its development is confirmed by the existence of an Air Ministry file, 'The Use of Television in Aircraft', opened on 24 November 1924,[65] to which Lieutenant-Colonel Hugh Lefroy, head of wireless research, contributed a note on 13 June 1926 to the effect that he had since April 1924 been making abstracts of accounts of Baird's work, and had discussed it with people who had examined the apparatus and attended demonstrations of it.[66] Lefroy, a career soldier with a glittering collection of awards for bravery as a wireless and intelligence officer, had specialised in wireless telegraphy since 1905. He joined the Air Ministry after retiring from the army in 1922, and worked on wireless development and research at the Royal Aircraft Establishment, Farnborough, from 1926 to 1927, when he appears to have taken a second retirement, and returned to the family estate in Ireland.[67]

Baird had swiftly moved on from the model which operated on the basis of pinholes and a screen of lights. The new transmission system was heralded in a patent for which he applied on 29 December 1923.[68] He sketched out the broad principles of the reception process in the article in the *Wireless World and Radio Review* in May 1924.[34] The transmitting disc is pierced with twenty holes staggered round its rim. The picture is displayed on the receiving disc itself, which has twenty torch bulbs arranged in the same formation as those on the transmitting disc and rotates in synchronism with it. The fundamental development, described in the patent, is that each hole in the transmitting disc contains a lens. It may be significant that someone who claimed to have witnessed the unsuccessful experiment in Falkirk in 1923 recalled a 'two-and-a-half-foot circular screen'.[51]

In the meantime Baird had found another supporter in W C (Bill) Fox, a Press Association journalist and wireless enthusiast whom Baird had impressed with his earnestness. Fox proposed that if Baird was able to transmit a wireless television signal from Hastings to his home in Golders Green, London, he would make a press report out of the achievement. The test took place on 8 April 1924:

Cinematograph by Wireless
Testing British Inventor's Device for Broadcasting Pictures

The invention of a young Englishman [sic], a wireless device whereby a cinematograph programme may be received by a valve set in a similar manner to musical pieces, was tested last night. The tests were carried out from a South Coast town and wireless amateurs listening in to the Paris 'Radiola' and other Continental stations, may have 'heard' the picture transmission although they were unable to see anything.

A Press Association representative who listened to the television transmission found that it was indicated to the ear by a curious high pitched whistle, with a hint of regular and very rapid interruptions. Almost inaudible it was quite distinct from the intermittent mutter of high speed telegraphy and was totally different from a 'howl'. With the necessary apparatus the signals could have been converted into a picture.[69]

'Seeing by electricity' was now firmly also in the realm of 'seeing by wireless'.

Baird had clearly managed to connect up his equipment to a local amateur radio station, whose owner would have kept quiet at the time for fear of losing his licence for broadcasting television rather than speech or Morse code. His identity is still a mystery, but it is most likely to have been Le Queux, who would have relished a covert operation.

There is some controversy also about the nature of the signals sent on this occasion. Baird would have had few problems at this time in transmitting a 'cinematograph programme', which was only marginally more complicated than sending a shadowgraph. Yet Fox later claimed that as the public did not then know the term 'television', his news editor had decided that the best way to describe it was 'cinematograph by wireless'.[70] In this case, the whole press release was by way of being a deception. The analogy with 'musical pieces' suggests movement. So does the description of the signal as being 'almost inaudible' and having 'a hint of regular and very rapid interruptions'. This is very different also from the sound of the transmission of the vision signals of the Maltese cross, described as a 'high-pitched scream' in an article published the same month.[71]

This article came from an interesting quarter. F H Robinson, editor of the Odhams journal the *Broadcaster and Wireless Retailer*, visited the Queen's Arcade laboratory with a photographer. He wrote a factual account of Baird's system in the April 1924 issue, with a photograph of himself, Baird, and the system, parts of which are covered up by drapes. Not only that. In *Kinematograph Weekly,* Robinson wrote a more journalistic article: 'Moving images may be transmitted ... and distance is no object, merely depending on the power of the wireless transmitter and the sensitivity of the receiver employed. ... The inventor is confident that no technical difficulties stand in the way. ... Undoubtedly wonderful possibilities are opened up by this invention, its very simplicity and reliability placing it well in front of many of the complicated methods which have been evolved to do the same work.'[72] It had the same photograph of the receiving disc, showing the positions of the 'quick-acting lamps corresponding to the holes in the transmitting disc',[71] but also one of it in action, with the shadow of a cross at its right-hand edge.

Things moved fast. Having seen the one article or the other, Wilfred Day, who ran a radio business from 19 Lisle Street, in London's Soho district, contacted Robinson. On 5 April, Baird wrote from 21 Linton Crescent to Day: 'I have heard from Mr Robinson of "The Broadcaster" that you are interested in my Television invention. I would be very pleased to meet you and expect to be in London tomorrow.' Day was a hard-headed and, perhaps for that reason, successful businessman. Baird, who has been described by former employees as shy, modest, approachable, polite, and entirely devoted to the progress of television, was at this time also a desperate man. A deal was struck, and an agreement signed on 17 April. In return for £200, Day received a share of one-third 'in the whole of the invention'.[73] Baird returned to Hastings, where he and Mephy celebrated with a slap-up dinner at a local restaurant.

The correspondence between Baird and Day during the next eighteen months, with the scanning disc from the receiving end of the apparatus used in the first public demonstration in 1926, fetched £70,000 when they were sold by auction to Hastings Museum in October 1999. Comprising hand-written letters by Baird and carbon copies of Day's letters to him, the correspondence demonstrates the dilemma, for the first but by no means the last time, of the practical engineer with a justifiable phobia of the piracy of his work, faced with an investor who wanted results, and the difficulties of a man of ideas competing in the business market place. It also illustrates the formality of the relationship. Throughout, they are to each other 'Mr Baird' and 'Mr Day', 'Yours faithfully'. Patent specifications accepted during the period of the partnership carry Day's name as well as Baird's, even though they may have been submitted earlier.

The partnership began as just that. Day supplied an amplifying panel, offered advice on optics, and lent Baird books on the subject. Baird sent a drawing of a disc for Day to have made up by a sheet-metal worker, and specified motors that he required, which had to be obtained from Holland.

Then a setback. Early in May, Annie Baird was sent home to Helensburgh on sick leave. When Jessie Baird opened the door, Annie could see that her mother was desperately ill. A doctor was called, but the cold which Jessie had neglected while she carried on with her household chores and her charitable visits had turned to pneumonia. She died at 9.05pm on 7 May. Baird was too late to see her alive. He sent a telegram to Day on 8 May explaining the situation. He travelled to Scotland for the funeral, and saw Jessie buried in the family plot in which now the bodies of his father and himself also lie. Day's letter of sympathy, sent to 'The Lodge', was grudging: 'Of course you could not do different than go to Scotland for a few days, at any rate, to see matters righted. We are very busy with your new apparatus but it is a time wasting job.'

Baird returned to Hastings immediately after the funeral to continue his work. His mother's death both shocked and depressed him. In her self-sacrifice and unstinting help to others, she had been his model of woman-hood. His father was now eighty-one. Annie gave up her work to come home and look after him. When he died in 1932, she stayed on in the house.

Jessie Baird had some savings of her own, mainly in debentures, exchequer bonds, treasury bonds, national war bonds, and deposit accounts. One-third of the value of her estate was left to her husband. The other two-thirds was divided equally between their four children, each of whom received in due course the sum of £206.14s.9d.* Baird's share must have been a considerable boost to his financial position, but would have been spent almost immediately on research and equipment.

On 5 June 1924, Day wrote to him, 'I note that you have got your article mentioned in "Popular Wireless", and hope you are not giving too much away in publishing these facts.' He also asked for Baird's opinion on 'the enclosed little work on Television', which he had been asked if he would sell. Baird replied that he could not recommend Day selling the book, 'there is practically nothing in it'; as for *Popular Wireless*, 'They got no information or photographs from me. I bought a copy this morning, the man who wrote the article seems to know very little about it.'

The main obstacle to true television was to get a cell which would respond to the minuscule levels of light reflected from an object. Baird was experimenting with both selenium and other types of photo-electric cells. The latter he obtained from a supplier in London, C F Elwell Ltd: the former from a Dr Roy, who may have been his contact in Tunbridge Wells. On 6 June Baird reported to Day that his latest photo-electric cell was a 'most delicate affair', but that he would need 'to screen the amplifier in a metal case to keep out induction from the mains'. Day replied rather superciliously: 'I note that you are well away with the new photo electric cells and that they are extremely delicate in their operations. This of course is a known fact, and do not risk the instrument for the sake of having a metal screen made which will earth any counter currents that may effect the photo microcell.' Ten days later, Baird had got the photo-electric cell 'sufficiently sensitive to work by reflected light'. This was a significant breakthrough, in that it put him ahead of other scientists who were still transmitting silhouettes. On 25 June he reported that he had been 'experimenting with colloidal [that is, fluid] solutions in the hopes of producing an improved form of light sensitive cell'.

The precise nature of the cell on which Baird finally settled constitutes an unsolved mystery. In an article in the *Wireless World and Radio Review* in 1925, Baird described it as being neither a photo-electronic nor a selenium cell, but a fluid cell 'of my own invention';[74] in another article, in *Experimental Wireless and the Wireless Engineer* in 1926, he refers to a liquid solution of particles of selenium.[75] This may have been what it was, or it may have been his way of putting competitors off the scent.[76]

The motors, after a few problems on the way, duly arrived. Day also supplied a Tungar rectifier at Baird's request, to obviate the need for and expense of continually recharging accumulators. Both men hoped it might be possible to mount a demonstration of television at the Cinematograph Garden Party in London on 19 July, but things were not far advanced enough for that, though they attended the event. On 23 July Baird acknowledged the receipt of a supply of batteries, but warned Day for the second time that he was having problems with the slots in the serrated disc at the transmitting end of the apparatus, which were not letting through enough light. Day expressed concern at the delay.

On Thursday, 24 July 1924, an explosion rocked the Arcade.

Baird wrote to Day on the Friday:

> I am pleased to say I managed to get a shadow of a strip of cardboard through yesterday very indistinct but more amplification will make it clearer.
>
> I also had a very unpleasant experience and I suppose should be thankful to be still alive. I got a shock from one thousand volts – it twisted me up and flung me across the laboratory, fortunately nothing was damaged except my hands which are badly burnt. The doctor was surprised I was still alive! however I seem shock proof.
>
> After this I will wear rubber gloves, electrocution must be a most fearful end. The people next door and round about thought there had been an explosion. I must have come down with a big bump but don't remember much about it.
>
> I don't think it will be necessary to alter the slots, they give the effect of looking through a grid iron but with proper amplification outlines will appear fairly clearly.
>
> Improvements can be made later. I will let you know as soon as I have more to report.

In the meantime Day, having seen a report of the accident in the paper, had written expressing concern: he hoped that Baird was 'progressing favourably and that no serious mishap has occurred'. He ended, 'I note in the report they say the instrument is badly damaged. I should be glad to know to what extent the instrument is affected.' Baird duly reassured him that the show would shortly be back on the road.

Whatever the damage to the equipment and to himself, Baird was on trenchant form a fortnight later, with a letter to the local paper:

> My attention has been drawn to a paragraph in your issue of the 26th ult [reporting the accident], in which it is stated that I have invented a machine by which 'I claim to see by wireless'. This statement is both misleading and damaging. May I point out that early this year I demonstrated to the Press and also to a number of experts the

actual transmission of moving outline images. Full accounts appeared in all the leading wireless journals and kinematograph journals and it is clearly described by Mr Wm Le Queux in 'The Radio Times' 25 April ('Television – A Fact!'). Also by Mr F H Robinson, Editor of 'The Broadcaster,' in the April issue ('Radio Television'). Both of these gentlemen were present at actual demonstrations.

The word 'claims' is, therefore, entirely out of place, and gives the wrong impression. I shall be glad if you will publish this letter in correction.[77]

On 6 August, he reported to Day that the images of moving shadows were 'broken and indistinct' and that he was going to have to alter the slots. He was also having trouble with extraneous noise, which he had resolved by 'keeping the valves well separated and enclosing the first three valves and the cell in steel cases connected to earth'.

On 14 August, he described a strange phenomenon. Having altered the slots, 'horizontal lines were quite clear but vertical lines were almost invisible. If a piece of cardboard was held in front of the transmitting lense its shadow was quite clear at the receiving end – as long as it was held horizontal. If it was turned to the vertical position it gradually faded. ... I have now got the proper size of slots and am going ahead.' Day replied that he was delighted with progress and sincerely trusted that 'before long you will have something tangible to put before me'.

On 21 August came a bolt from the blue:

Dear Sir

We herewith enclose statement of goods had by you, which we trust that you will find correct, and that you will see your way to oblige us with a remittance at an early date.

Yours faithfully

for WILL DAY LTD

The letter was signed by the secretary of the company and the bill was for £78.10s.2d.

Day visited Baird in Hastings on 5 September, to inspect the apparatus; he also appears to have mentioned the debt. The next day he wrote asking Baird to be quite sure that 'when we come down on Monday afternoon ... the Television effect is produced absolutely by wireless without a circuit in operation'.

It would seem that Day was trying to make a deal with the Sterling

Telephone Company for the commercial exploitation of the patent. As a result of the demonstration, attended by Mr Burney, a director of Sterling, the company then sent Captain Cohen, their technical expert and an advisor to the government on patents of this kind, to Hastings to inspect the apparatus.

Later in the month, in the course of a telephone conversation, Baird asked Day for a business loan. Day refused, and on 26 September wrote Baird a strong letter: 'You already have a substantial loan from me in the shape of the apparatus we have supplied to you; and for the benefit of yourself I may tell you that the agreement between us is that we pay one third (which we have done in the purchase of the apparatus) and you pay two thirds, and yet you calmly talk about selling the apparatus.' He then turned to the debt: 'I am sure I have helped you always, and so far have nothing in return.' He went on to threaten legal action if it was not paid, but offered a solution. He would pay Baird a further £100 (less the £78.10s.2d.), in return now for a half-share in the business.

Baird replied by return on 27 September:

I am sorry if my manner on the phone was abrupt, my nerves have been very much on edge with worry.

You will recollect that when you were at Hastings on your first visit you told me that if I needed cash to carry on to be sure to let you know, in view of this I was rather hurt by your refusal.

The apparatus I referred to was my own personal property. I should not sell any apparatus in which you have an interest without your consent.

With reference to the £78, although I have not paid any of this I have myself spent considerably more on Selenium cells, Photo Electric Cells, accumulators, amplifiers, receiving machines and other apparatus and one third of these costs will amount to a fair fraction of £78.

I have been giving my whole time to the invention, paying laboratory rent, cost of my patents and all sorts of incidental expenses without any salary. I know you have helped me and am grateful for your assistance but it is scarcely fair to say I have not reciprocated.

I demonstrated to Mr Cohen the instantaneous transmission of clearly defined images between two separate machines and he stated before leaving 'I am perfectly satisfied', this seems to me a very tangible and creditable result particularly in consideration of the confined and ill equipped laboratory and the complete lack of experimental facilities – It should be remembered that some of the best scientific brains in the world backed by highly trained staffs with the whole resources of modern science and unlimited cash at their disposal have been engaged on this problem for years without solving it. The chemical inertia of Selenium and the impossibility of synchronism are quoted by Professor Korn, Dr Fournier D'Albe and others as impassable barriers. The models demonstrated to Mr Cohen that these barriers had been overcome in a simple and practical fashion.

Up to the present the only other man who has been able to demonstrate anything has been C F Jenkins, his machine is immensely expensive and the shadows he transmitted were blurred and hazy. I cannot say whether Jenkins was first or not but as our systems are quite different it does not much matter.

I have spent every penny I possess on this invention and given my whole time to it and have produced results which have satisfied experts that the invention is thoroughly practical.

About the one half share I will come up and discuss this with you on Wednesday if this will be convenient to you.

On the same day, Day sent Baird a copy of a letter from Sterling, with his own comment: 'Evidently Capt. Cohen does not think very much of your invention, and consequently the company will not be inclined to do anything with the matter, and I am afraid it is not a very happy augury for the future.'

While there still seemed to be some room to manoeuvre with Sterling, Day's attitude in a subsequent letter (30 September) was uncompromising: 'I do not feel inclined to pander to Mr Burney or anyone else regarding this matter. I am anxious, for both our sakes to try and realize something tangible from this invention; and if after our conversation when you come up once more, we care to interest fresh people with this invention, then I think we can well afford to let Mr Burney stand aside.'

Baird and Day met on 1 October. The disagreement was patched up, and a new contract signed, which gave Day a half-share in the enterprise. But the writing was now on the wall. There is, moreover, no evidence in the correspondence between the two partners that Day made any further attempt to interest other parties in the invention. On the contrary, he seems from this point to be content to leave Baird do the marketing of the product as well as the research and development.

On 13 October, Baird reported that the Patent Office had accepted his 'Complete Specification':[18] 'So we have now a Full Patent, this should be an advantage in getting capital.'

Meanwhile, as a result of the explosion, Baird's landlord in the Arcade, whom Baird, with his habit of misnaming people of whom he disapproved, describes in his memoir as Mr Twigg, but who has since been identified as Mr Tree, had had enough. He informed Baird that unless he stopped experiments on the premises, he would be evicted. According to his own account, Baird ignored these instructions, and then was faced with an angry Tree demonstrating outside his lab. In the resulting fracas, Baird, having remonstrated with Tree before a crowd of onlookers in the Arcade, and then wheeled round to make a dignified return to his work, thrust his hands into the pockets of his threadbare trousers, and split them up the back.[78]

Tree, however, had the last word. His solicitor issued a threatening letter. Day set about finding alternative accommodation for the enterprise in London. Baird wrote to him on 13 October: 'As I dare not run my machines I have been experimenting with chemicals and managed to make a <u>Liquid</u> light sensitive cell, it is a novelty and may prove valuable.'[79]

It was, though, clearly time to move on.

4
Serendipity in Soho
1924–1925

On 30 October 1924, Baird reported to Day by letter that he had dis-mantled his apparatus, for the carrier Pickford's to uplift the following week.[1] The premises which Day had chosen comprised two rooms in the attic of 22 Frith Street, Soho, a building occupied by Cross's Pictures Ltd, film dealers. The rent, shared by Baird and Day, was £2 a week. Lisle Street was only a few blocks away, on the other side of Shaftesbury Avenue. This may readily explain why the surviving correspondence between them contains no further letter from Baird, who was in any case an unenthusiastic correspondent. It would seem that from this point Baird communicated with his partner by word of mouth; he may also have used the telephone in the office downstairs.

According to his memoir, Baird's first lodgings after his arrival in London consisted of a top-floor front room in Ealing, where he cooked his own food on a gas ring.

> The room was comfortable and quiet. On the wall was a framed poem: 'Short was the traveller's stay, / She came but as a guest, / She tasted life then fled away, / To everlasting rest. / Elizabeth Brown passed away aged three months.'
>
> Further along the wall was a photograph of an infant in a cot, evidently the dead body of little Elizabeth Brown. On the table were a number of books, Dickens, Silas Hocking and Annie Swan, also a book of press cuttings from Tit Bits and Answers headed 'Jokes and Teasers from various Columns'.
>
> The first night I stayed there the door handle of the bedroom was very slowly and quietly turned, and the door began to open. I watched spell-bound. The door opened about two inches and then stopped, there was the sound of someone moving stealthily away and then complete silence. Nothing more happened.
>
> Every night the same phenomenon occurred. I found at last that it

was the landlady's little boy who slept next door and suffered from night fears. He wanted to have the door open for company. Every night, for all the time I stayed there, this pathetic little ceremony took place.[2]

Ealing is a district some way out from the centre of London to the west. There was, however, a direct underground train from South Ealing to Piccadilly, which is a short walk from Frith Street. Perhaps the peacefulness compensated for the journey. It does not sound, however, the kind of place in which he could easily have entertained 'Alice'. Maybe he saw her out of London. There is a photograph, from about this time, of her in the garden of a house in a rural setting which is not Scotland, with a Pekinese in her lap. The photographer is Baird himself; his shadow, in overcoat and hat against the chill of summer, can clearly be seen (see plate 16).

In an article in the *Wireless World and Radio Review* in January 1925, Baird described a new development: the picture was now formed by a lamp traversing 'a ground glass screen'. He stressed the difficulties of producing true television, while being typically reticent about his own progress:

> The letter 'H', for example, can be clearly transmitted, but the hand, moved in front of the transmitter, is reproduced only as a blurred out-line. A face is exceptionally difficult to send with the experimental apparatus, but, with careful focussing, a white oval, with dark patches for the eyes and mouth, appears at the receiving end and the mouth can be clearly seen opening and closing.[3]

Bill Fox recalled, three years later, a demonstration of this very phenom-enon at Frith Street:

> Baird took me into a nearby room and introduced me to a small box, in one corner of which the image appeared. This was only connected by cable with the transmitting apparatus, and it proved the soundness of his method of synchronisation. When the two pieces of apparatus had settled down to their job the image was steady. There was no 'hunting' for it by varying the speed of the receiver in an endeavour to keep pace with the transmitter. They followed each other as faithfully as a man's shadow. On that crude apparatus I saw the first wink and other facial movements transmitted by television.[4]

As early as January 1925 Day and Baird were discussing the formation of a company to exploit Baird's invention. The problem of money as well as the bemused response even of the informed general public still persisted. The first is illustrated by the fact that on 3 February Baird was forced to borrow £8 from Day, to be 'deducted in full from any sums received from any syndicate in respect of Television being brought out as a company'.[1] The second is exemplified by Baird's own anecdote from the period 1924-5:

> Mr Gray, the General Manager of the Marconi Company, had once lived next door to us in Helensburgh. One day I thought I would call and see if I could get him to take an interest in what I was doing. I called at Marconi House, sent in my name, 'Mr Baird from Helensburgh,' and after half an hour in the waiting room was shown into a large office where an elderly man sat behind a large, important looking desk.
>
> I said, 'Good morning,' 'Good morning,' said Mr Gray. 'Are you interested in television?' said I. 'Not in the very slightest degree, no interest whatsoever,' said Mr Gray.
>
> His disclaimer was as emphatic and as disapproving as if I had asked him if he was interested in brothels.[5]

Someone else, however, was interested. Early in 1925, two men called at Frith Street. They were Anthony de Bosdari, who had seen Baird's demonstrations in Hastings, and his friend, Gordon Selfridge Jnr, the son of the founder of Selfridge's store, who was looking for an attraction for the firm's birthday celebrations in March. Baird produced a mask of white paper with holes for the eyes and mouth. By covering the gaps with strips of paper, he was able to transmit from one room to the other images of the mask winking and shutting its mouth. A deal was struck. For fifty guineas, Baird would give three demonstrations of television a day for three weeks, and answer questions from the public. In keeping with the company's policy that any customer who pointed out an error of fact in an advertisement received a financial reward, the store's handout for the 'first public demonstration of television' was a masterpiece of understated accuracy:

> For many years experiments have been conducted ... the apparatus that is here being demonstrated is the first to be successful. ... [It] is, of course, absolutely 'in the rough' – the question of finance is always an important one for the inventor. But it does, undoubtedly, transmit an instantaneous picture. The picture is flickering and defective, and at present only simple pictures can be sent successfully; but Edison's first phonograph announced that 'Mary had a little lamb' in a way that only hearers who were 'in the secret' could understand. ... Unquestionably

the present experimental apparatus can be similarly perfected and refined.

We should perhaps explain that we are in no way financially interested in this remarkable invention; the demonstrations are taking place here only because we know that our friends will be interested in something that should rank with the greatest inventions of the century.*

Only one person at a time could look down the funnel and see the outlines of different shapes transmitted over a distance of a few metres, by means of an apparatus that appeared to be constructed largely of cardboard and powered by means of a bicycle chain. The demonstration was seen by scientists and technicians, as well as by ordinary members of the public. Two visitors in particular recorded their impressions.

The first contributed an anonymous article to the distinguished scientific journal *Nature*, in which he concluded, 'Mr Baird has overcome many practical difficulties, but we are afraid there are many more to be surmounted before the ideal television is accomplished.' The description of the apparatus includes a new feature at the receiving end, a neon tube which 'causes light to appear on a screen in positions corresponding to the part of the object being dealt with'.[6]

The other was a stunningly attractive, dark-haired music student from South Africa. Just turned eighteen, she had been dragooned into attending the demonstration by her authoritarian mother. For her, 'The invention had the effect which all mechanical things have on me and gave me a feeling of bewilderment and faint nausea.'[7]

P R Bird, assistant technical editor of the *Popular Wireless and Radio Review*, gave a full account of the demonstration in the issue of 23 May 1925, illustrated with cutaway drawings of the system:

> At first the inventor was invisible, hidden behind his invention, which was spread out over half a dozen tables, and overflowed a floor space about the size of an ordinary room. Across the middle of the space provided an artificial wall had been erected. It was about a foot thick, with the transmitter on one side of it, and the receiving apparatus on the other.
>
> There were accumulators, arc lamps, switches, H. T. batteries, Ford coils, P. O. relays, neon tubes, chokes, two or three dozen L. F. transformers, a big biscuit tin (Rich Mixed), and several small electric motors which bore a strong family resemblance to electric fans, from which the blades had been detached. Evidently financial difficulties had

not deterred the inventor, and when his resources were low his resourcefulness was unbounded.

'How does it work,' I asked Mr Baird, when he was able to disengage himself from some interested old ladies, one of whom had incautiously touched the wiring, and almost succeeded in connecting 3,000 volts across herself.

'It's a long story,' he said.[8]

The article goes on to describe the system for the interested layman. Then by way of demonstration, Baird produced the paper mask.

'I'll make it wink,' shouted the inventor, covering and uncovering one of its eyes. The uncanny, flickering image at my end promptly winked at me in unison, shutting and opening one eye in the most flagrant and uncommonly knowing fashion. ... I am certain of one thing. However fair to behold the wireless pictures of the future may be, and whatever beauties Television may bring in time to come, I shall never forget the grinning gargoyle that Mr Baird showed me – the first face I had ever seen by wireless.[8]

The Selfridge's demonstration appears to have been followed immediately by one at the department store Whiteley's. Day wrote (4 April), 'I have been expecting a visit from you regarding the settlement of Whiteley's, and to know what has been done with the prospect to forming a projected company. I sent a large number of friends to Whiteley's from here, so that something should certainly transpire.'

That nothing seems to have transpired may well have been due to the fact that Baird, weakened by the strain of making so many public appearances, now had to spend three weeks in bed with a recurrence of his chronic problems. Day took it upon himself to dun Selfridge's for the money due to Baird for the demonstrations, half of which he seemed to feel was owed to him.

Technically, Day was probably right, though he later grudgingly agreed to waive his claim. In the meantime he had written to Baird (24 April), offering to sell out his share in the arrangement for £500, and giving his partner the 'option of dealing with this for four weeks from this day, and trust in that time you will have found someone that will be able to help you further the patent and your ideas for Television'. He pointed out also that he had so far spent between £400 and £500 on developing the 'idea'. If that is so, then Baird had spent at least that amount out of his own pocket.

It may have been simply frustration that prompted Day to make this move. He may, however, also have been influenced by the fact that Dr Fournier d'Albe had in the meantime given a private demonstration of his rival system, by means of which 'only rough outlines of moving images were transmitted'.[9] Instead of dividing the image into a series of little sections of light and darkness and sending these in very rapid succession, as Baird was doing and television still does, d'Albe, who had already invented the optophone whereby blind people could 'read' print, was attempting to send the whole picture at once, each spot of it being transmitted on a different frequency.

At this point an embattled Baird appealed to Buchanan, with Harris and Mephy, the third great ally of his youth. Buchanan was starring with Elsie and June Randolph in *Boodle*, a British musical comedy based on a celebrated farce, *The New Clown*, at the Empire Theatre, Leicester Square.[10]

> One night, early in 1925, as he was leaving the stage door after his show he was surrounded by the usual supplicants as well as fans. Elsie Randolph has recalled how he said, 'Gather round everybody – here comes another touch.' At this point one of the less presentable characters waiting at the stage door called out, 'Hello, Chump.' Recognising his old school nickname, Jack turned to find it was his boyhood friend, John Logie Baird. He told Jack of his difficulties in arousing any interest in his new invention, the television.[11]

Jack Buchanan responded with a gesture which may be unique in the chequered history of the relationship between art and science. On 1 May he gave a lunch for members of the press and wireless enthusiasts in a private room at Romano's restaurant in the Strand. At the end of the meal he made a short but eloquent speech.

> I have not heard many actors orate off the stage, and Jack Buchanan introducing his friend, John L Baird, the inventor of television, to a small company of us at lunch at Romano's yesterday was a surprise.
>
> He has a quiet manner, and he speaks in perfectly rounded periods with just a touch of brogue that adds attraction to a Sassenach audience. He was never at a loss for a word, and he talked sense.
>
> After lunch we were shown lots of pulleys and wheels and bits of cardboard, and told exactly how we were going to be able to see everything in the future by wireless.[12]

This sounds to be the voice of the arts, not the science, correspondent of his paper. Others who wrote up the event were appreciative not only of the introduction but also of the demonstration, in the course of which Baird went further than he had before, encouraging members of his audience to grimace in front of the transmitting end of the apparatus.

> Mr Buchanan said that Mr Baird had achieved his end by rough apparatus, and, unfortunately, he had exhausted his private means and could not go on. A few months now, with the necessary money, a perfected instrument would bring the invention to completion. Its possibilities were enormous. It made possible for 'seeing' what broad-casting had already made possible for hearing.
>
> Mr Baird, before showing his apparatus, explained that he was not sending a shadowgraph, but the actual picture of an object.
>
> The members of the party were then able to see each other's face in turn, in another part of the room, the winking of an eye or the opening and shutting of the mouth being plainly visible.[13]

Another report stressed that 'there is no reason why speech should not be transmitted simultaneously with action – an idea which opens up endless possibilities for the future'.[14]

The lunch received a lot of newspaper coverage, particularly in the more popular and the provincial press. As one set of headlines put it, 'Seeing a Wink by Wireless. Solving Problem of Television. Dawn of New Era. Scots Inventor's Big Forward Step.'[15] It was probably at this opportune moment that the prospectus was issued of a private limited company, to be called Television Ltd, with a nominal capital represented by 5000 ordinary shares of £1 each. The object of the company was to carry on with Baird's work and perfect a 'finished commercial machine'. The prospects were enticing.

> In a comparatively short space of time it is no rash prophecy to say that 'lookers in' will be almost as common as 'listeners in'. Picture houses will probably be the first to be provided with Television machines, and audiences in all parts of the country will be able to watch the finish of the Derby and other topical events at the moment they are occurring.
>
> The Company is the first to be formed to develop this coming industry, and holds out the prospect of very substantial returns to the shareholders.[1]

The description of the present state of the invention reflected precisely the situation Baird himself had described in the *Wireless World and Radio Review* the previous January.[3]

> The results are, of course, still very crude, as the apparatus is purely experimental, but they are sufficient to clearly prove the practicability of the invention. A face can be transmitted, and appears as a white outline with dark patches for the eyes and mouth, and the mouth can be clearly seen opening and closing.[1]

It may have been Baird's insistence on making such modest technical claims which was instrumental in an outburst on the part of Day, which he despatched the few hundred yards to Frith Street by registered post on 11 May; that, and the fact that Baird had presented him with a bill.

> I have assisted you in answer to your many requests, and your promises that you were going to achieve a definite result, which would mean that you had produced a commodity that would at least be marketable; but so far nothing has transpired, and you now bring before me a foolish statement charging me with all manner of items of which I know nothing whatever, and to which I am certainly not going to be made a party. ... So disgusted am I with you in your manner of dealing with money and accounts that I beg to give you notice that you cannot call on me for another penny piece to help you in your unfortunate speculations.[1]

He went on to say that he had cancelled his liability with regard to the rent of 22 Frith Street, and threatened legal action if Baird did not return the money he had borrowed and pay the account for goods supplied. He reminded his unfortunate partner that half the 'goods and chattels' at Frith Street belonged to Day's firm. He continued:

> It will be best for all concerned if you agree to purchase my holding in the patent of Television forthwith. ... I feel that you have told me a direct untruth when you state that you had no knowledge that I would not put any more money into your invention. ... I hardly think that you can say you have done your best towards forming a company or disposing of my share in your patent of Television. However, if you think your policy is a good one, I do not, and remember you will do nothing whatever with this patent unless you have my sanction so to do

in writing. I will rely no more on word of mouth, and I find that you are not a man of your word.[1]

It would also appear that Baird had been unduly secretive in not revealing his private address and in failing to be at home to 'vast numbers' of callers at Frith Street. Whatever the truth of the matter, it is difficult to see how Baird could continue under such provocation. He went to see Day, however, on Tuesday, 12 May, and an arrangement was agreed, though Day now asked that Baird should find a purchaser for his share in the patent by the end of the week.[1]

No purchaser materialised, or Baird had correctly assessed his partner's mettle. Television Ltd was registered on 11 June 1925, with its offices at 22 Frith Street. The two directors, Baird and Day, each took up twenty of the 2000 founders' shares of one shilling each – there were also 2900 ordinary shares of £1 each. On 12 June Baird and Day entered into an agreement with the company to sell 'the whole of the Vendors right, title and interest in or benefit of the Patents and Inventions'.[16]

It still, however, seemed to have been left to Baird to drum up support for the new company. He employed as promoter a Mr Brooks, the expenses of whose efforts to interest potential shareholders appear to have exceeded the amount of cash support he had managed to achieve. Baird's Inglis cousins, James and George, however, put up between them £500.[17] There was also, as a result presumably of the press coverage of the Romano's lunch, help of another kind. The managing director of Hart's Accumulators (no relation to John Hart of Falkirk, though he dealt with them)[18] donated £200 worth of batteries. The General Electric Company made Baird a present of £200 worth of valves. Said Baird, 'We subsequently bought thousands of pounds of valves and batteries from them. But for hard-headed business men to give £200 worth of goods to a dilapidated and penniless crank in a garret was a phenomenon worth recording.'[19]

For what the crank was doing at this time in the cramped confines of his garret we have only his own account:

> Light, light, more light to provide was the most serious problem with which I was faced. The photoelectric cells then available were quite unresponsive to the light given by my apparatus. In my efforts to increase this I built enormous discs. One was as big as eight foot in diameter and had fitted round it spirals of bigger and bigger lenses, until I got to using lenses eight inches in diameter. Light, light, more light. I soon reached a limit in this direction, my enormous wheels almost filled the little lab;

and as they had to revolve at an absolute minimum of 150 revolutions per minute, they were distinctly dangerous. The discs were made in sizes up to five feet in thick cardboard, and beyond that size I used three-ply wood. On more than one occasion lenses broke loose, striking the walls or roof like bomb shells. The apparatus would then get out of balance and jump from one side of the lab to the other until it was stopped or the disc tore itself to pieces. I had some exciting moments.[20]

It was exciting, if not also alarming, for the people working underneath. One day, there was a call for Baird on the phone in the office. A secretary climbed the stairs to fetch him. When the door was opened, her first sight was of a disembodied head, and she fainted away. The head was that of a ventriloquist's dummy; Baird called him Stooky Bill, which was later used as a telegraphic address by the Baird company. Stooky Bill was Baird's stand-in. No human could have coped with the heat of the arc lamps for more than a minute or so.[21]

The basic stumbling block, as Baird explained in an article in December 1926,

Did not lie in the mechanical or optical part of the apparatus, but on the electrical side of the problem, and essentially in the light sensitive cell. I made many attempts to improve this, including the construction of a cell made from visual purple out of a human eye. There was considerable difficulty in obtaining the eye, but at length I was fortunate in finding a surgeon with a keen scientific interest who supplied a fresh human optic. This cell when first constructed gave a quite appreciable reaction to light.[22]

There is a different version of this episode in Baird's memoir:

I decided to make an experimental cell using [visual purple], and called at the Charing Cross Opthalmic Hospital, and asked to see the chief surgeon. I told him I wanted an eye for some research work I was doing on visual purple. He thought I was a doctor and was very helpful.

'You've come at an appropriate time,' he said, 'I am just taking out an eye, and will let you have it, if you will take a seat until the operation is over.'

I was handed an eye wrapped in cotton wool – a gruesome object. I made a crude effort to dissect this with a razor, but gave it up and threw the whole mess into the canal.[23]

When he composed the latter account, Baird was living up to the image he had acquired of the eccentric inventor.

It is not known precisely by what accident, or by what sequence or combination of adjustments to his system, Baird arrived at his goal, but on Friday, 2 October 1925, the face of Stooky Bill appeared on the screen with absolute clarity, not, as hitherto, in stark outlines of black and white, but with proper tones and detail. Shaking with excitement, Baird stumbled down the attic stairs and grabbed by the arm the most suitable human guinea-pig: it was the twenty-year-old office 'boy', William Taynton.

A broad outline of what happened next can be pieced together from the accounts, written or recorded many years later, of both participants in this epoch-making experiment.[24] An intrigued but apprehensive Taynton was taken up into a laboratory in which chaos reigned, in the form of a hotch-potch of apparatus, with wires dangling all over the place. He was sat down in front of the transmitting end, and told to get in as close as possible, while Baird busied himself at the other extremity. Taynton stood the heat from the lamps for as long as he could, and then drew away from the whirring disc.

An agitated Baird emerged. When he saw Taynton mopping the sweat off his face and realised what the problem was, he delved into his pocket, thrust a 2s.6d. coin into Taynton's hand, and gently manoeuvred him back into position.

After a moment or so, he asked Taynton to put out his tongue. Taynton obliged, though he privately thought that this was a rather rude thing to do.

'That's fine,' said Baird. 'Now move your head about.' Then he shouted, 'William, I've seen you, I've seen you!'

Taynton was then persuaded to change positions, and, sure enough, he could recognise the flickering features of Baird's face on the tiny, two inches by three inches, screen.

Taynton was thus arguably the first person to be shown live on true television.[25] He was certainly the first to be paid for appearing on television.

There is, however, some controversy with regard to the first person to appear on television in public: not about whether he was the first, but whether he appeared at all. In about 1990, a retired Falkirk businessman, Robert Shaw, proposed that a plaque, which he had designed himself, be mounted on what corresponded to the wall of the old Temperance Cafe in the town, commemorating the fact that 'John Logie Baird demonstrated television in this building in 1925'. His story, the basics of which he stuck to for the rest of his life (he died in 1995), through numerous interviews with local and television historians, and journalists, was this.

In 1925-6, he was a continuation student in wireless telephony on a course held in Falkirk Old High School. This part is confirmed by his certificate, a copy of which is in the archives of Falkirk Museums; he attended the full fifty hours and was adjudged first class with eighty-five per cent. One day in November or December 1925, his tutor suggested he should go to a demonstration of 'seeing by wireless' at the Temperance Cafe. When Shaw arrived, there were just two men in the room, John Logie Baird and John Hart. Shortly afterwards there was an influx of men in civilian clothes. There was also a woman with a baby, which disturbed the proceedings and had to be carried out.

Baird gave an introductory talk, and then picked Shaw out of the audience, probably because he was the youngest person there, and took him into another room, which was darkened. Baird sat him down in front of a contraption which scanned his face with a flickering light. There was the sound of applause from the main room, and he was told that his face had appeared on the screen.[26]

Just before Jean, John Hart's widow, died in 1992 at the age of ninety, Shaw travelled to Tain in the Scottish Highlands with a list of questions for her. She confirmed that there had indeed been a demonstration at that time, for Royal Air Force personnel, and she had been the woman with the baby[27] – John Hart junior was born in March 1925. It may be significant, too, that John Hart senior served in the RAF during World War II.

In spite of exhaustive research, no documentary evidence has ever come to light to support Shaw's story.[28] In particular a search in the records of the Temperance Trust, which contain details of hall lets and bookings, has revealed nothing which 'could even tangentially refer to such a demonstration'.[29] The balance of probability, however, suggests that what Shaw claimed is true. Baird would hardly have proceeded with his plan to hold his first official demonstration in London without first organising a trial run. There was nothing in the press about any Falkirk demonstration because he did not want any publicity to dilute the effect of the London launch. And for this reason also, he would have chosen a place as far away from London as he could, before a specially invited audience.

Until or unless any corroboration of this demonstration materialises, the last word on the subject may perhaps be given to Shaw's former accountant, who heard the same story from his client: 'Mr Shaw's recall was very good. He was one of the old school, and certainly not given to flights of fancy.'[30] A man might dissemble to his wife, or even to his lawyer, but not surely to his accountant!

There could, however, be other contenders for the title of the first person publicly to be televised, if we knew their names. An inconspicuous, anonymous piece appeared in the Dundee *Evening Telegraph* in 1959, 'I Saw the Birth of British TV':

> [Baird's] trouble was that he was 'before his time'. When he had succeeded in transmitting the images of live people to the TV screen, sound broadcasting was still in its infancy.
>
> It was the end of 1925 when I saw the birth of British television in a Soho house at Baird's invitation.
>
> I had never seen anything in real life more like a Heath Robinson gadget. Parts of the apparatus were tied together with lengths of string. Cardboard was used instead of metal. Baird was showing himself, at least, to be a master of improvisation. ...
>
> I was a member of one of the groups to whom he showed the results of his work.
>
> He did not televise dolls, photographs or other objects – he televised us. He sent another man and myself up to the attic while the rest remained with him to watch the small screen. Upstairs, we stood close to a great electric light, the globe larger than our heads.
>
> Immediately in front of us was a double cardboard disc, 18 inches in diameter. All round the circumference at short intervals large circular holes were cut and the two discs – held together as one by pieces of string tied through each hole – revolved at a good speed.
>
> Below, Baird and the others watched a small-screen reproduction of our laughing, face-pulling and manual gestures. We changed over frequently to present the problem of identification and we shook hands as if to prove to the viewers that we were both really there together.
>
> Afterwards we two became the viewers, and the others the performers. ...
>
> Baird was delighted, in his dour way, at having succeeded in establishing the principle. 'You can see for yourself that there is no doubt about it now,' he said. 'I only need the money to develop it, to get rid of the flickering and improve the lighting, and then we shall be ready for public television.'[31]

Even though it was written at a distance of thirty-five years, there are reasons to trust the veracity of this account. The double cardboard disc, for instance, recurs in the reports of Baird's original apparatus that he demonstrated in January 1926, with the bits of string replaced by screws.[32] The rest of the account concerns a demonstration of cinema television in 1937 whose accuracy can be verified.[33]

Whatever progress Baird had made, the relationship between himself and Day had reached another crisis. Baird had asked Day to invest more money in the undertaking. Day wrote on 18 November:

> I am sorry I cannot take up more shares in this company, and rather than stand in the light of this wonderful patent, I would be inclined to sell out my share in the company for a sum of £500 cash. ... Therefore, you have my authority, if you can find a suitable purchaser who will be interested in the patent to further it, that you can introduce them to me, and I will dispose of my holding to them accordingly.[1]

This time, Baird did have a 'suitable purchaser'! He had met up again, and joined forces, with Oliver Hutchinson, now manufacturing as well as selling soap. On 16 December, Day formally resigned as a director of Television Ltd, and ceded his rights and his shares to Hutchinson.[1] Whether or not he knew about the breakthrough of 2 October is largely immaterial, and the same applies to any other developments on which Baird had quietly been working – on 1 September he had filed two patents which referred to transmitting images in colour.[34] Day wanted a marketable commodity, and in the eighteen months that the partnership had lasted, Baird had not produced it. Three further communications from Day to Baird survive, all written after the first official demonstration of true television.[1] They display a certain amount of exasperation, but they are not the letters of a man who believes he has been duped.

5
Vision on
1926

The official launch was fixed for Tuesday, 26 January 1926.[1] It was the cause of a great deal of heart-searching on the part of both Baird and Hutchinson. Baird's attitude was straightforward:

> I was definitely able to transmit the living image, and it was the first time it had been done. But how to convince the sceptical, hide-bound, select and exclusive scientific world? Would they admit that a wretched nonentity working with soap boxes in a garret had done something which many of them had stated was not possible? I wanted to show the results to the world, to nail down at once that I was first. I was extremely nervous in case while I waited, someone else achieved television and gave a show before I did.[2]

Surprisingly, it was the arch-showman Hutchinson, some of whose methods of publicity were to antagonise the very people he hoped to impress, who wanted to hold back. 'He was terrified that someone would copy my work, and particularly frightened (with very good cause) that the big wireless concerns would be given an impetus to take up television research, and use my work as a guide.'[2]

A compromise was agreed. Selected guests, including members of the Royal Institution, were invited, with a reporter from *The Times* to represent the press. In the event there were several controlled leaks to other papers in the weeks leading up to the demonstration,[3] of which a reporter from the *Daily Chronicle* had a preview on 26 January. His piece (27 January), in which he used the term 'Televisor', which Baird had coined to describe the receiving end of his apparatus, scooped *The Times*, whose brief factual account did not appear until 28 January.

The demonstration itself was a triumph of organisation over chaos. Bill Fox was drafted in to act as doorman. He was posted at the top of the several flights of narrow concrete stairs from the street, with orders not to let anyone through unless they had signed the visitors' book, and then only in batches of six. The guests, some with their ladies, arrived in twos and threes, in full evening dress. Once inside the workshop, having negotiated the clutter of cables and other equipment all over the floor, they saw, on the tiny screen, in thirty-two-line definition, the unmistakable but flickering and blurred image of Stooky Bill, transmitted from one room to another between two machines that were connected by land line. Then they were given the chance to see each other on television. Fox was able to overhear some of the guests as they squeezed themselves out of the workshop and down the stairs. One comment, by Sanger Shepherd, a man who had studied the telegraphy of photographs, in particular stuck in his mind: 'Baird has got it. The rest is merely a matter of £. s. d.'[4] If only it had been just a question of money!

The apparatus used in the demonstration incorporated, at the transmitting end, a lensed disc, made of a double layer of cardboard, about two feet in diameter with a double spiral of two sets of eight lenses, revolving three hundred times a minute. The lenses, each about three inches in diameter and secured by three screws, were the same as those used in bicycle lamps. Left to itself, this disc divided the image into eight strips. The final picture of thirty-two lines was obtained by passing the light impulses from the transmitting disc through a slotted disc, and then through a further disc, containing a single spiral slot, rotating once for every four revolutions of the lensed disc. This multiplied the number of strips by four. At the receiving end of the apparatus was an aluminium disc 17½ inches in diameter, containing a single spiral of thirty-two holes. The final picture was 2½ inches wide by 3¼ inches deep, though this was capable of being magnified.[5]

Baird himself later, in his typically deprecating fashion, stressed the hazards experienced by the guests:

> In one room was a large whirling disc, a most dangerous device, had they known it, liable to burst at any minute and hop around the room with showers of broken glass. … One of the visitors who was being transmitted had a long white beard, part of which blew into the wheel. Fortunately he escaped with the loss of a certain amount of hair. He was a thorough sportsman and took the accident in good part and insisted on continuing the experiment and having his face transmitted.[6]

There was the further potential hazard of the heat of the floodlights, estimated by an independent technician who assessed the system shortly afterwards at 500 candle power at a distance of one foot,[7] but by the first

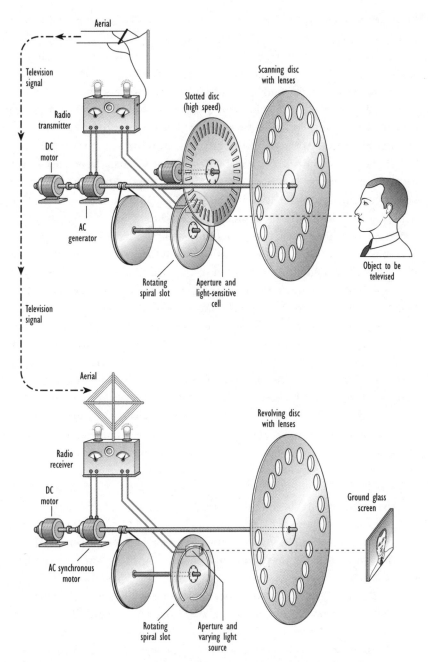

Figure 1: Basic principle of mechanical television, from Baird's lecture to the Physical and Optical Societies, 6 January 1927. The object to be televised was placed in a strong floodlight, and the image was then scanned by a spinning perforated disc. The system was capable of being modified by placing the light source *behind* the disc and scanning the object with the moving light beam. This is the spotlight system, which helped to overcome problems with the limited sensitivity of the photo-cells available, and with the heat of the floodlights.

honorary secretary of the Television Society at 16,000 candle power at four feet.[8] Officially it would be another two years before Baird employed an alternative means of scanning, which was less uncomfortable for the subject. Only a few days before the 26 January demonstration, he had applied for a patent for what became known as the 'flying-spot' method, which could be employed to scan either a subject or a piece of film.[9] This differs from the floodlight method of scanning in that the single source of light is focussed through the spiral of lenses in the disc onto the subject, from which it is reflected onto a light cell, or onto a series of cells working in parallel. In the case of film or other transparency, the light penetrates through the subject being scanned, onto the cell beyond it. Because the beam is focussed, far less light is needed than with the floodlight method.

Baird may have been experimenting with the flying spot during his Hastings period,[10] though he did not publicly describe it until 1928;[11] it illustrates the driving force and vision of the man that, at a time of the year and in a place where his appalling susceptibility to colds was most marked, he could be working ahead on improvements to a system of scanning which had not yet officially been demonstrated in public. Circumstantial evidence suggests that he tried out the flying-spot method at the debatable Falkirk demonstration in 1925.[12] This is consistent with the assertion of a modern authority that it was the flying-spot system which Baird used for the demonstration on 26 January 1926.[13] It would hardly have been diplomatic, still less safe, to subject members of the Royal Institution to such intensity of heat in the confined space of a Soho attic room. The secrecy can be explained as well as justified by the fact that though it was possible to patent a particular flying-spot working system, the method itself could not be protected.

The flying-spot technique was used by the Bell Telephone Laboratories of American Telephone and Telegraph on 7 April 1927, in the course of the next significant public demonstration of a working television system, to which it was estimated that almost a thousand engineers and other experts had contributed over several years.[14]

Another competitor was the American prodigy, Philo Taylor Farnsworth, who had been fascinated by television ever since high school. Barely out of his teens, he had got financial backing in San Francisco for the establishment of Television Laboratories, from which on 7 January 1927 he filed a patent for an electronic system using a cathode-ray camera tube (later known as an image dissector).[15] He demonstrated his system on 7 September 1927. He could at this time transmit only straight lines,[16] but the cathode-ray tube had come to stay.

It would be wrong to conclude that Baird was indifferent to electronic methods of transmitting and receiving television images, though it would appear that he did not know enough about electronics to devise such a system from scratch, or to guide effectively any purely electronic development of television.[17] In any case, he felt, quite rightly, that results could be obtained more quickly by mechanical means. He was, however, working with electronic systems from 1932 onwards.

After the Frith Street demonstration, Hutchinson soon got things moving. One day in February 1926 the operation was transferred to the fourth floor of Motograph House, Upper St Martin's Lane, WC1, which gave it more space, and probably more air. On 15 February proposals were adopted to restructure Television Ltd. These took effect on 4 March. The nominal capital was increased to £9050, made up of 8900 First Participating Cumulative Preference Shares of £1 each and 1000 new Ordinary Shares of one shilling each. By September, forty-three individuals or organisations had shares in the company, taking up all the ordinary shares and 7320 of the preference shares. George and James Inglis between them took up 1250 preference shares. Another individual with a substantial holding was Captain J Y M Broderip, a friend of Hutchinson, with 625 ordinary shares, and a further 625 held jointly with Baird and Hutchinson.[18]

Of the people who came to Motograph House to see demonstrations of television, two had qualifications which make their accounts particularly significant. E G Stewart, an engineer obviously of much experience, spent three hours with Baird and Hutchinson in April, after which he submitted a two-thousand-word technical report to his employers, the Gas, Light and Coke Company. The equipment that he inspected appears to have been the same that ostensibly was used in the 26 January demonstration, though that does not mean that Baird had not progressed in the meantime. As Stewart explained, 'The inventor declined to show me the interior of his apparatus as he has definitely decided to give a minimum of information upon the details of construction and operation to anyone.' He was able, however, to describe in some detail the principles of the system.[7]

Stewart was critical of the quality of the picture, which, he suggested, might be improved by the use of 'a more sensitive photoelectric cell. This cell is a closely guarded secret of the inventor and he told me only sufficient of its construction to demonstrate that it was entirely different from existing cells on the market.' He concluded that, subject to assurances that the picture could and would be improved, 'the invention is one worthy of financial encouragement and development. It is assumed of course that successful television is a needed and valuable invention.' He was, however, opposed to the notion that the apparatus should be put on the market as it stood. The public would quickly tire of such crude reproduction, and personalities who appeared would be positively 'scared off' by it.[7]

Dr Alexander Russell FRS, principal of Faraday House, was probably referring to a different system in his report in *Nature* in July 1926. At about this time Baird was working with a picture three inches wide by seven inches deep, consisting of thirty lines (or strips), with a picture frequency of 12½ per second, compared with a cinema film frequency at that time of sixteen per second.

> Naturally the results are far from perfect. The image cannot be compared with that produced by a good kinematograph film. The likeness, however, was unmistakable and all the motions are reproduced with absolute fidelity. ... This is the first time we have seen real television, and, so far as we know, Mr Baird is the first to have accomplished this marvellous feat. ... Those of us who remember the advent of the telephone in 1876, and remember also how little its importance was then realised, will hesitate to criticise this new invention.[19]

This last sentiment was one which some individuals might have done better to heed.

The 26 January demonstration had some far-reaching effects. The previous December, there had been a demonstration by the Admiralty Research Laboratory at Teddington, Middlesex, of a rudimentary television system, the work of Dr R T Beatty. Its purpose was to spot aircraft at sea. In the light of the comparative success and greater potential of the Baird system, both the Admiralty Research Laboratory and the Air Ministry abandoned their own developments in favour of following the progress of commercial systems.[20] Shortly after that, on 16 March, Harry E Wimperis, Director of Scientific Research at the Air Ministry, wrote an internal memorandum recommending the establishment of a permanent joint research programme with the Admiralty into wireless telegraphy systems for offensive pilotless aircraft and for defence against them, radio-photography and radio-vision (that is, television), and 'other applications of tele-mechanics'.[21] That Baird was involved in these activities is confirmed by a letter of 18 December 1926, marked 'Secret', from Wimperis to his opposite number at the Admiralty, referring to a letter from Television Ltd to Lieutenant-Colonel Lefroy (in his capacity as head of wireless research), proposing a demonstration of 'automatic spotting by radio transmission', and suggesting that the reply should come from the Admiralty. The letter concludes, 'I would add that the Air

Ministry would be very willing to give any assistance to you that might lie in their power in furtherance of any work of this nature.'[22]

The letter from Television Ltd was from Hutchinson, and followed a meeting the previous day at Motograph House attended by himself, Baird, Beatty, and Lefroy. The discussion centred on a television system for spotting and marking on a map things seen from the air.[23] On 15 October Baird applied for a patent[24] covering several methods of scanning. Out of this patent he extracted a further patent,[25] 'of value for military purposes', in which the position of what is being spotted appears on a transparent map at the receiving station in the form of a luminous cross.

For whatever reason, the Admiralty decided to cease taking any immediate interest in television at the end of 1926, and in February 1927 the Air Ministry followed suit.[26] The Army, however, was at this time looking into ways of utilising new inventions for signalling, and would have been scrutinising patent applications for any that might seem appropriate to military needs. Baird's application on 11 May 1927,[27] 'Improvements in or Relating to the Reception of Radio Signals', may well have come to the notice of the authorities in this way.

On 3 May 1926, the cinema production company Empire News Bulletins had announced that it had been granted exclusive cinema rights in news about television: 'All future information on the progress of the British invention – television – will reach the cinema screen exclusively through the Bulletin.'[28] Thus did one media organisation ensure that it kept track of what its upstart potential rival was doing. Empire News Bulletins was one of five such organisations (the others were British Paramount News, British Pathé, Gaumont British News, and Gaumont Graphic News), which, during the 1920s and 1930s, made and distributed newsreels which were shown as adjuncts to cinema programmes and in cinemas showing exclusively news and short films.

The television pictures being produced at this time were still undeniably crude, as was reflected on 25 June 1926, when Television Ltd notched up another 'first', with the publication of a photograph in the *Electrician* of a human face taken from a televisor. The picture is said to be of Hutchinson; if this is so, then one must agree with Baird's own judgment in *Experimental Wireless and the Wireless Engineer* that it was 'very imperfect but ... these defects were chiefly due to the mechanical and electrical imperfections in construction. They are being steadily eliminated. The quality either of the reception or of the photograph itself left much to be desired.'[29]

Somehow, however, Hutchinson had on 4 January 1926 conjured up from the prevailing technical situation a formal request to the Postmaster General for a licence to transmit television pictures from London, Glasgow, Manchester, and Belfast. Since there was no precedent, bemused officials were seeking legal advice when Hutchinson sprang into further action on 11 January, with a letter to the secretary of the General Post Office (GPO):

> The Television Company was hoping to hear from you stating that there was no objection as we have several important demonstrations to give. Also we are having made five hundred receiving sets and until we know officially that there is no objection we cannot offer these to our clients.[31]

These 'receiving sets' were simply a gleam in an Irishman's eye, if not a figment of his imagination, even though he boldly went into print with the claim.[32] Baird's organisation did not begin manufacturing them for general distribution until 1929; they first became available in January 1930.[33]

After considerable sparring between the company and the GPO, on 29 June Hutchinson tried a new tactic, similar to that used today in corporate differences of opinion with government:

> A tempting offer has been made for the world rights in our invention by a powerful American syndicate. Acceptance of this offer on our part would necessarily mean the transference of our apparatus to the USA. It is for many reasons our desire to keep control of television in this country, but if the necessary facilities for advancement are withheld we shall have no alternative but to make the best deal we can and allow the invention to go elsewhere.[34]

This certainly had an effect, and after some negotiation experimental licences to transmit on a wavelength of 200m and a power of 250W from Motograph House and Green Gables, the Baird laboratory in Harrow, on the outskirts of London, were issued on 5 August 1926. The call-signs allocated were respectively 2TV and 2TW. The latter was never used, as the station was only employed for receiving. From 5 August 1926 until late 1929, thirty-line transmissions were made from Motograph House. The 2TV call-sign is still operative; it is administered by Ray Herbert, a former employee of the Baird company, on behalf of the Baird Museum Amateur Radio Society.

According to Baird's own account, he had already satisfied himself that such transmissions were now feasible:

> With transmission accomplished in the laboratory I was anxious to transmit over a distance and got in touch with Mr [H L] Kirke, Chief

Research Engineer of the BBC. He was very interested and helpful, and several transmissions were arranged, the television picture being sent from my laboratory to the BBC by telephone line. Mr Kirke then put it on the ether through the BBC wireless transmitter. I received it again by wireless at my laboratory.

The picture came through the BBC practically unaltered, and it is interesting to record that the BBC actually transmitted television in 1926, although unofficially I was bound to silence and did not mention the matter at the time. It amused me to hear people say that while I could send television in the laboratory it could not be sent over the BBC. Unfortunately the transmission came to an abrupt end. Someone 'up above' at the BBC, Kirke would not say who, had ordered the transmission to cease.[35]

The 'distance', if he was referring to a transmission from the British Broadcasting Company's headquarters in Savoy Hill, was not very great (about six hundred metres), but the point had been made.

An intriguing sidelight on the sale of televisors had appeared in the *Falkirk Mail* on 16 January 1926, when it was reported that Hart's Radio Supplies 'have placed an order for the latest scientific marvel: The Television'. The order, for something that officially did not exist, had an even more intriguing outcome. In May 1926[36] Hart returned by train from a visit to London with a delicate piece of machinery, mounted on a wooden base. Shortly after this, he moved his premises in Falkirk to East High Street, where his son remembers the shop in the 1930s as having a framed and autographed photograph of Baird, as well as bronze-painted plaster busts of Marconi and Ramsay MacDonald, the former Labour prime minister.[37] Hart displayed the apparatus in the window of his new shop in September; fifty years later Margaret Gibb Scott recalled Baird's visits to Falkirk, and how she typed out cards for the display, explaining the workings of the various components.[38] An advertisement appeared in the *Falkirk Herald* on 18 September 1926:

> Mr Hart has just returned from the National Radio Exhibition at Olympia. During his visit he had the privilege of meeting Mr J. L. Baird (inventor of the astonishing 'TELEVISOR') who very kindly presented him with a model of his epoch-making instrument – this model was <u>ACTUALLY IN USE</u> at Mr Baird's London Laboratory.

The plaque attached to the exhibit was put on by Hart himself:[39] 'Presented to Hart Radio Supplies, Falkirk, by Mr J L Baird at 2 TV Studio – London,

September 5, 1926.' The odd thing about the date is that it was a Sunday. In selecting it for the plaque, was Hart trying to say something to posterity? The apparatus on its base was not something that could be tucked under one's arm and taken to the station in the bus or by underground railway.

That Hart should for the purposes of publicity suggest that in September he had only just acquired the apparatus is understandable if he felt that last May's news was no news. Further twists to the plot were introduced by the story in the same issue of the *Falkirk Herald* in which the advertisement appeared.

> This week Mr Baird was visited at Monograph House [sic] by Mr J Hart of Hart Radio Supplies, Falkirk, to whom he accorded a warm welcome. ... In conversation, Mr Baird said his father was born at Sunnybrae, Camelon. He himself had been in Falkirk once only, and then at the funeral of an aunt when he was very young. Mr Baird said that the instantaneous transmission of scenes or objects was now a reality. While explaining the working of the apparatus and giving a demonstration for Mr Hart's benefit, Mr Baird stated that the practical application of Television embraced a multitude of uses. All the possibilities were by no means exhausted in the few examples he gave. Simple costings indicated that a set for home use would be priced at about £30, no more than hundreds of thousands had paid to listen-in. Television would never supplant the legitimate stage or the cinema, but there was not the slightest doubt of the influence it would have on them both. Special Television theatres would spring into being. They would contain a screen, but neither orchestra or film. Each would be linked by wire to a central broadcasting station. ... Television, he believed, would have a pacific effect upon warring nations. It would show the hidden enemy. Aeroplanes would no longer wireless their scanty reports, but the electric eye within them would reproduce unerringly the entire field of action and the very shell-bursts. Stationary objects, moving troops, each tiny detail of hostile activity would be stripped of every shred of concealment. Tactics and strategy must inevitably vanish. ...
>
> [Mr Baird's] demonstration took place from Harrow-on-the-Hill. Another model he graciously presented to Mr Hart to exhibit in his premises at Falkirk. Later, he added, Mr Hart could hand the apparatus over to the local museum.[40]

It was reported the following week in the *Falkirk Mail*, whose piece was based on the story in its rival paper, that 'large crowds of people have visited the premises of Hart's Radio Supplies',[41] no doubt having been inspired by the stirring sentiments in the *Falkirk Herald*. The article in the *Herald* reads as though it was conceived, if not also written, by Hart as publicity for his shop. It must have been agreed with Baird that, for whatever reason, Baird's recent personal connections with the town would be kept secret. (That he had only been in Falkirk once, for his aunt's funeral, which took place in 1904, was repeated in the *Mail's* article.)[41] The rest of the account in the *Herald* is too glib to be accurate reportage of a chance conversation, and probably grew out of several discussions between the two friends. Nor would Baird himself have been likely to jeopardise his delicate relations with the Admiralty and the Air Ministry by discussing with a stranger the tactical uses of television in wartime; Hart, who had seen action during World War I, and was a man of technical intelligence and forethought, could well have been the source of these particular views. The article is also inaccurate in one significant respect, about which Hart might well have been ignorant. No demonstration could have taken place 'from Harrow-on-the-Hill', because the station was not being used for transmitting signals, only receiving them.[42]

The handing over of the apparatus to Hart was more likely to have been a business transaction than a gift: 'My husband visited Mr Baird in London where he helped him in some way financially and was given the transmitter on the promise that he would give it to the local museum as his grandfather had lived in Falkirk.'[43]

Baird was not concerned about the historical value of his early equipment. He could never remember what happened to his original Hastings apparatus; his wife later claimed that it 'disappeared, perhaps sold for a couple of pounds to pay the rent'.[44] Other machines were cannibalised and their parts re-used.[45] Had Hart not taken in hand this particular piece of apparatus, it would probably have been dismantled, as happened to the receiving end of the equipment which Baird demonstrated on 26 January 1926. The disc alone survives, having reappeared in 1999 and been sold to Hastings Museum along with the Baird/Day correspondence.

The Falkirk apparatus is not a televisor. Its basic components equate precisely to those at the transmitting end of the apparatus which Baird used early in 1926, if not actually at the 26 January public demonstration. A drawing of this model by Baird himself was used to illustrate his article in *Experimental Wireless and the Wireless Engineer* in December 1926, and his lecture at the Physical and Optical societies' annual exhibition on 6 January 1927.[46] In the 1930s the apparatus was on display in a room of Dollar Park House which was designated the Falkirk museum. After the curator moved on elsewhere, the museum was closed down and its contents put in store. When the museum reopened in different premises, it was under a series of curators who were more interested in the proximity of part of the Antonine Wall than in modern industrial archaeology, and the transmitter remained in oblivion. Jack Sanderson, who arrived as curator in 1973, found it among a collection of abandoned artefacts.[47] It was identified in 1975.[48]

The Falkirk transmitter is accepted as genuine,[49] or largely genuine. With the permission of Falkirk Council, it was for a few weeks in the 1960s taken out of storage and put into the temporary care of the newly-opened Falkirk College. It was found that the two circular sheets of cardboard holding the lenses had been damaged by water and had partly disintegrated. The college decided to replace these with identical materials; the lenses were then put back and fastened with the original screws.[50]

In November 1926 Ben Clapp was taken on as Baird's technical assistant – he became chief engineer the following year. Clapp was already a radio engineer of considerable expertise. His home in Coulsdon was equipped as an amateur radio station, for which he had been granted by the GPO permission to use the very high power of 1kW, enough to transmit signals across the Atlantic. The short waves (20m to 50m) used by radio amateurs could travel over much longer distances than the medium waves (200m to 500m) used for most of the British Broadcasting Company's broadcasts. One of Clapp's first jobs was to help Baird erect wireless aerials on the roof of Motograph House. Television transmissions were made to Harrow, and were also picked up as sound by radio amateurs in different parts of the country. In spite of his experience, however, Clapp was initially not made a party to the technical aspects of Baird's apparatus or even allowed into the transmission laboratory itself. Baird, by nature a generous man, was so paranoid about piracy that he could not bring himself to share his secrets even with a close colleague. Clapp also recalled that Baird perpetually suffered from the cold, 'frozen to the bone even with the windows shut tight and fires burning. He looked the part of the inventor with his great mane of bushy hair, but with him it was a necessity. If ever he had it cut, he caught a cold.'[51]

During 1926 Baird was involved in several other key developments.

> The idea occurred to me in 1926 that it should be possible to use infra-red or ultra violet rays in place of light, and so be able to send an image in complete darkness. I tried ultra violet rays first; at this time my only assistant was the office boy imported from Hutchinson's soap works. He was ignorant but amiable. The ultra violet rays affected his eyes, and he did not complain, but I got a fright and tried infra-red. I first used

electric fires to get these infra-red rays, which are practically heat rays. I could not get any result and added more fires until Wally was nearly roasted alive. Then I put in a dummy's head and added more fires and the dummy's head went up in flames.

I decided to try another tack and use the shorter infra-red waves. To get these I used ordinary electric bulbs covered with thin ebonite. This cut off all light but allowed the infra-red ray to pass. Wally sat under this without much discomfort, and after one or two adjustments I saw him on the screen, although he was in total darkness. That was again a thrill, something new and strange. I was actually seeing a person without light. Hutchinson was shown the wondrous phenomenon and great excitement prevailed.[52]

On 23 November 1926, Baird demonstrated his discovery, which he called 'noctovision', to Alexander Russell and two other observers. In a letter to *Nature* Russell stated,

The application of these rays to television enables us to see what is going on in a room which is apparently in complete darkness. So far as I know, this achievement has never been done before. We had the impression that the image on the screen was not quite so clearly defined as when visible rays were used, but we easily recognised the figures we saw, and made out their actions. The direct application of Mr Baird's invention in warfare to locating objects apparently in the dark seems highly probable, but I hope that useful peace applications will soon be found for it.[53]

A further demonstration took place on 30 December, when forty members of the Royal Institution took advantage of Baird's invitation to inspect his innovative process. Among them was the seventy-five-year-old Sir Oliver Lodge, who came with one of his six daughters (he also had six sons). He was a distinguished physicist who had made a special study of the ether and of radio waves, and had been the first principal of Birmingham University. He praised the invention but complained of the heat when he participated as a subject.[54] It could hardly have been convenient, either, to sit in the dark.

A demonstration of noctovision was a feature of the British Association meeting at Leeds on 5 September 1927, and it occupied Baird's thoughts for several years, though it contributed little to the advance of television *per se*. He saw what was at different times referred to as 'black light' and 'invisible smoke'[55] as a device which could be used in warfare as well as for navigational purposes in fog. Demonstrations were given to representatives from the Admiralty at Motograph House in April 1927.[56] Lieutenant-Colonel Chetwode Crawley, deputy inspector of wireless telegraphy for the GPO, wrote in an article in *Television* shortly afterwards:

> Mr Baird in his early experiments with television experienced much difficulty from the effect of powerful flood lighting on the person who was being televised, and it was this which turned his attention to the possibility of using infra-red rays in place of visible light rays. It is obvious that if the navigator of a ship were able to see objects through fog and darkness his greatest troubles would be things of the past, and it is hoped that the use of infra-red rays will lead towards this goal. The ship would direct a beam of infra-red rays, just as a searchlight would be directed, but instead of seeing the object with the eye as in the case of a searchlight, he would have it shown on a screen in his noctovision receiver.[57]

With regard to seeing through fog, this was to prove one claim too far!

While on the way to refining his spotlight scanning system, which would remove the prevailing obstacles to the full realisation of mechanical television and also have other applications, Baird devised an alternative method of using infra-red rays. Instead of a lensed disc, he employed two rotating slotted discs receiving an image broken up into dots or strips and sent through a honeycomb of hollow copper tubes, plated inside and packed closely together. He applied for a patent for this significant development in fibre optics on 15 October 1926.[58]

The same day he applied for a patent for an entirely different initiative, an invention which corresponds to today's video recorder.[59] He called it 'phonovision'. He described what led him to it in the course of the lecture at the Physical and Optical societies' annual exhibition on 6 January 1927, which met with such an enthusiastic response that it had to be repeated the same evening.

> In televising a scene, it is first transformed into a fluctuating electric current, the current variations depending upon the scene in front of the transmitting televisor; these fluctuating currents are sent through the ether in the form of a modulated carrier wave just as in the transmission of telephony the noise is carried, only in this case the modulations correspond to a scene instead of a sound.
>
> The vision modulations are also audible if received on an ordinary

wireless receiver and are heard as characteristic sounds, each scene having its corresponding sound.

Different faces make different noises and it is possible to distinguish one face from another by its sound.

I have taken a few phonograph records so that you will be able to hear these image sounds.

The first record gives the sounds made by the faces of three different people and by listening carefully it is quite possible to hear the different characteristic notes.

These sounds you have just heard are the sounds made by the faces of three members of the Physical Society who were kind enough to submit themselves to the experiment.

The second record gives the image sounds of a pair of scissors, a match box, a bowler hat and a cabbage.

These sounds form permanent records of the scenes they correspond to. They may be reconverted into electricity by playing the phonograph in front of a microphone, and by using this electrical output to actuate a televisor synchronised with the phonograph, the original image may be reproduced.[60]

The process was possible because with the low-definition television image of thirty lines, the highest vision frequency was still low enough to be audible and could therefore be recorded onto a gramophone disc in the same way as a piece of music. The first subject to be successfully transferred to a 78rpm disc was the now veteran performer Stooky Bill, on 20 September 1927. A recording of a woman smoking a cigarette was made on 28 March 1928; the label said she was a Miss Pounsford. When a copy of it was shown in a television documentary in 1993, Miss Pounsford's great-niece identified her as her Aunt Mabel, who had worked for the Baird organisation as a secretarial agency typist.[61] Though various forms of Baird's original phonovisor were marketed, he never developed this invention: 'The quality was so poor that there seemed no hope of ever competing with the cinematograph. If the cinema had never been invented, the phonovisor, as I christened the device, might have been worth developing; it was certainly an intriguing process. Vision into sound and sound back again into vision.'[62] He did, however, demonstrate his device to the press on 20 September 1928: 'The *Morning Post* gives a big story to Baird's experiment, which we put over yesterday; televising by gramophone – one needle for sound and another for picture. In other words, you both hear and see the performance! (A tiny image; "but a start"!)'[63]

Some privately recorded discs of television programmes survive, and pictures, without sound, have been retrieved by modern digital techniques.[64] Though recognisable, they tend to support Baird's own strictures. This was, however, not the only system of video recording which he devised. On 26 January 1927 he applied for a patent for a system of recording television signals by means of a magnetic disc.[65] Patent 324,904, for which he applied on 4 October 1928, describes the 'reproduction of the transmitted image' in sound as well as vision by means of a moving 'band of sensitised material'.[66] The recording on tape is replayed by traversing it with a scanning device, as is the case with videos today.

The diversity of Baird's innovations at this time has been attributed to various factors. The suggestion that already he was having to come up with new ideas to keep his backers happy is almost certainly mistaken. It is more likely that the moment he had a new idea, he would follow it up to see if it was feasible, and, having assured himself that it was, he went on to something else.

A F Birch, who was with the Baird company in 1928-9, first as technical assistant then as studio manager, confirmed this assessment:

> Never, in my experience, did Mr Baird discourage any technician work-ing for himself, nor did he let us see he was discouraged himself. At the same time, he was not a lavish praiser. He was the mind, brooding aloft in its clouds of pioneering ambition, which descended to earth merely to initiate his ideas through us, whom he trusted to set out their practical interpretation.
>
> JLB was undaunted by the appalling limitations which beset these ideas. In the same way that early radio waited for the thermionic valve, in order really to progress, so unknowingly our JLB awaited the cathode-ray tube to be harnessed to his inventions, to make them commercially practicable.
>
> He was always rather shyly pleasant to his staff, and would rather enjoy a laugh with us on occasions. To myself, he appeared very much the genius, with his untidy shock of hair, and spectacles. His prevailing fault, in our view, was a penchant for producing another idea for investigation before we'd reached any sort of finality on the previous one.[67]

Baird has also been described as 'quietly obstinate'.[68] Not only would he pursue new ideas before he had perfected the last one, but he would stick to any well-tried basic method which had served him in the past.

6
Hands across the Sea
1927–1928

The year 1927 opened with a broadside in the form of an editorial in the scientific journal *Nature*. Referring to Baird's lecture to the Physical and Optical societies,[1] it commented rather sourly on his omission of certain key elements in the description of his system:

> The attendance was a tribute to the intrinsic interest of the subject and to the expectations aroused by what little has become known of the lecturer's apparatus and achievements. ... From the information available – and it must be remembered that Mr Baird has not disclosed the essential details of his method – it appears highly probable that little further progress need be expected along the lines chosen by him. ... It is to be regretted that, possibly on account of patent considerations, Mr Baird has hitherto been unable to submit a proper authentication of his claims to a learned society. For aught his recent audience could say, the invention might be a mere plaything, with no more resemblance to television than a toy engine has to the real thing. That is not the way to convince a sympathetic audience of experts who are expected to judge of the merits and prospects of an invention. ... The policy of withholding publication of an essential item [the nature of his light cell] does not commend itself to modern inventors. It savours too much of medieval practice, and usually defeats its own object of securing to the inventor the fruits of his invention. It would be a source of satisfaction to us if one of our countrymen were the first to provide a practical solution of a problem of this magnitude. ... If the solution has been reached without the scientific, engineering, and financial resources at the disposal of rival inventors, it will appeal very powerfully to our sympathy and imagination. But for the present, and on the evidence supplied, the scientific world will prefer to reserve its judgment.[2]

The background to this particular effusion is that, since the establishment of the Royal Society in 1660, it had been an article of faith within the scientific profession to publish, for the scrutiny of other scientists, full technical details of any development. Baird had not done so and, to be fair to the pure scientists of the establishment, never did, though he wrote numerous articles for specialist journals. In the early years of the twentieth century, commercial pressures were beginning to conflict with the ideal of free and full scientific communication; the difference of opinion between Baird and *Nature* is a case in point. Today there is greater recognition, even in university circles, that ideas are intellectual property which may need to be protected for reasons of industrial or national security, but some pure scientists still bitterly oppose this trend. The question of whether to publish or patent remains a sensitive one.

Baird replied to the criticism. After pointing out that he had been asked to 'deliver a lecture suitable for a public audience interested in scientific matters generally, but not experts on television', he countered:

> I am further criticised for withholding technical details. The writer of the article is surely aware that my inventions are the property of a limited company. The disclosures by me of technical details likely to assist competing interests would therefore be a grave breach of trust to the shareholders. I may further add that we have demonstrated the invention to Government experts, and have received a letter from the Government requesting us to withhold publication of technical details.[3]

The editor of the journal could not resist a footnote:

> The further information given above by Mr Baird is precisely the kind which physicists were waiting for. In the absence of a clear description in technical language, many misconceptions are bound to arise, and it would be well for Mr Baird to consider the advisability of making such a communication at the earliest opportunity consistent with his other obligations.[4]

On 3 February Baird was invited to Glasgow, to give a public address in the impressive St Andrew's Hall; or, as he himself sardonically put it, 'The genius from the kailyard returns to lecture to the public dignitaries.' He arrived with Denton, as usual, in attendance. On the platform were the Duke of Montrose as chairman, the Lord Provost, the 'nobility and gentry' of the city, his father and Annie, and the Inglis cousins.

I had some simple apparatus to demonstrate light sensitive cells and other similar phenomena, a collection of lantern slides and a completely unsuitable lecture, far too technical. It was, I learned later, absolutely incomprehensible gibberish to the bulk of the audience, however, I was happily unaware of this at the time.[5]

Baird afterwards made, as he later admitted, a more fundamental error of judgment:

If an inventor reads these pages, let him by this be admonished to do what [Alexander] Graham Bell, inventor of the telephone, did, and sell at once for cash. Inventors are no match for financiers where stocks and shares are concerned, and will, if they hold on, find that the financiers have the cash and they have the paper.[6]

Beset by the Scylla of the scientific establishment, Baird now faced the Charybdis of the City. On the initiative of Hutchinson, a public company was floated to raise the necessary money for the development of the Baird inventions. The firm of E N Vowler and Company were enlisted as brokers, two of their younger members of staff having been given an impressive demonstration at Motograph House of Baird's systems, even though one of them remarked that the 'whole of his equipment was a most Heath Robinson affair, tied together with bits of string, bits of wire, old bicycle lamps, etc.'.[7]

Hutchinson estimated that £50,000 would be needed to purchase necessary equipment. Vowler's decided that they would raise £100,000, if Hutchinson would put up one-third of this sum. This he achieved within a week, the ever-loyal Inglis cousins having responded to a personal plea from Baird by promising £5000.[8] In the end it was decided to offer 100,000 Preferred Participating Ordinary Shares of £1 and 100,000 Deferred Ordinary Shares of one shilling at par. The business was to be called the Baird Television Development Company.[9]

The hand of Hutchinson is also to be discerned behind the wording of the company prospectus, which was issued on 8 April. 'Progress in development of inventions' included the statement, 'Demonstrations have been given from time to time before Government Representatives, Members of the Royal Institution, Leading Scientists, and to the Technical and Daily Press, the object of these demonstrations being to show the successful progress made in development.' More questionable was the assertion, 'The Science Museum, South Kensington, has also acknowledged the Invention by accepting Mr

Baird's original apparatus as an exhibit representing the world's first Television machine.' The Science Museum had certainly taken delivery of a machine that *resembled* the original; it had been hastily cobbled together for the purpose from components in Baird's laboratory, and, significantly, was minus its light cell.[10] It is now in the possession of the National Museum of Photography, Film and Television, Bradford.

The prospectus listed the 'uses of inventions' under four heads: the televisor, noctovision ('The fog-penetrating properties of these rays it is claimed will open up a great field of utility in rendering visible through fog to ships at sea light beams from a lighthouse, lightship or other shipping'), phonovision, and 'The distortionless amplifier used in conjunction with the Televisor and a novel type of loud speaker included in the inventions acquired by the Company, are, it is claimed, capable of being applied in the production of an improved form of speaking film.'

There followed an account of the 'anticipated sources of revenue out of which the Company should make considerable profits'. These included the sale of apparatus and fees for licensing its production, annual licence fees to users, two-thirds of the net proceeds from the sale and exploitation of the rights outside Britain, manufacture and sale of parts, and fees for government work. That Baird himself had some misgivings about the claims is attested by a copy of the prospectus in which the word 'should' in 'should make considerable profits' is underlined and glossed, in Baird's own hand, 'but will not'.[11]

The very day of issue of the prospectus, the news broke of the television demonstration of the Bell Telephone Laboratories of the American Telephone and Telegraph Company on 7 April. By the standards of the time, it was a very impressive achievement indeed, and broke the Baird monopoly, even if Dr Alexandre Dauvillier, the French physicist who had the previous year unveiled his own electronic system using a cathode-ray tube, commented in an article that the company had used the Baird system 'without acknowledgment'.[12]

The American demonstration, on which the laboratories had been working since 1925, comprised two transmissions. The one, by wire, involved the sending of the images of a face a distance of 250 miles (400km), from Washington, DC, to New York City. The other, by radio, was over a distance of 22 miles (36km). The resulting pictures were shown on two screens, one 2 inches by 2½ inches, and the other 2 feet by 2½ feet. There appeared to be no difference in quality between the two methods of transmission, though the large-screen pictures left something to be desired by way of clarity.[13] The method of scanning, by flying spot, differed from Baird's floodlight system, but was one which Baird was capable of using, if indeed he had not already done so.

The news of the American achievement, however, caused alarm and despondency among those who had agreed to underwrite the Baird issue. There were even accusations of deception. Baird commented in his memoir,

> They came round and agreed to carry on, but they were considerably shaken. I was shaken myself. I had begun to regard television as something which belonged exclusively to me and our monopoly was something inherent in the nature of things, and so the A T & T show was a blow, although I knew that a thing of this sort was inevitable sooner or later. ... It was surprising that we had had so long a run as fourteen months.[14]

The new company was duly established. The directors were Sir Edward Manville (chairman), chairman of the Daimler Company, Sir James Campbell Percy, an Irish businessman and publisher with a strong interest in television, and Francis Shortis, a banker who was a vice-president of the Guaranty Trust of New York, with Baird and Hutchinson as joint managing directors, each on a five-year contract at an initial salary of £1500 a year. The annual remuneration of the other directors was £300 net of tax (with an extra £100 for the chairman), plus expenses.[9]

The very fact, however, that A T & T had required several hundred scientists and technicians to put on their display[15] gave the Baird company directors much anxiety. Baird himself now had a few technical assistants, but they had no grounding or training in television; nor was he very keen to impart any detailed understanding of his unique systems, if, indeed, he had much aptitude for doing so. His perception tended to be instinctive. He did not make organised notes, preferring to work intuitively with a minimum of written communication. His brain was his notebook. It was therefore decided to insure him for £150,000, said to have been the biggest life insurance policy ever taken out. Baird was alarmed at what a medical examination might reveal, though the conditions listed on his 'unfit for any service' record of 1916 would not in themselves have disqualified him. 'Two doctors prodded me about, they whispered together, did more prodding and listening, whispered again, obviously they did not like the proposition, also obviously they were reluctant to turn down a magnificent bit of business.'[16] How far he was also at the time suffering from his periodic bronchial complaint is not known, but the policy was duly issued, at an annual premium of £2000.

Baird was now living in lodgings at 975 Finchley Road, close to Golders Green underground station, on what was then the Hampstead line to Leicester Square. Bill Fox was a neighbour. He got used to unannounced visits from Baird. On Christmas Day, either 1927 or 1928, Baird arrived unexpectedly early in the morning, and was invited in to join the family gathering. To Fox's surprise, he galvanised the party, playing games, making funny speeches, enthusiastically taking part in the solving of problems.[17] There was, however, another side to their relationship:

> It was common for the doorbell to go at midnight and to find Mr Baird on the doorstep looking as though he had been dropped there and did not know how it had happened, or else he was bubbling with ideas. He would come in and sit for an hour without saying a word some nights; on others we discussed everything under the sun.
>
> During the day it was not unusual to find him on a public seat at the end of the road looking like a tramp, lost, weary, and half dead. Time and place meant nothing to him when his ideas were moving. I found him a man widely read, interested in many things but devoted to the idea of getting television on to a practical basis. To that end he worked in a fashion I have never seen in another man. His whole life and time were television. When he was working on a problem it was impossible to get any sense out of him on any other subject. This was a peculiarity which puzzled many people and made them write him down as an impractical dreamer. But only a severely practical man could have taken up the bits and pieces of discarded apparatus and made them work to provide the answer to problems as Baird did.[18]

Commenting on these observations, Baird's wife later suggested that 'it is also possible that John was sunk in the Baird lethargy which alternated with the furious energy with which he pursued his ideas'.[19] Such symptoms are reflected also in clinical depression, such as could have been triggered off by the unsatisfactory nature of his emotional involvement.

> With his long hair, horn-rimmed glasses, and massive overcoats he became quite a character in London. He enjoyed dressing the part of the absent-minded inventor and he was shrewder than he looked. His private life was unsettled. His love affair was still in full swing, though both he and his lady were approaching their forties. His health varied with the seasons. In summer he was a reasonably handsome and lively man, but as winter set in he looked years older, his heavy black overcoat,

even a balaclava, always on. Each winter he was in bed for several weeks with a chill.[20]

Even when he was up and around he was continually trying to alleviate his catarrh by inhaling a mixture of ether and menthol, which he concocted in his own laboratory.[21] Baird saw several London specialists about his nasal problems, with results which seemed only to aggravate the condition.[22]

As one of the specialists diagnosed, Baird suffered from sinusitis, which renders the patient particularly susceptible to winter infections and viruses. Even today, with modern drugs, steroid sprays, and sophisticated operations, sinusitis can be, as it was in the case of Baird, a permanent condition.

Cold intolerance, lethargy, and weight gain (which affected Baird in the 1930s), together with other non-specific complaints such as constipation (from which Baird suffered for most of his life), depression, and eccentric behaviour, are among the symptoms which are consistent with hypo-thyroidism. This condition, which is particularly prevalent in Scotland, is caused by a deficiency of thyroid hormones. Proper testing methods for a clinical diagnosis were not available until the 1970s; even so, the progression of the disease is so slow that often neither the family or friends of the patient nor the family doctor see any changes. From the evidence available, it is possible that Baird could have been hypothyroid.[23]

Baird's immediate task after the formation of the new company was to restore confidence in the shareholders by demonstrating that anything A T & T could do, he could do better. Whereas they had sent pictures 250 miles by means of a special wire circuit, he would send them 435, using the ordinary telephone system. The receiver was set up in the Central Hotel in Glasgow, monitored by Clapp and Denton, and the show was seen by leading civic and scientific dignitaries, among whom was Professor E Taylor Jones, the professor of physics at Glasgow University, who reported on it most favourably in *Nature*.[24] There were two demonstrations, on 24 and 26 May. A person's face was readily recognisable on a screen about two inches square, though it was explained that there would be no difficulty in enlarging the picture to full size. It was bright enough to be seen clearly even when the electric lights were on in the room. On the second occasion, viewers could see Baird himself, while talking to him by phone on a separate line.

The inaugural board meeting of the new company took place on 18 July 1927. It was the first intimation to Baird of what the next years were going to be like. In his laboratory, now with adequate equipment, he was perfectly happy, pursuing whatever personal goal was on his eclectic agenda. Since his days with the Clyde Valley Electrical Power Company, he had never been responsible to anyone but himself. He resented the intrusion of people who knew less about television than he did, and he resented the time spent at board meetings. 'I was busy with my wheels and pulleys, and soon came to regard board meetings as analogous to going to church – functions to be slept through. Sometimes I woke up with a start at some of the proceedings at these meetings, and thought "God help the shareholders of public companies." However after a few squeaks I relapsed again into dreams of further permutations and combinations of wire and mirror drums and lamps.'[25] He thought nothing, if it was time to change his socks, of doing so at the board table.[26] He went to meetings primarily to watch what Hutchinson, who was fully at home at such gatherings, was up to. Baird particularly resented what he saw as the officiousness of Sir Edward Manville, who had an engineering background. His neurosis on this point was such that when the company moved to new premises at 133 Long Acre in January 1928, he had the door to his laboratory so constructed that the portly Manville would have difficulty getting through it. 'The first time he appeared there was a most heart-rending and embarrassing scene – he was an obstinate and determined man – he got through! But he lost several buttons from his waistcoat and dropped his cigar and tramped on it in the process. He never visited my laboratory again.'[27]

For the first time in his life, Baird was tasting high living. Lunch with Hutchinson at the exclusive Ivy restaurant across the road, was 'the high spot of the day':

> Commencing with cocktails we went through the hors d'oeuvres, rich pea soup, fritto misto, curried chicken and Bombe Gladys Cooper, washed down with copious draughts of Chateau Y'quem, followed by coffee and petits-fours washed down with Bisque d'Bouche Brandy. Gorged and bloated and belching, we tottered over to Motograph House and awaited afternoon tea.[27]

Baird's chronic bronchial problems were now complicated by a liver disorder and symptoms of an even more embarrassing nature: his nose swelled up and went a vivid crimson. He visited a succession of specialists. Strict dieting restored his nose to its normal proportions and colour, and did something, but not everything, for his liver. Baird had been a fairly heavy drinker in Glasgow, and still indulged heartily on occasions. Later, he had the strength of mind to become completely teetotal. At formal dinners, he would let himself be served with everything, aperitives, wines, liqueurs, but never took a sip from any glass.[28] It would appear, however, in the long run that the damage to his liver was irreversible.

Hutchinson had been continuing to goad the GPO into some positive action. On 17 August 1927, he wrote that the Baird organisation was investigating the establishment of a French company, and that an application had been made to the French government for a licence to transmit with 3 kW power, since it seemed doubtful whether the necessary facilities would be forthcoming in Britain. He now formally requested that such facilities should be made available. This time Hutchinson was not bluffing. He had written earlier to the French government asking for permission to establish a television transmitting and receiving station in or near Paris. The assistant secretary of the GPO, with whom the French government had been in touch about Hutchinson's proposal, replied by return of post. The application would be considered if the GPO's technical officials were given the chance properly to examine the 'present stage of development' of Baird's television system.[29]

Baird, however, had other things on his mind. He was giving innumerable public demonstrations of his equipment. He had also begun experimenting with both colour and stereoscopic television, and was preparing for the ultimate, and most spectacular, transmission in monochrome. In 1901 Marconi had managed to broadcast the sound of three feeble dots (the letter S) across the Atlantic from Poldhu in Cornwall to St Johns in Newfoundland, by bouncing radio waves on the ionosphere, the layer of ionised gas particles a hundred miles above the earth's surface. Baird proposed to send a complete television image by the same means.

One morning in September 1927, he approached Clapp in the laboratory, and in his measured and precise way asked him if he could go to New York the following day! Clapp always reckoned, considering he had to build the thirty-line televisor to take with him, obtain a passport, and complete other formalities, that he did pretty well to be ready to sail just a week later.[30] He arrived in New York on 5 October, and was put up in Hartsdale, a New York suburb, by a fellow radio amateur, Robert Hart, who maintained the radio link with London during the preparations and accommodated the receiving apparatus in the cellar of his house. In Britain, the transmitting apparatus would be at Clapp's home in Coulsdon, administered by a team of three technicians.

Over the next few months tests were conducted around midnight (the best time for transmission) three times a week in secret. Baird and Denton transmitted sound or vision signals by telephone line to Coulsdon, from where they were sent across to New York on a wavelength of forty-five metres. Finally, after fifty-eight such tests, Baird decided that he was ready to tell the world.[31]

The first attempt, however, was a failure, though it enabled Baird afterwards to claim that he had spent the night with the American actress Elissa Landi. She had been booked to be the first human face to be transmitted across the Atlantic, but though attempts were made throughout the early hours, the signals were not getting through to New York.[32]

The second attempt took place on 9 February 1928 (8 February in New York). In the USA, Hutchinson, Clapp, Robert Hart, and a representative of Reuter's press agency gathered round the two inches by three inches groundglass screen of the televisor, on which the signals, when amplified, were due to appear. Personalities and technicians stood by in the Baird studios in Long Acre, from which the images were sent to Coulsdon. A full-size pilot picture on a check receiver enabled the transmitting operator to adjust the signals.

Stooky Bill was called into service once again to open the proceedings. The sound of his image, it was reported, was like the drone of a huge bee.[33] When the message was received from New York that the face could clearly be seen, in black against an orange background, Baird himself took the stand. The time was 01.35 GMT, and it was appropriate that it was he who was the first human to be seen on television the other side of the Atlantic, less than six years after radio broadcasting officially began and thirty-four years before the Telstar satellite was launched to facilitate the transmission of television signals across the ocean. He sat for half-an-hour, moving his head about, until word came that the picture was satisfactory. He was followed by Bill Fox: 'It appeared that [his] features were particularly striking, from a television point of view, and transmitted better than those of the other sitters.'[33] Mia Howe, the wife of the Associated Press representative in London, was the final sitter. Though her features did not get through clearly enough for her to be recognised in New York, 'there was no mistaking the fact that a woman was seated before the transmitter'.[33]

The report in *Television* concluded,

> Atmospherics and other interference, and also fading of signals, marred the image as received at the New York end at times, but in spite of these disabilities, reception was, on the whole, very good. The demonstration proved quite conclusively that if a much higher powered wireless transmitter had been employed, the image would have been received in New York entirely free from atmospheric and other disturbances. An important feature is that only two operators were required to attend to the television transmission, one at each end of the circuit.[33]

The American press was particularly complimentary. An editorial in the *New York Times* commented,

> As a communication Marconi's 'S' was negligible; as a milestone on the onward sweep of radio, of epochal importance. And so it is with Mr Baird's first successful effort in transatlantic television. His images were crude; they were scarcely recognisable; they faded and reappeared, as the atmospheric conditions varied; but they were the beginnings of a new branch of engineering. ... All the more remarkable is Baird's achievement because. ... he matches his inventive wits against the pooled ability and the vast resources of the great corporation physicists and engineers, thus far with dramatic success.[34]

A similar point was made by the *Sun Telegraph* of Pittsburgh in describing the pictures: 'They were comparable to the visions brought in at the A T and T demonstration by air, from no farther away than New Jersey. The vision of the dummy, in fact, was clearer than those, but the moving faces were not so strong.'[35] And by the *New York Herald-Tribune*: 'If it be appreciated also that Baird is an experimenter of the most classic type, and that he has been struggling along for years with the crudest of equipment, built in the skimpiest shop, his recent stunt is nothing short of marvellous.'[36] Or, as the *Virginian-Pilot* said by way of headline, 'Sitting In Dark Cellar In New York, Group See Man and Woman In London'.[37]

But they hadn't seen anything yet! Hutchinson and Clapp, with the televisor, sailed for Britain in the Cunard liner *Berengaria*. On 6 March, in mid-Atlantic, without there having been any experimental tests, before an audience of ship's officers in uniform with black tie and others in evening dress, a grinning Stooky Bill appeared on the screen of the televisor, which had been set up in a state-room with its accompanying tangle of wires, batteries, amplifiers, and tubes. Baird then put a young woman in front of the transmitter in the Long Acre studio. The gathering on board picked out that the face was female. The ship's chief wireless operator, Stanley Brown, immediately identified her, from her hairstyle and her profile, as his fiancée, Dora Selvey, whom Baird had specially enlisted for the occasion.

By way of an extraordinary footnote to this *coup de théâtre*, two radio amateurs in the New York district of Queens not only picked up the transmission but, with the use of additional components and the assistance of a piano tuner, recorded it on a phonograph record. This they sent to the Baird company in London.[38]

At a lunch in the third week of February to celebrate the opening of a television department at Selfridge's, Baird announced that basic kits would be on sale from which a wireless amateur enthusiast could build a rudimentary televisor, which could then be upgraded to receive transmissions on a wavelength of 45 metres.

Meanwhile, things were moving at the GPO, whose representative wrote on 1 March to the Baird company asking for a firm date to be arranged for the official demonstration to its experts. Baird himself replied: 'Further contingencies have arisen which to some extent alter the situation. However I shall put the matter to our Board and will communicate with you further in due course.'[39] His motives for procrastinating can only be guessed at. The lead he had established over other scientists was being eroded. On 13 January the General Electric Company in the USA had given a demonstration of a forty-eight-line mechanical system using the flying-spot method of scanning, which transmitted an image at sixteen frames a second to three receivers set up in private homes.[40] Farnsworth was forging ahead with his electronic system, and Zworykin was about to come in from the cold to which his employers had assigned him. By the end of 1929, thirty television broadcasting licences had been issued by the authorities in the USA[41] to organisations which had development budgets totalling millions of dollars.[42]

The Baird company was dependent on its shareholders for money, and was answerable to its shareholders for results. It had only one research scientist of the highest quality, and he appeared to be concerned primarily with building up his record of 'firsts', to the detriment of the development of his basic product. There was some justification in the argument that the greater the publicity, the more would be the money invested in the company. More cash meant more reserves available for research and development. However satisfactory the present monochrome pictures were when demonstrated to the public, Baird knew that they might not pass muster as a public service when formally tested in the presence of experts and civil servants, some of whom might be hostile to the very notion of television, or to the inventor of the system, or to one or more of Baird's colleagues on the board of his company.

Any demonstration had to be on Baird's own terms. His standing was further undermined by Hutchinson's ambitious claims of company developments which were not realised. This was the background to the £1000 challenge issued in the March 1928 issue of *Popular Wireless*. For this, Baird was to transmit satisfactorily over a distance of twenty-five yards three recognisable faces, objects in motion (such as a tray of dice and marbles), some shapes, and the moving hands of a clock. The judges would be chosen by Norman Edwards, the editor of the journal, who, in an interview in the

Daily Telegraph, made a reasonable point: 'It is the opinion of scientists … that known television systems are not capable of sufficient development to warrant great optimism with regard to their early utility for television in the home.'[43] The stakes were increased by the fact that Peter Eckersley, chief engineer of the British Broadcasting Corporation, as it had become on 1 January 1927, was a regular contributor to *Popular Wireless*, in which he publicly expressed doubts about the present viability of Baird's system.

Baird declined the challenge, which, after an extension to allow him to change his mind, was withdrawn. If he had accepted, and only partly succeeded, there would still have been a bench-mark against which the practical possibilities of television could accurately have been predicted.

A damage limitation exercise was undertaken by Sydney Moseley, a professional journalist with a basic grasp of wireless technology and also, by his own account, an expertise in high finance. Moseley, a worldly man with a passion for music and sport, was just five months older than Baird. Their backgrounds, however, could hardly have been more disparate. Moseley's parents were Jewish immigrants 'from somewhere along the Baltic'.[44] His father, a violinist, died when Moseley was a baby, leaving his mother with seven children. She tried to make ends meet by opening a small millinery shop. Chiefly to help her, Moseley left school in 1903, when he was fifteen, to work in the counting house of the printers Waterlow & Sons. She died the following year at the age of fifty-four.

Moseley entered journalism on a full-time basis in 1910, when he worked briefly for the *Daily Express*, after which he was 'Dramatic Critic, Music Critic and everything else' for the short-lived *Evening Times*.[45] As editor in 1913 of the *Egyptian Mail*, an English daily paper published in Cairo, he inveighed against the Capitulations, an international law whereby any consul might order the arrest of one of his own nationals, which particularly suited the Russian agents of the Czar. For this Moseley was formally rebuked by Lord Kitchener, the British consul-general, who subsequently suppressed the publication in Egypt of Moseley's first book, *With Kitchener in Cairo*; it was finally published in London in 1917. Moseley was an official war correspondent for the Mediterranean Expeditionary Forces in the Dardanelles in 1915, and published a critical book about the conduct of the campaign, *The Truth about the Dardanelles* (1916). He finished the war as a junior officer in naval intelligence.

Though Moseley claimed to have become agnostic,[46] in 1921 he added a blockbusting Jewish novel, *A Singular People*, to his burgeoning literary output. It was followed by *A Much Chosen Race* (1922), a journalistic, and not uncritical, account of some Jewish shortcomings, which was notable for the fact that Moseley successfully took his publisher to court for insisting on going ahead with a cover of which the author disapproved. In the meantime he had established his own newspaper, the *Southend Times*, and sold it to Odhams Press. He stood as Independent Labour Party candidate for Southend in the general election of 1924, and lost his deposit. By 1927 he had become both feared and respected as a forthright investigative and crusading journalist, with numerous influential contacts in the press. He was not afraid of anyone. He was prepared to write critical articles about the BBC in the technical journal *Amateur Wireless*, while at the same time being employed by the corporation to broadcast on a regular basis. He was an inveterate player of the stock exchange, about which he had written a best-selling guide, *Money-Making in Stocks and Shares* (1927). His forte was the ability to write on technical subjects without using technical jargon.

This, then, was the man who not only was to see himself as the evangelist of the cause of television and the scourge of the sceptics, but also became Baird's business associate, as well as his confidant and closest personal friend.

Moseley first met Baird on 1 August 1928.

> The public are going crazy gambling on new companies. It seems that *anything* that comes out is oversubscribed. Prospectuses promise the moon. There are several gramophone companies whose issues were amazing successes. Many stockbrokers live at Westcliff [the district of Southend-on-Sea, Essex, where Moseley had his bachelor home], and the talk is 'new issues'. I met a pale young man named [T W] Bartlett, who is Secretary to the new Baird Television Company. *Television!* Anxious to see what it is all about. He invited me to go along to Long Acre where the new invention is installed. Now *that's* something! Television!
>
> Met John Logie Baird; a charming man – a shy, quietly-spoken Scot. He could serve as a model for the schoolboy's picture of a shock-haired, modest, dreamy, absent-minded inventor. Nevertheless shrewd. We sat and chatted. He told me he is having a bad time with the scoffers and sceptics – including the BBC and part of the technical press – who are trying to ridicule and kill his invention of television at its inception. I told him that if he would let me see what he had actually achieved – well, he would have to risk my damning it – or praising it. If I *were* convinced – I would battle for him.[47]

Hovering around the discussion was Hutchinson, 'a tall good-looking but highly temperamental Irishman ... nice but very nervous of chancing it with me. He was terribly anxious that I should be impressed.'

> Out went the lights. I sat before the primitive televisor and was asked to look through the tiny aperture. Suddenly there was a flicker.
>
> Hutchinson cried excitedly, 'You see, it's coming!' 'Look, Mr Moseley,' said Baird more calmly, 'at that object there!' I *could* see something and, truth to tell, my sympathies were so definitely enlisted on Baird's side that I was eager to be convinced.
>
> 'There!' he exclaimed. 'Can't you see that tree?'
>
> There were faint outlines of tiny objects which looked like trees, though I could not have sworn to them. What I did see with great delight was that the image of *something* in another room was coming through to me by means of Baird's contraption. He had managed to convey it *through* the walls even though little but a blurred outline was visible in the televisor. Baird looked anxiously at me and I nodded my assurance that I had in fact seen some sort of a picture.
>
> 'What you have here,' I told him, 'is certainly the beginnings of television. You have, in fact, transmitted a visual image and I shall certainly testify to that. I shall not be able to say that you have put over a perfect picture, but you have undoubtedly made a start.'[48]

To his diary Moseley confided, 'Liked the pair of them, especially Baird, and decided to give my support. I think we really have what is called television. And so, once more into the fray!'[49]

Moseley arranged with James Brown, the managing director of the publisher which controlled *Popular Wireless*, that the journal would print an article by him setting out the facts about Baird's television apparatus. This duly appeared on 22 September, even though Edwards countered by commissioning from Eckersley a reply to Moseley, which was printed on the opposite page. Baird was still thrilled with what Moseley had achieved. It was the beginning of a professional partnership between them, as well as a deep friendship.

Moseley, in Baird's words, was a 'stout and jovial man, with a merry and wicked twinkle in his eye'.[50] His precise status initially is unclear. According to him, 'From then on I devoted much of my time to acclaiming Baird's invention.'[51] He appears also to have attended board meetings of the Baird company, where his acute mind and inside knowledge was of inestimable value to Baird: 'Moseley was not the sort who fell asleep at board meetings or anywhere else where money was concerned.'[52] When the other board members had gone home, the pair of them would send out for fish and chips and hold a post mortem.

As Baird's professional associate Moseley acted as an adviser and a fixer. Baird's wife described their relationship: 'They laughed and fooled about, as much in public as in private. John had found someone whose sense of humour matched his own and with whom he could relax.'[53] They went on holiday together, and played practical jokes on each other. If Baird was the victim, he would treat Moseley to one of his favourite tokens of their friendship: 'Ach, Sydney, you *dirrty* dog!'[54]

In his quest for publicity, Baird had jumped at the suggestion the previous year that he should mount a demonstration of his apparatus at the British Association annual meeting at Leeds in September 1927.[55] Whether it was Baird's quirkish sense of humour that led him to choose to display the gimmick of noctovision rather than his latest achievements in more traditional, and viable, methods of transmitting images, he certainly achieved publicity.

> Mr Denton and myself with the aid of local carpenters erected in a hall in the Municipal Buildings a complete transmitting and receiving equipment. It was an extremely successful show. Successive parties were formed in the transmitting room which was in total darkness, and placed one by one in front of the transmitter in the dark room. They were seen on the screen in an adjoining room, a queue being formed to pass before the screen. The spectators were apt to linger and Hutchinson, who was acting as MC, made himself extremely unpopular by hustling many eminent dignitaries of the scientific world who were not accustomed to such treatment. 'Pass along, please. Pass along. Now then, sir, now then, you can't stand there all day – others wish to see as well as you.' The papers boomed the show and such a crowd gathered outside the Municipal Buildings that mounted police had to be called to control the crowd – a thing unheard of at a BA meeting.
>
> It was all, however, perhaps not quite at the level of dignity deemed desirable by certain of the scientists and did not do me much good in some academic circles.[56]

The most far-reaching outcome of the demonstration came at the end of a talk which Baird then gave to members of the association. W G Mitchell proposed that 'the time had come, owing to the enormous public interest and the success of Mr Baird's television development, for the formation of a society whose sole interest would be the study and development of problems associated with television and allied subjects'.[57] The Television Society (now the Royal Television Society) was established later that year. The president was Lord Haldane of Cloan, on whose death in 1928 Ambrose Fleming was appointed to succeed him, having initially refused the honour. Among the distinguished line-up of vice-presidents was Sir James Percy, who was a director of the Baird company. James Denton was honorary secretary (membership), and W G Mitchell honorary secretary (lectures). Baird was appointed the society's first, and sole, honorary fellow, and gave the lecture, followed by a demonstration, at the first general meeting of the society on 1 May 1928, at the Engineers' Club, Coventry Street, London. It was reported that 'Members attended in full strength, taxing the accommodation of the lecture room to the limit'.[58]

The lecture itself was largely a summary of Baird's personal progress, with slides of diagrams which were several years out of date. He referred to the use of infra-red waves in wartime as a 'means of vision which would enable the attacking force to be seen without them being aware of it'. He discussed his original method of large-screen reproduction. He also described the flying-spot method of scanning which officially he had yet to adopt for his systems. His party trick on this occasion was to transmit from Long Acre, about 750 metres away, into the room the image of the secretary of the Engineers' Club, which, it was reported, after 'some trouble due to interference [from a BBC radio transmission] … was successfully received'.[59]

A by-product of the establishment of the Television Society was the founding of the monthly journal, *Television*, 'The official organ of the Television Society'. Its first issue appeared in March 1928, under the editorship of A Dinsdale and the imprint of the Television Press Ltd, of which Moseley seems to have become a director shortly after throwing in his lot with Baird.[60] Since all the developments in television in the UK at that time centred on Baird, the journal, with its initial circulation of ten thousand, was effectively his company's house magazine. Early in 1929 Moseley became chairman of Television Press and managing editor of *Television*.[61]

Baird himself achieved another 'first' on or about 18 June 1928, by transmitting an image in daylight from the roof at Long Acre to a room four floors below. Among those who watched the demonstration was Ambrose Fleming, who wrote about it in *Television*.[62] From an article in *Popular Wireless*, it would appear that the means was to substitute short-wave wireless radiation for light, and a wireless receiver for the light cell.[63] This method of obtaining a picture by reflecting wireless waves from the image to be transmitted is described in Baird's patent 292,185, which, significantly, was officially accepted on 21 June 1928.[64]

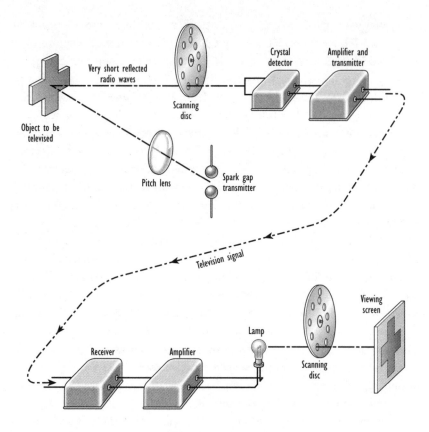

Figure 2: Radio wave imaging, redrawn from British patent 292,185 of J L Baird, application 21 December 1926, accepted 21 June 1928. The radio waves emitted from the spark gap act in the same way as light in a conventional mechanically-scanned television system. The wavelengths are very short, probably in the millimetre or centimetre range. Baird used a version of the system for his daylight television transmissions.

The publicity which Baird was generating encouraged the establishment on 25 June of a further company, Baird International Television, whose function it would be to license the Baird inventions and patents, and establish companies or obtain partnerships which would market them overseas or themselves act as manufacturers. Lord Ampthill, fifty-nine years old, a prominent freemason and former governor of Madras, who had served temporarily in 1904 as viceroy and governor-general of India, was appointed chairman. The other directors were Manville, Baird, Hutchinson, and Lieutenant-Colonel George B Winch of the brewing concern. Among the staff appointments which were now made was Lieutenant-Commander W W Jacomb as chief engineer and technical expert. He was a former Royal Navy communications officer who had served in the Dardanelles in World War I.

He had an instant grasp of anything to do with electrical systems, especially those involving signalling. The technical staff was reinforced by young, some of them very young, men such as T H Bridgewater and J D Percy, known as 'young Percy' to differentiate him from his father, Sir James. Young Percy later recalled the happy atmosphere at work, making receivers and amplifiers, and spoke of Baird himself as a shy, polite, pleasant, and popular employer.[65]

Percy, who opted to join the Baird company straight from school rather than go into his father's publishing business, was Jacomb's personal apprentice. The floor on which they worked was divided by wooden partitions into individual laboratories, which were full of components from earlier, more primitive apparatus. From screwing in screws, charging batteries, and making up and testing equipment, Percy graduated to creating apparatus to reflect Baird's visionary ideas, translated into potential hardware by Jacomb.[66] For Philip Hobson, who joined the company as a seventeen-year-old laboratory assistant in July 1928, his first task was soldering cables onto seven-pin plugs and sockets. 'The laboratories at that time were littered with the remains of the apparatus used by Baird for demonstrations of colour and stereoscopic television, Phonovision – and Noctovision. All [had been] more or less cannibalised, as no one then had any idea of their potential historic value.'[67] According to his recollections, there were about thirty people on the engineering staff during the years 1928-30.[68]

Significantly, and for whatever reason, no appointments were made of qualified scientific researchers or consultants. This differed markedly from the policy of other companies which were to become Baird's competitors in establishing a hold on the British market.

In the meantime Baird blithely continued to collect personal accolades, 'leaving the development of "straight" television to Jacomb'.[69] On 3 July 1928, he gave the first ever public demonstration of colour television, by the method of which he had first given notice in his patent applications three years before.[70] Each transmitting and receiving disc contained three spirals of holes, which were covered respectively by red, blue, and green filters. The transmitting disc, revolving ten times a second, broke up the image, and then passed it on in the form of ten red, ten blue, and ten green separated images every second. The complete image was reconstituted at the receiving end, having passed in front of a neon tube, for the red, and a tube containing mercury vapour and helium for the blue and green. The final picture was shown on a screen about 3 inches by 5 inches.

A reporter from the *Morning Post* was one of a group of enthusiastic spectators.

When the sitter opened his mouth his teeth were clearly visible, and so were his eyelids and the white of his eyes and other small details about his face. He was a dark-eyed, dark-haired man, and appeared in his natural colours against a dark background. He picked up a deep red coloured cloth and wound it round his head, winked and put out his tongue. The red of the cloth stood out vividly against the pink of his face, while his tongue showed as a lighter pink. ... The colour television proved so attractive that the sitter was kept for a long time doing various things at the request of the spectators.[71]

Dr Alexander Russell reported in *Nature*: 'The coloured images we saw which were obtained were quite vivid. Delphiniums and carnations appeared in their natural colours and a basket of strawberries showed the red fruit very clearly.'[72]

J D Percy commented on this demonstration with hindsight:

Astoundingly [it] worked – and not too badly. It is a standing tribute to the foresight and genius of a tall fair-haired Scot who in 1928 took little sleep and wore bedroom slippers all day, that by far the most pictorially successful system of colour television demonstrated in America just 20 years later, employed the very scanning principles used on the first British experimental machine.[73]

Baird's particular skill as an inventor lay in adapting his basic apparatus to perform a range of functions. Having used it for colour transmission, he now, on 9 August, at his Long Acre laboratories, demonstrated stereoscopic television, a process which over seventy years later has still never been made available to the television viewer. And as with all Baird's innovations, it was achieved by the simplest and most direct method. Two images, right and left perspectives, were obtained by an arrangement of mirrors and then transmitted simultaneously to the receiving station, where they appeared side by side. They were then merged by means of an ordinary stereoscope. Among those who saw the demonstration was Professor Frederic J Cheshire, director of the Optical Engineering Department at Imperial College, London; he wrote an article about the principles involved in *Television*.[74]

Both colour and stereoscopic television were demonstrated at the British Association annual meeting in Glasgow in September. While Baird supervised the demonstrations, helped by Denton and young Percy, W G Mitchell supported the cause by lecturing to the sixth forms of local schools. Denton's handwritten report of the occasion makes interesting reading:

A continuous stream of visitors inspected demonstrations of colour and stereoscopic television. ... Professor Gray kindly placed the Applied Physics Laboratory at the disposal of the operation, this floor being on a level with the main hall, near the Kelvin exhibits. It was interesting to find next to the experimental apparatus of Lord Kelvin a model of the First Television Transmitter made by Mr Baird, who is an ARCS of Glasgow Technical College, and an old student of Professor Gray. Visitors to the Television demonstration fully inspected the transmitting apparatus in operation in one room, and in an adjoining Photometric room, observed the received image. At times the operators responded to requests by making the demonstration to suit the visitor's demands; persons interchanged places, and varying coloured flowers, and fabrics, in turn were inspected as desired.

On the day following the meeting, a large audience assembled in the Physics Lecture Room as the result of an invitation sent out to the Educational authorities by the Television Society. Senior Students of the schools and leading educationists responded and Prof. Gray took the Chair. G W Mitchell lectured and the chosen subject was Television. After the lecture 500 senior scholars inspected the demonstration of stereoscopic television. Everyone voted the meeting a complete success.

An added interest was aroused amongst the operators just at the close of the meeting when Sir Donald MacAlister, Principal of the University, arrived with Lady MacAlister and family for a private view of the demonstrations which had achieved so marked a success.[75]

It would appear that it was on the initiative of Jacomb that progress was stepped up on the design and manufacture of prototype televisors. He also implemented the changeover from floodlighting the subject to scanning by flying spot. This enabled a smaller aluminium Nipkow disc, with pinholes instead of lenses, to be employed, which simplified the system and improved the quality of transmission.[76] In the July issue of *Television* there appeared (page 21) an editorial notice in a box: 'It has now been definitely announced that Baird Televisors ("seeing-in" instruments) will be on sale in this country at the annual Radio Exhibition, which will be held at Olympia, September 22nd to 29th.' In the event the company was not allowed to mount a stand at the exhibition itself. Visitors wishing to see television in action had to leave the main hall and cross over to Maclise Road.[77]

The first ever catalogue of television sets was issued at about this time. Three models were on offer. Model 'A' (£20) required to be connected to 'the output terminals of any ordinary wireless set which is capable of operating a loud speaker'. Model 'B' (£40) also required to to be worked in conjunction with a wireless set, one 'capable of operating a moving coil loud speaker', but gave a larger size image. The super set Model 'C' (£150) came with its own radio. 'Fitted in a handsome case', it formed 'a complete self-contained unit for simultaneous reception of vision and music, singing or speech.' Also offered was an optional 'Baird Three-Valve Amplifier' (£10).[78]

Shortly after the exhibition, William J Brittain, an acknowledged Baird-sceptic, saw a demonstration of the £40 televisor – a cost equivalent to about seventy-five theatre tickets at that time for the best seats in the house. He pronounced himself well satisfied.

The transmission was by land line. At the transmission end he 'saw the spiral-holed disc spinning before a bright light, and the beam of light covering rapidly and repeatedly the face of the sitter'. This is a clear reference to the flying-spot, or spotlight, method of scanning.

> At the receiving end I looked through the lens and saw tiny pink circles moving upwards as the disc in the televisor began to spin before the neon lamp. Soon the moving circles grew into images which flew upwards as the circles had done. A touch of the speed controlling device in front of the cabinet, and there behind the lens was an image of a man's face in detail – startling detail for me who had seen of Mr Baird's machines only his earlier or much simpler models. ... Later Miss Peggy O'Neil came. As soon as her image appeared behind the lens I realised that she had the perfect television face. I could have believed that I was looking into a mirror at her, only the image was in pink and black, due to the glow of the neon lamp.[79]

Peggy O'Neil was a star, described by the theatre critic W MacQueen Pope as a 'toast of the town; songs were written about this red-haired girl with the big eyes, and a brand of whisky was named after her'.[80]

Another convert was Bernard Jones, editor of *Amateur Wireless*. He had seen and reported on several demonstrations, and been much impressed: 'Such details as the whites of the eyes, the putting out of the tongue, and the passing of the extended hand over the face were clearly distinguishable.'[81] Now, nine weeks later, he had been given a special demonstration of new developments.

> We were very charmed with what we saw in the televisor. We saw a new dummy, we saw the face of one of Mr Baird's assistants and we saw also the faces of two young ladies who now provided speech and

song and 'vision' for Mr Baird's experimental work. ... A notable experiment ... was the reception, on a screen of translucent glass or paper approximately 3 ft by 2 ft, of the head of a model enlarged to at least double size. ... Obviously, the image on to the screen has been optically projected from a televisor [by means of a crater neon lamp].[81]

Experimental transmissions had begun in November 1928, from a specially built studio in Long Acre, using two transmitters mounted on the roof of the building. They went out at midnight (that is, outside normal broadcasting hours) on Tuesdays and Saturdays, and could be received in the London area on televisors such as had been displayed at various exhibitions. Members of staff were drafted in to provide the entertainment. 'Mr Baird's assistant', to whom Bernard Jones referred, was studio manager A F Birch, who had been initially employed as a technician. The 'two young ladies' were secretaries, Dora Caffrey and Connie King. Philip Hobson accompanied them on the piano. 'No extra pay, of course, let alone overtime, but it didn't matter and we all enjoyed doing it.'[77]

Caffrey and King performed for members of the Television Society at its meeting on 4 December 1928, the images and sound being transmitted from Long Acre to the Engineers' Club. 'This was the first time that many members had seen real television, and their comments on the action of the BBC in refusing facilities for broadcast purposes must have made many ears burn at Savoy Hill.'[82]

Apart from such homespun entertainments beamed to a limited range at inconvenient times, there was nothing for the home viewer to watch. The GPO had not still not granted a full licence for television transmissions, and the BBC, which had the monopoly of broadcasting, was, ostrich-like, keeping its collective head down and hoping that television would go away.

The GPO clearly reckoned that television was still at an experimental stage and therefore there was no cause to provide it as a public service. While lawyers for the Baird company tried to prove that no licence was required, the company itself made grandiose and often conflicting claims. The director general of the BBC, Sir John Reith (he had been knighted in 1927), issued statements which suggested a personal adversarial attitude and a state of some confusion within the ranks of his organisation.

Sides were taken. Scientists such as Ambrose Fleming and Alexander Russell supported the Baird company. For the BBC, its chief engineer, Eckersley, continued to argue in print that there was no proof yet that television was a practicable proposition.[83] His views were supported by the formidable Campbell Swinton, who had launched out with a letter to *The Times*.[84] He followed this up with an extraordinary document in the form of a letter, presumably to Eckersley, a typed transcript of part of which survives in BBC files:

> I fear that my view is simply that Baird and Hutchinson are rogues, clever rogues and quite unscrupulous, who are fleecing the ignorant public, and should be shown up. But there is a difficulty in doing so, I fear, because of the papers liking fat advertisements. *The Times* insisted in cutting out part of my letter which might have annoyed Baird and Co. ... Baird's advertisement in tonight's evening News and Standard [is] one of the most impudent efforts I remember, with its calm statement that they propose to 'broadcast their own programmes'. I cannot help wondering how the BBC is going to counter this advertisement, which, as it seems to me, can scarcely be allowed to stand.
>
> I think I have saved the Institution of Electrical Engineers having a paper by Baird, or at all events a discussion in which Baird would be invited to take part. One of the past Presidents was anxious for this, but I hope I have squashed the idea with the new President.[85]

Hutchinson, as we have seen, was quite capable of making extravagant predictions, but then shareholders in companies are used to this sort of blandishment. The Baird company had a licence to broadcast experimental programmes, and this they proposed to do, and did. The programmes would be received on sets sold for the purpose. That Campbell Swinton should have used his influence to persuade the Institution of Electrical Engineers not to give Baird a personal forum is peculiarly regrettable, especially in the light of the complaints levelled at Baird in *Nature* at the beginning of the previous year.[86]

Baird and Reith had first met, in what was probably 1907, at the Glasgow and West of Scotland Technical College (as it was then). Baird described the confrontation in his memoir:

> I was, and still am, very short-sighted and, at the beginning of one of the classes, the Professor asked if those who were short-sighted and wanted front seats would hand in their names. When I went up to the platform to give him my name, three large impressive young students were talking to him. They talked on terms of equality; in fact there was a distinct aroma of patronage. The young gentlemen were of the type we would today call 'heavies', and they boomed with heavy joviality at the poor little Professor who was distinctly embarrassed and ill at ease. I

interrupted timidly and handed him a piece of paper with my name on it. As I did so, the heaviest and most overpowering of the three heavies turned round and boomed at me, 'Ha! What is the matter with you? Are you deaf or blind?' I simpered something in inaudible embarrassment and he turned his back on me, and the three heavies walked out of the classroom booming portentously to each other.[87]

Whether or not they knew it at the time, Reith and Baird came from similar backgrounds. Reith's father, whose forebears had also been farmers, was a minister of the Free Church of Scotland, which had emerged from the Disruption in 1843 as a more austere movement than the Church of Scotland. George Reith had as his charge the influential College Church in Glasgow, and in the same way as did Baird himself, believed in the radical reform of abuses in the prevailing social system. Reith and Baird both idolised their mothers. Reith's was the daughter of a London stockbroker. Like Jessie Baird, she came from a well-to-do household, and was much given to good works in the community. Both Baird and Reith were youngest sons whose elder sister trained as a nurse. Beginning with the books in their father's studies, they were both widely read, though in this Baird had the edge. Reith, too, had a private education, but in his case it was cut short when his father could no longer afford the fees. Instead of continuing at school and going on to Oxford or Cambridge, he was sent to the technical college. He wrote in his autobiography:

> It was decided that I should become a mechanical engineer. A mechanical engineer. I knew it was all wrong; not at all mechanically minded; abhorrent the idea was. I wanted to go to a university – classics, philosophy, physics, literature, history; almost anything that was an intellectual rather than a manual pursuit.[88]

Reith was, then, a reluctant if not also refractory student, who did not believe he should be at the college. His behaviour towards Baird, who was a year older, could thus be interpreted simply as an isolated piece of loutish behaviour, to which Baird overreacted, though he remembered the hurt all his life. Reith tended to personalise his difficulties,[89] and it was equally in his nature to have taken an instant dislike to Baird, which he harboured for the rest of his life, his hatred being intensified in some perverse way by the fact that their backgrounds were so similar.

According to Baird's memoir, after the confrontation at college he met Reith just twice: once at the BBC, and once at a private lunch party with

Moseley at the Savoy.[90] Though Moseley also mentions the lunch party,[91] no firm date can be attributed to it. In fact, between January 1931 and December 1932 alone, Baird had no less than five personal meetings with Reith at the BBC; he also corresponded with him regularly.

Reith was also capable of what he himself referred to as 'insensate' jealousy,[92] and was prone to bouts of self-doubt and self-recrimination. In 1934 he confided to his personal diary:

> Tonight was so bored that having had a bath abt 7.15 I went to bed, getting up cocoa, toast and two eggs, reading Ian Hay's *David and Destiny*. It is about a Scottish boy of humble parentage more or less stranded in London, who determines to become a great man. There were bits every now and again which reminded me of myself, how ambitious I was and how certain that I was going to become famous. It was all profoundly disquieting and I am really very depressed, feeling that on an absolute basis I have become so little compared with what I expected, but quite definitely with what I might have become.[93]

It would be only too easy to cite Baird as an example of a Scottish boy of (more or less) humble parentage who became a great man in London. In 1934, at the time Reith wrote these words, Baird was the darling of the public and the press, the romantic inventor, the champion of the oppressed against the imperialistic attitude of the BBC; he was also ostensibly rich, and he had a young, glamorous, and talented wife. There is a story from much later in Reith's life told by Somerset Sullivan, who claimed to have got it from George Bernard Shaw in 1948. One summer evening, early in World War II, Reith was discovered by Shaw in a distressed state outside the bomb-damaged church where he had worshipped when he first came to London. Reith, who was obviously suffering from some emotional disturbance, expressed strong feelings of jealousy against Baird.[94] Though Shaw's biographer advises, with good reason, that the story should be treated with caution,[95] nevertheless both he and members of Reith's family agree that it has some ring of possibility about it.[96] There is, however, no evidence in BBC archives or in Reith's diaries of any personal animosity on his part towards Baird.

In one of his only two appearances on television, Reith, interviewed by Malcolm Muggeridge in 1967, was asked if he had originally seen the possibilities of television. He replied that he 'was frightened of it from the start'.[97] This had nothing to do with any lack of technical understanding. Though he claimed not to be mechanically minded, Reith ensured that he had on his staff leading experts on wireless technology, and he was brilliant at mastering a brief, however technical it might be. He was certainly frightened that television would compete for budget and attention with his plans for a worldwide wireless service, to be known as the Empire Service. There was, however, another aspect to his fear. He was a fervent believer, to whom the Word was God: the broadcast word should be without any ornamentation, as it was in his father's church, and as was his father's church itself.[98] In October 1928 he proposed to the GPO that if television transmissions were going to be licensed experimentally, it should be for pictures only, otherwise the BBC's monopoly would be infringed: 'The Corporation would, as you know, have the strongest objection to any infringement of its "sound" monopoly and if you must let the Baird company do something, however fatuous, I imagine it could be done within the terms of their experimental licence, but for pictures only.'[99] However ridiculous this may have sounded, to Reith himself it was perfectly realistic. It has also been suggested that Reith refused several invitations to walk the short distance to Long Acre to see television working.[100] If this is so, then it was because he did not wish to consort with the enemy of the unadorned word. So averse, indeed, was he to pictorial images, that he would never go to an art exhibition.[101]

In his 1967 interview, Reith described television as a 'potential social menace of the first magnitude',[102] an observation with which, with hindsight, many might agree. As for commercial television, in the House of Lords, to which he was elevated in 1940, he compared its introduction to that of 'smallpox, bubonic plague and the Black Death'.[103] His daughter recalls his being presented with a television set by the BBC just before World War II – one of those upright models, with the picture being projected from below on to the underside of the lid, which opened at an angle. It stood there, silent, never used.[104]

So it was amid a welter of recriminations from both sides of the argument that the GPO finally pinned down the Baird company to a demonstration to its engineers and other personnel on 18 September 1928. It took place between Long Acre and the Engineers' Club, by land line and by wireless. The faces of various individuals were transmitted as they talked or sang, and were received on a screen about 2 inches by 3½ inches, the picture being then magnified to about double that size. Reactions were mixed, but the general judgment in the GPO's report[105] by its superintending engineer was sufficiently favourable for the BBC to bow to the inevitable and prepare for an application from the Baird company for facilities to broadcast television. One genuine problem was the availability of suitable wavebands. Another was that no representative of the BBC had seen the demonstration.

In the meantime, Moseley had signified his entrance into the fray with a flurry of letters to (W E) Gladstone Murray, assistant controller (information) of the BBC. Murray, a Canadian, was a former air correspondent of the *Daily Express*. He was recommended to Reith by Lord Beaverbrook, the Canadian newspaper tycoon, and joined the BBC in 1924. He was appointed an assistant controller of programmes in 1935, but left the BBC under a cloud in 1936, after which he became general manager of the newly-formed Canadian Broadcasting Corporation. Moseley came to consider Murray as a close friend, and in 1935, when Moseley and his wife embarked on a Mediterranean cruise, Murray and his wife Ella came to see them off, with gifts of fruit and flowers.[106]

The day before the demonstration to the GPO, Murray gave lunch to Baird, Hutchinson, and Moseley at the Mayfair Hotel. Afterwards they repaired to Long Acre, where Murray was treated to a demonstration of television. To Moseley, 'The struggle to put Baird over with the BBC is more or less a *guerre à mort* – no holds barred, etc. ... Murray is sympathetic and will join me in fighting for Baird Television. ... He knows the line-up now – what we are up against – outside and *inside* the BBC, and he will help us.'[107]

The lunch was by way of being a sop, to judge from Murray's letter to Moseley four days later (21 September 1928):

> Further to my letter to you of the 13th instant, I was glad to recognise that you had withdrawn the absurd and offensive charges enunciated in your letter. In view of your apology and explanation, it gave me great pleasure to entertain Mr Baird, Captain Hutchinson and yourself at lunch. ...
>
> You remarked on Monday that many curious things seem to happen in connection with television, particularly in its relationship with the BBC. I noted your remark, and I have been endeavouring to eliminate any element of uncertainty or confusion so far as lies in my power. I had thought that I was being helped in this direction by your thorough disinterestedness. You will recall the emphasis which you placed upon the assertion that you had no financial interest whatever in television. I would not have been surprised, or would have considered it in no way discreditable, if you had admitted that you were engaged with the Baird Company. But you were quite clear and precise that your interest in television was purely altruistic. So I accepted this and resolved the resentment which had found expression in my letter to you of the 13th. ...
>
> Now today, in the 'Morning Post' there is a story about Television,

including a statement that you are a Director of the Company producing the paper 'Television'. This is nothing to be ashamed of. The
only thing is, if the story is true, why did you refrain from telling me
anything about your connection with the Baird Company? ... I would
be glad to continue a measure of collaboration with you provided that
you are able to define your position clearly, and provided also that in
connection with technical subjects you undertake to try to avoid the
pitfalls of ignorant and loose thought.[108]

Clearly, guidelines were being drawn up. By way of a footnote to this
particular exchange, shortly afterwards Moseley sent to Reith an article on
television by Ambrose Fleming.[109] The veteran scientist, inventor of the
thermionic valve which was a staple part of all radio and television transmitters and receivers, and president of the Television Society, would be
knighted in 1929. Reith circulated the article to senior members of staff.
Among the comments written on the accompanying internal memo were
'Soul selling. G[ladstone] M[urray]' and 'The old man's gone potty. P P
E[ckersley]'.[85]

A formal demonstration for representatives of the BBC was arranged for
9 October. In the meantime, Murray had on 1 October received an internal
memorandum on 'Television' from J Whitehouse, who seems to have been
acting as a temporary BBC mole in the Baird camp.

The Baird machine may be said to give a recognisable human head. It is
curiously unlike any particular face. ... Only very slow movements are
possible, any thing of even normal speed producing a wild blurr. The
impression is of a curiously ape like head, decapitated at the chin,
swaying up and down in a streaky stream of yellow light. ... The faces
of those leaving the show showed neither excitement or interest. Rather
like a Fair crowd who had sported 6d to see if the fat lady was really as
fat as she was made out to be. The image was held for 4½ minutes before
requiring adjustment which seemed a simple operation.[85]

Among Reith's first administrative steps in 1923 had been to appoint as
his deputy Rear-Admiral Charles Carpendale, who now had the job title
of controller. The following year Reith established a policy control board,
comprising the half-dozen or so most senior members of staff. Ralph Wade,
whom Reith had invited to join the organisation as an administrator in
1923, later committed to paper his thoughts about the BBC. He regarded
the control board as 'a shield against outside, or even government, criticism',

but which left much to be desired as the originator of speedy, intelligent, or original decisions:

> The members are at best exercising a remote control over what their executive staff are in fact doing and many of the decisions reached are really quite wrong ones. ...You can't sack a control board *en bloc*, but you can sack an individual director or head of department. The best test of suitability for headship of any group or activity is the willingness to accept responsibility. Once you have a board or committee which is technically responsible for *your* opinions, either you despair of getting things done *as you know they should be done* or, if you are that type, you nestle snugly down behind the protective screen of high level decision and become a 'Yes' man.[110]

The chips were stacked even higher against the Baird company when Eckersley largely prejudged the outcome of the demonstration by circulating to members of the control board on 8 October a memorandum, 'Suggested Attitude to Television', summing up 'what has been my point of view for a long while':

> Control Board will see tomorrow the demonstration of the head and shoulders of a man; it will be extremely interesting and quite likely better than what you have been led to expect. The question remains can the full length of a man be given adequately, or two men standing together talking, or a lot of men playing football, or a liner arriving at Plymouth, or any topical event? Can they, in fact, inadequately possibly, give running commentaries? If they say that they cannot at present give running commentaries, but will be able to later, our reply should be 'then we will wait until you can before we do experiments'. ...
>
> Perhaps on the other hand, some of the Control Board may take the view that the head and shoulders of a man is sufficiently interesting for us to do transmissions. If this point of view (which I personally do not subscribe to) is taken, it must be remembered that in effect an extra wavelength must be sacrificed for television ... and I think to take up so much aether in the broadcasting band simply to give the small picture of the head and shoulders of a man to people who can afford £40 sets, is rather ridiculous. ...
>
> I want to insist that in my opinion and in the opinion of many experts, the method of television at present used cannot be developed any further because quantities are against it. They can polish up the head

and shoulders as it were, but they can never give a complete man. ... If it is thought by Control Board that what they see demonstrated, i.e. *what has been done by Baird*, justifies in itself a service, then let us go ahead, but I warn everyone that in my opinion, it is the end of their development, not the beginning, and that we shall be for ever sending heads and shoulders.[85]

The following morning control board nominated six members of staff to attend the afternoon demonstration: Carpendale, Eckersley, his brother Roger, who was assistant controller (programmes), Murray, Noel Ashbridge, assistant chief engineer, and Major C F Atkinson, director of publicity. It was the first of several occasions on which Reith avoided attending a television demonstration or indeed any function connected with television.[111] The minute of the meeting stressed that 'No opinion is to be expressed either at the time of the demonstration or subsequently in response to enquiry.'[85]

On 10 October Murray addressed a memorandum to Carpendale, who was perfectly capable of coming to his own conclusions.

From the angle of service, yesterday's demonstration would be merely ludicrous if its financial implications did not make it sinister. The demonstration in terms of service might well be considered an insult to the intelligence of those invited to be present. ... The Baird method is either an intentional fraud or a hopeless mechanical failure. ... Keeping in mind the fundamental fact that the intrusion of Baird transmissions into the broadcasting band will gravely disturb our normal service and prejudice the Regional Scheme, I think it is our duty to resist or delay the suggestion in every reasonable and possible way. It is obviously the intention of the Post Office to dump the blame for further obstruction on our shoulders. This does not worry me in the slightest. We can carry well-informed and disinterested opinion with us. This is all that matters.

I think we should issue a carefully considered statement in which would be expressed our benevolent interest in all new inventions concerned with wireless and we should say quite frankly what we think of the Baird device on the scientific side, adding that in the future as in the past we shall be glad to see their results if they improve, and indeed to help them as long as this can be done without our being a party to misleading the public or disturbing our normal service.[85]

No announcement had yet been made when on 15 October Murray sent out eleven form letters, to the Press Association, Associated Newspapers, the editors of such papers as *The Times*, *Daily Express*, and *Daily Mail*, and to prominent individuals including Professor Edward Appleton, the noted physicist who was an adviser to the BBC.

> I am passing you in strict confidence a private tip to instruct your people to avoid accepting rumours of the favourable attitude of the BBC towards the Baird Television scheme. ... I owe it to you personally to tell you now that in my opinion there is a distinct element of 'ramp' either conscious or unconscious in connection with the Baird scheme and that this should be watched with extreme care.[85]

In spite of Post Office misgivings that an uncompromising attitude on the part of the BBC would simply result in the Baird company having to be granted permission for a more powerful station of their own, the BBC duly issued, on 17 October, the inevitable judgment: 'The demonstration was interesting as an experiment [but] failed to fulfil the conditions which would justify trial through a BBC station. ... The Corporation would be ready to review this decision if and when development justified it.'[112]

Shares in the Baird companies fell. Baird, no stranger to professional as well as physical adversity, was quoted as making a forthright statement:

> I regard the decision of the BBC to grant no facilities to television as a challenge which I mean to take up. The attitude of the Corporation, though not unexpected, is inexplicable, because it is a direct contradiction to that adopted by the Post Office and many leading scientists. Whatever may be behind the decision I intend to go forward independently. In a short time I shall be broadcasting vision on my own.[113]

This was no idle threat. On 1 November Baird himself announced through the press that he had negotiated an agreement whereby the Dutch government would make a transmission station available to him to broadcast television pictures from Scheveningen.[114]

There is an indication of Baird's state of mind at the time, and also of his personal concerns, in a letter he sent from Long Acre on 30 October to Mephy, now living on the outskirts of London in Clapham:

> My dear Mephy
> Sorry to hear you have been ill. Have had desperate worries up here over many things. Regret to hear of your worries, if they are of a finan-

cial nature please let me know if I can assist. While my '<u>wealth</u>' is still <u>entirely on paper</u>, I can raise a fair amount of hard cash. In any case call and see me next time you are in London.*

It is signed with the initials 'JLB'.

7
Sound and Vision
1929–1930

Shortly after Baird's letter to him, Mephy took charge of the domestic arrangements of them both. Mephy was an occasional actor;[1] nothing could have been more dramatic than the change he implemented in Baird's home life. In January 1929, having lived for a decade in a succession of lodgings or cheap hotels, Baird rented for three years, fully furnished, a former hunting-lodge in the grounds of the country seat of the Duke of Marlborough. It was called Swiss Cottage, on Box Hill in Surrey (telephone Dorking 219). The site was so spectacular that much of the land around was subsequently acquired by the National Trust.

Though the house was only a few miles from the town of Dorking, its only access was by a narrow road along the top of the ridge or by foot up a steep path.

> The road was very bad and on a foggy night the journey could provide adventure. On one occasion I fell asleep, and the taximan missed the road and took me nearly to Brighton before I woke up. On another occasion the taxi ran off the road and charged down the side of Box Hill, finishing up with a crash of glass and an oath of blasphemy from the drunken driver in a clump of bushes.[2]

Baird described the house as a 'most beautiful and romantic spot'.[2] The comparative isolation may also have appealed to him as a suitable environment in which he could entertain 'Alice', with whom he was still involved, when she came on her discreet visits. Mephy acted as major-domo, and supervised the staff, which comprised a Scottish housekeeper, a maid, a gardener-cum-chauffeur, and a cat called Winkle, who used to sit up with Mephy in front of the great log fire in the drawing-room waiting for Baird to arrive home in the evening.

When I was at home Mephy and I spent happy hours tramping over Box Hill, discussing the pre-established harmony amid the trees and recalling the past. Then we climbed the bridle path leading up to the chalky side of the hill. Mephy strode in front, a gaunt figure in a flapping black highland cape, his long grey hair floating in the wind, and grasping in his hand a great forked staff. One day we passed a lady with a little girl and I heard her whisper loudly, 'No dear, that's not Jesus.'[2]

It was a luxury existence at a time when Baird had begun observing, 'Money is no object.'[3] He had a hired chauffeur-driven Daimler, in which guests would be driven out from London and returned there. Sometimes, when there was no formal or informal dinner in London, he would get Moseley to accompany him home after work; the car would later take Moseley back to his London flat, 30a Primrose Hill Road, Hampstead. At other times Moseley would suggest lists of guests, including scientists and other prominent people, for small informal dinner parties at Swiss Cottage. Or Baird would invite the principal guest to bring a party of friends. One such supper party was held in July 1931 for Robert Pound, with whom Baird was in touch several times during that summer. Guests ate off the best china, with cutlery bought by Mephy from Mappin and Webb, while Baird, who used to be tongue-tied when facing members of his board of directors, acted the affable and interesting host. He also entertained at the Burford Bridge Hotel, a notable establishment at the foot of Box Hill.

People who knew Baird wonder why in the 1930s he never had or drove a car of his own. Considering his former penchant for unusual, and fast, motor vehicles, one might have thought that the first thing he would have done when he was in the money was to go out and buy the most powerful sports car he could find. It is possible that he could no longer trust his chronic short-sightedness when at the wheel. Or, as a former colleague observed, 'It may have been just another symptom of his liking to avoid tiresome detail. He would have to have thought about petrol quantity, radiator water and tube oil levels, tyre pressures and all the rest of it.'[4] This avoidance of detail was readily apparent in the laboratory, where he is recorded as beaming pleasantly at the newest recruit to the technical staff and saying, 'I want you to build me a ten-watt short-wave transmitter with plenty of sideband scope. Get what you need from the stores and let me have it in three days, will you?'[5] Baird no longer bothered to make lists of what to pack when going away, or even to pack. He used to buy what he needed when he got there. To a member of staff who asked him where his luggage was, for a forthcoming trip, he replied, taking a spare collar out of his pocket, 'This, Mr Percy, is my luggage.'[6]

As Moseley observed, one of Baird's personal vanities was to look 'the typical inventor':

> Consciously or unconsciously, he could *see* himself in this role. … I remember his arriving once at my hotel in Westcliffe-on-Sea in a large car complete with liveried chauffeur. It was a magnificent turn-out, but when the porters hurried up to his limousine to take his luggage, Baird pointed to an odd-looking bundle wrapped in a dressing-gown on the back seat. It contained all the wardrobe which he had brought with him on this visit, and it was not the hotel porter but the chauffeur who carried it into the hall with as much dignity as he could muster.[7]

Baird often worked until three or four in the morning in the laboratories. His method of encouraging his staff was mildly to ask, 'Well, have you anything to show me?' J D Percy said of him:

> My most vivid impression was his enormous toughness, underneath the quiet, dreamlike quality of his external personality. He would stop at nothing to achieve his end, which was always the furtherance of television. He had an unmatchable sense of humour and great courage, but I shall remember his resilience till I die. Underneath our professional relationship, affection was ninety per cent of what I felt for JLB.[8]

The year 1928 had ended with a flurry of rumours and press speculations. The *Daily Mirror* announced (5 November) that the Baird company would shortly be transmitting programmes from six stations on the continent, which would be sponsored by advertisers. The *Daily News* had had a report (29 July) that the Hungarian inventor Mihaly, who had lived in Berlin for ten years, intended to manufacture television sets and set up a company in Britain which would use a different system to Baird's, but much better.[9] In Britain the Marconi company and the Thomson–Houston company were rumoured to be developing television systems.[10]

The leaks, official and unofficial, gathered pace early in 1929. The price of shares in the Baird companies fluctuated in response to whatever rumour prevailed at the time. On 9 January Hutchinson was reported in the *Morning Post* as having stated that negotiations had been concluded with seven stations on the continent to broadcast programmes of music, singing, and speech, using the Baird system. He also indicated that the German government had recently sent a deputation to London to examine the Baird system. 'As a result we are installing a television transmitter in their Berlin studios for the purpose of public demonstrations with a view to their adopting the system generally.' This last statement was true.[11]

The BBC's management was under siege to justify its decision not to allow Baird facilities to transmit television programmes. In spite of various press reports that arrangements had been made for a further test of the Baird apparatus through one of the BBC's stations, the BBC issued a statement alleging that 'Baird Television Company has not yet intimated to the BBC any claim of improvement. Any such claim would be examined by the BBC with a view to determining whether the decision should be modified.'[12]

In the meantime Moseley had been quietly orchestrating support from notable members of the public. Demonstrations were given in Long Acre to people such as Sir Thomas Inskip, the attorney general, Lady Waley Cohen, wife of the industrialist, Field-Marshal and Lady Allenby, Sir Godfrey Thomas, personal secretary to the Prince of Wales, Lord Baden-Powell, author and journalist Rebecca West, and members of parliament who included Herbert Morrison, Minister of Transport, Charles Ammon, and Cecil Malone. Malone was one of the few members of the House of Commons with scientific experience, and he had in 1912 carried out the first experiments with wireless telegraphy from a naval aircraft.

Sir Herbert (later Viscount) Samuel came twice, on one occasion with his wife and thirty-year-old son, Edwin. Statesman, politician, philosopher, and reformer, Samuel had served both as an effective Postmaster General and, for ten years, an influential Home Secretary in Liberal and national governments. As a Jew of Reform sympathies, and, in the wake of the 1917 Balfour Declaration, from 1920 to 1925 Britain's first high commissioner in Palestine, he was no stranger to controversial assignments. He is also attributed with the aphorism about the civil service, 'A difficulty for every solution'. On 14 January 1929 he wrote to the Postmaster General, Sir William Mitchell-Thompson (later Lord Selsdon), enclosing a copy of a letter which he intended to send to the press, and suggesting that the GPO might wish to bring influence to bear on the BBC to change its attitude. As a former Postmaster General he felt that it was the function of the GPO to assist the cause of a new 'and perhaps useful' form of communication. The proposed letter to the press compared the facilities available in the USA and France with the complete lack of them in Britain. It criticised the attitude of Eckersley in denying that any progress was possible under the present circumstances. It concluded,

That the dead hand of monopoly should be laid upon a most remark-able invention, that the public should be denied access to it; that a brilliant inventor should be met, not with the gratitude and the active encouragement which are his due, but with an attitude of indifference and even of obstruction, this would indeed be in accordance with many precedents in the past, but it would not be in accordance with an enlightened view of the public need.[13]

Samuel's initiative[14] fell on receptive ears, for Mitchell-Thompson, with his assistant Viscount Wolmer, had already paid a private visit to Long Acre and had been favourably impressed by what they saw.[15] Discussions between the GPO and the BBC were now brought to a head, and a definitive test, on terms proposed by the BBC, which included absolute secrecy, was arranged for 27 February. To ensure that the BBC's conditions would be observed, Reith asked Hutchinson to see him on 30 January. It was their first meeting.[16]

Reith's private report of the meeting was distributed to Carpendale, Eckersley, and Murray.[17] Hutchinson hotly denied that either he or Baird, or any members of their boards, were 'market jugglers'; neither had he or Baird disposed of any shares, though they had purchased more. The BBC's press announcement after the last demonstration had, he suggested, jeopardised a deal with France which would have been, and still might be, advantageous to British interests. 'He spoke in general terms of the desirability of there being British control throughout the world and said we could help them to have this.' They discussed the conditions for the demonstration:

As [Hutchinson] was leaving, I reverted to the general situation and asked him how he could reconcile what he had said as to their integrity, etc., with last autumn's advertisement, which gave the public to believe that they would be able to 'look in' at Ascot, etc. He said that he was abroad and that the advertisement had been done by the Secretary, and he had got into trouble about it. I said that was not the only case and I thought it a pity that they should prejudice their technical case by exaggerated and unwarranted statements concerning the immediate commercial and public use. He said he quite agreed that their line had not always been wise, and mentioned incidentally that many newspapers were prepared to give them a great boost in return for criticism of the BBC at the time of the recent press attack, and he had refused. I told him I could not understand this, and that it would not have hurt us anyhow. I told him that it was absurd of people on his side to blame Captain Eckersley for the attitude of the BBC to them, and that they themselves were largely responsible, as above.[17]

Reith may not have been aware at the time that the condition of secrecy had been blown apart the previous day, when Cecil Malone asked the Postmaster General in parliament whether the GPO had ever suggested to the BBC that facilities for experimental television transmissions should be given to the Baird system. The minister replied that he had informed both parties several months before that, subject to suitable conditions, he would agree to a BBC station being used for this purpose. The BBC had implied that the system did not at present justify a trial, while expressing a readiness to review the decision if and when there had been sufficient development. He announced that a further demonstration was being arranged.[17]

Murray addressed a memorandum to Reith:

> The well informed gossip in the Lobby [of the House of Commons] makes no secrecy of the view that the BBC is being forced by political pressure to change its policy towards television. It is not suggested that the motive of pressure is an improper one, but rather that the previous policy of the BBC was unfairly reactionary in the technical sense. The verdict is almost certain to be cautiously friendly to television, with a recommendation to some further action on the part of the BBC. I think it highly important that this recommendation should be to the Baird company and not to the BBC; and should take the form of advising the Baird Company to avail themselves of the invitation contained in our last two official statements.[18]

The test took place not on 27 February, but on 5 March, beginning at 11.15am. The programme was to be transmitted from Savoy Hill, the BBC's headquarters, through its normal station 2LO. It would be viewed at Savoy Hill and at the head office of the GPO at St Martins-le-Grand, 1500 metres away, on a series of televisors of the kind that it was proposed to sell to the public. As Baird himself said later,

> It was a nerve wracking ordeal as we were to stand or fall by the result of one crucial demonstration. A wire slipping or a valve burning out at the critical moment, and the demonstration would be a failure and we would be faced with a devastating fiasco. I spent a dreadful nightmare night on the top floor of Savoy Hill where we set up our transmitter.[19]

The receiving station chosen at the GPO was a large committee room, hung with portraits of past postmasters, going back to the sixteenth century, and other historic pictures. Outside aerials were not possible, so the Baird engineers made do with lengths of rubber-covered wire hung from the picture rails, with a radiator brought into service as the earth. Two televisors were installed with their accompanying batteries, one a sound and vision set, and the other a portable without a loud speaker. These were tuned in to a BBC music programme and adjusted until there was a clear pattern of wavy lines representing the sound. When the wavelength became free for television after midnight, objects and faces came over quite clearly. Since no BBC wavelength was available for the sound, this was to be sent by means of a Baird transmitter. The BBC provided a piano.

The parliamentary advisory committee which had been appointed to judge the demonstration was led by the Earl of Clarendon, who was also, significantly, chairman of the BBC. He and half his team viewed the demonstration at the GPO, while the rest saw it at Savoy Hill. As the time approached, Baird, accompanied by Sir Ambrose Fleming, left the BBC for St Martins-le-Grand, where he found the televisors working properly.

The programme consisted of head-and-shoulders shots of singers and comedians performing; among them was Jack Buchanan, once again giving his time to his friend. At the end there was a surprise appearance by no less than Eckersley himself, making his first, and possibly only, appearance on television.

There appeared to be no hitch. One of the members of parliament at the GPO receiving end commented, 'This must be a swindle. You can't get this by wireless.' When being assured that you could, he remarked a few moments later, 'Extraordinary. Truly wonderful!'[20]

There were still the findings of the committee to be faced up to. These were indicated in a letter (27 March 1929) from the Postmaster General to the Baird company, which was published in *The Times* the following day. It contained several crucial observations, which can be summarised thus:

1   While it was not yet possible to transmit more than two or three people at a time, or any scene or performance that was not restricted to a few feet, the reproduction was of the required clarity.
2   The system itself represented a 'noteworthy scientific achievement', but because of the present limitations, there was no justification for transmitting television programmes during the normal hours of broadcasting. He would, however, certainly agree to this being done through a BBC channel outside broadcasting hours.

3   It was understood that for sound as well as vision, two transmitters would be required and two wavelengths. It anticipated that a second transmitter which would not interfere with crucial wireless services would be available in July, through the new BBC station at Brookmans Park in Hertfordshire.

4   In the event of television being transmitted within normal broadcasting hours it would be necessary to use wavelengths that were already much congested. The Baird company was therefore urged to experiment with a lower band, which he would make available.

5   Neither he nor the BBC accepted any responsibility for the quality of transmissions, and those who bought televisors did so at their own risk.

It was a personal triumph for Baird, whom Moseley described as having at this time 'the vision of a prophet, the happy confidence of a child and the business sagacity of a sheepdog, gazing with placid eyes through the shock of hair which his so much resembled'.[21] In the long term, however, it proved to be a Pyrrhic victory for his company. The BBC wavelength was so long that it could only accommodate a narrow bandwidth. While this was perfectly adequate for sound broadcasting, it limited the amount of definition that could be included in a television picture. Had Baird concentrated on the short wavelength (45 metres) which he had used for his transatlantic transmissions, there would have been more scope for improved picture definition. On the other hand, few people had radios which could pick up short waves.

Hutchinson now pressed the BBC for a quick decision as to how the advisory committee's proposals were to be acted upon. Eckersley replied that as the Brookmans Park installation, one of a series of twin-wave transmitting stations which were planned to cover the whole of Britain, would not now be ready until October, there was no point in having discussions until later in the summer. Hutchinson predictably blew his top. He also reminded Eckersley of the meeting he and Baird had had with him, at which Eckersley had apparently agreed that the Baird company should transmit daily between 11am and 12 noon, and also on three nights a week after midnight, when the BBC normally closed down.[22] This meeting could well have been the one described by Baird in his memoir, held over dinner at the Savoy. Noel Ashbridge, assistant chief engineer, who had joined the BBC, also from the Marconi Company, in January 1926, was present too.

Eckersley I found a most entertaining and human personality, and I got on extremely well with him. This was before the days of my total abstinence and we dined and wined lavishly. At about eleven, Ashbridge had to go and catch a train, but Eckersley and I remained over our old brandy until after one in the morning. 'If we had only met sooner,' said Eckersley, 'all this trouble over television would never have arisen.'[23]

Not only Eckersley was procrastinating. On 30 May, a Labour government had been narrowly elected into power, and a new Postmaster General, H B Lees-Smith, a fellow of The Queen's College, Oxford, and lecturer in economics, took office. This enabled Reith on 14 June 1929, to address a letter to Sir Evelyn Murray, secretary of the GPO:

> The corporation would have been glad had the late Postmaster General, after the definitely unconvincing demonstration which he and others witnessed, been able to deal with the Baird Company in such a way as would not have involved an early promise of co-operation by this Corporation, and without giving the Baird Company such increased facilities as might technically or otherwise, prejudice the Corporation.[24]

What the Baird representatives could not understand was why the BBC should be dragging its heels over the development of television programmes, when the corporation had since the previous year, out of programme hours, been supporting the Fultograph. This was a system for transmitting still pictures by radio which could then be reconstructed in the home with the help of a device connected to the normal wireless set. The fact that the Fultograph was a commercial failure did not help matters. With hindsight, the answer probably lies in Reith's personal attitude. Pictures without sound were marginally acceptable: it was the combination of pictures *and* sound that was anathema to him. It would also appear that two senior executives of the BBC had put money into Fultograph when its company's issue was floated in 1928.[25]

Meanwhile Baird continued with his private experiments. He was now investigating thirty-line horizontal, as opposed to vertical, scanning, assisted by Hobson and another technician, G B Banks. 'For demonstration purposes a boxing ring was constructed in the laboratory, and ultimately a press demonstration was given. As with so many of Baird's experiments, once it had been demonstrated to the press he lost interest.'[26]

To be fair, in his capacity as managing director, Baird had other things on his mind, and it was the initiative of his company and of himself, more than the blustering of Hutchinson, that forced the hand of the BBC. During the summer of 1929 Hutchinson and Moseley went to Berlin to return the

German visit, and were royally received by Dr Bredow and by President Kruckow of the German central post office.

> We were shown the up-to-date methods which characterise the working of this government department, and when (later) John Baird himself came over[27] he was enthralled with the excellent workmanship of the radio and television apparatus in the Post Office. ... All the more pleasing is it, therefore, that for the first time in history *the Baird apparatus has been installed in this building* [the central post office] so that the Baird engineers and our German friends will co-operate in further developments.[28]

Moseley went on gleefully to inform the British public that permission had been given for the transmission 'for the first time in history [of] a daily broadcast from 9-10am, sometimes between 1pm and 2pm, and after midnight'.[28]

On 21 June 1929 a new television company was established in Berlin. Fernseh AG was a joint foundation by the Baird company, Robert Bosch AG of Stuttgart (electric motors), Loewe Radio GmbH of Berlin (wireless parts), and Zeiss Ikon AG of Dresden (cameras and cinema projectors). The chairman was Emanuel Goldberg (Zeiss Ikon), a scientist as well as an administrator, who had himself researched aspects of television. The other members of the initial board were Hutchinson, David Ludwig Loewe, Erich Carl Rassbach (Bosch), and Eberhard Falkenstein (Zeiss Ikon's legal adviser).[29] The company headquarters was in Zeiss Ikon's Berlin factory at Zehlendorf. It was an uneven combination of forces. Bosch and Zeiss Ikon were large companies with substantial financial resources: Baird and Loewe were small organisations with specialist technical knowledge, and the Baird company was already in financial difficulties.

Back in London, the GPO stuck to its guns, and the BBC capitulated, with a singular lack of generosity and grace. Eckersley, having strayed from the paths of Reithian righteousness by flaunting his affair with the estranged wife of a BBC colleague, had been ordered to resign.[30] This left the BBC free to ignore any verbal undertakings that he may have given. On 26 June, Sir Charles Carpendale, the BBC's controller, wrote to the Baird company, offering transmission facilities for fifteen minutes three times a week at 11am. The respective chairmen of the Baird companies, Lord Ampthill and Sir Edward Manville, appealed to the new Postmaster General, asking for a minimum of six hours a week during normal broadcasting time, plus additional facilities outside normal hours. To his credit, Lees-Smith intervened with the BBC, and a compromise was agreed in discussions between Baird and Hutchinson and representatives of the BBC. Beginning on Monday, 30 September, there would be a regular half-hour programme at 11am every day from Monday to Friday, with additional facilities after midnight. The programmes would be transmitted from Long Acre to Savoy Hill and then broadcast on 2LO. For these facilities the Baird company would pay the BBC £5 for each half-hour broadcast, plus any capital cost in which the BBC was involved.[31] In addition, Baird, Hutchinson, and Bartlett (as company secretary) signed an agreement indemnifying the BBC against any claims by other parties arising out of the transmissions.[32]

As far as the BBC was concerned, their action came not a moment too soon. Without any fuss or publicity, Baird had already set up a powerful station at Kingsbury, a district of north London between Hendon and Harrow, with two 80-foot aerials set in concrete, capable of receiving television signals from the continent. In July, after seven months' work on the site, the first picture from Berlin appeared on the screen. It was the face of a gnome, with pointy beard and peaked hat, belonging to a doll which Baird had bought locally and named Albrecht.[33] By way of further experiment, the image of a person's face was converted into sound waves and sent from Kingsbury to New York, where it was successfully received.[34] The masts were dismantled in 1940.

On 17 July there was another memorable demonstration:

> I became a member of the Caledonian Club [then situated in St James's Square] early in 1928 through Lord Angus Kennedy [a vice-president of the Television Society] who was one of its staunchest supporters and oldest members. This led to my giving a demonstration to King Edward VIII, then Prince of Wales. We installed a receiver at the Club and arranged a special television programme to be sent over the line from Long Acre. I remember one of the performers was Gwen Farrar. I dined together with the other members of the Club at a dinner given to the Prince of Wales. After dinner, in the usual sweat of apprehension, I went up to the reception room. The image was coming through well. The Prince of Wales was ushered in by Lord Inverforth complete with double chins, bay window, pompous affability and a large cigar.
>
> The Prince of Wales shook hands affably, a smallish, thin, youngish man. He looked at the little flickering image and recognized Miss Farrar (she had a large cowslick wisp of hair which helped recognition). 'Very interesting – Amazing – Did you invent this? – Remarkable – Still a good deal to be done before it rivals the cinema. How is it Done? –

Must have taken you a long time.' Such were the nature of his remarks to which I replied in a sweat of embarrassment, and apprehension that the apparatus, which was developing precarious symptoms, would break down.

The gathering, after twenty minutes, departed in an atmosphere of cigars, white waistcoated corporations and a faint aura of old brandy. The cordial boomings and throaty laughter faded down the corridor. 'Damn good thing they have gone,' muttered the engineer who was looking after the apparatus. 'The bloody motor's nearly red hot.'[35]

Lord Inverforth was an industrialist and former wartime Minister of Munitions. That Baird should caricature him may have something to do with the fact that Inverforth subsequently became chairman of the Marconi–EMI company, which was to play such a critical role in the battle for the BBC contract. Gwen Farrar was a notable revue artiste, a comedienne with an eccentric appearance and a habit of doing the unexpected, such as suddenly taking a turn on a cello with perfect artistry. The programme on this occasion included two other turns. There was a demonstration of a 'tele-talkie', or talking film, of the head and shoulders of George Robey, known as the 'Prime Minister of Mirth', in his inimitable act as a much-married woman. A live performance was also given by Reginald S Shaw, a member of the Baird staff, who was making the first of a number of regular appearances as a black-faced minstrel.[36]

Lord Angus Kennedy was not at this private demonstration. At the invitation of the British Association for the Advancement of Science, he had sailed for South Africa with Clarence Tierney, chairman of the Television Society, and two Baird engineers, to demonstrate the Baird system at its meetings in Cape Town and Johannesburg.[37] These took place between 22 July and 5 August at Witwatersrand University, Cape Town Broadcasting Station, and the Engineering College of Cape Town University. At Witwatersrand, representatives of the press and others saw a man's face and heard his voice transmitted from another part of the building. The press reported, 'It was a living image and far more natural than the early results of transmitting the voice by wireless.'[34]

The Baird companies were spending a great deal of their shareholders' money, without, it would appear, any income from which to pay dividends. The value of the shares fluctuated as new market possibilities presented themselves or were developed from existing ones. Baird continued to demonstrate diversifications of television techniques while, with hindsight, he would have done better to concentrate on refining his mechanical systems for public broadcasting. He was also slow to appreciate the potential of electronic technology such as the cathode-ray tube.

So, on 9 August journalists were called to Box Hill for a demonstration of the latest development to that old standby, noctovision; this was the navigational version, prepared by Banks and Hobson. To set up the event, the technicians made a temporary home in two caravans on a site on top of the hill, and Hobson bought a small, second-hand Rover 8 air-cooled car, which he taught himself to drive in a convenient field.[38]

As always with Baird's public shows, the demonstration had about it a touch of the theatre. The apparatus, mounted on gimbals on a portable stand, was set up in the garden. When night fell, Hobson drove the car away from the house. The spectators could follow its lights as it joined the main road and reappeared in the valley below, coming to a stop about three miles away. The car was turned round, with one of its headlights pointing back to the house. Suddenly it went out. It had been covered by a sheet of ebonite, representing fog, which would cut out all but the infra-red waves. Up on the hill, Banks, acting the part of a ship's navigator, searched the valley with his noctovisor for the hidden light. The spectators, looking over his shoulder and through an opening in the back of the apparatus, suddenly saw a bright spot appear at the edge of the screen inside. Banks adjusted the apparatus until the spot came into focus as a brilliant orange light at the centre of the screen. From a circular graduated scale round which the noctovisor revolved, he read off the precise compass bearing of the invisible light.[39]

A national paper had a report:

> Mr Baird told me that several naval and mercantile officers have seen the noctovisor and believe it will be of enormous use to ships at sea.
>
> 'It should be of great use to fog-bound ships,' said Mr Baird. 'A ship in even the thickest fog will be able to see the lights of ships near by.'[40]

These words duly returned to haunt Baird shortly afterwards, when he arranged a demonstration for representatives from the Admiralty one evening in September, to be held at 11pm after dinner at Swiss Cottage. Hobson mounted a much more powerful lamp[41] on the roof of the porch of the Red Lion Hotel in Dorking, 1½ miles away in a straight line.

> As of course we knew the precise bearing, I then put the filter in place, and went back up the hill. For the demonstration the plan was to search for and find the bearing of the lamp from the scale provided on the instrument. But by about 10 o'clock the first of the autumn mists was

beginning to form, and to our consternation we could get no response when on the known bearing. I dashed down the hill, and had some difficulty getting back after having removed the filter, as the mist was developing rapidly. The worst had happened; we had a real fog to deal with, *and we could not find the light*! Banks had the nasty job of telling Mr Baird, and he must have had an even worse one telling his guests.

If that wasn't bad enough. Banks immediately afterwards developed rheumatic fever and I had a difficult job getting him back to his home in north London.[38]

Hobson was later employed at Long Acre to discover what went wrong. After days spent on the roof waiting for a suitable fog to descend low enough, and several abortive attempts chasing evening mists down Chelsea embankment in the firm's bull-nosed Morris, he decided to set up his own fog-making machine in the laboratory. By means of this, and help from the National Physical Laboratory and optical experts on the firm's staff, he concluded that 'noctovision as a navigational aid would not work unless very expensive quartz glass and lenses were used, and until photocells became available which were much more sensitive to the infra-red wavelengths which did penetrate fog'.[38]

On 19 August 1929, Baird repeated in public part of the private show he had given to the Prince of Wales. This was the first public demonstration of the transmission of talking films and their reception on an ordinary television set. As the reports indicated, the frequency bandwidth of nine kilocycles limited the amount of detail, but in spite of the picture being of the standard thirty lines, George Robey came over in sight and sound 'with a substantial measure of success'.[42] The transmission of a piece of moving film was not a great achievement in itself, being more straightforward than the 'true' televising of a living subject. An editorial piece in *Television* observed:

> Mr Baird experimented successfully with the transmission of ordinary silent films some years ago, and since then one or two foreign experimenters, notably C F Jenkins, in America, have conducted successful experimental transmissions of specially made silhouette films. In the recent Baird experiments ordinary standard talking films were used.[43]

What was new, however, was the fact that the sound and sound effects were picked up from the marginal record on the film and broadcast simultaneously with the picture, in the same way as in the cinema. The method had been proposed by Baird in a patent for which he had applied on 13 May 1927.[44]

He was also at this time involved in something quite different. In 1976 a letter arrived at the public library in Helensburgh. It was signed by James G Heath.

1 June 1976
                                        24 Myrtle Terrace
                                        Edinburgh EH11 1PG

Dear Sir or Madam

Concerning the paragraph in today's Scottish Daily Express – 'Did you know John Logie Baird?'

I have a distinct recollection of him in what I think must have been the summers of 1928 and 1929, when as a lieutenant in the Supplementary Reserve of Officers he joined us each manoeuvre season in Aldershot for 14 days.

I was then a young soldier (21) serving in 2nd Division Signals at Mons Barracks.

Mr Baird was conducting experiments in several types of army field communications and new systems. The main one at that time being his tryout in the back of a Morris six-wheeler truck to transmit messages through army field cables using an old Oliver green typewriter[45] and batteries. ...

Mr Baird's experiment I understand was not successful, due to the difficulty in obtaining balance in resistance in each of the two cable conductors.

Our section sergeant (Archbold), a very able man, said that Mr Baird was experimenting with an invention to send pictures through the atmosphere. To us, and to Sgt Archbold, this sounded as impossible as sending a man to the moon.

My impression of him in those days – when a soldier's two ideals were strong discipline and a smart appearance, was of a very untidy man. His hair was long and unbrushed, and his uniform uncared for. He stood out a mile among the smart young officers of the times. He was very quiet, and rarely spoke to anyone – including the officers.

This graphic piece of reportage has caused more, and more vociferous, controversy than any other first-hand account of Baird at work. Since no mention of Baird's army service could be found in Ministry of Defence records, doubts have been cast on Heath's testimony, especially as it was never checked with him – he died on 10 February 1978.[46] To be fair to the sceptics, the Ministry of Defence has no record either of Heath's service, while stressing that 'he could have served, but it would appear that the record did not survive the passage of time'.[47] At his death Heath was being paid a small pension by the Paymaster General[48] which, it has been confirmed, corresponds to an army pension of some kind, probably in relation to a short-term period of service.[49] The description of Heath as a 'retired telephone engineer'[48] further supports this hypothesis, in that such work would represent a natural progression from his training in army signals.

Ministry of Defence records do, however, confirm that Sergeant J R Archbold served in 2nd Division Signals in the years 1928 and 1929.[50] It is also known that during 1928 and 1929 2nd Division Signals exercised regularly in the Aldershot area and that a number of supplementary reserve personnel attended these operations.[51]

How, then, did Baird come to be serving with the Royal Corps of Signals as a uniformed officer, at the age of forty and twelve years after being unceremoniously declared unfit for army service?

A military historian has suggested an answer to this conundrum: 'My guess is that after the importance of his work became known he was given a post-war general service commission – it is quite common for the army to take on civilians and give them the necessary military rank if their work is deemed essential. As such it is most unlikely that their names would appear on the Army List.'[52]

Whether or not the sounds of a typewriter heard in Baird's boarding house bedroom in 1923 represented early experiments in signalling, he had certainly been thinking since about the employment of his systems for relaying messages. Patent 298,582 ('Improvements in or relating to the Reception of Radio Signals') refers specifically to the use of the designated apparatus 'when it is desired that the reception should be highly selective, and it may also be used for the purpose of maintaining secrecy'. It had been applied for on 11 May 1927, and was accepted on 11 October 1928. Patent 324,029 ('Improvements in or relating to Television and like Apparatus') was applied for on 3 October 1928; it specifically refers to the use of 'a typewriting device' to produce an image. These dates are significant, because they fit in with the sightings of Baird in army uniform.[53] The War Office would have been keeping an eye on any patent submissions which had potential military applications.[52]

A further Army link with Baird's systems, if not also with Baird himself, can be detected in a letter of 1 November 1929 from A[rthur] H[enry] Hall, chief superintendent, Royal Aircraft Establishment, Farnborough, to Harry

Wimperis at the Air Ministry.[54] Hall served in this post from 1928 until his retirement in 1941; he is even better remembered as the co-author of the phenomenally successful *Hall and Knight's Algebra*. The letter describes a visit to the Signals Experimental Establishment at Woolwich on 25 October to see a demonstration of the 'area system of telegraphy', which, in the opinion of Colonel [A C] Fuller, 'represents the only useful application of television principles to service requirements':

> A message written on a tape is passed slowly in front of an aperture at the transmitting end and an image of this message is seen passing slowly across a similar aperture at the receiving end. The message can be read out by an observer and written down by a second person. The system has advantages in that it will operate through considerable jamming and gives quite a large measure of secrecy.[54]

Fuller, the inventor of several telegraphic devices, was a member of the Royal Engineer and Signals Board from 1920 to 1933, after seeing active service in World War II and being experimental officer at Woolwich from 1916 to 1920. He subsequently held directors' posts at the War Office and the Ministry of Supply, having been promoted major-general from 1937.[55]

The method of transmission referred to in Hall's letter corresponds so precisely to that described by Baird in his patent 299,076,[56] that one may presume that it had been licensed to the Army for this purpose. The same system of transmission was still being used by the Army in 1932, to judge from a Signals Experimental Establishment secret report.[57]

Baird utilised the results of his early experiments in sending written messages to devise Television Screen News. Letters, each 2¼ inches wide by 3 inches deep, were put into slots in an endless roll of varnished linen passing over a series of rollers. When it was time for the news, an oblong panel was slid aside, and the lettering passed across the field of vision from right to left.[58] A further development of the process was the adaptation of a typewriter to produce a message on a continuous roll of white, opaque tape, which was then scanned by a drum with apertures in it (see figure 3).[59]

Towards the end of 1928 Hutchinson was on an extended visit to New York, where he established a luxurious television studio at 145 West 45th Street, staffed by two Baird technicians, Desmond Campbell and Frank Bingley. There they demonstrated on 2 September the transmission of talking films sent by wire from the Paramount Building. A further demonstration, attended by the Mayor of New York, Jimmy Walker, took place on 20 December. It is said that Desmond Campbell was most put out when, of

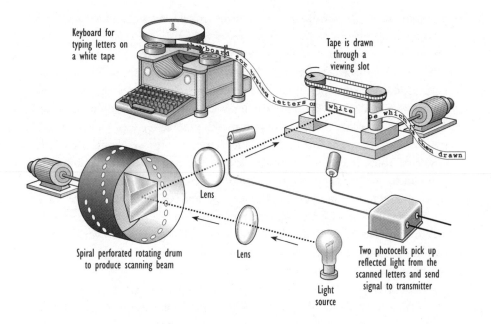

Figure 3: The Baird telewriter (1929) transmitted text on a line-by-line basis. It was a precursor of his much higher-definition fast facsimile system (1944), which could send documents rapidly page by page (see figure 11).

three young women who were auditioned to appear on television, the one he favoured was not selected. His choice was currently appearing in the Broadway show, *Girl Crazy*; her stage name was Ginger Rogers.[60] Hutchinson's ambitious plans for establishing a Baird Parent Corporation in USA and for a link between his companies and the Radio Corporation of America, however, came to nothing.[61]

There was also at this time an attempt to establish an Australian presence. Clapp and Bridgewater had arrived in Melbourne on 3 December 1928 with seven crates of equipment. The apparatus was successfully demonstrated privately in Melbourne on several occasions, and two local engineers were trained. The operation appears to have foundered on the personality and eccentricities of a retired major who had been sent out by the Baird company to act as business manager. He knew nothing of the technical side, and conducted morning briefings from his bed, with a parrot perched on his shoulder. Bridgewater and Clapp gave up the unequal struggle to cope with his temperament and returned to Britain in the summer of 1929. Work continued, however, and the first public demonstration of television in Australia duly took place on 30 September. After an enjoyable and no doubt bibulous lunch, the company saw and heard the singer Mollie MacKay, accompanied by violin and piano. Thereafter neither the equipment nor the major were ever heard of again.[62]

The thirtieth of September 1929 was also a historic day in Britain. The BBC made its first experimental television broadcast, in the absence of its director general, who was on holiday in Scotland.[63] The proceedings began at 11am, with Moseley as self-appointed presenter. A letter was read out from the President of the Board of Trade, and then Sir Ambrose Fleming and the physicist Professor E N da C Andrade spoke. There followed a programme of entertainment by Sydney Howard, comedian, and Lulu Stanley, soubrette, who sang 'He's tall, and dark, and handsome' and 'Grandma's proverbs', and the Baird company's Connie King, who sang 'Mighty like a rose'. There was also an impromptu appearance by Baird himself. As only one wavelength was available, those appearing first performed in front of the television transmitter, and then repeated their words to a microphone, in two-minute stretches. The pictures appeared on a circular screen about eight inches in diameter, against a reddish-orange background. There was one slight hitch when a negative rather than a positive image appeared on the screen, but the defect, caused by two wires being wrongly connected, was swiftly put right. The standard of reception was compared to the early flickering cinematograph.[64]

Baird appeared triumphant, with a dreamy look in his eyes. Moseley's attitude was more realistic, especially after Baird took a question from the press as to how many people had been able to see the programme. He answered, counting on his fingers:

> There is one receiving set at my home on Box Hill, and I believe the BBC and the Post Office each have one. That makes three and I should say there are half-a-dozen other sets in the country. Add to these the receivers which clever amateurs have built for themselves from our directions and you might count another twenty. That makes twenty-nine in all.[65]

Initially the programmes went out without sound, as only one transmitter was available. Sound and vision together arrived on 31 March 1930, when both Brookmans Park transmitters were made available, on 261.3 metres for vision and 356.3 metres for sound. There was a televised ceremony, as usual presented by Moseley. Lord Ampthill and Sir Ambrose Fleming spoke. The real entertainment should have kicked off with a song from Cicely Courtneidge, then appearing with her husband, Jack Hulbert, in a revue at the Adelphi Theatre called *The House that Jack Built*. Moseley, an opera aficionado, thought otherwise:

> As Director of Television Programmes, I have turned down Cicely Courtneidge's song – a silly thing, which runs something like this: 'Sing a cadenza, I've got influenza!' Cicely told a reporter that she had been singing that song with success at the Adelphi, and added, 'If Mr Moseley won't let me sing that song, I shall not sing any!' And she didn't – and thus lost the opportunity of becoming one of television's first artistes. (We have been sweating blood to put television over – not for this kind of muck I hope.)[66]

Cicely Courtneidge was made a dame in 1972. Her place on this occasion was taken by another future Dame of the British Empire, Gracie Fields, the reigning queen of the music hall stage. She sang 'Nowt about Nowt' and 'Three Green Bonnets', but not without some difficulties in the run up to her performance:

> I was put in this little room, it seemed as big as the smallest telephone kiosk you see in the street, and they put me in there and they said, 'You're going to sing through here.' Well, all I could see was, well, it looked like a brick wall. 'Are you kidding? Are you pulling my leg?' They said, 'No. You see. It goes in there and it's going to be seen miles away.' Somebody is pulling my leg. Well, all right, I'm used to singing in so many places, and I go in there and get myself locked inside and start to sing.[67]

The musical-comedy star Annie Croft also sang. The proceedings closed with a ghost appearance by R C Sherriff, the thirty-three-year-old oarsman and author, whose play, *Journey's End*, set in the trenches in World War I, was the theatrical sensation of the decade. *The Times* reported that Sherriff was 'unavoidably prevented from performing'.[68] Moseley, in his biography of Baird, states that Sherriff made a brief speech, in the course of which he said, 'I am afraid if this invention became too perfect it would cause most people to spend their evenings at home instead of visiting the theatre.'[69]

The Baird company was now a maker of television programmes as well as of television systems and receivers.

> Our little studio was thronged with artists to whom we usually paid one to two guineas, but many of our best turns were unpaid, the novelty and

excitement were sufficient inducement. Our studio manager was Mr
Bradly, a brother-in-law of Sydney Moseley. He had a wide experience
of the stage, and ran the studio on professional lines. I remember
how strange it was to come down from the cold austere laboratory to
the exotic atmosphere of the studio, mysterious with young females
floating about in tights, red nosed comedians applying grease paint, and
colourful figures in wigs and lurid costumes, pianists and violinists
rehearsing, and all the colourful chaos of back stage.[70]

One of the pianists was Margaret Albu. She had been the unwilling
teenager who had recorded her aversion to the Selfridge's demonstration in
1925. Now a struggling classical pianist, she was there to accompany a singer.

It was some time after midnight, and we were preparing to leave when
the studio announcer said in an awed whisper, 'Here is the Inventor
himself,' and John came into the studio. He was in his heavy overcoat
and carried his hat, and his appearance at once showed an unusual and
striking personality. Although outwardly quiet and dignified, he gave
the impression of great energy. He had a mane of fair hair and horn-
rimmed glasses – behind which were blue eyes which were either
extremely penetrating or very vague.

We young artists were solemnly introduced to him by the announcer,
but I had the feeling that he was deep in thought and did not really see
any of us. A rather embarrassed and prolonged silence followed our
introductions, until I, unable to bear it any longer, asked what must have
seemed a banal question, 'How long have you been working on this
amazing invention?' He turned his gaze on me and very slowly and
clearly said, 'Seven years.' Then we all left to find our various ways
home.[71]

Each half-hour programme usually comprised three solo turns, ranging in
appeal from the light to the very light. There was an occasional sketch, and
an even more occasional educational item, such as 'Sydney A Moseley,
Director of Programmes, a talk on Television'.[72] The walls of the studio were
hung with heavy curtains, and the artists looked into a small aperture in one
wall, behind which the flying-spot scanner operated. Technical assistants
doubled as announcers, dinner-jacket tops at the ready to cover their over-
alls. To save expense, wherever possible the entertainment was home made.
'Great Expectations', a sketch performed on 25 November 1930, was written
by Ruth Maschwitz, Moseley's secretary, and produced by Harold Bradly,

with Maschwitz and Bradly also taking two of the four parts. Staff members E B R Benson demonstrated 'some curious knots and their uses' (26 March 1931), and T H Bridgewater the 'deaf and dumb language' (27 March 1931). By juggling its schedules and print deadlines, the BBC managed to avoid printing the full television programmes in the weekly *Radio Times*, even though they could be received in most parts of Britain. The public learned of them through information sheets released to the press by the Baird company.

For twenty-five guineas, the equivalent of fifty tickets for the best theatre seats including tax, the public could buy a television receiver; or, you could make your own from a sixteen-guinea do-it-yourself kit, to work in conjunction with a radio set. The thirty-line reddish-coloured picture, on a screen 2½ inches high by two inches wide which could be magnified to about four inches by three inches, needed regular adjustment to prevent it bouncing up and down, a problem of synchronisation of the motors at the transmitting and receiving ends.[73]

It was probably Moseley's idea for Baird to present a receiver to the Prime Minister, Ramsay MacDonald, who wrote him a personal note on 5 April 1930 in his own hand:

Dear Mr Baird

I must thank you very warmly for the Television instrument you have put into Downing St. What a marvellous discovery you have made! When I look at the transmissions I feel that the most wonderful miracle is being done under my eye. I congratulate you most heartily & send you my sincerest hopes for your further success. You have put something in my room which will never let me forget how strange is the world – and how unknown. Again & again Thank you.

With kindest regards

Yours very sincerely

J Ramsay MacDonald[74]

The July 1930 issue of *Television* gave a list of 'some of the principal stockists' of televisors. They numbered seventy-seven, in places as far away from London as Aberdeen, Belfast, and Jersey. Hobson, who described himself as 'the first television service engineer dealing with commercially available television sets', was sent out on a roving commission which took him to suppliers in many parts of Britain between 1 April and 10 July 1930. Most of the problems that he encountered related to interference. He concluded in his final report,

Television will not be very popular in the north of England until some local source of transmission is available. ... Owing to the large amount of amplification required to receive London at sufficient strength to operate a Televisor most customers have found that the interference in big towns makes reception during the morning transmission for demonstration purposes impossible. ... Interest in television seems considerable, but customers naturally find it a considerable drawback being unable to demonstrate during the daytime.[75]

In May 1930, the two Baird companies were merged into one. The official reason was that it had proved impossible to separate their functions; less officially, the Baird Television Development Company was in financial trouble owing to its considerable outlays. There is a fairly authoritative account that when the merger was first mooted, with Baird and Hutchinson being appointed joint managing directors at a salary each of £10,000 a year, an outside company offered them each £125,000 for their share holdings. They both refused to sell, Hutchinson because he did not regard it as being enough, and Baird because he had no idea what he would do with so much money.[76]

The new company was called Baird Television Ltd. This was probably the occasion referred to in Baird's memoir on which he had another falling out with Hutchinson, who had wanted it to be called British Television.[77] The board now comprised Lord Ampthill (chairman), Sir Edward Manville, Baird and Hutchinson as joint managing directors, Winch, and Francis Shortis, an Ampthill supporter.

One casualty of the merger was Bill Fox, who had joined the Baird company in 1928 as information officer. Having the previous year been paid by Hutchinson a bonus of £25 as expenses (so, free of income tax) 'in appreciation of [his] efforts and work in connection with the Pamphlet',[78] he now found himself made redundant, 'in consequence of the reorganisation and rearrangement of the staff', and given a month's salary (£27.6s.) 'in lieu of notice'.[79]

It was a wide-ranging purge. In Berlin, Dr Alfred Gradenwitz, who seems to have been an agent for or consultant to the company, wrote to Fox commiserating with him for losing his job, and enclosing a copy of the translation he had just personally made for Baird of a report of the German Wireless Commission's visit to London: 'That men so reluctant to acknowledge any advance of a British inventor over German achievements should have so candidly to admit the superiority of Baird's work is in my opinion the most eloquent proof of a satisfactory state of affairs.' Two days later Gradenwitz wrote again. He, too, had been sacked by the company.[80]

Over fifty-five years later, Fox claimed that he had resigned because of Baird's attitude to publicity:

> He was an irritating and inconsequential character to work for. My job was to keep the press informed. He'd say to me, 'This is secret. Not a word to anyone.' So I wouldn't mention it. Two days later a reporter, it might be from some insignificant, cheap paper, would say, 'Here, Bill, have you heard this?' 'Where did you get it from?' I'd ask. 'Oh, Baird told me himself.' So I'd lose the chance of going first with the news to the London papers.[81]

Clearly this rankled with Fox, and it has more than a ring of truth about it. Baird was a self-promoter who could only play the game by his own rules. Fox returned to journalism. According to him, he and Baird never met again.[81]

The occasion of the first play to be televised, from 3pm to 3.30pm on 14 July 1930, was also that of the first public large-screen presentation. It was a joint production by the BBC and the Baird company. The one-act play, *The Man with the Flower in His Mouth* by the contemporary Italian dramatist Luigi Pirandello, had been first produced in London in 1926. It was chosen for this occasion because it only had three characters (two male, one female) and not much movement; it was also popular with amateur and student dramatic clubs. The producers were the BBC's Lance Sieveking and (who else?) Sydney Moseley, and the production was transmitted from the Long Acre studios to Savoy Hill and broadcast from there. The male parts were originally intended to be played by the BBC's thirty-year-old head of drama, Val Gielgud, and his younger brother John Gielgud.[82]

Val Gielgud had joined the BBC in 1928 as a junior editorial assistant on the *Radio Times*. In 1929 he was catapulted by Reith into the post of director of all radio drama and variety, which he graced for thirty-five years. Reith used to take part in BBC amateur theatrical productions. At a rehearsal for Ian Hay's *Tilly of Bloomsbury*, in which he played a drunken broker's man, he was bawled out by Gielgud, the producer, for being late. When the BBC required a new radio drama director, Reith immediately thought of Gielgud: 'I've found just the man for the job,' he announced to Carpendale. 'If he can be rude to me, he ought to be able to tell actors what to do.'[83]

In the end, John (later Sir John) Gielgud was unable to take part – in 1929 he was already playing lead Shakespearean roles at the Old Vic. Val Gielgud had to drop out at the last minute because of illness. This may have been a blessing, for he himself used to suggest, with what was said to be a combination of modesty and sound judgment, that while his brother was arguably the best actor in Britain, he was undoubtedly the worst.[84] The final cast was Gladys Young, Earle Gray, and Lionel Millard. In order to compensate for the lack of definition, they wore heavy make-up of yellow, with blue-black lips and eyebrows, and lines around the eyes and down the sides of the nose. Viewers saw only head and shoulders, or the hands, of one actor at a time.

On the flat roof of Long Acre, four storeys above the studio, a select audience of scientists and representatives of the press saw the transmission from Savoy Hill on a screen about five foot high by two foot wide consisting of 2100 tiny flash-lamp bulbs, set up in a tent. The day dawned stormy, and Baird was worried that a sudden gust of wind might carry away tent, screen, which was on wheels, and audience. As it turned out, there was another hazard with which to contend. Two-thirds of the way through the play, a frantic message was relayed from the roof to the studio below: the screen was overheating and in danger of meltdown. The transmission must be halted immediately. Sieveking recalled the experience:

> I appealed to Baird, who was there with us. He was a man with a tremendous sense of occasion. He said, in his soft Scottish voice, 'Tell them to go on, and let it melt!' Then he grinned at me. The screen was in fact red hot and melting at the edges by the time the play ended![85]

The play was also received at Selfridge's store, where Hobson set up and tested in the morning two ordinary televisors for the public, and one for Gordon Selfridge himself in a separate room. Hobson reported on the experiment to his sales manager:

> The reception of the play in the afternoon was an utter failure. A large crowd of people were present, who consequently had to be hurried through so fast that they only caught a very fleeting glimpse of the picture. I am sure a large number of these only saw the curtain.
>
> It was difficult to make out what the scenery was intended to represent and all the fine detail on the actors' faces was absent, due no doubt to the kind of make up. Synchronisation was excellent.[86]

The critic in *The Times* the following day wrote elegantly and realistically about the problems faced by the producer, as well as by the viewer:

> The Baird system of television was yesterday applied, for the first time in England, to a public, though still experimental, broadcasting of a play.

The piece chosen – and, having regard to the circumstances, very perceptively chosen – by Mr Val Gielgud, was Pirandello's *The Man with the Flower in His Mouth*. It is a forbidding study of emotion in the shadow of death, which the BBC might not ordinarily choose as part of an afternoon's programme, but its qualifications for the present experiment are overwhelming, for where else shall we find a play that is almost without action, that demands no depth of perspective, and that can be performed without grave loss though but one actor (and then only his head and shoulders) is to be seen at a time? ...

If the process has still a long way to go before every subscriber to the BBC is fully satisfied by seeing and hearing plays in his own library, the difficulties that have been overcome are many and remarkable. ... The space in which the actors have their being ... is half of a small cube, sliced through on its diagonal. ... When another actor's turn comes a chequered screen must be passed across [his] face ... while he withdraws and his colleague takes his place. ... These are conditions such as the most intimate of Intimate Theatres have never dreamed of. Mr L de G Sieveking, the producer, working in inches where other producers work in yards, has made an extremely ingenious use of his material. ...

What the audience sees in the televisor is an image of about the size of a postcard. The clearness of the image greatly and rapidly varies. At its best it allows slow gesture, such as the moving of The Man's hand to his mouth, to make its effect, and even admits the more striking changes of expression. At its worst, when the apparatus appears to have taken leave of its senses, the whole world of television leaps into the air and the actor oscillates violently between the room above and the cellars beneath, not deigning to pause in the little rectangle on which our attention is fixed.[87]

The BBC control board was nothing like as understanding:

The experimental play performed for Baird Television on 14th July under the Director of Productions was discussed. Whilst this provided material of interest to the Productions Department and no doubt to the Baird Co. and showed our willingness to co-operate to the limits of which their system was capable, no material technical progress has been made such as would justify our Programme Branch co-operating any further; such co-operation, with attendant publicity, would mislead the public as to the possibilities of the system now or as now foreseen. Our future action therefore would be only that the Engineering Branch holds a watching brief. ...

It was decided that the substance of [the above] paragraph of this minute is to be a definite instruction to members of the Programme Branch concerned, lest interest in any cases carry them beyond the discretionary point.[88]

Sieveking, who was then thirty-four, went on to have a long and distinguished career as a BBC producer. After this production he wrote a long memorandum on the future of television. He was critical of the amateur approach of the Baird company to the development of artistic and technical ways of exploiting the new medium, and recommended that the BBC should cooperate with them in planning and producing programmes. A wider waveband should be allocated to television transmissions to support Baird's own development of facilities for showing a number of people at once. The BBC should institute a five-year research programme into television, and give the Baird company and its technicians advice and encouragement.[89]

The memorandum was read out and 'discussed at length' at a meeting attended by Reith, Carpendale, Ashbridge (now chief engineer in succession to Eckersley), Murray, Commander V H Goldsmith, director of business relations, Gielgud, and Sieveking. Ashbridge 'said he would like to express his views in writing'.[90] These views were effectively that the BBC should simply keep in touch with any research that was being conducted into the improvement of commercial standards and technical developments. No money should be expended on licence fees until the best system emerged, or on developing a service for a minority of the public which could afford a receiver. There should be no cooperation with the Baird company over programmes, though limited technical assistance might be offered in connection with the present experimental service.[91]

Ashbridge's views prevailed. Control board agreed:

(i)   that the Baird television transmissions should continue for the present.
(ii) that there should be no programme co-operation with Baird.
(iii) that the technical liaison should be closer.[90]

Of all the decisions regarding Baird television made by the BBC over the years, expressly to forbid the BBC production team to share their expertise with the Baird company at this time is perhaps the most genuinely shocking. Towards the end of his life (he died in 1972) Sieveking wistfully wrote, 'In three-quarters of a century no one in any field of activity has been anything but friendly and cooperative – except in the field of television. Why?'[92]

Ashbridge was later knighted. There is a story behind this. In 1934 Reith was offered the higher degree of knighthood, the GBE. He wrote to Ramsay MacDonald, whose party returned to government in 1931, declining the honour on the grounds that Ashbridge, for whom Reith had earlier recommended a knighthood, had not yet been recognised. The Prime Minister replied, pointing out that honours were not attached to offices. Reith had earned his GBE: Ashbridge was not yet deserving of an honour. Reith consulted H J Whitley, chairman of the board of governors of the BBC, who said he must accept the GBE. Ashbridge received his knighthood in 1935.[93]

Baird Television Ltd and Baird himself, without the support of any kind from the one national institution which had the necessary expertise as well as the broadcasting monopoly, had begun to lose their way. Tony Bridgewater, a member of Baird's staff at the time, summed up the situation in his John Logie Baird memorial lecture in Glasgow in 1959:

> In retrospect one can see that the odds were against Baird; and of course he was only human and made mistakes. He was not astute enough in the selection of staff – particularly those who could have helped him on the electronic side – and in the framing of a research programme. Too much time was spent on adventurous sidelines and in exploiting the 30-line system – largely in pursuit of publicity which, rightly or wrongly, was considered necessary for the attraction of public interest and capital. Too little time on essential technical improvements.[94]

Therein lies also one of Baird's particular predicaments. The thirty-line transmissions on a medium waveband could be received throughout Britain and also on the continent of Europe.[95] In theory, a wider range of transmission meant more television sets sold. Baird himself, in his memoir, suggested that by mid-August 1932 the company had sold a thousand receivers, which did not take into account the 'immense number' of amateur enthusiasts who, because of the simplicity of the apparatus, had been able to construct a set for themselves.[96] On the other hand, higher definition pictures would require a short waveband, which had only a limited radius of reception. Moreover the cost and complexity of a short-wave receiver would discourage many potential viewers and constructors.

Baird had, however, another public demonstration up his sleeve, which, if it did not have dramatic subtlety, made up for it with sheer panache. The large screen was demonstrated to the booking agent for the London Coliseum, a noted variety theatre of considerable audience capacity, now the home of English National Opera. When it opened in 1904, it was the first London theatre to have a revolving stage. 'The New Radio Sensation / First Public Presentation in Any Theatre / TELEVISION / The Baird British Invention' was top of the bill for three performances a day for a fortnight, opening on 28 July 1930.

There must be no question of the screen overheating! As the opening performance neared, Baird was in what for him was a state of considerable apprehension. Moseley described it:

> He was rushing from the laboratory to the office and home again and continually exhorting his grand team of technical colleagues to work faster. He was no slave-driver in the ordinary sense of the term and all his colleagues and assistants held him in great affection. But once he was on the trail of any fresh development he could think and talk of nothing else, and he could not understand why everybody else was not as excited, as devoted and as tireless as himself. Toiling electricians and mechanics would look after his tousle-headed figure with wry amusement. He was always asking them: 'Well, how's it going? What have ye now?', but he never expected much in the way of an answer, for the dreamy eyes behind the glasses could take in every mechanical detail at a glance.[97]

The principle which he employed was that which he had outlined in his first patent (222,604), seven years earlier almost to the day. Each of the lamps, arranged in thirty vertical rows of seventy, was energised in turn twelve-and-a-half times a second behind a ground glass cover. The switching mechanisms were housed in a caravan on the revolving stage. Hobson had the job, when the signature tune 'Happy days are here again' was played, of jumping off the stage as it rotated, plugging in the loudspeakers, and turning up the volume at the right moment.[98] The screen stood out in bright illumination from its setting of black curtains. It was reported in *The Times* that in spite of its comparatively small size, it 'could be seen by everybody. The definition was not quite so good as that obtainable on the small televisor, but it was noticed that the photograph of Mr Baird which was put before the televisor at the end of the demonstration came over much more distinctly than the images of actual faces in relief.'[99]

The programmes were transmitted from Long Acre. In organising and, with Bridgewater, presenting from the studio the thrice-daily, ten-minute slot, Moseley was in his element. The opening programme included appearances by the veteran actress Irene Vanbrugh, the popular romantic novelist Ruby M Ayres, and A V Alexander (later Earl Alexander of Hillsborough), First Lord of the Admiralty, who made a short speech in which, significantly, he pointed out the possibilities of such an invention for naval signalling, though he hoped 'it would be used for peace and not for war'.[100] Audience participation was encouraged. 'Bombardier' Billy Wells, the boxer, who at one point succumbed to stage fright, was asked questions by people in the theatre which were relayed to him by telephone. The Lord Mayor of London, on screen, enquired of his wife, who was in the theatre, what time dinner would be. She replied, by phone, 'Eight o'clock.' Came the answer from the screen, 'I'll be there.' It was a gala occasion, to which the press testified. Ashbridge and his wife accepted the free tickets Moseley had sent them, but refused his invitation to go 'behind the scenes' after the show.[101]

During the fortnight Moseley inveigled numerous celebrities, including several members of parliament, to appear in front of the transmitting apparatus at Long Acre. More ingenious was the act of the 'Charming Belles in Harmony', Helen Yorke and Virginia Johnson, who were starring on the bill in the normal course of events. Yorke, on stage, performed a duet with her partner on the screen, televised from Long Acre. George Robey began his act live, and then left the audience watching a piece of talking film of him on the screen, while he took a taxi to the studio, where he carried on by television.

The screen, with its caravan and four dedicated engineers, now went on a continental tour. Twenty-six demonstrations were given between 18 and 30 September at the Scala Theatre in Berlin, the city's largest music hall, from a studio several kilometres away. The 'circus' went on to Paris, for several performances a day for two weeks at the Olympia cinema. The tour ended in Stockholm, with two performances a day for a fortnight in December at the Red Mill Theatre.[102]

The takings from the Coliseum performances amounted to a gross profit of about £1500. There were some small profits accruing from the sale of television sets in Britain. To Baird, it was looking now as though the big money was going to come from large-screen television and from abroad.

In August, both Baird and Moseley were in Berlin for the radio show from 21 to 31 August. Baird took the opportunity to call on Manfred von Ardenne, a young research scientist who had the previous year written a paper on his development of a new cathode-ray tube for photographically recording images.[103] A photograph taken of them with a television receiver shows that Baird, in his overcoat, had at that time a rather puffy face (see plate 34).[104] When interviewed over sixty years later, von Ardenne spoke about the meeting, and about the photograph:

> This is a historic image. The moment is frozen. Namely, the television pioneer Baird is looking here for the first time at a television image on the screen of a Braun tube at the Lichterfeld Institute where the equipment was set up and worked. At the time, I tried to persuade Baird to switch to electronic television with Braun tubes because I wanted to win him over as a customer for my electron beam tubes, amplifiers and reflecting instruments. For financial reasons. But Baird couldn't be persuaded; he saw the future in mechanical television with the Nipkow discs.[105]

There equally well could have been financial reasons for Baird's unwillingness to be persuaded to make the change.

Moseley recorded in his diary:'(Berlin again) This time to induce Germany to accept television.' Of the following day, 26 August, he wrote:

> A terribly busy time. If I am able to put over British television in Germany what a triumph that would be ...!
>
> Despite all, I manage to pursue my one and only recreation – opera – and no other country produces opera better. I forego parties and even a solitary dinner at the hotel in order to get to the opera house in time. Some of the young Baird engineers sent over here from London were down in the mouth; they had been kept hanging around until I arrived. They certainly needed pepping up. I said:'All right! I'll give you all a good time tonight.'They thought I meant a night club. Instead I took them to the opera. Surprisingly it worked! They revelled in it.[106]

Moseley stayed on in Berlin after the radio show. A confirmed bachelor of now forty-two, he had been giving time and thought to the affairs of Win Williams, widow of his great friend Graeme, who had died suddenly in 1923, leaving her with three sons. 'It has suddenly struck me: "I wonder whether Win would marry me." Wrote her!'[107]

Win obviously agreed.

> SEPT 7: (Berlin) Wrote to my incomparable aide Walter Knight in London to see Win and fix up the whole thing – everything ... flat ... ring ... notice of marriage at the Hampstead Registry Office. Romance in a hurry. 'Just like you,' I can hear Win saying, 'getting someone to go along with me to help choose the ring.'[107]

Plate 1
Jessie Baird at the front gate of 'The Lodge' in about
1900, photographed by Baird.

Plate 2
Baird, aged about twelve, in the garden of 'The Lodge'.
A rare picture of him in a natural pose.

Plate 3
Rev. John Baird poses for the
photographer (almost certainly
Baird himself) outside 'The Lodge'
in about 1900, unaware that beside
him Jack Buchanan is acting up
to his nickname of 'Chump'. An
elderly Helensburgh resident plods
along on the other side of Argyle
Street, oblivious to the fact that he
is in the picture.

Plate 4

Baird and his 'reaper and binder' (see page 11) outside 'The Lodge' in about 1908, with his pretty cousin Jeanie Coates in the passenger seat. The model is a 1904 Humber Olympia tri-car, maximum speed 17½mph.

Plate 5

Climbing the 'Rest and be Thankful', at the head of Glen Coe, between Arrochar and Inveraray, in about 1910, in a later model of tri-car (see page 11). The identity of the intrepid passenger is unknown.

Plate 6

The wedding reception at the Queen's Hotel, Helensburgh, for Baird's sister Jeannie ('Tottie') and her husband, Rev. Neil Conley, on 6 June 1922. Jessie Baird is on the bride's left, and Rev. John Baird on the bridegroom's right. Baird, looking remarkably fit after his sojourn at a health spa, is first from the right in the back row. His sister Annie is immediately behind the bridegroom. Far left, back row, is Anna Snodgrass (née Inglis), aunt of Arnold Snodgrass.

Plate 7

Glasgow street scene in 1918, with two of Baird's 'sandwich women' on parade (see pages 14–15). Using women for this kind of advertising work was unprecedented, but the two men behind seem unimpressed.

Plate 8
Mephy (Gavin Fullarton Robertson) in the sidecar of Baird's motorcycle, summer 1919 (see page 17), though the intention was doubtless to take 'Alice' on trips. The machine, of which Baird was the second registered keeper, is a 1910 Excelsior Auto-Cycle, built in Chicago by the Schwinn company. With a capacity of 1000cc, it was capable of a speed of 100mph, presumably without sidecar. The third registered keeper was J A D McLean, of Port Bannatyne, Bute, who acquired it on 10 October 1919.

Plate 9
Bad news for Baird! 'Alice', Easter 1920, between two men, of whom the one on her right with the pipe is identified on the back of the photograph, in a female hand-writing, as 'Sid'.

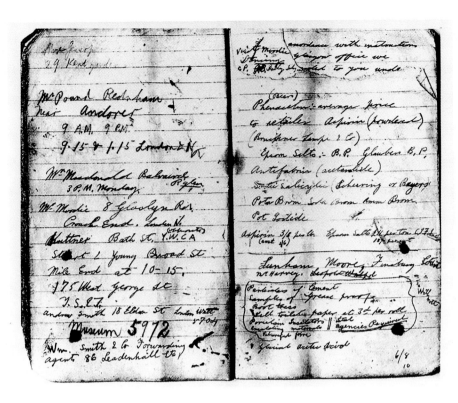

Plates 10/11
Two spreads from the notebook that Baird kept in Trinidad in 1920 and then in London until the end of 1922.

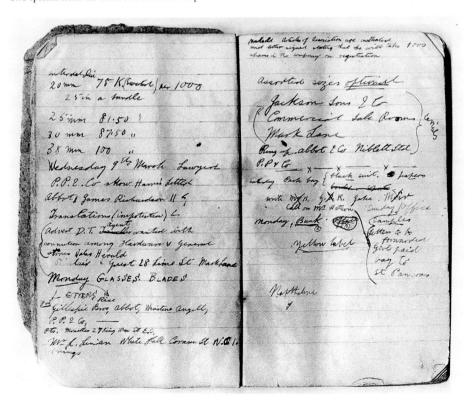

Plate 12

'Alice' in the front garden of 40 Upper Grosvenor Road, Tunbridge Wells, November 1923. The support for the equipment strongly suggests the 'pedestal framework' described by Helena Walker (see page 40). Since Baird may well have been more concerned on this occasion with capturing the image of 'Alice', for once he did not bother to cam-ouflage his equipment. This is thus the only known genuine picture of part of his original apparatus. The arrangement follows that described in his first patent (222,604) and in the article in *Chambers's Journal* (see page 43). The smaller white disc is the pulley wheel of the transmission disc. The lens in the centre of the picture focuses the image through the serrated light chopper onto the transmission disc, which has a spiral of pinholes round the outer edge. Part of the apparatus can be seen again in plate 13.

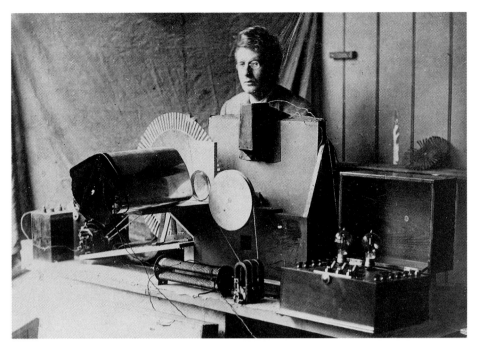

Plate 13

January 1924, and Baird, with his apparatus, is installed in 21 Linton Crescent, Hastings. Baird sits at the far side of the transmission disc, which is obscured by plywood. The serrated disc is now larger, but an identical, or at least very similar, disc to the one in plate 12 is on the shelf to Baird's left, beside the candlestick. The wooden frame in which the transmission disc sits, with the viewing aperture just below the pulley wheel, is the same in both pictures. (Royal Television Society)

Plate 14

The Queen's Arcade laboratory, April or May 1924. The large circular object is the receiving disc with light bulbs round the rim (see page 46). On Baird's right is William Le Queux, and on his other side is Claud Frowd, a member of the local radio society. (Royal Television Society)

Plate 17a
Lake of Menteith, Scotland, 1934. Jean Hart, who became thirty-three in September of that year, is in the hat. Her friend is Mrs Andrew Hunter. (John Hart)

Plate 17b
John Hart, in cap, with Andrew Hunter, who had a large draper's shop in Falkirk's Cow Wynd, known as Falkirk's Bargain King. (John Hart)

Plate 18
The Falkirk 'transmitter', as it is today and much as it was when John Hart brought it from London on the train – the remains of the baggage label are on the upper surface of the base, just below and to the right of the pulley wheel (centre). For the wording of the plaque, see pages 77–8. The apparatus equates precisely to that in figure 1, and comprises, from left to right, scanning disc with lenses, slotted disc, disc with spiral slot (partly obscured), motor to drive slotted disc, pulley wheel for disc with spiral slot, motor to drive scanning disc and disc with spiral slot. (Royal Television Society)

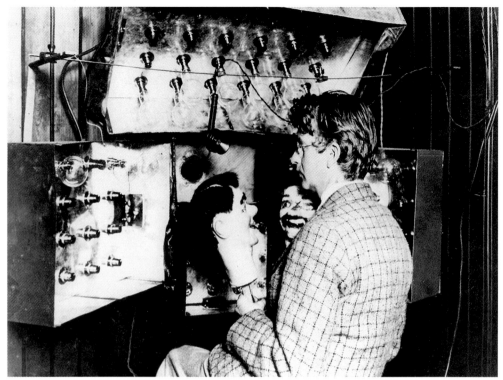

Plate 19
Baird and two Stooky Bills (the original is the one on the right) face the batteries of forty-watt floodlights at Motograph House in September 1926. The apparatus is now closed in, and the subject is scanned through a lens in a four-inch aperture in the wall. A telephone system carries the sound. (Royal Television Society)

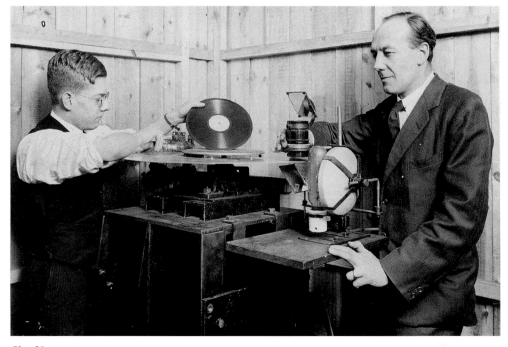

Plate 20
Percy (left) and Bill Fox pose with some early phonovision apparatus. (Royal Television Society)

Plate 21
James Denton controls the transatlantic transmission by phone from Long Acre to New York, 1928. (Royal Television Society)

Plate 22
On board the *Berengaria*, March 1928. Hutchinson is on the far left, with beside him (behind the four-striper) S W Brown, the chief wireless operator whose fiancée appeared on the screen. The ship's captain, Sir Arthur Rostron, is leaning on the television receiver. (Royal Television Society)

Plate 23
Hutchinson, Baird, and Sir
Oliver Lodge, in about 1928.
(Royal Television Society)

Plate 24
Baird, at the peak of his success
in 1928, poses on the front steps
of 'The Lodge' with his father
and Annie. The dog was called
Jinky. Note the spats, for style
and for warmth!

Plate 25
Dora Caffrey in 1929. (Nick Jackson)

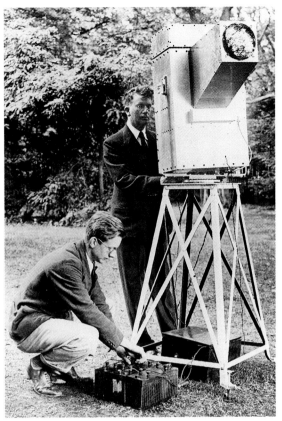

Plate 26
Noctovision in the garden of Swiss Cottage, 10 August 1929. Baird stands behind the camera, while Philip Hobson attends to the rotary converter.

Plate 27
Swiss Cottage, Box Hill, Baird's home from 1929 to January 1932, and scene of noctovision outdoor experiments. (Ray Herbert)

Plate 28
A relaxed Jack Buchanan sits before the daylight camera on the roof of the Long Acre building. Baird looks on. The technician is Thomas Collier. (Royal Television Society)

Plate 29
In the street outside the Long Acre building, May 1931, the setting of the first outside television broadcast. The caravan, with its mirror-drum camera inside, is angled so that images can be picked up of people on the pavement. Moseley is standing with his back to the used car specialists. (Royal Television Society)

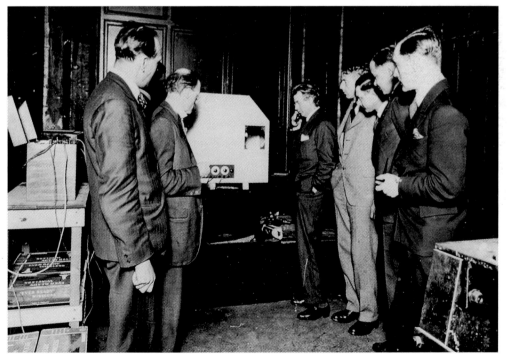

Plate 32
Baird televisor, 1930.

Plate 33
Baird telewriter, 1929. The printed tape passes in front of a lens, behind which it is scanned by a rotating drum. See page 134, and figure 3. (Reproduced with permission from Graham Winbolt, *John Logie Baird: a Pictorial Record of Early Television Development 1924–1938*, Kelly Publications 2001)

They were married on 4 October, with a wedding lunch afterwards at the Savoy. It was a small, mainly family, party, to which Baird and Gladstone Murray were invited as 'close friends'. Afterwards, giving Baird a lift, the couple drove down to the Burford Bridge Hotel, Box Hill, for a honeymoon weekend.

> [Baird] put on a special party for us at his charming house atop of Box Hill. He had invited a number of distinguished 'gentry' (his favourite term) to greet us. Win was flattered when Sir Richard Gregory said to her: 'Well, I thought I'd remain a widower but after this – I'll think again.'[108]

As a footnote, Moseley later added, 'He really did, not so long after; he married one of the guests at the party.'

Richard Gregory (he was created a baronet in January 1931) was then sixty-six, and had been since 1919 the distinguished editor of *Nature*, in which he had published if not also written the editorial in 1927 criticising Baird.[109] His first wife died in 1926. His new wife, who was clearly also among the guests if not the gentry, was Dorothy Page, only daughter of William Page, archaeologist and editor of the extensive *The Victoria History of the Counties of England*. They had met once, two years earlier, but from now on it was a lightning courtship. Baird was invited to a reception at the Ladies Army and Navy Club ('Morning Dress') on 20 January 1931, and to the wedding at Felpham, Sussex, on 27 January 1931.[110]

Towards the end of 1930 the Baird company's business on the home market was looking so unpromising that Lord Ampthill asked for a private meeting with Lord Gainford, vice-chairman of the board of governors of the BBC. This took place at Brooks's Club on 7 November 1930. Gainford reported to Reith:

> [Ampthill] had been told we were not prepared to even continue the very inadequate facilities now given and for which the Baird company paid us £2000 a year. In America the process was being warmly taken up, and he contrasted the difference of our attitude to that of other governments and countries. I told him at the moment we were not proposing to reduce the facilities we had given the Baird Company, and that our Corporation's broadcasting operations could not be compared or contrasted with the advertising methods pursued in the USA or by Government or interests on the Continent. ...
>
> He asked whether he and his principals could come and meet the

Board. I said it would be better to know what proposals they wished to discuss, and that any request should be put in writing *for our consideration*, but I could hold out no prospect of any more facilities being afforded than were now given, unless there was some real advance in the production necessitating some revision of these facilities.[111]

The meeting between the boards of the respective organisations never took place, though the two noble lords corresponded with each other several times. The BBC refused to be drawn by arguments that more facilities for television would result in more televisors being sold, which would be in the interests of Britain and the British Empire, or by comparisons with the situation in USA, and also in Germany, where the Baird company was already fairly comfortably entrenched.

It was at this point that Baird decided that he must personally confront the hated ogre of his student days.

8
Meeting Difficulties
January to October 1931

For the year 1931 there survives Baird's engagement diary,* maintained largely by his devoted personal secretary, Dora Caffrey (later Jackson). She had originally been taken on in November 1928 as Bill Fox's assistant. She became Baird's secretary in May 1931. From a letter she wrote to a BBC programme researcher in 1957,[1] it would appear that Moseley and Baird were not only in the habit of having supper in the boardroom after the regular Monday afternoon meeting; they sometimes had their fish and chips there for lunch beforehand. On these occasions, Caffrey and Moseley's secretary, Ruth Maschwitz, would rush round the room fanning the air before Lord Ampthill arrived. One day, on which there was no meeting, Baird brought back from lunch a packet of Mexican jumping beans, which Caffrey helped him organise into races up and down the boardroom table.

Baird was now sole managing director. Hutchinson had returned from his extended visit to the USA with nothing tangible having been achieved except a mound of expense claims and a potential lawsuit. He had subsequently tried and failed to forge any commercial links with other major companies in Britain.[2] His fellow directors were not amused, and he resigned.

The appointment of a business, or general, manager, L Napier, on a part-time basis after Hutchinson's resignation was instrumental in things going from bad to worse. With, in Baird's words, 'cash becoming dangerously low', Moseley, who was already the company's official liaison officer with the BBC as well as 'Director of Programmes' and much else besides, was appointed to the board as full-time business manager. He effected some drastic staff cuts and other economies, which included persuading Baird to accept a fifty per cent reduction in his salary.[3]

The first few days of 1931 illustrate the multifaceted role that the Baird company expected its managing director to perform. It combined the functions of chief executive, leading negotiator with commercial, national, and government institutions and officials, and with ministers of the crown and members of parliament, marketing director, and principal if not sole research scientist. Baird's experience in all but the last of these areas was limited. He had run successful small businesses, and he had a proven record as a salesman of socks, soap, honey, and television. He could express himself fluently and persuasively in writing, or when dictating, but he lacked confidence in the board room or when face to face with anyone but the most ardent supporter of his views.

On Friday, 2 January, Baird had a meeting with Lord Marks, chairman of the Columbia Graphophone Company, in Lincoln's Inn Fields. The seventy-year-old peer, who had been ennobled in July 1929 for his role in politics and government, was also an engineer and authority on patent law. Hutchinson had unsuccessfully been making advances to the Gramophone Company.[2] It is possible that Baird's purpose in seeing Marks was to try and open negotiations for some kind of alliance with the Columbia Graphophone Company. Alternatively, he may have been consulting Marks on a point of patent law.

During the afternoon Baird presided at a press demonstration in the Long Acre laboratories of his company's latest development, zone, or multi-channel, television, with a mirror drum as the scanning device. A fairly detailed picture could be produced by sending it in three sections over three separate telephone lines, and projecting the sections, side by side, on a cinema screen. At the transmitting end, scanning was done under ordinary floodlights or in daylight, the mirror drum causing a series of images to pass over three photo-electric cells, one for each section of the final picture. There was nothing startlingly new about the mirror drum; it had first been proposed by the Frenchman Lazare Weiller in 1889, and a working system incorporating it had been demonstrated by Telefunken at the Berlin radio show in 1928.[4] The introduction to the Baird laboratories of a drum with thirty mirrors, corresponding to the thirty-line picture and canted at slightly different angles, was, however, fraught with anxieties. Desmond Campbell recalled the experience:

> Baird said to me one day that we ought to try to do twenty-five pictures a second instead of twelve and a half and asked me if I'd like to try. I said, 'No, I don't think it's safe.' 'Oh, yes, it's quite safe.' 'No,' I said, 'I don't think it is. When these bits of glass strip start going round fast they're going to fly off. I don't want to touch it.' So he got someone else and the result was they nearly got cut in half.[5]

The someone else appears to have been Clapp.

> We blew up the whole mirror drum. All the glass mirrors fell off because of the speed it was running and Mr Baird said, 'I think we'd better go home now, Mr Clapp. I think we'd better go home.'[5]

No such accidents blighted the press demonstration on 2 January 1931, which was hailed as a 'new revolution in our industry'.[6] Baird could not have stayed long to acknowledge the plaudits; at 5pm he had an appointment with the Postmaster General at St James's Palace. The subject of their discussion would emerge the following week.

After the weekend at Swiss Cottage, Baird had a Monday lunch appointment at the Ivy with Major (Archie) Church and Colonel Moore-Brabazon (later Lord Brabazon of Tara), pioneer aviator, politician, and president of the Radio Manufacturers Association. Major A G Church DSO MC MP had been a keen supporter of television and a personal friend of Baird since the transatlantic transmissions in 1928.[7] His function at this time seems to have been that of unpaid adviser and supporter in high places. Several lunches are recorded, at which he would set up a meeting between Baird and an influential figure. Described as 'small and dynamic … a delightful companion, full of innumerable suggestions and ideas',[8] Church had in 1920 become general secretary of the newly-established Association of Scientific Workers. Through the organisation, he met Richard Gregory, editor of *Nature*, and through Gregory he met H G Wells. Gregory and Church openly supported Wells as Labour candidate for the University of London in the general election of 1922, and signed his letter of support:

> Scientific method is business and production, systematic progress in health and education, pitted against the methods of adventure and scramble: that is why the advent of a Labour Party will mean a greater obligation to sustain and extend scientific subjects and scientific research not only in physical, but also in financial, economic and social science.[8]

Wells was not elected. Instead Church himself was persuaded to stand as Labour candidate for the London constituency of Leyton (East) in a by-election in 1923, and was elected, becoming parliamentary private secretary to the President of the Board of Trade, the notable economist Sidney Webb, in the first Labour administration. He was returned to parliament again, for Central Wandsworth, in 1929, when he was appointed parliamentary private secretary to the Secretary of State for War. His powerful contacts in Germany included Heinrich Brüning, chancellor of Germany 1930-2, to whom he introduced Baird, who recalled going with Church 'on many occasions' to meet Brüning, a 'quiet, studious impressive figure, more of a scholar than a statesman'.[9] Church was appointed to the board of the Baird company in September 1931, after he ceased to be a member of parliament on the establishment of a national government under Ramsay MacDonald to deal with the country's economic problems. He also became a member of the board of Fernseh.[10]

Also on 2 January, Baird had dictated to Margaret Leslie, Caffrey's predecessor, a letter to Reith at the BBC, Savoy Hill, saying that there was a 'rather important matter which I should like to have the opportunity of discussing with you personally'.[11] The response was immediate, and a meeting fixed for 2pm on 6 January.

Reith was an awesome figure, six foot six inches tall; on his left cheek 'the scar of his war wound added to his gauntness'.[12] His office manner could be unnerving, as his daughter recalls:

> His actor's set is the playing field scale of his desktop, curiously devoid of papers and of the paraphernalia of process. The pens and inkwells are arranged with geometrical precision – he is pathologically afraid of disorder – and he quaintly believes that to get to heaven your affairs must be in perfect order. He has a gold fountain-pen which lies across his desk like a telegraph pole (only the best will do for John Reith) and as he strides quickly to and fro, his audience – because that is the form that meetings with Reith take – has to follow his movements back and forth uneasily and feel vaguely disadvantaged, knowing that he could dispense kindness, vision, misery and small mindedness in equal measure.[13]

Baird certainly would have been recalling their previous confrontation at college. It appears now that Reith remembered it too. In his personal diary, which he kept up for sixty years until his death, he wrote, 'I had my first meeting with J. L. Baird, and found him most reasonable'. Later he added into the typescript, in his own hand, the word 'business', between 'first' and 'meeting'.[14]

In the meantime, information seems to have been leaked from the GPO, because it was reported by Murray to a meeting of the BBC control board on 6 January that Baird was likely to make an approach, after a meeting with the Postmaster General, for an allocation from the revenue from the broadcasting licence fees in order to pay the artists used in his television transmissions. Murray also, however, pointed out sourly that as the amount charged to the Baird company for the transmissions did not cover all expenses, it was likely that the company would be asked for a further monthly sum.[11]

In the light of that meeting of control board, several recommendations were drafted to be put to Reith:

(1) Nothing has happened in the way of development or improvement which would justify any extension of facilities or change of attitude towards Baird Television.

(2) It is essential to avoid the admission of Baird Television to programme time in any circumstance that can be envisaged at present.

(3) There is no case for relieving the Baird Company from the burden of the expenditure involved by the experimental transmissions.

(4) There are various directions in which the BBC can help the Baird Company to make more effective and more economical use of the existing facilities within the limits of the present policy. It is recommended that the Director-General should write to Mr Baird on the lines of the attached draft, being careful to omit any particulars of the methods whereby through consultation in the ordinary way the BBC may implement its friendly attitude.[11]

Whatever the tone of the draft, Reith's letter (15 January 1931) was couched in friendly terms:

I was glad of the opportunity the other day of discussing your problems. As I believe you recognised at the time, there is really no case from our point of view for subsidising your activities or for bearing part of the cost of the experimental transmissions. I am advised that the development of your system of television has not yet advanced sufficiently to justify any change of policy on the part of the BBC. At the same time, however, I want you to realise that the BBC is anxious to be as helpful as possible in the solution of your different problems. There may be ways in which within the present policy this friendly attitude may be made more effective than at present. Anyway, you can take it that there is here the maximum goodwill towards you personally, and I am asking those concerned to continue to explore with you and your colleagues the various avenues of constructive co-operation.[11]

Baird, who had been away 'with a severe chill', replied on 27 January:

I am pleased to say that I am feeling better now, and therefore hasten to express my appreciation of your letter, and for the steps you have taken to ensure constructive co-operation in the future.

I am sorry to hear your view that the development of television has not reached a sufficiently advanced stage to justify any change of policy, for, as I told you, I do think that the extension of hours of broadcasting, for instance, is vital to our development. Our technique has improved tremendously as a direct consequence of broadcasting facilities you have granted, but we are dependent on obtaining more convenient and longer hours to demonstrate the greater public interest which we know to be in existence.

With regard to the financial side, the word 'subsidy' is hardly a correct description of the suggestion I put forward, but perhaps it would be as well to leave this over for a further discussion when we next meet.[11]

Reith wrote at the bottom, 'He doesn't seem to have taken up the point of joint investigation. Shd I write to him and make it clearer? If so please give me a letter to sign', and passed it to Ashbridge for advice. Ashbridge replied that 'no answer to this present letter' should be sent.[11]

That Reith's letter was intended to be taken at its face value is attested by a memorandum from Murray to Carpendale (4 September 1931) in which he commented, of the meeting between Baird and Reith on 6 January, 'Baird's mission was to secure financial help from the BBC. There was also a general talk on very cordial lines and I remember the DG at the next meeting of the Control Board expressing a special desire that everything possible should be done to help Baird.'[15]

The severe January chill was only one of Baird's health problems. Between 6 January and the end of June, he paid eighteen visits to his dentist, G Holloway in Weymouth Street, on some occasions three times in a week. Baird did not have good teeth. Though he was supremely indifferent to his personal appearance, he was very rarely caught smiling by the camera. Occasional appointments are recorded, however, with his tailor, J Conroy, of Kenton, Middlesex, possibly at the instigation of Caffrey.

Meanwhile, other organisations were demonstrating their interest in the development of television techniques. In Britain, the Gramophone Company (His Master's Voice), in which the giant Radio Corporation of America (RCA) had a principal interest, had shown its new equipment at the Physical and Optical societies' exhibition in the first week in January. With this, images on cinematograph film were transmitted by multi-channel techniques onto a screen measuring 24 inches by 20 inches to make a picture of 150 lines. Strictly speaking, this was not 'true' television as envisaged by Baird, since the subject itself was not scanned. Baird was sufficiently alarmed, however, to present himself at one of the shows, where he was allowed to examine the apparatus. The Baird company subsequently brought an unsuccessful action against HMV for infringement of its rights.[16]

Also among the audience for one of the shows, but incognito, was Hobson. He reported back to his laboratory manager at Long Acre.

> The general flicker of the picture was very noticeable owing to the fact that it was flickering in five sections instead of the whole picture. Detail seemed to be very good indeed, the various views of London being very clear and easily recognisable. Synchronising was very good, as was to be expected with the use of synchronous motors. A very noticeable point was the very neat layout and also the smallness of the apparatus. ... Although the size and scope of the complete 5-zone picture was better than anything I have seen here, the detail actually in one zone did not seem to be much better than our standard single zone land-line picture.[17]

In USA, the Bell Telephone Laboratories also had a multi-channel system, details of which were announced in the scientific press in January.[18] The gap between Baird and his rivals was narrowing, but he sprang a surprise on 7 January with a demonstration at Long Acre to the scientific and technical press of a system of 'direct arc modulation'; with this technique the light source was an electric arc between two carbon rods, and the picture on the screen appeared with increased brilliance, in black and white instead of the black and orange produced by a neon lamp.

Baird was having regular meetings with Edward (later Sir Edward) Appleton, who in 1924, at the age of thirty-two, had been appointed to the Wheatstone chair in physics at King's College, London, after, it was said, having in 1923 turned down the offer to become the BBC's first chief engineer. He was a friend of Eckersley, the man who took the job, and significantly was a member of the BBC committee which met from 1927 to 1929 to consider the erection of high-power regional stations. His advice and cooperation were still frequently sought by the BBC, not least when the initial broadcasts of Baird's thirty-line system were being made. Appleton recalled:

> [I told] Baird that I was expecting two pictures to be received – one above the other – at places on the edge of the service area. This was due to the action of the Heaviside Layer which caused a second picture to arrive at the receiver a little later than the main one which had travelled along the ground. Eventually I received a drawing from a Bristol viewer

of a man with two heads one above the other – and from the displacement I was able to get a nice determination of the height of the Heaviside Layer. I got excited about all this but I naturally didn't find Baird sharing my enthusiasm at all.[19]

This effect is a form of radio location which detects an object and enables its distance from the observer to be calculated. Appleton was, however, a natural scientist, and Baird was almost exclusively focussed on television, so the practical significance of this observation was not appreciated at the time.

From February 1932 Appleton was retained by the Baird company as a consultant at £400 a year plus two guineas an hour for written work.[20] His enthusiasm for the quality of picture that could be obtained by ultra-short-wave television transmission was shared by Baird, who acknowledged Appleton's encouragement to him to proceed with experiments.[21] To make this a commercially viable proposition for home viewing, however, would require resources that the Baird company did not have, and the cooperation of the BBC, which controlled all national broadcasting, regardless of wavelength. In the light of the fact that no provision had been made under the Geneva Convention for the proper expansion of television within the broadcast band of wavelengths, new radio techniques needed to be developed. A solution might well lie in serving local areas by means of ultra-short-wave transmitters. There were still difficulties to be resolved, however, in that these waves could be affected by buildings, steel structures, trees, and ground contours.[22]

In between business meetings and lunches, weekly board meetings, visits to the dentist and to a Dr W J O'Donovan of Harley Street, Baird was holding discussions with other scientists, including, on 20 February, the thirty-four-year-old Hungarian inventor, Kálmán Tihanyi, who had patented a fully electronic television system in 1926. RCA were to purchase his patents in 1934. Baird was regularly in touch with Sir Ambrose Fleming, inventor of the diode valve, who was also a personal friend and was entertained at Swiss Cottage. On 26 February technical staff at Long Acre gave Fleming a private demonstration of a whole range of processes: transmission by land line with and without a noctovision filter; thirty-hole and sixty-hole telecine reception on a televisor; transmission by portable disc to a televisor; floodlight three-zone transmission and reception; mirror-drum receiver; modulated arc; Kerr cell.[23]

For some of the staff, including Hobson and Banks, the demonstration for Sir Ambrose was almost their last job at Long Acre. As a part of the economy drive, about a dozen of the thirty technicians were now made redundant.[17]

One who survived the cut was Richard Vince, who had joined the company in August 1928. He was to be closely involved in another Baird technical initiative in conjunction with the company's French partner, Television-Baird-Nathan, which was established in 1932. Previous public demonstrations, by the Reichspostzentralamt in Berlin in 1929 and the Bell Telephone Laboratories in USA in 1930, of a television link between two people speaking on the telephone had been less than successful because a caller at one end of the line was too dazzled by the light from the flying spot to see on the screen the caller at the other end.

By using noctovision methods incorporating an infra-red beam for scanning, Baird-Nathan resolved this problem. The apparatus was built at Long Acre and taken by Vince to Paris, where he organised a demonstration on 19 May 1932 between the Galeries Lafayette and the offices of the newspaper, *Le Matin*, about a mile away. It was witnessed by the Minister of Posts and Telegraphs and by members of the press, including a representative of *The Times*:

> The receiving screen, some 10 in. long by 5 in. wide, showed the head and shoulders of the sitter. Although the image was fairly coarse the features of the sitter were clearly recognisable, while the movement of the lips could easily be followed. From the offices of Le Matin your Correspondent carried on a brief conversation with an engineer at the Galeries Lafayette. The whole play of expression on the face of the speaker was remarkably clear, and when he obeyed a request to put out his tongue the organ in question popped out from the face on the screen.

Subsequently, the experiment was repeated between Paris and the Lyons offices of the Galeries Lafayette, 250 miles away.[24]

On 12 March Baird virtually cleared his bank deposit account by withdrawing £5306.13s., a sum representing £175,000 in today's money. One can only assume that the money was used to try and shore up his ailing company. Moseley records that when the company was drastically cutting its outlays, Baird paid Caffrey an increase in salary out of his own pocket.[25]

Caffrey seems to have been worth her weight in gold; so are the memories of Baird she set down in 1957:

> He was, on the whole, a mild-tempered man, but simply could not bear to be interrupted when dictating. Letters to friends and business acquaintances were leisurely affairs, but technical matter was invariably

dictated at high speed, and noise, especially, irritated him. I remember one day some 'musicians' were performing beneath our window, and he broke off and said, 'Miss, if they smell as bad as they sound …!' Another thing which annoyed him was an open window, at any time except, perhaps in the height of summer. He would rush across and shut the offending panes, saying something like, 'Miss – d'yer want me to catch my death?' On one occasion press photographers wanted a photograph. It was winter and he was swathed, as usual, in thick woollen muffler and ditto overcoat. He held up his hand to them and said, 'WAIT!' – fished into the depths of the coat, and produced a hot-water bottle! Thereby slimming himself considerably for the photograph. Apart from the fact that he was oblivious to time (he frequently came into the office just before 6pm and said, 'Good morning, Miss,' and oh, how often I have made appointments for Saturdays or Sundays, tennis, etc., only to have to cancel them; I had to take down a Provisional Specification, or on one occasion go to the office and get the passport from his rolltop desk.)

Although he most certainly had a great sense of humour, he appeared lacking – or at least quite unaware of – the ridiculous. When he took me round the beautiful garden at Box Hill, I admired a great bush of buddleia; he immediately broke off just one branch and handed it to me. Imagine me sitting in the London train, holding a long curling branch of lilac flowers, rather like an angel who should have had a lily, but something had gone wrong somewhere! I found him always kind and considerate, and although the typical inventor – the long-haired, carelessly dressed inventor beloved by the fiction writers – his comments were frequently most pertinent. Before his marriage I used to see that he was properly dressed for important occasions, dinners, etc. and he once turned to a friend and said, 'You know, I shall be sending for Miss Caffrey every time I want to blow my nose, soon.' He always had trouble with his feet, sometimes walking around barefoot. There was a private drawer in his desk and one day he opened this and said, 'Miss, you had better DO something about these.' 'These' were socks – dozens and dozens; they oozed out and flopped to the floor, rather like pips from a gooseberry.

His poor health frequently sent him in search of the sun and, staying at Worthing once, he sent for me to take dictation. I went down by train, did the work, and after typing my notes at a local bureau, returned to the hotel. This was, of course, a four-star place, and Mr Baird asked me to join him for dinner. He drank only mineral water himself, so I had half a bottle of wine with my seven courses. Now I am one of those who cannot travel in a closed car or bus for long journeys, and I realised, too late, how foolish I had been to accept his invitation to return to town in the Daimler, instead of by train. When I had weakly asked for a window to be opened, then crawled – just in time – round to the back of the car, he was kindness itself. Was I completely recovered? Took me to my door, etc. BUT, in the morning, and for several weeks afterwards, he found great joy in disbelieving my story of travel sickness. 'Miss, *how* are you going to get on if you throw up every time a young man takes you out and gives you a drink?'[1]

In April the news broke of a merger, largely brokered by Lord Marks,[26] of the Columbia Graphophone company with the HMV Gramophone company, to form Electrical and Musical Industries (EMI). RCA had a stake of some twenty-seven per cent in the new company, on whose board was David Sarnoff, executive vice-president of RCA. A significant appointment was Russian-born Isaac (later Sir Isaac) Shoenberg, now fifty-one, of HMV, who became director of research and head of patents of the new company.[27] He decided not only to persuade his board to pursue an expensive research programme into television, but to concentrate all the company's efforts into electronic scanning, for which no conclusive solution had yet been achieved. He saw no future for mechanical methods.[28] Baird, on the other hand, was still dedicated to them. As J D Percy observed, 'Optics and mechanics were his very life blood.'[29]

Monday, 4 May was a bank holiday. An emergency meeting of the Baird company's board was called for the following day, presumably to discuss the financial situation. Outwardly, though, matters progressed as usual, with three further Baird 'firsts' being notched up within four weeks.

On 8 May, after a rehearsal the previous week from the roof of the Long Acre building, the mirror-drum camera, housed in a wooden caravan, was used to make the first outside television broadcast, from the street below. A reporter inside the building viewed it on a receiver. 'He saw images of people passing to and fro in the street below. There was considerable variation in the quality of reception, due to varying degrees of cloud and sunshine, but the panorama of the streets was there – small boys looking at the transmitting machine in the road, a white-coated seller of chocolates, and so on.'[30]

Baird was in the habit at this time of eating in the evenings at a restaurant at 79 St Martin's Lane, just across the road from 133 Long Acre. One night he found Percy, also working late, making adjustments to equipment in the van in the street.

'Would you like your supper, Mr Percy?'

This was a regular arrangement, but, as usual, there was a catch. When they had finished eating, Baird took out a pencil and said, 'Now I'd like you to make up this bit of equipment by eight o'clock tomorrow morning because I want a variation in the lens system.' When Percy protested that he hadn't any paper on which to make notes, Baird drew a diagram on the spotless white tablecloth, which he pulled off the table and presented to Percy. The waiter was told to put it on the bill.[31]

The first interview by television took place on 13 May. The subject was Ethel Snowden, wearing a hat. She was a governor of the BBC and the wife of the Chancellor of the Exchequer, from whose official residence at 11 Downing Street the interview took place. The interviewer was the ubiquitous Moseley, sitting in the editor's room in the offices of the *Daily Herald*, of which he was radio critic.[32] They communicated with each other by phone, Mrs Snowden's picture being received on a televisor on Moseley's desk.

Their coy exchange was printed in the *Daily Herald* the following day. In the course of it Moseley inveigled her into observing, 'This interview itself proves how the broadcasting of sound will soon develop to include the broadcasting of all the eye can see.'[33] Reith would have been, and probably was, incensed. He did not like television, he did not like Moseley,[34] and he did not like Mrs Snowden, to whom he referred in his private diaries as the 'Red Woman'. He even wrote the beginning of a play about the rows generated by her and his other *bête noire* on the board, the chairman Lord Clarendon, with which he used to amuse dinner guests. One of them, the formidable politician and writer Mary Agnes Hamilton, herself a governor of the BBC, wickedly told him in 1935 that it was 'very good' and that he should continue with it![35]

On 3 June, shortly after a week of cancelled appointments, suggesting yet another bout of illness, Baird achieved what he had first forecast in 1923. Apart from croquet on the lawn at Helensburgh and, it would seem, social tennis with 'Alice', Baird was no sporting type, and it is doubtful whether he had ever seen a horse race until he televised the Derby. The entry in the diary for 6 May, '3.30 Epsom (Major Hill)', suggests that on that day Baird reconnoitred the ground. He seems to have been satisfied, because on 19 May Moseley wrote to Gladstone Murray at the BBC asking if the Baird company could have 'five or ten minutes on Derby Day for a television broadcast during the race'. The BBC duly responded with an offer of the London national wavelength (261 metres) between 2.45 and 3.15pm, provided that the voice commentary would be on a separate telephone line from any rented by the BBC, and that there was no interference with the BBC's radio running commentary.[36]

Tests were run. On the day itself, the van, with its mirror drum, was parked opposite the winning post, with a wooden scaffolding round it for the engineers and for Moseley, who was to do the commentary. Baird, having satisfied himself that all was well at that end, returned to Long Acre for the transmission. At Epsom, Moseley shared his perch with a crowd of adults and bawling children who seemed to be under the illusion that the temporary stand had been put up for their benefit. At Long Acre press representatives and other interested parties crammed into two rooms to watch the proceedings on normal commercial receivers. They heard Moseley's commentary broadcast over a land line. Along with other viewers who were able to tune in to the images sent by land line to Long Acre and then transmitted via the BBC, they saw flickering representations of the crowd, the parade of horses before the race, and the finish. Much was ill-defined because of interference.

The vision and the overall planning were Baird's. The technical side was in the hands of his engineering staff, Jacomb, Campbell, Percy, and Bridgewater, who after World War II became chief engineer of BBC Television, but without getting a knighthood. Baird publicly pronounced himself satisfied with the transmission. The opinions of the press were divided between those who criticised the reception and those who applauded the fact that anything had been achieved at all.[37]

In July, a significant research trip was undertaken by someone who has already appeared in this narrative. A G D West, the BBC's assistant chief engineer who had gone down to Hastings on behalf of Odhams, had in May 1929 left the BBC for HMV, to develop the design of radio sets and gramophones. Now, he was sent by his company to the USA, primarily to visit the RCA laboratory in Camden, New Jersey, where Zworykin had been experimenting with cathode-ray tubes since 1930.[38]

On his return West submitted a report to the board of EMI, his employers, recommending that they should purchase the complete RCA television transmission system. His proposals were accepted by the board, but were stoutly opposed by Shoenberg, who wanted them to buy a Marconi transmitter instead. He had his way, and the transmitter was delivered in January 1932.[38] Also in January 1932, West typed up his curriculum vitae,[39] presumably to support his application for the slightly curious career move he was shortly to make: to become chief recording engineer at the Associated Talking Pictures studios in Ealing, which had been opened in 1931. There is also some evidence that HMV was not a very happy place at which to work. Eckersley, after leaving the BBC, was employed by HMV as a consultant. Reith recorded in his diary, 'PPE in at tea; he said he hated the HMV ... no one is allowed to see Clark except the General Manager, and all kinds of rules about the use of the telephone, memoranda, etc.'[40] Alfred Clark was Chairman of HMV and subsequently of EMI.

Margaret Albu was also poised to return to the action.

I was twenty-four and beginning to get good engagements as a pianist. I did not find life in England congenial, but there were a few friends from home in London at that time, and one of them was Grace [Mitchell].

One day Grace telephoned me and said: 'I've been asked to go and have tea with a man who lives on top of Box Hill and I'd rather not go alone.'

I agreed to go with her.

'It will be quite easy,' Grace said, 'He is sending a car for me. I'll pick you up and we'll be back by half-past six.' Grace was an optimist.

The following Saturday [1 August 1931] Grace arrived in the car. Near Box Hill the chauffeur lost his way and it was not until he asked someone the way to Mr Baird's house that I realized who it was that we were to visit.

We arrived at Swiss Cottage and I was introduced to John and Mephy. We sat around the log fire in the drawing-room although the August sun was blazing outside.

Mr Baird was a tousle-headed man of forty-two, with wide blue eyes, a courteous manner, and an air, which impressed even me, of being someone in some way different from the majority of men. As the afternoon drew to a close he said in a voice that beseeched us: 'Will you two girls give me the pleasure of coming down to Worthing for dinner? The chauffeur will drive you straight home afterwards.'

He could usually persuade people to do what he wanted and the drive to the coast was pleasant in the clear evening.

As we climbed into the car after taking our leave he ran down the steps of Warne's Hotel and asked for my telephone number. Hoping that this meant an engagement for television, I gave it to him. His parting words were, 'I wish I was returning with you girls instead of spending the weekend alone here.'

The following Monday [a bank holiday] I was out teaching when my mother's maid, Doris, telephoned me, saying: 'Oh, Miss Margaret, do be home by eight o'clock. Mr Baird has phoned you five times today and will be phoning again at eight.'

I went home and took the call. It was not for an engagement for television but an invitation to dinner at Swiss Cottage.

We saw each other every day, and by the end of the week the die was cast. Although there was nineteen years' difference in our ages, although our backgrounds and upbringing were so different, there was an instant sympathy between us. I knew he was loyal, without guile, and could give me the security and companionship I wanted. As for him, he said I gave him a feeling of youth.[41]

Baird's engagement diary for that week, with postponed lunch dates and entries set down simply as 'lunch' or 'dinner' with no name, would appear to confirm her account of a whirlwind courtship.

Margaret Cecilia Albu was born in Johannesburg on 13 March 1907. Her younger brother, Gordon, was born in 1909, by which time the family had moved to Kimberley, where her father, Henry Albu, was a manager at the De Beer's diamond mine. Henry's father, Berthold Albu, was a musical rabbi (he played the violin), who came from Britain in the 1870s to be the first rabbi of the diamond field in the Kimberley and Barclay West area. He brought with him his wife Bella (née Silverston), described on her marriage certificate as a manufacturer of Honiton lace, whom he had married in Exeter.

They had two sons, Henry and John, and four daughters, three of whom had musical careers as pianists or opera singers. Berthold had a heart attack at a concert and retired to Durban, where he played the violin in the Philharmonic Orchestra. When he died at the age of 57, he was the first Jew to have an official burial in Durban.

Henry, a Liberal (or Progressive) Jew who went to synagogue just once a year on the Day of Atonement, was born in Sheffield, and worked for an uncle in the East End of London, sticking labels on jars of jam, before himself emigrating to South Africa. He prospered in the diamond business and as a stockbroker, but lost most of his money before meeting Cecilia Reid, a headmistress sixteen years his junior, who had come from England to South Africa as a qualified teacher in 1903. She was born in Ripon, Yorkshire, the eldest of four daughters (there were also two sons) of Thomas Reid, head gardener at Copt Hewick House, near Ripon, and Sarah Fitzwilliam. Cecilia was what Margaret called an 'Anglican of the High Church variety', but she and Henry Albu married in 1905, and Henry used to take Margaret to church on Sundays.[42]

Margaret discovered her vocation when she was three.

At a tea party I was asked whether I should like some tea. I shook my head at the hostess. 'Would you like some cake?' Another shake of the head. 'Would you like to go and play in the garden?' Another shake of the head. 'Then what would you like to do?' This question brought a definite answer: 'I should like to play on your piano.'[43]

She had her first lesson when she was eight, at the convent near the house in which the family was living in Klerksdorp. When she was ten, she went to Miss Harrison's Conservatoire of Music in Johannesburg, where she spent seven years as one of 450 pupils who were taught by forty certificated music teachers. Though, like her father, she was supposed to have a weak heart, which necessitated packing up and moving sometimes twice a year from the six thousand feet of Johannesburg to sea level at the Cape or in Natal, she passed her teacher's diploma and started to perform in public when she was sixteen.

Just before my eighteenth birthday it was decided that I should go to London. I did not want to go but I had little say in the matter, and in 1925 my mother took me to England. Her idea was to arrive in the spring, so I nearly froze to death. My mother and I eventually took a small flat in Kensington. I hired an upright piano, horrid after my Steinway, and practised eight hours a day.[43]

Later that year, as a solo performer, she became an associate of the Royal College of Music, and in 1926 a licentiate of the Royal Academy of Music.

Mother and daughter returned to South Africa in October 1926, but Henry Albu died shortly afterwards at the age of seventy. Cecilia's one thought now was to get herself and her children back to England; she always held out for the English way of life against what she saw as the rougher colonial and commercial atmosphere of South Africa. It did not matter that Gordon was within a few months of taking his matriculation, which would qualify him for entrance to a university. She packed up and took both protesting children to London. Gordon, with no academic qualification, took a job as an apprentice teller in a bank. Margaret saw him one day through the bars, and burst into tears.[42]

Soon after the family's arrival in London the stock market collapsed and the depression set in. Henry Albu had left quite a considerable estate in the form of equities. Cecilia made the mistake of holding onto the shares for sentimental reasons. There was nothing for it but to rent a small house in suburban Sutton, and settle down to a life of faded gentility. What money there was, went towards Margaret's musical education. After an audition, she was accepted by the pianist Lev Pouishnov as one of his five pupils. Understanding her circumstances, he sent her pupils to teach who had not made the grade with him.[44]

It is not recorded, even in Baird family folklore, what Cecilia thought about Margaret's romance, of which she must have been aware shortly after the start. There is no doubt that she would have asked searching questions. They would have been even more searching if she had known that her daughter's beau had for ten years been having a relationship with a married woman which was still going on. If 'Alice' stayed at Swiss Cottage in 1931, it would have been during the summer, and it appears that Mephy moved out temporarily into lodgings in Hanwell, Middlesex, at about this time.[45] While Baird did not at the beginning have any thought of marrying Margaret, as a son of the manse he craved respectability. He was forty-two. The position with 'Alice' was hopeless, and there was always the risk, especially for a man in the public eye, of his affair, which seems to have been conducted with supreme discretion, becoming public knowledge.

Margaret was young and beautiful. She was also a good conversationalist and, even more to the point, a good listener. There was from the start a chemical attraction between them. She was rather in awe of this public figure with the staring blue eyes that sometimes appeared to be looking right into you. Whatever the reason for Grace Mitchell being invited to tea, he established an immediate rapport with Margaret. He liked to take her out and be seen with her, and she with him. He would send a car to pick her up from Sutton and drive her down to Brighton or Worthing for dinner, and back again the same evening. It did not matter to her that he talked incessantly about television, and never about music. They may have discussed religion, both having been brought up in a Christian tradition. When she first mentioned her Jewish ancestry, he observed, 'The Jews are the salt of the earth.'[46] He also had certain strong philosophical views, which he would happily air with anyone.

It was at about this time, too, that Baird put to Moseley a suggestion that escalated, in Moseley's mind, into a fixation. The controlling interest in Baird Television Ltd was represented by a block of 997,300 deferred shares in the original Television Ltd, which had gone into voluntary liquidation. The means by which Moseley managed to buy these shares from the receiver for £16,500 occupy three out of the twenty chapters of his biography of Baird,[47] with the titles 'A Matter of Life and Death', 'The Fight in New York', and 'The Fantastic Deal'. Suffice here to say that after several frantic weeks buying up voting rights from residuary shareholders and several more in New York in August and September trying to raise the necessary capital,[48] Moseley managed to obtain the funds in Britain through a loan from Alfred Bates, an advertising agent and newspaper owner. The cash to enable him to mount his campaign, in the form of an advance of £5800, came from Isidore

Ostrer, president of the Gaumont–British film company. Ostrer had begun his working life as a stock exchange clerk, and was an old boyhood friend and former neighbour of Moseley.[49] A year younger than Moseley and Baird, he was a poet and economist, as well as a financier.

Moseley's fare to New York, where he arrived on the German Lloyd liner *Bremen* on 19 August, was funded by Nathan Goldsmith, an American dealer in real estate, and his associate Leon Osterweil. The pair of them had materialised in London in July, with the idea of negotiating the purchase of some of the deferred shares in Baird Television Ltd.[50] It now appears that they also discussed with the board of the Baird company a proposal for financing an American company to promote the Baird interests and market the Baird products. 'Mr Moseley said it was the intention to have American manufacturers produce 1,000,000 television sets a year and there was no reason why they could not be sold as easily as radio sets. They will be the Baird patent commercially built televisions sets, and will have the modulated light used in the English market instead of the neon lights.'[51] Matters had progressed to such a point that Moseley was given the company's power of attorney to conclude a deal on the spot when he arrived in New York, though as it turned out he did not use it for this purpose.[52]

Moseley was in New York when the deal for the Television Ltd shares was concluded by transatlantic cable without any American support.[53] He now effectively controlled Baird Television Ltd, and he appears to have been appointed vice-chairman of the company,[54] with Ampthill still as chairman. For his own holding of shares, which at one time was worth a quarter-of-a-million pounds, Baird eventually received just £3000.[55] Bates subsequently sued Ostrer and Moseley on the grounds that Moseley had been acting as Ostrer's agent; Ostrer generously agreed to settle out of court because 'I think it will relieve Moseley of all this bother.'[56]

Soon after Moseley had sailed for New York, Baird had a meeting, at 3pm on 17 August, with Rt Hon. J H Whitley at Whitley's Chelsea home. Whitley, a former speaker of the House of Commons who had presided over five administrations in seven years, had in 1930 been appointed chairman of the governors of the BBC when, to Reith's huge delight, Lord Clarendon had become governor-general of South Africa. Baird wrote to Moseley at the Biltmore Hotel in New York on 24 August:

> I saw Whitley and had quite a long talk with him. He seemed extremely
> well disposed and anxious to help us, and I am hoping that we will soon
> get extended hours and better treatment generally from the BBC. I

am having dinner with Gladstone Murray on Thursday, and generally keeping in close touch with him.[57]

The dinner, for 'Mr Gladstone Murray and party' duly took place at 8pm on 27 August, probably at the Burford Bridge Hotel, as in Baird's engagement diary the words 'Box Hill' are crossed through.

Baird's letter to Moseley concluded on a personal note: 'I hope you are not going to stay away long, as I have no one to lunch with and altogether things are becoming very depressing without your unbounded optimism, magnetic personality, strength and guidance.'[57]

While there is no record of Baird's meeting with the chairman of the governors of the BBC, Whitley apparently made some notes which were discussed by Ashbridge and Murray in their now habitual state of obduracy. They agreed between themselves that the Baird company should have no slots in BBC programme time. They denied that television, by any process, was within 'measurable distance of its service stage'. They concluded that it was no part of the function of the BBC to be involved in the development of 'commercial inventions' or to be used 'by outside concerns as an instrument of research'. As token concessions, they put forward some 'constructive proposals', conditional on 'it being understood (a) that all Baird transmissions continue to be experimental and described as such, and (b) that the Baird Company defray all expenses incurred'. These included reducing the five half-hour transmissions to a total of two hours 'at times not inconvenient to the BBC but more suitable to the Baird Company', and transmitting a regular programme, 'such as Jack Payne's Band'.[58]

One may wonder whether this attitude was compatible with Reith's 'special desire that everything possible should be done to help Baird'.[15] It is likely that Reith, because of his personal aversion to television, resolved not to become closely involved in the decision making. More than with other significant issues, he seems to have left major matters of television policy for his senior staff to work out, and collectively and individually they were either not competent enough to cope on their own, or were unwilling to make crucial decisions in case they proved to be the wrong ones.[59] It would also appear that as late as the end of 1932, Carpendale and Ashbridge, at least, simply did not realise the potential interest that television would generate.[60] Moseley, who was nobody's fool, seems to have put his finger on the problem, without realising what lay behind it, when he referred to the 'curiously negative role of the BBC's Director General throughout our protracted negotiations with the great monopoly which he controlled'.[61]

All this would seem to be borne out by a confidential memorandum to

Ashbridge, typed by Murray at his home. It is undated, but is likely to have been written on or about 16 August 1931.

> The agreed policy is to keep the pace as slow as is compatible with the maintenance of decent relations. It has been a considerable relief not to have to deal with a guerilla warfare on that front. At the same time we are careful not to concede too much for peace.
>
> You will recall that towards the end of last year, we had to encounter a threatened breach of the Baird peace, over some absurd demands on their part for programme time. The situation was smoothed over largely as a result of the DG seeing Baird himself. The DG envisaged various methods of extended cooperation which were mentioned at Control Board and you and I were left to work them out. We definitely resisted the idea of intrusion into programme time certainly at this stage but we recommended the indefinite continuance of the present facilities. Then to implement the effect of the cordial interview between the DG and Baird, I suggested, you concurred, and it was agreed that we should not press for the extra charge which Chief Accountant wished made on the heading of engineers expenses.[11]

The 'absurd demands' were made by Lord Ampthill in his letter to Lord Gainford (17 November 1930): 'What my Company desires is extended facilities and a closer co-operation of your Corporation, which would be of immense assistance to us, and I would suggest regarding the hours of transmission that half an hour every evening from 10 to 10.30 should be granted for television broadcasting.'[11] Also it was Baird who had taken the initiative and asked for the interview with Reith, a man whom he had a deep-seated reason to dislike and of whom he was in awe.

Murray's private memorandum to Ashbridge goes on to discuss the portable transmitter which the Baird company had asked Ashbridge and Murray, at a demonstration in the company's laboratories at the end of 1930, to be installed in the BBC for experimental purposes. It was at present stored in 'No. 10', an external BBC studio to which it had been transferred after being used for the Snowden interview.[56]

> We fenced a bit, but indicated that we might do something about using the portable in one of our studios as an auxiliary to one of the ordinary television transmissions outside programme time. Subsequently I actually arranged for the portable to come over here during the first week of January. Then there was some technical hitch at their end. This I exploited

to the maximum with the result that several months elapsed before we actually accepted delivery. I liked your idea of the 'silent exhibit' in No. 10, partly because if their attitude were still purely political, they would be satisfied. Not so however. I have discovered that at a recent Board meeting, the staff were taken to account for making the Company appear ridiculous and amateurish. This being the case, I think we should take the initiative in moving the portable to Savoy Hill so that it may be used actually in connection with an ordinary Baird transmission. If this could be done early this week, then I would like you to meet Baird again, preferably apart from Moseley who is in one of his vicious periods and requires specialised separate treatment and temporary segregation.[11]

Baird's engagement diary notes that there was a test demonstration of the portable transmitter at No. 10 studio on 19 August. The identities of the true villains of this particular piece are beginning to emerge.

On 1 September, five days after Baird had privately entertained Gladstone Murray and his party, the two men met again at the Carlton Grill, with Ashbridge. On 8 September Murray wrote to Baird, ostensibly to pick up the points that Baird had discussed with Whitley. After reiterating the BBC's policy towards the Baird company, which was in fact the policy Murray and Ashbridge had agreed between themselves on 24 August, Murray refused to entertain any reduction of charges, or any suggestion that the company might have a half-hour's transmission on a Sunday afternoon or be allowed rent free a studio at Savoy Hill, or that the Baird programme department be put under the control of the BBC director of programmes. Consideration would, however, be given to the two midnight transmissions being replaced by a single half-hour weekly feature, but only when the London national frequency was available for vision, or by a weekly programme featuring a hotel dance band, transmitted from the hotel itself, 'it being understood that all negotiations and difficulties with the dance bands and hotel authorities would be the concern of the Baird Company'. In addition line tests to the North Regional transmitters in conjunction with BBC engineers could now be entertained, at the Baird company's expense.[11]

Baird replied by return of post, 9 September:

I appreciate your frankness but I must confess to some surprise at the note of suspicion which still permeates BBC communications. One might deduce that the Baird Company was a kind of predatory monster engaged only in trying to embarrass or demolish the BBC. I hope some day to gain even BBC recognition of the *bona fides* of our effort to contribute materially to the progress of science and the happiness of mankind, not to mention potential British supremacy in a new field of activity. Meanwhile, however, I am not unmindful of the personal cordiality I encounter at Savoy Hill, and I am in complete sympathy with the peculiar difficulties you encounter by virtue of your monopoly and public service constitution. ...

The new weekly feature transmissions replacing the two half-hour midnight transmissions will be of a studio subject, such as Jack Payne's band, put on not later than 10.30 p.m., vision on 261 metres. I note that you give the hotel transmissions as an alternative. I agree that there should not be both in any one week, but I suggest the real reason for including the hotels is to provide the possibility of change within the very narrow compass of opportunity you have prescribed.

These two variations in conjunction with the five half-hour morning transmissions are accepted as a basis of development.

It is suggested that the first of the new weekly transmissions should be arranged to take place during the first week in October. We have in mind Jack Payne and his Band, but we understand that the acoustical properties of Number 10 Studio may not be adequate for this purpose, and that the aural programme may suffer. Therefore, it will be necessary to experiment, and if Number 10 Studio is found to be unsatisfactory, another Studio would have to be tried. Meanwhile, we shall begin negotiating with Hotels, as suggested in your letter.[11]

Baird, with the promptness of his response and the nature of his reaction, clearly finessed one of Murray's aces. In a memorandum to Ashbridge, and to Reith (marked 'To note, please'), Murray admitted, 'The last paragraph of Baird's letter is very clever. My attempt to scale over this point did not succeed.'[11] To have put one over the assistant controller (information) of the BBC, by return of post, was a feather in Baird's cap, at a time when he was assiduously courting Margaret and dealing with the day-to-day matters which are recorded in his engagement diary: 7 September, '2.30 Board Meeting, 5.30 Mr Dalton (high speed cable telegraphy)'; 10 September, '1.15 Lunch with Major Church, 4.0 Mr Brown (shareholder), 4.15 Dr Cooke, 5.0 Tea with Mr Snodgrass'.

The reference to 'high speed cable telegraphy' suggests a further diversification of Baird's activities at the time. Dalton was almost certainly John (later Sir John) Dalton. He had served throughout World War I as an officer in the Royal Engineers (Signals), and later joined W T Henley's Telegraph

Works, of which he was subsequently chairman for many years until his retirement in 1958.[62]

Arnold Snodgrass, Baird's second cousin on his mother's side, was an alcoholic with a private income. He and his wife lived in Helensburgh opposite what was now called Larchfield Academy. The poet, and future poet laureate, C Day Lewis, who taught English and rugby football at Larchfield for four terms during the years 1929-30, recalled being taken on pub-crawls in Glasgow by Snodgrass. 'When in drink, the admirable Mr Snodgrass reverted to his 1914-18 days: he saw me now, not double, but as a whole platoon or even a company of men, drilled me on the station platform, entrained me, and when we returned to Helensburgh, marched me with ear-splitting words of command along the sleeping avenues homeward.'[63] Snodgrass could not stand Day Lewis's successor, the poet W H Auden, who taught at the school from 1930 to 1932, but Mrs Snodgrass worshipped him and used to feed him vast suppers.[64]

On his return to Britain in late September, a triumphant Moseley immediately waded into the confrontation between the Baird company and the BBC. He wrote in his radio column in the *Daily Herald*, 'If this country loses the lead in television, the responsibility will be [Reith's].'[65] He sent a strong letter to Murray about the 'concessions' that had been offered and threatened to solicit from the Postmaster General a licence and wavelengths to operate an independent television service. The BBC's control board considered the letter at its meeting on 6 October and decided that they did not understand the company's dissatisfaction and that no further concessions could be made. The minute concluded,

> During the discussion it was decided that in communication with Baird no reference should at present be made to the ultra-short wave experiments which we are undertaking, but that should they make application to the Post Office and our comments be asked for we should resist permission for them to operate separately, pointing out the concessions recently made and referring to the possible value of ultra-short wave experiments to television.[11]

In other words, while continuing to oppose the establishment of an independent television channel, which might well have been subsidised by advertising on the American model,[66] and in spite of Reith's explicit offer of technical cooperation, the BBC was keeping from Baird and his company any information about its own work on ultra-short waves. Baird was also experimenting with ultra-short waves, though he did not then see them as a commercial proposition for his firm. If the BBC had acted openly in this, the future of the Baird company might have been different.

There was, however, a sort of gesture the following week. On 12 October Ashbridge decided to take up a long-standing invitation to visit Long Acre to see what was new. He reported verbally to Reith afterwards, and confirmed his account in a five-page memorandum on 14 October.[67] He saw a demonstration of a receiver using a mirror drum and Kerr cell, which projected a picture onto a screen about four feet by two feet: 'easily the best television I have seen so far.' The next piece of apparatus was 'an application of television to the "singing arc". ... I was not able to gather exactly what they have in view. ... Both these pictures were grey in colour, instead of the rather objectionable reddish colour which one obtains from the ordinary Neon lamp type of picture.'

He examined a mirror-drum televisor showing, without magnification, a picture of about nine inches by six inches, which was 'fairly good'. With regard to the demonstrations, he concluded that 'definite laboratory progress is being made, which should lead in a few years' time to Television becoming of definite programme value, but my opinion has not changed in connection with the transmissions which are being sent out now, namely that they are worth very little from the point of view of entertainment and interest, apart from scientific consideration'.

Ashbridge then had a talk with Moseley, one of whose proposals was that selected BBC radio programmes which lent themselves to being viewed should also be televised, initially 'three or four times a week, without charge'. Ashbridge pointed out that those who did not have televisors would complain, and that the only way he could see such a thing happening, 'even if Television developed sufficiently, would be by sending vision on ultra-short waves. Being entirely non-technical [Moseley] did not comment very much on this.'

Ashbridge finally concluded that 'we should not visualise the abandonment of television':

> I would be inclined to encourage the Baird company to a reasonable extent in what they are doing now, because I feel that someone must develop Television for broadcasting, and if they do it adequately so much the better, if not sooner or later the BBC will be forced to do it, at great cost to the listening public.
>
> During the last two years [Murray and I] have endeavoured to apply the policy decided at Control Board meetings. Generally speaking this has been on the lines of minimum possible concession because it did

not seem that progress was being made. ... We now agree that the situation has changed to an extent, and that the tendency should be for the BBC to take the initiative, in some degree. The point is that if Prime Ministers, Postmasters General, and Members of Parliament were impressed with the Baird Television of two years ago, it is obvious that they would be very much more impressed by a demonstration of the latest improvements, which the Baird Company might give at any time. [Murray] considers that the Post Office might conceivably grant the Baird Company facilities in the shape of wavelengths outside the broad-cast band, which might be unsound from our point of view. This would seem to be another reason for anticipating such a manoeuvre.[67]

The devastating ingenuousness if not also duplicity in the tone of this memorandum is apparent in the light of the fact that Baird was not at Long Acre to present this vital private demonstration or to participate in the subsequent discussion on policy. Did Ashbridge deliberately set up the visit at a time when he knew Baird would not be there to answer technical questions about development plans? How might Baird himself have reacted at that time to the leading comment about the use of ultra-short waves?[68]

Baird was not even in the country on 12 October. Six days earlier he had sailed for New York.

New York, and Marriage

1931–1932

B aird sailed for New York on Tuesday, 6 October 1931, in the Cunard liner
Aquitania. He was accompanied by a minder, Moseley's personal assistant
Walter H Knight, who had begun his association with Moseley in 1922 as
advertising manager on the *Southend Times*.

At this time the general situation in the USA with regard to television
was, compared with other industries, positively vibrant. Nervous investors, hit
by the stock market crash in October 1929 and subsequent further depreci-
ation of their holdings, were looking to the brash new broadcasting system of
television as a potential growth area through which they might recoup their
losses. In 1931 there were twenty-two licensed television stations in operation
in the USA, broadcasting in channels between 2000 and 2950 kHz (150 and
100 metres).[1] All these stations employed a mechanical system, with a flying-
spot camera in the studio and some form of Nipkow disc at the receiving
end. The signals could not be received on ordinary radio sets, and television
sets were marketed with a built-in radio. The less expensive Baird televisor in
Britain could be connected to a normal radio set to pick up the BBC signals
on the medium waveband. The American system operated on a higher
frequency. This allowed higher definition pictures to be broadcast, even by
mechanical methods; most stations transmitted sixty lines and twenty pictures
per second.

Almost unnoticed amid the hype, research towards electronic television
was being undertaken in two laboratories on opposite sides of the continent.
David Sarnoff, head of RCA, was taking a personal interest in the work
Zworykin and his team were doing at the RCA laboratories in Camden,
New Jersey. In San Francisco, California, Philo Farnsworth was developing
the image-dissector camera which was to become an integral part of the first
electronic systems. Zworykin himself had in 1930 visited the laboratory
where Farnsworth was conducting his experiments, and had written an
enthusiastic report. In April 1931, Sarnoff followed up with an offer of

$100,000 for Farnsworth's business. Farnsworth turned him down in favour of an arrangement with the Philadelphia Storage Battery Co (Philco). This relationship ended in 1934, when Farnsworth again became a free agent. Throughout the 1930s Farnsworth maintained a legal battle with RCA over infringement of his image-dissector patents. An agreement was reached in 1939, as a result of which RCA paid royalties to Farnsworth for the use of his technology. This was the first time that RCA ever paid for the use of any patent in the fields of radio or television.[2]

In his biography of Baird,[3] Moseley lets the man himself give the reason for his expedition:

> Our company in New York, 'Baird Television Incorporated', was proving a very expensive affair. We had to pay for expensive offices and staff and the chief result of all these activities appeared to be lengthy reports holding out hopes of big deals just about to mature. The Board, urged on by Sydney, decided to send me to USA to investigate the situation.[4]

Subsequent writers have accepted this explanation, while expressing surprise at what on the face of it seems a curious decision on the part of the London board, especially in the light of Hutchinson's failure to make any impact on the American scene.[5] The truth is somewhat different.

There were in 1931 four principal television stations broadcasting in the New York area. Jenkins Television had since April been broadcasting twenty-six hours a week, divided about equally between live programmes and films. Columbia Broadcasting System (CBS) was on the air forty-nine hours a week, almost entirely live shows. National Broadcasting Company (NBC), owned by RCA, had opened new studios in the Empire State Building in July. Their experimental programmes, showing for thirty hours a week, consisted of moving test images. By speeding up their sixty-aperture discs and interlacing the pictures, they achieved a 120-line definition at twenty-four pictures a second. (Hogan's) Radio Pictures operated from Long Island. It was a small, primarily experimental outfit.

Donald Flamm, the thirty-two-year-old go-ahead owner and operator in New York of WMCA, the 'largest regional station in the entire country',[6] which he had founded in 1927, was planning also to broadcast television programmes, using the Baird system. These would include Broadway musicals, and sports' events from Madison Square Gardens, including the weekly boxing match, ice-hockey, and six-day cycle races, to which he had the exclusive rights.[7] WMCA stood for William MacAlpine, the name of the hotel from which the radio station first operated. Flamm, in the same way as many

Americans, had first learned about Baird in 1927 from the *New York Times* Sunday edition, which carried a full-page feature, with an interview, extolling him and his invention.[8] He had followed Baird's progress ever since, and early in 1931 he made contact with the company's New York office, and witnessed a demonstration of the Baird system.

On 3 June 1931, significantly the same day that Baird succeeded for the first time in transmitting pictures of the Derby, Flamm, in the name of his principal company, Knickerbocker Broadcasting Co, filed with the US Federal Radio Commission an application for a radio station construction permit of 1kW power, 'For the purpose of inaugurating in this country the most advanced form of television experimentation as developed by the associated Baird companies in England, France and Germany, utilizing however American made apparatus constructed entirely by American labor, and supplied by the Baird Television Corporation of America.'[6] An additional application was made on 27 August for a construction permit for a television station using 500 watts; on the same day the RCA-Victor company of Camden, the RCA in New York City, and two other concerns applied for licences to develop television stations.[9] Moseley, while in New York, had on 8 September discussed with Flamm the terms of a draft agreement between the Knickerbocker Broadcasting Co and the Baird company for the rights to use the system. A copy of this agreement was despatched to London for consideration by the Baird board.[10]

Moseley left New York for London on 11 September.[11] It may be assumed that he attended the company board meetings which took place on 21 and 28 September, according to Baird's engagement diary. It was decided that Baird and Knight should go to New York to complete the negotiations that Moseley had started on the two fronts. There seems to have been some delay in confirming the final arrangements, because on 30 September Captain William J Jarrard, the Baird company's representative in New York, cabled Moseley in London: 'Flamm's attorney making completion extremely difficult by insisting on indemnification for patent infringement and other points which I have refused. ... Absolutely essential that I know the date of arrival of Mr Baird.'[10] According to Baird's engagement diary, it was not until Monday, 5 October that he and Knight met at the US consulate, presumably to obtain their visas. They sailed the following day.

There was urgency on the other front as well. When he was in New York, Moseley had become disenchanted with Goldsmith and Osterweil, and had entered instead into discussions with Carroll O'Toole and Company to take over the Baird company's New York operation. He had returned to London with a proposition, which the board of the Baird company, by now no doubt very confused about the position, had tentatively approved subject to further negotiations by Baird and Knight. Knight's position was a delicate one. He was not an employee of the Baird company, though the company was paying his expenses. He had first met Baird about three years earlier, but did not know him well. He had, however, a thorough grasp of business affairs, and was trusted by Moseley, though this in itself did not make him any more reliable in the eyes of the board.

Baird, at a critical time in his personal life, with a New York winter approaching, was being despatched to a country he did not know, to negotiate concurrently two separate legal agreements with principals whom he had never met, and to conduct whatever technical discussions and demonstrations might be required. He also needed to uphold the supremacy of his television systems in the face of the advance in the USA of alternative methods.

For Baird himself, spice was added to the voyage by the fact that twenty years earlier he had been involved as an apprentice in the building of the ship, and by a meeting which, however, did not live up to expectations:

> Among the passengers was H G Wells and I was quite excited at the prospect of meeting a man who in my youth I had regarded as a demigod. The invaluable Mr Knight soon arranged a meeting and Mr Wells and Mr Knight advanced together along the deck to meet me. Mr Wells proved to be a substantially built man of medium height with a cap pulled over his eyes, utterly devoid of any affectation or any effort at effect. A great anticlimax after the magnificent Sir Oliver Lodge and the overpowering Sir John Reith. No formal facade here, only a poor vulgar creature like myself. We had a short chat about youth camps. I said these organisations appear to ignore sex. 'Oh well,' he said, 'every Jack has his Jill,' and that is all I remember about the conversation with my demigod.[12]

Poor Baird, tongue-tied as usual when in the presence of someone of whom he was in awe! From his enigmatic, or just inane, remark about Jack and Jill, it is possible that Wells felt the same about Baird. Here was a man who had put into practice, with apparatus constructed with his own hands, a scientific marvel which Wells himself had predicted in his fiction.

By his own account, Baird's arrival on 13 October had about it several touches of the surreal:

> As the boat approached New York harbour I was surprised to see on the pier a body of highland pipers marching up and down with great elan

to the skirl of the pipes. These wretched men proved to be a gang of comic opera pipers from the Ziegfeld Follies. A misguided but enthusiastic American publicity agent had arranged to give me a real Scottish reception. I was to ride in front of this procession with a police escort to my royal suite at the Waldorf Astoria. I could not face it. I slipped away and and reached the Waldorf unobtrusively in a taxi; a few minutes later the Highlanders (from Czechoslovakia, Louisiana and Hollywood) arrived. It was an expensive matter pacifying them. The royal suite was overpowering, particularly the bathroom which was an enormous hall with a vast black marble bath set in the floor and a great assortment of sprays and showers and gilded WCs. The flat was filled with press men, flashing bulbs and taking notes, egged on by the dynamo publicity man. They stayed on but gave me the impression that they had no interest whatsoever in myself or my work, but concentrated on the whisky and refreshments. At two in the morning the last of them had reeled out or been carried out and I returned to my gilded bedroom.[13]

A press report gave the purpose of Baird's visit as being 'to expand the offices of the American branch of the Baird Television Company and plan for the production of television sets on a large scale. ... Mr Baird said he would sign contracts with Donald Flamm, president of WMCA, for transmission by the Baird system in this country. The application will come before a Federal court for approval in November, he added.'[14]

One of the press interviews Baird subsequently gave was with the radio editor of the *New York Times*, Orrin E Dunlap Jr. It may have been his own conviction, or it may have been to bolster the negotiations with Flamm, that led Baird firmly to nail his colours to the mast:

[Baird] sees no hope for television by means of cathode-ray tubes. He has developed what he calls a 'mirror scanning drum' which empowers him to cast images on the wall or screen. ... He asserts that the neon tube will remain as the lamp of the home receiver. For theatres he has developed a special arc light, which can be made to fluctuate rapidly in accordance with the incoming television signal.[15]

A second prediction was also just as wide of the mark:

I observe that there is a movement towards the utilisation of ultra-short waves in America. I am rather sceptical about their success in television because they cover a very limited area. I am of the opinion, based upon our tests in London, that the regular broadcasting channels are best adapted to carry the television pictures. We have not done much with the very short waves, although I may later experiment with them using an aerial on top of the Crystal Palace.[15]

In America, RCA, which held a large stake in the British company EMI, was instigating a research programme which was intended to pave the way towards very high-definition television pictures. In Britain, unknown to Baird, the BBC was already investigating the implications of sending vision by ultra-short waves.

On Baird's first full day in New York,

> The roundabout started at 8 o'clock with three business visitors to join me at breakfast to discuss a very important proposition. The proposition seemed to me incomprehensible nonsense but the gents ate heartily and drank enormous quantities of rye whisky. At 11 am one of them collapsed on the couch and lay as if dead with glazed eyes. The prohibition spirit had got him. He was removed for an application of the stomach-pump.
>
> This seemed to be quite a commonplace part of the business routine. More businessmen arrived, more press men. I had ten guests whom I had never seen or heard of to lunch. They talked incessantly; when I went to the WC they followed me still talking; at dinner time, two more arrived accompanied by their dames with a spare dame for my use. They stayed apparently with the intention of staying the night, dames and all! I wanted to do my best to be friendly and hospitable to everybody but these hard faced drunken pussies were the last straw. I told Knight if he did not clear them all out I would go to another hotel. He had them out in ten minutes; he was the soul of tact and determination.[16]

Baird's account may not have been intended to refer to any specific individuals, but there are affinities with the initial discussions which he and Knight had with Mr O'Toole of Carroll O'Toole. Carroll O'Toole had proposed spreading the financing of the new company over a period of five years. The Americans would have six months in which to find the first $60,000; the Baird company would receive a block of shares for its American patents, but could not deal in them until six months after the conclusion of the financing of the American company. At the end of June 1931, the Baird company's assets in cash and securities were worth about seventy thousand pounds, against an expenditure of that same amount over the previous twelve months. Baird and Knight had concluded that on this basis the company could not wait for five years and six months before getting a return on its American patents, and that something better would have to be negotiated.[17] Knight reported:

> In accordance with instructions, the first person we interviewed was Mr O'Toole, who was in a state bordering on hysterical fright caused by some rumour that was going about that on 9 November RCA were going to demonstrate some wonderful new system of television which would render all existing systems obsolete. He was not then in a position to improve upon his original scheme, and in fact he was not prepared to commit himself definitely to anything. He talked and talked and wandered miles from the point, with lectures on American methods of finance, and each time we brought him back to the point he had nothing concrete to offer.[18]

Exhaustive and exhausting attempts to find an alternative backer were frustrated by the fact that though the Baird name carried some weight with the American investing public, the Baird company was not in good odour with the market on the grounds that such a proposition had been hawked around for some years. In particular, Charles Izenstark, who reckoned that he had had a raw deal from Hutchinson, was taking the opportunity forcefully to express his opinion of the company.[17] There is more than merely a suggestion that he had an interest in the establishment of the new company in the form of a legal option.[19]

While these initial negotiations were going on, there was a formal reception by Mayor Jimmy Walker at City Hall, to which Baird's car was was conducted by a police motorcycle escort with sirens at full blast.

> When we arrived at City Hall, a small band of Ziegfeld Follies Highlanders were marching up and down playing outside 'The Barren Rocks of Aden'. I was ushered into the Mayor's Parlour, and after some little delay, Mayor Walker appeared, shook me cordially by the hand and then immediately began an address to the press representatives who were present in force. He evidently did this sort of thing regularly. 'We have with us today,' said the Mayor, 'a man who has given us his world famous invention of —', here he hesitated for a moment and his secretary whispered in a stage whisper, 'Television'. The Mayor then went on to give a dissertation chiefly on the wonders of New York, and

kept referring to me as an Englishman, although here was a band of pipers outside.[20]

Flamm took no part in the frenetic welcome. He met Baird for the first time after the mayor's reception. Sixty-five years later, he recalled Baird as 'soft-spoken, a gentle, kind man who thought carefully before saying anything. He had a sense of pride in what he had achieved, and with good reason. I felt that this was a man I could do business with.'[7]

Any business discussions between the two men at this time must have been both constructive and conclusive. On 18 October,[21] only five days after the *Aquitania* had docked in New York, Flamm himself went on air over the WMCA and the Inter-city Networks with a surprise announcement:

> Within a very few moments I shall introduce to you John Logie Baird, the Father of Television – a man who, like so many other great inventors, was confronted with difficulties which a lesser spirit would have deemed insurmountable. ... In regard to television, this eminent Scotch scientist stands much in the same relations as James Watt does to the steam engine, Robert Fulton to the steam boat, or Marconi to radio. As Vulcan stole fire from the heavens and gave it to mankind, so Baird reached into his brain and gave us the ability to witness scenes and events transpiring thousands of miles away. ...
>
> Now, Mr Baird is to bring his system of television to America. Here, with upwards of five hundred stations to choose from, he has selected WMCA as the American station best suited to use his system. ... Sensational though the televising of the finish of the Derby was, I can assure everyone that we have plans under way for even more startling broadcasts. ... It remains only for certain legal formalities to be met – for a television wave to be assigned to us by the Federal Radio Commission – before WMCA starts to broadcast its television programme.*

Baird, who had never been invited by the BBC to broadcast on radio in his own country, made the most of his opportunity to do so to an American audience. With his fluency of expression on paper, it would not have taken him long to compose his own script.* In his elation, he even spoke warmly of his first impressions of New York, including the pipe band, and of the city's 'go ahead vigour, welcoming of novelty and enterprise', though in the event his initial euphoria wore off before the end of the month. He went on to explain to his audience,

> Our company is installing the necessary television transmitting appa-
> ratus and we hope in a very short time to be sending out from this
> station television programmes similar to those we are now sending out
> in London, but with this difference that through WMCA we will have
> a much longer time available.*

Outside broadcasts would be transmitted by means of 'apparatus similar to
that being used by us abroad, for broadcasting daylight scenes such as the
British Derby classic'.

He concluded,

> Television is only in its infancy and big developments are pending.
> Television images which have been seen by the general public offer no
> criterion to what has been achieved in the laboratories. And, our work
> now is to simplify and cheapen our present laboratory apparatus so
> that it can be made available to the man in the street. The problem of
> television is solved. What remains to be done is entirely a matter of
> technical development. There are startling results being achieved behind
> the closed doors at the laboratory and I think that the severest critics
> of television would be convinced by a demonstration of what can be
> done under perfect conditions, but at the present time I can make no
> disclosures.
>
> Throughout the world the highest scientific thought is being
> devoted to television. Vast strides have been made and will be made in
> this new art. I myself look forward to seeing at no distant day television
> theatres supersede the talkies, and the home television become as
> common as the home radio is today.*

World War II would upset his projected timescale, but he was right about the
television in the home, and almost right in that television, particularly the
video, a working concept he himself was the first to introduce, largely super-
seded the cinema. He was right, too, about the startling results, but they were
not emanating from the Baird company laboratories.

As far as Baird and Flamm were concerned, apart from final negotiations
between the respective lawyers of their two companies, the only hurdle
remaining was the licence hearing on 30 November and 1 December before
the Federal Radio Commission in Washington, at which Radio Pictures Inc,
of Long Island, had given notice of an objection.[22]

Meanwhile, on the day before the broadcast, Knight had been contacted
by Samuel R Rosoff, a millionaire New York contractor. Rosoff, an associate

of Goldsmith and Osterweil, had sat in on one of the abortive discussions with potential backers and had been impressed by Baird's account of what he had achieved in Britain, notably the daily BBC transmission, the Coliseum show, and the televising of the Derby. So impressed, indeed, was he that he had telephoned a contact in London, who confirmed that the claims were true.[18]

An immediate meeting was set up with Rosoff, as a result of which a three-hundred-word cable was despatched the same day to the board of the Baird company with details of a proposition. A group headed by Rosoff would pay $50,000 on signature of contract. A public issue would be made immediately after a demonstration of a mirror-drum home receiver and large screen.[23] A million one-dollar shares would be allocated to the American company, and 750,000 each to the English company and to the promoters of the issue. If Moseley wished, an additional 300,000 shares would be issued which he could exchange for his block of deferred shares in Television Ltd. Knight was to be appointed to the board of the American company to represent the Baird company's interests, with Baird as chief consultant; the other directors would be nominated by the promoters of the issue.[18]

While waiting for his board's reaction, Baird set up in his hotel suite a demonstration of his available equipment for Rosoff's lawyer.

> Our agent Pockrass endeavoured to instil some enthusiasm into the cynical [lawyer] who watched our picture with an appearance of disinterested contempt and finally with an 'It ain't up to the pictures' took his departure. *'There's no pleasing that guy,'* said Pockrass. *'If you was to show him Jesus Christ walking out of the garden of Eden he would say it was lousy!'*[24]

The litigious Izenstark was also ready to offer his opinions and his advice. He warned Rosoff that the Baird company, having got Rosoff's signature and his money, would then do nothing. A perturbed Rosoff demanded to know when the mirror-drum apparatus was being shipped.[18] The board in London insisted that the agreement had to be signed first. Rosoff changed his mind about parting with $60,000 without first seeing a demonstration, but offered to pay the cost of bringing the apparatus out, which Baird calculated would cost $1750, including the services of an engineer. To this Rosoff agreed, on the understanding that if the demonstration was successful, he would have an option to set up the new company on the agreed basis, with an initial commitment of $60,000; if the demonstration was not satisfactory and he did not take up the option, he would forfeit his $1750. To this, the board agreed, while informing the company's attorney in New York, Milton Winn of Wise & Seligsberg, that any agreement entered into by Baird must first have the board's approval. When Rosoff heard that the company's managing director did not have the authority to finalise a deal, even though its basis had been agreed by the board, he cried off.[17]

Goldsmith and Osterweil now came back into the picture, and offered to put up the $1750 in return for an option on the same terms as had been agreed with Rosoff. Baird and Knight had now been in New York for just over a fortnight, and already the company was querying their length of stay and the cost involved. Though the name Goldsmith was apparently anathema to Moseley, they felt that they were bound to put the Goldsmith–Osterweil offer to the board. This they did by cable on 31 October, using the agreed codeword Fradogubet to represent Messrs Goldsmith and Osterweil. The board accepted, subject to the agreement incorporating any safeguards which Winn recommended.[18]

On 3 November Baird cabled London: 'Winn withdrawing option to meet your stipulations. ... Send Richards with daylight.'[25] Winn had met Baird and Knight for breakfast earlier that day; a stenographer was provided for him, and he spent the whole morning redrafting the original agreement. The result was approved by Goldsmith and Osterweil and their attorney, and signed the following day, 4 November. Baird and Knight cabled London: 'Option signed as redrawn by Winn. Mailing copy. Cash paid.' A delighted Ampthill was all for firing off a congratulatory cable, but a more cautious Moseley suggested that this should be postponed until the first payment of $60,000 had been received![17]

Baird was now stuck in New York. He was waiting for the hearing in Washington, at which he was due to give evidence in support of the Knickerbocker company's application, and he was waiting for the transmitter to arrive from Britain so that the agreement with Goldsmith and Osterweil could be ratified. Before he left for New York, he had agreed with Margaret that if he had to stay for any length of time, she should join him.

> John hardly ever wrote personal letters, though I do have two brief letter-cards sent from the *Aquitania* and complaining of feeling cut off, missing the telephone. When he had been in New York for three weeks he telephoned me and, with a touch of Scottish thrift, reminded me that the call cost a pound a minute. He asked me to come over on the next ship.[26]

She agreed, and a passage was booked on the White Star liner *Olympic*. She was only two days from New York when on 9 November Baird received a cable from his board: 'Very perturbed at prolonged stay yourself Knight and heavy expense involved. Consider that negotiations should be left Jarrard Winn.' Baird left the reply to Knight (10 November): 'Baird very ill, pneumonia feared. ... Your message upset and hurt him deeply. Considers such criticism in his absence without knowledge of facts grossly unfair especially as certain show of affluence was essential to counteract opinion widely prevalent here Company on last legs. ... My only fear Baird will publicly resign.'[11]

According to a subsequent newspaper report,[27] Margaret arrived the following day, 11 November.

> I ... had some difficulty in disembarking at New York, due to some law about women travelling alone, something to do with the white slave traffic, I believe.
>
> Just as I was expecting to be put on Ellis Island John came aboard and threatened officials with all sorts of things, including Mayor Walker.[26]

Baird was certainly not at all well. It sounds as though the heated atmosphere in the hotel, and the dust and fumes in the streets, were playing havoc with his sinuses. Also, weakened by days, and nights, of intense negotiation on matters with which he was unfamiliar, he had caught an infection. Flamm was consulted, and recommended the salt sea air of Coney Island, where a new hotel, the Half Moon, had just been built on the Boardwalk. In or out of New York was a five-cents' ride on the subway.[7] That same day or the next, Knight and Margaret transferred the patient to the Half Moon. Baird must have been glad to get away from the Waldorf for other reasons. Shortly after the end of World War II and only a few months before his death, he wrote to Moseley: 'What a vision that brings of those nightmare New York days – with gangster bell boys, hard faced insolent inhuman waiters and all the hard brassy vulgar discomfort of those "Luxury" Hotels.'[28]

Margaret and Baird decided to get married, at once, though Baird was in bed with flu-like symptoms. Knight, for the second time in a year, was called upon to make wedding arrangements. He bought a ring, and had a clerk of the Marriage License Bureau to come to the hotel to make out the licence. The wedding ceremony was conducted in a suite in the Half Moon by city magistrate Alfred E Steers on Friday, 13 November. The date had no malign significance for either party. Margaret was born on 13 March, Baird on 13 August, and he had arrived in America on 13 October. For good measure, the second witness with Knight was Thelma Wallace, a reporter on the *Brooklyn Eagle*, whose birthday was on 13 November.[29]

Baird struggled out of bed and into dressing-gown and slippers for the ceremony,[30] during which he was so nervous that he could not prevent himself sidling away. At one point, it seemed that Knight, standing much closer to the bride than Baird, might have been married to her by mistake.

To the couple themselves, there seemed no reason to give any explanations to family, friends, or business colleagues.

> John sent a telegram to Helensburgh, saying, 'Married Margaret Albu today.'
>
> Old Mr Baird exclaimed, 'Margaret Albu? Never heard of her!' He was ninety by then and had long been retired from the ministry, while John's last visit to Helensburgh had been in January 1930.[31]

There was still, however, the problem of 'Alice'.

> We also had to cope with John's old love affair. It had become hopeless, from his point of view, but he was kind and loyal and did not want a violent and painful break with her. He thought he would hurt her less if he could write from New York and say he was already married, and we spent several hours on our wedding day drafting this letter, until the room was a mass of crumpled paper. It was a waste of time. She read of the marriage in the newspaper the same day, while she was in a restaurant, and the news was a violent shock.[31]

After that, Margaret spent her wedding night and much of her four-day honeymoon filling hot-water bottles. She did manage to get the bridegroom out of his sick bed and into a suit again for a wedding reception at the hotel on 15 November. Twenty-nine people sat down to eat at a horseshoe table decked with flowers, bootleg champagne and what looks from the official photograph suspiciously like bootleg spirits. The affair was organised by Knight, who sat on the bride's left. He had invited, according to Baird, 'all our business contacts in New York',[32] a gathering so eclectic that forty-five years on Flamm could only recognise in the photograph himself and his then wife, and his lawyer, William Weisman, and wife.[33]

Jacomb was now in New York, too, presumably to add a touch of technical expertise to whatever was going on. He cabled London on 17 November:

> Situation like comic opera in spite of Baird. Option is legal commitment

here and cannot be altered except by consent. Jarrard and self kept in complete darkness by Knight, who rules over Baird at Coney Island. Latter proceeds to Washington for radio license. Neither serves any useful purpose here and are apt to be expensive with mad demonstrations. Understand Richards arrives soon – what for? Am going ahead with demonstration in Waldorf for Goldsmith and public. Who pays for this anyway? Understand Rosoff will not participate. Remove Baird and Knight and things will progress as smoothly as is now possible.[10]

The cast was augmented on 23 November by the arrival, in the *Olympic*, of Moseley and the company's business adviser and stockbroker, Ian Anderson. Moseley was initially a good deal less supportive of Baird's marriage than Baird had been of his, and was very suspicious of Margaret.

His arrival was stormy. Brushing me aside and brandishing his brief-case he shouted: 'John! What the devil is going on here?' That was my first meeting with Sydney. He cooled down a little when he understood the situation.[31]

That same day Roberts, secretary of the Baird company, received a cable from Knight, which concluded, 'Your Managing Director and your nominee to represent your interests on Board of new American company are stranded with hotel bill and other accounts unpaid, entirely without funds, and compelled to borrow a few dollars from practical strangers to meet immediate necessities.'[11]

Roberts cabled Moseley (23 November): 'See Knight's amazing telegram of 22nd and report. Have remitted Jarrard $1000.'[11]

Anderson and Moseley had a meeting with Baird and Knight in Anderson's rooms at the Plaza Hotel on the evening of Friday 27 November. It was not a success. Anderson stormed at Baird and Knight, accusing them of entering into a scandalous and disgraceful agreement with Goldsmith and Osterweil. He railed at the company's board for acquiescing to it, and threatened to expose the directors at the next annual general meeting for throwing away the American rights and paying an exorbitant price for securing capital for the American company. He claimed that now he was in America he could arrange with leading New York stockbrokers to underwrite the whole of the American issue at a fraction of the cost. Knight said that in that case he had better go ahead and do it![18]

Moseley was caught up in a complex conflict of interests. Baird, Knight, and Anderson were his personal friends, and he had travelled out with

Anderson, one of whose reasons for being in New York was to obtain the best price he could in the USA for Moseley's personal holding of shares in Television Ltd.[17] Moseley was also vice-chairman of Baird Television Ltd, in which capacity his duty lay in obtaining the best deal he could in the USA for the shareholders in the English company.

He and Anderson visited the company's lawyer, Milton Winn, to try to establish whether there were grounds for advising the London board that the 4 November agreement was inimical to the company's interests or had somehow been concluded in a way which was open to challenge from the board. Moseley cabled Roberts: 'Have asked Baird return home immediately. Richards returns tomorrow. Situation satisfactory and very hopeful. Remit $2000 under my supervision.' Richards sailed for Britain on 29 November, without apparently having conducted any demonstrations, but having fallen out with Jacomb, who objected to Richards having been instructed to send confidential reports.[11] Baird and his wife left for Washington on 28 November for the federal hearing.

In other respects the situation with regard to the proposed financing of the American company was anything but satisfactory and hopeful. Knight explained the position to Goldsmith and Osterweil. They were adamant that no-one in New York at that time could obtain a firm underwriting contract for television or for anything else. Rather than put the directors of the Baird company in an embarrassing position if Anderson were allowed to make a fuss to the shareholders, however, they generously agreed to stand aside and give him a week's grace in which to come up with a concrete proposition. If he did succeed in doing so, they would surrender their option in exchange for compensation for the time and expense they had put into the negotiations.[18]

The Federal Radio Commission hearing in Washington on 30 November and 1 December took place before Ralph L Parker, examiner. William Weisman and Paul D P Spearman appeared for the applicant, the Knickerbocker company, and Louis G Caldwell for the respondent, Radio Pictures, with George G Porter representing the Federal Radio Commission.[34] Baird found the proceedings strange:

> The complete lack of formality was astounding to one accustomed to the dignity and red tape of British procedure. Reporters, witnesses, solicitors and a smattering of the public sat all together in a large hall. The Commissioner proved to be a young man, I should think anything from 20 to 28 in appearance. He lay back in his chair gazing abstractedly at the ceiling, throughout the proceedings.
>
> Everybody in the hall seemed to give evidence at interminable length.

When my turn came the subject had been so thoroughly exhausted that there was little left for me to add; however, I did my best and the proceedings terminated without comment from the Commissioner. Donald Flamm was however quite happy about it, and told me that we were certain to get permission.[35]

The applicant presented five witnesses: Baird, Jarrard, Douglas West (Jarrard's deputy), Frank Marx (Flamm's chief engineer), and Flamm himself. There were 238 pages of sworn testimony, and numerous exhibits, including copies of Baird's patents registered both in Britain and in the USA. Flamm, in the expectancy of a favourable recommendation, encouraged Baird and Margaret to stay on for a few days' honeymoon in Washington.[36] It was a lull before the storm.

Moseley had cabled Roberts on 30 November: 'Baird's heavy expenses are partly personal and should certainly be recovered. You should nevertheless cable me in the following terms. "Board satisfied your report but cannot be responsible Baird's expenses beyond his passage home not later than Friday [4 December]."'[11]

A cable was handed to Baird on 2 December: 'Board surprised no report from you personally explaining situation and reasons for your prolonged absence from duties London. Opinion you should return immediately. Telegraph today.' He did so: 'Very important developments render my presence here imperative. Situation critical but very hopeful of successful issue. Sending full personal report.'[37]

The week's grace for Anderson to underwrite the American share issue expired on Friday, 4 December, whereupon he asked for and was granted an extension of a further four days. Knight's feelings were decidedly sour; Baird's are not recorded. Goldsmith and Osterweil were now, with some justification, complaining that Anderson had spoiled the market for their issue. Moseley sent a cable to Roberts (3 December): 'Have had incredibly difficult time but believe things straightened out so that I may leave with Baird early next week.' He sent a further cable on 7 December: 'You should make an issue of Baird's return with us Berengaria Friday [11 December]. Anderson confident launching bigger better scheme than present one.' Roberts replied the same day: 'Telegraph names of individuals returning Berengaria. How does Anderson's scheme affect option? Absence of detailed information and Baird's telegram of 2nd, yours of 3rd, makes your suggestion regarding Baird incomprehensible.' Moseley replied, 'Anderson Baird myself. Hope report by Friday completed revised scheme. Anderson returning New York after preparations London.'[11]

Anderson, at a conference on 9 December, suggested that he had a conditional offer from a group of unnamed people which would be more advantageous to the English company. Knight was not impressed. The following day he addressed to the Baird company board a fifteen-page single-spaced letter on foolscap.[18] It damned Anderson for derailing the existing negotiations; it damned Anderson's alternative scheme, especially the provision that the voting rights in the nine hundred thousand deferred shares should be vested in the board of the English company. '[Anderson] has thrown mud at Baird, Goldsmith, Osterweil, the directors of the English company, individually and collectively, and at myself in particular.' For Baird, however, Knight had nothing but praise:

> Anderson's attack is directed mainly at myself, personally, for having entered into this option, and he regards Mr Baird as having given placid assent to all that I did. He contends that I was the moving spirit in the transaction, and I, and I alone, am responsible.
>
> I am content that this should be so. ... [But] if, as I believe, this arrangement will eventually turn out to be in the best interests of the English company and the English shareholders, and that it was the best arrangement that could possibly be made with the conditions prevailing to-day, then I ask that a full share of the credit for that transaction shall be accorded to Mr Baird, who, I unhesitatingly say, fully deserves it.
>
> As, under present arrangements, Mr Baird returns to England tomorrow and I am remaining in America, it is just possible that he and I may never meet again, and I want to put now on record the high esteem in which I hold Mr Baird and the very sincere regard that I have for him.
>
> Although, of course, I had been acquainted with Mr Baird for nearly three years before we came out here, I did not know him, nor did I get to know him even while we were on the boat coming across. It was only during those first three weeks in New York, when we stood together with our backs to the wall, trying to hold our own against some of the keenest brains of America, and upholding, as we believed, the interests of the English shareholders whom we had come here to represent, that I really learned to know Baird as a man and to realise the strength of purpose and tenacity that is in him and his ability to dissect a proposition.
>
> By the time the option was signed, Mr Baird was as nearly dead from exhaustion as any man could possibly be. He had had three weeks of the most strenuous mental strain that could possibly be put upon him. From

nine o'clock in the morning until two or three o'clock the next morning he had joined in the arguments, and had taken part in conferences in a manner which would have astounded those people in London who regard him as a placid quies[c]ent person, who allows himself to be driven against his will and against his better judgment. Whether or not the agreement we finally made was a good one, Mr Baird put his whole heart and soul into the work in which we were engaged, and no living person could have been actuated more keenly than he was by the interests of the English shareholders.[18]

The letter also revealed that Knight and Baird already had an additional scheme up their sleeves, which would strengthen the efficacy of the existing option. During the week before Anderson and Moseley's arrival, Knight had had a conference with Count Anthony de Bosdari, who owned or controlled forty-nine per cent of the stock of the Sanabria company.[38] The company had been showing television pictures on a ten-foot screen in New York and other cities.[39] Baird had concluded that Sanabria was infringing one of his early patents. This de Bosdari did not dispute, while pointing out that it was one thing to claim that there had been an infringement, but quite another to prove it in court. Baird and Knight had pursued an 'if you can't beat them, join them' policy. After talking to Sanabria himself and to some of his engineers, they proposed that the new Baird company in America should acquire a controlling interest in the Sanabria company. This would avoid litigation and also give the American company the nucleus of a young, keen, technical staff among whom there was already a sense of team spirit.[18]

Bosdari saw the sense of the proposal, and agreed to exchange fifty-one per cent of the stock of the Sanabria company for 100,000 shares in the new American company. The long-suffering and patient Goldsmith and Osterweil agreed that the proposal was within the terms of the option agreement that they had signed, and said they would surrender 100,000 of the 750,000 promoters' shares. This, Knight fluently argued, would give the 'new American company a most valuable additional asset, without the cost of one single dollar to either the new company or to the present American company or the English company'. The snag was that Anderson had contrived to assume responsibility for negotiations with de Bosdari, and was attempting to draw him into his alternative scheme.[18]

In the end, only Moseley and Anderson sailed on 11 December, after a flurry of further cables. To Moseley, 10 December: 'Directors Report will soon be in print. Cable fully before your departure so that an adequate statement may be made therein.' From Moseley, received 11 December:

My report about conditions in America being favourable for development of Baird Television is fully borne out by Baird. There is definitely
far more interest in Baird Television here than in London. Negotiations
proceeding now must result in strengthening the financial structure
here and in London. Americans have vision enough and confidence
enough to support our plans. Suggest references to important broadcasting agreement should not be printed Chairman's Speech but given
verbally to the Meeting because premature publication here must be
avoided. Facilities afforded to television over here are immense and
London must not lag behind, but in any event Baird Company will not
only share in these developments but will be well to the fore. Is this
what you want? What date meeting? Flash reply.[11]

To Moseley, 11 December: 'Your telegram too general. Essential we should
have definite statement regarding negotiations. Meeting probably thirtieth.'[11]

Baird cabled Roberts on 14 December: 'Have postponed sailing on urgent
advice of Anderson and Winn and option holders. Important public demonstrations at Waldorf on Wednesday [16 December].' Roberts cabled, 'Imperative
you should attend shareholders' meeting 30th. Please cable exact reasons for
postponing departure. Can you return Adriatic sailing 18th?' Baird's reply
was received on 15 December: 'Reason postponing departure strong repre-
sentation made by option holders who wish me to supervise demonstrations
and interview capitalists, and consider my presence of utmost importance.
Fox of Fox films expected to see demonstration this week. In view of Board's
opinion imperative me to attend General Meeting am returning by Adriatic.'[11]

Baird and Margaret duly sailed on 18 December. According to Knight,
Jacomb stayed on for a further three weeks, and then returned to London
'without giving any demonstrations – an unfortunate reminder to the
Optionholders of Izenstark's prophesy that the English Company would take
Rosoff's money and, having got it, he could whistle for his demonstrations'.[17]

Allowing seven days for the voyage, the Bairds would have got into
Southampton on Christmas Day.

I was determined to be a good housewife, [but] we had agreed that I
should continue my career as a musician.

Mephy solemnly handed over the keys of Swiss Cottage and went to
live in a boarding-house in Dorking [the nearby town].

I made a start as a housewife by checking all the household's account
books, something strongly resented by the housekeeper, who had her
own way of housekeeping. And when Mephy caught flu, she told me

that if he died it would be my fault because I had turned him out of his comfortable home. So swathing him in blankets and keeping him warm with hot-water bottles, I put him in a car and brought him back to Swiss Cottage and nursed him until he was well.

On the top of Box Hill I was lonely, with John going off to London every day in his hired Daimler; the only way for me to leave the house was to slip and glide down the hill through snow a foot deep. For company I got a black labrador from the dogs' home at Battersea, but John did not like dogs and one day when I was out he sent poor Sambo to the vet to be destroyed. I still feel it was a cruel thing to do, but John had been a bachelor for so long that he was not used to considering other people's feelings. What is more, his father had dominated 'The Lodge', and no doubt he expected to do the same as his father in his own home. But I had been brought up in a very different tradition, where women were given every consideration.[40]

By the end of January 1932 Margaret knew she was pregnant. In February the Bairds gave up Swiss Cottage for a more convenient house near Hampstead Heath and close to the Moseleys: The Cottage, 84 Lawn Road, London NW3 (telephone Primrose Hill 4014). Here they settled for the time being into a routine that suited them both. There was money to pay for domestic staff, while Margaret kept up her piano playing with a view to breaking into the concert circuit. She enjoyed too the cachet of being the wife of a famous man. Baird's irregular hours and dedication to the various roles he was expected to perform meant that they saw comparatively little of each other, while each respected, if not necessarily understood, what the other was doing professionally.

Margaret was twenty-five and Baird just forty-four when their first child, Diana, was born on 5 September 1932. According to her own account, Margaret was still in the nursing home when Baird's father died on 14 September, at the age of ninety.

John came in very upset, having learnt of his father's death. John and his father were alike in their tenacity, determination, and fierce independence. But as a father, John was never remote and Godlike in the manner of a Victorian father. As [our] children grew he played patiently with them and told them stories which he made up. His simplicity and directness of mind made him a perfect companion for children.[41]

10
Baird and his Company
October 1931–May 1932

The shares of the Baird company, having opened the year 1931 at 1s.3d. and dropped to 1s. on 23 January, had risen to 2s.6d. at the end of March. After erratic falls and recoveries they reached 2s.½d. on 3 September and again on 30 October. On 17 November they achieved a high for the year of 6s.4d., but fell back to 2s.7½d. at the year's end.[1] On 19 November EMI filed its first application for a television patent, for a system employing a cathode-ray tube. This, the first of numerous EMI patents to emanate from RCA in America, gave the company the ability to manufacture in Britain the picture tubes and a complete electronic system based on them.[2] It was the shape of things to come.

In Baird's absence, there was at last some constructive progress in the relations between the company and the BBC. The concern of Ashbridge and Murray that if the BBC did not take some initiative, and be seen to be coop-erating, the Baird company might be granted its own broadcasting licence, was reiterated by Murray in a memorandum to Reith on 19 October.[1] It concluded, 'Once the initiative is passed to us, we should be in a position not only to counter any hostile use of television but also to determine the rate and manner of applying it to broadcasting. ... With the Baird system under control, it could be developed side by side with the ultra short-wave work which [the Chief Engineer] has in hand.'

The BBC control board, at its meeting on 27 October, decided by 'a majority of opinion', in favour of cooperation with the Baird company, which included equipping a studio in Broadcasting House for the programmes, and dropping the charges to the Baird company for running the 261-metre trans-mitter for the visual signals. At the end of the discussion, Ashbridge 'asked that a note be made of the fact that the ultra short wave might later present a more suitable medium of transmission'.[1]

Reith wrote (12 November 1931) inviting Lord Ampthill to come and see him. 'I have not had the pleasure of meeting you, but recently we have been giving renewed careful consideration to the relationship between the Baird Company and this Corporation.'¹ Their discussion took place on 17 November; it may have been the news of, or a leaked report on, the meeting which caused the company's shares to reach their 1931 peak that day. Two days later Reith wrote, 'summarising the proposals for collaboration between the Baird Company and this Corporation as mentioned to you then'.¹ Broadly speaking, these were that the Baird company should install and maintain at the BBC complete transmitting apparatus in return for a nominal hire rent; the BBC would pay for alterations to the premises, lighting, extra cables, etc., and supply additional engineering staff. The BBC would provide a weekly one-hour programme from 11am to 12 noon, or 12 noon to 1pm on a Saturday. If the company desired, it could continue the present five half-hour programmes a week from its own studio, paying the cost of these, and the BBC would reduce its charge for transmitting them. In this case the BBC might later be prepared to pay the cost of two of these programmes and transmit them at 11.30pm; on the office copy Reith wrote against this paragraph, 'This was not intended to be given away unless absolutely essential.' The BBC was free to give an agreed number of months' notice to terminate the arrangement, 'either abandoning television transmissions or carrying them on by some other method', and to employ other television methods whether or not the Baird transmissions were continued. Finally, if the Post Office were to institute a licence fee of ten shillings for the use of a television receiver, all the net proceeds would come to the BBC, 'the principle being that your Company would make its money from the sale of Television receiving apparatus and from licences to manufacturers'. No mention was made of ultra-short-wave transmission.

Ampthill replied on 24 November, having read the letter to his board the previous evening. Moseley was not present, because he was at sea on his way to the USA. Baird was in New York. This left Shortis and Church, besides Ampthill himself. In his letter Ampthill suggested that it would be more advantageous to both sides if all transmissions were from the BBC studio. A weekly programme on a Saturday was inadequate to stimulate and maintain public interest, or encourage manufacturers. The regular morning or afternoon transmissions should continue, because that was when the trade held demonstrations for potential customers. Allowance should also be made for special features, such as the Derby, 'statesmen addressing public meetings, and other events of general interest'. The cost of all programmes should be borne by the BBC, which should in addition be prepared to make 'some definite annual payment in consideration of what is in effect a service to the public'. A three- or five-year agreement would have been desirable; failing this, at least one year's notice of termination should be given. Ampthill closed by asking for a meeting between his board and Reith and any members of his governing board 'to discuss the present position of Television broadcasting and the proposed agreement'.[1]

Reith passed the letter round and asked Murray to draft a reply for him to send. Murray finally did so on 16 December, with a note: 'I am sorry it has taken so long, but there has been a good deal of deliberation. [Chief Accountant] and [Ashbridge] suggested that Lord Ampthill should be rebuked for the tone of his letter, but left it to me to find a formula. On mature consideration I have concluded that no useful purpose would be served by introducing a rebuke.'[1]

The letter that Reith sent on 22 December followed the terms but not the precise, sometimes peremptory, wording of Murray's draft. Its main thrusts were that the programme proposals must stand; no guarantee could be made beyond six months; the BBC would make no payment to the Baird company. It concluded:

> The matter appears now to have become one of consideration of detail and perhaps you will agree that the next step should be that the discussion be carried on between officials of the two concerns. It is not felt that any purpose would be served at the present stage by a meeting of your Directors and our Governors.[1]

Thus, at Murray's prompting, was Reith able for the moment to distance himself from matters also of policy.

It was doubtless on Murray's initiative that a thoughtful and highly significant article appeared in *The Times* on 29 December, two days before Baird finally returned to his desk. As a statement of the prevailing situation with regard to the BBC and the Baird company, the only British firm at that time officially engaged in the development of television, the article can only be faulted for the suggestion, 'Recently the BBC has participated more actively in originating television programmes, using the ordinary studio material at Savoy-hill, at no cost to the Baird Company.' As a forecast of where, after several vicissitudes, British television would ultimately lead, it was uncannily accurate, in spite of the disclaimer, 'The immediate future of television is very difficult to foresee.' The writer, the paper's wireless correspondent, made a point of the fact, 'Among the less ambitious television systems which lend themselves to television in the home, it must be claimed for the British system of Mr Baird that, considering the relative simplicity and cheapness of the receivers, the results are better than with any other system of a comparable type.'[3]

After questioning the entertainment value in the long term of the current broadcasts, the article went on to summarise what appeared to be the present attitude of the BBC:

> Here is the only British system of broadcast television. Let us explore its possibilities so far as we can in experimental transmissions, bearing in mind our other contracts, giving the public as good an opportunity as possible of judging it. If it turns out that the ultimate solution of television in the home is to be found in quite a different process from that of Baird – and naturally we must be prepared to change to some other British system if a better one is invented – the present transmissions will by no means have been wasted, for much will have been learned technically as well as in connexion with the choice and possibilities of studio material.[3]

As far as broadcasting wavelengths were concerned, there was no place for television within the normal range. 'Fortunately ... we have in the ultra-short wavelengths of five to 10 metres transmission media admirably adapted for local television broadcasts, and it is now generally agreed that the television of the future will be accomplished by means of ultra-short wave transmitters elevated on a tower or on a hill radiating to local receivers run and synchronized by means of a common electrical alternating-current network.'[3]

If Baird did not see this article at the time, someone would have drawn it to his attention in the office: Ampthill himself, the publicity-conscious Moseley, or the technically-aware Church, who was deeply concerned about the direction in which the company should be going and was already taking steps, independently of Baird, to investigate the viability of alternative systems and wavelengths. Anyway, Baird chose for the moment largely to ignore the message. Shoenberg, on the other hand, acted upon it, if indeed he had not already done so.

There is nothing in Baird's office diary for 30 December, so one may assume that the shareholders' meeting that his directors were so insistent that he attend on that day did not take place. On Thursday, 31 December, he had afternoon meetings with an inspector of taxes and a journalist from the Sunday *Observer*, and Church arranged for Baird to lunch the following Monday, 4 January, with him and Robert Watson Watt, before a board meeting.

Watt, who took the name Watson-Watt when he was knighted in 1942, was born in 1892. Since 1927 he been superintendent of the radio research station at Slough, a meteorological outstation of the National Physical

Laboratory. His particular expertise lay in the use of cathode-ray tubes to locate the sources of radio signals as well as atmospherics.

In a letter to Moseley in 1951, Watson-Watt recalled meeting Baird on two occasions, once in connection with an early demonstration of nocto-vision, and the other at lunch, at which they talked 'generally about television'.[4] This was obviously the lunch with Church on 4 January 1932. The conversation may have been generally about television, but it was also more specifically about cathode-ray tubes.

The previous December, Appleton, as consultant to the company, had been asked by Church to obtain reliable technical information about the current status of cathode-ray television in Germany, and in particular on the processes and apparatus with which von Ardenne was working. To enable him to do this, Appleton asked the Department of Scientific and Industrial Research if it would be prepared to nominate and supply one of its officers to go to Berlin and report on von Ardenne's television receiver. The depart-ment agreed to second Watt for the four-day trip. The previous March he had paid a private visit to von Ardenne's laboratories, and seen a preview of a demonstration which was later given publicly at the Berlin radio show in August of that year.[5]

The research party, which comprised Watt, Church, and H Barton-Chapple from the company's technical staff, arrived in Berlin on Saturday, 19 December 1931. Church, for some reason, was forced to return to London the follow-ing evening, and Barton Chapple left Berlin late on 21 December. The Sunday was taken up by a visit to von Ardenne's laboratories, to which Watt and Barton Chapple returned on the Monday, after which they went on to the Loewe radio works,[6] the Goertz optical works, and Fernseh. Watt, now on his own, visited the Heinrich-Hertz-Institut für Schwingungsforschung on the Tuesday, and the television laboratory of the German Reichspost the following day, before himself returning to London.[5]

Von Ardenne demonstrated a different system to the one Watt had seen before. Watt reported that von Ardenne 'shares the opinion, universally held in Germany, and held also by competent critics in this country, that the only practicable channel for television of acceptable entertainment value is to be found in a radio link in the 5-10 metre waveband'. A single knob on the receiver enabled the viewer to select any part of the picture to be viewed in close-up, and the angle of viewing was much wider than by mechanical means of reception. In contrast to a mechanical receiver, the working was completely silent. Watt himself was unable to comment on the quality of picture, but Church and Barton Chapple professed themselves satisfied on this point. It was the general opinion shared by Dr Loewe and Dr Goertz,

Professor Karl Willy Wagner, Professor Leithauser, and Dr Krahwinkel of the Reichspost that within two years the transmission of aesthetically and technically satisfactory pictures from film would be practicable for home reception over a limited metropolitan area on a wavelength of about seven metres. There was no intention in Germany for the time being to transmit by any other means than by standard cinematograph film, for which Fernseh held patents which would enable developing to be done in two seconds, making the delay between the event and its transmission only about five seconds.[7] In none of the transmissions seen by the British team was the picture frequency as low as the 12½ per second employed by the Baird company. All were between twenty and twenty-five pictures per second, comparable to the standard talking-picture figure of twenty-four pictures per second. The definition was measured not in terms of lines but of 'picture points' or pixels; in this case the received picture, 11cm by 8cm, was made up of five thousand points, all of the same size, but varying in brightness.[5]

In the second (less technical) part of his report, Appleton stressed the higher quality of picture that was being aimed at and achieved in Germany:

> Before the question of cathode-ray versus mechanical methods is even touched on, it is important to realize that the opinion of foreign workers is that only pictures having a higher grade of detail than those at present transmitted by the Baird system have the required entertainment value necessary to retain public interest. This is a point which I emphasised in a previous report to the Company.
>
> To send pictures of high-grade requires a channel of communication which will permit of the transmission of high modulation frequencies. The idea of Sir Ambrose Fleming that a television station needs only a single frequency, not a frequency band, is quite erroneous, and his letter to *Nature*[8] one of the most mischievous ever published by a scientific journal, in that it raised hopes that were entirely false.[5]

Appleton went on to quote the remarks of the wireless correspondent of *The Times* on the employment of ultra-short waves for television,[9] and made a further point:

> As is well known the BBC intends to build an ultra-short wave transmitter on top of Broadcasting House and there seems to be no reason, if the present relations between the BBC and the Company continue, why experiments on ultra-short wave broadcasting of television should not be carried out.

After listing the advantages and disadvantages of the current von Ardenne system, he presented his conclusion:

> On the whole therefore it would seem clear that the cathode-ray system, because it provides satisfactory pictures with the minimum of technical burden on the receiving installation, is destined to provide one satisfactory solution of the television problem and it seems to me wise for the Company to deviate from what the outside world regards as its somewhat rigid adherence to a system providing very limited detail and which embodies a synchronising system which does not eliminate vertical swing. This, naturally, does not mean dropping the methods entirely, for it may turn out that a satisfactory solution embodies both systems. The technical staff of the Company is in possession of a lot of valuable technical data and would doubtless make rapid progress if the field of investigation were somewhat widened.[5]

In a covering letter to Church, Appleton hammered home his main point:

> The crux of the whole matter appears to be this. The broadcasting of television on normal broadcasting wavelengths has been taken as far as is physically possible by the Company. Little further progress can be made in this direction because of the limitations of the channels. The use of ultra-short waves appears, in my opinion, to be inevitable, and the Company should be widening its technical interests so that it is prepared to make the fullest use of the channels.
>
> The first chapter in the history of television appears to be ending. Using the normal broadcasting wavelengths Baird television is the best in the world, and it does not look as though any other company can produce better under the same limitations. But the advent of ultra-short waves changes the situation entirely and there is now going to be a new race for supremacy in this field. Can the Company repeat its success using the newer channels of communication?[10]

The report was received too late to be circulated before the company's board meeting on 11 January, but it would have been studied by all the directors before the following meeting, on 21 January. Baird was not there; he had been laid up in Berlin with yet another of his habitual winter doses of flu, but had telephoned the office to say that he hoped to return later that day. In his absence, he was nominated as one of the 'officials', with Moseley, Roberts, and R S H Boulding, laboratory manager,[11] to attend a meeting with the BBC on 22 January, with a subsequent meeting on 4 February. The BBC fielded Murray, Ashbridge, and Roger Eckersley, eldest brother of Peter. Eckersley, a former professional golfer and chicken farmer, now director of programmes, was reputedly a favourite of Reith, who had set him up with a select London house in which to entertain, at the BBC's expense, 'pillars of society, politicians and other public figures'.[12]

The injection of Baird and Moseley into the discussions produced some positive results for the company. The BBC would produce and transmit four half-hour programmes of its own at 11pm on Monday, Tuesday, Wednesday, and Friday, on a sound wavelength of 398.9m, with vision on 261.3m. These transmissions would not be 'entirely discontinued' before 31 March 1934, and after that date the BBC would give six months' notice before pulling out the plug. Later, it was agreed that there would be at least two programmes a week until the end of March 1934. Some such assurances were vital to the Baird company if it was going to sell its receivers, even though there had to be a warning notice with each one to the effect that the programmes might be terminated within a year. The company was also, however, now able to hire out sets. The BBC retained the right to broadcast by alternative television systems, if any materialised that was of proven and unquestionably superior character.[13]

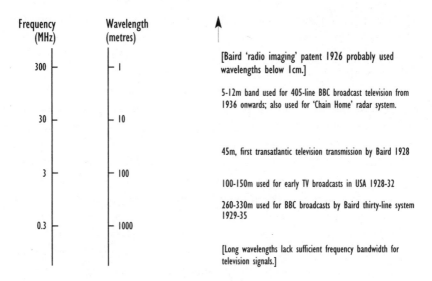

Figure 4: Chart of broadcast frequencies and wavelengths, showing early television and radar applications. Frequency and wavelength are inversely related to each other. A high definition television signal requires a bandwidth of at least 0.5 MHz, whereas the original Baird thirty-line system required only about 0.01 MHz. Thus the early television stations could operate on the same medium wavelengths as sound broadcasting without causing interference. Modern television systems use ultra-short wavelengths.

Space and facilities for the necessary equipment would be made available in the BBC's new home, Broadcasting House, Portland Place, which was officially opened on 2 May 1932, and the transmissions would begin as soon after that as was practicable. The final programme from Long Acre, after over two years of continuous transmissions in sound and vision, went out on 17 June.[14]

★

In the meantime, Moseley had on 27 January 1932 secured the immediate future of the Baird company in some form by effectively delivering up control of Baird Television Ltd to Isidore Ostrer. The deal was arranged by the purchase, through one of the Gaumont-British subsidiary companies, of 800,000 of his block of deferred shares by a syndicate, LVT Ltd, whose directors were to be Ostrer's brother Maurice and Moseley himself.[15]

The intentions of Gaumont-British, now that it had voting control of Baird Television, were a subject of great speculation and suspicion to the board, some of whose members were already in a state of ill-disguised hostility against each other. This erupted during the continuation of the delicate and controversial American negotiations.

The report to the Federal Radio Commission of the examiner investigating the Knickerbocker company's application for an American licence was published on 23 January 1932. As Flamm had forecast, it recommended that the licence should be granted. There were three grounds for this conclusion. The applicant was financially qualified and had available the necessary technical expertise which might be expected to develop the art form (Baird had testified at the hearing that he would spend half of each year in the USA). Experimental work by Radio Pictures would not be 'curtailed to an unwarranted extent'. Therefore 'public interest, convenience and necessity will be served by the granting of this application.'[16]

Goldsmith and Osterweil, fed up with all the comings and goings and changes of mind and direction, had lost their trust and interest in the Baird company, though not in the option agreement that they had legitimately and in good faith signed. Knight, still in New York, was now negotiating not only with de Bosdari and his associate, Oliver C Harriman of Harriman International Corporation, but also with a further group led by John Sherman, with a view to the one or the other taking over the option. He now cabled for Moseley and Baird to return to New York to conclude a deal. Instead the board sent Church and Anderson, who arrived on 31 January. After several conferences, they managed to persuade the two groups to join forces, and to agree that Goldsmith and Osterweil would receive substantial compensation if and when the new company's shares were sold. Knight commented rather sourly, 'This new agreement provides increased benefits for the English company and it provides increased watered stock to furnish those increased benefits, although the main objection to the 4th November option is sup-posed to be that there is too much water.'[17]

Instead of registering a new company, the consortium acquired an existing company, Television Corporation of America, which had not functioned. There would be nine directors, of whom Harriman (president), Church, and Sherman would comprise an executive committee. Three of the other directors would be nominated by the Baird company and three by Harriman International, all six being subject to approval by the executive committee. A draft of a new twenty-eight-page agreement was taken to London by Harriman and Anderson on 16 February, for execution not later than 29 February.[17]

On 24 February, while Ampthill was having breakfast at the Bath Club in London, where he had been staying the night, he received a phone call from Roberts to say that two cables had come in from Church. One of them was in code: 'Suspect attempt purchase Gaumont's deferred holding thus control British company from America. Situation wants watching.' Ampthill replied: 'Shall treat your coded telegram as personal. This must have been your intention. Watching situation.' Church confirmed this: 'Intention rightly interpreted. Hope realized my enforced stay here complicating my affairs at home and board must be prepared make arrangements with me.'[18]

Ampthill wrote from his home, Oakley House, Bedford, to Church at the Plaza Hotel, New York, on 26 February. It was a very personal letter, which concluded, 'I think that you would do well to destroy this letter as soon as you have read it as you are amongst people who would not hesitate to search among your papers!' Church, for some reason, did not do so; indeed, he preserved it. Mainly, it was about Moseley:

> I shall of course make it my business to see that you do not suffer pecuniary loss through your prolonged absence from home. I had thought of this even before I received your cable but you must leave it to me to choose my own time and manner for proposing some fair arrangement to the Board. As you know, I shall be up against Moseley's jealousy which rises to insane intensity whenever there is a question of paying anyone for services rendered. ...
>
> It has been no easy task dealing with Moseley since your departure and I should be in a very awkward position if Shortis were ever absent from a Board Meeting. In spite of great pressure from his wife and

daughter who want him to accompany them abroad for his own health as well as for their sake he has decided to stay at home until your return. This, however, could not be accomplished until I had acted upon his own suggestion and written him a very strong letter that he could show to his wife.

Moseley's attitude about the Agreement which you and Anderson have negotiated is characteristic of the man himself and extremely unpleasant. He is determined, by hook or by crook, to avoid taking responsibility for accepting the Agreement. He has managed to dodge out of giving his signature to anything in connection with the Agreement and he has even resorted to the expedient of leaving the Board Room, on the plea of having to keep an engagement at the BBC, when the moment arrived for coming to a final decision.[18]

While Ampthill's impression of Harriman was 'not by any means un-favourable', there were problems with Guedella, Harriman's London lawyer.

We did not let Guedella come into the Board Room because we knew that if once he got there it would be impossible to get him out again. We had good reason to suspect that he wanted to have a hand in the drafting of the Agreement itself and to share the pickings with the New York Attorneys. We were, therefore, at great pains to keep him to his actual task which was that of insuring that we gave you a valid author-ity to sign. In the end we were even obliged to suggest that Guedella should accompany Roberts to the Post Office and hold his hand while he posted the letter containing your Power of Attorney! All this distrust was very unpleasant but we cannot justly say that it was excusable in view of Baird's appalling blunder over the signing of the Agreement of the 4th November.[18]

This was the option on which, according to Knight, Ampthill had at the time wanted to send Baird a telegram of congratulations.[17]

As far as the Gaumont-British company was concerned,

They have *not* got control of our Company and I do not think they want to get control. I also think it quite unlikely that the Ostrer Brothers should try to sell their Deferred Shares in America. So far as I can judge, their present policy is merely to 'wait and see' and I am not at all inclined to invite them to take an active part in the affairs of the Company at this stage.[18]

Ampthill was right about the shares, but wrong about the Ostrers's intentions. He signed off with a gratuitous observation, the virulent anti-Semitic
sentiment of which was unusual even for those times: 'I can only hope that
you have got into touch with some really pleasant people in New York and
that you will not have been confined to the society of Goldsmiths, Osterweils,
Izenstarks "et hoc genus omnes" [sic].'[18]

There is no record of whether the American agreement was ever signed
by all parties. It was probably better that it should not have been, for on 18
March the Federal Radio Commission in Washington issued a nine-page
document rejecting its own examiner's recommendation.[19] Radio Pictures
had successfully appealed against the commission's earlier decision on the
grounds that Baird Television was a foreign company. There would be no
broadcasting in the USA by the Baird television system. The Baird office in
New York was closed down. West had already left to form his own company
in Canada.[17] Jarrard will reappear in our history.

Isidore Ostrer stayed his hand until May, when he nominated two new
directors to the board of the Baird company. Harry Clayton was his accountant. Harry Greer, who was fifty-six, had been knighted in 1922 after serving as
a Conservative member of parliament from 1918 to 1922. He was managing
director of the Mercantile Marine Finance Corporation Ltd and chairman of
the Lord Roberts Workshops. His main interests were quoted as being
'Colonial and Far East trade and development'.[20]

Church, who had been invited to see Ostrer on 26 May to discuss these
appointments, subsequently drafted a report on their meeting:

> Mr Ostrer stated that he had nominated Sir Harry Greer and Mr Clayton
> in order that he should be advised of the conduct of the affairs of the
> company, in which Gaumont-British had a large share interest through
> a subsidiary, with a view to securing fuller cooperation between
> Gaumont-British and the Baird company.
>
> Mr Ostrer stated that he was well aware of the financial position of
> the company and he anticipated at no distant date that further financial
> assistance would be necessary. The fact that he had nominated Sir Harry
> Greer and Mr Clayton to serve on the board, he hoped, would be a
> guarantee that he and his company would be prepared to lend assistance
> of this kind when it was required.
>
> He stated that his interest in the Baird company was due to the need
> for safeguarding the position of television in Great Britain against the
> creation of an American monopoly. He had considered the position of
> other television companies in Great Britain but had finally decided to

support the Baird company in view of its relations with other companies abroad, as the most likely company to achieve a satisfactory position for television. He expressed the opinion that everything should be done by the Baird company to strengthen its relations with patentees in television companies operating in Germany, believing that with cooperation between Germany and Great Britain we could successfully hold our own against American competition.[21]

Baird found Ostrer difficult to get to know:

> He was totally unlike any other successful business man I have ever met. I liked him but never felt at home in his company and was, even if indirectly, in the position of an employee. When I did see him I invariably had some goose to cook. These influences served to destroy freedom of conversation. There remained an undercurrent of uneasy alertness, I was on guard all the time and unable to speak freely.[22]

No doubt Ostrer found Baird's unpredictability and general demeanour equally distracting. Margaret Baird recalls an occasion when Baird was invited to Ostrer's house in Hamilton Place:

> On the way he stopped off at Fortnum & Mason's and bought a haggis, to be a surprise for me. At Hamilton Place the butler took hat, coat, and haggis, and when John left he forgot the haggis. When he reached home he sadly told me what had happened, and I could hardly stop laughing. My laughter hurt him because he could see nothing funny in an absent-minded Scottish inventor leaving a haggis behind in the mansion of an illustrious Jew.[23]

11
Baird and the BBC
March 1932–June 1933

The arrangement that had been hammered out with the BBC[1] ensured simply that there was a temporary market for television sets, with restricted viewing times. The Baird company publicity machine put a brave face on it:

> With the Baird 'Televisor' in your home you can sit in comfort and see the programmes broadcast by the BBC. And as the Baird Research Department, under the guidance of John L Baird, develops the transmission of films, one may predict that the day is not far off when owners of the Baird Home Reception Set will be able to witness a whole film performance and hear a complete talkie in conjunction with their wireless set.[2]

A set, 'complete, finished brown metal casing, artistically lined', to be used in conjunction with a radio, was being offered at £26.5s.; a 'complete kit of parts for the home constructor' cost £16.16s., with 'other spare parts' as extras. While the transmission of standard cinematograph films was technically feasible, their adequate display on a miniature, upright, thirty-line screen was in the realm of fantasy.

It has been estimated that in the early 1930s the BBC's television programmes were seen on about five thousand sets.[3] The sale of these represented a modest return on the company's investment, but with the collapse of all American negotiations, and the cost of these, there was still the problem of funding the necessary research into future development, particularly the use of cathode-ray tubes, to say nothing of paying dividends to shareholders, which the company had never done, and salaries to staff. Baulked at trying to obtain any research and development assistance from the BBC, Baird turned his attentions to the GPO, with support from a surprising source.

The campaign began with an invitation to the Postmaster General, Sir

Kingsley Wood, to visit the Baird headquarters on 23 March. It was arranged by Cecil Malone, no longer a member of parliament but now president of the Television Society. Wood was a lawyer who had been in politics as a Conservative since 1918; at the general election in 1931, which confirmed the national government in power, he had become the fourth Postmaster General in that year. Reith, after a meeting with Wood on 5 April, described him as a 'feeble little creature. ... He talked a lot about giving the public what it wants. I was quite disgusted with him.'[4] He had arranged on this occasion for Ashbridge to be one of the party, and to accompany Wood to Long Acre.

Ashbridge reported back to Reith:

> The PMG was received by Baird and Moseley. The former described the technicalities and said nothing on policy questions. Moseley, on the other hand, said a great deal on such policy questions and was inclined to suggest that the BBC had been obstructive, but that things were better now, although he certainly did not give the impression that he was altogether satisfied even now.[5]

After a successful demonstration of a new small, home machine, and of a large (three foot by two foot) screen, the party repaired to the board room, where 'most of the talking was done by Moseley, who delivered a long harangue about the development of a great British Industry, suggesting that the whole question was more than a mere commercial proposition, and concerned the building up of a great public service. ... It should be noted that Moseley was very careful not to say anything at all concrete.'[5]

A concrete proposal was put to the Postmaster General by Baird in a three-page letter dated 6 April 1932. He asked that one penny out of the total radio licence fee of ten shillings should be paid to the Baird company: 'this, small sum though it is, would mean the difference between continuing our research work in a crippled and drastically restricted fashion, or going ahead vigorously.'[6] He went on to point out that in Germany Fernseh had supplied the post office with transmitting apparatus based on the Baird system, and in France Television-Baird-Nathan would shortly begin transmissions by the Baird system under licence.

He went on to describe the American situation as 'interesting'. After explaining that the US Federal Radio Commission had refused the Knicker-bocker corporation a licence to broadcast by the Baird system, he continued:

> While in America a British controlled invention is prevented from functioning, in this country [EMI] has already obtained permission to

broadcast on short waves. Both [EMI] and the Marconiphone companies are controlled by the Radio Corporation of America, and it is common knowledge that the Radio Corporation of America is making strenuous efforts to enter the television field in England. ... You will see that there is a very grave danger of the whole television industry falling into American hands unless this Company receives the financial support for which I am asking. This, I hardly need emphasize, would be a great blow to the country from every point of view.

I beg therefore that you will discuss the situation with the Prime Minister who, I believe, is not unsympathetic. It is imperative that some action be taken immediately, otherwise I should not have addressed my request to you in these urgent terms.[5]

Baird took a copy of his letter to the BBC on 18 April to give personally to Reith, who annotated it in his own hand, and wrote in his private diary, 'Saw Baird. The television affairs are evidently in a bad way. A great deal of trouble is due to Moseley, whom nobody seems disposed to trust, certainly not I!'[7] Reith's suggestion to Baird, which ensured that there would be no tampering with the licence fee and thus possibly with resources due to the BBC, was that instead the Baird company should apply to the GPO for an annual grant similar to the subsidy which the government paid to the BBC for the broadcasting of opera.[8] He even offered to write to the GPO in support of such a claim. When, perhaps predictably, the GPO threw out Baird's request for a mite from the licence fee, Reith wrote to Baird on 28 April, suggesting a meeting at the BBC's new headquarters in Portland Place to discuss his alternative proposal.[9]

Relations between Reith and Baird, and between the BBC and the Baird company, were just settling down into a state of amicable agreement when it was revealed that the GPO, without consulting the BBC, had granted an experimental licence to the Baird company to broadcast on ultra-short waves. Carpendale wrote to the GPO on 28 April:

It has come accidentally to our knowledge that a licence has recently been granted to the Baird Television Company to transmit television experiments on what are usually called ultra-short waves.

We cannot trace having received any communication from you in connection with this licence. In the past you have been good enough to advise us of such proposals and to give us an opportunity of expressing our views, and we venture to think that this is a desirable procedure in order that we may be fully in touch with developments of this kind, particularly in view of the co-operation which now exists between the Baird Company and ourselves.[10]

F W Phillips, assistant secretary of the GPO, replied on 7 May, pointing out that it had not been his organisation's practice to consult the BBC where no public service or use of a BBC station was involved, but that in future the BBC would be kept informed of any facilities granted to the Baird company for experimental purposes.[5] By this time Baird himself, with maximum publicity, had gone ahead with his experiment. Billed as 'Television by Ultra Short Waves. A New Departure. First Public Demonstration in the World',[11] it took place between Long Acre and a receiver installed at Selfridge's store 1½ miles away. Two actors were televised, Marie (later Dame Marie) Tempest and Leslie Mitchell. The sixty-seven-year-old Tempest, who still had the figure of a girl of sixteen, was especially known for her starring roles in comedy. Mitchell (twenty-six), who in 1936 became the BBC's first full-time television announcer, had played the lead role of Captain Stanhope in R C Sherriff's *Journey's End* on tour in South Africa and also in a BBC radio broadcast.[12] He later commented on his first television appearance:

> We were, I am afraid, most inexpert, as at that time one had to stand rigidly in one spot, otherwise one's face bulged out of one side of the screen or the other, or one's forehead went over the top, or one's chin went below the screen. Dame Marie's comment indicated our reaction: 'Well, Mr Mitchell,' she said, 'I must say that your *voice* was reasonably distinct.'[13]

Of even greater significance than the wavelength was the nature of the receiver. It was a mirror-drum type, employing a Kerr cell, with the picture being displayed on a screen (12 by 4 inches) rather than in a lens. Through the medium of a company press handout, Baird informed the public that the ultra-short-wave transmissions could still be received easily on the existing televisors, if these were fitted with an adaptor. The existing range of 5 to 10 miles could be extended in due course 'with the collaboration of the BBC'. He also stated that the company had been conducting experiments with cathode-ray tubes, but he reiterated that 'mechanical television is far superior'.[11]

There was some hype involved here. The standard televisor could only show thirty-line pictures, regardless of whether they were transmitted by medium or ultra-short waves. The main advantage of ultra-short-wave transmissions was that they could accommodate 180-line pictures, which could be handled better by cathode-ray receivers than by mechanical receivers. Regardless of the pros and cons of employing cathode-ray tubes, Baird, it would appear, was now looking to the BBC as a partner in the development of public broadcasting by ultra-short waves.

There is no record in BBC files of what the BBC thought about this proposal, which suggests that it was ignored. Reith and Baird duly met, and Reith drafted a letter to the Postmaster General to which the Baird company's board gave its approval. It was sent on 23 May.

> I understand from [Mr Baird] that unless they can get some money – he says about £15,000 per annum – from some unusual source, their activities, in particular those of research, will be most severely crippled. He feels, in fact, that they will not be able to carry on at all for more than two years and that, during that time, a great deal of work would have to be suspended.[5]

Reith's solution was an arrangement similar to the 'opera grant':

> I pointed out to Mr Baird that if this were done it might necessitate some reconstitution of his company, for instance to the extent of a limited dividend (they have never paid any), but he says he foresees no difficulty in complying with any alterations that might be required.[5]

The difference between the opera grant and what Reith was proposing was that the former was intended specifically to encourage the production of quality opera in the country, whereas the funds which he was suggesting should be made available to the Baird company were for research for commercial purposes. The application would probably have failed anyway for this reason. Baird did not do his cause any good, and risked jeopardising his personal relationship with Reith, by seeking a meeting with Wood and Sir Evelyn Murray, secretary of the GPO. This took place on 31 May. Baird arrived at the BBC for another session with Reith on 15 June, bringing a copy of a letter he had written to Wood after the meeting. It was a remarkable document in that it proposed a completely different scheme to raise money for his company to the one Reith had suggested, at a time when Reith's proposal was still under consideration:

> The Baird Television Company has developed television to its present stage at very heavy expense; the BBC in taking over a Baird television transmitter and installing our equipment in Broadcasting House is

receiving the fruits of those years of unremunerative labour, and in return they intend to pay us a nominal fee for the hire of the apparatus. For this nominal fee they are also to receive free broadcast user rights in all our patents, inventions and developments, both in the past and all we may do in the future.

In March 1929 a Committee of Members of Parliament, the Post Office and the BBC, after a demonstration of my invention reported that in the Postmaster General's opinion the system represented a 'noteworthy scientific achievement', and recommended that the BBC should give experimental transmissions. I take this opportunity of stating that this was the first official encouragement I ever received, and helped me in surmounting the extraordinary obstacles that were placed in my way from many directions.

I am anxious now that the results achieved should be used to the best interests of this country, and I feel that co-operation with the Post Office would have this desired effect.

The suggestion I put forward is that the BBC pay us £5,000 per annum, and that a further £10,000 per annum should be paid to us out of the proportion of the proceeds from the licence fees which goes to the Post Office. In return for this the Post Office and the BBC have the right each to appoint a Director to the Baird Company and the grant is made upon the condition that the representatives are satisfied that the cash is spent on research likely to prove useful to the Post Office; such an arrangement would be subject to yearly revision since the additional income likely to accrue to the BBC and Post Office may be considerable as television becomes more popular.

My personal desire is that this company should, in future, devote itself entirely to research work and that the broadcasting of television should be taken over entirely by the BBC, the function of this company being to supply them with the latest improvements and apparatus, the results of our research.[14]

Presumably Baird also had in mind that these payments, representing in today's money a total of something over half a million pounds, would supplement income from the design if not also manufacture of receiving sets. In proposing that the BBC should assume total responsibility for television broadcasting, Baird was a little ahead of his time: in forecasting that the 'additional income likely to accrue to the BBC and Post Office [in television licence fees] may be considerable as television becomes more popular', two decades ahead. In suggesting that the Baird company should in effect be the exclusive supplier to the BBC of television technology, he was, did he but know it, already too late!

Reith's personal reaction, apart from annotating his copy of the letter with underlining and exclamation marks, was surprisingly restrained, and also constructive. His account of their meeting took the form of an internal memorandum:

> Baird came to see me today to say that he had had a talk with the PMG since my letter had arrived. The latter was quite sympathetic and Baird, of course, was most grateful to me for writing the letter, which he said he thought had been very helpful.
>
> The only thing about his meeting with the PMG which he told me was that the latter asked how much the BBC was paying him and Baird got the idea that if we paid him £5,000 the PMG might pay him £10,000.
>
> Baird said as usual that he thought we were benefitting from the free use of their apparatus, but I told him I thought the boot was entirely on the other foot. Of course he saw my point of view, and when I see him he is always reasonable. He admitted that we were now carrying all the expenditure which they were carrying before, namely programme items, power, etc. That had cost them, he said, £[5],000 or £6,000. I do not know how much we estimate for our television costs.
>
> His specific proposal was that we should pay him, not a nominal rental, as the letters say, for their use of the apparatus, but £5,000 a year. I put that suggestion in its proper perspective by saying that that was what we paid for the whole of the wireless patents owned by Marconis, Standard Telephones, RCA, etc.
>
> It finally came down to this, that he thought it might pay us to fix a reasonable annual sum now for all time, thereby safeguarding ourselves against any considerable change in the situation, which might put them in the position of being able to demand a higher rent.
>
> Obviously if we can get all the other patents for £5,000, the television ones are never likely to be worth that, and the ordinary patents are not going to increase in price to us. But there is an element of rationality in the suggestion in that whatever sum we pay now should be not merely for the length of the contract but indefinitely.
>
> Of course I not only gave Baird no encouragement, but made him agree with the unreasonableness of the suggestion – except if something unlikely happened. But he is now expecting to hear whether we are prepared to pay him anything – in fact what we are going to

mean by the nominal rent referred to. Then he is going back to the PMG.[15]

Wood's response to Baird's representations was brief and frank. There was no chance, particularly at a time of economic uncertainty, of any additional government funding for scientific research, and even if there were, other claimants might get priority. Any question of payment by the BBC was a matter entirely between the company and the BBC.[16] A copy was sent to Reith, with a covering letter. He replied briefly:

> I understand how the matter now stands as between the Post Office and the Baird Company. Perhaps you would not expect us to endorse all that Mr Baird says in his letter, particularly his observation to the effect that we are receiving the fruits of years of unremitting labour.[5]

This last statement was not unfair. There would be no 'fruits' for the BBC until the issue of television licences.[17]

★

With his plans in tatters for breaking into the American market, the very future of his company in the balance, and while personally conducting the ongoing negotiations with the GPO and the BBC, Baird was also engaged in the most nerve-wracking and most sensational public demonstration of them all. He undertook to televise the Derby in such a way that it could be seen by a cinema audience on a large screen and also transmitted by the BBC to viewers with their own receivers. This constituted the first public viewing by closed circuit television of a national event, and the first general transmission by the BBC of an outside television broadcast.

As usual, Baird conceived the overall technical plan and the general logistics of the operation. Inside the Baird caravan, parked opposite the Epsom grandstand by the winning post, a mirror on the door reflected the scene onto a mirror drum with thirty mirrors. There were several reasons why Baird chose his standard thirty-line format, comprising pictures of a ratio of seven high by three wide, transmitted at 12½ pictures a second. It represented the best compromise between the conflicting considerations of light sensitivity, detail, and flicker that he could achieve within the limitations of the hardware available to him at the time. The transmission bandwidth could just be accommodated by standard GPO telephone lines.[18] And the BBC could broadcast pictures of the race to those who had receivers in their homes over its normal medium-wave channel.

The vision signals, with the sound picked up by a microphone at the course, were to be sent through 25 miles of telephone cables to the Metropole Theatre, 15 miles from Epsom. A connection was also to be made to the control room at Long Acre, where the vision and sound would be amplified and relayed to the BBC. Estimates of the audience at the Metropole vary between two and five thousand, but to meet the needs of such numbers required, in Baird's eyes, a screen 10 feet high by 8 feet wide. Since a single thirty-line image magnified to this size would result in an extremely coarse picture with the vertical strips being emphasised, he employed the zone system which he had first demonstrated in January 1931. Three adjoining thirty-line images were focussed by the mirror drum at the course onto three separate photo-electric cells. At the Metropole these images were amplified, reconstituted by individual light valves (developed from the Kerr cell), and back-projected onto the theatre screen via a second mirror drum, to form a composite picture of ninety lines. The ingenuity of the system enabled the BBC to transmit just the centre portion of the television triptych to the home viewers.

So much for the theory. At the Metropole, Paul Reveley spent three days setting up and adjusting the apparatus. He slept there, too, so concerned was he that everything should be right on the day. For the running of the race, Baird himself and Clapp became part of the Metropole team. At Long Acre, Bridgewater and Campbell held the fort. For Campbell, the transmission came alive early on the day before the race:

> I was checking the test pictures from Epsom. Faintly I saw a little black dot – it might have been anything. It got bigger and I peered closer at the screen, wondering what it was. For all I knew it might have been some defect in the equipment. Then suddenly I realised what it was! It was a policeman, walking along the racecourse. It was raining and I could even see the sheen on his cape.[19]

The 1932 Derby was run on 1 June. At the course, Percy was for the second time in charge of the mirror drum in the caravan, which demonstrated on this occasion an alarming propensity to sink down into the mud beside the winning post. Stabilising it was the job of one of the firm's carpenters, who on the day itself was more interested in drinking and laying bets. He returned from one of his extended forays, shouting, 'April the Fifth, Mr Percy! April the Fifth!' Percy, who by now had had enough, sacked the carpenter from his assignment, handed him a pound note for his fare home, and returned to his post inside the caravan.

At the Metropole, proceedings began fifteen minutes before the 'off' with an introduction from the stage by the theatre's manager, Mr Sowden. He gave way to the announcer from Epsom, John Thorne, who was heard over a loud speaker:

> After a rather lengthy description of the ground and the crowds, the audience began to wonder whether the television pictures would appear at all. But a few minutes before 3pm, when the horses came within range of the transmitter, the screen was illuminated, and it was possible to distinguish the grandstand and a section of the course in the flicker-ing images which flashed across the screen. Then the famous parade began, and horse after horse was clearly seen as it passed in front of the television apparatus. It was difficult to distinguish details, and some-one was heard to remark that the horses looked more like camels! Each jockey and horse appeared as a single moving object, but the general impression was excellent. At one moment three or four horses were seen on the screen together, and showed the greater range covered by this open-air transmission compared with the usual studio images.
>
> An interval of some minutes followed, during which the announcer again described the scene, and then a great shout went up from the crowd, which was being faintly heard all the time as a background to the speaker's remarks. The race had begun! Immediately the screen was exposed again, and the audience was rewarded by seeing the winning horses flash neck to neck across the screen. A few seconds later the runners-up followed in twos and threes, these being more distinct than the winners, as they passed at a more leisurely speed. After the race, it was possible to see the crowd moving on to the course, rather like a swarm of ants, and the winners were led past by their owners, though this was the least satisfactory part of the transmission.[20]

In going for the most famous of all flat races, Baird had also chosen one of the fastest sprints in the racing calendar. The national press was unanimous in its commendation of the way that the atmosphere and the excitement of the occasion had been captured. The Metropole audience, who 'probably witnessed more of the race than 50 per cent of the people on the course',[21] cheered the winner, April the Fifth, and the man who had brought them this thrilling innovation: 'Marvellous! Marvellous! shouted men and women around me. ... Mr J L Baird, the inventor who made the marvel possible, stepped on the stage and received a bigger cheer than April the Fifth. He was too thrilled to say a word.'[22] Baird was totally drained by the experience: 'Baird was standing beside me on the stage and he suddenly said: "Mr Clapp,

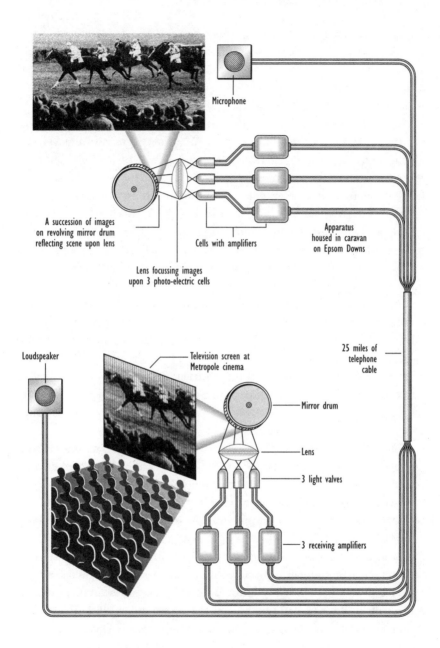

Microphone

A succession of images
on revolving mirror drum
reflecting scene upon lens

Cells with amplifiers

Apparatus
housed in caravan
on Epsom Downs

Lens focussing images
upon 3 photo-electric cells

25 miles of
telephone
cable

Loudspeaker

Television screen at
Metropole cinema

Mirror drum

Lens

3 light valves

3 receiving amplifiers

Figure 5: The mirror-drum system used to televise the Derby in 1932.
Three pictures, each of thirty vertical lines, were transmitted separately,
and then recombined on the screen to give a picture of ninety lines.

I'm finished." And there was a chair beside him and I pushed it under him and I think he'd have gone on the floor if I hadn't done so, he was so exhausted.'[23]

Back on the course, Percy was astonished to see, weaving towards him, the drunken carpenter, who thrust into his hand a sheaf of bank notes: 'Your winnings, Mr Percy!'[24]

There is no mention in BBC files of the historic transmission, only a note of an angry and inconclusive meeting on 12 July between Baird and Moseley for the company and Ashbridge and Murray for the BBC, 'to consider what action, if any, should be taken as a result of a decision by the Postmaster-General against a Government subsidy for the Baird Company'. Baird suggested that Reith had indicated to him verbally that if the request failed the BBC might contribute £15,000 a year to the company. The representatives of the BBC responded that an annual payment of ten shillings for user rights would be more appropriate, and that there would be no commitment to any one system of television.[5]

Meanwhile, Bridgewater and Campbell had been seconded to help the engineers set up and man the apparatus for the thirty-line BBC transmissions.[25] This had been largely designed by J C Wilson, one of the Baird company's best technical brains, and constructed by the firm of B J Lynes. It employed the latest in mirror-drum scanners, 8 inches in diameter, carrying thirty mirrors, with an additional lens being brought into play for close-up shots.[26] The studio, in the bowels of the main building, was amply provided with space, dressing rooms, and sound equipment.

The engineer appointed in charge of BBC television was the talented Douglas Birkinshaw, with Eustace Robb as producer. Robb was a former Guards' officer, recruited from the gramophone industry, where he had had production experience with Brunswick Records: 'With his background and commanding presence he soon impressed us as the obvious man for this key position.'[27] Though neither had worked with television, they learned fast. Robb in particular used his administrative abilities to circumvent petty incidents of BBC bureaucracy, his artistic imagination to evolve the most effective means of achieving contrast in make-up and costumes, and his organising ability and drive to put on the first show at what turned out, thanks to his BBC masters, to be just three weeks' notice. There would then be a daily programme from 11pm to 11.30pm on Mondays, Tuesdays, Wednesdays, and Fridays on 398.9 metres for sound (via the BBC's transmitter at Daventry) and 261.3 metres for vision (via Brookmans Park).

After six test transmissions, each of forty-five minutes, had been approved by the Baird company, the technical arrangements were pronounced on 8 August to be complete, though it was a further week before Robb had unrestricted use of the studio for his auditions and rehearsals. Cyril Smith, a concert pianist who had regularly performed behind the scenes at Long Acre as accompanist, was engaged as resident pianist.

Robb kept a personal diary, of which entries from 20 October 1933 to 29 January 1936 survive. The story which emerges is not only one of continual struggles against the pettiness of the bureaucracy – trouble with the ventilation, having to move office to another building without being consulted, the loss of a curtain, and the supply of a daily paper for reference, a basin for the extra dressing-room, and fireguards after an artiste's dress had caught fire. It also confirms that there was little or no direction from the top, and considerable confusion and antagonism lower down:

> 11 September 1934. Saw [Reith]. Mentioned unhappy owing to uncertain policy asked his advice. No answer. ... A Dept official [had said to me], 'You can't expect us to show enthusiasm when it means disruption of our depts.' [Reith]: 'Do you mean to tell me that people in this building think that they will be pushed out of a job with adoption of television?' I said from their remarks I could only suppose they did.[28]

There were problems even with his closest colleague:

> 18 May 1934. Whitehouse of EMI met Birkinshaw and let slip that he saw him the previous day at [the EMI factory] experimenting with make-up. Birkinshaw admitted this to be true. This is a Gilbertian situation. Programmes have no entertainment value. Programme people have no say in television matters. It is an engineering matter pure and simple. The programme man's (myself) invention of special make-up to overcome colour dissemination of photo cells is used surreptitiously by engineers in making experiments of new systems. It is bad enough that I should not be given equal facilities for the study of new progress in studio apparatus but that my activities in experiment should be carried out behind my back by another hand is intolerable.[28]

The question of 'entertainment value' was a real one. Robb became unpopular with the management because his programmes, instead of merely satisfying the corporation's criteria of edification, were actually entertaining. '4 May 1934. [Gielgud] rang to mention displeasure at reports "Pop[ular] Wireless" that I considered my programmes had entertainment value.'[28]

There were problems also with Robb's own staff. An assistant called Whitworth was foisted on him in January 1935, to be responsible for helping with programmes and auditions. Whitworth announced that he would not audition for variety or music hall items as he was out of sympathy with them. Then there was the temperamental Miss Bartlett, who graduated from secretary to assistant producer. Gielgud, whose secretary she had previously been, instructed Robb to make her an announcer, ignoring the BBC's official disapproval of women announcers. The appointment was overruled.[28] Matters could not have been helped by the fact that in November 1934 Jean Bartlett became Mrs Tony Bridgewater.[29]

On 15 August 1932, Baird passed through Calais, en route to the Berlin Radio Exhibition, where Fernseh was demonstrating a new, and revolutionary, method of transmission which the Baird company was to employ signally in various forms and for various purposes later in the 1930s.[30] The intermediate-film process was especially suitable for transmitting outdoor or large indoor scenes. The scene was photographed and the sound recorded on cine film, which was then developed, fixed, and washed in about thirty seconds. The moving image, in the form of a photographic negative, was then scanned in the normal way, with the sound being picked up off the film and transmitted in exact synchronism. Subsequently, Fernseh surmounted the problem of the amount of film needed by employing a continuous loop about a hundred feet long. After scanning, the emulsion was removed, the film was cleaned, and new emulsion applied; the film was then dried, and passed through the camera again.[31]

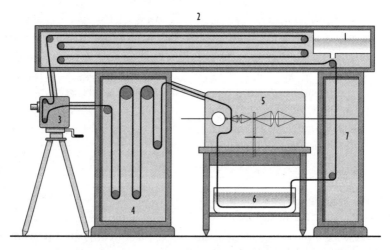

Figure 6: Intermediate-film process, as devised in Germany by Fernseh AG for television outside broadcasts. A loop of film is continuously coated with emulsion (1), then dried (2), before entering the cine camera (3). The exposed film is processed (4) before passing through the television scanner (5). The used emulsion is washed off the film (6), which is then dried (7) before being coated again (1). The Baird company later used fresh film, so that only steps 3-5 were needed. This gave better picture quality, but greatly increased the cost.

Of this German trip, Baird recorded:

> When I first visited Berlin, like most English visitors I went directly to
> the Adlon, being told that it was the best hotel in Berlin. Church
> however dispelled this illusion and pointed out that the Adlon was built
> and run with the express purpose of exploiting the US and English
> tourists and that the real leading hotel was the Kaiserhof. So there I
> transferred myself and there I saw Hitler for the first time ... when he
> was beginning to make himself a power in Germany.
>
> Hitler was a man built on exactly opposite lines to the dreaming
> studious Brüning. He sat near me in the lounge of the Kaiserhof where
> every afternoon he took tea surrounded by some dozen of his sup-
> porters; Göring and Goebbels were no doubt amongst them, but I
> had not recognized them. At that time, they had not blazed into
> prominence. Hitler however could not pass unnoticed. He sat at the
> head of the table and his eyes stared in front of him with a strange fixed
> look from under a shock of black hair. He sat erect and silent and
> unmoving except occasionally when some member of his party
> whispered respectfully to him, when he would bow or shake his head.
> The gathering regarded him as a god. I gaped fascinated at the scene.
> The maitre d'hotel approached and warned me discreetly to look else-
> where. Nazis in brown shirts came to Hitler's table, gave the Nazi
> salute, took instructions and departed briskly. It was the first time I had
> seen all this! I was told it was a lot of nonsense and would soon fade
> away! The man was simply a fanatic followed by a few out-of-works and
> others of no importance.[32]

The inaugural BBC television broadcast took place on 22 August 1932,
fourteen days before the birth of Baird's first child, Diana. It began two
minutes late and overran by five minutes. That apart, Birkinshaw was able to
report:

> Everything went off without a hitch of any sort either technically or in
> the programme – a result I had hardly dared hope for in view of the
> appalling lack of time for preparation – excepting that we got a howl
> back for a moment owing to the loudspeaker being fully faded up and
> also the picture was momentarily obliterated as one photoelectric cell
> group-plug was pulled out of its socket during the shifting of the cells
> about in the studio.[33]

Care was taken that there would be no inadvertent transposition of connections resulting in a negative instead of a positive picture being shown,
such as had marred the opening broadcast in 1929.[34]

A reporter from *Television* was in the studio.

> Moving [between the groups of people] were the stage directors in
> faultless dinner jackets, jostled by engineers in shirt-sleeves and
> headphones, and carefully avoiding the wires which connected up the
> photo-electric cells. Through a long window in the wall of the studio
> the transmitter was pointing, and as Mr Baird said to me while waiting
> to open the broadcast, it looked 'just like a machine gun'. Five feet away
> from the window was a large white screen, forming a background to
> the television 'stage'.[35]

The show was opened by Roger Eckersley, who concluded his few words,
'As it is the Baird process which is being used, we are glad to welcome its
inventor in the person of Mr John L Baird, who will now be televised.'[35]

Baird, clutching a sprig of white heather,[35] now stepped into the range of
the flying-spot scanner, and said even fewer words, composed for him by the
BBC:[34]

> I wish to thank the BBC for inviting me tonight and express the hope
> that this new series of television transmissions will lead to the develop-
> ment of broadcasting, increasing its utility and adding to the enjoyment
> of the great listening public.[33]

To the BBC, television was still an adjunct to listening, not a broadcasting
medium in its own right.

The entertainment which followed was precisely of the kind which had
been pioneered by Harold Bradly, and included two youthful veterans of
the Long Acre transmissions. These were Betty Bolton, singer and dancer,
with her short, dark hair and distinctive kiss-curls, and the blonde Betty
Astell, who sang, 'Is I in love, I is', 'When we're alone', and 'Living in
clover'. Visual as well as cultural contrast was provided by Fred Douglas, in
'black-and-white' make-up, who sang a Negro spiritual and performed
some conjuring tricks. For the benefit of maturer viewers, the musical-
comedy actress Louie Freear sang one of her hits from the 1901 show,
Chinese Honeymoon.

Whereas at Long Acre it had been regarded as the height of sophistication
and daring to vary the standard head-and-shoulders shots with some of the

legs from the knees down of Bridgewater's sister Ailsa demonstrating ballet steps, Robb had already worked out how to use the projector for 'full figure' pictures. Three hundred miles away, a reporter in Newcastle was much impressed, in spite of 'adverse conditions, including considerable morse interference, and considerable fading and very bad atmospheric disturbances', by the sight of Betty Bolton first in a Spanish outfit and then in shorts. 'I am therefore hoping that full figure transmissions will fill a fair share of the future programmes from Broadcasting House.'[36]

The projector incorporating the scanning system could be panned to a certain extent from side to side, but not up and down, though Wilson had devised a method by which the beam of light could be raised or lowered. Robb divided the studio space from front to back into three zones, close-up, semi, and longshot, in which he disposed his performers according to the image required. With 'longshot' the entire figure could be shown, but with unrecognisable features. Features became recognisable in close-up. His further ingenuity knew no bounds. Within a few months of the start he produced a pantomime of Dick Whittington with a cast of eight. He also brought ballet to the minuscule screen; the Ballet Russe de Monte Carlo with Léonide Massine, Anton Dolin, and Alicia Markova all danced for him.[37]

There were boxing matches, fashion parades, acrobats, and revue and musical comedy turns. Josephine Baker, sensational singing and dancing star of the *Folies Bergère*, appeared in October 1933. Sammy the sealion played the saxophone on screen in 1932. Birkinshaw brought her from the Victoria Palace, where she was performing nightly, in his open touring car, since no taxi would accept her as a fare, and marched her up the steps of Broadcasting House and through the main entrance. This provoked an internal memorandum: 'For Your Information: Performing animals will, in future, only be admitted to the BBC by the goods entrance.' Apparently it has never been countermanded.[38]

One of Robb's difficulties was the lack of feedback from the very source from whom he should expect it, the Baird company and in particular Baird himself. On 24 November 1932, he addressed a worried memorandum to the director general. Reith himself took this up with Baird, regarding the matter of such importance that he dictated a letter over the telephone from his home in the country on Saturday, 26 November. It was as courteously expressed as always in the correspondence between the two men:

> I am sure you must be more than satisfied with the energy which is being put into the television transmission here. ...
>
> The situation with regard to the number of people looking-in on

these transmissions may be better than we think, but unless we have full facilities and are given all the information that you possess, it is just as likely that we shall imagine it to be less hopeful than it is.

I am therefore suggesting to you that there should be no secrets whatever between us – that all the information you have available in every respect should be at our disposal, and vice versa. I think your correspondence from lookers-in should come to us, and whatever estimate you have of the number of receiving sets in operation we should know – and as accurately as possible.

We should also know what the manufacturing position is. I gather that there is some new apparatus – the Kerr Cell Mirror-drum – to be put on the market. Mr Robb says he has been enquiring for two months past for news of your negotiations with manufacturers, but has never got anything more definite than that an agreement was on the point of being signed and that a new apparatus would be on the market within a few weeks. Can we not have complete confidence shown in this and all other matters?[5]

The BBC's director general may temporarily have forgotten, or may have chosen at this time to ignore, the fact that as a matter of policy his organisation had been keeping secret its research into the effective use for television of ultra-short waves.

Baird replied by return of post, asking for a meeting at which he hoped 'to be in a position to make the whole situation clear to you'.[5]

They met on 2 December. Reith noted in his diary: 'Baird to see me about television, and I told him I was annoyed as they were still keeping us in the dark about what was happening at their end.'[39] After the meeting Reith sent a copy to Baird of the internal memorandum to Murray which he wrote the same day:

[Mr Baird] entirely accepts my view that there should be complete frankness on his side, and that all the information available to them with regard to reaction on the television transmissions, and with regard to their plans, should be available to us.

On the other hand, I entirely agree that this should only be to someone such as yourself in the BBC.[5]

There would be regular reports of enquiries about apparatus and of correspondence about the transmissions, and information about plans 'with regard to the future, eg on the matter of manufacture'.

With regard to the latter point, [Baird] tells me that there is to be a meeting, tonight or tomorrow night, with some of the Ostrer people to decide what they are going to do with respect to the manufacture of their new apparatus. Mr Baird says that he has made six experimental sets, and he said he had no doubt that it would be agreed to proceed with a manufacturing programme, carried out partly by licence and partly by the radio firm [of Bush] associated with the Gaumont firm.[5]

There is quite a history behind these six experimental sets.

In spite of Ostrer's assurances to Church, the situation within the Baird company had continued to be volatile. Late in May or early in June, Roberts, the company secretary, had resigned. Moseley wanted his nominee, a man called Powell, to be appointed immediately in Roberts's place. Ampthill wrote privately to Church on 11 June 1932:

Personally I think it would be a mistake if we did anything in a hurry and I think it is certainly desirable that our new Colleagues [Greer and Clayton] should become acquainted with Mr Roberts before they are asked to come to any decision. They will want to know, and they have a right to know, why Mr Roberts has resigned, and when it comes to those explanations at the Board Table there will be an inevitable recurrence of the old ructions.

As you know, I regard it as disastrous to let Mr Roberts go and I should like to try to get him to retract his resignation. I do not know whether this is possible as I have not consulted him on that point, but it is quite certain that he would have to have some assurance that Mr Moseley and Mr Baird would no longer intrigue against him. So far as I am personally concerned, you will remember that I have stated explicitly that I am not willing to retain the responsibility of Chairmanship unless I have Mr Roberts with me.

The matter is really not so pressing as Mr Moseley will no doubt make out. If there should be any interregnum there is no reason why we should not go on for a while with Mr Layzell acting as Secretary and General Manager as he seems to be doing very well and gaining experience. A complete stranger would inevitably be completely at sea in our office for a month or two, and that would be during the most critical period.[40]

In the event, R E Layzell was in due course confirmed as secretary of the company.[41] On 12 July 1932 Ampthill wrote to Baird enclosing his formal resignation as chairman of the company.[42] Shortis resigned from the board on 21 July.

Moseley, holidaying in Brittany in August, wrote in his diary, 'Note from Baird urging me not to delay my return, as apparently things are happening. Sir Harry Greer has been elected Chairman of the Company.'[43] Greer, also chairman of Stephens Ink,[44] was, Reveley recalls,

> A stereotype City potentate, accustomed to running businesses by delegation, through the well understood clutch of standardised inter-mediate departmental responsibilities: company secretary, production manager, sales manager, research manager, etc., all dutifully delivering in coordination what convention expected of them. Baird Television certainly did not fit into any such comfortable mould.[45]

Nor did Baird himself, as Moseley recorded in his diary:

> NOV. 20 [1932]: The struggle for Television still goes on. It amuses me to see how my business colleagues on the Board of directors are trying to discipline a genius – JLB. Sir Harry Greer, the Company's Chairman, sends me a copy of a letter he has sent to John:
> 'Dear Baird
> 'With reference to the conclusions arrived at on the occasion of our Board Meeting on Tuesday last, I do trust that you are not allowing yourself to be in any way interrupted by ordinary routine matters, and that you are, as arranged, entirely concentrating on the special Test Sets. As arranged, you will not trouble about any Board affairs for next Tuesday, but I should be glad, however, if you would just spare 5 minutes some time on Tuesday morning to dictate what I might term a Progress Report regarding the special Test Sets, which the Secretary can read at the meeting.'
> In his covering letter to me, Sir Harry wrote:
> 'I would, as a favour, ask you to see that as far as is humanly possible, Baird's time and attention will not in any way be distracted from the special work of getting ahead with the Test Sets.'
> The fact is that Baird's mind is *very much* on Board affairs, and the last thing in the world he proposes to do is to let them run the business side of his television without him. ... The Board thinks he should concentrate on technical affairs. There is something in this – but Baird is shrewd enough to know that unless he keeps an eye on the business – he'll be out! Besides, who are these wonder men who want to run

him? As a matter of fact, Baird and I have quiet fun about some of the people on the Board, and we both pretty well know the score.[46]

Greer was obviously taking charge, in the only way he knew. Moseley's observations were to prove remarkably prescient.

Percy described the test sets on which Baird was working:

In order to confound the critics who argued that pictures by the Baird system on television sets using Neon tubes and discs were 'too small to have any entertainment value', Baird decided to build six super home receivers giving a picture 12 inches by 6 inches, and employing the mirror-drum Kerr cell principle. The Kerr cells were actually made by Jacomb, and were put into test tubes, Jacomb and one assistant performing all the intricate assembly and glass work which was necessary. In addition to the five receivers which were privately allotted in the London area, one was presented to the BBC and was installed in one of their press listening halls at Broadcasting House.

These sets were probably the ultimate in 30-line receivers, and they were bright, presenting a black-and-white picture, and exceedingly stable in operation. From them was developed the well-known Bush mirror-drum receiver which was in fact a scaled-down version of the original six sets laid down in the spring of 1932.[47]

So, writing eighteen years after the event Percy was under the impression that these experimental sets were almost, if not actually, completed in the spring of 1932. Robb's information from the company was that the new apparatus would be on the market during the autumn. Yet on 20 November, the prototypes were still being constructed. Greer's frustration becomes understandable.

Baird, however, was now up to his eyes in a controversy which in due course would destroy any vestige of good relations between his company and the BBC, and change the relationship between him and his company. In a letter to Reith (6 December) he raised the subject of ultra-short waves:

We have spent considerable time developing apparatus for use with ultra-short waves, both with cathode ray and mechanical systems and have gone as far as 240-line scanning. This apparatus is, however, entirely unsuitable for the medium waveband owing to the immensely high frequencies involved, but the pictures produced are, of course, immensely superior. I am drawing your attention to this point as I understand the [Radio Corporation of America], through its associated companies in London, has been giving demonstrations of apparatus *under laboratory conditions*, but this must not be taken to imply that this shows an advantage over our British systems. ... Our own results in the laboratory are far superior to those which we are sending out through the BBC, but such results are of academic interest until the ultra-short wave channel is sufficiently developed to pass the very high frequencies involved. ... I am stressing this as I have reason to believe that the [Radio Corporation of America] through its subsidiaries, is endeavouring to create the impression that it has something which is superior to ours.[5]

Reith underlined this last sentence and marked the letter for Ashbridge's attention, with an exclamation mark. As well he might!

The sequence of events had begun innocently enough with an invitation from Shoenberg, director of research of EMI, to Ashbridge to witness a private demonstration of television. According to a memorandum Ashbridge wrote in 1952, he had known in about 1930 that Shoenberg had begun work on a new television system, and that EMI had been energetically developing it ever since. The company had been unwilling, however, to give any kind of demonstration until something commercially useful had been achieved.[48] The demonstration for Ashbridge took place at the EMI factory at Hayes on 30 November 1932. A series of excerpts from silent films and newsreels were transmitted by ultra-short waves over a distance of about two miles. The pictures were displayed on a cathode-ray receiver with a screen about five inches square, though another machine was available with a screen four times the size. Ashbridge was quite impressed:

> The method differs considerably from the Baird system, in particular three times as many lines per picture are used,[49] and there are twice as many pictures per second. The apparatus is developed only for the transmission of films and I am informed that the development of the system for studio transmissions might not be very easy. ... I think I ought to say that although these pictures give a measure of entertainment value, they are hardly likely at the present stage of development to command sustained attention over long periods. On the other hand they represent by far the best wireless television I have ever seen, and are probably as good, or better, than anything that has been produced anywhere else in the world.[50]

EMI were asking the BBC to 'take up this system at first on an experimental basis, for about 7 or 8 months, and later for use in our programmes'. Ashbridge suggested that 'film is the only way in which we can develop the televising of actualities. I cannot see any method developing in the immediate future so as to allow of the direct televising on a satisfactory basis of, say, the finish of the Derby, or the Wimbledon Tennis Matches, at any rate within the next few years,' though film would be satisfactory for plays. A system of films would involve the costly establishment of an alternative programme, on which everything would be transferred onto film. 'Provided that sufficient apparatus were available, a film could be made and re-transmitted within a matter of only a few hours.'[51] He was doubtful as to whether the system could be developed to enable direct television of a studio performance. If, however, the BBC took responsibility for the transmission, there would be no problems about the receiving end, for which EMI would make, market, and supply all the television sets and other apparatus.[50]

Ashbridge went on to make some general comments on television and the BBC. Television was nothing like as far advanced as was radio broadcasting when the British Broadcasting Company was formed. He did not agree with those who said television would completely revolutionise broadcasting. There would be no point, for instance, in televising a newsreader or an orchestra. Indeed, he doubted whether a television programme could 'last usefully for more than two hours a night on average'. Transmission would have to be by means of ultra-short waves, and would therefore be 'patchy' and expensive. It would be a luxury service, and 'it can hardly arouse the steadily increasing enthusiasm such as sound broadcasting has enjoyed, on account of cost alone'. Also, television had to be watched 'in darkened rooms. ... In fact, I am inclined to think that the great importance of television, and its enormous far reaching effects, are a good deal exaggerated.'[50]

On the other hand, the BBC should not 'hold back in developing a new invention of this type to its greatest extent', as long as the financial aspects were carefully monitored, but 'in taking this development we should have to accept the financial risk of another method superseding the one under review'.[50]

Reith initialled the memorandum, to indicate that he had seen it. Carpendale wrote on it, 'Most interesting, I do so agree of [sic] his opinion of the small possible interest television can ever have for the reasons given.'[50]

How Baird so soon got wind of what had been developed in secret and demonstrated in confidence is not known. There may have been a mole in EMI or, possibly, a leak to a journalist.[52]

In alluding to EMI as a subsidiary of RCA, Baird was overstating his case. EMI, at its inception as a result of a merger between the Gramophone

Company (HMV) and the Columbia Graphophone Company, was, to be sure, almost two-thirds under American ownership: the majority shareholders were J P Morgan, the American investment bank, and RCA, whose founder and president, David Sarnoff, was on the EMI board. Also EMI's chairman, Alfred Clark, formerly chairman of the Gramophone Company, was American.[53] EMI did, however, have access to RCA's television technology, in particular the iconoscope camera, but Baird was glossing over the fact that EMI's initiative was essentially a British effort, conducted by British scientists and technicians.

While the BBC decided how to deal with Baird's assertions, EMI's chairman, Alfred Clark, saw Reith to ask the BBC to set up in the autumn an experimental ultra-short-wave service, which would show filmed material through the EMI system. In doing so, Clark was acting precisely as Appleton, in his commissioned report a year earlier, had proposed that the Baird company should do. At a control board meeting on 3 January 1933, Reith asked Ashbridge to prepare a report on television developments. This Ashbridge did on 5 January – Reith's handwritten annotations are printed in brackets in italic type. On the future of Baird Television, Ashbridge came to a number of conclusions:

> A year ago we agreed to go ahead with the regular production of programmes on the Baird 30 line process for transmission by ordinary broadcast wavelengths, in order to see –
> (1) Whether a good producer could make anything of it from the programme point of view, in relation to public interest.
> (2) To gain experience of television problems, both on the technical and programme side.
> (3) To give Baird (as the only Englishman who had produced anything) the opportunity of progressing further in his researches.
> I will not go into the various safeguards which we laid down in connection with these arrangements, but the important fact is that now Baird's are considering going into mass production for sale to the public. ...
> What I should like to do, therefore, is to tell the Baird Company that so far as we are able to see at the moment, there is a distinct possibility of terminating the agreement on the specified date, and of possibly reducing the number of transmissions in the meanwhile, in accordance with the agreement. Secondly, that they should concentrate on the production of 120 line pictures, or at any rate pictures of greater detail, for transmission by ultra-short waves. *(This is also my view.)* Thirdly, they

should concentrate on the production of studio scenes, as this has not been done by anybody else. Baird states that he has done this, but no demonstration has been forthcoming so far.[54]

On the question of Alfred Clark's request for a regular service to start in the autumn, Ashbridge stated, 'I think that we ought to make it clear that we are not in favour of this so far as we can see at present. *(I agree. When and how?)'* Suitable talking films would have to be found, and two short-wave trans- mitters would be required. These would have to be of higher power than any that were then available, though the Marconi firm was looking into this on behalf of EMI.

> Altogether I must say I dislike these rush tactics, they are too much like the Baird Company's tactics in the early days, and their object I think, may be the following. To try and rush us into establishing a service as quickly as possible, so that they can get well ahead in the receiver market for television sets, although no doubt they would be prepared to license other people when it paid them to do so.[54]

If it cost the BBC £20,000 a year to operate the service, and EMI sold a thousand receivers a year, 'they would be making a small profit and we should be making a large loss, even if an extra licence fee were paid for television reception. *(This is what I said very emphatically to Clark.)'*

> What I dislike is the danger of our paying out a very large sum of money in order to let EMI make a profit of a few thousands a year for a year or two, with the possibility of making a much larger profit later on, but with practically no risk whatever, except the danger of losing the sum they have spent on development. ... However, you may say that we are entirely justified in making what may amount to a loss of £100,000 in order to establish television at the end of a period of three to five years. *(I certainly don't.)*
> I am entirely in favour of doing research because I believe that many years of experimenting are necessary before television becomes a definitely established service. In this connection it must be remembered that they are concentrating entirely on films, and I feel doubtful whether a programme service of films *only* is a satisfactory policy as a permanency. For this reason I feel very strongly against trying to dump another doubtful service on the public as soon as next autumn.[54]

If Ashbridge, at this crucial juncture in the development of British television, was hoping that Reith would give some firm direction, he failed to get it.

On 13 January Baird wrote a long letter to Ashbridge, confirming that he hoped 'to be in a position to show you a 240-line picture in the second week of February'. He suggested that Ashbridge had previously agreed that it was the duty of the BBC to develop the wireless aspects of ultra-short-wave transmission, with the Baird company concentrating on the transmitting and receiving apparatus. 'Obviously, until ultra-short wave broadcasting is perfected it is necessary to proceed on the medium-wave as we are now doing.' He hoped 'next month, to be in a position to show you also our latest results with the cathode ray tube, although I do not think it by any means supersedes mechanical systems'. Baird went on to ask if the BBC would install at Broadcasting House a Baird cine-projector capable, through the BBC's short-wave transmitter, of sending pictures of 240 lines.[55]

Ashbridge, in true BBC fashion, responded by proposing a meeting to discuss matters. It took place on 27 January between Baird and Moseley for the Baird company, and Ashbridge and Murray for the BBC. According to Ashbridge's notes, the Baird line was that the BBC should not 'transmit by any other method than the Baird system unless the proposed new method showed an improvement of a revolutionary nature'. That if the BBC were to do so, it would deal 'a heavy blow at British industry, and [be] helping an American concern'. And that 'they could produce as good television of the high definition type as could EMI'.[55]

The BBC's predictable response was that the agreement with the company referred to regularly advertised transmissions, not those for the purposes of research, that the EMI system could not be said to be American, and that it was a pity that the Baird company had not demonstrated its developments in high-definition transmission before. At this point Moseley, who was convinced that the reason for the EMI approach to the BBC was that EMI was considering a share issue in the near future, got so heated that it was agreed that the meeting should continue only between Baird and Ashbridge.[55]

Baird asked if the BBC would suspend its tests with EMI until after his February demonstration. Ashbridge replied that it was not his decision, but that if the Baird system were to prove superior there was no harm done. Ashbridge then asked Baird for his opinion on the future for thirty-line television:

> Mr Baird did not care to give his own personal opinion, but stated that the Ostrer brothers had receivers in their houses, and had decided to go ahead with the production of sets for the public. CE [Ashbridge] stated

in answer to this that he considered the latter was a wrong move, in view of the fact that Mr Baird had said that he would soon be in a position to demonstrate 240 line television of objects in a studio and of films. It was, in fact, most unfortunate if they contemplated proceeding with the production of receivers for the public designed only for 30 line television on a medium wavelength. Mr Baird answered that this matter had been decided by the Ostrer Brothers, and he had nothing further to add.[55]

The meeting took place on a Friday. On the following Monday, Ashbridge wrote to Baird:

> You will remember that during our conversation we discussed the question of the mass production of receivers for the public on a basis of a 30 line picture intended for transmission by the medium broadcast wavelength. In view of the fact that towards the end of February you are going to give us a demonstration of 240 line of both films and studio scenes, we feel strongly that it would be a mistake to take the somewhat irrevocable step of selling numbers of receivers to the public for television reception by a method which was already obsolescent.
>
> We feel, therefore, that you should consider this step very carefully indeed, and we shall be glad to receive your comments in due course.[56]

The BBC control board minutes of 31 January included the note, 'It was stated that a warning had been sent to the Baird Company against going into mass production of thirty line receivers in view of the fact that they expect to be demonstrating a 240 line transmitter to us in a few months time.'[55]

Ashbridge sent his notes of his meeting with Baird to Reith, accompanied by a memorandum: 'I suppose we can take it that there is bound to be a certain amount of further trouble. In the event of your wishing to go ahead with EMI straightaway, I attach a draft letter to Mr Clark.' After speaking to Ashbridge, Reith wrote on the memorandum:

(1) Advisable to send Baird a letter indicating policy in <u>lines and numbers</u> etc otherwise we shall be blamed if Ostrers go into production on 30 basis. CE agreed.

(2) Is it advisable for us to write officially to Baird re EMI. CE thought not necessary.[55]

According to a handwritten note below, these words were 'Noted by Chairman'. In Reith's judgment, the BBC should spell out to Baird in terms of lines and the number of pictures per second precisely what its plans were for the transmission of television images by ultra-short waves. It does not appear that this was done.

The 'further trouble' that Ashbridge foresaw duly materialised. It was intense and vociferous, and, perhaps surprisingly, had some effect in the short term. This phase of the campaign was opened by Moseley, who wrote in strong terms to the Postmaster General:

> I am not satisfied that the BBC realises its duty to the country in this respect. My own relations with the executives are of the friendliest, but I think it is a matter for the Government rather than for the BBC to lay down a policy with regard to the future of British television. The BBC, which holds the monopoly by virtue of a Charter granted by HM Government, seems to me to be extraordinarily cynical where the rights of a British sister science are concerned.
>
> I have been fighting extremely hard to prevent the tying up in any shape or form of the fastest known means of communication with this foreign body, but I fear that unless you take steps immediately the Radio Corporation of America, through one of its controlled companies in London, may force a means of 'muscling-in' through the back doors of the BBC. Were this done it would be a public scandal and as I told the Shareholders of the Baird Television Company on Monday last, I would not hesitate to call together a public meeting were such an attempt made. It is because I wish to avoid such a step that I would ask you, in the interests of this country, to take immediate steps.[57]

On the face of it, it is not easy to see precisely what the government was being asked to do. This is obviously what the civil servants felt too, and a letter incorporating these statements of Moseley was sent on 1 February by the GPO to Carpendale at the BBC, asking for his views.[57] Reith himself signed the reply to the GPO, on 3 February. He did not comment on issues of national identity and responsibility; he reiterated the BBC's position about the test transmissions:

> The Baird company claims that this is not in accordance with our arrangement with them, which I should mention is not in the form of a definite agreement, although this fact does not affect the situation in any way. On the other hand we maintain that we did not undertake not

to carry out *research* on television by any method, distinct from *public transmission* of advertised programmes, and that, therefore, the question as to whether the Electrical and Musical Industries system is at this stage fundamentally superior to the Baird system does not arise. ...

Our proposal is that we should proceed to compare the results obtainable by any system which showed promise, and then consider what, if any, system should be adopted on a more permanent basis for programme purposes, having regard to technical and policy considerations.[55]

Moseley's blustering tactics are understandable: they were the only ones he knew. Baird, faced with competition in the back yard that he had regarded as his own, and realising that by locking himself, and effectively his company, into the thirty-line system, he had put himself several years behind the times, panicked. He began to bombard Reith with letters. On 31 January he again complained that the BBC was 'in direct contravention of the agreement arrived at between us', and that it was the BBC which was holding up development: 'We have contented ourselves at present by sending out transmissions only on the 30-line machine, waiting until such time as your engineers had developed the ultra-short wave to such a pitch that it could handle pictures with a larger number of lines.' He concluded,

It is of the utmost importance that broadcasting in this country should not be under foreign influence, directly or indirectly.

Mr Ashbridge maintains that he had nothing to do with this and that it was a matter for the Board. I trust therefore that this matter will be discussed fully by your Board of Governors, because the very last thing I desire is a repetition of the early friction between ourselves when we had to fight tooth and nail in order to get the BBC to realise that the development of television was a matter of concern not only for the BBC but for this country.[55]

On the same day he acknowledged briefly Ashbridge's letter of 30 January, saying that he had written directly to Reith.

Reith replied to Baird on 3 February:

I think there can be no doubt that the undertaking ... did not apply to research or test transmissions. I might say that it is obviously essential to conduct research with apparatus of any kind in order to obtain information bearing upon all phases of our work.

If your claim to superiority over other systems can be demonstrated on a practical basis, I cannot see what you have to fear from the procedures explained to you at the meeting last Friday 27 January.[55]

On 4 February Ashbridge wrote to Baird pointing out that neither in his letter to him of 31 January nor in his letter to Reith had he 'commented on the question of 30 line television, which I raised in my letter'.[55]

On that same day of 4 February, which was a Saturday, Baird wrote two letters to Reith. The first was dictated and signed at the office:

I do not quite understand what you mean by "the procedures explained to you at the meeting last Friday, 27th January". ... I have written to Mr Ashbridge [31 January] suggesting that we agree notes of the meeting. I think that is the best thing to do in order to clear up what is obviously a misunderstanding.[55]

The second, marked 'Private', was handwritten from 84 Lawn Road:

Since writing to you I have heard an alarming report from the city which states that an attempt may be made in May to raise money from the public on the strength of an arrangement with the BBC in regard to television.

I do not know the company referred to but it certainly is not ours.

May I remind you of the harm done to the BBC through a similar arrangement made by 'Wireless Pictures' [the Fultograph people] in which the public lost every penny it invested.

I tell you this of course in confidence and in all friendliness.[55]

Within the BBC there now circulated a flurry of internal memoranda between Reith, Ashbridge, H Bishop (assistant chief engineer), and Murray. There were also letters to and from Clark, and discussions with post office engineers. In the light of these, various conclusions were drawn and decisions taken. As Reith indicated to Baird (9 February, draft approved by Murray), 'I do not quite understand why you say that you have just heard of an alarming report, since I noticed a reference to this effect at the meeting which was held here on 27th January. If it concerns Electric & Musical Industries, Ltd, I am assured that there is not a vestige of truth in it.'[55] Baird replied on 14 February:

I do not know whether the rumours in the City refer to the Company you mention. This Company, by the way, according to a letter from the

City editor of the 'Times', which has been shown to me, is virtually controlled by the Radio Corporation of America – (27% which, as you know, is virtual control) which surely controls quite enough of the world's communications without the home of British broadcasting taking it under its wing.[55]

It was also decided that Murray should send Baird a version of Ashbridge's notes on the 27 January meeting. It was virtually identical to the report given by Ashbridge to Reith, except that two references to the 'Ostrer Brothers' now appeared as the 'Baird Company' and a sentence had been added: 'It was mentioned that only 27% of the capital of Electric and Musical Industries Ltd was in American hands.'[55]

In response, Baird returned to the fray (18 February) with yet another letter to Reith. He did not agree that the original arrangement did not refer to experimental transmissions. There was no need for the BBC to transmit by means of the EMI system of 120 lines. His company could install a 120-line transmitting apparatus, and EMI could use these transmissions for their reception tests; the German post office was already experimenting very satisfactorily with a Fernseh 120-line transmission apparatus. 'It is universally agreed that 27% gives virtual control of a public company.' The BBC's ultra-short-wave wireless transmitter could not transmit even thirty lines perfectly; when it could do so with more lines, the Baird company would immediately install the necessary transmission apparatus.

> Great injustice and harm could be done to our Company by the BBC using another system for ultra-short wave tests. We have abandoned our own ultra-short wave [wireless] transmitter, relying upon the under-standing that for two years we would not be either wholly or partially displaced by any other system.
>
> What our legal redress would be, only legal action could decide. I trust this position will not arise and I can see no reason why it should, particularly as I understand that the EMI have no desire to be concerned with the transmitting end, and there is no reason why our 120-line transmitter should not fill all requirements and enable them and the BBC to conduct any tests they desire.[55]

The significance of the BBC wireless transmitter was not only its power, but that it was set high up on a tall building in a city. No experiments in ultra-short-wave transmission with anything more than thirty lines had been conducted in Britain from a city site, with its hazards such as other buildings in the line of transmission. Only by experimenting in this way could the difficulties inherent in developing a national ultra-short-wave television broadcasting service be ironed out.[58]

Baird's letter circulated within the BBC for a fortnight, at the end of which it was decided (3 March) that it might remain unanswered,[55] both because the BBC had said all it had to say on these points, and because the circumstances had been largely overtaken by events.

Baird had also been writing to the Postmaster General, who seemed less intractable to his claims. The assistant secretary of the GPO wrote to Reith (1 March) saying that Baird had promised to demonstrate his ultra-short-wave apparatus now in the first week of April, and that perhaps it might be wise to defer a final decision about the EMI transmission equipment in the BBC until after that. A meeting between representatives of the GPO and the BBC was held to discuss the situation.[55]

Baird had in the meantime responded to Ashbridge's specific question about the thirty-line television receivers:

> It is not my opinion that this is already obsolescent. The ultra-short wave is still a long way from having reached the public service stage.
>
> Even when the BBC [wireless] transmitter reaches the stage where it is capable of transmitting say 90 or 120 or even 240-line pictures, it will be necessary to duplicate this station all over the country so as to provide a reasonable service area.
>
> I can therefore see many difficulties still to be overcome before ultra-short wave broadcasting becomes a service in any way comparable or competitive with the present medium waves and I think you will agree with me that there is still a great deal of work to be done before this stage is reached. Even so, are you prepared to stake your reputation that ultra-short waves *is* definitely the solution to perfect television? Until the fact is proved it is dangerous to minimise the opportunities of a system that at any rate has proved to severe and experienced critics that it has a definite entertainment value. I would, however, very much appreciate any comments you care to make.[59]

Ashbridge may or may not have seen this letter before going to Brussels for a fortnight. Whether he did or not, Bishop replied on 13 February:

> [Ashbridge's] object in raising the question of receivers for a 30-line picture was that mass production plans for such receivers would doubtless be planned for some period ahead, and in view of your forth-

coming demonstration of 240-line television it seems to us decidedly unwise to create extensive obligations in connection with a system which, if your demonstration is successful, will at least tend to become obsolescent if the new system is to develop.

It is of course agreed that to cover a large area on ultra short waves means a number of transmitters. However, it is too early in our opinion to forecast what will be the final solution to television. Much research work has yet to be done and we feel strongly that the sale to the public of receivers suitable for a system liable to be displaced would be most undesirable at this stage.[55]

It is difficult to fault the BBC's attitude on this particular issue. It was a function of the corporation to respond to the needs of the public and to ensure that the public had the facilities on which to base a judgment. If and when the scientists came up with a foolproof high-definition television system, then it was the BBC's responsibility to devise ways in which it could be broadcast as widely as possible. Baird had not demonstrated such a system. In any case, the Baird company desperately needed sales of receivers now; without sales there would be no money for its research.

On the question of the intrusion of EMI into the equation, Baird had even written to the Prince of Wales asking him to intervene, on the grounds that the BBC was 'crushing a pioneer British industry' and 'giving secret encouragement to alien interests'. A puzzled private secretary, Sir Godfrey Thomas, consulted Roger Eckersley, asking for a note on the general situation which would enable him to reply in the prince's name.[60] Eckersley's report to him was detailed and fair. It rehearsed all the issues and concluded, 'We take the view that it is our duty to determine what is the best method of doing television from a technical point of view, wherever the system might originate. The question would afterwards arise as to whether the best system could be adopted from other points of view.'[55]

★

Ashbridge was not the only continental traveller at this time. Margaret Baird records that in February 1933 she went with Baird to Berlin. It was not a good time to go. On 30 January Hitler had, quite constitutionally, been appointed Chancellor.

It was very cold and soon John was ill. One of my many relations in Germany, a Dr Platau, an ear, throat, and nose specialist, attended John and told me sad stories of the difficulties put in the way of Jewish professional people, how they dreaded a knock at the door during the night, when one of the family, chosen at random, would be taken away to a concentration camp. Storm troopers stamped through the streets, swastikas hung from every window, and my relations had good reason to be terrified.[61]

This must also have been the visit to which Baird refers in his memoir:

The last time I saw [Brüning] was shortly after Hitler came into power when his life was in extreme danger. Church and I visited him in a villa outside Berlin where he was staying with a friend. I remember the talk ranged on the reformation of the race by sterilizing the unfit. His friend opposed it. 'It is,' he said, 'too great a shock to the soul.' Brüning nodded in agreement. I was struck by the use of the word soul in a discussion of this kind until I remembered that Brüning was a devout Catholic.[62]

The trip must have taken place after 18 February (a Saturday), on which day Baird wrote to Reith. On 27 February the Reichstag, the German parliament building, was set on fire by agents of the Nazis, who were then able to denounce the act of arson as a Communist plot. At the end of May Brüning was warned that he had been listed by the Gestapo to be murdered; the following month he silently left the country in disguise.[63]

Gladstone Murray was also away from his office at this time, on a three-month study of the Canadian broadcasting commission and Canadian broad-casting affairs in general. For this, the Canadian government paid him $7200, most of it to compensate him for loss of income. It was rumoured, however, that he spent $8000 drinking his way across the country while conducting the investigation.[64]

★

Much to the fury of EMI and the frustration of Reith and Ashbridge, the BBC was forced to concede to the Postmaster General's instructions, incorporated in a letter from the GPO of 13 March, to postpone the final decision on the EMI tests until after Baird's demonstration 'of his short wave apparatus by the first week in April', and after a further demonstration that EMI should be asked to give. Both demonstrations were to be witnessed by representatives of the GPO and the BBC. Reith scribbled at the top of the letter, 'Chairman to see / Protest against interference'.[55]

Reith's protest (21 March), dictated by Ashbridge, was addressed to the secretary of the GPO. It repeated that the EMI proposals 'were intended to be purely of a research nature'.

> Had we been allowed to proceed with the EMI transmissions, our intention was also to test new television transmitters put forward by the Baird or any other Company, provided they gave promise of better results. In this connection, we understand that at least two other firms are doing work of a somewhat similar nature.
>
> In these circumstances, we are unable to see why you should find it necessary to ask us to delay the tests with EMI apparatus, having regard to the fact that this apparatus has been ready for some weeks past, whereas, no other similar apparatus is yet ready for installation in this building, so far as we are aware. ...
>
> However, we gather from your letter that you do not propose to issue a licence for these tests, until after the demonstrations have taken place. Presumably the Baird Television Co will communicate with us concerning the date of the proposed demonstration, not later than the first week in April.[55]

Baird was finally ready on 18 April. His demonstration would be at Long Acre, with EMI's the following day at their works in Hayes, Middlesex. On 19 April Baird wrote to Ashbridge:

> I do not wish to anticipate your report, but I hope you will understand that all I was concerned in showing you yesterday was that we have a transmitter capable of sending a 120-line image with 25 pictures per second.
>
> Naturally the receivers do not yet show the perfect picture as there is still work to be done on the reception side before this stage is reached. I may add also that the results shown to you were not up to the best we can do, as in order to keep faith with you, I rushed this demonstration through.
>
> The whole purpose of the demonstration was to show what I promised, that is, a transmitter with reception either by mechanical or cathode ray system up to any number of lines practical through ultra-short wave channels.
>
> It would assist us very greatly if we could have one of our 120-line transmitters installed at the BBC at an early date so that we can develop the receiving apparatus; we have at present no facilities for our own ultra-short wave transmissions.

If other concerns wish to receive these transmissions to develop their own receiving apparatus and would prefer a different number of lines, this could always be arranged by merely changing the transmitting disc.

I was glad you came yesterday and I hope you were interested.[55]

It was a forlorn, last-ditch throw of the dice to wrench the initiative from EMI.

A meeting, under the chairmanship of L Simon, director of telegraphs and telephones of the GPO, of five senior representatives of the GPO and Carpendale, Ashbridge, and Bishop for the BBC, was held at the GPO on 21 April to consider the results of the demonstrations. Bishop took careful notes of the proceedings. On the main point there was no discussion at all. The results of the EMI demonstration 'were immeasurably superior ... and the EMI equipment was far in advance of its competitor'. The Baird company, however, reported the chairman, had represented to the Postmaster General that it would be unfair, in the light of its pioneering work, to install any other company's high-definition equipment in Broadcasting House. There had not been time to develop suitable equipment since 'they had frequently been told by Mr Ashbridge that there was no need to develop on these lines, since the future of television did not lie in this direction'. Ashbridge, as he had every right to do, 'strongly refuted these allegations and said that he had constantly suggested to Mr Baird himself that the future of television lay in high definition television on ultra short waves'.[55]

The rest of the meeting, during which no decision was made with regard to the experimental broadcasts, was taken up with discussion about the implications of giving EMI the facilities for which the company had asked.

Mr Phillips [GPO] then asked whether the BBC would be willing to have both systems installed at the same time in Broadcasting House, giving each system equal access to the ultra short wave transmitter. Mr Ashbridge replied that such an arrangement would be impracticable since space in the building was at a premium and two competitive systems in close proximity would hardly be a workable arrangement. Mr Phillips said he appreciated the BBC's point of view, but thought that the Postmaster-General would not be willing to exclude Baird's entirely since they existed solely for television, whereas EMI had other interests, and if it became known that the BBC had allowed the EMI system to be installed it would be very damaging to the Baird Co.[55]

The nub of the matter, after all, lay in politics:

> In conclusion, Mr Phillips said that the Post Office were afraid that if the Baird Co. were prevented from installing high definition equipment, questions would be asked in Parliament and in the Press which would be difficult to answer, and the Post Office mainly, and the BBC to a lesser extent, would be blamed for the inevitable bankruptcy of the Baird Co. The latter would be bound to distort the facts leading to the decision to install another maker's apparatus. The Post Office wanted to protect themselves against any such trouble, and this was the real reason for their anxiety that the BBC should afford the Baird Co. rather than any other firm, facilities for research in television of the high definition type.[55]

Or, as Carpendale rather cynically put it in a handwritten note on the memorandum accompanying the minutes:

> I have rather forgotten the words of their unsatisfactory reply when I asked them 'If they felt that way about Bairds all the time why are we here and what was the object of having a demonstration?' I think they said 'the demonstration was to show if Baird could produce anything on multitive [sic] short wave pictures' – no matter how bad – even so they did admit that if he had produced nothing they might have told us to go ahead with EMI – personally I'm sure they would have pleaded for some months extension of time.[55]

In the meantime the Baird company had been blithely going ahead with an operation which might have been specially devised to drive Reith apoplectic. Moseley wrote to Reith (21 April 1933):

> Bush Radio, an Associated Company of the Gaumont-British Group, told me this morning that they are going to inaugurate the placing on the market of the first consignment of new 'Televisors' by a Dinner to be given in two or three weeks time.
>
> In order to celebrate the birth of this new British industry, the Group is inviting many of its friends prominent in public life to this Dinner. Naturally we would all like you to be present, and I am writing to you privately to know whether any particular date would suit you. If you cannot fix the date now, I may be able to give you further information later, telling you the names of some of the people who are likely to be present.[55]

Reith's reply (25 April 1933) was brief and to the point:

> In answer to your letter of 21st April, I am afraid I cannot associate myself with the launching of a receiver by a particular company. Any public interest from officials here in the reception of broadcasting should be rather in connection with associations of manufacturers than with particular ones.[55]

As Moseley should have known, and probably did.

Reith unburdened the BBC's other concerns to the Postmaster General, in a letter dictated by Ashbridge (27 April), accompanying a copy of Moseley's letter. With regard to the thirty-line transmissions,

> It was agreed at the time that if, in our opinion, the interest taken by the public was insufficient, they should be terminated in March 1934. ... Up to the present time I think I am right in saying that no receiving sets have been put on the market on any considerable scale, but apparently, a year late, it is intended to do so.
>
> For some time past it has seemed most unlikely that we should be able to see our way to continue these transmissions beyond March 1934, having regard to their programme value and the limited interest which they have evoked. Our opinion has been strengthened considerably by recent developments of the high definition type of television, which as you know can only be transmitted on 'ultra short' wavelengths.[55]

He enclosed a copy of Ashbridge's letter to Baird of 30 January 1933 referring to the 'somewhat irrevocable step of selling numbers of receivers to the public for television reception by a method that was already obsolescent' and Baird's reply (9 February 1933) disagreeing with this view. Reith concluded his letter:

> I understand that you have under consideration the various questions which have arisen in connection with the recent demonstrations given by Electric and Musical Industries, Ltd, and the Baird Company. I therefore hasten to call your attention to the possibility of a difficult situation arising from the recent activities of the Bush Radio Company, inasmuch as we are anxious to stress that there is insufficient programme value to justify a permanent service of this type.[55]

Reith was right about the ultimate validity of transmitting high-definition images on ultra-short wavelengths, but wrong about the present interest in the thirty-line programmes. They were not discontinued until September 1935, and then only after a parliamentary committee had considered all the issues relating to a public television service.

It may have been the distraction of having to think about television at all that led Reith now to make one of his more preposterous interventions into BBC business. The day after his letter to the Postmaster General, an article by Filson Young, programme adviser (music department), appeared in the *Radio Times*, urging readers to prepare themselves 'for the realisation, in our own day, of television as an accomplished fact'. Not just watching sporting events 'on the glass panel of some parlour cabinet a thousand miles away':

> Suppose that I were broadcasting this article by word of mouth instead of by means of the printing press. That which is commonplace today would have seemed sheer miracle twenty years ago. Add television, and what do you get? ...
>
> So you see it is about time that we began to prepare ourselves for what will be a new technique in broadcast reception. I am always hammering away, as you know (I fear) to your cost, about the duty of cultivating the art of listening; but it seems not unlikely that before you have learned to be perfect listeners you will have to begin to learn a new technique – the art of looking.[65]

It was obviously this suggestion that the art of looking might take precedence over the spoken word which caused Reith to erupt. He attached a handwritten memo to the offending article and sent both to Carpendale:

> Is it desirable to give some instructions to our weekly journals as to what line to take respecting Television? Never to refer to it – or to have all references pass through CE or what? If you prefer and can give a formula and so avoid either expedient above, please let me have it.[55]

Carpendale ducked the issue by passing it on to Ashbridge, with the comment, 'What formula can you suggest?'

Ashbridge recommended a somewhat wordy one:

> It is probable that television will become a practical proposition within the next few years, and will take its part in the daily programmes. On the other hand it is bound to start on a limited basis owing to the fact that at first receivers, whether purchased or hired, are likely to be expen-

sive. For many years it is not likely to revolutionise broadcasting to the extent which many writers have stated. For the present it should be looked forward to more as a possible addition or aid to what we are doing now rather than as a feature which will revolutionise the whole art. Any substantial change in the character of our programmes resulting from television is almost certain to be more in the nature of evolution than revolution.[55]

Carpendale, on reflection, did not agree with there being a formula at all:

I think this is too optimistic, I would change [the first sentence] as 'It is possible that television may become a practical proposition within the next few years, and may take its part etc —
But in view of all the graft intrigue etc. is it not best to drop the subject in our publications. I would prefer this course.[55]

The bizarre exchange was ended by Reith himself, who decided, in a memorandum to Murray (3 May), that the 'best plan would be for you to issue an instruction to all editors not to mention Television at all without referring the proposed observations to Controller or CE.'[55] The editors of the *Radio Times*, *World Radio*, and the *Listener* were duly informed of this new regulation, which, however, 'does not refer to publication of our televised programmes or comments on them'.[55]

The two controversies, the imbroglio with regard to the launch of the new receivers, of which only a hundred would initially be put on the market,[66] and the ructions between the BBC and the GPO, and the BBC and the Baird company, over the ultra-short-wave experiments, rumbled on. The former was partially resolved in a discussion between Baird and Bishop which took place on 26 May. Sixty journalists were to be invited to a dinner at the Dorchester Hotel on 12 June. At 11pm the ordinary BBC television programme would be shown on several of the new receivers, though the programme would be enhanced by 'turns which will be specially suitable for the demonstration'. The receivers were de luxe models, incorporating a receiver and loud speaker for the sound, and a second receiver and screen for the vision, and would be offered to the public at £75 each. A notice warning the purchaser about the limited period of the transmissions, whose wording had been agreed by the BBC and the Postmaster General, would be issued with each set sold. Bishop expected Baird to propose that some distinguished person should be televised speaking on the progress of television, but Baird did not do so. Bishop ended his report to Reith, 'There will no doubt be a good deal of embarrassing publicity following Baird's demonstration. I consider that the market for these luxury sets will be very restricted indeed.'[67]

The BBC tried to resolve the EMI controversy by proposing that EMI and the Baird company pool their resources as far as transmitting television signals were concerned, and develop the receiver side separately. Ashbridge reported:

> Baird at first thought this was impossible, and afterwards rather came round to the idea that it should be considered. Shoenberg, on the other hand, would not listen to to the proposal at all, on a basis that Baird had nothing to offer.[68]

Ashbridge could not understand why the Post Office was so keen to test both systems at the same time, which would create problems of accommodation, rather than start with the more developed system.

> Later, if Baird brings his system up to a standard which is comparable with that already obtained by EMI then we could try his system afterwards. There is no question of Baird not being given a fair trial, he has been connected with us for years, and even in connection with ultra-short waves we are not throwing him overboard.[68]

Considering the difficulties in establishing the connection in the first place, this was slightly overstating the case. Ashbridge moreover was still adamant that nothing should threaten the BBC's monopoly:

> In connection with any negotiations with the Post Office ... we must not allow either Baird or EMI to be given any facilities which will lead to the establishment of a broadcasting system of either television or sound, or a combination of the two, on ultra-short waves.[68]

The Postmaster General, however, continued to press for the two systems to be tested simultaneously. In a telephone message on 23 May, Reith was informed that Baird had that afternoon been to see the Postmaster General, who would 'probably arrange for an experimental transmission by the two competing systems. He also told Mr Baird that he must face up to the possibility that the other system might prove superior, as there was some reason to believe, and promised to communicate with him in due course.'[55]

Reith responded to the Post Office by letter on 25 May. It was unfair,

he said, to keep EMI waiting any longer, and in any case it would be inconvenient to have simultaneous experiments. Might the BBC proceed with
EMI, on the understanding that if Baird could within the next two or three
months give a satisfactory demonstration, further experiments would be
carried out with his equipment?[55] Wood replied (27 May) that he understood
Baird to have said that he only needed a fortnight's notice, but that he
would check this with him.[55] Baird wrote to the Postmaster General on 6
June, having discussed the matter with his board. He offered to give a further
demonstration, on the grounds that,

> Considerable progress has been made by us since the last demonstra-
> tion, and secondly, since our last conversation I have been going very
> carefully into the possibility of adapting our present 30-line apparatus
> to receive 120-line images, and I find that if our transmitter is used it
> will be possible to do this with a comparatively cheap alteration when
> (and if) ultra-short wave broadcasting supersedes or supplements the
> present medium wave service.[69]

On the basis of this statement, Wood set the proverbial cat among the pigeons
by informing Baird that he was prepared to 'accept these assurances without
a further demonstration', and would give the BBC permission to begin
experimental transmissions with both systems on 1 July.[70]

The BBC learned about this two days later. Phones rang! Reith made a
note, 'Napier [private secretary to the Postmaster General] by phone 15th
said he didn't take the PMG's waiving of a demonstration to preclude our
having one before installation.'[55] Carpendale added, 'Spoke Napier again 23
June. He clearly confirmed the above adding that he had immediately after
the conversation with D[irector] G[eneral] spoken to PMG who agreed that
our insistence was reasonable – I told him that we would now go ahead with
EMI and as and when Baird produces something to our satisfaction he will
be allowed here too. Napier added that if we have any difficulty with Baird
he hopes we will let him know so that he is aware of it before they come
blasting into the Post Office.'[55]

On 15 June Baird wrote to the Postmaster General:

> Thank you for your letter of 13th June.
>
> We are ready to commence installing our transmitter at the BBC at
> once.
>
> I take it that we shall now get in touch with the BBC to make the
> necessary arrangements.

His letter was read over the phone to the BBC by Napier, who added that Sir Kingsley Wood was not replying to it.[55]

It is the last official document written by Baird in the files of the BBC. It was another four months before the Baird transmitter was installed in Broadcasting House. By that time Baird himself was no longer working from his company's premises or playing any part in its day-to-day affairs.

12
Crescent Wood Road
1933

By the late summer of 1933 several significant and, in some ways, dramatic changes had taken place in Baird's personal and professional life, and in the constitution and location of his company.

Baird had been relieved of the duties but not the title of managing director, and had moved to a house near the Crystal Palace, where he established his own private laboratory. Moseley had resigned from the board and ceased to have any links with the company, though his personal bond of friendship with Baird continued as strongly as ever. The company's studios, workshops, and general offices were now in rented accommodation at the Crystal Palace at Sydenham. A head office was maintained at 66 Haymarket, near Piccadilly Circus, with the registered office of the company at 58 Victoria Street; some meetings were held in the Gaumont-British offices at Film House, Wardour Street, off Oxford Street.

The spectacular Crystal Palace had originally been designed by Joseph Paxton, head gardener of the Duke of Devonshire, for the Great Exhibition of 1851 in London's Hyde Park. Two thousand workmen completed the job in four months, whereupon one prophet of doom pronounced, 'The finger of the Almighty will infallibly descend on so presumptuous an enterprise.'[1] (As indeed it did, in 1866 as well as in 1936.) Between May and October of 1851 there were over six million visitors, not far short of a figure equivalent to the total population of England at that time. After the exhibition the halls and galleries were purchased by the Crystal Palace Company and re-erected on a permanent site specially created on the crest of Sydenham Hill. To the engineers of the Baird company, the particular attractions of the complex were the two water towers, originally constructed by Isambard Kingdom Brunel.[1] These towers, each 275 feet high, commanded a view over seven counties, and were ideal installations from which to transmit by ultra-short waves.

Gaumont-British money ensured that the grand design of the facilities was unrivalled anywhere else in Europe. In addition to offices and laboratories, resources were available on the one site for the manufacture not only of receivers, but also of transmitters and related electronic equipment such as cathode-ray tubes, photocells, magnetrons, and microwave links. Significantly, there were also four fully-equipped television studios, the largest of which, 60 by 40 feet, could house lavish productions involving up to forty artists. Professional stage performers took part in what were still ostensibly experimental transmissions, while members of the Baird staff filled in as bit-actors in sketches with elaborate sets, or participated, for real, in boxing matches in a miniature ring. The high-definition, 180-line, pictures were beamed from aerials on the top of the South Tower, which was 680 feet above sea level.[2]

According to Margaret Baird, the company moved to the Crystal Palace in July 1933.[3] She had already returned to work herself, and had given two performances in Glasgow in March. Needless to say, Baird 'had not realized what a career as a concert pianist entailed and tried everything, even feigning illness', to prevent her going. Eventually he gave up but stipulated that she stay at the Central Hotel, then the most expensive in the city.[4]

Her introduction to their new home was as bleak as it was unexpected:

> I knew nothing about a new house until John said one day that he had bought a house, adding: 'I hope you will like it.'
>
> With nanny and Diana I went by taxi to Sydenham, which I saw for the first time as a wilderness of broad and empty streets among large and decaying houses. Before 1914 Sydenham had been a fashionable suburb where the wealthy had built Gothic or Georgian houses for themselves, but fashion had long since passed Sydenham by.
>
> The house which John had bought was Georgian, vast, with acres of bare floors and windows high out of reach. The old kitchen, with its pantry, maids' sitting-room, larder, and cellars, took my breath away. Weakly, I sat down on the steps. Nanny chose that moment to say, 'Of course, madam, if you live here I'll have to give notice: all my friends are in Hampstead.' Diana chose the next moment to cry.[5]

The house, with an eighty-foot frontage, had been built in about 1850. It comprised a hall, three reception rooms, sun room, conservatory, seven bed and dressing rooms, two bathrooms, and kitchen quarters. The whole area covered 2½ acres.[6]

The attraction to Baird of the rambling house at 3 Crescent Wood Road was more than just that it was close to the Crystal Palace. He was looking also for laboratory space. There was a coach house and stable, with a coachman's

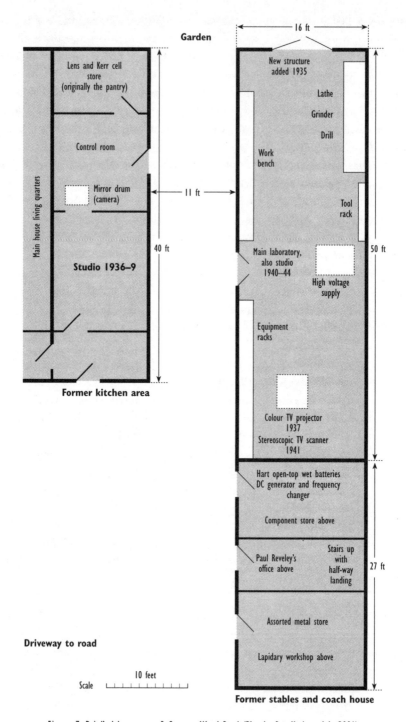

Figure 7: Baird's laboratory at 3 Crescent Wood Road (Plan by Ray Herbert, July 2001)

flat above. These, with what had been the maids' sitting-room and the larder, together with an enclosed working area of a thousand square feet (constructed in 1935), became his place of work.[7]

The chain of circumstances which led to Baird's change of status within the company would seem to have begun with a meeting between Greer and Church on 6 April, which Church followed up with a forthright letter to Greer about the position of the company. It is also a devastating critique of the role of Baird himself in the company's affairs.

In Church's opinion, Baird's concentration on his mechanical system had resulted in only two patents now being of value to the company: the original flying spot, used only at the transmission end of the process, and one dealing with synchronisation, employed at both ends of the process.[8] Church did not see, however, that there would be any revenue from these 'until thousands of television sets are being manufactured'.

> Our income must be obtained from the manufacture of sets for the Baird company, and the sale of these sets will depend upon (1) their entertainment value, and (2) their price. I am still of the opinion that the 30 line picture on which Baird has concentrated so much effort, has nothing except novelty value. For entertainment value we must produce pictures on at least 120 line basis, which, in the present stage of research, means that these must be transmitted by ultra short waves. I still feel too, that there is more immediate hope of transmitting 120 line picture by the cathode-ray system than by the mechanical system at present in use by Baird, owing to the difficulties of synchronising a heavy mirror drum, and the difficulty of getting the mirrors optically perfect.
>
> Baird has allowed over fifteen months to elapse since I first emphasised the need for developing the cathode-ray system (on which there are practically no patents), side by side with the mechanical system. Only after repeated attempts on my part, has he set up cathode-ray tubes in the laboratory; and the pictures he obtained he demonstrated to Professor Appleton yesterday, when Professor Appleton, having regard to the progress made by HMV said to Baird quite frankly that he thought he had 'missed the bus'! – adding that Baird should have gone ahead with cathode-ray work when he and I first reported on its possibilities in December 1931.
>
> I do not feel hopeless about the position, or even pessimistic, provided we can get a real move on, and bring to bear upon our problem some of the best brains in the radio technical field.[9]

He went on to insist that the board must have 'definite information as to the aims of the researches which Baird proposes to carry out'. There must be a research programme and the board must be told about the progress of each item. There should be a 'livelier liaison' with Fernseh with regard to technical development. Contact should be maintained, as far as was possible taking secrecy into account, with the research establishment under the Post Office at Dollis Hill, London, with His Majesty's Signals Department at Portsmouth, with the Radio Research Station at Slough, with the National Physical Laboratory, and with the Royal Aircraft Establishment at Farnborough.[9]

> But to take advantage of the work which is being carried out in allied fields, we must be sure of the quality of our research and technical staff. Some of our men have left us in the last two years, and taken service with rival concerns here and in America. I am not in a position to appraise the merits of those who are left, but I do feel that they lack purpose and direction. In fact, they are always being 'messed about', first for one stunt and then for another. There has been much improvement since you came on the board, but I am convinced there is room for much more. ...
>
> Above all, we must get a move on. We cannot afford to go on in the old way, stunting, making optimistic statements in the press, attacking everything that is being done by other companies, and wasting money on activities of this kind. We should not have to chase the press: the press ought to be chasing us, and their enthusiasm kindled by our reticence to talk of achievements until they were achievements, and not merely pious hopes! If you think it worth while, I should be prepared to put in far more time, and particularly as regards liaison work [and] in the formulation of a research programme in consultation with Mr Baird and my co-directors at Fernseh.[9]

The first intimation outside the company of what was going on at board level came in Bishop's memorandum to Reith of 30 May 1933, to which reference has already been made:[10]

> After my meeting this morning [26 May] with Mr Baird, I gleaned the following information which may be of interest:
> The Ostrers having obtained control of the Baird Co., Sidney Moseley has severed his connection with the Company, and apparently the important work is done by Sir Harry Greer and Mr Clayton. It is

the intention of the Ostrers to keep Baird himself very much in the background, and confine him to technical research work. They are proposing to strengthen their technical side by taking on A D G West, who is at present employed by a film company in Ealing.[11]

The full reasons for Moseley's resignation have never been established. Baird's version of the affair has, as usual, elements of drama and romance:

> It was not long before trouble began to blow up between Sir Harry and Sydney. This came to a head over our negotiations with the Marconi Company. Before Sir Harry came on the Board we had commenced negotiations with the Marconi Company for a merger. These negotiations had reached an advanced stage and if this merger had been completed it would have been, in my opinion, greatly to our advantage. The Marconi people were very keen and little but drawing up of the agreement remained to be done; they had shown us through their research laboratories, there had been successions of meetings and dinings and winings and with Sydney in the forefront, it looked as though it would go through. Sir Harry's first action was to attempt to freeze Moseley out of the negotiations; Moseley retaliated by a stiff note to Sir Harry and non attendance at the next board meeting. Then Sir Harry buttonholed me and said that either Moseley would resign or he would and asked me to convey that message to Moseley. I told Moseley, and in high dudgeon he went to Ostrer to get him 'to kick the old fool out'.
>
> He was astounded by Isidore Ostrer's reception. Isidore said that he thought Moseley would be more useful to the Company off the board than on it. The thing ended by Moseley going off, with very adequate compensation from Isidore Ostrer, and Sir Harry being left in control. Then the fun started for me. I had been giving full support to Moseley and this had completely antagonised the rest of the board. With Moseley gone they turned on me. Daniel in the Lion's Den was a poor show compared to Baird in the Baird board room. The first thing the boys did was to smash up the Marconi negotiations, and then they turned on me. Everything I did and had done was faulty.[12]

Moseley, writing nearly twenty years later with the benefit of the documentation which it was his custom to keep or copy for his personal diaries, gives a different slant to the episode:

Here I must part company with Baird. It is true that we had begun negotiations with the Marconi Company for a merger before Sir Harry Greer joined the Board, and equally true that I was heartily in favour of such a merger. But Baird was, I feel sure, mistaken in supposing that we had reached anything approaching a final agreement. ... When he wrote that the Marconi Company was 'very keen' and that 'little remained to be done except to draw up the agreement', the wish must have been father to the thought. ...

The new Board was fast losing patience with Baird and his dilatory methods. Baird the visionary was still occupied in development, whereas the practical men of the Board wanted results. They wished to sell receivers, whereas Baird was still reaching out. This difference in conception led to hostility which developed and reached a climax, and I decided that my usefulness to British television was at an end. ...

Still, after discussion with John, and at his insistence, I agreed to have lunch with Ostrer and talk things over with him. ... However disappointed I might be personally at the turn which things had taken in the Board room, I owed it to both Ostrer and Baird to stick to my post. But there had to be a choice between 'the Baird faction' and the newcomers. What then was my astonishment, my relief and my amusement (I experienced all three emotions at this fateful meeting) to hear my friend Ostrer remark that, after all, he believed I could wield more influence *off* the Board than on it![13]

Nothing has been found in the records of either the Baird or the Marconi company to support the view that a merger had even been discussed. There is only a Marconi board company minute to the effect that, in the light of press reports that the Baird company was applying for an injunction for breach of patent rights, conversations had taken place between Baird himself and the Marconi management with a view to the exchange of rights.[14]

Moseley himself, in his biography of Baird, gives as the reason for his resignation:

I felt certain that if I left at this juncture it would clear the way for a fresh beginning between the Baird Company and the BBC. The Board seemed to sense this, too. They had the impression that if they were able to go to the BBC and say that the firebrand Moseley had taken his departure they could begin a fresh, innocent friendship where they could receive fair play from the BBC.[15]

In its particular context, this has been accepted as a reasonable explanation, for Moseley's tactics had certainly not endeared him either to Reith or to Ashbridge. He was, however, a personal friend of Murray, who, it appears, when the issue of EMI's experimental transmissions first surfaced in December 1932, was leaking information privately to Moseley about the BBC's attitude, and advising him on how to deal with Ashbridge: 'I think you should arrange without delay to put a set into Ashbridge's house: he probably has heard I have one, and this would anger him. So, if there is not another available, I suggest moving mine to his place early next week.'[16] In any case, the campaign to bring round the two BBC principals most important to the company's cause, Reith and Ashbridge, had been and was being waged by Baird, and even he was shortly to be removed from the firing line.

In the light of Church's report to Greer,[9] and Bishop's memorandum to Reith,[11] a different scenario emerges. Moseley almost certainly would have seen, and was intended to see, a copy of the former, as indeed would Baird have done. Moseley's reference to the new board 'fast losing patience with Baird and his dilatory methods'[17] reflects precisely Church's revelation about the pace at which Baird had implemented the development of the use of cathode-ray tubes and of ultra-short-wave transmission. And according to Bishop, it was the intention of the Ostrers 'to keep Baird himself very much in the background, and confine him to technical research work'.[11]

It does not require much stretch of imagination to envisage Greer, armed with Church's report, consulting Isidore Ostrer about the situation with regard to Baird's position with the company. Whether it was on Greer's or Church's initiative that Baird was relieved of his management responsibilities, removed from the task of directing research into and development of the company's basic techniques and products, and banished to his private laboratory, it was all clearly done with the firm backing of Ostrer. It cannot be mere coincidence that Baird, now ostensibly free to develop his own lines of research, should decide to concentrate from the outset on large-screen cinema television. Through Gaumont-British he had the outlets, and also, if he required, the availability of cinema films. It may even have been at Ostrer's instigation that he chose this course.

It is easy to see how Moseley might have reacted to his friend and closest business associate being sidelined by the board of the company that Baird himself had founded, at a critical point in its affairs. And being Moseley, he would have resigned on the spot, and then gone to see Ostrer to complain. As we have seen, whatever the nature of their discussion, he got no change out of Ostrer, because Ostrer was behind the measure.

The terms of the deal between the company and Baird were probably negotiated by Church, who was Baird's friend.[18] Baird would operate entirely independently of the company, with his own private laboratory, and with technical staff supplied by the company, one in 1933 rising to six in 1936.[19] He was also able to call on company services, such as workshop facilities, stores, and the assistance of the various research departments,[20] though it would appear that he preferred largely to be self-sufficient.[7] And it was under these conditions that he conducted his successful experiments in cinema television, and also laid the foundations of his research into colour television, stereoscopic television, and ultimately stereoscopic television in colour. It was probably Baird's vanity that caused him to insist on his retaining the title of managing director, and Church's personal loyalty to him that was responsible for this being granted. It was an anomaly which the company could well have done without.

No personal link has been established between Gaumont-British and A D G West, then working for Associated Talking Pictures at their Ealing Studios. He may have come to the notice of Michael Balcon, since 1931 head of production of his own film company, Gainsborough Pictures, and also of Gaumont-British. Suffice to say, he was appointed technical director of the Baird company at the instigation of the Ostrer brothers. West had a distinguished academic record, and had specialised in acoustics and in radio transmission while working for the BBC and EMI. Effectively, his job was both to manage the staff and to be ultimately responsible for research and development, in place of Baird. Though he was never managing director, he appears to have used that title when it suited him; indeed, the twenty-one-year-old Gilbert Tomes, who joined the staff of the company in 1935 as a junior in the cathode-ray research department, thought West was managing director but 'sometimes called himself technical director'.[21] Perhaps understandably, West and Jacomb, who had been the senior technical presence in the firm since 1928, did not hit it off together,[22] and Jacomb left.

A list of the staff at this time compiled from memory by Paul Reveley suggests that the total number was about thirty-five,[23] of whom Bridgewater and Campbell were shortly to be transferred to the BBC. The fact that four years later the number had risen to 382[19] attests certainly to the resources made available through Gaumont-British, and also to the direction that the company's activities had been given in the meantime.

Of the others whose names have already appeared in this account, Caffrey was transferred to the Haymarket office,[24] leaving Baird without a secretary, and Banks, Boulding, Clapp, Percy, Richards, Taynton, and Vince were among those who went to work at the Crystal Palace. Reveley, who had operated the mirror-drum equipment at the Metropole for the 1932 Derby transmission and had subsequently demonstrated the single-screen version in Derby and in Denmark, was, to his immense pride, appointed Baird's single technical assistant at Crescent Wood Road.[7] J C Wilson, in his capacity as head of the patents department, managed to establish a discrete office in central London for himself and his assistants. He came to Crescent Wood Road primarily to discuss patent matters with Baird, with whom on these occasions he would spend many hours alone, a reflection also of the bond of affection and respect between the two men.[25] Though the Baird and the West families became friendly, and visited each other's houses, West himself in his official capacity never visited the Crescent Wood Road laboratory.[26]

In addition to West, the company appointed as a full-time director Jarrard, its former head of operations in New York. Baird, in his memoir, gives the impression that Jarrard had been dismissed from that post by himself and Moseley.[27] There is a record of a cable from Moseley in New York to the board, sent on 30 November 1931 at the height of the confused American negotiations: 'Accept Jarrard and [West] resignation if tendered. American company in any case will not require them.'[28] From the company letter heading, it would appear that Jarrard had a science degree and was an associate of the Royal College of Science.

★

On the domestic front, Margaret did what she could to make the house into a home:

> The dining-room and the drawing-room opened into each other and measured sixty feet from end to end. The heating system required a man in the cellar all day, feeding coal into the furnace with a long-handled shovel. We never really warmed the house in winter.
>
> I bought acres of Wilton carpeting and haunted auctions buying the largest pieces of furniture I could to fill the rooms. The final effect combined Jacobean and Chinese. We had a magnificent sideboard and table of dark oak, Chinese carpets and rugs, the decoration completed by Chinese bowls and vases then fashionable.
>
> The grounds covered three acres and contained four enormous beech trees, which John named Bach, Beethoven, Brahms, and Baird. He had the rose garden dug up and sweeping lawns laid out, probably because the garden of 'The Lodge' at Helensburgh was mainly grass.[29]

Nanny, as she had threatened, could not stand Sydenham after Hampstead, and left. Diana records:

Her place was soon taken by a young girl, Nursie Basham, with whom I quickly established a satisfactory modus vivendi. There was a sandpit in the garden – rather muddy because it was under trees – and playing in that and with the pools that collected in the roots of the four great beech trees, or going for walks past rhododendron 'houses' – nothing grew under them – through the woods to the stile leading to Dulwich Common (I think we always turned back at the stile) provided plenty of entertainment. My mother used to read bedtime stories and help me collect series of cigarette cards and make scrapbooks, and JLB was also on the premises – I remember him saying, 'Take that child away,' when I was having a temper tantrum at about age two.[30]

Other staff included two maids, Molly and Barbara, who were sisters.

When Reveley first arrived at Crescent Wood Road, his only colleague was George Day, the gardener–handyman. Anything which could be done with hand tools on the site, they did between them. JLB worked mainly from his bedroom, where he used the telephone to order standard components and materials direct from their suppliers, and to keep in touch with his numerous technical and business contacts. Items which required making under machine-shop conditions were produced by B J Lynes, who ran the prototype and model-making business which had made the scanning equipment, to J C Wilson's design, for the first BBC television broadcasts. Non-mechanical construction work was done by a local building contractor. Small fittings were obtained from local hardware stores. All invoices for goods and services went direct to Baird, who signed them and then passed them to the company's accounts department for payment.[7]

The basis of television is progressive line-by-line scanning which depends on the persistence of human vision to provide an illusion of continuity. Any development to apparatus must respect the characteristics of the human eye. Baird's immediate objective was to improve the quality of the illusion which he had achieved at the Metropole. 'Inspired by his repeated exhortation, "Results, Mr Reveley, not reports," we proceeded with a conforming pro-gramme to construct a complete hardware system of greater capability.'[7]

As was his practice, Baird aspired to what he believed was possible.

He aimed to increase line scan rate from 375 to 2000 per second and frame frequency from 12.5 to 100 per second, to change the aspect ratio to five and one half high to four wide, to retain vertical scanning, and to interlace frames of 20 evenly spaced lines each sixfold to comprise 120 lines in all, at a picture repetition rate of 16.67 per second. These advances implied increasing mirror drum speed from 750 to 6000 rpm and driving with 100 cycle synchronous motors.[7]

Running his personal laboratory with only one technical assistant did not change Baird's ways. He would wander in and ask, 'Have you anything to show me, Mr Reveley?' The general directive was his, the detailed working out of the means he left to others. To be fair, Reveley revelled in this method of working. Baird's failing, however, was an inability to see the need for detailed work preparatory to putting a project in motion. He would ring up a supplier: 'Oh, Mr Lynes, we need a water-cooled box for a motor that is getting a little hot, say about X by Y by Z inches. Could you make one, please?' Reveley then had to make do with whatever the supplier had thought might be suitable, which often it was not, because the implications had not been worked out on paper beforehand.[31]

Writing during World War II to Moseley in the USA, Baird commented, 'The war is making things very difficult, but is less harassing than the wars that used to rage between me and the old B[aird] T[elevision] L[td] board!'[32] Whatever he thought about board meetings, however, he assiduously attended them, and equally assiduously respected the confidentiality of boardroom discussions, though he was not averse to passing wry comments on some of his colleagues.[33] It is not clear whether the reference in his memoir to the board's attitude, 'Everything I did and had done was faulty,'[12] relates to the period before or after he was relieved of management duties in June 1933. Certainly there was a breakdown of confidence the following October, when the board took him to task for withholding from its members certain information about the company's relations with the BBC. It would seem that this referred to the meeting on 27 January 1933 between Baird, Moseley, Murray, and Ashbridge to discuss EMI's ultra-short-wave transmissions, of which Baird was sent the BBC's report on 15 February,[34] and to correspondence relating to the meeting and the report.

Baird's response, which appears to have been dictated over the telephone, had about it an air of aggrieved innocence:

> While a Director of this Company Mr Moseley acted as Liaison Officer with the BBC. All correspondence from the BBC I placed before Mr Moseley and disposed of as directed by him.
>
> The letter of 31 January last and the notes on the Meeting were shown to Mr Moseley who composed the reply.
>
> With regard to not placing these matters before the Board, I had been in the custom of handing all such matters to Mr Moseley for

attention, and did not concern myself in regard to whether any matter was of sufficient importance to be reported to the Board. I realise that the letter and Meeting in question were of such importance that they should have been reported, and consider that Mr Moseley's action in with-holding the information was deliberate, as he did not want to cause complications in the minds of the Board, who at that time were endeavouring to raise new finance.[35]

The meeting and correspondence have been discussed in chapter 11.[36] Moseley could hardly himself have reported in full on that meeting, since for half of it he was excluded. All the correspondence with the BBC about and arising from the meeting was written by Baird; Moseley would have been unable to comment on the technical aspects of the exchange. The truth is more likely to lie in the fact that Baird was an individualist whose nature was in any case to play things close to his chest. If he thought about the matter at all, he probably concluded that the board, as it was constituted at that time, was incapable of making an informed judgment on the issue of ultra-short-wave transmission.

★

In August 1933, Baird had visited Berlin, where he found

> Nazis everywhere, Nazi officials on guard and every stall in the Radio Exhibition, swarms of them in the streets, Heil Hitler resounding on every side. Hitler was no longer to be seen at the Kaiserhof: he was in the Chancellery. The former Chancellor of Germany, Brüning had fled for his life and the old regime had vanished completely. A grim reign of terror had taken its place. The yearly visit to Berlin had in past years been a delightful period, with charming happy friendly people and hotels with every comfort and smiling waiters anxious to please. This had suddenly vanished; no smiles remained. The people had become grim and hostile, not openly so, but in a way it was obvious. Those who were friendly and who disliked the Nazi regime (and they were many) were terrified. The streets were filled with marching men, saluting and 'Heil Hitlering'. It got so much on my nerves that I took the first train I could back to London and heaved a sigh of relief as we steamed out of the Frederic Strasse Station.[37]

For Baird, it was the end of an era in more ways than one.

13
The Baird Company
1933-1939

The first recorded meeting between West, in his new capacity as technical director of the Baird company, and Ashbridge took place on 13 July 1933 at the BBC. The two had worked together from 1926 to 1929 as assistant chief engineers to Eckersley. Ashbridge, born in 1889, was the elder by eight years. Both served in World War I as wireless officers. Against Ashbridge's degree in engineering at King's College, London, and training with two engineering firms,[1] West had a first-class honours degree with distinction in mathematics at Cambridge, as well as a BSc degree at London University with first-class honours in mathematics, and had been a research student at the Cavendish Laboratory in Cambridge under the supervision of Sir Ernest Rutherford and Appleton. He had joined the BBC three years before Ashbridge, and in addition to being an assistant chief engineer, was also designated chief research engineer.[2]

Eckersley left the BBC in May 1929, and was succeeded by Ashbridge. That same month, West resigned from the BBC, and joined the Gramophone Company (HMV). It is impossible not to speculate whether West's resignation was connected in any way with Ashbridge's appointment as chief engineer.

There are two accounts of the meeting. Ashbridge dictated one immediately afterwards, for internal circulation:

> [West] told me that he had been appointed a technical member of the board of the Baird company, and that he was in effect Technical Director, having been put in by the Ostrer brothers, who virtually own the Baird company. He added that Moseley was out of the concern altogether, and that Baird was in the process of going out, but would probably be retained in a kind of secondary capacity for detail research. He said that the past was to be wiped out entirely, and he fully realised that the conduct of the company and its relations with the BBC in the past had been appalling.

He mentioned that the board did not know anything about the letter which we wrote warning them of the danger of placing receiving sets on the market for 30 line television, having regard to the obsolescence of the latter,[3] and that had they known this they would not have gone ahead through the Bush Company with the production of expensive receivers. They had made £5,000 worth of such receivers, which would probably be wasted. He agreed that there was no future for 30 line television, but said that they would like somehow or other to try to sell the 100 receivers which they had made, with some arrangement by which they were changed for ultra-short 'multi-line' receivers when that system replaced the 30 line transmissions on ordinary wavelengths. I expressed the opinion that this was not an altogether satisfactory arrangement, seeing that we did not at present know when, if ever, regular programmes would be transmitted on ultra-short waves. ...

He said that they were working from the Crystal Palace, and had a research licence for various short wavelengths for that purpose, and that we could co-operate with them there if we liked. This was all a little vague. ...

I gave my views in general on the subject of television, and said that ultimately the commercial possibilities would only be in connection with the sale of receivers. ...

There is no doubt that the Baird company has received a fresh fillip, and is in entirely new hands from a technical point of view. Whether, however, this will lead to anything tangible or not is impossible to say.[4]

West's report, done at Ashbridge's request and sent to the BBC on 17 July, put a slightly different slant to certain aspects of the matter:

Mr West said that he had come to see Mr Ashbridge to tell him that the Baird company had recently had a complete change of management and that it was the intention of the company in future to place before the BBC complete information as to their immediate and future plans in their television development work. The Baird company was now putting in hand a very definite programme of experimental work, with a view to bringing television out of its somewhat vague and indefinite technical situation into a commercial reality. ...

Mr West then referred to the position with regard to 30-line transmission and reception. Owing to the fact that no member of the present management had heard of the request of the BBC to the Baird company to change from a 30-line to some better form of transmission, in January last, until the request was revealed to Sir Harry Greer and Mr Clayton in an interview with Sir John Reith early in June [Ashbridge wrote in the margin at this point, 'Baird had'], the Baird company had as a gesture to the BBC put on the market a complete 30-line mirror drum 'Televisor' set [Ashbridge's handwritten note in the margin, 'He hasn't got this right at all']. ...

The Baird company propose putting in hand immediately designs for television receivers of the most modern type, which will be manufactured in quantity production by Bush Radio Limited.[5]

Ashbridge sent to Carpendale what he referred to as 'West's idea of the meeting', adding, 'I am afraid that [his] version is a very inaccurate account of what actually transpired, but I do not think that we need take this as being intentional.' Carpendale wrote his own comments on the accompanying memorandum:[6]

Thankyou. I don't know what are his implications re his 5000£ for 30 line receivers – he tries to throw blame on to us which is akin to the old crafty policy of Bairds with which I understand the new management dissociated itself –

Also re mass production of new receivers ... he must be definitely choked off this – or we shall again be blamed.

This tripartite exchange epitomises the failure of confidence on both sides, the lack of any consistent and comprehensive policy within the BBC, almost certainly the result of an absence of direction from the top, and the continuing confusion within the Baird company about commercial prospects and research and development policies. If West really said that the company's conduct in regard to its relations with the BBC had been 'appalling', this is demonstrably untrue. Though Moseley's adversarial tactics had at times been infuriating, even the BBC, in its official letter to him when he left the company, admitted that there may have been some justification: 'The Corporation has heard with regret of your resignation from the Board of Baird Television Ltd. Although there has not always been agreement either in policy or method, it should be recognised that your consistently active advocacy has been an important, perhaps even the decisive factor in the progress that Baird Television has made to date.'[7]

As for Ashbridge, it would appear now that he was prepared to admit that the BBC 'did not at present know when, *if ever*, regular programmes would be transmitted on ultra-short waves' (our italics), when five months earlier he had declined to respond at all to Baird's challenge: 'Are you prepared to stake your reputation that ultra-short waves *is* definitely the solution to perfect television?'[8] At that time, Baird had really no alternative to pursuing the only policy which would bring some earnings to the company for whose finances he was ultimately responsible, in the form of sales of thirty-line receivers. The missing, suppressed, or subsequently overlooked letter which was the cause of so much agitation, and to which Baird had replied,[8] was certainly not a request 'to change from a 30-line to some better form of transmission', merely an enquiry as to Baird's thoughts on the wisdom of 'selling numbers of receivers to the public for television reception by a method which was already obsolescent'.[3]

The truth of the matter seems to be that the BBC wanted to reduce the number of television broadcasts, if not dispense with them altogether, and West's admission about the future of thirty-line transmission played into Ashbridge's hands. Indeed, the writer of an unsigned memorandum asserted, 'Ashbridge openly boasts that he has West "in his pocket".'[9] Yet to someone of West's technical and intellectual understanding, with the experience of his research trip to the USA two years before, it was perfectly natural that he should in effect agree that sooner or later thirty lines would give way to higher definition on ultra-short waves, and he was quite right.

It is impossible, however, not to conclude also that the prospects of the Baird organisation had been adversely affected not only by uninformed overall direction on the part of the board, but also by the fact that, as first in the field in Britain, the company had no bench-mark against which to measure its aspirations.

The position with regard to the installation at the BBC of 120-line transmission was discussed at the meeting between West and Ashbridge, but not fully resolved. The apparatus, which Baird himself had developed, was demonstrated at the British Association annual meeting in Leicester on 12 September 1933, transmitting films at twenty-five frames per second to a cathode-ray receiver.[10] Subsequently, experimental transmissions were undertaken from the Crystal Palace on ultra-short waves of between 6 and 6.25 metres.[11] Permission had had to be obtained from the GPO to transfer the experimental stations from Long Acre and Kingsbury. The GPO, mindful of the fuss made by the BBC over the previous application,[12] invited the BBC to comment. Ashbridge dictated a letter for Reith to sign (21 July):

> We have no objection to the transfer of the experimental stations ... to the Crystal Palace, provided that it is definitely understood that only

research will be carried out, and that no series of programmes will be sent out which could be taken by listeners as being regular transmissions intended for public reception.[13]

The BBC was still strenuously, but blindly, maintaining its monopoly of public broadcasting, without having much idea as to where television was destined to go.

What could have been an ongoing awkwardness in the relations between the BBC and EMI was unexpectedly resolved on 8 August. Reith confided to his diary:

> Alfred Clark to see me about television of course. To my surprise he said that they would be quite content to let the Baird people come in first and have a run for some months. No doubt he thinks if they are in second there will be no definite date for getting them out.[14]

West and Ashbridge met on 1 September to discuss the conditions under which the experimental transmissions would take place, which were confirmed in writing.[15] The Baird company had no difficulty with these, but offered two further conditions. Any 'rival firm or firms who are allowed to make tests of a similar nature' should do so under precisely the same conditions, including the removal of their apparatus at the end of the period which had been assigned to them. At the end of all such tests, the Baird company should be given a further opportunity to demonstrate what it could do, in the light of any further developments that had been achieved in the meantime.[16] Carpendale replied, very reasonably, that the first point was understood, but that the BBC could not bind itself 'indefinitely' to it. All improvements incorporated into apparatus since the actual test would be taken into account in the final analysis, but he did not think it would be necessary to re-install each system. He ended on a note of understandable weariness:

> The accommodation at Broadcasting House has been ready for some time and we shall be glad to know when you propose to begin the work of installing.[17]

On 27 September the Baird company issued a statement to the effect that 120-line experimental broadcasts would be transmitted from the BBC for three months from 1 October. In the meantime the BBC would continue to broadcast programmes on the Baird thirty-line apparatus. 'A decision has not been reached regarding the continuance of such broadcasts subsequent to

31st March 1934 until such time as a regular programme service of high definition pictures can be guaranteed for lookers-in throughout the country.'[13] The BBC duly responded with a press release of its own (12 October 1933), confirming that the Baird company and then EMI would each carry out experiments through the BBC's ultra-short-wave transmitter, and that other companies might then be given the same opportunity. 'The present thirty-line transmissions will be continued until … March 31 1934. No decision in regard to a further series … has yet been made.'[13]

The BBC was now having to give serious thought to the future of television. This is attested by a confidential memorandum written by Bishop, in Ashbridge's absence. It was occasioned by a letter from the television firm of Scophony. Scophony Ltd had been founded in 1930 by Solomon Sagall, a Hungarian-born economist who had the previous year snapped up the British rights in Mihaly's system, after reading about it in the London *Observer*.[18] Now, it would appear, the company was enquiring what was the BBC's long-term thinking, if not also its policy, on television.

Bishop pointed out that while there was not enough technical data available on which to base a published policy, it could fairly confidently be stated that the future lay in 'high definition work'. Though Scophony apparently agreed with this, the company was still working on a thirty-line receiver, as were other firms. Though the Baird company was bound by an agreement to put a notice in all its receivers that transmissions were about to be discontinued, there was no obligation on Scophony and the others to do so. Should not a firm line be taken on this immediately?[19]

High-definition transmission was at present limited to film, though the Baird company was on the verge of being able to transmit studio scenes. At what point would the system become practicable for reception by the public, and how would the BBC provide permanent facilities on ultra-short waves, bearing in mind that with the present transmitter the range was limited to five to ten miles, not more? It might be expedient to continue the thirty-line transmissions for a short period after March 1934. 'I see no objection to maintaining public interest in television, but I submit that if we are not careful we shall be maintaining it under false pretences.'[19]

Scophony's concern was echoed by other British manufacturers of television receivers and components. In August the BBC had conducted a census of viewers, who were asked to send in postcards with comments. The manufacturers saw this as a move to stop the transmissions altogether. Whether they were right or wrong, and they may have been right, they made a statement collectively recording their 'deep resentment' at the possibility, and deplored the census at this time of the year as being 'of very doubtful value, if not definitely misleading'.[20]

On 22 September Goldsmith wrote to the Baird company giving notice of the termination of the agreement on 31 March 1934, as the BBC was entitled to do, but offering a lifeline: 'Any other arrangements at which we may arrive with your company would be the subject of a fresh agreement.'[13] The Baird company asked for a meeting to discuss the future of thirty-line television. It took place on 30 October. The company was represented by Greer, Church, Baird, and West, about as strong and knowledgeable a line-up as could be imagined. The BBC's team was Whitley, chairman of the board of governors, Carpendale, and Ashbridge. One might have expected Reith himself in place of either Whitley or Carpendale, but he presumably preferred to keep aloof from the proceedings, though he reported on the meeting to the Postmaster General.[21]

After a further meeting on 4 December, a press statement was issued to the effect that if high-definition television was not sufficiently developed by 31 March 1934 to justify regular transmissions by any of the systems that had been tested, thirty-line transmissions would be continued, probably twice a week, but 'with no guaranteed duration', to 'assist those members of the public who are experimenting with television'.[13]

In the event, this is what happened. In April 1934, programmes were reduced to two a week, on Tuesday and Friday at 11pm. Six months later, there was a change to Saturday (4.30pm to 5.15pm) and Wednesday (11pm to 11.45pm), with the extra fifteen minutes being a 'continuing bonus'. In 1935, the Saturday programme was moved to Monday at 11.15pm.[22]

In the meantime, however, the Baird company's experimental transmissions had run into trouble. On 19 October, West was still not ready to go ahead, but hoped to do so within a few days. Percy would be in charge of the transmission on the eighth floor of Broadcasting House, assisted by two maintenance engineers. Banks and a technician called Howarth would observe the results at a receiving station set up at the nearby Regent Street Polytechnic. West and Baird himself would make daily visits to the installation.[23]

The tests began in late October, but there were further delays in implementing what should have been the Baird company's *pièce de résistance*, the transmission of studio shots. The problem seems to have had more to do with the facilities than the apparatus. In order to send studio scenes with both sound and vision, a second wireless transmitter was required for the speech. The Baird system employed this sound channel also to send the synchronising signal. It was early December before suitable equipment was available to be installed in the new BBC television studios at 16 Portland Place, an elegant Georgian house that had recently been acquired. Because of the delay, the BBC offered the company an extension of three weeks, to 20 January 1934. Until then there was no need to remove the 120-line and 180-line spotlight transmission equipment for the televising of studio scenes that it was proposed to install in 16 Portland Place. The apparatus on the eighth floor of Broadcasting House could also remain in place, and the ultra-short-wave wireless transmitter would be available for further experiments until the new deadline.[24]

At this point, the Baird company not only refused to install any apparatus in 16 Portland Place, but immediately set about dismantling the equipment in Broadcasting House without, according to the BBC, ever having officially demonstrated its capabilities.[25]

There were the usual recriminations and counter-recriminations, largely conducted between Greer and Carpendale.[13] In the meantime, a situation evolved which on the face of it was even more extraordinary. After Ashbridge had on 12 January 1934 seen an impressive demonstration by EMI of the transmission of films on 150 lines, using their own ultra-short-wave transmitter, Shoenberg told him that his company did not wish after all to install its apparatus in Broadcasting House. Instead, he proposed that the BBC should conduct experiments with a wireless transmitter of a higher power, which EMI would provide, together with the equipment for transmitting films. He added that EMI was spending a large part of its £100,000 a year research budget on television.[26]

Ashbridge began to see light at the end of the tunnel. He realised that the BBC would need separate premises for television, with facilities for transmitting on short waves at higher powers than could be managed from Broadcasting House. Either he did not know about the Baird/Fernseh intermediate-film technique, to which EMI would not have access, or he preferred to ignore it. He dreamed of programmes entirely consisting of cinematograph films and of newsreels such as were produced for the news theatres. He foresaw the BBC establishing a chain of transmitting stations, first in London, and then in cities throughout the rest of Britain. The small matter of finance still needed to be considered, however, especially as there might be some opposition from the film companies.[27]

The hand, and commercial potential, of EMI were at this crucial point considerably strengthened by an alliance with Marconi. The establishment of a separate company, Marconi–EMI, specifically to develop television systems, was not formally announced until 22 May 1934,[28] but had been known to the BBC in March.[29] It gave Shoenberg, a shrewd operator as well as an outstanding scientist, not only the Marconi expertise in wireless transmission, but also access to a wide range of patents relating to television.

The Baird company was now further isolated. According to Baird himself, there was at some point an attempt to form an alliance between the Baird company and the General Electric Company (GEC) which was vetoed by Ostrer.[30] Whether or not this is so, the two companies did in 1933 make a two-year arrangement for the supply by GEC of cathode-ray tubes, which ran into difficulties towards the end of the period.[31]

In contrast to EMI, which preferred to develop techniques in secret and demonstrate them in private, the Baird company was still bent on pursuing its policy of ostentation. At the beginning of March, Greer tried to pin Reith down on the phone to choose a date on which to see a demonstration of the company's latest developments in high-definition television. Reith simply referred him to Carpendale. On 7 March Greer wrote one letter to the BBC, inviting the board of governors to the demonstration, on 12 March at 12 noon, and another personally to Reith:

> The actual time of the demonstration has been fixed to suit the convenience of the Prime Minister, who informs me he will be present. I hope in view of the importance of the occasion you will accept my cordial invitation to be present. We shall not detain you long, as the programme we have arranged will not occupy more than half an hour.[13]

Reith replied:

> I am sorry I have engagements which make it quite impossible for me to come along on Monday, but I can assure you that my absence will not make any difference at all. We shall always be adequately represented at any demonstrations such as those to which you invite us.[32]

The demonstration comprised 180-line pictures of living subjects and on film, displayed by means of a cathode-ray tube manufactured by GEC and enlarged to about 12 by 18 inches by a water lens. The transmission from the Crystal Palace was on an ultra-short wavelength with a power of about 500 watts. The sound and picture-synchronising frequency were sent separately by land line. Ashbridge found the studio shots 'disappointing' and the film transmissions 'somewhat indifferent'. His conclusion, however, was fair: 'No opportunity has been available so far to compare a demonstration under absolutely strictly comparable conditions, moreover the EMI company have not so far attempted a demonstration with living objects.'[33]

If any irony was intended in Reith's reply to Greer, it was missed, for Greer issued a second invitation both to him and to Carpendale to attend a further demonstration, which was being given for members of parliament. Reith declined on behalf of them both, pleading that he had an 'engagement which I cannot very well alter', and in the case of Carpendale, 'I imagine it would be substantially the same [demonstration] as that which he saw recently'.[34]

The annual general meeting of the Baird company at Wardour Street on 20 March provided an opportunity for another stunt. As shareholders waited for Greer to arrive, he appeared on one of Baird's large screens to give his opening address, which was televised from one of the Crystal Palace studios. Then, while a car whisked Greer through the streets for a personal appearance, the shareholders and the press were treated to a programme of short films and a live variety performance. They are likely to have been less amused by the balance sheet, signed by Baird and Church, which the chairman presented. At 30 June, the effective funds of the company amounted to £39,700. During the previous year spending was £27,500. Of this amount, a miserable £13,600, compared with the resources available to EMI, had been spent on 'laboratory, experimental, publicity, and sales expenses'. Directors' fees had cost the company £2800, less £620 which had been waived. The managing director's and administrative salaries amounted to £6200, less £1241.13s.6d. which Baird had declined to accept. On this basis, without injection of further capital, the company could not survive much beyond the end of the year.[35]

The sum of £1000 in the accounts as 'remuneration of a director for special services' is likely to have been awarded to the indefatigable Church, who had, however, earlier in the year suffered a most humiliating experience. The occasion, on 7 February 1934, was an election for membership of the Athenaeum, the prestigious London club which since its foundation in 1824 had catered for 'individuals known for their literary or scientific attainments, artists of eminence in any class of the fine arts, noblemen and gentlemen distinguished as liberal patrons of science, literature, and the arts'. The result was unprecedented and totally unexpected. Reith wrote in his diary that night: 'Lunched at the Athenaeum for the purpose of black-balling a man whose sole qualification appeared to be that he was a Director of Baird Television. I was afraid, however, that he would get in as we had not organised anything.'[36]

The candidate was Church, who had been on the waiting list for membership of the club for over four years. He was proposed by Sir Richard Gregory, editor of *Nature*, and seconded by Sir Percy Nunn, the first director of the University of London Institute of Education. No less than twenty-five distinguished members of the club, from their personal knowledge of Church, signed his ballot form in support of his candidature. They included Lord Passfield, whom, as Sidney Webb, President of the Board of Trade, Church had served as parliamentary private secretary, Sir Ian McAlister, secretary of the Royal Institution of British Architects, Major-General Sir Frederick Maurice, principal of Queen Mary College, University of London, Professor Sir Frederick Keeble, botanist, Sir Edwin Deller, principal of the University of London, O J R Howarth, secretary of the British Association for the Advancement of Science, Sir Julian Huxley, zoologist, Sir Frank Smith, secretary of the Department of Scientific and Industrial Research, the Very Rev. John T Mitchell, residentiary canon, Liverpool Cathedral, Sir John Evelyn Shuckburgh, deputy under-secretary of state, Colonial Office, Professor Sir Charles Sherrington, Nobel prizewinner in medicine in 1932 and former president of the Royal Society, Professor H E Armstrong, the doyen of British chemistry, and Sir Philip Hartog, educationist and former member of the Indian Public Services Commission, and a pillar of the Liberal Jewish movement in Britain.[37]

Under club rules a candidate failed to be elected if ten per cent of the votes were blackballs. Out of 119 votes cast on this occasion, a massive thirty-four (over twenty-eight per cent) were blackballs.[38]

Church's proposer and seconder must have been mortified, his personal supporters stunned. While Church himself probably never knew the extent of his rejection, to fail at all must have been a severe blow to his self-esteem, to say nothing of the fact that he was now effectively banished from the club as the guest of a member, a privilege he would have enjoyed on many occasions. Even Reith, if he was aware of the figures, must have been agreeably surprised at the extent of Church's defeat, for he could not possibly himself have raised so much opposition during the course of a single lunch.

If the man had been generally disliked, that would have been a reason for his rejection, but the backing of his personal supporters and other sources suggest that this was not so.[39] One must therefore look to his directorship of the Baird company, which he cited as his main occupation, as the probable source of discontent. Part of the opposition almost certainly reflected the malign influence of the former member of the Athenaeum, Campbell Swinton, even though he had been dead now for four years. Other blackballs may have been cast by those who deprecated the company's aggressive marketing tactics and attempts to influence the political process.[40]

The apparent impasse in relations between the BBC, the Baird company, and EMI, which depended also on the GPO for any resolution, was partly broken by Reith, who wrote to the Postmaster General on 15 March 1934, proposing a conference 'between some of your people and some of ours to discuss the future arrangements for the handling of television'.[41] It took place at the GPO on 5 April, with Phillips, assistant secretary of the GPO, in the chair. The GPO was represented by Colonel Arthur S Angwin, assistant engineer-in-chief, and J W Wissenden, senior staff officer, and the BBC by Carpendale and Ashbridge.

The meeting discussed the relative standards reached by the Baird company and EMI, with a side glance at other systems, such as Cossor and Scophony. Angwin stressed the reluctance of EMI to demonstrate 'direct television, ie instantaneous transmission of the images of moving objects'. Ashbridge said that this was because the company regarded 'its present development as inadequate for commercial exploitation'. He added that EMI manufactured 'well constructed and workmanlike apparatus', whereas that made by the Baird company was 'distinctly amateurish in construction and finish'. Questioned by Angwin, he did, however, admit that Baird/GEC cathode-ray tubes were superior to those used by EMI. Ashbridge reported on EMI's proposal that the BBC should build a new television transmitting station from which to produce and send out programmes. There was discussion also about press statements that the Baird company intended to apply to the GPO for a licence to operate an independent television service. It was decided that a committee should be appointed at once to advise the Postmaster General on all questions appertaining to television, which would have sufficient authority to be a support to the GPO and the BBC in subsequent decisions which would need to be made.[42]

Reith later claimed that it was all his own idea that such a television committee should be established. 'Television – I suggested to Kingsley Wood that he should appoint a committee to recommend what system should be used, and how a service was to be financed; there might be representatives of Post Office and BBC with a manufacturer and one or two disinterested members. He liked the idea; acted on it at once.'[43] Reith was not happy, however, with the Postmaster General's choice of chairman, Lord Selsdon. As William Mitchell-Thompson, Selsdon had been Postmaster General from 1924 to 1929; Reith described him as a 'miserable cad'[44] and the 'most unfriendly PMG there had been'.[45]

The committee's vice-chairman was Sir John Cadman, public servant and former professor of mining engineering at Birmingham University, and now chairman of the Iraq Petroleum Company, and a director of the Suez Canal Company and the Great Western Railway.[46] The other members were Phillips, Angwin, Carpendale, Ashbridge, and O F Brown, representing the Department of Scientific and Industrial Research. The Secretary was J Varley

Roberts, a GPO staff officer. Reith, when he began to realise that perhaps it would not deliver what he wanted, called it a 'poor committee'.[47]

The constitution of the Television Committee was announced in the House of Commons on 14 May 1934, and it had its first meeting on 29 May. It was not a moment too soon. A month earlier, Church, having been refused a face-to-face meeting with the Postmaster General, had written him a long letter about the future of television in general, and the present and future position of the Baird company, with particular reference to the thirty-line and high-definition controversy. There was also the hint of a threat, of which the Postmaster General was fully aware:

> Your technical experts and those of the BBC have attended demon-strations of our latest results. You have seen them yourself, and with all respect we submit that you are in a position of judging whether our contention is correct that we are technically ready to provide a programme of 180-line television from our station at the Crystal Palace, to serve the whole of the Greater London area.[48]

The Crystal Palace station had since 1933 been operating a vision trans-mitter with a power of 500 watts. In December 1934, its effectiveness was vastly increased by the installation of a ten-kilowatt replacement, designed and built by a team of Baird technicians, which was the most powerful ultra-short-wave transmitter in existence. To avoid infringing a Marconi patent which related to the neutralisation of power amplifiers, the company used the constantly pumped, demountable tetrode valves made by Metropolitan Vickers, which did not need to be neutralised. The CH (chain, home) coastal radar stations which became operational in 1938 used identical valves in a similar circuit, and the Baird vision transmitter seems strongly to have influenced the design of this equipment.[49]

The Television Committee did its work thoroughly and with commend-able speed. Reith recorded in his diary: 'The Television Committee had their first meeting on Tuesday [29 May] and today they came here and saw the obsolescent 30 line system. I went into the Board room and had tea with them, and they all seemed pleased to see me.'[50]

For Robb, however, the occasion was traumatic:

> 30 May 1934. Warned at 10.30am demonstration to be arranged to Television Committee at 3.30 next aft. Memo [Goldsmith] to me handed personally. Protested at short notice and disorganization of plans. Gielgud took opposite view. Said nothing unethical. Friday's transmission billed

in the Radio Times didn't matter even if it did not take place. I maintained that had Carpendale and Ashbridge considered my work (which they have never done), the Committee could have accepted another day at a later date. Either Friday 1st or almost any day next week. Or could have postponed their visit for 1 hour to 1½ hours and seen the results of Thursday rehearsal at the run through. [Goldsmith] refused to listen to anything and took the attitude that it was insolence and futility on my part to question the request. ... I told Gielgud that I regarded this short notice as another instance of disregard of myself and that it was more than possible that this action was intentional in order to prejudice the success of the demonstration.[51]

The following day:

Demonstration took place. I was introduced to no one. [Goldsmith] seemed surprised that I was at the reception end. [Carpendale] did not recognise me. Sir John Cadman however introduced himself and appeared to take great interest. Somewhat diffidently I followed the party into the lift, though I was not asked to do so, in order to show [Carpendale] the way, as I knew he did not know our lay out. In fact he started to go down to No. 16 P[ortland] P[lace] basement. The programme was stopped in order to show the party the studio. Mr Baird, West, Jarrard were present. Also Ashbridge, Birkinshaw, Bishop. I was asked to explain something of methods of operation. I had just begun when I was interrupted and Baird was asked to do so. Subsequently I took Sir John Cadman into the Control Room and explained technicalities to him. He was not allowed to remain long however. The whole affair was rushed and distressing.[51]

All told the Television Committee interviewed thirty-eight witnesses, some of them several times. Among these were representatives of the television companies, Baird, Cossor, EMI and Marconi–EMI, Ferranti, GEC, Plew, and Scophony, the Newspaper Proprietors' Association, the Radio Manufacturers' Association, and the Television Society, and specialist journals. Baird was not invited to give evidence, nor did he offer to do so, nor did he appear on behalf of the Baird company, which was represented by Church and West. If anything, this illustrates the extent to which he was at this time isolated from the mainstream of his company's developmental research. The EMI companies were represented not only by Clark and Shoenberg, but also by G E Condliffe, manager of research, the television scientists A D Blumlein and C O Browne, and three other witnesses. The committee examined all the television systems being developed in the United Kingdom. A delegation went to the USA and also to Germany to investigate progress there in television research, and obtained information from other countries. The twenty-eight-page report was published on 14 January 1935, incorporating Appendix I, the list of individuals and organisations that gave evidence. The remaining appendices were withheld from publication for reasons of confidentiality; they comprised Appendix II (four volumes), the evidence itself, Appendix III, reports on the USA and Germany, Appendix IV, descriptions of each system in the UK, and Appendix V, financial details.[52]

The committee made a number of recommendations. High-definition television should replace the thirty-line system as soon as possible. An advisory committee should be appointed by the Postmaster General to guide the development of such a public service, which should be the responsibility of the BBC. Ultimately, half the population could be served by ten ultra-short-wave transmitting stations, but a start should be made in London. A service should be established there, with the Baird company and Marconi–EMI alternately operating the television system, and supplying the apparatus for it. The cost of the service, at least during its experimental period, should be taken out of the existing ten shillings radio licence fee, and shared between the Treasury and the BBC.[53]

Reith became even more incandescent with rage when he discovered that the Treasury was suggesting that the whole cost should be borne by the BBC. He received some sympathy in high circles:

> 2[½] hours this afternoon with [Sir] Warren Fisher [permanent secretary to the treasury and official head of the civil service]. We talked about governors [of the BBC], about the Committee, and about the Television Report. I told him how annoyed we were with the attitude of Phillips, of the Post Office, and as a result of what I said he read me a memorandum he had dictated to the Chancellor of the Exchequer, following on a recommendation by the Treasury officials that we should be made to pay the whole of the £180,000 television costs likely to be incurred in the next year and a half. I might almost have dictated this note myself. It said he fundamentally disagreed with the attitude towards the BBC in this instance and elsewhere; that we were a sort of nest egg and that the attitude had been wrong from the beginning.[54]

The new committee, known as the Television Advisory Committee, had its first meeting on 5 February 1935. Its constitution was the same as that of the original committee, with the addition of Sir Frank Smith, secretary of the Department of Scientific and Industrial Research, who had been one of the ill-fated personal sponsors of Church for membership of the Athenaeum. The original committee's report had been rather ambivalent as to when the thirty-line transmissions should finally be abandoned, and relations between the BBC and the GPO sank to further low levels on this very issue. In a change round within the national government early in June 1935, Stanley Baldwin had become Prime Minister and Ramsay MacDonald Lord President of the Council. Wood now became Minister of Health, and was replaced as Postmaster General by Major G C Tryon. The Television Advisory Committee had proposed that the service should cease on 10 August 1935. Carpendale spoke to Phillips of the GPO on the phone on 14 June:

> I spoke to Phillips today on the subject of closing down the 30-line television, he is being just as difficult as ever, and bases his objection on the PMG being shot at for causing such a hiatus between the two services. ... I told him I was frankly disappointed with his attitude and he said it was only his opinion, and if the rest of the Committee took our point of view we should get what we wanted, ie closing on 30 July. In regard to this I said it was not fair, because he always had the whip hand in influencing the Chairman if he said the PMG strongly objected to it. I am convinced the new PMG knows nothing about it and cannot be so keen on the political business as Phillips makes out.[55]

On 27 June Bishop reported to Ashbridge:

> Mr Varley Roberts tells me that Mr Phillips has so far been unable to get this date [10 August] agreed by the PMG. I said we were anxious to have it confirmed because we do not wish to commit ourselves on programmes after that date and also we wanted to arrange staff holidays after that. I urged him to press the PMG for a decision as quickly as possible, and he asked me to ask [Carpendale] to write a further letter to Mr Phillips.[13]

Carpendale commented: 'Phillips has been priming new PMG up to the "awful risk" of stopping 30 line – I've told him politely what I think of him!'[13]

In the event, the last thirty-line transmission did not go out until 11 September 1935, ten weeks after the birth of Malcolm, the Bairds' second child. The programme, at 11am, comprised a piano solo by Cyril Smith

(Chopin's 'Polonaise in A flat'), two violin solos by Daïsy Kennedy, songs by Morgan Davies and Olive Groves, and dances by Algeranoff and prima ballerina Lydia Sokolova, who brought down the curtain and the house with her rendering of Moussorgsky's 'Bacchanale'. There was champagne, presented by Robb, whose connection with television was now severed. The technical staff were transferred to Alexandra Palace, the new site of BBC television.[56] The service had presented 650 broadcasts, in which 1700 performers had taken part.[57] It had come to have an audience of between eight and fifteen thousand viewers, in most regions of the United Kingdom and in many parts of the continent of Europe.[58] From September 1935 until November 1936, when the first regular transmissions went out from Alexandra Palace, the only live television programmes in Britain were those transmitted by the Baird company from the Crystal Palace, with the original call-sign G2TV.[59]

There was a closed circuit broadcast from the Crystal Palace on 8 November 1935, on the occasion of a Press Club television dinner. Sydney Moseley was in the chair. The two hundred guests included Baird, Greer, Gerald Cock, the new director of television at the BBC, and Sir Stephen Tallents, recently appointed controller (public relations) at the BBC. Moseley wrote up the event in his usual egocentric, but pungent style:

> Being Chairman is not difficult. I like the job. Yet having to make speeches you haven't thought out beforehand can be a trial on important occasions. The anticipation is worse than the reality. Once I get to my feet I become – outwardly at least! – as cool as a cucumber. ... Delightful, taciturn Baird, whom I put on my left, kept on repeating: 'Ach! Dear old Sydney has put it over again!' He was tremendously amused at seeing 'his old pal and defender' officiating (with a big hammer!) while Greer and the BBC crowd (his critics, he still insists) *had* to applaud. Sir Stephen Tallents, whom I placed on my right in preference to Greer, is an interesting old chap who loves the country – a nice fellow, but why he has his present job at the BBC – search me![60]
>
> We had installed the first television set ever to be seen at the Press Club, and had a special relay from the Crystal Palace. After I had proposed the Royal toast the television experiment began. Horace Sanders, my old friend, now Chairman of the Club, came through on the set, addressing himself to 'Master Sydney Moseley'. The picture was by no means perfect, but very much larger and more impressive than I have seen before. That damned flicker, however, is in my view the curse of the thing, and some new invention will be necessary before it is perfect – just as the thermionic valve was needed for radio. ...

Baird made a first-class, bright little speech. Much to my surprise, he thanked me *publicly* – and with fervour! – for what I had done for him. 'Television had needed a fighter, and Sydney was and is a fighter!'. ... He really paid me a touching tribute.[61]

The Baird company's German interests had received a death blow in August 1935, with the announcement that, under a decree signed by Hitler, television in Germany had since 12 July been under the control of the Air Minister, General Hermann Göring, 'in view of the importance of television for the security of aircraft and for national defence'.[62] Church managed to negotiate a deal which gave the company some cash compensation for its share in Fernseh,[63] but that was scant satisfaction.

In preparation for the now inevitable changeover to a national system of high-definition television in the United Kingdom, the company made a licence agreement with the Farnsworth Corporation in the USA enabling it to manufacture copies of magnetically focussed cathode-ray tubes, which gave a screen size of 15 inches square.[64] Farnsworth's image dissector tube was also called into service as the basis of the electron camera, to be used for larger studio scenes in the system which was designed to represent the company's bid for the BBC contract.[65]

The BBC had begun work in February 1935, under Birkinshaw's direction, to convert two floors and a tower of Alexandra Palace, north London, into a broadcasting station which could house and operate two different television systems, each with its studio, control rooms, and equipment. The surrounding park area had been opened in 1863 as a place of recreation. The palace was rebuilt in 1873, the first building having been destroyed by fire. When Campbell first saw it in 1935, he found 'an old tyre, no roof, no doors, and I could see the sky. The smell of cat in the old banqueting rooms nearly made me sick and the whole thing looked the most dreadful mess.'[66] He and Bridgewater were among the engineers recruited to man the technical side of the operation for which the BBC was responsible, while gaining experience of the two different technologies which would be involved in the initial transmissions. Whichever system was ultimately chosen, the BBC would have to be able to operate it.

The Marconi–EMI all-electronic system centred on the handy emitron camera, a version of Zworykin's iconoscope. Shoenberg gambled on being able to resolve the dreaded 'tilt and bend' scanning pattern distortions inherent in the system, while going for an unprecedented 405-line scanning specification giving twenty-five pictures a second. His company had the equipment, it had the technical know-how, and it had cash.

Paul Reveley, who was a spectator of the events, has concluded that 'the contest for the BBC contract was a head-on commercial struggle between Marconi–EMI and Gaumont-British Film Corporation, in the guise of Baird Television.'[67] The Baird company's system was not designed by Baird himself, but by West, and it was West who led and directed the Baird company team. 'Baird had to keep quiet and go along with this, because his livelihood as nominal managing director depended on it.'[67] West's view was that the standard to be aimed at was a 240-line picture, with twenty-five pictures a second. With far less resources by way of suitable patents available to him than to Marconi–EMI, he settled for a combination of two well-tried techniques and one fairly unknown quantity.

Close-ups of speakers and announcers would be transmitted by means of a mechanical spotlight scanner, designed by J C Wilson, with a disc running at fifty revolutions a second. For large scenes, and for medium distance and deep scenescape shots, he would use the intermediate-film technique developed by Fernseh, with a film camera which could be panned to take in three sets. As the apparatus was noisy, bulky, and required to be connected to the mains water supply and drainage, he would also employ for such scenes an electron camera based on the Farnsworth image dissector.[68]

It would appear that in 1933, possibly at the instigation of Church and Appleton, the Baird company board made approaches to Philo Farnsworth. Farnsworth's widow wrote a colourful account of her husband's life and achievements. She described how Farnsworth and several colleagues took an immediate crossing, with the equipment travelling with them in crates as personal baggage. The ship did not dock at Southampton, so passengers for Britain, with their luggage, had to be loaded onto a British boat at sea. Gaumont-British sent a private launch for the Farnsworth party and equipment. As the crates were being lowered by crane, a wave heaved the launch upwards. There was a sickening crash, as deck met crates. Though much of the ancillary equipment was damaged, enough of the tubes and other components survived to put on a demonstration. Greer tried to negotiate a licensing arrangement without royalties, but Farnsworth stuck out for an advance of $50,000 against royalties, to which Ostrer was persuaded by his scientific advisers to capitulate.[69]

The two companies began installing and testing their equipment at Alexandra Palace in March 1936. Though the launch would not be until 2 November, both systems went on public view at the Radio Manufacturers' Association annual exhibition at Olympia from 26 August to 6 September. The programmes, organised and produced by the BBC, were transmitted from Alexandra Palace to a series of booths containing initially eight but subsequently twenty television receivers, manufactured by eight different companies: Baird, Cossor, Ediswan, EMI, Ferranti, Philips, Pye, and Scophony. The Baird receiver, manufactured by Bush, had the Farnsworth 15-inch magnetically deflected tube. That the operation was mounted at all was due more to the enthusiasm of individuals than to that collectively of the BBC or the RMA, both of which organisations had reasons for regarding the new phenomenon as a threat to the status quo.[70] Indeed, there was an attempt at industrial sabotage the night before the exhibition opened, with a wad of lead being inserted into a crucial plug point supplying power to the booths.[71]

Though the Baird spotlight scanner had only been installed the previous day, Marconi–EMI too had its share of problems, with the emitron cameras having an off day as regards distortion of the image.[70] It is instructive to note, however, that on the basis of the first day's showing both systems earned high praise from cinema critics, with the Baird pictures, apart from a tendency to flicker, being regarded as no inferior in quality to those produced by Marconi–EMI.[71]

The Baird company won the toss of a coin to decide which company should have first innings proper, and televise the programmes for the initial week of the trial, including the opening ceremony. As a result of tests of both systems during October, the Television Advisory Committee expressed doubt as to whether the Baird system was functioning satisfactorily enough to provide the sole means of transmission on 2 November. It was therefore decided to televise the proceedings twice, once using the Baird system, and then again with the Marconi–EMI apparatus.[72]

The *Radio Times* had already gone to press when the decision was made. This resulted in a series of confusing instructions on the part of the announcers, Leslie Mitchell and Jasmine Bligh. Viewers were requested to 'be ready to switch your sets over from Baird to Marconi–EMI, after Buck and Bubbles have finished their performance and we have made a further announcement'. To meet the requirements of the competing systems, Mitchell was required to change his make-up between the two performances in an interval during which the BBC Television Orchestra played on sound only. Bligh was instructed 'to remove her spotlight make-up and proceed to the Restaurant for Hostess duty'; her place on the set was taken by Elizabeth Cowell.[73]

The platform party was R C Norman, chairman of the governors of the BBC, Major Tryon, Postmaster General, Selsdon, chairman of the Television Advisory Committee, Greer, chairman of the Baird company, and Lord Inverforth, chairman of Marconi–EMI (by a late change taking the place of Alfred Clark, chairman of EMI). There would be brief speeches by Norman, Tryon, Selsdon, and Greer, followed by a news film and some light entertainment. The party would then troop into the Marconi–EMI studio and repeat their performance, except that Inverforth would speak instead of Greer.[73]

The Baird company used a spotlight camera for the announcements, and the intermediate-film technique for the speeches and the entertainment. Marconi–EMI employed three emitron cameras to cover the speeches. The schedule incorporated a 'standby gramophone programme' in the case of an emergency caused by a technical breakdown.[73] It was not needed.

On this momentous day for British television, Baird, its initial architect, sat in the audience and fumed.

> All the notabilities in any way connected with television appeared on the platform and were televised, all except Mr Baird, who was not invited but sat in considerable anger and disgust in the body of the hall among the rank and file. Thus is pioneer work recognized. This little episode was but another addition to the host of slights and insults given me by the BBC. What the devil had they done for television. But there they sat, sunning themselves in the limelight as the men responsible for this great achievement, for so they apparently wished to appear. While I, the best part of whose life had been given to television, who had transmitted the first television image ever seen, who had first introduced television to the BBC, who, year after year, had forced the pace and pushed Britain and the BBC into the position of leadership sat snubbed and humiliated among the audience![74]

These impressions, dictated five years later in what obviously was long-simmering heat, were only partly true and partly fair. The single BBC personage on the platform was the corporation's chairman. (On this momentous day for British television, and at the height of the abdication crisis involving the King and Mrs Simpson, Sir John Reith, the BBC's director general, was on holiday in Scotland.)[75] The Baird and the Marconi–EMI companies were also represented by their chairmen. For all his pioneer work, Baird was not involved in planning or setting up his company's apparatus for the trial, nor had he given evidence to either television committee. If Shoenberg, who had masterminded his company's system and had given evidence to both committees, was present, he too was in the audience!

Both sides had problems from the outset of the trial. Marconi–EMI's answer to the transmission of cine films was to pick up the images by means of an emitron camera pointed at a film projector through which the film was travelling at twenty-five frames a second, instead of the normal sixteen. Some distortion was inevitable, especially if the original image was dark. By contrast, the Baird method, using the spotlight mechanical scanner, was simplicity itself. In the judgment of Percy, who was in charge of the intermediate-film process, 'With our straightforward scanning device with no electronic storage, nothing except a photocell, we had a perfectly square, plain, beautiful clear picture.'[76] Though Marconi–EMI had devised 'tilt and bend' correction circuits whose function was automatically to rectify scanning pattern distortion, their close-up shots were still markedly inferior to those produced by the Baird Nipkow disc scanner.[67]

On the other hand, the Baird six-foot-high intermediate-film machine, rooted in its special unit, often proved too inflexible for the occasion. The fifty-four-second delay during which the film was processed and transmitted was too short a time for comfort for the engineers, but far too long for the announcers, whom Percy described as spending 'most of their time apologising for breakdowns because everywhere you looked down the long chain of fifty-four seconds, you had disaster staring you in a hundred places'.[77]

> A lot of us were standing on a wet floor with 10,000 volts running through the machine; the cameraman was hanging over the Nipkow disc spinning at 6000 revs a minute and if you absentmindedly sipped some of the cyanide fixing fluid which splashed on the floor, you were dead for a certainty. Liz Cowell generally trailed her long frock into it and had to be hosed down quick so, as all this was happening in the cramped little scanning room, you can say rehearsals and transmissions were always exciting.[77]

The Baird company's electron camera proved so temperamental that West sent a SOS message to Farnsworth in Philadelphia to come to London at the company's expense to help sort out the problems. Farnsworth's mother flew in from San Francisco to look after the two boys, seven and one, and Farnsworth and his wife sailed for the UK on the German cruise ship *Hansa*. Having spent over a fortnight in London, the couple went on to France and Monte Carlo on a trip which was both rest cure for Farnsworth and a celebration of their ten-year marriage.[78] Whatever it was he managed to do to the electron camera, however, it remained largely unused.[79]

The company's problems were compounded on the night of Monday, 30 November, in the most spectacular fashion. The Crystal Palace, long the regular site of firework displays, became itself a public fireworks' show.

The fire began at about 7.30pm, in what is now believed to be a fractured earthenware flue from a boiler room which provided heating to the offices towards the north end of the central nave. It quickly travelled towards the centre of the building under the asphalt-covered floorboards. By 7.45pm the blaze was apparent, and a crowd had begun to form, yet no-one had called the fire brigade.[80] The first alarm call was received at 8pm, and brought the whole of the London fire service into action. By the time the first fire engine arrived on the scene at two-and-a-half minutes past eight, the central transept was ablaze, and a large part of it collapsed a few minutes later. The fire, fanned by a bitter north wind, began now to threaten the south end of the building.[81]

Baird was at dinner when the phone rang, and a frantic voice told him that the Crystal Palace was on fire. From the window he saw the sky lit up with a red glow. He rushed out of the house in his slippers, without bothering to find his hat. The main road was blocked with cars. He forced his way through a dense crowd of sightseers, and gazed astonished at what he later called the 'seething mass of flames'.[82] Back at the house, someone lifted up sixteen-month-old Malcolm to the window, so that he too could see the conflagration.

At Sutton, eight miles away, Margaret, who was staying at her mother's house with Diana, watched the glow in the sky from the garden, and wondered what it was.[83]

Tomes, who was working on the night shift, travelled as usual by train from his home in East Dulwich. At the station he was told about the fire. As he approached the laboratories at the south end of the nave, he saw smoke coming from the centre of the building, but as it was so far away he went straight to his bench and got on with his work. Suddenly, it seemed, the whole building was alight. He and his colleagues in the laboratory swept up their technical notes to take them outside. Tomes grabbed their latest cathode-ray projection tube and the office cat. As they left the laboratories, they saw the fire moving along the roof towards the South Tower. Tomes went through the gate at the south end of the building, and walked round to Crystal Palace Parade, which ran along the west front. There he handed the cat to someone who worked in the grounds. At 11pm, with the building burning from end to end, he left and walked home. There was nothing more he could do.[84]

Tom Nuttall, a research engineer on the electron camera, had only joined the company two months before.[85] The day after the fire he wrote a long letter to Elsie, his fiancée in Lancashire, describing the experience. He had finished work at 6.30pm and returned to his lodgings in Westow Street, a few hundred yards away, where he had his tea as usual. At eight o'clock someone shouted down the stairs that there was a fire. The sky was alight as he went to investigate. He worked in the same part of the complex as Tomes, but his laboratory was locked, and someone had to climb over a gate to get in.

Everything looked quite normal, except that at the end of the corridor the heat was beginning to seep in from the fire above. He and colleagues removed dangerous items such as gas cylinders and flasks of liquid air, some papers, and valuable pieces of small apparatus. They evacuated the premises on the orders of the firemen.[86]

Nuttall could not bear to stay to watch. He had to use force to get through the crowds of sightseers. Hundreds of cyclists thronged the area, their machines jammed together in the press. The glare was painful. Aeroplanes taking photographs and shooting newsreels circled above, their red and white lights flashing like fireworks around a vast bonfire. The manageress of the café where he usually had lunch let him use the telephone in her house at the back to ring Elsie. When he returned to his lodgings, the street outside had been turned into a car park for sightseers.[86]

H C Spencer, who had joined the department on the same day as Nuttall, was one of those working late in the laboratory under the main building. The first thing they knew about the fire was the roof beginning to cave in above them, with an enormous noise. Firemen appeared, and ordered them out of the building. It was only the next day, when he saw the weird shapes made by pools of molten glass on the ground outside, that he realised what a close call they had had. He had watched helplessly until the fire brigade blew up the passageway between the main building and the School of Arts to prevent the fire reaching it, and had then returned to his lodgings in Church Street, the rear portion of which was an all-night café the other side of the road from the south end of the Palace. It was doing a roaring trade, and he spent much of the rest of the night helping out there.[87]

Clapp, the longest serving and third highest paid member of staff,[88] had left the office at six o'clock to go into London in his car and collect his father, who was coming to stay with him. On the way back he heard fire engines. At a petrol station, he was told that the Crystal Palace was on fire. In the absence of West, who was out of London that day, Clapp was the senior manager. He was stopped at Streatham, a couple of miles to the east of the Palace, and told by the police that he could not drive any nearer. He explained his position, whereupon a senior uniformed officer jumped onto the running board of the car, and directed him through the traffic. Clapp stood below the South Tower, fearing for its collapse, while the fire completely consumed the office block. The only thing that survived was a filing cabinet, which someone had bodily thrown out onto the grass.[89]

Where the fire had passed, the damage was indescribable. The area was a mass of smoking twisted metal and glass, the smell of which hung around for a month.[90] The Baird offices and laboratories in the main building were gone, together with the equipment and records that were housed there. Farnsworth, who paid a visit to the site the following January on his way back to the USA, found in the ruins the charred, contorted remains of one of his own image dissectors.[91]

The South Tower had been saved, however, along with a small building containing apparatus, near the foot of the tower, and the workshop which housed the receiver production unit. The company issued a statement the day after the fire, which was also read out on the BBC six o'clock news. The receiver production unit and the service and testing department were undamaged, and delivery of television sets should not be affected. Property and equipment were fully covered by insurance. The transmissions from Alexandra Palace would continue uninterrupted.[92]

The damage to morale, however, was incalculable, and displaced staff had to be relocated in cramped conditions in the South Tower, the School of Arts, and the Rotunda. According to Tomes, after the fire two hundred staff were made redundant.[93] This was a temporary panic measure which may have been related to the next savage blow which the company received. On 9 December, Gerald Cock, director of television at the BBC, wrote a report on the Alexandra Palace trial for the Television Advisory Committee. It was scathing about the unreliability of the Baird apparatus. By contrast, Marconi–EMI, with its standardised equipment, had already demonstrated that its system 'would make a service of general entertainment interest immediately possible'.[94]

While nobody has ever questioned the superiority of the Marconi–EMI system, there are suggestions that the difference in quality between the two at the receiving end was not so great as has sometimes been made out. Some weeks earlier, Church had made an extraordinary approach to Shoenberg, suggesting cooperation between the two companies, and been rebuffed. Now, on 11 December, he wrote to Shoenberg. After some time spent 'looking-in on different receivers at our respective transmissions', he gave his opinion on them:

> There is still much research work to be done before television in the home reaches a stage of popularity to make it a commercial proposition. Apart altogether from the programmes, the present transmissions, yours and ours, are not really satisfactory. Making every allowance for possibly inexpert handling of the apparatus installed at Alexandra Palace the fact remains that the transmitters are uncertain in performance, the detail in extended scenes is far below that demanded by a public used to the cinema, and the main difficulties in transmitting outdoor scenes by electrical 'pick-up' have still to be surmounted.[95]

The ostensible purpose of the letter was to persuade Shoenberg to join in an approach to the Television Advisory Committee to call a conference of interested parties to discuss a joint programme of research between the television manufacturing companies, the BBC, the GPO, and the Department of Scientific and Industrial Research. Alternatively, he suggested that the four principal firms, Marconi–EMI, the Baird company, GEC, and Cossor, establish a television cooperative association, which would allocate problems to the respective staffs and pool the results of their research.

Nothing seems to have come of this approach, or it may simply have been that it was too late. At its meeting on 16 December, the Television Advisory Committee decided to recommend to the Postmaster General that the trial should be abandoned, and that the Marconi–EMI system should be adopted by the BBC.[96] In doing so, its members were taking a chance on the last of the emitron's 'tilt and bend' problems being exorcised, and they were to be proved right.[97]

The Baird company met the decision philosophically. Baird took it as a personal affront.

> To be thrown out of the BBC after all these years of pioneer work, to be displaced by newcomers, was to me a bitter blow. Clayton and Greer did not seem to appreciate this. 'I can't understand,' said Clayton, 'why you place such importance on this transmission. After all, the money is in the sale of receivers. I understand of course, that from the sentimental angle it must be a blow to you. If you will pardon me speaking freely, it hurts your vanity. But simply looking at the thing as a business man from a purely business angle, I think that it's the best thing that could have happened. We have done nothing but lose money in transmission. Now we can leave it to the BBC and concentrate on the receiver market.'[98]

The previous summer Church had produced a memorandum, 'Publicity on Television', in which he stressed that the company's object in this aspect of its activities was 'to make the public believe that (1) our system is the best, (2) our commercial articles are superior to those produced by other concerns'. He continued:

For (1) we have certain assets among which are the facts that:
  i.   Baird is the true and first inventor of television.
  ii. Baird Television Limited have exclusive rights on Baird inventions.
  iii. Baird Television Limited have a greater experience of television than any company in the world.

iv. The Baird Television Limited technical staff has a longer experience of the practical problems inherent in the transmission and reception of television than any other company's staff.

v. Baird Television Limited was the first company in the world to produce television pictures (a) for home receivers, (b) for large screen reception.

vi. Baird Television Ltd was the first to demonstrate
    (a) cathode-ray reception as well as mechanical reception.
    (b) It is the only company which has transmitted pictures across the Atlantic – etc.
    (c) Its cathode-ray receivers are the largest in the world.

vii. Baird Television Limited can demonstrate large screen television images, clear likenesses of the persons and objects transmitted, on a screen large enough to provide entertainment for cinema audiences.

viii. Baird Television Limited are well ahead of their competitors in every department of television.[99]

Readers may judge for themselves how many of these statements were valid once the results of the Alexandra Palace trial became public. It would also require something exceptional simply to survive the aftermath of the fire.

It was probably Baird and West, under Church's chairmanship, who now sat down and very quickly produced a company document on 'Future Technical Development'. Its main conclusions were:

1. We can beat the iconoscope if we can settle down to quiet research. We have only done exactly one year's work on our electron research, and this has already yielded very satisfactory results. If we had concentrated on this four years ago we would have been ahead.

2. Our receivers are recognised as fundamentally good, and if we could get the price down we should score heavily.

3. In all this we must not forget that experience counts more than anything. The last two or three years experience combined with a selection of the best imaginative brains should put us in a strong position for the future.

4. We should, with careful planning, be able to manufacture and market many sidelines such as cathode-ray tubes, time bases and photo-electric cells. With technically good products the success of such ventures depends on the efficiency and enthusiasm of a Sales Department, which need only be very small for this purpose.[100]

The document went on to suggest specific lines of research, contributing to the development of a 525-line electronic system of transmission. These included 'New forms of electron camera for direct pickup as present camera has come to the limit', microwave transmission and reception, and electron multipliers. A new receiver should be designed, giving a picture 18 inches by 12, to operate on 405 or 525 lines, with only two knobs. It should have 'improved freedom from interference', be simple to erect, and sell at thirty guineas, 'with all wave radio, forty guineas'. Research would be conducted into shortening the present size of cathode-ray tube, and developing tubes to give a picture 4 feet by 3, for the cinema, and small tubes to give, with a cheap lens, a picture 18 inches by 12. The compilers of the document noted, 'Much of the research work described is directly of value for Air Television and similar applications.'[100]

The company had already demonstrated that it could install a working television receiver in a commercial aircraft. On 4 September 1936, a KLM flight carried the 420lb apparatus, on which passengers saw, while travelling at 170mph at 4000 feet, live pictures transmitted by the BBC from Alexandra Palace, and also a Gaumont-British newsreel of the maiden voyage of the liner *Queen Mary*.[101] There is an Air Ministry record of 30 April 1936 to the effect that the French air attaché in London had approached the Baird company about installing a television reconnaissance system in an aircraft. On 26 May, West obtained permission from the Air Ministry research department to deal with foreign governments as long as any television equipment supplied had no specific military application.[102] The Baird company accordingly went ahead with specifications for the French Air Ministry and also the government of USSR for systems for transmitting images from aircraft, and for mobile and ground receiving equipment. These were set out in an internal company document dated 12 April 1937. Both specifications incorporated the use of the intermediate-film technique at each end of the process.[103]

For the French, the images would be recorded on 16mm film by a camera with two lenses, and developed in twenty seconds. This would then be scanned by electron camera or cathode-ray tube, 405 lines, twelve-and-a-half pictures per second, with a check picture reproduced on a 30cm cathode-ray tube. The pictures would be transmitted to a mobile van on the ground up to a distance of 23 kilometres away, reproduced on a cathode-ray tube, and recorded on 16mm film, which would then be processed in thirty seconds and projected, wet, onto a screen 6 feet by 4. The film would also be passed through a second projector which could show a still picture at any point. The French had asked for delivery in six months; the specification was for nine months.[103]

The specifications for the Russian air-to-ground system were much the same as for the French, except that the Russians wanted the film developed in fifteen seconds at each end, and sound recording and transmission built into the process. In addition, the USSR asked for specifications for a ground-to-ground system involving two mobile transmitting stations, one for scanner and sound receiver, one for vision and sound radio transmitters, and a mobile receiving station. Alternative specifications were offered for the use of intermediate film and for an electron camera with the picture reproduced on a cathode-ray tube of 38cm diameter. There were also specifications for large-screen television equipment, with vision and sound recorded on 16mm film, scanned by the interlaced method 405 lines, fifty pictures per second, and projected onto a screen 6 feet by 4½.[103]

Allowing for overheads at one hundred per cent of the cost of materials and labour, the contract price of £10,500 to the French showed a net profit of £3000, and the price of £47,000 to the Russians a net profit of £12,800. In order to fulfil both contracts in their entirety, a move to a new factory was essential, design and testing engineers, wiremen, and instrument makers would need to be redeployed, and some new staff taken on. Development would continue unabated, however, on existing research projects, including electron telecine for the BBC, new radio receivers for autumn sales, a new light-scanning camera, multiplier cells especially for receiving sets, projection tubes, and microwave links.[103]

The French contract duly materialised, being known for security reasons as job number 4141,[104] but the potential deal with USSR appears to have sunk without trace. It seems that the French government was also negotiating at this time with EMI, whose television equipment was fitted into a French air force bomber at Hendon in 1937.[105]

EMI had also installed cameras in a British warplane, to judge from a memorandum from Church:

> I saw Colonel Worledge, head of Signals Dept at the War Office, by chance yesterday evening. He tells me that it is difficult to get the general staff interested in television, but he is keeping in touch personally with developments. He implied that EMI had many friends at the Air Ministry and had managed to get an order from the Air Ministry for the installation of emitrons in a plane. The emitrons have been fitted up and experiments have been carried out for some time past, with what results Worledge could not say, but he believed that they had not been too satisfactory. He himself thought that neither the emitron nor the electron camera were suitable for the kind of

work which the Services required for aeroplane cooperation owing to the speed of the plane, which made it difficult to concentrate upon any particular point on the ground. For this reason, he favours the installation of intermediate-film apparatus in the plane and on the ground, so that any pictures taken could be enlarged later. He says the Air Ministry informed him that they were in touch with our negotiations with the French Military Authorities and would wait until we had got some results with the French Services before doing anything much with us.[106]

Early in 1937, Clayton, in addition to his function as deputy chairman, had been appointed joint managing director with Baird,[107] in an obvious attempt to rationalise decision making and clarify the chain of command. Church's memorandum, which was addressed to Clayton, with a copy to West, provides confirmation, if any is needed, that Baird was not in any way personally involved in this aspect of the company's activities.

There is a curious episode relating to the Crystal Palace premises, which took place a couple of months earlier. In March 1937 the company received one of a series of visits from Samuel Hecht, a civilian radio engineer in the department of communications research and development of the Air Ministry. On this occasion he was accompanied by Dr R V Jones, who had proposed to the Air Ministry an infra-red imaging scheme to which the company might be able to contribute a thermal image converter. It appears that they first paid a courtesy visit to Baird, in the studio in the South Tower which his personal staff used for transmissions. Then they talked with West, who during the discussion suggested that reflected radio waves penetrated fog much better than the infra-red variety. Since this was precisely the basis of radar, the highly secret system of detection officially proposed by Watson Watt in 1935, Hecht warned West to keep his ideas strictly to himself,[108] but the incident suggests that the Baird company was not party to the British radar programme at this time.

Later in the year there was an attempt to strengthen the public image of the board, by inviting Moseley back as a director. The emissary was Church, to whom Moseley replied on 1 November 1937:

My dear Church

I was unable to get you on the telephone.

I gather that you are proposing to the Board that they should invite me to become a Director again. I appreciate this and have written to Sir Harry expressing a similar appreciation of the intimation given me by him and by Mr Clayton some time ago that they too would welcome me on the Board, but surely you can see that it would be hardly fair to ask me to come back at the present juncture.

Would you be good enough to ring me or if it is impossible to have a chat, postpone putting the matter forward.

All the best,

Yours sincerely[109]

It is necessary to quote this letter in full because it contradicts Baird's own account of the sequence of events, and of the events themselves,[110] which has been followed by subsequent biographers and which, to be fair, Moseley himself did not fully deny in his life of Baird.[111]

Moseley's diary entry for that same day of 1 November confirms the evidence of the letter.

NOV. 1 1937: The complexities of the Baird Company are worrying John Baird, particularly since I went abroad [to USA]. He was rather bitter. Finally I said: 'Well, you always *talk* a lot about your treatment: why don't you write down what you feel – now?' He said he would. Instead, he dictated to me what he felt, and I wrote it in my diary. Slowly and deliberately he said:

The exhibition of jealousy, malice and spite which I witnessed during the past three years will live with me to my grave. Nor shall I ever forget the damnable intrigue which culminated in trying to force me to sign a document which might have landed me in a prison cell.

I put the paragraph before him. 'If that is what you feel,' I said, 'read it and sign it!' He made a pretence of doing so, but instead of signing his name he put – his *mark*! Typical, cautious John![112]

Typical and cautious, but also loyal!

There was a further reorganisation of the board in January 1938. Baird was appointed president (at a salary of £4000 a year),[113] and ceased to attend board meetings.[114] Clayton now became managing director. The company moved a mile-and-a-half away to new premises in Worsley Bridge Road, Lower Sydenham, in the summer of 1938. This left at the Crystal Palace a small team in the School of Arts working on the French contract, the cathode-ray tube production department in the Rotunda, and Baird and his select staff of technicians using part of the base of the South Tower, with an aerial at the top, for his large-screen, and also colour, television transmissions. From

1936 the manufacture of television receivers was undertaken by the Gaumont-British company of Bush Radio.[115] As an economy measure, salaries were frozen. Many staff left of their own accord; the more skilled among them found related work with the Air Ministry and other government organisations, including radar and Army signals, the BBC, and rival companies such as Marconi. About a hundred remained to see out the last months of peace.[116]

One of the engineers involved with the airborne project was Ray Herbert, whose interest in television had begun in November 1933, when he constructed a television receiver from bits of Meccano and old radio components. A four-year day course at Faraday House Electrical Engineering College included a final period of work experience, which Clapp (a family friend) arranged for him to spend with the Baird company. By moving from department to department, he gained an overall knowledge of television engineering. After qualifying in 1938, he continued with the company, in the transmitter research laboratory, to replace an engineer who had left to work at Watson Watt's radar research station at Bawdsey. The original transmitter for the aircraft was not powerful enough to satisfy the specifications. Herbert's first job on the project was to design and build a new transmitter in a week, to meet the deadline for acceptance tests.[117]

The full apparatus, weighing 363kg, was installed in a French Marcel Bloch twin-engined bomber stationed for the purpose at Hendon airport. The crew of five, a French air force pilot and mechanic, and three Baird engineers, tested the equipment over the English countryside during June and July 1939. The results were spectacular. From heights of between 3000 and 5000 feet, and travelling at speeds up to 150mph, the transmitter in the forward gun turret sent, even in poor conditions, clear pictures of the film to the ground of tennis-court lines, moving cars, water rippling on reservoirs, and even the names on buildings. These were viewed on a receiver with a 20-inch diameter cathode-ray tube, housed in a specially-adapted Renault van, and are claimed to be the world's first live television transmissions from an aircraft in flight. The tube, the largest then available, was designed and constructed in the Baird company's vacuum laboratories. An additional feature was the video-recording system on the ground which enabled pictures to be recorded on 35mm film. At the press of a key, the operator could view a single frame or one in every three frames as a continuous series. The strength of the signal was fully satisfactory, and the specified range could be exceeded by a considerable margin.[104] Fifty years later, film-based air-to-ground reconnaissance systems employed by many national air forces were functionally identical to that devised by the Baird company for the French air force in 1938.[118]

Herbert became a permanent member of the crew, making all fifteen flights from Hendon, and a further two over northern France when the plane returned to its base at Villacoublay in August 1939. After the outbreak of World War II, it was moved to Orleans and then to Toulouse. Its subsequent fate is unknown.[104]

In an article published on 26 August 1939, Baird reviewed television progress since 1925 and predicted its future:

> Millions are being spent in research laboratories and on technical development in the United States and Germany with the object of forestalling British manufacturers in the world markets. This competition can be met only if our own home market is adequately developed, and this depends entirely upon the development of a network of television transmitting stations to cover the whole of Great Britain. Without this network of stations, making television programmes available to all, plans for mass production of receivers cannot be carried out. It is time officialdom acted more energetically.[119]

On 1 September, at noon, because of fears that the short-wave signal from Alexandra Palace would be used by German bombers as a navigational aid, the BBC, without warning, closed down its television service just as an exciting television promotion was about to be launched at the annual radio exhibition at Olympia.[120] Estimates of the number of television receivers in use at this time vary between sixteen and twenty-three thousand.[121] Not only were these sets rendered useless at a stroke, but manufacturers and distributors had invested heavily in new ranges of cheaper sets in anticipation of the extra sales that the promotion, sponsored by the BBC, would generate. These were now unsaleable. Companies such as Baird and Scophony had contracts to supply large-screen systems for cinemas, which were now cancelled.

Britain and France officially declared war on Nazi Germany on 3 September 1939.

The Baird company, which had seemed about to turn the financial corner after piling up losses of over £100,000 in each of the two previous financial years, was put into receivership by the action of Gaumont-British, which held £300,000 in loan stock of the company's total capital of £1,080,000.[122] The intention of Gaumont-British was to take over the assets of the Baird company in payment for its bonds, and invest them in Cinema-Television, the specialist subsidiary of the Baird company, which had been formed in 1937.[123]

On 20 October, afterwards known as 'Black Friday', many of the members of the staff of the Baird company received dismissal notices. Isidore Ostrer personally guaranteed the wages of the remaining staff, mostly at ninety per cent of the original amount.[102]

Greer wrote to the company's shareholders, explaining the position. The letters were addressed personally. Annie Baird received one, at 'The Lodge'.* Baird must have had one as well. Three years earlier he had held 1822 preferred ordinary shares and 443 deferred in Baird Television Ltd.[124]

On 4 November W Harrison, of the accountants Price Waterhouse, was appointed manager and receiver of the company.[102] On 17 November West presided at a lunch for all those staff who had lost their jobs, and also those who had survived.[64]

Towards the end of December, Moseley received a cable in New York: 'Company unable to carry on through lack of funds. Noteholders have installed Receiver. A merry Christmas and happy New Year. JLB.'[125]

14
Crescent Wood Road
1933-1939

Just as one should not look too closely for hard facts in Baird's personal memoir, so his wife, in her biography of him, and also Moseley in his, tended to emphasise extremes of behaviour of one kind and another:

His sense of humour could be coarse, cruel, and wounding. In 1934 I was in poor health and hoped to raise my spirits by having a new hat specially made, a hat with a brown crown and a brim of brown fluted velvet. When it arrived I put it on at once and turned to him for approval. He said: 'You look like a whore!'

John was even rather proud of his command of bad language. As an apprentice he had worked among the lowest of what was then called the working class, with the fear of poverty and destitution never far away. In moments of stress he was liable to break into Saltmarket eloquence, in his rather high-flown words, 'sufficient in its foul brutality and obscene imagery to cause a Billingsgate porter to stop his ears in horror'.[1]

What I found more depressing was his lack of enthusiasm for anything but television. He had no hobbies. He worked himself into a state of exhaustion and then recuperated in a state of complete inertia, lying in bed half the morning. Even then he kept in touch with his work through the telephone beside his bed.

Any kind of social life was impossible. One day a friend of my father's called and I had a happy afternoon hearing news of old friends. After he had gone I said to John: 'Do you like him?' The reply was: 'No. I thought he was a horrid man.' My father's friend was a courteous and civilized gentleman. ... With friends, when [John] relaxed, he was the kindest and most charming of men. But he took an unreasoning and acute dislike to some people, and much of his unhappy relationship with the board [of his company] stemmed from this.[2]

Asked to comment on observations such as these, Reveley, who worked at Crescent Wood Road for five years, suggested a rather different persona, anyway in public:

> In my presence JLB always treated Margaret with the utmost courtesy, and never under any circumstances made jokes or derogatory remarks of any kind at her expense. On the other hand of course the open physical displays of affection that are commonplace today were absent, since the maintenance of strict formality in company was then the accepted norm of polite social behaviour. I think it would have been at JLB's initiative that I was asked to join them for dinner on some occasions when I had been working late. Margaret ran a tight household ship, and cooking and serving was done with smoothness and precision by her domestic staff to five star hotel standard. She was in herself a very attractive person both in appearance and also personality, and presided over her dinner table with considerable distinction.
>
> JLB never exercised his Saltmarket eloquence in my presence. There was only one occasion in the whole period of my association with him on which he reproved me roughly. I cannot now recall the words, but still remember the outline of the incident. I had unguardedly let fall a remark to the effect that our effort had not pushed hard enough against the boundaries of readymade technology. This triggered a response the vehemence of which I realise in retrospect must have reflected his own frustration with the circumstances with which he had been surrounded in his progression up to that point.[3]

Of the times when he dined with the Bairds, alone or in company, Reveley recalled, 'These were most pleasant and gracious occasions, since both host and hostess were very civilised persons indeed. Baird was well educated to Scottish standard, and widely read also, and could and did maintain a sophisticated level of conversation. He was compassionate of poverty, but was a natural gentleman who I think by no means thought of himself as anything but middle class, despite having experienced hardship.'[4]

Baird had a cultured mind, and a sardonic, dry wit such as informs *Sermons, Soap and Television*. He was, however, a private person who rarely opened up in company. He wrote, ostensibly of a period which included the late 1920s and early 1930s,

> I had no business friends, plenty of acquaintances, plenty of contacts, yes, but no friends … none who spoke my language, none with whom

I would willingly have spent a minute more than was necessary for the purpose in hand. I was uneasy and bored in the company of my colleagues, with the exception of Moseley. Why was this? Firstly I think because Moseley had an outstandingly shrewd and acute mind and a keen sense of humour; secondly he was utterly devoid of dignity and decorum and self-respect, and so free of the hypocrisy, cant, humbug and vanity which unfortunately are the invariable accompaniments of dignity, decorum and self-respect.[5]

Diana's bedroom window at 3 Crescent Wood Road overlooked the front drive. She recalls watching her father and Moseley, arm in arm, walking up to the house, talking and laughing together. Often she was kept awake in the evenings by the sounds of her mother practising Rachmaninov and Bach in the drawing-room below, on the Steinway piano which Margaret's father had given to her. The piano remained with Margaret through most of the many moves she made during her life. The room directly underneath Diana's bedroom was the morning-room. This was Baird's subsidiary laboratory in his early years at Crescent Wood Road. Entry was strictly forbidden. Occasional surreptitious glimpses revealed a litter of papers and television components, and a strong smell of dust. Baird claimed that he knew exactly where everything was, as long as no-one disturbed anything.[6]

In the spring of 1934 there was a family outing by taxi to Southend, to see the illuminations. Diana wore a fluffy pink coat. She was a very late walker, and still had to be carried. She sat on her father's knee in the taxi, as they drove slowly along the promenade. On the way back it poured with rain. Baird announced that it would go on raining for forty days and nights, and they would have to build an ark.[6]

Reveley, who was fond of children, gave Diana a doll, Madam Paris, by Raynol. 'She was an exotic creature with real blond hair, dressed in a black and gold taffeta gown and a black velvet picture hat.' Diana called her Raynol, and kept her right through childhood, during which the doll gradually became an elder sister, with a wardrobe made by Margaret, who was a skilled seamstress.[6]

Reveley was joined in the laboratory in 1934 by S J Squire,[4] who had been taken on by the company in February 1933.[7] Squire's particular expertise was cutting and polishing the specially designed square-ended calcite prisms for the single-zone mirror-drum back projector which the team built in the new coach house extension. In this, as in other things, Baird took his specifications to the limit of what was then the constraining factor, the largest size of naturally occurring calcite crystals of the required optical quality.[4]

The complete mechanical system was demonstrated to members of the Baird and Gaumont-British boards, and well-disposed scientists such as Appleton and Fleming, in 1935. The two mirror drums were designed by Reveley and machined by B J Lynes from duralumin forgings. The mirrors themselves were glass, formed and toughened before silvering, and attached with clamps and screws which had been fabricated from the highest tensile steel available. Reveley himself assembled the drums, so as to be assured of meticulous balance and resistance to stress required when they were revolving six thousand times a minute. Each drum had to be fully enclosed to reduce air turbulence. The power came from air-cooled drive motors, also enclosed to reduce noise.[4]

One drum formed the scanning element in a flying-spot type of camera set up in the former larder of the house; the maids' sitting-room was the studio. A coaxial cable was the link with reception in the old coach house across the alleyway, where the pictures were back-projected by mirror drum onto a single-zone frosted-glass screen 12 feet square. For ease of handling, the heavy screen was suspended from sliding runners, with a pair of tracks parallel to the longitudinal walls of the laboratory. Baird found that he could just squeeze himself sideways between two of the columns which supported the tracks, and on his visits to enquire about progress would take the opportunity also of checking his girth.[4]

In the light of the private demonstrations, it was decided to upgrade the technical components of the receiving apparatus and install it backstage at the Dominion Theatre, the Gaumont-British cinema in Tottenham Court Road. At the same time, space in an annex of the base of the Crystal Palace South Tower on its west side was partitioned off to make a studio and control room, to which the sending apparatus was transferred. The link between 'send' and 'receive' was no longer a cable, but a short-wave radio transmitter which had been developed to West's specifications. The transmitting aerial was cantilevered out from the balcony at the top of the tower. Line of sight was made to a receiving aerial mounted on a wooden mast on the roof of the Dominion Theatre. Half a kilowatt of power was sufficient to achieve a satisfactory signal to noise ratio. The whole system was ready for public demonstration during the autumn of 1935. At the same time, Baird and Reveley had developed a mobile version of the six thousand revolutions per minute mirror-drum mechanical camera, mounted on a truck in the same way as a studio film camera (see plate 51). When this was stationed at the wicket-gate by the South Tower, which opened onto Anerley Hill, very clear black-and-white pictures were obtained of the trolley buses going up and down, even in adverse weather conditions.[4]

In the meantime the theatre-going public was being introduced to the further possibilities of television through an adventure story of a struggling inventor who has to go abroad to find a buyer for his system. *Glamorous Night*, a lavish musical by Ivor Novello, who also played the lead, opened at the Theatre Royal, Drury Lane, on 2 May 1935. The inventor, Anthony Allan, rejected in Britain, finds himself in the Ruritanian kingdom of Krasnia, where he falls in love with Militza, a prima donna. After many convolutions of plot, he loses his girl to the king, whom she has to marry to save her country from anarchy. At least the king does buy Allan's television system, and it is by means of this, on a huge screen which dominates the stage in the final scene, that Allan, back in Britain, sadly watches Militza's wedding.[8] When Novello agreed to supply book and music for a new show at the Theatre Royal, he had no idea for it.[9] Television was being thrust before the notice of the public, and Baird was much in the public eye. It is more than possible that Baird, who did not himself appreciate musicals, provided some of the inspiration for what became the first of several notable Drury Lane successes for Novello.

Baird was now a father for the second time. It had initially been Margaret's decision:

> In 1934 I looked out of an upstairs window and saw Diana, then about two, alone on the vast expanse of lawn and decided that she was not going to be an only child. John was against my going through it all again, but I talked him round and, on 2 July 1935, our son Malcolm was born.
>
> I had no sleep for three months before the birth, a breech presentation, but Malcolm was healthy and energetic. For my recuperation my mother took me first to Tunbridge Wells and then to the South of France, where we stayed at my aunt's flat at Cagnes-sur-Mer.
>
> My constitution showed none of the former resilience present after Diana's birth and it was a long time before I could return to normal life. While I was ill my sister-in-law, who had been on her own since her father died, came down to Sydenham.
>
> A week after Malcolm was born John told me that the strain of my confinement had been so severe that he needed a holiday and was going to Morocco with Sydney. They also visited Tangiers.[10]

Margaret both overstated and understated the difficulties. The Tangier holiday after Malcolm's birth is one of her less felicitous contributions to the Baird legend. Even though she inscribed on the back of a photograph of Baird (in cap) standing by a palm tree, 'JLB in Morocco recovering from

Malcolm's birth',* Baird's passport has him in Tangier from 26 to 31 December of the previous year.* There is no passport entry for July 1935, but on 20 December 1935 he entered the continent via Boulogne. If this was for a holiday, it was without Moseley, whose published diaries show that he was in London at this time.[11]

Margaret had, however, suffered a complete breakdown, from what is now known as postnatal depression. On her return from her 'recuperation', she went to live with her mother in Sutton. This must have been a difficult decision both for Margaret and for Baird. He did not like his mother-in-law,[12] and 'Grannie Albu did not like little boys'.[13] The separation lasted two-and-a-half years. Diana stayed most of the time with her mother, while Malcolm remained at Crescent Wood Road. Malcolm was looked after by Miss Yarker, Nursie Basham's replacement, who came from Yorkshire, while Baird and the house were looked after by Annie Baird and her treasure of a housekeeper, Margaret Scott, who came down from Helensburgh for the duration of Margaret's illness.[14] For the whole of this time, Baird telephoned Margaret every night regularly at nine o'clock.[13]

To Reveley, 'Annie had all of JLB's charm of manner, but my impression was that she used this to cover a much more practical and basically competent personality, deriving I imagine from her nursing career.'[15] Since postnatal depression was then not recognised as a clinical condition, the domestic arrangements puzzled Reveley, and others who came to the house. Among the visitors at this time were Farnsworth and his wife, for whom Baird and Annie gave a dinner party in November 1936, during the frantic efforts to make Farnsworth's camera operate smoothly. Elma Farnsworth wrote that she was especially charmed by the graciousness of Lady Greer, compared with the 'rather chilly reserve' of the other wives. In her experience 'only those who had attained the higher rungs of the social ladder could afford to fraternize with those whose status was yet unclear'.[16]

Another visitor to the house while Margaret was away was Joan Hilton, who had joined the company early in 1936. Years later she responded to Margaret's request for information for her biography of Baird:

> In those days we hardly ever glimpsed sight of your husband, at least in the south wing where we were mainly working. He didn't even have a secretary of his own, and ... one lucky day I'd gone into the typists' pool with some work that had to be done, and heard that he'd rung over for a typist, so – having long admired him and his work from afar – I went over instead. He was writing a short autobiography as a framework for someone who wanted to write his life, and I think had been having

heavy weather of it with a succession of typists; anyhow, he kindly asked me to keep coming over and work on this with him. I could at least spell, and write an intelligent-sounding paragraph from a few odd phrases and notes. He was so shy and retiring, as far as most of us were concerned, that we knew nothing about his private life. I met a very charming lady there, but had the impression she was his sister, and there was also a duck of a small child running in and out, to his delight and mine. ... He used to be quite apologetic about calling me away from my work in case he interrupted something important! I remember sunlit afternoons and Mr Baird stopping so that I could have a glass of orange juice (I don't drink tea), and similar thoughtfulnesses.[17]

In the autumn of 1936 Baird had personal staff of six technicians: Reveley, E G O Anderson (who joined the company in October 1936), C F Oxbrow, A (Curly) Sayers, Squire, and Vince.[7] While West and his company's team were preparing for and participating in the Alexandra Palace trial, Baird and his team were finalising arrangements for another Baird spectacular, a press demonstration of the big screen at the Dominion. It was intended to use the Crystal Palace transmitting facilities, but the fire put paid to that. Though the installations were intact, there were no electricity or telephone services. The mobile mechanical camera was transferred to a dressing-room in the Dominion Theatre, which served as a studio. Transmission was by land line to the receiving apparatus on the stage.[4]

The demonstration, on a screen 8 feet high by 6½ feet wide, with very little flicker, was held on 7 December 1936.[18] L Marsland Gander, an experienced critic newly appointed to the post of television correspondent of the *Daily Telegraph*, was a member of the select audience. Sitting in the dress circle, which he estimated was 150 feet from the screen, he was most impressed by the 120-line picture:

> The face of Mr John L Baird, inventor of the system, was clearly recognisable. Mr Baird was actually seated in a small studio in a remote part of the building. His face enlarged to the dimensions of a cinema close-up appeared on a screen over the stage.
>
> Using a telephone in the dress circle, I asked Mr Baird a number of questions about the system. He could be seen on the screen picking up the receiver, and his answers to my questions boomed through loudspeakers alongside. ...
>
> The picture seen at long range was surprisingly effective. Dark

vertical lines, varying in intensity from time to time, were, however, noticeable on the screen.[19]

The 'entertainment' was introduced by Will Hay, with performances by Betty Astell and Horace King. Because of the exigencies of the improvised studio, it was only possible to show close-ups. With a display of ingenuity worthy of Baird in his plywood and biscuit-tin days, lengths of black cotton were stretched across a wooden frame to indicate the correct distance of the face from the lens.[19]

The demonstration was repeated for the public on 4 January 1937. Members of the cinema world also took up tickets, to size up the potential opposition. The specialist film press was less than enthusiastic about the quality of the pictures, which, it was felt, were inferior to those on the small screen.[20]

Nothing daunted, later that month the Baird company, represented by Church and Clayton, met the Television Advisory Committee to enquire whether permission might be forthcoming for experimental transmissions to cinemas. In May the company applied to the GPO for a licence for such transmissions, pointing out that Baird himself had been specifically experimenting with large-screen television for several years. After discussion with the Television Advisory Committee, the application was refused on the grounds that no bandwidth was available.[21]

The company's response was audacious. The Palais-de-Luxe in Bromley, Kent, a Gaumont-British cinema, was fitted out with Baird's large-screen equipment. The press were invited on 7 December 1937. 'Late one night, looking like conspirators in some sinister plot we entered a dark narrow alley-way in the main street to go in by the exit door.'[22] What Baird did was to pick up the normal BBC transmission from Alexandra Palace, 15 miles away on the other side of London, and project it onto his screen. 'The picture was excellent, even the smallest detail of a Mickey Mouse cartoon being clearly identifiable. Sound was good, too.'[22]

The cloak-and-dagger stuff may be related to the fact that the following day, 8 December, Scophony gave a demonstration at British Industries House. BBC images from Alexandra Palace were picked up and clearly shown not only on a large screen (6 feet by 5 feet) but also on a home receiver with a screen whose dimensions were 2 feet by 18 inches.[23]

Whatever the implications of this for the Baird company, Baird himself had another trick, and another 'first', up his sleeve. He had perceived that he could convert his personal apparatus to colour. Both the scanning drum and the receiving drum incorporated a revolving disc containing twelve slots. By fitting blue-green and red filters alternately to these slots, he had a simple colour system. There was some loss of brightness at the receiving end because the complete two-colour picture repetition rate was halved to 8.33 per second, but the result still gave the appearance of full colour.[4] It was during this period, when he was experimenting with colour, that Baird taught Diana how to mix the primary colours to make orange and mauve, which she practised for herself in the shed in Sutton which she used as a playroom.[6]

Baird has been criticised for obstinately sticking to outmoded mechanical techniques, which is partly justified in that in the early 1930s he was slow to adapt his systems to the cathode-ray tube. He was, however, unfairly made a scapegoat for his company's failure to obtain the BBC contract in 1936, since he was not involved in the operation and his company used the best methods that were available to it at the time.[24] In the case of colour television, he was, on 27 July 1939, the first person to demonstrate a system incorporating a cathode-ray tube, in conjunction with a mechanical scanning device.[25] The National Broadcasting Company and the Columbia Broadcasting System in the USA, with vast resources, were still using mechanically-rotated colour filters in 1941. And in the end, it was Baird who produced the world's first all-electronic colour television receiver, in 1944.[26]

The press were invited to the Dominion to view the new phenomenon of cinema television in colour during the week beginning 5 December 1937.[27] The screen, 12 feet by 9, was even larger than Baird had used for monochrome pictures. The programme was transmitted from the Crystal Palace South Tower on a wavelength of 8 metres.[28] The sound was conveyed by telephone line rented from the British Post Office Telephone System Authority; a second identical land line allowed the technical staff at each end of the process to talk to each other. There was nothing to be proved by using radio for this purpose. On the other hand, the bandwidth requirement of high-definition vision signals could not then be compressed within the capacity of an ordinary telephone line. So the use of wireless transmission for the vision was a necessity in itself, and demonstrated the availability of a bandwidth adequate for high-definition vision on wavelengths much shorter than had become customary for sound broadcasting purposes.[29]

The public were introduced to large-screen colour television for the first time anywhere on 4 February 1938. There was no fanfare. The partly-live programme, transmitted by wireless from the Crystal Palace, was simply inserted into the Dominion's evening performance before an audience of three thousand.[28]

Between the two demonstrations, Baird had taken a holiday with Moseley in Cannes. According to Baird's passport,* they crossed to Calais on 5 January

1938. Moseley published two accounts of the trip, a brief one in his diaries[30] and a longer one in his biography of Baird, which is for once more revealing about Baird than about himself:

> We were both sun-worshippers, John and I, and that is how it came about that during one spell of dismal English weather we took a holiday together on the Riviera. The farther we travelled south, the more his spirits rose, and when we arrived at Cannes – where people with overdrafts had no right to be! – he was in the mood to ignore his business worries. And although cables, telegrams and telephone calls began to shower upon us, we dismissed them summarily and set out in brilliant sunshine to walk to Golfe Juan.
>
> That was the beginning of a carefree spell such as Baird had not enjoyed for many years. It liberated his mind from the obsession of television, and we had long talks about religion, the pursuit of happiness, the purpose of this life and the riddle of a life to come.[31]

It was an occasion, too, of *haute cuisine* and practical jokes. The manager of the Gallia Palace, where they stayed, turned out to be the brother of the man who had run the Grand Continental Hotel in Cairo, in which Moseley had lived twenty-five years earlier when editing the *Egyptian Mail*. After a celebratory lunch (pâté de foie gras, specially flown in from Strasbourg, filet de sole bonne femme, and the chef's speciality, soufflé en surprise), Baird retired for a siesta while Moseley wrote a cable to his stockbroker in New York. Having decided to deliver it personally to the post office during their stroll before dinner, he went to Baird's room to tell him this. Baird was stretched out on the bed, rigid, with his eyes staring blankly at the ceiling.

> I rushed from the room in search of aid. Failing to find anyone, I rushed back to make certain that my fears were justified. Baird was still in the same position, lying rigidly with fixed eyes. Then I remembered the obvious thing – the telephone, of course! I picked up the receiver. ...
>
> 'Oi! Ye're *daft!*' came in a broad Scots accent from the bed, shaking me to the very core. I dropped the instrument and turned, to see John sitting up, as lively as a cricket!
>
> Later he confessed to me that he had been experimenting in Yoga. 'I have often succeeded,' he said, 'in leaving my body and standing by and watching it. Today I succeeded in doing it far more effectively than ever before. Then you came in and spoilt it. In fact, you nearly chased my spirit away!'

'In point of fact, then,' I said, 'I was looking at your dead body.'
'The empty shell,' he replied simply. 'The empty shell. ... '[32]

Baird put one over his friend again, when they were out walking. He dawdled behind, and then, when an exasperated Moseley went on ahead, he suddenly appeared in front of him, laughing, on a grassy knoll. Moseley's retaliation struck at one of the central issues of Baird's being:

> Baird's hair had grown even longer than even he cared to wear it, and so, a day or two later in Cannes, he decided to have it trimmed, and I went with him to the barber's shop to act as interpreter. My knowledge of French was limited, but Baird could speak no French at all.
>
> Directly he was seated in the barber's chair – with the white cloth tied behind him and his back to the mirror – an impish urge came upon me to make sure that, for once in his life, he should have a really good hair-cut. But the French 'artist' engaged upon this memorable job was not allowed to make more than a few preliminary snips before Baird said to me anxiously: 'Tell him not to take off too much, Sydney, just a wee bit.' At the same time he made vague gestures of protest with his hands beneath the cloth, followed, in unusually broad Scots, by a succession of instructions of which the barber could not understand a single word. Scissors aloft, the man turned to me with an eloquent questioning shrug of the shoulders.
>
> I ought, of course, to have told him to go easy, but actually all I said was: '*Oui, Oui; beaucoup, beaucoup!*' At the time, I admit, beaming at Baird with my most reassuring smile.
>
> The barber bent to his task again and the scissors went through that tousled mane like a scythe through long grass. John grew more anxious still. 'Tell him to be careful,' he implored, but once again I said to the barber: '*Continuez – beaucoup, beaucoup!*'. And the fell work proceeded.
>
> I could bear it no longer. I ran from the shop to let loose a shout of laughter and was still laughing when an infuriated Baird came out looking like a shorn lamb. He had seen himself in the glass and could not find words strong enough to express his horror and indignation. He stood spluttering before me, waving his clenched fists.
>
> 'What's all the fuss about, John?' I asked, with an air of innocent surprise. 'Why, you look ten years younger than you did!'
>
> Then the floodgates opened and I turned away to escape a stream of abuse couched in the most lurid language of the Glasgow engineering shops, where he had served his apprenticeship.

It took him quite a long time to cool down and he did not altogether forgive me for a long time. Indeed, he never trusted me in a hairdresser's salon again and did not visit one at all until his hair was long enough once more to flop over his eyebrows.[33]

Back in London, Baird gave a further demonstration of large-screen colour television on 17 February 1938, to members of the Television Society, the press, and some distinguished guests. Among them was Selsdon, who, considering the low frame rate for each colour, allowed that, 'with all its defects, [Baird] is producing a colour picture'.[34]

The following week, Baird and Margaret set off on an adventure which marked the re-establishment of their married life.[35] The occasion was the World Radio Convention in Sydney, Australia. According to Baird, the keynote address was to have been given by Marconi, 'but his death [in July 1937] left a vacant place and I was chosen as a substitute'.[36] If this is so, then Baird would have been the first to appreciate the honour, and the irony! He was not too happy about leaving London at this time, but the chance of seeing Australia was too good to miss, the Australian government was paying his expenses, and the company representatives there felt that his presence would do a lot for potential business.

While waiting at Victoria Station on 24 February to travel overland to Marseilles, Baird gave a press interview in which he suggested, 'In Australia I shall go into the question of perfecting television, particularly for the large screens of cinemas. Television has not yet been introduced to Australia but it is hoped to start activities there in a reasonably short time.'[37]

They sailed from Marseilles on the P & O liner, *Strathaird*. His invitation to Margaret to accompany him had been made in his typical offhand fashion, with a touch of Scottish thrift:

> 'If you come I shall have to pay your expenses, whereas if I take Sydney he will be paid for!'
>
> I am glad I went with him, for that was the first time in our lives together that we were able to escape from the business worries of television. His cares diminished with every mile we travelled until he became like a young man.
>
> He had not given me any details of what was to happen in Australia, and it was only when unpacking in the cabin in the *Strathaird* that I found an itinerary crowded with functions, luncheons, and dinners, in Perth, Adelaide, Melbourne, and Sydney, in fact wherever there was a branch of the Institute of Radio Engineers. I did not have appropriate

clothes with me, but in Bombay I managed to buy some evening frocks at the Army and Navy Stores.[38]

In Bombay they were invited to be guests of honour at a dinner given by the Maharajah of Kutch, at the Taj Mahal Hotel on Malabar Hill.

> His Highness the Maharajah, an elderly man, was cultured and distinguished, and as the only woman present I was seated at his right hand. The elegance of the occasion, the frangipani on the table with its beautiful appointments, fairly took my breath away. This was the first time I had sat at table with any but white-skinned people. Fortunately I had been reading Rabindranath Tagore and was able to say so by way of conversation with the maharajah. 'Ah, yes,' he said. 'He was an intimate friend of mine.' I could not help thinking that this race of people was civilized when the inhabitants of Britain were practically savages.[39]

Baird's memories of the occasion were less romantic:

> What a meal! All other banquets pale before it! Dish followed dish, delicious and exotic. I ate heartily and was horribly ill for nearly a week afterwards. In fact we had reached Perth in Australia before my internal organs had got back to normal.[40]

They stopped off in Colombo. During the latter part of the voyage smallpox broke out on board. After being vaccinated, Baird and Margaret were allowed to land at Fremantle, according to Baird's passport on 22 March,* and to take the train across Australia to Sydney, missing out Melbourne and the arrangements that had been made there for them. The company's Australian representative was L P R Bean, chairman and managing director of Stromberg–Carlson and vice-president of the Institution of Radio Engineers (Australia). He arranged for Baird to address the Perth Radio Society, and a professor from Perth University took the couple exploring the region in his car.

Baird was impressed by the country, which seemed to him to approximate to one in which his moderate socialist principles were observed:

> I saw no acute poverty and no 'slums' as we understand the term, and on the other hand I saw no evidence of flaunting wealth, and found indeed an almost startling absence of anything in the nature of class

distinction. It was a country entirely inhabited by petty bourgeoisie and as I myself belong to that class I was pleasantly at home. It reminded me of what the USA might become if it could be purged of its gangsters, its crooks, its horrible film magnates and upstart millionaires and all its strident screaming vulgarity.[41]

What also impressed him were the two parallel broadcasting systems, the Australian Broadcasting Commission and the private stations with their advertising.[42] This is what he had in effect been advocating in Britain for television for over ten years now. It would not happen until 1954, eight years after his death.

Of Baird's reception in Sydney, Bean wrote to the company board that it 'had never previously been accorded to any visitor to Australia, not even the most distinguished royalty'.[43] The warmth of the reception is confirmed in an air letter Baird wrote to Moseley from the Australia Hotel, Sydney:

> I got your notes on toilet paper and sent a reply which I hope you received. From what you tell me things are still in the same state as when I left London.
>
> I have had a most hectic week in Sydney. Lunches dinners speeches from morning to night. I wish I was back on the 'Strathaird' in peace.
>
> We leave on the 16th and will be back in London on the 27th May. If you want peace try a sea voyage.
>
> This is a very pleasant place, warm summer sunshine, beautiful sandy beaches and no rain. I have been too busy however to get in any paddling although the water is warm and the sandy beach tempting. <u>My paper was a great success</u>. I hope some business will result.[44]

He had delivered his 'paper' in the Great Hall of the University of Sydney, dressed in white tie and tails, with beside him on a table a large cathode-ray tube, the Baird 'cathovisor', which he had brought with him from London for the occasion. In the course of a detailed technical account of television developments, with illustrations and diagrams, he gave credit to other pioneers such as Jenkins, Farnsworth, and Zworykin. He did not, however, mention Marconi–EMI by name, describing the current BBC television cameras as having been 'first developed by V K Zworykin of the Radio Corporation of America'.[45] This brought down on his head something of a corrective tirade from the chairman, Sir Ernest Fisk, president of the Institution of Radio Engineers, who appeared to be 'just a trifle upset by the amount of publicity the president of a rival concern was receiving'.[46]

The subsequent discussion was closed by Bean, who referred to the inscription on the memorial tablet in St Paul's Cathedral:

> If you want to know about Sir Christopher Wren's life work, 'look around you'. These words apply to Mr Baird; examine his work and you see him as a scientific genius. As a pioneer, Mr Baird has done stupendous work and has blazed the trail for hundreds of other research workers.[45]

On the return voyage the *Strathaird* again docked at Colombo. To Baird the ship had 'become by this time a second home. I thought life on board ship ideal and would have continued cruising through these tropical waters indefinitely.'[40] As Margaret put it, 'The nearer we got to London the more John's spirits fell.'[47]

According to Baird's passport,* they passed through Calais again on 21 May. They had been away for three months. During this time Hitler had overrun and taken over Austria, and the British government had announced that all school children would be issued with gas masks. Also, Grannie Albu had fallen down stairs and broken her leg.[48]

The Bairds were briefly a family again. Margaret was convinced that war was imminent. So was Moseley, who attempted to inject into Baird a sense of alarm:

> John is still absorbed almost exclusively in television, and when I warn him of the approaching international catastrophe he takes it all in his stride. 'Och! We'll away to the Scottish hills, Sydney,' he says, 'and stock up with ... (and here he mentions some Scottish make of tinned food). One can forgive an inventor with his head in the clouds for such absurdities, but not our leaders, who are craven and confused.[49]

Margaret tried to persuade Baird to take the family to South Africa. Baird finally compromised by renting a furnished house for her and the children at Minehead, on the Somerset coast. They went there in July. Miss Yarker, now promoted to governess of the two children, came too. Diana recalls a winter walk on the beach. She and Malcolm wore tweed coats and angora berets, blue for her, red for her brother. Miss Yarker collected pieces of quartz to make a necklace, and Malcolm fell in the sea.

They were briefly back at Crescent Wood Road in September for Diana's sixth birthday. At breakfast, a large brown paper parcel was solemnly handed through the serving hatch into the dining-room. Diana asked, 'Is that for me?'

'No,' replied her mother, 'It's your father's shoes!' When opened, however, it revealed a workbasket for Diana, which she kept until it disintegrated, long after she married.[6] Baird was in Minehead in October,[50] and again at Christmas, when he arrived 'loaded with parcels, stout for once and looking healthy'.[51] Margaret organised six concerts locally, one for each month that they were there. The artists included the violinist Brosa, Garda Hall, a South African singer, Gaby Valle, the soprano, and Betty Humby, who in 1943 became the second wife of Sir Thomas Beecham, the conductor.

The international crisis seemed to be temporarily eased in the light of the Munich agreement in September 1938, and the family was reunited at 3 Crescent Wood Road in January 1939. Though the situation worsened in March with the Nazi occupation of Czechoslovakia, and the subsequent admission by Neville Chamberlain, the British Prime Minister, that he had been duped, Baird and Margaret managed a three-week holiday on the continent, at St Tropez, at the end of April and beginning of May.

Meanwhile, the Television Advisory Committee had continued to vacillate about the status of cinema television. The Baird company and Scophony had developed and were publicly demonstrating their systems. On 1 June 1938 both showed the Derby as it happened to invited audiences, the Baird company at the Tatler, a Gaumont-British news cinema in Charing Cross Road, and Scophony at the Kensington store, Derry and Toms.[52] The Baird company too was now using electronic methods of cinema projection. Its equipment incorporated a powerful cathode-ray tube which projected the picture onto an 8 foot by 6 foot screen from in front. At the same time an even more powerful tube, known as the 'teapot tube', operating on forty thousand volts, was being designed and manufactured in the Baird company laboratories. This enabled paying customers on 23 February 1939, at both the Tatler and the Marble Arch Pavilion, to see live, broadcast by the BBC from Haringey Arena, the British light-heavyweight title fight between Eric Boon and Arthur Danahar on a screen which was 15 feet by 12.[53] The fight could also be seen at a rival show put on by Scophony at the Monseigneur News Theatre, conveniently next door to the Marble Arch Pavilion, back-projected onto a 6 foot by 5 foot screen.[54] The police were called out to control the crowds trying to get in to the performances. At the Marble Arch Pavilion every seat was taken, and about seventy people stood along each wall. Two cameras were used, and the blistering fight, which was won by Boon when he stopped his opponent in the fourteenth round, was wildly applauded by the cinema audiences.[55]

Baird was now working on his colour television system. He no longer had the services of Reveley, who had resigned from the company in November

1938 to join the post office department of the government of Hong Kong. Reveley had come to the conclusion that the resources available to Baird were too small for the problems to be resolved on a commercial basis. Even so, he 'took this step with the greatest reluctance because [Baird] was the best boss as a person that anyone could hope to work for'.[56]

Baird was either too preoccupied with his personal research to consider how he might be of benefit to the war effort, or he simply assumed that his capabilities, and his work, were so well known to the relevant authorities that he would be called upon when the time came. This attitude infuriated Moseley:

> Many a time I was tempted to shout at him: 'Blast your inventions, John! What do they matter when the whole world is likely to go up in flames at any moment?' But I could not be angry with him for long; and so, with a sigh, I would resign myself to letting him talk 'shop' and do my best to force my own thoughts back into channels which were fast becoming too narrow to contain them.[57]

Moseley's response to the seemingly inevitable onset of total war was typical of the man. 'I am going to join up. ... Have been writing to the Services. ... The only way. ... Acknowledgment from the Admiralty. Offer to serve "noted"! It would be a relief to get back into uniform. I am fat and fifty, but could be useful.'[58] 'In these days of intense nationalism it occurred to me – *me*, a one-time pacifist! – that perhaps it would be as well to collect any medals due to me from the last war! So, after twenty years, I wrote to Admiralty and War Office Records. ... Surprisingly came – four medals!'[59]

Early in February 1939, frustrated at hearing nothing further from the Admiralty, Moseley obtained an interview with Rear-Admiral John Godfrey. Godfrey, who commanded the battle cruiser *Repulse* in the Mediterranean from 1936 to 1938, had just been promoted and appointed director of naval intelligence, Moseley's old outfit in World War I. On 15 February, Moseley wrote confirming their discussion, adding, 'I assume, of course, that the Admiralty has realized the great potentialities of Noctovision? After seeing you, I had a word with my friend, John L Baird, who is the British television pioneer, and we should be very happy to help you in any possible way.'[60] In his reply, Godfrey wrote,

> It is very good of you to offer your services in such an open-handed way. I am taking up the suggestion contained in your letter, and am making enquiries of various Departments regarding the possibility of

making use of your services in war-time. In the meantime, your name has been noted as an applicant.[61]

On which Moseley commented, 'Promising!'[61] It is impossible to tell from what survives of the exchange whether Godfrey took seriously Baird's offer, or indeed did anything about it. It was probably an error of judgment on Moseley's part to mention noctovision, in the light of the fiasco of the Admiralty demonstration in 1929. In the end, there was no naval job for Moseley either. He wrote, 'Still on tenterhooks – ever waiting for the post-man. What a terrible thing it is that one must wait until the war is on before one is told where and when he is wanted.'[62]

He further recorded in his diaries the countdown to world conflict:

[August 31]: Mobilisation and evacuation ordered.
SEPT. 2: This night scarcely slept, after Chamberlain's amazingly inept speech. I *felt* it would create anguish in [Parliament]. Apparently it did. 'Speak for *Britain!*' a member cried. ... Other members joined in.
    A British (*not*) a Franco-British ultimatum to Germany.
SEPT. 3: (Sunday morning) Up at 6, waiting for the seven o'clock news. No change. ... at eight o'clock it was announced that there would be important news at nine. I guessed what that was. ...
    WAR!![63]

Margaret recalled:

The first thought was to get the children out of London because every-one expected that Hitler would use gas. John took a map and a ruler and drew a line westwards from London. The line ended at Bude on the Cornish coast, almost two hundred and fifty miles away. By persistence on the telephone at two o'clock in the morning he had us booked into a small hotel there. I hated leaving him, but there was no choice and, with suitcases packed in haste, we left the next day.[64]

With the collapse of Baird Television Ltd a few days later, Baird lost his position as president, and his salary. His shares in the company which he had founded were worthless. He had no job, no income, and no war work, but he owned a house and a private laboratory, and there was £15,000 in his bank deposit account.[65]★

15
Carrying on: Bude and London
1939–1942

B aird had ruled out the southwest coast as a refuge for his family because of its proximity to channel ports such as Plymouth, which could be targets for bombers. Bude, north Cornwall, was a town of five thousand people which largely owed its existence to the tourists who flocked in by train for summer holidays. Its main attractions were the fine sandy beaches with good surfing conditions, and a wind-blown golf course around which the town was built.

Miss Yarker had returned home, and Margaret decided that as she no longer had the house in Crescent Wood Road to run, she would look after the children herself. After a fortnight in hotels, the Maer Lodge and the Penarvor, she found a furnished house, Glenside, 25 Killerton Road, within walking distance of the station. Grannie Albu, now sixty-seven and lame from her fall, was prevailed upon to leave her rented house in Sutton. She arrived in Bude in a hired car, with her black half-Persian cat (Titus), her black labrador (Sultan), and several canaries and budgerigars in cages. Schools were found, in Malcolm's case a nearby kindergarten. When asked by a neighbour if he was not very young to be going to school, he replied insouciantly, 'Oh no, some of the chaps come in prams.' Diana started at St Catherine's, quite a large school, where roller skating in the asphalt playground was the current craze. Margaret decided it was too rough, and when Malcolm was five moved both children to Sandown, a Bexhill private preparatory school which had been evacuated and now occupied the Penarvor Hotel.

Conditions at Glenside were cramped, and the ménage moved to a larger house known as Little Manaton, and then, in the summer of 1940, to one half of a farm house, Maer Farm, a mile or so out of Bude. Margaret bought a grey Hillman with red seats, which she drove until forced to give it up because of the petrol restrictions. She then acquired a green lady's bicycle, called Harriet, on which she wobbled precariously along rutted Cornish lanes, with loads of shopping hanging from the handlebars. Diana records: 'The life of the English countryside, with the tearing winds off the Atlantic, the winter squalls, the mud and the general isolation, was not [Margaret's] scene. She consoled herself with frequent visits to the cinema on the Headland, where the programme changed three times a week.'[1] One day Margaret returned from the shops laughing hysterically. As she had emerged from the butcher's with the family's weekly ration of a few ounces of cooking fat, the paper bag containing it was caught by the prevailing westerly wind and blown irretrievably across the dunes of the golf course. It was directly facing the golf course that the family finally settled: Thymeland, an Edwardian terrace house at 7 Flexbury Park Road.

Baird was more concerned about the safety of his family than he was about his own. 'I was in the middle of some extremely important work on colour television and, rather than see this stopped, I continued this work at my own expense, keeping on two assistants and working in [my] private laboratory at Crescent Wood Road.'[2] Initially, it was three assistants, Anderson, Oxbrow, and Sayers, but Oxbrow left for war work at the Royal Aircraft Establishment early in 1940, and Sayers on 5 April 1941.[3] Anderson stayed on. Baird also used the services part time of an expert glassblower, Arthur H Johnson. On other occasions he was able to call, just as he did in his Hastings days, on volunteer helpers, who included Squire, Richard Head, and Geoffrey Bernard, who was waiting to be called up.[4]

Most of the rooms in the main house were closed, with windows shuttered and furniture under dust sheets. The principal drawing-room remained in use for occasional press conferences. Of the servants, only Bill Woodley, part-time gardener and handyman, remained. Initially Margaret travelled up to London to put the house in order. The journey took eight hours, on trains so crowded with servicemen that at Exeter she would go into the guard's van with her sandwiches and sit there until she got to London. When family pressures at Bude prevailed and the risks from bombs increased, she had to give up the trips. A part-time housekeeper, Mrs Bennett, was engaged for a while, but later in the war Mrs Woodley helped out. Baird would eat sketchy meals prepared by them, or make himself a pot of tea to wash down the Scottish oatcakes of which he kept a supply in the house. He took to spending the night at one of the shabby residential hotels nearby, the Toksowa on Dulwich Common, or the Beulah Hill, Norwood.

Baird carried a pocket diary as an engagement book and *aide-mémoire*. The diaries for the years 1940 to 1946 survive in the possession of the Baird family.* Cryptic as the entries are, they help to provide a first-hand record of his activities and contacts during the war years. In 1940 in particular, he was closely in touch with some of the key technical people at Cinema-Television, whose factory at Worsley Bridge Road, and the workshop which had been maintained in the Rotunda, were within walking distance of his house. He did not, however, have security clearance to visit the premises, and had to be accompanied all the time by West,[5] now chief engineer of Cintel, as Cinema-Television came to be called early in 1940. West's name appears forty-four times in Baird's diary for 1940 alone.

The absence of security clearance is understandable in the light of the work on military projects West obtained for the company, and the fact that Baird was not employed either by Cintel or by the British government. In May 1940 an arrangement was made between Gaumont-British, Cintel, and the receiver of Baird Television Ltd, to the effect that Cintel was financed for the purpose of carrying out government contracts.[6] At that time Cintel had one factory and a staff of forty. In December 1944 there were three factories and a thousand staff, ninety-five per cent of whom were engaged in the production of equipment for the armed services which had originally been designed by the company, and five per cent on further development.[7]

During the first year the work was mainly developing types of equipment associated with television techniques, such as electronic instruments, cathode-ray tubes, photographic recording equipment, and specialist radio receivers. Subsequently the company branched out into the design and construction of other types of military hardware. Prominent among these were thirty thousand landmine detectors of different designs for different circumstances, many of which were used in the fighting in North Africa, and in the landings in Sicily and Italy. Also produced were devices for detecting unexploded bombs, photo-electric cells for a variety of purposes including monitoring the change in colour of blood of pilots flying at high altitudes, and equipment for measuring the time between a shell being fired and its explosion in mid-air, and for calculating the blast power of super bombs. Among unusual pieces of radio apparatus was a receiver which indicated on the screen of a cathode-ray tube the operating frequency of any enemy radio station which started transmitting, so that a message could be intercepted or jammed, and a miniature transmitter/receiver which was strapped to a paratrooper's chest, so that he could maintain contact with his aircraft or with his headquarters.[7]

In the course of the war, Cintel manufactured and supplied over 110,000 cathode-ray tubes.[7] A tube coating, developed by Constantin Szegho, provided a 'slow-fade' image lasting several seconds after being scanned by the electron beam, and was extremely useful in radar receivers.[8] It enabled images to be recorded more easily, and even traced out by hand. This technique of Szegho's was probably incorporated in the Skiatron dark-trace cathode-ray tubes used in Britain's radar defences, of which Cintel was a supplier. Szegho was also a leading member of a Cintel team working on improved projection cathode-ray tubes, which could create a small but very bright image. Many private meetings with Szegho, who went to the USA in October 1940, are recorded in Baird's diary. Baird was at that time working towards a colour television receiver which also used projection from a small, high-powered cathode-ray tube, with the screen being an integral part of the set.

Two other Cintel scientists whose names often appear in Baird's diary for 1940 are K A R Samson and A H Sommer, who had joined the Baird company in 1935 and 1936 respectively. Their expertise lay in the development of sensitive surfaces which could amplify an electrical image (electron multipliers) or a light image (photomultipliers). Though they had left Germany because of Hitler, nevertheless when war broke out their status in Britain was that of 'alien'. Initially West arranged for them to work somewhat in isolation from colleagues in the laboratories, to avoid jeopardising potential government contracts. Cintel described Samson and Sommer as 'probably the world's chief experts' on the photo-cells used in proximity fuses. In July 1940, the Admiralty issued indefinite exemption from internment to both men, as long as they were under 'strict surveillance outside their employment'.[6] Later in the war Samson was put in charge of the mass production of the Skiatron tubes. Baird's particular interest in their expertise would have involved the sensitive photo-cells at the transmitting end of his electronic colour television system.

Tomes recalls being asked by Baird to meet him towards the end of 1942 at the Beulah Hill Hotel. Tomes was thinking of establishing his own business, and Baird wanted to know if he could make for him a particular kind of photomultiplier. When Tomes explained that this would be impossible in wartime, Baird advised him, when he started on his own, to file as many patents as possible to 'dress the shop window'. He also recommended that Tomes should take on Sommer.[9]

Another source of information about Baird's wartime activities is a small collection of surviving letters from him to Moseley.[10] Moseley, frustrated at the British government's signal failure to call on him to participate in the war effort, had gone to the USA on his own initiative to conduct a personal campaign to make Americans aware of the British situation. He had been in Canada in November 1939 on a broadcasting trip when his former associate Leon Osterweil cabled him: '*Here* is where you are wanted, you are preaching to the converted in Canada. Come on over and plead Britain's case to America.'[11] So he went.

Baird wrote to Moseley on 2 January 1940. There had obviously been a breakdown in communications between them, because Moseley had written to Baird care of their mutual friend Lindsay Carstairs, who had read the letter to Baird over the phone.[12] Baird was upset about this: 'Surely it is not a very <u>gentlemanly</u> thing to send an open letter to be forwarded.' The reason for this outburst was probably that Moseley had suggested he should come to the USA, and Baird did not want anyone else to know.

> The company is in the hands of a receiver (Price Waterhouse). It will be bought from him I expect by G[aumont] B[ritish] but this may take some months. My salary has stopped and I don't know whether G B will re-engage me or not.
>
> I can't possibly come to USA on 'spec' and am amazed that anyone would suggest it. The last time I was there it cost a small fortune and proved a loss.
>
> If the USA has anything for me and will pay me my fare and expenses that would be a different story. My position is a very unhappy one here. I can only hope the position will clarify in the next two months. It all depends on the war.
>
> I am endeavouring to cut down expenses and try and last as long as possible. Can you recommend a good workhouse?[10]

He was still hoping he might be re-employed by Gaumont-British when he wrote to Moseley on 14 January 1940, having had a 'bad attack of influenza'. In the meantime Moseley had found, probably through Flamm, the money for Baird's fare.

> I am very far from busy and prosperous but am continuing research and paying my three men and buying material <u>out of my own pocket</u>. I have still got faith in my work!
>
> If you would let me know what the project or programme is which you have in mind, I might be able to fix things, but so far all you have mentioned is the fare. Before taking a decision which might well be a matter of life or death (financially if not otherwise) I feel I should know something about what the proposition is.[10]

He wrote again on 4 March:

> The company is still in the receivers' hands but G B will probably take it over within the next two months. I have a strong impression that there will be no great anxiety to include me in the new concern! However the whole situation will reach a climax shortly.[10]

Moseley persisted with his invitation. Baird wrote on 3 April:

> I ... hope when this business clears it may be possible to come out and spend next winter in California.
>
> What part had you in mind for me to play? Lectures or acting in the Pictures! (I did a little in this for a film the Post Office were making on the History of Television.) Or had you in mind the formation of a new company in the USA or Canada? Everything here is in the melting pot. I don't know what will emerge. I hope there may be a revival. This waiting is a nerve wracking business but I must hold on. ... I wish I could come, another winter like this one may finish me. ... The company is still in the receiver's hands and likely to remain so for two or three months more. We <u>may</u> be clear at the end of May at the very earliest.[10]

With this letter he enclosed a list of his patents and a brief history of the Baird company, converting pounds sterling into dollars for easier understanding.[13]

In addition to his worries about his family and about himself, Baird was also concerned for Mephy, who had since the mid-1930s been in the Isle of Wight, living in lodgings and running a herbalist's shop. He was in touch with Mephy during the week beginning 14 April 1940, with the suggestion that Mephy might come and stay at Crescent Wood Road the following weekend, but that does not seem to have happened. According to his diary, Baird wrote to Mephy on Sunday 16 June. On the following Tuesday, while he was sitting in the garden, he received a letter from Ryde:*

> Dear Sir
> I am taking the liberty of writing to you, knowing that you were an old friend of Mr Fullarton Robertson.
>
> I am sorry to say he committed suicide on Friday June 14th. He had been very depressed lately owing to the War, and the few air raids we have had have seemed to upset him very much. He seemed to take no interest in anything. He is being buried on Wednesday the 19th.
>
> I have known Mr Robertson for five years, and have lost a very dear friend. He had no other friends besides myself, and I thought perhaps you might like to attend the funeral.
> Yours sincerely
> Stella Jaye[14]

Baird later recorded his anguish:

I could not for a moment realize it. Mephy, whom I had just written to and had arranged to visit, dead! Suicide! Impossible – why should he commit suicide? Why, without one hint or suggestion suddenly take this irrevocable final step out of everything? The hopeless finality, the tragic terrible loss, struck me with brutal force, a terrible loss indeed, and one that could never be replaced. Why did I not go to Ryde sooner? I could have stopped it. Why did I not write earlier? He never received my last letter. Poor Mephy! Ryde being opposite Portsmouth, had been having continual air raid alarms. He could not sleep and his nervous system must have given way completely. On the Friday morning he took no breakfast and went to his little studio in Herb Cottage, locked himself in and attached a tube to his gas ring, turned on the gas and, lying down, covered himself and the tube with a blanket and went to sleep never to wake again! The next day, when he did not return to his lodgings, the police broke down the door and found him.[15]

Baird arrived in Ryde in time for the funeral, exhausted and drained. As Mephy's oldest, and closest, friend, he retrieved from his lodgings some of his own letters going back twenty years,[16] and made arrangements for storing Mephy's effects until he could deal with them. He wired to Margaret to meet him in Salisbury, where they spent a night before going to Bude, from which Baird returned to London the following Wednesday.

Mephy was buried in Ryde cemetery. According to a report in the Isle of Wight *County Press*, he died of carbon monoxide poisoning in the basement of his shop, Herb Cottage, St Thomas' Square. It was described by the coroner as a 'ghastly hole' which must have contributed to his depression. His state of mind was attributed to his reaction to the fall of Paris, which happened on 14 June. Evidence was given by Mephy's sister, Iris Bell, from Stone, in Staffordshire, and by Lilian Hodson, daughter of his landlady at Arabian Lodge, 20 Castle Street, where he had lodged for six years.[17]

Mephy died intestate. It is not known whether he owned or rented Herb Cottage, but his estate was valued at £2894.17s.3d net, the equivalent of about £120,000 today. Everything automatically went to Iris, the 'lawful sister of the whole blood and the only person entitled to the estate of the said intestate'.[18]

The position with regard to Mephy's personal effects exercised Baird for some time. The entries in his diary 'Crates' (30 June 1940) and 'Empty Mephy's crates' (22 August 1942), also 'Mephy's clothes' (31 August and 13 September 1941), taken in conjunction with references to telephoning and visiting Ryde in between times, clearly refer to this ongoing process. His contact in Ryde turns out not to have been Stella Jaye, but H Pearce, Barfield Lodge (tele-phone Ryde 2423), by whom the crates must have been stored. H Pearce was Helen Marigold, one of two daughters (there were also three sons) of William Charles Pearce, Barfield Lodge, owner of the Ryde and Sandown wine merchants, Yelf and Company, and his wife Helena. Helen, who was probably born in about 1910, was the only one of the Pearce children living at home when Mephy died.[19]

There are also in Baird's diaries reminders to 'Send picture to Ryde' (2 October 1940), 'Send on picture H Pearce' (12 October 1942), and 'Photo to Ryde' (17 October 1942).[20] Whether these refer to a signed photograph of Baird as a gift in return for Helen's help, or perhaps the photograph of Mephy and his shop reproduced in this book (see plate 46), has not been established.

Mephy was much in Baird's mind when he wrote to Moseley on 24 June 1940. The letter, written in Bude but with the Crescent Wood Road address, is scrawled in pencil on several small sheets of paper. After describing Mephy's death and the shock of it, Baird continued:

> We are still dragging along here. ... I am continuing my research work at 3 Crescent Wood Road and we have now my own apparatus and equipment so that I am in fact a separate company, paying my own staff of three men. I think we are doing good work and I will hold on as long as possible in the hope that the war stops soon and it will be possible to raise funds. If the war continues too long I will be sunk but I don't suppose I will be the only one in that state!
>
> I have sometimes thought of moving the whole menagerie to Canada or the USA but it bristles with difficulties. I would not like to leave my assistants in the lurch nor do I like the thought of leaving the country. ...
>
> I am glad to see you are keeping the flag flying but let me tell you that you are missing something by being away at this time and knowing you I think you would be really happier here than in the States.[10]

The entry in Baird's diary for Saturday, 7 September, is just, 'Bang!' This was no explosion in the laboratory, such as had happened in Hastings, but the devastating air raid on the east end of London and the docks, only a few miles from Sydenham, which marked the beginning of the blitz. The house and laboratory at 3 Crescent Wood Road survived, but windows were blown out and there was some structural damage. It is probably to this period that belongs the anecdote which is recorded by Moseley as having taken place at the outbreak of the war,[21] but in Carstairs family folklore set during the blitz.[22] Lindsay Carstairs was taking Baird for a drive in the country when air-raid alarms signalled a raid on London. Baird insisted on being driven at once to Crescent Wood Road. Carstairs assumed that there was a vital piece of equipment or a set of drawings that he needed to preserve. When they arrived at the house, Baird dashed into the laboratory, from which he emerged a few minutes later with a grey and white kitten called Smoky. He later took Smoky to Bude on the train, where it became a member of the family's collection of pets.[23]

Because of the blitz, Baird spent a few weeks lodging with friends in the village of Jordans, Buckinghamshire, from which he commuted to Sydenham by hired car, at considerable expense, to continue his experiments with colour television. He was back at Crescent Wood Road more permanently on 13 November, when he dictated to Moseley the only surviving letter in the series which is professionally typed:

> I can't very well come over to New York during the war, but will probably come over when the war finishes. I spoke to Churchill about letting you run the war, and he tells me he will consider it.
>
> I am glad to say things here are looking a little brighter. I have a very fine colour television picture, and also I am working on a large screen which should give a picture ten to a hundred times as bright a picture as the present system, and furthermore the projector will be able to go in the operating box and not in the auditorium as at present. Perhaps something can be done in the States, if not now, later. If you have any ideas in the matter, let me know. Things are developing more rapidly, and I will probably have some news for you within the next three weeks.[10]

As things turned out it was to be about seven weeks, but it was news which, but for the war, would have made headlines. The key components in both the transmitter and the receiver of Baird's new system were the powerful projection cathode-ray tubes which had been developed a few years earlier by Szegho and others at the Baird company for large-screen cinema television. At the transmission end, a small but very powerful projection cathode-ray tube produced a plain pattern of scanned lines on its screen. This intense pattern was projected through a lens as a flying spot, which scanned the person or object being televised. The scanning of the complete image was carried out alternately with red and with blue-green (cyan) light by placing a rotating wheel, containing filters in the two colours, in front of the projection tube. Light reflected from the two-colour scans was picked up by sensitive photo-cells. The signals went by cable to the receiving end of the process, where they were amplified and sent to another small projection cathode-ray tube. The picture was re-created in colour by means of synchronously rotating red and blue-green filters, then magnified by a lens and back-projected on to the ground-glass screen of the receiving set.

The main step forward was the use of electronic scanning by cathode-ray tube, instead of mechanical scanning by disc or mirror drum. The high speed of electronic scanning gave a 600-line picture with a frequency of twenty-

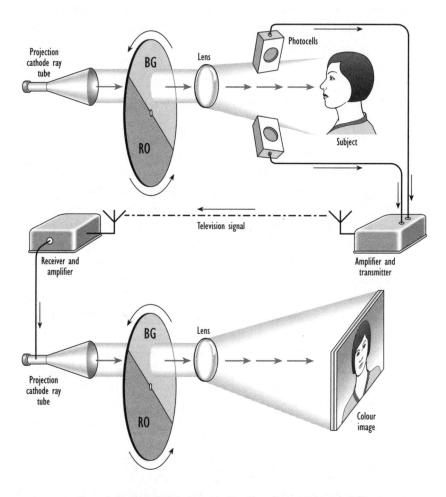

Figure 8: Diagram of Baird's colour television system, demonstrated in late 1940.
A grid (raster) is traced out very rapidly by scanning beams projected from a cathode-ray tube through a rotating colour filter (BG = blue-green, RO = red-orange), onto the subject being televised. Reflected light from the subject is picked up by several photo-cells and the amplified signal is transmitted to the receiver, where the picture is built up through a cathode-ray tube and rotating colour filter, and projected onto a ground-glass screen.
A good 600-line picture was obtained by having the lines transmitted alternately in different colours (interlacing).

five pictures a second on a 2½ by 2 foot screen, the complete result being achieved by interlacing the two basic colours.[24] From the normal viewing distance, the human eye was unable to distinguish between the lines and saw only the mixture of the two colours. Despite only two colours being used, instead of the more usual red, blue, and green, picture quality was excellent.

In the memo section of his diary for the week beginning 9 December 1940, Baird wrote, 'Invite all the press for Thursday. Technical press by special arrangement.' The demonstration took place on 19 December, and earned a four-hundred-word piece in *The Times*: 'Flicker has been almost eliminated, and definition is extremely good. ... Because of the war this country has had to abandon for the time being the leading place in the broadcasting of television, but it is well that the invention of Mr Baird should keep Britain in the front line of technical development, so that when peace comes she may be able to present the world the best, and maybe the first, commercial colour television set.'[25] Baird bought copies of the issue for friends and potential backers. He sent one to Moseley: 'A Merry Xmas. From the enclosed you will see I am still working. Can you do something with it in USA? Observe Carstairs among the audience in the photograph.'[10] (See plate 56 for the photograph.)

Baird took a brief Christmas holiday at Bude, and then hurried back to London to give more demonstrations of his system. He kept in touch with Margaret mainly by phone, but a few of his scrawled and rather impersonal letters survive, including one written shortly after his return to London:

> Dear Margaret
> I enclose a cheque. The demonstrations have all gone off without a hitch but no person seems to want to put up any money, however I have one or two more to try. We have deep snow here and very cold. I hope you all keep well, this is the most dangerous time of the year. Mrs Flannelfoot and Izzy and Dizzy send their kind regards.
> John[26]

According to Margaret, 'When Diana was born [Baird] tended to regard her as another experiment, but he gradually became aware that she and Malcolm would very likely be with us for a long time.' He would quote to them from Edward Lear and *Alice in Wonderland*, and make up stories for them. These included a saga about a pair of flies, Izzy and Dizzy, who lived with their mother, Mrs Flossy Flannelfoot, in a series of hotels and lodgings, and reflected his own sufferings from cold and wartime accommodation and food.[27]

Baird was still keeping Moseley in touch with his progress. He wrote to him on 14 February 1941:

> I have got a really good picture – the best I have ever seen – and as my overheads and other expenses are very small (total staff 3) there will be a fortune in it after the war. I intend to back Baird to my last penny – but may have to bring in others to get sufficient finance and these others may prove a curse later on. Can you do anything in USA? I hope to give another show with very impressive results and will send you full particulars.[10]

At the show the previous December, photographs were taken direct from the screen by Dufaycolour film and colour plates made of the subject, Paddy Naismith, who may have been a journalist. Her red hair was her asset on this occasion, and her picture on screen was published, unretouched, 6 by 4 inches size, with no scanning lines visible, in the April 1941 issue of *Electronics and Television & Short-Wave World*. The article concluded optimistically: 'We can be assured that when the war ceases Britain will once again hold the leading position in the television field.'[28] This was not to be, and after Baird's death in 1946 the leadership in colour television passed to the USA, where Peter Goldmark of the Columbia Broadcasting System had been developing a workable field-sequential system somewhat similar to Baird's. In a lecture on colour television in 1944, Goldmark gave full credit to Baird's contribution.[29]

Baird was delighted with the article and photograph in *Electronics and Television & Short-Wave World*, which he immediately sent to Moseley on 2 April:

> I enclose a copy of 'Electronics' with the first Television photo in colour. Can you do anything with this in USA? A syndicate to buy the rights for USA? Donald Flamm to broadcast colour television? I may form a small private company in England. I am running on very economical lines total staff consists of two junior assistants (even less than the old Long Acre days when you chopped off all the heads!) Do you know anyone likely to be interested? I live the life of a recluse at present and see nobody. Carstairs however is on the phone frequently. He seems to be keeping his head above water – no easy matter at present.
>
> Do you ever see I[sidore] O[strer]?
>
> Hutchinson has a small farm outside Brighton. I met Mrs H (Rosie) looking very prosperous in Scott's. She told me she did the milking and

asked me down for the week end. If you were here we might start another Television Ltd!![30]

Moseley replied on 16 April. Baird responded (9 May) by sending further copies of the 'colour television picture' and giving additional details about his present situation:

> I have a staff of two, total wages £12. We make everything ourselves. I have a fully equipped laboratory. I have a complete colour and mono-chrome Television Transmitter (600 lines). I have Colour Television receivers developed to a commercial stage. I have 8 Provisional Patents covering inventions which I believe to be of importance. Still have to take these out in USA. I have the goodwill and reputation resulting from twenty years of work.
>
> These are the assets. My suggestion is that you form a small syndicate with Flamm, Wiseman and possibly others to acquire the rights for USA. I would be prepared to come over after the war and bring my apparatus and give demonstrations. I might be able to come sooner but this would probably present considerable difficulties. I have in mind the possibility of opening a television station in California where it would be possible to work in comfort and avoid the awful English winter.
>
> With regard to my position over here. It is very difficult but I can still carry on for a time on my own and have hopes of raising a small amount from my friends. I am considering forming a small syndicate (£10,000). ... Before closing I should mention that I have now developed a cheap colour television set with a small screen (4 inches by four) to sell at £15. I have not so far given a public demonstration as at present there are too many other demonstrations of a much more spectacular nature going on.[31]

The 'demonstrations' to which Baird was referring were the renewed air raids on London, culminating on 11 May with the most terrible of them all. In bright moonlight, 550 German planes indiscriminately dropped hundreds of high explosive bombs and a hundred thousand incendiaries in a few hours, destroying the chamber of the House of Commons, setting ablaze the roof of the twelfth-century Westminster Hall, and almost tearing the heart out of the city of London. Two days later, Baird entered Tempsford Hall, near the village of Sandy in Bedfordshire, some fifty miles north of London, as a patient.

In his memoir, which he began a few weeks later, Baird wrote, 'My whole position was becoming very distressing. I had not only been badly hit financially but I had been in bad health for some time and the continual air raids, which had blown out the windows of my house and brought down all the ceilings, were very upsetting.'[32] The pace of his work, the strain of his life-style, the irregularity of his diet, the worry about his finances, and the shock of Mephy's death, to which was added the responsibility of dealing with his effects, had combined to weaken his health still further. The signs begin to appear in his diary in July 1940, in the form of initials which almost certainly relate to his symptoms. On 13 December 1940 he noted down, underlined, 'See doctor re liver'.

Tempsford Hall stood in a large estate which had formerly belonged to the Stuart family, of Scottish royal descent. It advertised itself as a 'Country House for Medical Treatment'. Among the medical conditions treated were heart disease, obesity, and 'general exhaustion resulting from overwork and asthenic states'. The fees were expensive for the time, ranging from 15 to 25 guineas a week.[33] At first Baird was bored and depressed. He drafted in his diary an ironic letter to Buchanan: 'Very quiet, a few old ladies and gentlemen sit in the lounge. I have been here for five days and have not heard them speak.'

The entry in Baird's diary for 21 May simply reads, 'Coronary thrombosis'. Dr Miles examined him and told him bluntly that he was overweight, the fat was pressing against his heart, and he could drop dead at any moment. His heart attack, coupled with his liver condition, called for drastic measures. Baird's stay at Tempsford Hall was extended and he underwent a complete fast: two weeks on raw carrot and mustard and cress, then two weeks on only water (the first fortnight had given him acute sickness and indigestion), and then just twelve grapes a day. Other treatment included massage, pyretic baths, gentle walks in the grounds, and plenty of sleep. Baird kept in touch with Margaret and the family in Bude and with Anderson at the laboratory by telephone, but time hung heavy on him.

On his slow meanderings round the tranquil estate he made friends with Philip Morrell, who had been a prominent barrister and member of parliament, but whose pacifism during World War I effectively ended his political career. His wife, Lady Ottoline Morrell, a half-sister of the Duke of Portland, shared his views. Their house at Garsington, near Oxford, and their later home in Gower Street, London, were gathering places for the young, and not so young, literati, especially the Bloomsbury set. Lady Ottoline had died in 1938 at the age of sixty-four. Morrell himself was ailing, and he would die in February 1943. He and Baird had long philosophical talks, in the course of which he strongly urged Baird to write an autobiography before the memories faded. Baird had already begun thinking about such a project,[34] and this seemed just the way to alleviate his boredom and forget his symptoms. A shorthand typist, Miss Griffin, was called in, and Baird dictated 'Sermons, Socks and Television'. Almost fifty years were to elapse before the chapters were published in 1988 as *Sermons, Soap and Television*.[35]

By mid-July Baird had lost over three stone, dropping from 164lb to 112lb, and had to arrange for a local tailor to make him a new suit. He began to make occasional visits to London. Some of his friends said he resembled an 'emaciated scarecrow', others that he looked a hundred per cent better.[32] Margaret, who met him off the train at Exeter, was horrified. Baird, however, was very pleased with himself, and said he felt much better, though he merely nibbled some biscuits instead of eating a meal. On medical advice he went back to Tempsford Hall for observation, from where he conducted television business by telephone and letter. He returned to Crescent Wood Road in early September with renewed energy. He dutifully continued to diet on porridge, fish, whatever fruit was obtainable, and oatcakes without butter. The initials in the diary entries almost disappear.

On 15 September 1941 a friend of Moseley rang, with a message from Moseley asking why Baird had not written to him. Baird immediately dashed off a note, explaining that he had written twice since receiving Moseley's last letter. Both communications, one sent 'by air mail at great expense', had obviously gone astray.

> I am continuing research work here and have a complete Television concern of my own, we can and do make everything <u>including our own cathode ray tubes</u>. When the war is over I hope to regain all I am spending and also [make] a vast fortune![10]

Though Baird's physical health had improved, there were considerable worries over the health of his finances. Since the beginning of 1940 he had made regular withdrawals from his deposit account of £500 about every two months. On 9 September 1941 he withdrew £1500, leaving him now with only £8000 of the £15,000 which he had at the beginning of the war. Despite the publicity he had achieved for his electronic colour television system, no financial backer had come forward. He had no grants for war-related work, and apparently no war-related work either. In his memoir, dictated during the summer of 1941, he says, 'I sent in my name to the authorities and expected to be approached with some form of government work, but no such offer materialized.'[36]

The government was facing an acute shortage of physicists and radio engineers, and many of the Baird company's technical staff had gone into radar or other military work. Vince, from Baird's personal staff, was working at the radar establishment at Bawdsey Manor. At the very least, Baird held patents in radio imaging dating back to the 1920s, and this and his related work were known to H E Wimperis, who had directed the surveillance of Baird's early experiments,[37] and had in 1934 been instrumental in the establishment of the Tizard committee under whose auspices Watson Watt's radar system was developed. Although articles on the detection of objects by reflected radio waves had appeared in several countries, and patents been lodged, since 1904,[38] the first operational use of radio direction finding (later to be known as radar) was begun by the British government in 1935. Watson Watt had met Baird in 1932,[39] and had been technical consultant to the Television Advisory Committee. He is recorded as having visited the Baird company laboratory in the School of Arts at the Crystal Palace in 1937 to examine a transmitter.[6]

The British radar programme, however, was a closely guarded secret, and it appears that Baird was not let into it. A possible reason for his exclusion is that he was too much in the public eye. If his well-known figure were to be seen in or around radar establishments, it could cause security problems. The technical writer Maurice Exwood pointed to other aspects of Baird's work: 'One would have expected a man who had done a lot of practical work on television by infra-red rays and the fog penetration properties of these, had something to contribute to the war effort, but perhaps his name was still tainted in high circles.'[40] It is by no means clear to what Exwood was specifically referring, but it is possible that Baird's links with Germany in general and Fernseh in particular could have been a matter for concern, despite his detestation of everything that Hitler stood for. Yet Church had been a director of Fernseh, and he was appointed in 1941 assistant director of fighting vehicle production at the Ministry of Supply. Maybe the Baird company's aggressive marketing tactics in the late 1920s and early 1930s still rankled. It could, however, simply be that in the eyes of the authorities Baird's name was, unfairly, associated with old-fashioned, and thus out-of-date, technology, such as mechanical scanning.

There is little or no indication in Baird's wartime diaries of any activity that corresponds to war work, apart from some unexplained blanks, and a few instances of initials which may represent a substitution code. It has been suggested that he took part in some of the informal weekend brainstorming meetings of senior government and service personnel, known as the 'Sunday soviets'.[41] There are two second-hand but authoritative reports of visits by Baird to Whaddon Hall, the MI6 radio station at Bletchley, Buckinghamshire.[42] Not the least interesting theory is that Baird may have been at some time a member of a committee which vetted proposals for new inventions that might have a military application.[43]

Baulked of any cash return from his newest developments, Baird gave thought to one of his earlier preoccupations. At several points in his diaries for the winter of 1940/1, the words 'secret signalling' appear. He was also regularly at this time meeting Church, who it was that probably put Baird in touch with Cable and Wireless Ltd. As early as 1927 Baird had realised the potential value of television for sending messages at high speed in the form of a succession of images. The standard means of sending radio messages in World War II, however, was still the Morse code, by which only a few hundred words a minute could be sent; it could also be read by anyone with a Morse operator's training. Morse transmissions could be made more secure by means of complex codes, but with enough effort these could be deciphered; the classic example of this was the breaking of the German Enigma ciphers by the skilled staff at Bletchley Park, which helped to win the war. Secret, or 'scrambled', television images, on the other hand, are virtually impossible to decipher. They can be achieved, for instance, electronically by scanning the lines of the image out of sequence, such as is done today for pay-TV. Moreover, a message of several hundred words could be sent in just a few frames of high-definition television requiring a fraction of a second to transmit.

Cable and Wireless had sole responsibility for Britain's external telegraphic communications. The growing volume of traffic created by the war had put the company's systems under severe pressure. Its management was interested not only in secrecy, but also in any means of speeding up the traffic, and so increasing the capacity of the company's cables and radio channels. On 30 July 1941, Baird travelled to London from Tempsford Hall to have lunch with Sir Edward Wilshaw, the chairman and managing director of Cable and Wireless (Holding) Ltd, and Admiral H W Grant, chairman of the Marconi Wireless Telegraph Company. Grant was also on the board of Cable and Wireless, which had a controlling interest in his company. It was not the first time that Baird had come to Wilshaw cap in hand, as Wilshaw revealed to Moseley in a letter in 1951:

> Away back in the old Eastern Telegraph Company days, when I was secretary, Baird came to see us with his then manager, to see if he could interest us in his activities.
>
> We went into the matter and found that, although a genius himself from the scientific point of view, he was no financier, and he had placed himself from time to time in the hands of others. It was therefore not possible for us to help him.[44]

From entries in Baird's diary it has been deduced that in 1941 he subsequently offered Wilshaw an option to buy control shares in a company for £25,000, later raised to £30,000, in return for a salary for himself of £1500 for five years. Instead he accepted simply a contract as 'Consulting Technical Advisor' at £1000 a year for three years, beginning on 1 November 1941.[6]

Surprisingly, perhaps, in the light of the fact that his contribution could well be on the secret list, the appointment was announced in the press. Baird sent the cuttings to Moseley, with a letter with the printed heading, 'JOHN LOGIE BAIRD / *Television Engineers*', and the Crescent Wood Road address and telephone number (Forest Hill 4678):

> This [position with Cable and Wireless] does not interfere with my research, which is quite independent (and entirely my own property) and I am still going ahead at 3 Crescent Wood Road. ...
>
> I don't see how I can leave London now, but after the War is over I would very much like to come across. Perhaps you can see some way this could be arranged.[10]

Baird told Margaret that his consulting work amounted to a couple of meetings a month at the Cable and Wireless head office, Electra House, an impressive building known as 'The Fortress', on Victoria Embankment. There are, however, in his diaries eighty-nine references to his consultancy between November 1941 and October 1943, including visits to the Marconi transmitters and research laboratory at Chelmsford from March 1942 onwards. His main contact was a Mr Jacob, but there were meetings also with Wilshaw.

During 1941 and 1942 Baird had been quietly experimenting with high-definition stereoscopic television. Since his demonstration in 1928 of thirty-line stereoscopic television, no-one, not even in America, had seen fit to study its possibilities. At the transmitting end, he was using the flying-spot scanning principle, as he had in his colour demonstration in December 1940. The object being televised was scanned at very high speed, and the reflected light was collected by photo-cells. The stereoscopic effect was achieved by two different methods: one process giving a full-colour picture, and the other, on the anaglyphic principle, involving scanning the object from two view-points, for monochrome viewing.

By the anaglyphic method,[45] the object was was scanned by a rapidly moving beam of light, from a high-intensity projection cathode-ray tube, in two colours, red and blue-green. A system of mirrors enabled the scanning of each colour to be done from a slightly different position. Thus each image (anaglyph) was transmitted in a different colour and from a different viewpoint. At the receiving end the process was reversed. Another projection tube produced a high-intensity image. This was passed through a rotating colour filter disc and a lens, and projected onto a ground-glass screen, to form alternate pictures in the two colours. To the naked eye, the screen image was blurred and strangely coloured, because of the slight displacement between the two anaglyphs. When the viewer wore special glasses, however, with one eyepiece tinted red, and the other blue-green, the picture sprang into three dimensions. The red filter cut out the red image, showing the blue image in black and white; the blue-green filter cut out the blue-green image, showing the red image in black and white. Thus each eye of the viewer saw a slightly different black-and-white image. The brain then combined the two images to give the sense of depth. A similar effect could be achieved by using polarised light, which can be split into two directions using polaroid glass or a transparent mineral called Iceland spar, but this was more expensive than the two-colour method.

Baird's stereoscopic system gave a high-definition (600-line) picture. Fifteen years later, the anaglyphic stereoscopic principle was introduced into cinemas in the USA and Britain, but the special glasses proved unpopular with audiences. Modern colour television equipment can quite easily be adapted to transmit in stereo, as is done occasionally in the USA and Canada for late-night movies. There is, however, again the drawback that the viewer must obtain and wear the special glasses.

Baird developed an ingenious alternative, which required no glasses, and gave a full-colour picture (figure 9).[46] The flying spot from the projection cathode-ray tube at the transmission end of the process was passed through a disc with red, blue, and green filters. The three-coloured scanning ray then went through a rotating shutter and a mirror arrangement which allowed the televised person or object to be scanned alternately from two positions. The separation of the scanning positions was about three inches, the distance between the human eyes. The reflected light was picked up by three special multiplier photo-cells, one for each colour. At the receiver, the process was reversed. It was simply necessary for the viewer to keep his or her head in a certain precise position relative to the screen, to get the benefit of stereoscopic television without the need for glasses. The picture was of 500 lines definition, consisting of a succession of 100-line frames, in the primary colours, red, blue, and green. The frames, at a rate of 150 a second, were interlaced five times to make up the 500-line picture. All the apparatus, including the projection tubes, was constructed by Anderson on site.[47]

A few years earlier, high-definition colour and high-definition stereoscopic colour television would have been lead news items. Under wartime

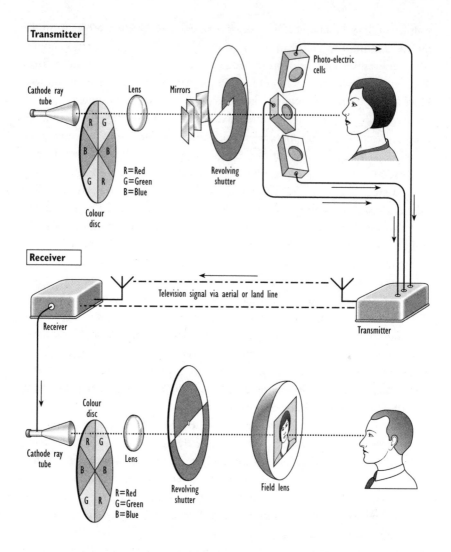

Figure 9: Baird's stereoscopic colour television system, demonstrated in late 1941.
The detailed picture was formed by scanning beams from a high-power cathode-ray tube; the colour and stereoscopic effects were obtained by mechanical means. The rotating colour filter was similar to the one used a year earlier (see figure 8), but with three primary colours. A stereoscopic effect was produced by transmitting two alternating pictures, viewed from slightly different angles which corresponded to the separation of the human eyes. This required an arrangement of mirrors and a revolving shutter at the transmitting end, and another revolving shutter (but no mirrors) at the receiving end.

conditions, Baird had to go out and generate his own publicity. He cultivated the press by means of a series of meetings and lunches in central London, often at his club, the Caledonian, or at Scott's restaurant, then in Piccadilly. The person most often cited in his diary for this period is still Church. Other names which crop up regularly are Geoffrey Parr, editor of *Electronic Engineering*, and N Maybank, editor of *Wireless World*. Popular journalists such as James Spence, who was writing Baird's biography, and Tom King are mentioned several times. There are meetings with John Gordon, editor of the mass-market *Sunday Express*, and also E V Knox, editor of the humorous and satirical weekly, *Punch*.[48] Lunch meetings with editors were usually followed by a demonstration at Crescent Wood Road. A few days before a general demonstration to the press, Baird's diary would contain a reminder to buy whisky.

Richard Head, in his part-time voluntary capacity, assisted at two of these demonstrations, on 17 and 18 December 1941, the first for the daily papers, the second for the weeklies. He had somehow acquired some ham and tongue for sandwiches, but all the reporters wanted was whisky. While they waited for the demonstration to begin, he provided an impromptu musical interlude on Margaret's Steinway. The test picture was a red Mickey Mouse smoking a yellow pipe against a blue sky. When the apparatus was started up, 'one was quite likely to see a yellow Mickey Mouse smoking a blue pipe against a red sky – it was necessary to "slip" a pole on the motor until the sky came out blue'. Head was impressed by the picture, though there was an amount of background noise. At the end of the demonstration, Baird handed out a press release to each journalist, with the injunction, 'That is all you can print.' Faces fell, until it was revealed that the scripts were all differently worded. Baird had laboriously typed out each one himself.[49]

Baird was pleased with the resulting press coverage. He wrote to Moseley on 23 December:

> In spite of the war things are still moving in Television. I enclose cuttings of latest development. It gives very remarkable results and is quite unique although I expect now that it has been made public there will be plenty of imitations, as there were with colour television.[10]

The *Illustrated London News* published a full-page feature illustrating the anaglyphic system and referring to the colour system. It was drawn by G H Davis, who had also produced the page in *Popular Wireless* celebrating Baird's demonstration at Selfridge's almost exactly seventeen years earlier.[50] The caption to the *Illustrated London News* feature concluded on a note of high optimism which was to be sadly misplaced: 'Baird's invention will be of the greatest entertainment interest to thousands, if not millions of "lookers-in" after the war is won.'[51] There were, as usual and as only to be expected, words of caution from a BBC team, to whom Baird gave a demonstration on 22 April 1942. The representatives of the BBC on this occasion included Birkinshaw, Campbell, and Leonard Schuster, who before the war had been Gerald Cock's administrative assistant and keeper of the purse strings. Schuster, in his report, objected to having to wear glasses to view the monochrome system, and suggested that its effectiveness varied according to an individual's sight. Some of the colours in the colour system were poor, and the definition was unsatisfactory.[52]

Church, who was now working at the Ministry of Supply, arranged for Baird to demonstrate his stereoscopic systems to Herbert J Gough, director of scientific research, Ministry of Supply, in the hope of obtaining badly-needed financial help from government. Gough's responsibilities were very wide, and included the radar research station at Worth Matravers (moved to Malvern in 1942), the chemical station at Porton, and the rocket station at Aberporth.[53] The demonstration took place on Saturday, 13 December 1941. The following week Baird received a letter from the Ministry of Supply:

> Since visiting your laboratory with Major Church on December 13th I have gone most carefully into the question of finding a Service application for the stereoscopic technique you are developing, but I have come to the conclusion that there is nothing that would warrant official support for the continuation of the work, even to the extent of helping you retain the services of technical staff liable for national service.
>
> I thank you for an interesting demonstration of your method of stereoscopic presentation which I hope may find its proper peace-time application.[54]

In other words, the British government regarded television as having little or no relevance to the war effort. This attitude was in direct contrast to that of the German government, which had placed television research under military control in 1935.

There is an interesting sequel to this comprehensive rejection of Baird's plea for official support. In 1948 a long technical paper on three-dimensional cathode-ray tube radar displays was published by Parker and Wallis of the Admiralty Signal and Radar Establishment.[55] According to the introductory section of the paper, the Admiralty had started to work in this area of electronics in 1942-3. The technique resembled Baird's anaglyphic system, with the operators wearing special glasses. Baird's patents on stereoscopic television are not cited in the list of references, nor is any mention made of the press articles on the subject. It seems that Baird's concept, which in December 1941 had been stated by the Ministry of Supply to have no military application, had nevertheless been taken on by the Admiralty shortly afterwards. This episode further supports the conclusion that Baird was deliberately excluded from the radar effort during World War II, despite some degree of overlap between his research and the development of radar.

Writing in 1941, Baird regretted that in the early days of television he had 'turned down all sorts of invitations and continued to shuffle around in the lab ... absorbed in my bits and pieces'.[56] During World War II he set out to remedy this omission by cultivating significant public figures, and making them aware of his progress, ready for the time when plans would be made for postwar television. There were meetings with Sir John Wardlaw-Milne, a senior Conservative backbencher and the son of a Helensburgh banker. Another parliamentary contact was Captain Leonard Frank Plugge, a charismatic figure who had been interested in Baird's work since about 1926.[57] Plugge had been one of the prewar promoters of British commercial radio, broadcasting programmes of dance music across the English Channel from Radio Normandy on Sundays; the BBC, under Reith's direction, eschewed such frivolity on the Sabbath. During World War II, Plugge was chairman of the parliamentary science committee, and he had long been interested in the use of television for the purpose of signalling.[58] He listed among his inventions 'radio two-way telephone in car, television glasses, stereoscopic cinematograph, Plugge patent auto circuit'.[59] Entries in Baird's diaries, 'set in Parliament', suggest that he and Plugge had discussed demonstrating colour stereoscopic television at Westminster, but it would appear that nothing came of this.

One of Baird's most influential contacts was Sir Harry Brittain, an energetic and articulate Yorkshireman who had had a long career in politics and journalism, and served on innumerable public committees. 'His gift for instant friendships was counterbalanced by intense egotism, impatience, and ruthlessness, which less than endeared him to others.'[60] He lived into his 101st year, but was only a sprightly sixty-eight when he brought the Postmaster General to see Baird's demonstration at 3 Crescent Wood Road in April or May 1942. Many years later he wrote to Malcolm:

> Your father was not only a prophet but he was a genius and it was my good fortune to know him well. I remember one instance ... he told

me he was getting on splendidly at Sydenham, and would like me to come up and see the progress he was making. My reply was – of course, but wouldn't it be helpful if I brought some cabinet minister with me?

'Indeed it would,' he said.

'Well,' I said, 'I think I know them all. Who would you like?'

He replied that the Postmaster General would be the most useful, so Morrison and I went up together. He was at that time, I remember, trying to get the perspective, then colour, and marry the two; he had made splendid progress. 'Shakes' Morrison ... was as interested as I was. That day left many a happy memory. I would it had been more fruitful in results.[61]

Plate 34
Baird, in an overcoat to combat the chill of August in Berlin, with Manfred von Ardenne, who is demonstrating his receiver with cathode-ray tube (see pages 147-8).

Plate 35
Hero-worship. Baird with H G Wells on board the *Aquitania*, October 1931 (see page 179). (Royal Television Society)

Plate 36
Sir John Reith and his wife Muriel, on their way back from the USA in June 1931. Lady Reith's mother was a sister of Baird's benefactor, W J B Odhams. The Reiths were married in July 1921 after an engagement which had lasted two years and three months. (BBC)

Plate 37
The happy couple, photographed in USA on their wedding day, 13 November 1931, with Baird in his bedroom slippers (see page 188, 420). They were never formally engaged, and had known each other for little more than three months.

Plate 38
The Bairds' wedding reception at the Half Moon Hotel, Coney Island, 15 November 1931. The top-table line-up from the left is Donald Flamm, his first wife Rhoda, Baird, Margaret, and Walter Knight. Margaret said of this photograph, 'We look like a couple of sheep among a lot of wolves' (M Baird, p. 111; see page 188).

Plate 39
Gladstone Murray, photographed in 1939, when he was general manager, Canadian Broadcasting Corporation. (Gibson/National Archives of Canada)

Plate 40
Noel Ashbridge speaking at the Television Society's lecture in 1930, with the chairman of the society, Sir Ambrose Fleming, beside him. (Royal Television Society)

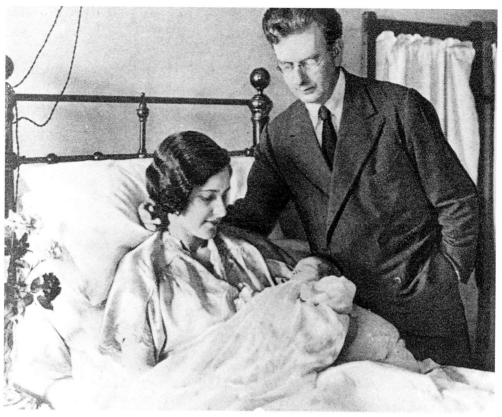

Plate 41
Fatherhood, a new challenge for Baird. The photograph was taken at the Lawn Road house on 26 September 1932, when Diana was three weeks old. (Science Museum)

Plate 42
The house at 3 Crescent Wood Road, Sydenham. Baird's laboratory is just out of picture, to the left.

Plate 43
The Bairds, soon after their marriage. The suggestion that Baird is following the music is erroneous, as he was tone deaf. One night, when they had been sitting up late listening to the wireless, he observed to Margaret, 'I think I recognise that tune.' It was 'God save the King.' (Science Museum)

Plate 44
The Crystal Palace 1933-39; the towers are 1608 feet apart.

A Area destroyed by fire, 30 November 1936 (within dotted line)

B Baird's house

C Fire started below here

D First floor. Original vision transmitter 1933, used for sound 1934-35, and finally for Baird's colour TV 1937-39

E Baird's studio for colour TV 1937-39

F Baird company offices, laboratories, and studios July 1933 to November 1936

G Rotunda. TV tube production 1936-39. Transmitter department on balcony 1938-39

H School of Arts. Receiver design and production 1935-38. Offices and general use after fire. Airborne TV group 1937-39

I Transmitting aerial for Baird's colour demonstrations 1937-38 (8.3 metres)

J Transmitting aerial 1938-39 (2 metres)

(Photograph: Crystal Palace Foundation. Map: Ray Herbert 2000)

Plate 45
Baird, well wrapped up against the rigours of spring, with Diana, Malcolm, and Baird's sister Annie. Crescent Wood Road, 1936.

Plate 46
Mephy (Gavin Fullarton Robertson) outside 'Herb Cottage', Ryde, Isle of Wight, in the mid-1930s. The photographer is almost certainly Baird. This may well be the photograph which Baird gave to Helen Pearce in 1942 (see page 324). If so, it is likely to have been presented by her to Radio Rentals Ltd in the 1960s, after that company acquired the use of the Baird name. (Alan Montgomery)

Plate 47
Cecilia Albu (Grannie Albu), Margaret's mother, in the garden of her house in Sutton, about 1935. The paper in her hand is probably folded over at the crossword puzzle, a form of intellectual exercise to which she was addicted.

Plate 48
Captain A G D West with Baird at the British Association meeting in Leicester, 1933. (Richard West)

Plate 49
Baird at the controls at
the Dominion Theatre,
in about 1937. He kept
his hair long for warmth.

Plate 50
Baird and the short haircut (1), Cannes, January 1938, shortly after Moseley's practical joke (see page 309).

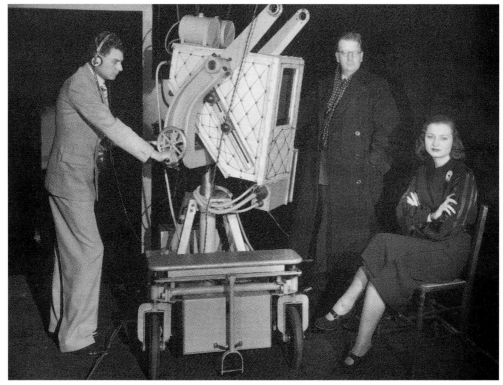

Plate 51
Baird and the short haircut (2), and also with overcoat and scarf indoors, February 1938, taken in one of the dressing rooms of the Dominion Theatre. Reveley is at the mobile mirror-drum camera (see page 302), converted to two-colour work. Seated is a Miss Sabry, daughter of an Egyptian diplomat, who was assigned to the task by the Royal Academy of Dramatic Art, in response to Reveley's request for a model for a colour television demonstration. (Royal Television Society; information from Paul Reveley)

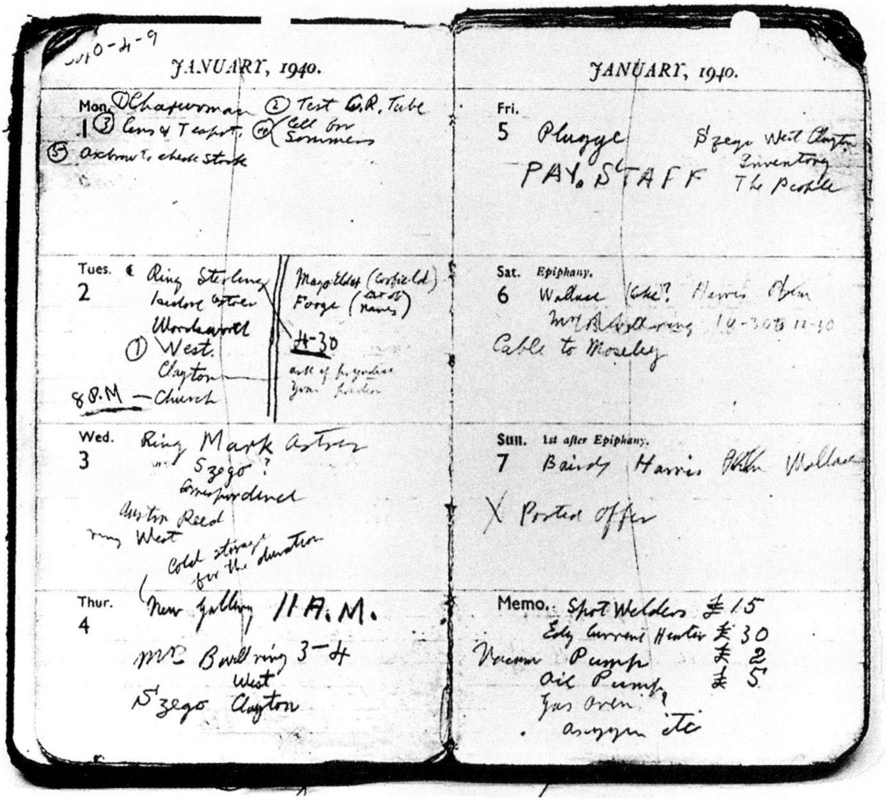

Plates 54/55
Two spreads from Baird's wartime diaries.

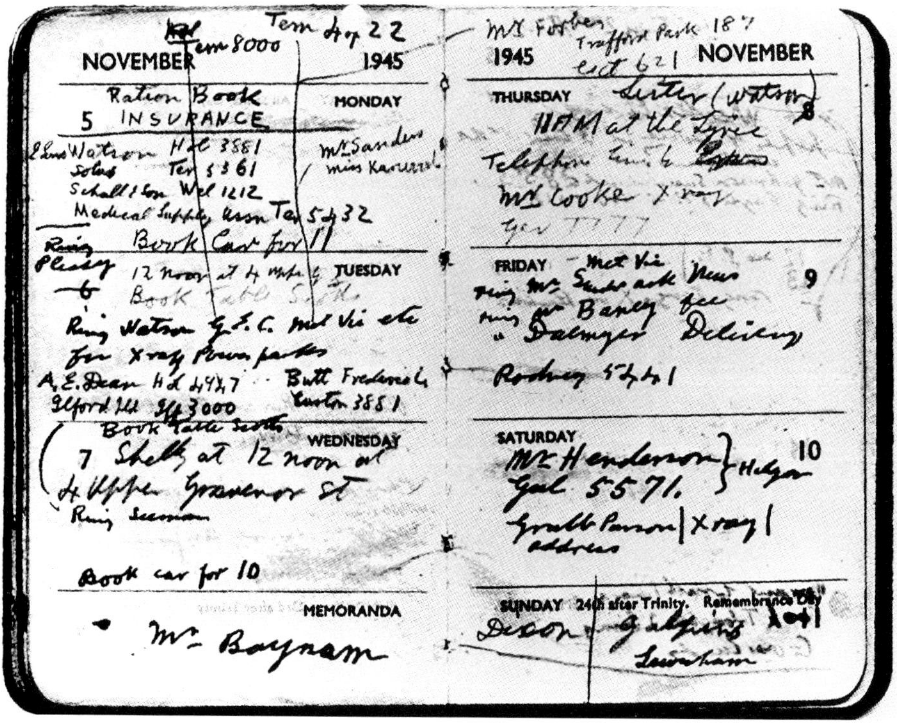

Plate 56
Baird demonstrating his 600-line colour television system in the drawing-room at Crescent Wood Road (note Margaret's Steinway on the right), 19 December 1940. Paddy Naismith is seated nearest to Baird. Anderson is far right (back to camera). Standing on the left is Geoff Bernard. Below him (sitting) is Lindsay Carstairs. The picture on the screen is a photograph. See pages 325-7. (Ray Herbert)

Plate 57
Sir Edward Wilshaw, in about 1942. This is the only known example of a fast facsimile image sent by Baird. The original is printed on light-weight photo-sensitive paper, and measures 5¾ x 4 inches. The 180 scanning lines are just visible, as are (at the bottom of the picture) the sprocket holes from the cine film on which the image was recorded. The number of scanning lines is com-paratively low, but may have been dictated by bandwidth limitations. See pages 354-5. 'Photo of Wilshaw' is mentioned frequently in Baird's diaries for 1942-43, and in a series of notes at the end of 1944 is a refer-ence to 'Show facsimile photograph'. (Hastings Museum and Art Gallery)

Plate 58
Baird in his Sydenham laboratory in 1942-44, working on a cathode-ray tube. This rare photograph of him without a jacket suggests that it was a very hot day. (Hastings Museum and Art Gallery)

Plate 59
The Grosvenor television receiver, incorporating wireless and gramophone. With its screen of 22 inches by 17 inches, it was the only one of its kind ever built (see pages 353-4). It was used to show the Victory Parade at the Savoy Hotel in 1946, and was shown at the *Daily Mail* Ideal Homes Exhibition, 4-29 March 1947, and also at the Radiolympia exhibition the same year. (Royal Television Society; reproduced from *Television*, March 1948, p. 153)

Plate 60
Tea with Mr Snodgrass, 1957. From right to left, Arnold Snodgrass, Annie Baird, Annie's housekeeper Margaret Scott, Annie's old school friend (from Ministers' Daughters' College) Louisa Irvine, photographed by Malcolm Baird.

16
The End of the Road:
Bude, London, and Bexhill
1943–1946

Baird spent on average about one week in four with his family in Bude. During these visits the sequence of diary entries – reminders, letters to write, telephone calls to make – usually continued. Many years later a tabloid journalist asked Diana, then in her sixties, about her 'deprived' wartime childhood. She had to disappoint him, because she and Malcolm remember the five years at Bude as quite a happy time. Baird himself frequently remarked to Margaret, 'What a paradise for children; some good is coming out of this evil.'

Margaret was thirty-two when the war began. Though life was not easy for her, in the same way as millions of others she adapted to wartime conditions and shortages. She proved to be an imaginative cook who could do 'wonderful things with sardines and spam', and she managed to acquire supplies of unrationed luxuries such as duck eggs ('rich and succulent') and rabbit. She also made all the children's clothes.[1] She maintained her musical interests by piano teaching at the independent school, Clifton College, which had been evacuated to Bude from Bristol. She also gave some public piano performances at towns on the south coast, under her professional name of Margaret Albu. The strictly non-musical Baird broke the habit of a lifetime and attended a Sunday afternoon concert at Bournemouth in July 1943.[2] Margaret recalled, 'He was amazed, he was thrilled, he hadn't heard me play with an orchestra and he was as proud as Punch.'[3]

Diana and Malcolm settled in to the private preparatory school, Sandown, to which they walked from Flexbury Park Road. They had a small circle of friends, mainly middle-class evacuees like themselves. Their best friend was Noel Harrison, son of the actor Rex Harrison and his first wife, who was living with his maternal grandparents just up the road from the Bairds. There were parties for birthdays and Christmas, capably organised by Margaret. The sandy beaches were within walking distance, and occasional motor excursions were arranged into the countryside. Skadge Hill was superb for picking blackberries. The secluded Coombe Valley, with its thatch-roofed inn, was a reminder of the old, slightly sinister Cornwall depicted in the novels of Daphne du Maurier. Nearer to home, the Bude golf course was not much used by regular players, and Malcolm and his friends taught themselves the rudiments of the game, swinging an old club. Golf balls could be found on the bed of the stream that meandered through the course.

The senior member of the household, Cecilia Albu, was a strong figure, despite being lame from her fall and somewhat hard of hearing. She gave Margaret invaluable moral support; Diana remembers her as a friend, who introduced her to knitting and helped her form her literary interests with books borrowed from Boots' Library. Malcolm's memories of his grand-mother are less happy. To him she was an irascible character, not unlike Bertie Wooster's Aunt Agatha. She was very insistent on correct table manners and social etiquette. When Malcolm acquired a Cornish accent from playing with local children, Grannie Albu, in spite of her deafness, was quick to spot the change and sternly rebuked him: 'Malcolm, you must not speak like the common boys!'

The arrival of Baird for his monthly break was eagerly anticipated. The family would wait on the windy platform for the arrival of the 5.09, watching for the first puffs of smoke a mile away along the single, straight track. He would emerge from the train, a somewhat dishevelled figure in his habitual overcoat, hat, and scarf, lugging a heavy suitcase containing clothes and working papers. The family, reunited, returned to the house by taxi. Supper might be fish or rabbit or that classic British standby, bubble and squeak, from which Malcolm got his lifelong aversion to cabbage.

At Bude, Baird would relax, though he still spent a lot of time on the telephone. He would say to Margaret, 'Can you wait the dinner? I must ring Carstairs.' Or it might be Church, or Spence, or Anderson, always referred to by their surnames. He had time, however, to show the children some simple things from his work, such as a large lens through which, in a darkened room, perfect images could be obtained of the view from the window. The lens could be used, too, to focus the sun's rays on a sheet of paper until it caught fire. Baird also produced slabs of Iceland spar, the transparent mineral through which polarised light could be formed. He increased Diana's expertise at mixing colours by showing her how any required shade could be produced from the primary colours in a paintbox. She also remembers long walks with him along the sands, sometimes as far as Sandymouth, two bays to the north of Bude. This was her ultima Thule! It only took twenty minutes to get there along the sands when the tide was out, but several hours getting back along cliffs heavily indented by coombes – deep valleys which ended in small bays.

Malcolm's greatest interest was a large glass prism which, when placed in a ray of sunlight, produced a complete spectrum of colours.

At other times, although Baird was only in his fifties, he had the air of an older man. His speech was soft and slow, and punctuated with sighs. He would walk slowly along the beach in his coat and hat and scarf, even in summer, carrying a notebook in which he jotted down ideas as they occurred to him. Sometimes Margaret would accompany him, taking down patents in long-hand from his dictation. One day his walk was interrupted by a young military policeman who had presumably been warned about spies reporting back to the Germans on Britain's coastal defences. The defences at Bude consisted of nothing more than a few concrete blocks as tank traps, but the zealous young man stopped the muffled figure carrying a notebook. In response to his questions, Baird was at a loss for words. The situation began to look ugly, until Margaret, who was further along the beach, came up bran-dishing Baird's ration book as proof of identity.[4]

As Baird had effectively been warned would happen in the unhelpful letter from the Ministry of Supply,[5] early in 1943 Anderson, his senior full-time technical assistant, received his call-up papers. Initially, Anderson thought about declaring himself to be a conscientious objector, but the authorities were known to be exceptionally strict in dealing with such pleas. Instead, Baird, as Anderson's employer, set out to make a convincing case that he should be exempted because he was doing essential work. Baird, accompanied by Margaret,[6] went before the tribunal and described Anderson's invaluable contributions to colour and stereoscopic television, but exemption was denied on the grounds that television had nothing to do with the war effort. Baird appealed against the decision. It may be that he obtained the support of Wilshaw with regard to the research work that he and Anderson were doing for Cable and Wireless. Anyway, the appeal was upheld, and Anderson stayed on at Crescent Wood Road.

Money was still an acute problem. Though Baird cashed in a life insurance policy with Eagle Star for £650.12s in December 1942,[7] and despite his retainer from Cable and Wireless, the regular withdrawals of £500 continued, and his reserves dropped from £8000 in September 1941 to £4500 in April 1943. In June 1943 he made a note in his diary to approach Watson-Watt and a General Whitaker for consulting work on 'radiolocation' (that is, radar), but nothing seems to have come of this. He told Margaret that his financial situation was 'like watching himself bleed to death'.[8]

In December 1942 the sculptor Donald Gilbert had asked Baird to sit for him. The sittings took place in a room taken for the purpose in the Aeolian Hall, Bond Street, during lunch hours, which was when Gilbert could get away from his army duties at HQ, London District. They continued every few days through January and February 1943, and finished on 3 March.[9] To judge from the sculpted image, Baird kept his overcoat on throughout. The clay bust was exhibited at the Royal Academy summer exhibition in 1943 (no 952).[10]

Gilbert made a cast in plaster from the original bust. In January 1959, thirteen years after Baird's death, Gilbert's prospective son-in-law wrote to the BBC on his behalf, offering the sculpture of Baird for the new television centre which was under construction.[11] The attitude of the BBC is contained in an internal memorandum: 'I can say officially that we would not be interested in acquiring a bust of "Baird" for the new Television Centre.'[12]

Six months later, Gilbert submitted the plaster to the trustees of the National Portrait Gallery in London, whose committee commissioned a bronze casting from him.[10] Before delivering it, Gilbert kept it for a while in his studio: 'I worked on the colour, which did not satisfy me when it came from the foundry. The colour of bronze is natural and improves with the passage of time, but there are certain little things which can be done to help it to a good start, knowledge of which I have inherited from Sir Alfred Gilbert and my father.'[13]

Gilbert handed over the finished casting personally to Kingsley Adams, director of the National Portrait Gallery, on 7 December 1959. The following day, in a letter accompanying his account, he wrote,

> For many years, through the vicissitudes of the war and the difficult period which followed, I preserved the fragile plaster cast of the original model, firmly believing that the day would come when the genius of Baird and the value to posterity of his lifelong pursuit of the vision in which he had so great a faith, would be recognised.
>
> That this recognition should take the form of the placing of my portrait of him among the Nation's own collection of the Immortals is something I hoped for indeed, but only in those secret thoughts which inspire to achievement.[14]

A second bronze casting was donated to Helensburgh by one of Baird's old friends, J Arnold Fleming, the expert on Scottish pottery. It was unveiled in the Hermitage Park, Helensburgh, in 1961 by Annie Baird, and was later moved to a plinth on the seafront, looking across the Firth of Clyde. Gilbert died on 17 June 1961 at the age of sixty-one. A third casting was commissioned from Gilbert's widow in 1965 on behalf of the University of Strathclyde,[10] and presented to the university's Baird Hall of Residence, in whose entrance hall it stands, to commemorate the twentieth anniversary of Baird's death.[15] A fourth casting was presented anonymously to the University of Strathclyde in 2001, and is displayed in the Collins Gallery of the university; it is likely to have been commissioned by, or as a gift for, Lindsay Carstairs.

Throughout the war Baird kept his name before the public by offering news items to the national and technical press, and sometimes by writing them himself. On 28 October 1943, he made one of his rare public appearances before a specialist audience. The occasion was an early-evening lecture on 'Colour and Stereoscopic Television', sponsored by the British Institution of Radio Engineers (London Section), and given in a packed hall at the Institution of Structural Engineers. He described the development of his systems from 1928 to those he had demonstrated in 1941-2, and referred to the parallel work of Peter Goldmark on colour television that had been going on in the USA under the auspices of the Columbia Broadcasting System and the General Electric Company.[16] A member of the audience that day recalls that Baird was 'rather nervous and flushed in the face. ... There was some scepticism [in the audience] about what he said; undeserved, but he was still inextricably linked to mechanical scanning and the failure in 1936 to get it adopted by the BBC.'[17] That such an audience, which included members of the staff of the Bush organisation which manufactured receivers for the Baird company, should, so comparatively soon after the event, associate Baird with a company failure for which he was not responsible, may explain why in certain quarters unjustified blemishes have attached themselves to his reputation.

The lecture also attracted the attention of the Soviet embassy, and soon afterwards Baird was contacted by one of the counsellors, Arkadiy Aleksandrovich Sobolev, who had studied electrical engineering in Leningrad.[18] The USSR and Britain were now staunch allies against Hitler. As a token of fraternal good will, Baird received an invitation to an afternoon performance of the Russian Ballet de la Jeunesse Anglaise,[19] which he accepted out of courtesy, for ballet was certainly not his cup of tea. On several occasions later Sobolev and some technical colleagues visited Crescent Wood Road, where they were shown the colour and stereoscopic systems. In November of the following year Baird and Margaret were guests at a reception at the Soviet embassy.

On 3 August 1943 Baird wrote to Moseley:

> I have been approached by a syndicate (of Highlanders) to form a big post war company. Whether anything will come of it or not I don't

know but it occurred to me that you might know of someone who wanted to acquire the American rights for my inventions viz –
1) Colour television (without revolving discs)
2) Stereoscopic television (without coloured glasses)
In addition I have other inventions coming along *which will revolutionize the whole art!!* [These last six words crossed out.] The inventions mentioned (colour and stereo) have already been demonstrated and I think you have received press cuttings describing the demonstrations but if you want more particulars let me know.[20]

Since the other half of the correspondence with Moseley has long disappeared, we cannot know how energetically Moseley responded to Baird continually urging him to form syndicates on his behalf or sell US rights in his systems. There is, however, the comment in Moseley's biography of Baird:

> Was there ever another such a lovable and yet maddening fellow? He *knew* I was doing work of vital importance in the States; knew it left me no time for other business and knew, too, that the only way I could help him was to have him in America with me then, not after the war was over. But he could not leave London, and so would I form a syndicate to acquire his patent rights![21]

Moseley did make some effort:

> FEB 8 [1944]: Rose early to keep appointment at RKO in order to try and 'sell' Baird to them. Saw the boss and told him the best thing to do was to get Baird over, when he would be able to put them into television 'on the ground floor'. He thought it a good idea. But one must keep on at these moguls to get anywhere. And John [Baird] needs pushing from behind. If only I could be with him I could help him again.[22]

There really was, however, a potential syndicate in Britain. The journalist Tom King, who figures regularly in Baird's diaries, began communicating with Irving Harris, a journalist and also the owner of an entertainment business, about the possibilities in January 1943. In June Baird used this as a peg on which to hang a request to Cable and Wireless for further funding: '[He has] been approached by a Syndicate with an offer of £7000 a year for 2½ years; the Syndicate would then have the right at the end of that period to form a company to take a fifty-fifty interest in Mr Baird's inventions.'[23] The company did not respond to the tactic. The potential syndicate, however, encouraged by a press report to the effect that when the war was over, the BBC's monopoly of broadcasting would cease, brought in a third backer in September. The proposal was to form the Baird Holding and Development Trust, which would buy all Baird's existing and future patents. An initial investment of £50,000 would then enable significant patents to be developed and manufacturing facilities to be provided, with television receivers as the first priority.[24]

According to Margaret's engagement diaries for 1943-4, the family spent Christmas 1943 together at the Riviera Hotel, Torquay, where Baird went down with flu. She travelled to London from Bude on 11 January, and was present at Baird's demonstration to 'Cable & Wireless experts' two days later. On 16 January Baird's diary shows a return of the mysterious initials which may denote symptoms of illness. On 17 January, Margaret reports, 'Logie ill', and the next day she called in the doctor. The entry for 19 January in her diary, 'Demonstration to Russians: Carstairs and self for Logie', and Baird's in his, '3.30 pm Russian minister',[25] suggest that he was not well enough to be present. This is almost certainly the illness to which she refers in an epilogue ('Chapter Ten') to *Sermons, Soap and Television*, which she wrote in 1948. She was staying with Baird in London, when 'he had one of his strange attacks, followed by a feverish state which lasted about a week. His doctor advised me to take him out of London to Crowborough [in Sussex]. So we left the air raids and stayed for a time in the invigorating air.'[26] It appears that she went back to Bude on 24 January, leaving Baird at the Beacon Hotel in Crowborough. She returned to Crowborough on 13 March, and reported, 'Logie not too bad'. In the meantime, it would seem from his diaries that Baird had continued, while based in Crowborough, to undertake a limited range of commitments and to keep in touch with his business associates. He returned to London, with Margaret, on 14 March.

On 13 March 1944 Baird noted in his diary: 'My agreement with B[aird] T[elevision] L[td]. My agreement with C[able] & W[ireless]', presumably to ensure that he was free to sign up with the syndicate. On 26 March he wrote down, 'Ring Tom King, I think we are at the beginning of a very big thing.' Baird and Margaret travelled down to Bude from London on 27 March. Baird was ill again. So, according to Margaret's diary, was Grannie Albu: 'mother very ill'. It is likely that the entries every day from 28 March to 2 April, 'Dr Holtby', refer to calls to see both her husband and her mother, who had suffered a heart attack.

In the meantime King had reported to Harris on 31 March that Baird had 'gone into hiding'. Neither would he sign legally binding documents until he had assessed all the implications: '[He] has a strong antipathy to putting things down on paper because of his previous experiences.'[24] Baird probably remembered the difficulties he had with Will Day in Hastings, twenty years earlier.

Matters came to a head on 4 April. Baird wrote to King from Bude:

> I am sorry about the delay. The explanation is ill health. I have been far from well and am here under strict medical supervision. The position is that the questionnaire is such that it raises matters which can only be dealt with by personal interview which I can't give owing to my state of health. As I don't want to appear discourteous, or you to keep these people hanging about any longer, perhaps your suggestion to discontinue negotiations is the proper course. I enclose the questionnaire and the letter.[27]

This letter crossed in the post with one from King to Baird which demanded an explanation for his silence, and suggested a meeting between Baird and his prospective backers. When King received Baird's letter of 4 April, he apologised and suggested that negotiations should be renewed when Baird had recovered.[24]

Baird appears to have stayed in Bude until 9 May. Though he lunched with King at Scott's on 17 May, and met members of the prospective syndicate on 24 May, that was the end of the Baird Development Holding Company. It was, however, the beginning of a period of renewed creative energy on the part of Baird, and of some welcome financial relief. Baird had kept in touch with Jack Buchanan, who had been fully occupied during the war years in his star capacities as stage and film performer, and also producer. His half-hour, completely unrehearsed, comic dialogue with Bing Crosby at the opening of the Stage Door Canteen club in Piccadilly for the forces of the allied nations has gone down in theatrical history.[28] So has his first playing of a straight part, at the age of fifty-four, in Frederick Lonsdale's *The Last of Mrs Cheyney* at the Savoy Theatre in June 1944.[29] Since 1937 he had owned Riverside Film Studios in Hammersmith, where comedy films such as *Happidrome* were being produced to cheer up wartime audiences.[30] With the end of the war in sight, Baird urged Buchanan to start thinking about cinema television. As a first step, Buchanan took on his old friend as consultant on cinema television to Riverside Film Studios for a year, starting on 2 June 1944. The salary was £30 a week, payable in share options, which for income tax purposes was the equivalent of £1290 for the year.

Meanwhile, at Crescent Wood Road, Baird, who was suffering increasing bouts of illness, and Anderson, with the help of glassblower Johnson, had been working on a form of colour television receiver which would entirely eliminate mechanical moving parts: an all-electronic system.[31] The essential element was a cathode-ray tube of a rather special type, incorporating a screen which was semi-transparent and was bombarded with electrons from both sides. The cathode-ray tube was spherical, and actually consisted of a modified mercury arc rectifier tube. Modifying the spherical bulb was a major challenge for Johnson. Mounting the screen inside the bulb was like the old trick of getting a 'ship in a bottle', a phrase which recurs several times in Baird's diaries.

In the simplest form of receiving tube described in the patent, there were two electron guns, one on each side of the screen. The guns were aimed at the screen from an angle of about forty-five degrees, producing an electron image on each side of it. The surfaces of the screen were coated with thin, semi-transparent films of colour phosphors which produced light when bombarded by electrons. In the two-colour tube, one surface had a red phosphor, and the other blue-green. When there was a semi-transparent phosphor coating on each side of the mica screen, the observer saw the red and the blue-green images superimposed, and the result was a picture in natural colours. The screen was ten inches in diameter, with a picture definition of six hundred lines. An advantage of the tube was that the screen could be viewed from either side, though in this case one side was a mirror image of the other. The patent specifications describe several variations on this scheme, including an ingenious three-colour arrangement, with three electron guns and three different colours of phosphor.

Once the patent had been accepted, Baird could demonstrate his invention to the press. He still had one problem, what name to give his tube. In his diaries he had always referred to the system as 'line by line', to distinguish it from his earlier 'frame by frame' (field sequential) system with the rotating colour filters. He wrote down 'Chromotron' and 'Electrochrome' in his diary, and finally settled for the 'Telechrome' tube.

The press demonstration of the first all-electronic colour television receiver using a single cathode-ray tube took place on 16 August 1944. The visitors, some of whom were televised and saw themselves on the receiver, were agreeably surprised by the quality of the pictures.[33] The *News Chronicle* reporter noted that,

> The image was in colour as natural as any colour film I have seen. The light wood grain of my pipe stood out clearly, a bead of perspiration on my forehead was highlighted, and the book in my hand was pictured so plainly that the coloured title of it could be read.[34]

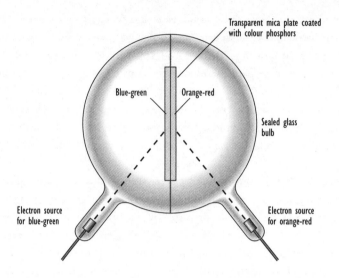

Figure 10: The Telechrome tube in its basic form, redrawn from British patent 562,168 of J L Baird, application 25 July 1942, accepted 21 June 1944.

In December, the family were briefly in London and saw the Telechrome in action. Malcolm, who was then nine, still vividly remembers the clear, bright picture. Eddie Anderson was the model, and Malcolm was much impressed by the realistic way in which the Telechrome showed the smoke drifting from his pipe.

Late in 1943 a government committee was formed to investigate the future of television after the war. It became known as the Hankey committee, after its chairman, Rt Hon. Lord Hankey, a former civil servant and cabinet minister, who in the course of nearly a lifetime of public service chaired, and produced the reports of, fifteen government committees between 1943 and 1951.[35] The members of the committee were Sir Stanley Angwin, engineer-in-chief, GPO, Sir Edward Appleton, secretary, Department of Scientific and Industrial Research, Sir Noel Ashbridge, now deputy director general, BBC, Sir Raymond Birchall, deputy director general, GPO, Professor J D Cockcroft, Air Defence Research and Development Establishment, Ministry of Supply, William J Haley, director general, BBC, and R J P Harvey, assistant secretary, Treasury. The establishment of the committee was formally announced in parliament on 18 January 1944 by the Deputy Prime Minister, Clement Attlee. Its objective was to study and report on 'the re-instatement and development of the television service'.

Evidence was taken from representatives of General Electric, Marconi–EMI (Shoenberg), Scophony, Standard Telephones and Cables, Board of Trade,

BBC, British Film Producers Association (J Arthur Rank), Ministry of Education, Radio Industry Council, REP Joint Council, and from one private individual, 'J L Baird Esq FRSE'.[36] John Logie Baird, Fellow of the Royal Society of Edinburgh, was invited by personal letter from Hankey to give his advice on certain specific matters.[37] He responded in writing, in a memorandum of some two thousand words.[38] Broadly speaking, the following were his views on the points on which he was consulted:

1 *War research and television development*
On applications of television to war, his experience was limited to infrared rays to render objects visible in the dark and in fog, and his company's installation of transmitters in aircraft. His current work on stereoscopic and colour television 'has no application to war ... [but] is of importance to the National effort'.

2 *Re-opening of television service on the 1939 standard of definition*
Broadcasting should begin as soon as possible with a guarantee of the use of the prewar system of 405 lines for three years. The BBC's monopoly should cease, and an arrangement on the Australian model introduced.

3 *Television research*
The range of the transmissions must be extended, to which relay stations are only a partial solution. Extending the service to the continent of Europe and the USA should be investigated. The quality of picture should be improved to 1000 lines, with colour and stereoscopic depth.

4 *New television service of radically improved type*
Colour stereoscopic television of 1000 lines definition should operate on an international standard in conjunction with an international worldwide television service. Baird then outlined the development of his own research, and suggested that the most effective start would be to use his two-colour all-electronic stereoscopic system, which dispensed with special glasses and could be viewed from any angle. The definition could be 600 lines, or reduced to 405 to be consistent with the prewar transmissions and receivers.

5 *Home market*
Extend broadcasting to the 'provinces', make available a cheap, mass-produced receiver, and introduce free competition in broadcasting.

6 *Foreign market*
From his experience the Soviet Union represented the largest potential market. To encourage export an international system should be introduced, radiating from London.

In July 1944 Baird demonstrated the progress he had made to some of the members of the committee at Crescent Wood Road.[39]

The Hankey committee's report was delivered to the Privy Council on 29 December 1944, and published in March 1945. It was only a few pages long. Baird's general ideas were accepted as the long-term objective, though his suggestion of a three-year timescale to develop colour television was quietly ignored.[40] In the event, the development of British television was much slower than Baird's expectation: the 405-line standard was not improved upon until 1964, and colour was not introduced until 1967. The market is still awaiting stereoscopic pictures. On the other hand, his plea for the introduction of commercial television was acted upon in 1954.

Baird was already in 1944 thinking seriously about his role in the postwar television business. He had long discussions with Buchanan, and also with K E Shelley, about setting up a new company, John Logie Baird Ltd. Kew Edwin Shelley was a charming, astute, and successful barrister specialising in patent law, whom Baird had first met in 1931. According to his entry in *Who's Who*, Shelley, born in 1894, was educated at Rugby School and New College, Oxford, served as an officer in the Royal Sussex Regiment and as a flying officer with the Royal Flying Corps in World War I, was called to the Bar in 1921, and played croquet for recreation.[41] The fact that he was appointed KC (King's Counsel) in 1937, comparatively early in his career, testifies to his skill as a lawyer.[42] He was certainly at Rugby and New College, to which he won a mathematical scholarship. His name, however, was not Kew Shelley, but Krishna Kumar Edwin Bonnerjee, and he was the only son of Kamal Shelley Bonnerjee, barrister and old Rugbeian, of 1 Ballygunge Park, Calcutta.[43] In 1920 he changed his name by deed poll, shortly before passing his final Bar examination.[42] Shelley was also to become the Baird family's lawyer, and executor of Baird's will.[44]

On 22 July Baird wrote to Buchanan: 'I think the sooner the company is formed the better as things are beginning to move in the television field ... also if the war comes to a sudden end there will be a boom in television and we should be ready to take advantage of it.' On a more personal note he added, 'I have wanted to get you in with me in television for a long time and am glad to see it come about at last.'[40]

John Logie Baird Ltd, the fifth British limited company to bear his name, was registered soon afterwards; the company's scope included cinema television as well as the design and manufacture of television receivers. The initial financial support came from Buchanan and the financier J Donaldson-Hudson. Baird provided his expertise and access to his patents and equipment. The other members of the board were Shelley and H Norman Letts.

In late 1944 Baird was advertising for technical assistants,[45] and further advertisements appeared in the latter part of 1945. The technical work took place mainly at Crescent Wood Road. Board meetings were held at three- to four-week intervals, sometimes at the company's registered offices at 4 Upper Grosvenor Street, but more often at Buchanan's office in the Lyric Theatre, Shaftesbury Avenue. Baird's salary of £1250 a year was adequate for that time, though far below what he had earned before the war.

The Upper Grosvenor Street premises included a studio and control room on the ground floor, and a large gas oven for extra glass work, though what little glass work was done was on a part-time basis by Johnson. There was a workshop area and offices on the floors above, but no machinery except for hand-held tools and welding equipment. There was no drawing office as such, but Sayers acted as draughtsman when he returned from war service in 1945, with another technical assistant to run the workshop, where some television and projection tubes were made.[45]

The development of cinema television was a delicate issue, as many cinema owners were suspicious of television. A notable exception was J Arthur Rank, who had acquired control of Gaumont-British in October 1941 and of the Odeon cinemas early in 1942. He had testified to the Hankey committee that a cooperative approach between the two industries could be mutually beneficial.[46] Strong support for cinema television also came from Samuel Seeman, head of Capital and Provincial Cinemas, which owned the 'Classic' circuit of London cinemas. Seeman had visited the USA, and reported that American big-screen television was 'not as good as ours', and that there was no colour. He suggested breaking the BBC's monopoly by setting up a television station which broadcast exclusively to cinemas.[47]

In the area of domestic television receivers, Baird persuaded the board of his new company to support the design and construction of a 'super set', which would dwarf any existing model and put the Baird name firmly back on the map of British television. It began with an innocent enough sounding question from Baird to Anderson:

> I remember him asking me how large could one build a sealed-off cathode-ray tube. My reply was, 'Well, how large can you get a bottle?' A few days later Mr Baird arrived complete with large car and driver, who dragged out the largest glass bulb I think I have ever seen. When I had recovered from the shock, ways and means were discussed as to how to proceed to make this into a tube. It was decided to make the first one continuously evacuated, to enable alterations to take place. After many trials and tribulations the great day arrived when the pumps

had been operated all night and the flask of liquid oxygen topped up, the filament heated and the scanners switched on, leaving only the EHT off. Click went the switch, and the largest and brightest scan I have ever seen appeared on the screen.[48]

The device was at that time the largest sealed-off cathode-ray tube ever known, 27¾ inches in diameter, giving a picture of 22 inches by 17. This is large even by today's home viewing standards. It gave a picture with an area of about three hundred square inches, compared with about eighty for the normal twelve-inch tube available in the years following the war.

The prototype was constructed to Anderson's design at Crescent Wood Road, and Baird's diary contains reminders about installing a special vacuum pump, a large glassblower's lathe, and an annealing oven. The Plessey company provided the chassis, the radiogram, and the cabinet. The set was named the Grosvenor, and its assembly was completed early in 1946. As events turned out, this model was the only one of its type ever made.

From 1942 for the next three years, Baird had quietly continued as a consultant technical adviser to Cable and Wireless, alongside his much publicised television projects. Baird's diary shows that he was in frequent contact with Jacob and Wilshaw. Periodically he visited the Marconi transmitters and laboratories at Chelmsford in Essex. Sometimes Chelmsford is specifically mentioned; sometimes a visit can be inferred from an entry such as, '2.15 from Liverpool Street', the London terminus for trains to the eastern counties.

Cable and Wireless used the term 'facsimile' to describe their process for transmitting a still picture by telegraph or radio.[49] A photograph or document was attached to a rotating cylinder and slowly scanned, with the image being transmitted over a period of several minutes. A modern fax machine works on somewhat the same principle, sending scanned pages by phone line at the rate of about one every ten seconds. Baird proposed a very fast version of the facsimile process, in which images were sent at the same rate as television images, twenty-five per second. His method has never been fully described, and no patents were ever taken out, but from entries in his diaries the process involved the intermediate-film technique.[50] During the 1930s the Baird company had developed a facsimile system using the intermediate-film technique which could send a page of five inches by four inches every ten seconds, about which Baird, as a member of the board, would have known. This was demonstrated to members of the Admiralty Research Laboratory and the director of H M Signal School on 26 May 1938.[51] It may be assumed, then, that Baird's personal system consisted of photographing the pages one frame at a time onto cine film, then processing the film continuously in a chemical bath, and rapidly scanning it wet for transmission on 180 lines at twenty-five frames a second (see plate 57).[52]

On 13 July 1943 Baird reminded himself in his diary to 'show facsimile to Colonel Lee'. This would have been Lieutenant-Colonel Sir George Lee, engineer-in-chief, GPO, from 1932 to 1939, and now director of communications research and development at the Air Ministry. There was a demonstration also to Angwin, who had succeeded Lee at the GPO in 1939, and been knighted in 1941. Early in 1944 Baird discussed with Wilshaw the possibility of patenting the fast facsimile,[53] opinions being obtained from Angwin and from Francis J Mortimer, doyen of British photographers and editor of the *Amateur Photographer and Cinematographer*.

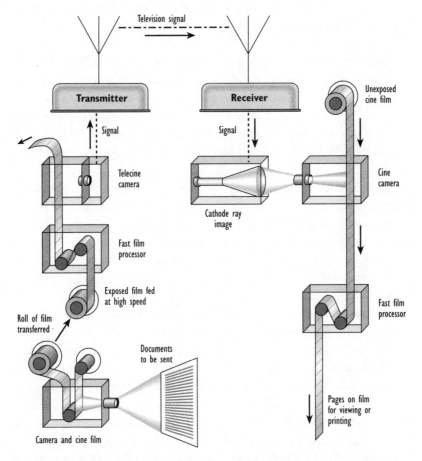

Figure 11: Fast facsimile method for high-speed transmission of images such as pages of text or maps. This is a conceptual diagram, based on a drawing by Malcolm Baird of what is known of his father's work for Cable and Wireless 1941-4. Neither J L Baird nor Cable and Wireless took out patents on this system.

In May 1944 Baird appears to have been allowed to publicise parts of his fast facsimile work in the press. He jotted down in his diary ideas for a press release as they occurred to him: 'A speed undreamt of by other methods became possible by Fac Tele'; '[Images on] film have been transmitted by Baird at the rate of 25 per second'; 'Facsimile Television opens a new era in communication'; 'At present the range is restricted by the range of television [signals] but it requires little prophetic vision to see that the range will be extended to cover the Globe'; 'Communications will give us the newspaper man's dream The International Daily Paper'.[54]

The *Daily Telegraph* ran a piece on 18 July 1944, under the headline '5 novels per minute', referring to the extremely high rate at which information could be transmitted, estimated at 750,000 words a minute. It would appear that journalists were first shown a piece of the actual apparatus on 16 August, at the same time as Baird demonstrated his Telechrome.

> Mr Baird yesterday exhibited the sending instrument. It looks rather like a magic lantern. 'I cannot show you it in operation because I cannot at the same time have the other instruments in the room,' he said. 'The instrument makes an international newspaper seem probable. A whole newspaper could be transmitted about the world in a matter of seconds.[55]

Baird's coyness about details was worthy of his secretive attitude during the 1920s, and for much the same reason. An American journalist who interviewed him in 1944 on the future of television included two brief paragraphs on his facsimile, ending, 'The details of … this new electronic device were not revealed, however, owing to the wartime embargo on technical inventions which may benefit the enemy.'[56] Baird did, however, reveal to journalists that his system involved the intermediate-film process and that it operated on ultra-short waves, which would require a series of relay stations every fifty miles along the route.'[55]

The Germans had in fact also been working on the fast transmission of images, though this was not revealed until many years after the war. The Fernseh company, operating under the disguised name of Farvis, carried out a major research programme on the fast transmission of maps, diagrams, and other graphical information. In the Fernseh–Farvis system, a page was scanned by the flying spot from a cathode-ray tube, and the signal directly transmitted in a fraction of a second as a single short burst which would be unintelligible to anyone without sophisticated receiving equipment.[57]

It is probable that Baird was allowed to reveal to journalists such details as he did because in terms of the technology available in 1944, his apparatus was ahead of its time. To experiment with it, he needed one of Cable and Wireless's main transmitters, which was not practicable in wartime because of the amount of government and service traffic.[58] Consequently, when Wilshaw reported to the court of Cable and Wireless in September 1944 that Baird had produced nothing of advantage to the company during his three years as consultant, the board decided not to renew his contract, and gave him three months' notice.[59] Wilshaw, however, found the funds to continue to pay Baird £500 a year, right up to his death.[58] Of Baird's work, he wrote to Moseley:

> We had the satisfaction of knowing that we did our best to help a genius during his time of financial difficulty. Had he lived longer, I had no doubt, and I still have no doubt, that the ultimate end of telegraphy will be some form of picture transmission of the written word rather than the mechanical process of the punched slip. ...
>
> I consider that Baird was a genius – his premature death was a great loss to science. I have the happiest recollections of him and some satisfaction in knowing that my company, through kindness of heart and on purely humanitarian grounds, eased his path during the war up to the date of his death, and enabled him to carry on with his experiments.[58]

Wilshaw died in 1968 at the age of eighty-eight. His prophecy has come true. The clattering teleprinter, fed by punched tape, is now a museum piece, and the Morse code itself, after 140 years of useful service, is no longer a requirement of the training of radio operators. The fast transmission of images, as envisaged by Baird, is commonplace, thanks to modern technology such as microwave transmitters, fibre-optic cables, satellites, and the internet. His prediction in 1944 of the 'international newspaper' has been fulfilled in that all major newspapers have internet editions which can be read all over the world.

There have been major changes, too, in the sensitive area of secret signalling. By 1975, the transmission of messages by characters in Morse code was obsolete, and the 'Ultra' codebreaking operation at Bletchley Park during World War II could be revealed without any damage to security. On the other hand, very little has been divulged about secret signalling by means of images. In 1984, Tom McArthur, one of Baird's biographers, asked the Ministry of Defence about his wartime experiments, and was told, 'No comment. Much of his work is still classified.'[60] A similar approach sixteen years later to the director of public relations resulted in the disappearance of the letter of enquiry,[61] but a follow-up letter was sympathetically dealt with by the head of DG Info XR1, though no information could be found.

Radar contributed even more to the war effort than the Ultra code-breaking project. As has been explained, Baird's work overlapped with radar in various ways.[62] Baird Television and Cinema-Television had contributed personal skills and components to the radar effort, but Baird himself had been excluded. After the victory in Europe in May 1945, details of British radar began to appear in the popular and technical press. Baird's thoughts went back to his early work on radio imaging which had been entirely ignored in the publicity for Watson-Watt and his team. He probably did not want to initiate a public controversy which might adversely affect the new company, John Logie Baird Ltd. Instead, he approached Parr and Maybank of the technical press. The October 1945 issue of *Electronic Engineering* (edited by Parr) ran a short piece entitled 'Radar Anticipated?'.[63] The December 1945 issue of *Wireless World* (edited by Maybank) contained a full-page feature under the heading 'Radar Prehistory', in which a claim was made on Baird's behalf:

> British Patent No. 292,185, applied for as long ago as 1926, describes an arrangement that bears on the face of it, a remarkable resemblance to H2S, one of the most refined and developed applications of modern radar. Baird pointed out that wireless waves can be reflected and refracted like visible light waves and contemplated a method of viewing an object, consisting of projecting upon it electromagnetic waves of short wavelength.[64]

In the 1980s a bitter controversy erupted about Baird's role in radar, which still flows on. It does not appear, however, that anyone in 1945 wrote disputing either of these articles published in widely-read technical journals. On 16 October 1945, Baird made an entry in his diary, 'Secret Patent Radar', and later reminded himself to consult his patent agents, Boult, Wade and Tennant, about 'radar renewals'.[65]

In the summer of 1944, the Bairds started to think about moving closer to London. There was no need now to be so far away. On the other hand, the bomb damage (a flying bomb demolished the house next door) and general dilapidation ('dry rot mushrooms growing in the dining-room') at 3 Crescent Wood Road, whose lease was in any case running out, meant that the family could not return there.[1] A search was undertaken for somewhere healthy for Baird which was within reasonable travelling distance of London. Newbury in Berkshire was considered, but the final choice was Bexhill, a resort on the east Sussex coast just a few miles from Hastings. In September 1944, Baird made an offer for the lease of a three-storey semi-detached house named 'Instow', at 1 Station Road. The name of the house never appealed to the family; Margaret remarked that 'stow in' would have been more appropriate. As the address suggests, the house was very near the station, from which frequent electric trains went to London's Victoria Station. The commuting time was one-and-a-half hours, rather on the long side, but an improvement on the journey of seven or eight hours between Bude and London.

The move was a long and complicated process. According to Margaret's diary, their own furniture was transferred from Bude on 15 December, and she began packing personal belongings the following day. She left for Bexhill with Diana on 22 December, putting up at the Granville Hotel. Baird's diary for 23 December has the entry, 'VERY ILL', so it is to be supposed that Margaret organised the move single handed. Not that the logistics of moving house would have been very much in Baird's line! The furniture arrived at Instow on 28 December. On 1 January 1945, Margaret returned to Bude to collect her mother and Malcolm, who stayed with her en route at the County Hotel, Salisbury.

The move made little difference to the lives of the children, except that Margaret made it clear to Diana that a girl of thirteen could not wander round Bexhill as she had done at Bude. Sandown School had evacuated from Bexhill to Bude in 1939, so that when it moved back to Bexhill, Malcolm was simply able to continue there. Diana was now too old for Sandown. At first she attended a school nearby which was basically a cramming establishment for girls who would leave at fourteen to go into offices. This was a new slant to her education, and its practical aspect appealed to her.[1] She started to study book keeping, business letter writing, and other useful skills, until she was sent to a more fashionable school at Cooden, a few miles west of Bexhill.

Cecilia Albu's physical health had worsened as a result of her heart attack the previous April, although she was still mentally sharp and won the occasional crossword prize. At Bexhill she remained effectively confined to her bedroom on the first floor. Margaret's workload in the house increased. There was a series of domestic helps, who proved to be incompetent or dishonest, or both.[1] The shops were close at hand, however, there was less rainfall than at Bude, and buses and trolley buses plied their way along the coastal road. The family went to occasional entertainments at the De La Warr Pavilion in Bexhill and the White Rock Pavilion in Hastings.

There was no doubt, however, that Baird's health was deteriorating. Doctors were consulted, specialists examined X-rays and cardiograms. All gave opinions, mainly that rest was essential. None foresaw the tragedy that lay ahead. Physical inactivity when his mind was active was to Baird anathema. Margaret saw what was happening:

> A misleading factor was the fascination of his conversation, especially with men of intellect. A doctor might begin by treating him as a patient, but in a few minutes the professional atmosphere would disappear, Logie's eyes would twinkle and brilliant talk would ensue, irrelevant to his illness but full of wit and humour. Every doctor who saw him must have thought, 'Here is a genius, undoubtedly highly strung, but a mortally sick man – no!' His powers of recuperation were tremendous, especially if he could get into warmth. He dreamed of going abroad into what he called 'bursting, bubbling sunshine'. He said to me once, 'My days are numbered; I have shot my bolt. I expect this feeling of general malaise must be age creeping on, yet I do not feel old, any older than I did when I was twenty-five.'[26]

There was a happy day in Bexhill when Seeman unexpectedly dropped by. He talked television animatedly with Baird, and offered him a seat on the board of Capital and Provincial News Theatres, together with facilities at the Classic news cinema in Baker Street for the new Baird company's experiments with large-screen cinema television.[26]

The war in Europe ended in May 1945, and in the Far East in August. When he was able to do so, Baird commuted between Bexhill and London, sometimes staying the night at the Palace Hotel or in a private hotel near Crescent Wood Road, where he still spent most of his working time. Moseley, back in England for a few days, made contact with him by letter. 'The next morning [Baird] was on the phone to me. He was evidently excited and yet, before he uttered a word, there came to me the old deep-drawn, familiar sigh with which he nearly always prefaced such conversations.'[66] Moseley and his wife met Baird at the faded residential hotel ('for decrepit old *rentiers* and aged ladies') in Sydenham where he was staying. From a 'cold and lifeless drawing-room occupied solely by a grey-haired old woman, busy with her knitting, but not too busy to listen to every word we had to say', they moved to Baird's room, 'indistinguishable from a dozen others in which I had visited him over more than twenty years. The windows were closed, the electric fire was full on and on the bed was an untidy heap of clothes.'[67]

> We started fooling at once and the hotel's aged inmates must have been surprised to hear Baird's gusty laughter and my own chuckles. When we

first arrived he had walked softly and spoken in low tones, almost as though he were afraid of waking the dead-alive to life. Soon afterwards he was his old self again, boisterous as a schoolboy and inclined to horseplay. Eventually we drove to a tea-shop he recommended down the road and there we talked about the past and the future, yarning interminably about old friends and new opportunities. Baird, who was looking older and more tired than when I had last seen him, shed his cares for once and, laughing at my sallies, responded to them in his best vein of pawky humour.[68]

It was the last time the two old friends ever met.

Baird wrote to Moseley on 10 November:

It was like a breath of old happy times to see you again. But those care-free days are gone for ever.

With regard to the business with USA, judging by my experience out there I think it is a mere waste of time and can be a source of extreme irritation. It is here in London I will win or lose.[20]

Clearly, at their meeting, Moseley had diplomatically explained the difficulties of doing business at long distance with the USA at the present time.

Baird's hotel was probably the Woodhall, near Sydenham Hill station, which was where he had a visit in November from Reveley. When the Japanese overran Hong Kong, Reveley had been the head office assistant to the senior wireless engineer of the colony. Initially, he was held in a hotel, along with the postmaster general, assistant postmaster general, and the senior wireless engineer. Subsequently he was interned in Stanley prison camp, where he served as section quartermaster, in which capacity he was called upon to divide inadequate quantities of food equally among some eight hundred very hungry and critical prisoners.[69] 'He never failed, at the six-monthly meeting, to be selected as one of [the district's] leaders by a community labouring under semi-starvation conditions and considerable mental strain.'[70] After the Japanese surrender, Reveley was flown back to England. He was shocked at the physical change in his former employer, but recorded that his mind was as alert as ever.[71] For Reveley, too, it was his last sight of Baird, for he then returned to the Far East.

Also in November, Baird had other visitors. Margaret brought the children up from Bexhill for a treat.

He was proud to show us all over the new premises [at Upper Grosvenor

Street] where all the new apparatus was gradually being installed. Unfortunately, there was no lift in this four storey building and I have a painful memory of his slow ascent of the staircase, pausing and gasping on each step, but joking to us that he would 'join us in a quarter of an hour'. His weakness was increasing apace now, but few people could have realised it, so brave and indomitable a show did he put up.[26]

This is, too, the impression one gains from the entries in his diary. There was the same level of activity as in previous years, with many meetings in London, and technical reminders about cinema television and the Grosvenor model receiver which was under construction. The entries continue into the new year, with a company board meeting at the Lyric Theatre on 8 January 1946. There are several reminders also to send for 'Livadex', presumably liver pills, from Bexhill. Then, on 14 January, there is the ominous entry, 'Ill'. He stayed on in London at the Palace Hotel, trying to fight his illness. There are only a few more entries in January, the last of which is a note of a meeting with Buchanan on the 25th. Margaret came up to London to bring him back to Bexhill on Saturday, 26 January. He went straight to bed, and for a few days seemed to be rallying. On 2 February he insisted on going for a short walk. He came back exhausted, and went to bed. During the night he suffered a stroke.

For the next four months the main bedroom at Instow became a hospital ward. A night nurse was brought in to enable Margaret to get some sleep, and an oxygen cylinder and breathing apparatus were set up beside the bed. The single light socket in the room had a spider's web of wires descending from it, feeding electric blanket, bedside light, electric fire, and wireless, around which the family used to gather once a week to listen to Tommy Handley's *ITMA*. The fire was on continuously, and Margaret was alarmed when the quarterly electricity bill amounted to £65. Baird was weak, but fully conscious, and for the first time began to realise that he might not survive this bout of illness. The diary entries cease between February and the end of May 1946, but he was often in touch with Anderson and with the company office from the telephone by his bed.

Shortly before Baird had his stroke, a letter had arrived from SIGESO, a government agency attached to the Ministry of Aircraft Production, in answer originally to an enquiry he had made about fluorescent coatings for cathode-ray tubes. He was invited to view documents recently captured from Fernseh, which he had helped to found, and to interrogate Professor Heimann,[72] who was being brought to Britain from Germany. Baird was too ill to take up this invitation; had he done so, his feelings would have been of amazement, perhaps tinged with frustration, at the Germans' progress in developing the military applications of television, while the British interest in airborne television had faded soon after the outbreak of war. Fernseh had not only been working on secret signalling by television, but also on airborne television cameras for guiding flying bombs.[73] The system was known as Tonne A. The camera, which used miniature valves, occupied a chassis 17 x 17 x 40cm, not much larger than a shoebox. It provided a 441-line picture and was placed in the nose of the missile, which could then be guided to its target by a controlling operator who viewed the screen display in a mother aircraft. Fortunately for Britain, Tonne A was only built late in the war, and was never put into operational use. Meanwhile, the Americans had been working on a television-guided gliding bomb known as the GB-4, in which the camera used a miniaturised iconoscope tube (type 1846) developed by RCA. The GB-4 was actually used a few times in the bombing of German naval installations in August and September 1944.[74] Many years later, in 1991, the American advanced television-guided missile system was employed to great effect in the Gulf War.

As Baird tried to gain strength in the spring of 1946, his attentions were focussed on the resumption of television on 7 June, and the televising of the Victory Parade on the following day. His new company had arranged to feed the BBC television pictures of the parade to projector receivers at the Classic Cinema in Baker Street and the News Theatre in Agar Street. At the Savoy Hotel the programme would be seen on a 5-foot projection screen, and also on the 28-inch screen of the Grosvenor receiver, strategically placed 'in a room surrounded with lots of mirrors',[45] most probably the ballroom now known as the Lancaster Room.[75]

Working from his sickbed, Baird seemed to get a new lease on life as the date of the parade approached. Wilshaw wrote on 31 May saying that he was 'glad to hear you are very much better', and asking for tickets for the show-ing at the Savoy. Margaret gladly arranged for these to be supplied to him through the company. She and Baird talked about the possibility of going to some sunny spot in southern Europe so that he could convalesce. There is a note in the diary for 4 June: 'passports'.

On the day of the parade, the showing at the Classic had to be abandoned because of interference from the BBC broadcast.[45] Reports of the Grosvenor prototype, however, suggested it had worked well, and Baird noted in his diary, '12 sets by Plessey, 12 sets by our own factory', and 'another 28 inch tube for Eros', a London cinema. The last entry written by him is on 13 June: 'ring Post office re line to Eros'.

That evening, the night nurse was away, and Margaret made up a bed for herself in Baird's room. He was restless during the night, and at about two o'clock in the morning she gave him a drink of water. He looked up at her and, adapting a line from Cowper, said, 'In spite of all thy faults, I love thee still.'[76] He settled down, and she waited until he was breathing quietly before going to sleep herself. When she awoke, the room was unnaturally quiet. She went over to Baird's bedside, and knew that he was dead. She herself wrote into his diary the last entry, on 14 June: 'John died in Bexhill.' His death certificate cites the causes of death as coronary thrombosis and arteriosclerosis, and gives as his occupation, 'Company Director. Inventor of Television.'

Years later, when television reached the Sussex coast, reception at 1 Station Road was consistently reported to be bad.[77]

17
Epilogue
1946–2002

Baird's death in the early hours of 14 June 1946 had a devastating effect on his family. Although he had been ill for several months, he had always hoped that he could hold on, and he eagerly looked forward to seeing the postwar growth of the industry he had helped to create. Margaret and his sister Annie arranged that he should be buried in Helensburgh, and the funeral took place on 17 June. Many local people attended the ceremony at which Baird was buried in the family grave, next to his father and mother. Because of the distance and the fact that there would be a memorial service in London, few people from his professional life were present, though William Taynton and his wife made the long journey from the south of England. After the funeral, a distraught 'Alice' appeared at 'The Lodge', and had to be consoled by Margaret with a cup of tea and sympathy.

A public memorial service was held on 26 June at St Saviour's Church, Walton Street, Chelsea, at which an address was given by Rev. Dr R F V Scott, minister of St Columba's Church of Scotland, Pont Street. Margaret brought Diana and Malcolm, who had not gone to Scotland for the funeral. For ten-year-old Malcolm, it was the first time he properly realised that his father had been a person of significance in the outside world.

At Bexhill Margaret faced a difficult financial situation. Baird, in a will made not long before he died, made Shelley and Margaret joint executors of his estate, the whole of which he left to Margaret. Probate was granted to Shelley, 'with power reserved to the other Executor', in respect of a net value of £7102.1s.10d.[1] Over the next few years Shelley found excuses to retain the money. In 1953, Margaret's brother Gordon, on a visit to London from South Africa, threatened to report Shelley to the Law Society. Margaret was then paid about eighty per cent of what was owing to her. Through a solicitor, she was still trying to extract the remaining £1500 in 1961, by which time Shelley himself was in serious financial trouble.[2] There was some relief in the form of a modest pension of £500 a year from John Logie Baird

Ltd, authorised by the board of the company at the urging of Buchanan and also Seeman.

In addition to her financial difficulties, Margaret was physically and emotionally exhausted by Baird's illness and death. She also had to look after her very sick mother, who died of heart failure in October 1946, leaving a bank overdraft of £400 to add to the family woes. At short notice, Annie Baird and her housekeeper Margaret Scott came to the rescue again. They travelled from Scotland, and helped to look after the house and household. Annie, with her nursing background, was a brisk and firm character, and it was perhaps inevitable that Margaret should feel that her children were being taken out of her care. During the bitterly cold winter of 1946/7, she fell into a state of acute clinical depression.

Clearly the family could not remain at 1 Station Road, and Crescent Wood Road was uninhabitable. In April 1947, the whole ménage, including Diana's cat (Minnie) and several canaries in cages, moved north to 'The Lodge', Helensburgh. The house, which had belonged to Annie since her father's death in 1932, had changed little since the early 1900s. Old books, pictures, papers, and the primitive telephone switchboard were constant reminders of John Logie Baird. In a drawer, Malcolm discovered an old stereoscope and a few of the special double-imaged cards which could be viewed with it to give a three-dimensional effect. Much later, he realised the connection between this device and Baird's research into stereoscopic television in the 1940s. On one of the windows, Baird had scratched his name with a diamond cutter. The children were fascinated by the memorabilia and the Victorian atmosphere of the house. Annie was very much a Victorian herself, having been born in 1883, but behind her brisk and forthright manner was a kindly character with a dry wit.

Margaret's state of depression continued. She was unhappy in the cool, damp climate of Helensburgh, and often said that the house was haunted by ghosts from the past. She pined for the warmth and sunshine of South Africa. On medical advice she voluntarily entered the Crichton Royal Hospital near Dumfries (now a campus of Glasgow University and other institutions) for full-time psychiatric treatment. This continued for several years, during which she only made occasional visits to Helensburgh.[3] Diana continued her education at St Bride's School, and Malcolm at Larchfield School (the 'Academy' designation had been dropped).

The household in Helensburgh had neither the benefit nor the distraction of television, which did not reach Scotland until 1952. In the years immediately after the war, television was broadcast by the BBC for an insignificant number of hours a day from Alexandra Palace to a few thousand viewers in the London area, using Marconi–EMI equipment which had been mothballed since 1939. Television manufacturers were scrambling to get production started, but faced difficulties with labour and components. The retail prices of new television sets were high, relative to average earnings, and carried heavy purchase tax; they were regarded as interesting toys for the wealthy. It was a time of general shortages, and in February 1947 the BBC shut down television for a month as an electricity-saving measure.

Against this discouraging background, John Logie Baird Ltd, under Buchanan's chairmanship, began to produce television sets for the London viewing market. The receivers were built at a factory in Rayner's Lane, Harrow, and at Buchanan's suggestion were named after London theatres: the Lyric, the Garrick, the Adelphi. The top of the line was intended to be Baird's creation, the Grosvenor, but with a price tag estimated at £1500, only the one set was ever produced.[4] The Lyric, with its superb cabinet of bird's-eye maple, survives as a collectors' item.

Buchanan was keen that the company should enter the richer and less heavily taxed American market, for patriotic as well as business reasons; Britain was desperately in need of dollar earnings to help pay off her debts under the US lend-lease programme. Baird's former assistant Anderson, who had continued with the company as technical partner, was asked to develop a table-top television set for the American standards. A major selling point was that it did not require an external aerial (antenna in American English), but could use the mains lead for the purpose. In March 1948, Buchanan and Anderson travelled to New York with a prototype of the set. It was not very efficient, but Buchanan's future wife, Suzzie Bassett, in whose Park Avenue apartment it was first tested, recorded in her journal that the 'signal came through and then a perfect test picture. The sound reproduction was excellent.'[5] Whatever failings the set may have had, Buchanan returned to Britain with large orders, including one from Jack Strauss, head of Macy's department store, but he was unable to raise the additional capital to mass-produce the sets.[6] But for this, John Logie Baird Ltd might have established a firm presence in the USA at the beginning of the television boom in the 1950s. Soon afterwards, in November 1948, Buchanan relinquished his interest in John Logie Baird Ltd, which merged with Scophony.

John Logie Baird Ltd had not continued with any of Baird's lines of research after his death, and the fate of his equipment in the Crescent Wood Road laboratory is uncertain. Several of his patents and published results, however, proved useful to American scientific researchers. Anderson was in the USA in 1946, when he almost certainly visited RCA.[7] Whether or not he passed onto RCA details of Baird's work for Cable and Wireless on fast facsimile, and a cryptic observation he once made in writing suggests that he did,[8] it seems to have been the basis of RCA's Ultrafax system.[9] Donald S Bond of RCA started work on the system at the company's research laboratories in Princeton in what seems to have been June 1947,[10] and it was publicly demonstrated in October 1948 by RCA and Eastman Kodak at the Library of Congress.[9] In the Ultrafax system, the intermediate-film process for recording the images had been speeded up by using hot processing solutions. For a capacity of 540,000 words per minute the system required a large bandwidth of 4 MHz; it was suggested that television facilities should be used to send images in off-hours when regular programmes were not being transmitted. The enthusiasm of the Americans is in some contrast to the attitude of Wilshaw and his colleagues at Cable and Wireless, that Baird's fast facsimile system was impractical.

In the area of colour television, Peter Goldmark of the Columbia Broadcasting System had praised Baird's work on field sequential colour, such as he too had been developing, with considerable financial support. Between 1950 and 1953 the CBS system was adopted by the Federal Communications Commission as the US standard for colour broadcasting.[11] It comprised a cathode-ray tube, which showed, in black and white, a rapidly repeating sequence of three images viewed through a large rotating 'color wheel' containing filters in the three primary colours, thereby producing a picture in full colour. A full-size cathode-ray tube was used, rather than Baird's method, which employed a small tube with projection and magnification of the picture. The CBS receivers gave an excellent picture, but the rotating color wheel had to be about ninety centimetres in diameter, which was a decidedly awkward feature. Meanwhile the Radio Corporation of America with the National Broadcasting Company had been working intensively on an all-electronic system in which the cathode-ray tube screen was coated with special coloured phosphors; the system was eventually adopted by the FCC in 1953. The RCA patents cite Baird's work on the Telechrome as prior art. Britain had no colour television until 1967, when a modified form of the German PAL system was introduced. The PAL system had in turn been developed from the RCA system by Walter Bruch (1908-90), the same man who had been in charge of the guided-missile Tonne A programme.[12]

The company formed by the merger between John Logie Baird Ltd and Scophony in 1948 was called Scophony–Baird.[13] Scophony had been in some financial trouble, and the previous year Seeman had been brought in as managing director.[14] The head office was moved from Upper Grosvenor Street to Lancelot Road, Wembley, Middlesex. The new company continued to manufacture Baird television sets, but they were of a plainer and less expensive design than before. The names of the models were less exclusive, too: the Townsman, the Countryman, the Everyman. One of the most popular was the Baird portable, with a screen of 9 by 6 inches; at fifty-five guineas, about three months' wages for the average worker, it was still expensive.

The postwar progress of the television industry had little impact on the Baird family in Helensburgh. In 1951 Margaret was making a gradual recovery from her mental breakdown. Malcolm was at Fettes College, Edinburgh, on a foundation scholarship, and Diana was reading English at Glasgow University. One day in June, Annie received a letter from John Swift, asking for help with his projected biography of Baird. Swift was a young BBC producer who had published a very full, and by all accounts very good, history of the first twenty-five years of British television.[15] His research for that book had stimulated his interest in Baird.

A few days later Swift travelled to Helensburgh, where, over one of Margaret Scott's delicious and substantial teas, Annie gave him an interview and lent him some early photographs. She also suggested he should contact some of Baird's former associates, including Moseley, who was now living in Bournemouth. When they met, Moseley put it to Swift that they should write the book together. Both Swift and his publisher, Phoenix House, owned by J M Dent & Sons, refused to consider the suggestion. Moseley wrote to Annie:

> I have been asked to write a book about John Baird and I am at present engaged upon it. I am told that John left a number of notes, which I am sure he would like to set before the public in his own way.[16]

The emergence of two biographers within a few weeks bewildered the family.

During the next few months the professional journalist Moseley set out to achieve a scoop over Swift.[17] He contacted Shelley, and obtained from the estate's papers an uncorrected copy of 'Sermons, Socks and Television'. He interviewed Lord and Lady Samuel, Wilshaw, Anderson, and Buchanan.[18] He obtained papers from his publisher, Odhams Press, relating to the contact in 1923 between Baird and W J B Odhams, who had died in 1943. Swiftly and skilfully, Moseley cobbled together a 256-page biography, which appeared in March 1952.[19] Swift was at that time moving to the Cyprus Broadcasting Corporation. He tried to pick up the pieces of his book, but his publisher decided not to go ahead with it. Swift had a nervous breakdown, and never resumed work on the biography.

The appearance of Moseley's book set alarm bells ringing in the BBC.

Sir William Haley, director general, wrote an internal memorandum to Ashbridge, who in a reorganisation of senior management in 1948 had relinquished the title of deputy director general and become director of technical services:

> I see in this morning's papers that Moseley has got out a book about Baird and apparently makes all sorts of allegations against the BBC. I do not think at this stage there is anything we should dream of replying to them. But: (1) some Tory MPs may raise them in the forthcoming Charter [of the BBC] debate as a wicked example of a monopoly trying to kill a financial enterprise, and (2) I think they should in any case be in the BBC archives if there is to be a statement of the case from the BBC's point of view.[20]

Ashbridge sent an anguished appeal to the registry: 'Is there any hope of tracing my papers on this?' The registry sent up what it had, though it would appear that some documents had been destroyed by a bomb. Ashbridge finally wrote to Haley on 9 June: '[Moseley's book] is not, I think, what one would call a balanced appraisal of the circumstances surrounding Baird's work in relation to the BBC.'[21] Since these circumstances were seen from Moseley's point of view it would have been extraordinary if it was. Nevertheless Ashbridge was unable to put his finger on anything in the book which justified an objection in public. Moseley was far too wily an old bird for that!

Moseley's biography of Baird was no best seller, but he received a few hundred pounds in royalties which he transferred to Margaret's bank account. Though the book was an affectionate and revealing portrait of his old friend, with interludes which were more about Moseley than Baird, it conveyed the message that Baird had been a romantic failure because his system of mechanical television appeared to have led nowhere. Surprisingly, because he had been kept posted with letters and press cuttings, Moseley said little about Baird's work on electronic television during the war.

Moseley's biography was well intended, but the notion of Baird as a failure had already been propounded in other, less sympathetic quarters. In July 1946, only a month after Baird's death, the chairman of EMI had written to the *Sunday Times* stating that modern television had nothing to do with Baird and was due to the prophecies of Campbell Swinton and the expensive research efforts of his company.[22] EMI, and in particular the former members of Shoenberg's research team, felt that they had not been given enough credit for their development of electronic television, and, in order to get it, they had first to discredit mechanical television, and thus also Baird. This anti-Baird movement (as it became known in the family) gave rise to some painful experiences. Margaret was infuriated by a scurrilous and inaccurate piece about Buchanan and Baird in the *Tatler*, which described Baird as an 'odd and honest little man who liked to go around in carpet slippers'. It went on to claim that he 'died during a dinner given in his honour at the Holborn restaurant'.[23] Margaret wrote a letter of complaint, but it was not published.

More serious was the impression, given in a paper read at a six-day convention of the Institution of Electrical Engineers on 'The History of British Television', that Baird contributed nothing of practical value.[24] This particular issue resurfaced in 1975 in the correspondence columns of *Electronics and Power*, where the anti-Baird movement (G R M Garratt and W T O'Dea) came off second best to the Baird supporters' group (Professor R W Burns, Malcolm Baird, I A Shanks, L C Jesty, and Reveley).[25]

A certain air of mystery attends the failure of an attempt to turn Baird's birthplace, 'The Lodge', into a television museum. In 1957 an approach was made to the family on behalf of William Harries, a Welsh businessman whose electronics outfit had made him a millionaire. He had been a lifelong admirer of Baird, and felt that it was scandalous that there was no major memorial to him. At a Scottish Radio Industry Club luncheon on 4 December 1957, Harries announced that he was launching a fund for the preservation of Baird's home as a 'museum and monument to a great Scottish genius'; later in the day live interviews with him about his plans were broadcast on the radio and on television by BBC Scottish region. At a dinner at the House of Commons on 17 December, a council of trustees was appointed under the chairmanship of Harries, with Sir Robert Boothby as honorary president. Boothby was one of Britain's first television personalities, 'which did not endear him to colleagues lacking his eloquence and engaging personality'.[26] It was arranged that he would address forty leading television manufacturers at a lunch at the House of Commons on 30 January 1958, in an endeavour to swell the coffers of the £30,000 appeal.

The job of public relations was entrusted by Harries to Harry Traynor, of the advertising agency Napper, Stinton, Woolley. Traynor wrote to Cecil McGivern, the BBC's deputy director of television, inviting him to the lunch, and asking for McGivern's personal views on the fund.[27] McGivern replied cautiously. He declined the invitation on the grounds that he would be in Scotland. As for the fund, 'I would not like to commit myself at present. We are forced to have strict rules with reference to appeals, which on television are few in number and decided by the BBC Appeals Committee.'[28] Whether McGivern knew it or not, the BBC's board of management had already decided that the corporation 'should not be associated with this memorial';[29]

members of the television programme board were warned at their meeting on 5 February 'that the BBC was not proposing to cooperate'.[30]

According to Traynor's recollection, early in January 1958 he was called to Boothby's prestigious Chelsea residence. There, Boothby, wearing pyjamas and dressing gown, with his silver hair in disarray – in sharp contrast to his suave television persona – informed Traynor that he had advised the council of trustees that the lunch on 30 January was cancelled. He had apparently discussed the proposal for the fund with a wide circle of acquaintances, the majority of whom believed that Baird's scientific contribution had been matched by other British and American engineers. These acquaintances included Lord Brabazon of Tara, a former president of the Radio Manufacturers' Association, to whom, as Colonel Moore-Brabazon MP, Church and Baird had given lunch at the Ivy in 1931. When subsequently contacted by Moseley, Brabazon said, 'Baird was a most imaginative, hard working, enthusiastic visionary and he certainly brought television along as a practical proposition. Unfortunately the mechanical system of scanning never turned out a success and they shifted to electronic scanning with the gun, which was something entirely different to the Baird invention.'[31] According to BBC files, however, the fund was still very much in existence on 5 February, when Traynor replied to McGivern's letter, suggesting an informal meeting; all that had happened in the meantime was that the lunch had been 'postponed' because of a 'mass exodus of television heads to foreign parts. Many were away on business trips, others in search of sunshine.' These included, of the members of the council, Harries, Boothby, and Stephen McAdden, the secretary.[32]

This was one further step in the decline of Baird's reputation. In 1962, Shoenberg's contribution to television was recognised by the award of a knighthood, which thus appeared to set the seal on the establishment view of British television history. Although the general public still associated Baird's name with television, officially he was being consigned to a minor role.

Meanwhile the fortunes of the Baird family were improving. Diana completed her studies at Glasgow, and married in 1956. Malcolm became essentially self supporting in 1957, with a research grant in chemical engineering at Cambridge. Margaret had emerged from her years in depression with a new philosophical outlook on life. Although she never attached herself to any specific religious faith, she claimed that her recovery had been helped by religious teachings.[33] In July 1953, she attended her first public event since Baird's funeral, the unveiling of a plaque at Kingsbury Manor, where the Baird company had built its receiving and transmitting station in 1929. In October 1957, she was the principal guest of the BBC television production, *This is Your Life*, whose subject was Baird.[34] Among those who contributed to the programme were Moseley, Clapp, and Taynton. This is the only time the long-running series has ever featured someone no longer living. The programme closed with a tribute in verse by Christopher Hassall, poet, dramatist, and librettist, who had composed the lyrics for Ivor Novello's *Glamorous Night* in 1935.[35] Two months later Associated Rediffusion TV screened Geoffrey Scanlan's play, *A Voice in Vision*, which was largely based on Moseley's biography of Baird.[36]

With the release of some of the capital from Baird's estate, and the economic independence of her children, Margaret was at last able to make trips to her beloved South Africa, to which she moved permanently in 1959. She tried to persuade Diana and Malcolm to join her, but they preferred to make their own lives elsewhere. Before she left Britain, she gave several outspoken press interviews about the lack of financial and official recognition of Baird's contributions to the British television industry. One headline was, 'I'm sick of the way Britain treated my husband, says TV widow.'[37] Rather to the embarrassment of Margaret's family, a newspaper established a fund on behalf of her and Baird's other dependants, to which some contributions were made by the television industry. The BBC, when asked for a donation, unearthed a ruling to the effect that the corporation did not contribute to funds for individuals other than members of staff, and suggested, 'Mrs Baird and her son were not, apparently, in any serious financial difficulty.'[38] While this last observation was strictly true, Margaret was not well off, and the fund did at least enable her to receive a minute share of the fortunes that were being made at that time from the manufacture of receivers and from commercial broadcasting, which finally began operating in 1955, following the Television Act 1954.

The public demand for television had received an enormous boost from the coronation in 1953. Television sets were still too expensive for outright purchase by the average consumer; the solution lay in hire-purchase or rentals. In return for a rental charge of a few shillings a week, a householder had the use of a set with no worries about repairs, and the growth of television viewing began to have an impact on cinema audiences. The leading British television rental company was Radio Rentals, whose founder, Percy Perring-Thoms, had started in a small way by renting out radio sets in the 1930s. One day in 1960, the point was raised at a company staff meeting about the confusion in the public's mind between the company's name and its main business of television rentals. Someone suggested, almost facetiously, 'We need a name which will be recognised, like Baird.'[39] Perring-Thoms seized on the idea, and a search was put in hand for the person or organisation who had the rights to the name.

The trail was somewhat labyrinthine. Late in 1949 or early in 1950, Baird Television, a division of Scophony–Baird, had been formed, with a board which included Seeman (managing director) and Percy. Scophony–Baird was acquired early in 1951 by EMI Engineering Development Ltd, and took on the name of Baird Television Ltd on 14 August 1952.[40] Two years later, Baird Television was bought by A W M Hartley and became Hartley–Baird Ltd. Radio Rentals acquired the Baird name under licence from Hartley, and as part of the agreement undertook responsibility for Margaret's pension, which was handsomely increased. In May 1961 Margaret was guest of honour at a reception and dinner at the Dorchester Hotel to meet the directors. Also among the guests was Taynton. The manufacturing division of Radio Rentals was renamed Baird Television Ltd, and a few days after the Dorchester dinner Margaret paid a much publicised visit to the newly opened Baird factory in Bradford. Baird television sets were available for sale as well as by rental, and soon the factory was producing sets for the new 625-line British standard, with the ability to receive the BBC's new channel, BBC 2. Radio Rentals set up an exhibition of early television sets, including a televisor, at its head office in Swindon, and changed its telegraphic address in London to 'Rentabaird'.

The company's most spectacular public recognition of Baird was in April 1964, with a one-night 'Baird Festival of Television' at the Albert Hall in Kensington. Margaret flew in for it from South Africa, and Malcolm from Edinburgh University, where he was at the time a research fellow. There was a lavish buffet supper and dancing to three leading jazz bands: Ted Heath, Johnny Dankworth, and Mister Acker Bilk. Margaret presented special medallions to thirty outstanding personalities from the early days of television: among these were announcers (Leslie Mitchell and Sylvia Peters), entertainers (Gracie Fields and Arthur Askey), and pioneers (William Taynton and Ben Clapp).

Perring-Thoms died suddenly in July 1964. Radio Rentals was taken over by Thorn Electrical Industries in 1968, but the company's shops continued to operate under the old name. The Baird factory in Bradford was reorganised, and for a few years was the largest producer of colour television tubes in Europe, until it was closed down in 1978 owing to Japanese competition. The Baird logotype, however, was still to be seen on television sets and on videotapes in Radio Rentals shops as recently as 1985.

Meanwhile Margaret, in South Africa, had returned to her music, giving some public performances and making a full-time career as a teacher of the piano. At the same time she began to look back calmly on the circumstances and drama of Baird's life and their life together. She wrote letters to former members of his staff, and collected notes and photographs for a personal biography. In 1966 she began approaching publishers in London, without success. The usual reply was that there was not enough public interest in Baird; one publisher told her that 'anyone who was interested could find out the story by looking up back numbers of newspapers'. Eventually her short book, *Television Baird*, written with assistance from Eldred Green, was published in South Africa by Haum of Pretoria. In the same way as Moseley had done with his biography of Baird, she drew uncritically on Baird's still unpublished memoir, and added personal insights. Sales were limited because of the small market, but when she returned to live in Scotland in 1986, she arranged to have the unsold copies shipped to her; these were distributed to Scottish booksellers and found a ready sale.

One hot morning early in 1974 Malcolm, who was escaping the Canadian winter by taking a sabbatical at the University of Queensland, received a letter from the University of Strathclyde. The writer, Dr Peter Waddell, explained that the university was planning an exhibition in the winter of 1975/6 to mark the fiftieth anniversary of Baird's first demonstration of television. Could Malcolm provide any relevant information? A detailed correspondence ensued, which is still going on. The exhibition duly took place, and was well attended. Jean Hart, whose husband had died in 1973, was among the visitors. So, according to a newspaper report some years later, was 'Alice'.[41] The exhibition marked the renewal of a long-standing connection between the university and the Baird family. Baird had graduated from the university's precursor, the Royal Technical College, in 1914, and Malcolm had taken courses there in chemistry and chemical engineering in 1955-7.

Waddell has played a key role in the continuing connection between the university and Baird. A member of the department of mechanical engineering, his research field is optical imaging, backed by an understanding of mechanics and optics, and other elements of early television. With the publication of her book, Margaret felt she had done all she could, and Diana and Malcolm had become somewhat blasé about their father's contribution to television history. Waddell's pervasive enthusiasm did much to reawaken the family's pride in Baird's accomplishments.

Waddell, with his technical background, was also able to supplement what had been written about Baird by Moseley and Margaret, and he was the first in the public arena to re-establish Baird as a serious achiever rather than an impractical eccentric. With the Glasgow journalist Tom McArthur, he wrote a controversial biography of Baird, the thrust of which was that although Baird was associated in people's minds primarily with mechanical television, he had contributed to other areas such as electronic colour and stereoscopic television, electronic large-screen television, radar, fibre optics, and secret signalling.[42]

Baird studies have also benefited from the unobtrusive efforts of Ray Herbert. Since retiring, at the age of seventy-three, from being consultant electrical engineer to the management services division of NatWest Bank, he has enhanced his reputation as a television historian, often called upon to authenticate a document or record a soundbite. He has contributed to specialist journals over fifty articles relating to Baird, and written, and himself published, an illustrated book about Baird's achievements, and the Baird company's involvement in airborne television.[43]

Academic research into Baird's life and work has been undertaken by Professor Russell Burns, formerly of Trent Polytechnic (now Nottingham Trent University),[44] and at University of Strathclyde by Douglas Brown and Adrian Hills. A Scottish engineer, Donald McLean, has in his spare time managed, by using modern computer enhancement techniques, to play back images from some of the original phonovision recordings made on 78rpm wax or aluminium discs, going back to 1929.[45] His restorative work has made a practical contribution to the debate about the picture quality of mechanical television. Still photographs of mechanical television pictures tend to emphasise any distortions or inadequacies, and support the lingering view that Baird's system was inadequate, or was not television at all. Moving pictures, however, come over much more realistically because the human eye's persistence of vision tends to overlook or compensate for flaws in the technique. It is still possible to view live mechanical television through the work of the Narrow Bandwidth Television Association, a group of enthusiastic amateurs who build their own mechanical television transmitters and exchange ideas by means of a quarterly newsletter. Members can record their television signals on audio cassettes, which provide quite enough bandwidth for the low-definition pictures. Most of the members of the association are based in the UK, but Peter Yanczer, of St Louis, USA, built a working model of Baird's mechanical colour television system, which he showed in public in 1998, seventy years after Baird's own demonstration of it.

The anniversary in 1976 was the stimulus for Flamm to reappear on the scene. Since his all too brief association with Baird in 1931 he had pursued a distinguished career in American broadcasting, in the course of which he had helped, during World War II, to found the 'Voice of America'. Subsequently he became a successful backer of stage plays, though he ruefully bemoaned the fact that he had turned down Agatha Christie's *The Mousetrap*, which became the longest running play ever.[46] Now Flamm contacted Malcolm in Canada, and wrote to Margaret to reintroduce himself after forty-five years.

As a first step in re-establishing the name of Baird in the USA, he arranged that every 26 January an announcement was made on his radio stations WMMM and WDJF in Connecticut, celebrating the anniversary of the first public demonstration of television.

Most Americans believed that television dated from April 1939, when it was publicly introduced at New York World's Fair by David Sarnoff, head of RCA. Between 1976 and 1997, Flamm gave many interviews to American newspapers and magazines to promote the fact that Baird's television achievements predated the pioneering efforts of RCA and Farnsworth. In 1984 Flamm even brought his crusade across the Atlantic, and gently rebuked the British television community for its lukewarm attitude to Baird's achievements.[47] He also provided generous financial support to the University of Strathclyde, in recognition of which he received an honorary degree of the university in 1994. Because of his age, he could not travel to Glasgow, but a television link to his home in Florida was specially set up so that he could participate in the ceremony.

Margaret made occasional summer visits from South Africa to the UK and Canada to see Diana and Malcolm and their families. Thorn Electrical Industries continued to pay her pension, with adjustments for inflation, after it had absorbed Radio Rentals. In 1980 Thorn merged with EMI, to form Thorn–EMI. Margaret's pension was now in effect being paid by the company which had defeated Baird Television in the BBC trials in 1936, and whose chairman had written to the *Sunday Times* in 1946 asserting that Baird's work had nothing to do with modern television. By 1980, however, EMI had been out of the television business for many years,[48] and the new company treated Margaret with the greatest respect and consideration. When in 1986 Margaret, now seventy-nine, decided to move to Scotland to be near Diana and her family in Hamilton, Thorn–EMI helped financially with the move and acquired for her a small but comfortable house within walking distance of Diana's. Her presence in Scotland meant that she was more able to give interviews and participate in ceremonies. She tirelessly unveiled plaques and opened new buildings, on one occasion insisting on making an appearance when she should have been in hospital after a fall earlier that morning.[49] When asked what she thought about modern television programmes, she would give a charming smile and say that television must be a good thing because it provided employment for so many people.

As the centenary of Baird's birth on 13 August 1988 approached, the family began to realise that Baird was no longer the forgotten man of television history. The BBC, which had often demonstrated a negative attitude to Baird, put on a fifty-minute docudrama under the title *I Chose Madness*, in which dramatised passages were interspersed with interviews with people who had known Baird, such as Flamm, Clapp, Loxdale, and members of the family.[50] Another gratifying event was the publication at last of Baird's memoir, under the title of *Sermons, Soap and Television*,[51] made possible by financial support from the BBC and the Royal Television Society. There was also a special service in Helensburgh, to mark the unveiling of memorial stained-glass windows in the West Parish Church. This church had a few years earlier absorbed the congregation of St Bride's Church, known also as the West Established Church, the first minister of which had been Baird's father. The service and subsequent lunch were attended by the Baird family and by some of the surviving figures from the early days of television, including Clapp and Herbert.

Margaret was now in her eighties. Her life had been intense, with high peaks and deep, deep valleys, and she was now slowing down. She had always smoked, and as she grew older her consumption increased. Malcolm arrived from Canada one Monday with a carton for her of two hundred duty-free cigarettes, and was alarmed when on the Thursday following she asked him to go out and buy her a fresh pack. She spent an increasing amount of time in front of the television, on which one of her favourite programmes was Terry Wogan's chat show. To her delight she was invited to London on 10 August 1988 to appear on the show, during which she was outspoken in her criticism of Reith, and cannily presented Wogan with an autographed copy of her biography of Baird. In May 1992, she was awarded an honorary degree of the University of Strathclyde, in a salute to the memory of her husband, whom the university regards as its most famous alumnus. The award also recognised Margaret's own efforts, for five decades, to keep the flag of Baird's achievements flying and to encourage ongoing research.[52]

That degree ceremony was her last public event. She became more frail and in 1994 she was moved from the house to a nursing home. She died on 14 July 1996, fifty years and one month after the death of her husband. Her ashes were placed in the family grave in Helensburgh.

Margaret's death ended a chapter in the story of Baird and of almost all of those most nearly associated with him. Captain A G D West was killed in a climbing accident in Switzerland in 1949. Of Baird's closest friends, Archie Church died in 1954, Jack Buchanan in 1957, and Sydney Moseley in 1961. Lord Reith, a disappointed man to the end, died in 1971, and Sir Noel Ashbridge in 1975. Gladstone Murray was relieved of his post of general manager of the Canadian Broadcasting Corporation in 1942 after a parliamentary commission had questioned his claims for expenses. He became a public relations consultant to business, and died in 1970 at the age of seventy-seven.[53] Isidore Ostrer died in 1975, and Donald Flamm in 1998, at the age of ninety-eight. Of Baird's close working colleagues and staff, Hutchinson died, of a heart attack, in 1944, at the age of fifty-three, William Taynton in 1973, E G O Anderson in 1989, and Ben Clapp in 1990.

Paul Reveley finally returned from the Far East in 1991, having for the previous forty-five years worked on electrical and mechanical engineering projects in Hong Kong and Malaysia. His most recent job was in 1997, when he was employed temporarily by the National Hospital for Neurology and Neuro-Surgery to rationalise and stocktake its building service technical stores.[54]

Nearing sixty years after his death, Baird is still a central figure, if not the central figure, in the history of television. He was also one of the last private inventors. Most of his research was paid for out of his own pocket. These factors rank higher than the controversy among television historians as to whether mechanical television is television at all.[55] A poll of those listed in *Who's Who in Scotland 1999*,[56] to which 1608 individuals responded, placed Baird second only to Sir Alexander Fleming, discoverer of penicillin, as the greatest Scot of the twentieth century.[57] His technology, as well as his name and reputation, live on at the University of Strathclyde, where, in collaboration with an American company,[58] a stereoscopic imaging system is being developed which is descended from the system demonstrated by him in 1941.[59]

Baird's life story could have been written by his idol, H G Wells. He was indeed, a Wellsian kind of character: single-minded, eccentric, and no plaster saint, caught up in triumphs, setbacks, and business intrigues. Perhaps because it would require a Wells fully to do his life justice, some of the attempts to re-create it have ranged from the fanciful to the absurd.

Baird was an optimist, with a supreme faith in television, and in himself. He was also obstinate, and had more than a touch of vanity. He was a maverick, he was an electrical wizard, whose closest friends and business associates often did not know in which direction to point him. In the whole of his career, perhaps only one person of influence with him, Church, understood what he was up to at any one time, and even Church could not prevent him from piloting his firm even closer to the brink. Despite the war and the loss of his income, Baird continued his research in the belief that his colour and stereoscopic television would be adopted after the war. He achieved technically brilliant results, but the effort wore him out and contributed to his premature death. He sold his life insurance policy in December 1942 to support his research, and then placed his trust in the lawyer Kew Shelley. These actions brought his family, after his death, close to poverty, from which they were effectively rescued by Annie Baird.[60]

Baird was soft-spoken, civilised, and well read. He disliked intensely any form of pomposity, class arrogance, or fussy officialdom. This put him at odds with some figures in the British establishment, and even with members of his own board. On the other hand, his quiet charisma commanded the respect of people ranging from humble technicians to public figures such as Sir Frederick Wilshaw and Sir Harry Brittain. Though Baird did not know it, the evidence of Reith's diaries and BBC internal files is that Reith had great personal respect for him. The loyalty to him repeatedly expressed by surviving members of his staff is intense.

He seems to have made many friends, even if he lost contact with some, such as John Hart and Bill Fox. The close friends of his Helensburgh youth returned his loyalty to them. Gavin Fullarton Robertson played a vital part during his Hastings period, and organised his life at Swiss Cottage. Jack Buchanan, effortless stage performer and a person of great integrity, was a lifelong friend who gave him much personal and financial backing. The role played by Archie Church, shrewd soldier and politician, with a technical brain, in giving Baird realistic support between 1930 and 1945 has been little noticed by earlier biographers. Baird's unlikely personal relationship (friendship is too superficial a term) with Sydney Moseley lasted from 1928 until the day of his death. The genuine affection in which Moseley held him is evident not only throughout Moseley's biography, but also in his published diaries.

Though there is no published evidence of any animosity between Baird and A G D West, and though they were frequently in contact with each other from 1933 onwards, there are suggestions that all was not sweetness and light between them. If this is so, then it is hardly surprising. West was called in by Ostrer effectively to sort out a mess for which Baird was largely responsible. Baird would have regarded West as having usurped his position within the company. In the eyes of the world, at the time and since, Baird was seen as having failed to secure the contract in 1936 for the BBC's high-definition system, but the failure was the company's and West's, not his. The advertising campaign of Marconi–EMI the following year could not have helped his relationship with West. Baird's fury at this campaign, in which the Marconi–EMI publicity department tried to write him out of television history at the expense of Marconi, who, he judged, 'never knew one end of a television apparatus from the other', shows up clearly in his memoir.[61]

In his youth, perhaps influenced by the revolutionary social thinking of H G Wells, Baird had embarked on a highly unconventional love affair. The social climate in the early years of the twentieth century, and indeed until quite recently, was very different from what it is today, and the affair had to be kept a deep secret. At heart, Baird was a Victorian who practised the

Presbyterian work ethic, believed in the importance of family values, and occasionally suffered guilt feelings. His courtship of and marriage to Margaret were also unconventional, but he did the conventional thing in marrying her rather than compromise her position even for a day. For a few years at Crescent Wood Road and in Bude he became, in his spare time from television, a family man. Margaret was a hugely talented and independent-minded woman who had largely to give up her musical career when she married. In her biography of Baird, there are some sardonic remarks about him, but neither Diana nor Malcolm, nor Reveley (who spent much time in the house between 1933 and 1938), remembers anything which could remotely be called a family row. At home Baird had a civil but vaguely preoccupied manner; he would spend much time on the telephone, or in meditation. He could be infuriating to colleagues and friends alike, and even to those he loved and who loved him, but he was a difficult man with whom to have a quarrel.

For many years reporters and interviewers have besieged members of Baird's family, asking short, simplistic questions in their search for a convenient headline or soundbite. Was Baird a victim of ruthless business manipulation or was he a manipulator himself? Was he a success? Was he a failure? Research for this book has suggested that it is after all impossible to fit him to any stereotypical image. He does, however, seem to have been at heart a thoroughly decent, straightforward man, of whom the veteran radio and television critic L Marsland Gander, in a review written shortly before his own death, said:

> John Logie Baird was an eccentric visionary with a passion for gadgetry who had also inherited some of the mystical character of his father. ... I interviewed [him] many times and found him a modest man of inflexible resolve, ready to try anything but constantly in financial trouble. Quiet, humorous, always approachable, he never made extravagant claims.[62]

APPENDIX

John Logie Baird
and the Supernatural

Baird was an ingenious experimenter with a basic knowledge of and respect for the laws of physics, and a strong sense of the practical. Yet throughout his life he also had an interest in supernatural and psychic phenomena which has been difficult to fit into the main narrative of this book. This side of his character may have originated from his childhood in the religious atmosphere of 'The Lodge'. He recalled that he 'thought that God was actually floating somewhere overhead, a stern man with a beard, something like Papa only of enormous dimensions, infinitely powerful and fearsome'.[1] The atmosphere of the Victorian Scottish manse also affected Baird's contemporary, John Reith, who came to believe that he had been divinely chosen for some great work. 'I used to think … particularly when there was a wind and a sound of music in the trees, that there was a message for me, but I couldn't quite make it out, couldn't quite make it out.'[2]

Baird's strongest literary influence, H G Wells, had a scientific training and was no friend to organised religion; his short stories often have at their centre dreams and the supernatural.[3] By the time he was in his teens, Baird had reacted against religion, and would take on in theological argument earnest young clergymen who visited 'The Lodge'.[4]

He could not, however, entirely shake off the Presbyterian notions of guilt and eternal punishment in the after-life. This shows clearly in a dark and chilling story that he wrote for the Technical College magazine. The main character, Dominic McSharkey, is an idle student who is late for lectures and spends his time 'at roller skating rinks, music halls and other dissipations'. One day he is killed in a skating accident, and finds himself taking notes in a vast lecture room. The lecturer is a fearsome apparition, the bench on which McSharkey is sitting is hard, and the clock in the room is marked in years and centuries. The lecture itself is 'duller than any he had ever heard but still he must write, and he is writing yet'.[5]

Shortly after Baird graduated from the college, World War I started. He was deeply affected by the deaths of so many people of his age, including some of his college friends. He would have been aware of the carnage from the experiences of his sister Annie. The senseless destruction of life led him, and many others at the time, to become interested in spiritualism and psychic phenomena. In his memoir, he cites Sir Oliver Lodge, the distinguished scientist to whom he demonstrated noctovision,[6] and the noted author Sir Arthur Conan Doyle as believers in spiritualism. Lodge was, however, very chary about entering into any public confrontation on the issue, and in 1927 refused Moseley's invitation to write an article for him on spiritualism.[7] Doyle was more open in his support, which led to errors of judgment such as in the affair of the Cottingley fairies,[8] and the 'masked medium', about which there was a court case in 1920 in which Moseley appeared as a witness.[9]

Moseley himself, as good journalists should, kept an open, but sceptical, mind.[10] His book on the subject, *An Amazing Seance and an Exposure* (1919), had a preface by Doyle. Lodge and Doyle were members of the Ghost Club Society, founded in 1851 and devoted to the serious and impartial study of 'subjects not fully understood or accepted by science, especially psychical phenomena'. So too, interestingly enough, was Kew Shelley.[11]

The three episodes in *Sermons, Soap and Television* which relate to the supernatural appear in the book out of chronological sequence. We have rearranged them in order. The Sea of Azov episode (pp. 70-1) falls during Baird's time with the Clyde Valley Electrical Company, in about 1916. The piece referring to noctovision and the 'professor of entomology' (pp. 66-7) suggests a time soon after soon after the demonstration to Lodge in December 1926. Thomas Edison died in October 1931, so the seance in which he communicates by Morse code (pp. 67-8) would have taken place after that.

The spiritualistic seance endeavours as its object to prove the survival of personality after death. I had an intriguing experience not connected with the survival of personality but connected with the problem of what this personality is.

A supernatural mechanic could make a very good imitation man. Memory would be supplied by a library of talking picture films. The creature could easily be made to react to light and to the spoken word, so that it could guide itself. Its movements could be activated by some kind of television device which would make it able to move without striking the furniture. It would be able to answer questions, the sound of the voice operating a device which would turn on a gramophone arrangement giving the proper answer. Real man might be considered as some sort of very perfect mechanism of this type, plus something else. This something else is usually designated as the personality or sometimes, by the old fashioned, as the soul.

I had a very startling experience of seeing a body with the soul absent. When I was an engineer I shared a room with another man; one night when I was just going to sleep he woke me by asking if I knew anything about the Sea of Azov. I said I fancied it was very shallow.

'Ah yes,' he said, 'but is it wet?' 'Of course it's wet.' 'Oh well,' said he, 'we must use armoured cable.' I realised he was dreaming and I found that as long as I answered him in accordance with his dream we could hold lengthy conversations. That night in the dream in which I co-operated we called in Stibbs and his gang of navvies and solemnly laid a cable across the Sea of Azov. Night after night, I took part in these extraordinary conversations. In the morning he remembered absolutely nothing of what had taken place. His sleep personality was utterly distinct from his waking personality. Sometimes in the middle of his dream state he would come awake with a sudden exclamation, 'What was that, did you speak?' He had no recollection whatever of what he had said a moment before. While he was in the sleep state it was possible to conduct him from one scene to another by easy stages by making suggestions to him. He had no will whatever of his own.

Unfortunately for the experiment he got mixed up with a young lady and this ultimately brought the whole thing to an abrupt end; but before it did so it provided one very interesting incident. They had a quarrel and he wrote a letter, in great trepidation and mental anguish, breaking off their engagement. That night in his sleep he began talking about this. 'I do not think I should have written that letter,' he said. I answered in the proper spirit and suggested he should write again. To my amazement, there and then in the middle of the night, in almost pitch darkness he proceeded to write a letter, and put it in an envelope, put this in a drawer, and returned to bed. Next morning he remembered nothing whatever of this. That evening the young lady arrived at our digs and the quarrel was made up. They married shortly and my investigations came to an end.

★

The newspapers gave [noctovision], which I called 'seeing in the dark', great publicity which had one rather amusing result. At that time I was staying in a small residential hotel and one morning when I came down to breakfast a young lady resident asked me, 'Is it true, Mr Baird, that you have an apparatus which can see through brick walls and in the dark?' I said 'Yes' and she said, 'That explains the queer tickling sensation I had last night.' That is, of course, a quite exaggerated and wrong view to have of the powers of television as it is today but some time in the future it may be possible to do what the young lady dreaded, although if this does happen it will be a very doubtful blessing for everyone concerned.

It was not long before another very peculiar application was suggested. One day a bent up elderly man appeared in the board room. He was a professor and a distinguished entomologist and he had a very strange story to tell. It appeared he had been called in to investigate the activities of a medium called 'Marjorie', this was the name the medium was known by, although more strictly speaking it was the name assumed by her controlling spirit. The earthly 'Marjorie' was a respectable married lady who in early life had lost her only son in tragic circumstances. This boy 'Jack' one morning in a fit of depression had gone into the bathroom and cut his throat, leaving the razor with bloodstained thumb marks on the floor; this razor had been locked away untouched. 'Marjorie' was heartbroken and in an effort to speak again to her son joined a spiritualistic circle. She was discovered to have astounding mediumistic powers.

In the darkened silenced room of the spiritualistic circle she sank into a trance; in this state her body exuded from its orifices a strange vapour called ectoplasm. This extraordinary substance floated about her like a cloud and was of such a fine and mysterious nature that it could be used by the spirits to build ectoplasmic bodies. It was now that the spirit of Jack her departed son appeared and made his presence felt. Not only did he speak and answer questions, but he used the ectoplasm to materialize his hand and shook hands with the audience, wrote messages and moved objects and did all that a hand floating in space could do. It was at this stage of the proceedings that the professor was called in as an independent scientific observer to test and report on these astounding phenomena.

He approached the whole matter with complete scepticism, and went to work with the careful thoroughness of a highly trained scientific observer. He was however badly handicapped as all manifestations had to take place in a completely dark room, ectoplasm being highly sensitive to light which instantly destroys it, with dreadful results to the medium, profuse bleeding and even death — such was the tale. Nevertheless the professor persevered, the mystic hand materialized and the professor shook hands with this ectoplasmic manifestation. The hand, he said, felt hard and cold like the skin of a serpent, but of its existence there was no doubt.

Then he was struck with a really brilliant idea, no two thumb prints were alike, why not get Jack's ectoplasmic hand to make a finger print and compare it with the prints on the carefully preserved razor. This extraordinary experiment was carried out, Jack was readily persuaded to press his ectoplasmic hand on a piece of carefully prepared wax. The prints so produced were compared with those on the razor and they were identical. The professor had heard that I had a device which enabled a person to see in the dark. He wanted to borrow this so that he could watch the whole process of materialization without destroying the ectoplasm.

I agreed at once to take part in this and he went off to arrange matters. I never saw him again. He was killed in a motor accident. A spiritualist told me that this was undoubtedly the action of the spirit forces and the result of his effort to pry into sacred secrets.

★

This was not, however, the end of the matter. Sometime afterwards a caller arrived at the company's office with an invention for me to examine. It was a little electric motor controlled by a tuning fork. He had it with him but had some difficulty in making it run properly. I suggested he should come back when the troubles were overcome. He rose to go and as a parting shot said: 'Would you care to have definite and irrefutable evidence of the survival of the personality after death?' I said, 'Yes, I would give everything I possessed for such evidence.' 'Well,' he said, 'I can give it to you if you do not mind making a journey.' I said, 'I would go to the ends of the earth for such a cause.' 'There is no need for that,' said he, 'you only have to go to West Wimbledon.'

This was arranged and I duly arrived at the address given, a small highly respectable villa; here I was welcomed by a party of elderly ladies and gentlemen and given tea. Then the medium arrived, a neurotic nervous looking woman of about 35. We trooped up to the seance room. Here there was arranged a circle of chairs and in the centre of this a small box like a sentry box, draped in black, provided with a chair. The medium was handcuffed to this chair. The audience sat round on other chairs provided, each person held a hand of each of his neighbours and put a foot on one of his neighbour's feet, so that any undetected movement of hand or foot was impossible. Lights were then extin-guished. The leader, an impressive elderly gent with side whiskers, then led the singing of a hymn, 'Tis a beauteous belief that spirits round us throng'. This was followed by a prayer. Then darkness and silence, broken only by a steady humming sound, which I learned afterwards came from an electrical tuning fork. The rhythmic sound was found to assist manifestations (also possibly to mask any noise made by the medium).

We waited and waited, the darkness and silence had a most eerie effect, then the old lady next to me squeezed my hand and whispered in an awestruck whisper, 'Look it's coming.' Sure enough in front of the booth, faint and almost invisible a wavering purple coloured cloud was forming. It grew denser and then the silence was broken by the irregular tapping of a morse key; the spirit was signalling by tapping in the morse code. The message was directed to me and it came from no less a person than Thomas Alva Edison. Edison had, it appeared, been experimenting with noctovision in his home in the astral plane, and he was convinced that it would in time prove of great use in assisting communication between the living and those who had passed over, but the time was not ripe, and to attempt to use it now would incur grave danger. He was however continuing his research and would communicate with me when the time came to use noctovision. Here his message stopped and Edison left and gave place to another control called Lily.

Lily was more domestic in her messages and gave detailed advice to one of the circle upon what to do for her rheumatism and how to handle various family troubles. I remembered that I had a lunch appointment and time was passing, so I whispered to the leader that I had an engagement and if he would excuse me I would slip out. A horrified whisper replied to me, 'If you move you may be struck dead.'

I murmured that under the circumstances I would wait, however, the spirits took the hint and a few minutes afterwards heavy groans came from the medium. She was coming out of the trance, and the lights were turned up. The leader hurried into the box with a large glass of something hot and steaming, and soon the medium was sitting up looking about her in a dazed way. I slipped out, bade a hurried and apologetic good-bye and arrived at the Dieu Donne restaurant nearly an hour late.

My guests, two hearties from Scotland, were still waiting, drinking beer over lunch. I told them where I had been and what I had seen. 'It seems all tosh to me,' said Mr B. 'I wonder how sensible people can waste time with all that nonsense,' said Mr M. 'Well,' I said, 'what about Sir Oliver Lodge, Conan Doyle and other men of similar standing, you can't brush them aside with vulgar noises.' 'Oh,' said Mr B, 'they are people who are perfectly sane except on one point. I once knew a man who was not only sane, but extremely clever, but he was under the delusion that one of his legs was made of glass.' 'It's not that,' said Mr M, 'old Lodge and these other boys wanted to get into the limelight, the press won't give any prominence to their ordinary activities, but they get a good show for spooks, the public will always read about spooks. Of course the whole thing is a lot of damned rot.'

I might have agreed with him but I have witnessed some very startling phenomena under circumstances which make trickery out of the question — and also unfortunately publication. I am convinced that discoveries of far-reaching importance remain waiting along these shadowy and discredited paths.

The Manuscripts of Sermons, Soap and Television: A Brief Account

In February 2002, Hastings Museum and Art Gallery acquired privately, from the family in whose possession they were, two typed manuscripts of the nine chapters of Baird's autobiographical memoir (which we shall call MSS A and B), and a holograph manuscript of 'Chapter Ten' by Margaret Baird. This has enabled comparisons to be made with the only other known typescript (MS M), which belonged to Margaret Baird and is the basis of the version published in 1988 as *Sermons, Soap and Television*. As a result, certain tentative conclusions can be drawn.

Manuscripts A and B are carbon copies of the same typescript. The lines are short, and the spacing is generous, to allow for changes to be written in. Manuscript A has marginal comments and suggestions, and sometimes also corrections, by several hands, and alterations by Baird and by his wife. The only comments in MS B are for chapter 3, in one of the hands that annotated MS A. No comments in this hand appear in chapter 3 of MS A. It would appear from this that at some point, before the other commentators and Baird worked on it, chapter 3 of MS B was inadvertently transposed with chapter 3 of MS A.

Manuscript M is now seen to consist of carbon copies of chapters from two separate typings. Chapters 2-4 and 6-9 are identical with the same chapters in MSS A and B. Chapters 1 and 5 are all that survives from an earlier, presumably the original, typing, which we shall call MS M(1).

The title of MSS A and B is 'Sermons, Socks and Television', but at the head of the first page of the first chapter of MS M(1) is the title 'Sermons, Soap and Television'.[1]

In her biography of her husband, Margaret Baird states that 'he worked on [his notes for an autobiography] up to the last months of his life'.[2] It is now possible to see what this work comprised.

Some of the marginal comments in MS A and chapter 3 of MS B are very critical indeed, and were obviously written for Baird himself to see by someone who knew him well. They largely relate to points of style or are adjurations to avoid clichés or repetitions of phrases. Baird has responded to some of these by making alterations in the manuscript. Surprisingly, perhaps, considering the nature of the narrative,[3] and the conditions under which MS M(1) was composed,[4] there are very few factual queries, and from this point of view the revised script is virtually the same as the published version.

Two crucial passages which appear in the published version have been deleted from MS A. The first concerns the circumstances of Moseley's resignation from the Baird company board in 1933.[5] The other, also only a few lines, is the description of Mephy's suicide.[6]

At some point, possibly shortly after it was typed from Baird's dictation, MS M(1) was retyped in the form of MSS A and B. There are many references in his wartime diaries both to his 'book' and to the journalist James Spence.[8]

Baird was also actively collecting photographs to illustrate the book, some of which were acquired by Hastings Museum at the same time and from the same source as the manuscripts (see plates 57 and 58). Some of the annotations in MS A must be in the hand of Spence; it was probably also he who arranged for the script to be read by the others whose comments are on it. Spence died on 13 April 1944, and Baird marked the tragedy by shading over the diary page on that day. A week later Baird wrote in his dairy, 'Ring [William] Spence ask for MSS?' William was probably James's brother, and the entry must refer to MSS A and B. Between then and his death, Baird and Margaret went through MS A, making corrections.

Kew Shelley, Baird's lawyer and executor, is known to have had MSS A and B in his possession when he died in 1964. Though his personal legal practice ceased to exist on his death, no attempt was made to return the manuscripts to the Baird family. It may be surmised that on Baird's death in 1946, Shelley had taken them into safe keeping, and Margaret made up a third, uncorrected version for herself (MS M) from carbon copies of two chapters of the original typing (M(1)) and seven from a further carbon copy of the second typing.

It is possible to date Margaret's composition of 'Chapter Ten' to a visit Shelley made to Helensburgh in July 1948. He might well have brought MS A with him, and suggested to Margaret that she go over it finally, and add a chapter of her own to finish the narrative. At this time Margaret wanted the book published. Maybe Shelley promised he would try and find a publisher; maybe he suggested the exercise purely as therapy. Though Margaret was already in dispute with him about Baird's estate, she had no choice but to give or send the manuscript back to Shelley with her 'Chapter Ten', because it was from him that it had come. 'Chapter Ten', which is in pencil, is not a draft; though it has passages crossed through, or rubbed out and written in again, it has been carefully worked over, and is easy to follow. Margaret did not herself type, and her script is clearly intended for typing. 'Chapter Ten' may now be seen, therefore, as an integral part of the revised autobiography represented by MS A.

Margaret did not tell her children at the time that she had written this chapter, probably because their father's death was still a recent memory. When matters between her and Shelley grew increasingly bitter, she may have felt it was pointless to ask for the return of the material. After Shelley's death, she assumed that it was lost, and worked on her biography of Baird from her own script (MS M) and without benefit of 'Chapter Ten'. Latterly, she was opposed to the publication of *Sermons, Soap and Television*, but was persuaded by Malcolm that it would be in the public interest that it should be published. By this time she had either forgotten that there had ever been a revised manuscript, or felt it would serve no purpose to say so.

Reference Notes

*When a source recurs within the notes for a chapter,
the original note number is repeated.*

★	Baird family papers and related items
Abramson	Albert Abramson, *The History of Television, 1880 to 1941*, McFarland 1987
Baird/Moseley	Letters from John Logie Baird to Sydney Moseley 1931-1945, BBC, S2/2 Moseley/Baird Correspondence
BBC	British Broadcasting Corporation, Written Archives Centre, Caversham Park
Bridgewater	T H Bridgewater, *Just a Few Lines: The Birth and Infant Years of BBC Television – a Personal Memoir*, British Vintage Wireless Society 1992
Burns (1986)	R W Burns, *British Television: The Formative Years*, Peter Peregrinus 1986
Burns (2000)	Russell Burns, *John Logie Baird, Television Pioneer*, Institution of Electrical Engineers 2000
Church	Papers of Major A G Church, in the Sindell Collection (not catalogued)
Exwood	Maurice Exwood, *John Logie Baird: 50 Years of Television*, Institution of Electronic and Radio Engineers 1976
Hastings	Baird/Day correspondence, Hastings Museum, HASMG 999.40
Herbert	Ray Herbert, *Seeing by Wireless: The Story of Baird Television*, PW Publishing, Broadstone, second revised edition 1997
Hills	Adrian Hills, 'An Early History of British Military Television, with special reference to John Logie Baird', thesis presented in fulfilment of the requirements for the degree of PhD, University of Strathclyde, 2001
Hobson	Papers relating to Baird Television Development Ltd 1928-1931, presented by Philip Hobson to Glasgow University Library, MS Gen 1606/1 and 1606/2
JBLD	Private engagement diaries of John Logie Baird 1940-1946★

M Baird	Margaret Baird, *Television Baird*, Haum (South Africa) 1973
McLean	Donald F McLean, *Restoring Baird's Image*, Institution of Electrical Engineers 2000
Moseley	Sydney Moseley, *John Baird: The Romance and Tragedy of the Pioneer of Television*, Odhams Press 1952
MS A	'Sermons, Socks and Television: Autobiography of John Logie Baird', annotated typescript, Hastings Museum, HASMG 002.1. See Postscript, p. 389.
Norman	Bruce Norman, *Here's Looking at You: The Story of British Television 1908-1939*, British Broadcasting Corporation and the Royal Television Society 1984
Percy	J D Percy, 'The Founding of British Television', Royal Television Society Memorial Paper, March 1950
PRO	Public Record Office, Kew
Radio 2	*Seeing by Wireless: The Life of John Logie Baird*, BBC Radio 2, 21 October 1997, programme presented by Joan Bakewell and produced by Kenris McLeod.
Reith	Personal diaries of Lord Reith, BBC
Reveley	Paul V Reveley, 'Some Memories of John Logie Baird', unpublished manuscript 1995
Robb	Diaries of Eustace Robb, courtesy of Early Technology
SMDiaries	Sydney Moseley, *The Private Diaries of Sydney Moseley*, Max Parrish 1960
SS&T	John Logie Baird, *Sermons, Soap and Television*, Royal Television Society 1988
Waddell	Tom McArthur and Peter Waddell, *Vision Warrior: The Hidden Achievement of John Logie Baird*, Orkney Press 1990, new edition of the authors' *The Secret Life of John Logie Baird* 1986

Chapter 1: Helensburgh Days 1888-1919

1 In her biography of Baird, however, she refers to him as John.

2 SS&T, pp. 5-6, 15-17

3 SS&T, pp. 17-18. Buchanan married his second wife, an American, in 1949. A few years later they visited Scotland, and hired a car so that he could show her Helensburgh. As they drove slowly through the sleepy streets, he suddenly called out, 'It's still there!' It was a tree-house, built like a ship's cabin, in one of the gardens (Susan Dillon, formerly Mrs Jack Buchanan, telephone conversation with Malcolm Baird, 10 September 2001).

4 Margaret Menzies Campbell, personal letter to Peter Waddell, 3 June 1975. She and her husband, a dental surgeon, were friends of Mephy.

5 SS&T, p. 18

6   David Daiches, *Glasgow* (1977), p. 152

7   SS&T, p. 21

8   The actual year is not given in SS&T, p. 21, because it does not appear in the particular copy of the text from which that book was typeset. MS A has, 'It was about this time, that is to say in the year 1903, that the idea of trying to produce television originally occurred to me.'

9   Abramson, p. 23

10   SS&T, pp. 22, 116

11   Dollar Academy Archives

12   The passage from his memoir which follows does not appear in the published version.

13   'Laß in den Tiefen der Sinnlichkeit / Uns glühende Leidenschaften stillen!' (Goethe, *Faust*, part 1, Studierzimmer ii, lines 1750-1). Baird's adaptation of the lines is from the translation by Albert G Latham for the Everyman's Library edition (1908), p. 80: 'Our glowing passions in a sensual sea / Now will we quench, nor in the shallows dabble!'

14   Abramson, pp. 13-15

15   Waddell, pp. 73-4

16   *The Royal Technical College Magazine*, Christmas 1913, p. 82

17   *The Technical College Magazine*, January 1910, p. 93

18   *The Royal Technical College Magazine*, February 1913, pp. 122-3

19   *The Royal Technical College Magazine*, January 1913, p. 21

20   SS&T, p. 3

21   'Visions: The Life and Legacy of John Logie Baird' (1999), a CD-ROM researched and written by Adrian Hills

22   Gavin S Hamilton, letter to Baird, 11 October 1913★

23   SS&T, p. 27

24   Dollar Academy magazine, June 1915

25   Dollar Academy magazine, March 1917. The information about his service with both regiments recurs in the records of the Dollar Academy Edinburgh Former Pupils' Club. The 10th Battalion served almost continuously in France between 1916 and 1918. Robertson would be unlikely to have supplied the school with misleading information while the war was going on. At the same time, neither the Argyll and Sutherland Highlanders Regimental Museum, Stirling Castle, nor the Scottish National War Museum, Edinburgh Castle, has any record of his serving as an officer at all. There are further mysteries about Mephy: his name does not appear on the electoral roll either in Hastings, where he is known to have been living from 1922 to 1924, or in Ryde, Isle of Wight, where he was from about 1935 to his death in 1940. Nor is there any mention of his paying rates on the property in Ryde that he owned or rented. It is almost as though he managed to avoid his existence being recorded.

26   SS&T, p. 28

27   SS&T, p. 23

28   30 November 1915 and 7 November 1917★

29   SS&T, p. 29

30   This description has been compiled from SS&T, pp. 29-30, and an account of the episode Baird gave verbally to Richard Head, who worked for the Baird company 1937-9, and for Baird personally on a part-time voluntary basis during World War II. Head comments, 'It is a pleasure to me to think that someone had the courage to try something like this, instead of just thinking about it' (Richard Head, 'The Power Station Affair', handwritten note, 8 January 2001, courtesy of Ray Herbert).

31   Describing the original launch of the product, MS A refers to a 'pamphlet describing their advantages and a number of carefully prepared home made testimonials'.

32   A Hartley, 'John Logie Baird: Written about One Year Ago', January 1959*

33   General Register Office for Scotland, stamped 12 September 1918, number 15348

34   See M Baird, p. 63.

35   The Scottish comic Tommy Lorne used to say, 'Me and Jack Buchanan are the only ones who can tour in England, because we can both talk English' (Jack House, *Music Hall Memories* (1986), p. 40).

36   William Smith Inglis (b 1885) was the son of William Smith Inglis, master grocer, of Rutherglen, whose father was Robert Inglis, farmer, the brother of John Inglis senior.

37   Information from Vintage Motorcycle Club and Glasgow City Archives. The authors are grateful to Ian Love and Bob Simpson for delving into this arcane area of research.

38   SS&T, p. 33

Chapter 2: Entrepreneur with Problems: Trinidad and London 1919-1923

1   Moseley, pp. 49-50

2   Waddell, pp. 91-2

3   Malcolm Baird, 'Life with an Inventive Father', in Antony Kamm and Anne Lean (eds), *A Scottish Childhood* (1985), p. 155

4   See Waddell, pp. 100-2.

5   SS&T, pp. 19-20

6   SS&T, p. 36

7   M Baird, p. 37

8   Diana Richardson, interview with AK, 25 August 2000

9   JLB notebook 1920-2*

10   W MacQueen Pope, *The Footlights Flickered* (1959), p. 69

11   W MacQueen Pope, *The Footlights Flickered* (1959), p. 79

12   SS&T, p. 38

13   SS&T, pp. 37-8

14   The sole evidence for Baird's stay in Buxton is SS&T, p. 38. It is difficult to

associate any specific condition for which the Buxton facilities were noted with any of the particular symptoms experienced by Baird, except possibly colitis or 'high arterial tension' (see *The Spas of Great Britain: The Official Handbook of the British Spa Federation*, 'For the use of the medical profession' (n.d.), pp. 34-7). Exhaustive research by Buxton Museum through lists of visitors to Buxton in the local press, and an examination by Derbyshire Record Office of the X-Ray Department report book of Buxton's Royal Devonshire Hospital, which at the end of the 1920s was treating four thousand patients a year, have failed to turn up his name. One must conclude either that twenty years later he was mistaken about where he took the cure, or, on his arrival at the station, he slipped through the press cordon unnoticed and stayed at one of the more exclusive establishments, such as the Buxton Clinic, 'Terms from 4 Guineas to 6 Guineas weekly' (*Buxton Aquae: The Spa of Blue Waters*, 'Official Guide' (n.d.) pp. 12-13).

15   M Baird, p. 37

16   SS&T, pp. 39-40

17   Documents relating to John L Baird and Company Ltd, PRO 72022, ref. BT 31/27521/185166

18   Waddell, p. 72

19   'Visions: The Life and Legacy of John Logie Baird' (1999), a CD-ROM researched and written by Adrian Hills

Chapter 3: The Beginning of Television: Hastings and Other Places 1923-1924

1   'Hastings Honours Baird', *Television*, December 1929, pp. 487-8

2   SS&T, p. 42

3   M Baird, p. 41

4   M Baird, p. 37

5   Burns (1986), p. 15

6   SS&T, p. 54

7   Abramson, p. 38

8   Abramson, pp. 42-3

9   Abramson, pp. 53, 60

10   Abramson, p. 50

11   Burns (1986), pp. 37-8

12   Abramson, p. 84; Burns (1986), pp. x, 47

13   SS&T, p. 42

14   Moseley, pp. 65-6. The claim in Burns (2000), pp. 46-7, that the negotiations between Baird and Odhams occurred in January 1924, is interesting, but raises as many questions as it attempts to resolve.

15   P P Eckersley, 'The Achievement and Failure of John Logie Baird', *Electronics & Power*, April 1962, pp. 197-8

16   Moseley, p. 67

17   SS&T, p. 44. There is a tradition in Odhams's family that though Odhams felt he could not take up the offer in his official capacity, he did give Baird a donation out of his own pocket (Marista Leishman, telephone conversation with AK, 18 January 2001). This is confirmed by Odhams's grandson. It is said that Odhams's words were, 'Young man, I do not see how your invention would fit in with publishing.' Another investment opportunity which Odhams turned down was cats' eyes, since he could not see the point of investing in bits of reflective glass which were destined to spend their lives being run over by motor cars. He did, however, purchase a huge television receiver in about 1936, 'about the size of those early HMV radiograms or a small chest deep freezer', for his house in Chalfont St Giles (Hew Naylor, personal letter to AK, 19 March 2001).

18   222,604, accepted 9 October 1924

19   230,576 and 236,978, both accepted 19 March 1925

20   'Seeing by Wireless', *Chambers's Journal*, November 1923, pp. 766-7

21   'Wireless Invention at Hastings', *Hastings & St Leonards Observer*, 19 January 1924

22   *Daily News*, 15 January 1924

23   Information from Gavin Fullarton Robertson, in Margaret Menzies Campbell, personal letter to Peter Waddell, 3 June 1975

24   For the subsequent history of the manuscript, see Postscript, p. 389.

25   Ray Herbert, personal letter to AK, 19 May 2000

26   V R Mills, 'Inventor of Television', letter to *Electronics & Power*, May 1976, p. 310, describes his own contribution. Later in the year he recorded an account of the roles played by other members of the local radio society.

27   V H Mills, Radio 2

28   Ray Herbert, 'Radio Amateurs and Early Television', *Radio Communication*, October 1996

29   Norman Loxdale, personal letter to Malcolm Baird, 10 March 1980. He became one of Baird's mechanics, making discs and brackets.

30   Norman Loxdale, interview with Thornton H Bridgewater, 8 April 1981. See Adrian R Hills, 'Eye of the World: John Logie Baird and Television, Part 1', *Kinema*, No. 5 1996, p. 5.

31   Cyril N Pamment, letter to BBC, 29 October 1957 (BBC file T12/505/1, 'This Is Your Life – Baird J L')

32   Ray Herbert, personal letter to AK, 19 May 2000

33   Waddell, pp. 104-5, 125-7. The account of this experiment is separately confirmed in Loxdale, personal letter to Malcolm Baird, 10 March 1980.

34   *Wireless World and Radio Review*, 7 May 1924, pp. 153-5

35   292,185, accepted 21 June 1928. Cited as a reference in Robert H Rines, US patent 2,696,522 (7 December 1954), which incorporates a radio location system whereby the range of an object can be deduced.

36   'A Coming Wonder / The Genius of a Helensburgh Man', *Helensburgh and Gareloch Times*, 7 November 1923

37   Waddell, pp. 120–1

38   Burns (1986), p. 20.

39   Sydney H Walker (Mrs Grinyer's son-in-law), letter to Century Hutch-
      inson, 11 April 1987, courtesy of Peter Waddell. Tunbridge Wells is about
      40 miles inland from Folkestone and 25 miles from Hastings.

40   *A Guide to Tunbridge Wells* (1923), pp. 42–3

41   Sir David Lionel Salomons, *Wireless* (1925), p. 21. Biographical details
      from *The Dictionary of National Biography: Missing Persons* (1993), edited by
      C S Nicholls, pp. 581–2, *Kent and Sussex Courier*, 4 July 1980 and 19 April
      1985, and *Country Life*, 8 August 1991, p. 59. The authors are grateful to
      Melanie Machin, Tunbridge Wells Reference Library, for pointing out
      this connection.

42   Helena Walker, personal letters to AK, 2 May and 14 December 2000

43   Information from Isabel Mackay, a cousin of John Hart

44   Jean Hart, personal letter to Peter Waddell, 24 May 1975

45   298,582, accepted 11 October 1928

46   John Hart (junior), personal letter to AK, 11 April 2000

47   Jean Hart, personal letter to Jack Sanderson, 14 January 1975

48   John Hart (junior), in a telephone conversation with AK, 3 November
      2000

49   John Walker, 'The Curious Case of John Logie Baird', *Journal of the Falkirk
      Local History Society*, May 1996, p. 59

50   Honor Trojanowska, quoted in personal letter from John Walker to Peter
      Waddell, 14 August 1989

51   Robert Mitchell, letter to John Walker, 19 February 1989

52   300,679, accepted 19 November 1928, with addition to it (328,315),
      accepted 28 April 1930

53   'Aeroplane with Eyes', *Daily Express*, 18 November 1924

54   Information from Portsmouth and District Registry, 12 June 2000

55   It is described in *Wireless World and Radio Review*, 7 May 1924, p. 154, and
      in patent 235,619, accepted 12 June 1925, for which Baird did not apply
      until 12 March 1924. Perhaps he could not afford to do so before.

56   SS&T, p. 45

57   *The Dictionary of National Biography: Missing Persons* (1993), edited by C S
      Nicholls, p. 397

58   *Wireless World and Radio Review*, 23 April 1924, pp. 114–15, 118

59   Abramson, pp. 79–81

60   William Le Queux, 'Television – A Fact', *Radio Times*, 25 April 1924

61   Abramson, pp. 64–5

62   William Le Queux, 'The New Spy Menace to Britain', *Ideas*, 3 May 1924

63   See p. 337.

64   Paul Reveley, telephone conversation with AK, 12 May 2000

65   PRO, Air 2/S24132

66   Waddell, p. 127

67   *Who's Who 1943*, p. 1819

68   230,576, accepted 19 March 1925

69   P A London News Agency, 9 April 1924

70   'The transmission was successful and a short paragraph was written about it. However, the Press Association sub-editors had *never* heard of "Television" and as talking films in the cinemas were just making their appearance they insisted it was cinema film which was being used and altered my paragraph to read that way' (Bill Fox, 10 October 1978, Royal Television Society Archive 5/30).

71   F H Robinson, 'Radio Television: An Invention which Solves the Problem Satisfactorily', *Broadcaster and Wireless Retailer*, April 1924, p. 47. That Baird was also at this time experimenting with transparencies is suggested in the letter he wrote to Wilfred Day on 16 June 1924: 'I have got the cell sufficiently sensitive to work by reflected light – that is actual objects not transparencies' (Hastings).

72   F H Robinson, 'The Radio Kinema', *Kinematograph Weekly*, 3 April 1924

73   Hastings

74   'Television. A Description of the Baird System by its Inventor', *Wireless World and Radio Review*, 21 January 1925, pp. 533-5

75   'Television: A Paper by Mr J L Baird', *Experimental Wireless and the Wireless Engineer*, December 1926, pp. 730-8

76   Ray Herbert, 'Baird's Lost Letters', *Practical Wireless*, January 2000

77   *Hastings & St Leonards Observer*, 9 August 1924, reproduced in Herbert, inside front cover

78   SS&T, pp. 45-6

79   See p. 49.

Chapter 4: Serendipity in Soho 1924–1925

1   Hastings

2   SS&T, p. 47

3   'Television. A Description of the Baird System by its Inventor', *Wireless World and Radio Review*, 21 January 1925, pp. 533-5

4   W C Fox, 'A Love of Scientific Adventure; and Where it Leads', *Television*, April 1928, p. 18

5   SS&T, pp. 47-8

6   *Nature*, 4 April 1925, pp. 505-6

7   M Baird, p. 51

8   P R Bird, 'Wireless Television. A Review of the Baird System', *Popular Wireless and Wireless Review*, 23 May 1925, pp. 622-3. The drawings are by G H Davis.

9   *The Times*, 18 April 1925

10   W MacQueen Pope, *The Footlights Flickered* (1959), p. 144

11   Michael Marshall, *Top Hat and Tails* (1978), p. 204

12   'Visions of the Future', *Daily Graphic*, 2 May 1925

13   'Seeing by Wireless. Novel Experiences at Luncheon Party', *Sheffield Daily Telegraph*, 2 May 1925

14   *Daily Chronicle*, 4 May 1925

15   *Daily Herald*, 2 May 1925

16   Burns (1986), p. 40

17   SS&T, p. 52

18   Personal letter from Jean Hart to Peter Waddell, 24 May 1975

19   SS&T, p. 53

20   SS&T, p. 55

21   Ray Herbert, Radio 2. Stookie in Scots means stucco or plaster.

22   'Television. A Paper by Mr J L Baird', *Experimental Wireless and the Wireless Engineer*, December 1926, p. 736

23   SS&T, p. 56

24   SS&T, p. 57; William Taynton, Radio 2, and in *This is Your Life*, 28 October 1957 (BBC T12/505/1 Baird J L). Taynton, who had a physical disability, was brought up in an orphanage (Margaret Baird, personal letter to Alan Montgomery, 4 November 1973 (Hastings Museum, HASMG 001.57)). Baird assured him that he could always have a job with his firm, if he wanted one. Taynton was working with the Baird company in 1929, and in 1936 is listed as being 'stationery, stores and reception clerk' at a salary of £156 a year (Baird company staff list, 17 November 1936 (Church)). Subsequently, between 1937 and 1939 he kept the records of production of television tubes from an office on the ground floor of the Rotunda, Crystal Palace (Ray Herbert, personal letter to AK, 13 September 2000). When Taynton contracted tuber-culosis in the early 1930s, Baird paid for him out of his own pocket to recuperate in a sanatorium (Joan Woodcock, personal letter to Margaret Baird, 8 February 1960).

25   This was later confirmed both by Baird (John L Baird, *Television – A General Survey*, Proceedings of the World Radio Convention, Sydney April 4 to 14, organised by the Institution of Radio Engineers, Australia (Hastings Museum, HASMG 002.1)) and by Margaret Baird (Margaret Baird, personal letter to Alan Montgomery, 4 November 1973 (Hastings Museum, HASMG 001.57)).

26   John Walker, 'Did a Falkirk Cafe Host the World's First Public TV Demo?', *Falkirk Advertiser*, 11 July 1990

27   Robert Shaw, interview with Jan Leman, February 1994, for the film *TV is King* (1994), directed by Jan Leman

28   Unless it be the report (*Falkirk Mail*, 16 January 1926) that Hart had placed an order for the 'Television'. Might this have been on the basis of a successful demonstration he had organised a few weeks earlier?

29   John Walker, personal letter to AK, 3 November 2000

30   Frank Imrie, personal letter to AK, 1 September 2000, and telephone conversation, 4 September 2000

31   'I Saw the Birth of British TV', *Evening Telegraph* (Dundee), 10 August 1959

32   A similar disc with screws can be seen on the apparatus on view at Callendar House, Falkirk.

33   See page 306.

34   Patent numbers 266,564 and 267,378

Chapter 5: Vision on 1926

1   Both SS&T and Moseley give the date wrongly as Friday, 27 January.

2   SS&T, p. 59

3   These included the *Daily Express*, 8 January, and the *Evening Standard*, 8 January.

4   SS&T, p. 60; W C Fox, 'A Love of Scientific Adventure: And Where it Leads', *Television*, April 1928, p. 20

5   Description of the apparatus compiled from the following sources: *Daily Chronicle*, 27 January 1926; E G Stewart, 'Television', unpublished report, April 1926; J L Baird, 'Television: A Paper', *Experimental Wireless and the Wireless Engineer*, December 1926, pp. 153-5; P Waddell, W V Smith and J Sanderson, 'John Logie Baird and the Falkirk Transmitter', *Experimental Wireless*, January 1976, pp. 43-6; Jim McCue, 'Sale of Logie Baird's Disc Reveals Television's Hidden Tale', *The Times*, 15 October 1999.

6   SS&T, p. 59. A journalist reported a demonstration at which there was a 'galaxy of lights', a 'great disc-studded wheel began to whirr', and his face appeared in another room on a 'screen some six inches square' (*Spectator*, 31 July 1926).

7   E G Stewart, 'Television', unpublished report, April 1926

8   W G W Mitchell, honorary secretary of the Television Society, 'Developments in Television', a paper read to the Royal Society of Arts, 25 February 1931, *Journal of the Royal Society of Arts*, 22 May 1931, p. 621

9   269,658, application 20 January 1926, accepted 20 April 1927

10   Captain A G D West, technical director of Baird Television, stated in 'A Practical Outline of Television', *Television and Short-Wave World*, August 1935, p. 466, that Baird was using the spotlight method of scanning 'as far back as 1923'. The authors are indebted to Peter Waddell and Adrian Hills for this reference.

11   Television Society, Report of First General Meeting, *Television*, June 1928, p. 12

12   John Walker, 'Did a Falkirk Cafe Host the World's First Public TV Demo?', *Falkirk Advertiser*, 11 July 1990

13   Abramson, pp. 83-4. The dates of the patent application and the demonstration could be significant in that the Patent Office advises that no

public demonstration of a new technical development should be given before a patent application for it has been lodged.

14   Abramson, pp. 99-101

15   Abramson, pp. 95-6

16   Albert Abramson, 'The Invention of Television', in Anthony Smith (ed.), *Television: an International History* (1995), p. 24

17   Paul Reveley, letter to T H Bridgewater, 28 September 1958, courtesy of Paul Reveley

18   Burns (1986), pp. 43-4

19   *Nature*, 3 July 1926, pp. 18-19

20   Abramson, pp. 84-5

21   PRO, Air Ministry file, memorandum dated 16 March 1926, courtesy of Peter Waddell. In 1934 Wimperis was instrumental in the establishment, under the chairmanship of Henry Tizard, of the committee for the scientific survey of air defence. It was under this committee's auspices that Robert Watson Watt's radar system was developed.

22   Reproduced in Waddell, p. 215

23   Burns (2000), p. 99

24   289,307

25   295,210, 9 August 1927

26   Burns (2000), p. 100. As Hills points out, however, an internal memorandum from Wimperis dated 6 December 1927 suggests that the Air Ministry continued its research, but with the lowest priority rating (PRO, AIR 2/2743).

27   298,582

28   Empire News, ENB 1(7), on Video V300R1, reference courtesy of Jan Leman

29   J L Baird, 'Television: A Paper', *Experimental Wireless and the Wireless Engineer*, December 1926, p. 737

30   Reproduced in Exwood, p. 8

31   Quoted in Burns (1986), p. 50

32   O G Hutchinson, interview in *Amateur Wireless*, 30 January 1926, p. 179

33   Sydney A Moseley, 'More Facilities', *Television*, January 1930, p. 535

34   Quoted in Burns (1986), p. 54

35   SS&T, pp. 71-2. In Exwood, p. 11, it is suggested that these tests took place in June or July 1927.

36   Jack Sanderson, Museums Manager, Falkirk, personal letters to AK, 20 December 1999 and 13 July 2000. The apparatus is registered in the original museum catalogue as having been donated by John Logie Baird in May 1926. It is now displayed in Callendar House, Falkirk. The remains of the original luggage label are still stuck to the upper surface of the base: 'Lon[don North Eastern Rail]way / EXC[ESS BAGGA]GE / TO / FAL[KIR]K'.

37   John Hart (junior), personal letter to AK, 9 March 2000. Hart sold the East High Street shop in the winter of 1936/37 to Samwell, Smith and

Co, which had an associated company, Scottish Radio Industries, in nearby Denny. He then, at the instigation of his wife, opened another shop at the west end of the High Street, appropriately enough opposite the Temperance Cafe. Jean ran the shop after he enlisted in the RAF in 1938.

38 Margaret Gibb Scott, letter to Jack Sanderson, 11 October 1975
39 Jean Hart, personal letter to Peter Waddell, 24 May 1975
40 *Falkirk Herald*, 18 September 1926
41 *Falkirk Mail*, 25 September 1926
42 J L Baird, 'Television: A Paper', *Experimental Wireless and the Wireless Engineer*, December 1926, p. 737
43 Jean Hart, personal letter to Jack Sanderson, 14 January 1975
44 M Baird, p. 49
45 J D Percy, interview with Bruce Norman 1980, courtesy of Ray Herbert. Bill Fox, who worked for the Baird company 1928-30, recalled in an interview with Ray Herbert (30 January 1986) that Baird was a most difficult man to keep pace with. 'One day he would see something and say it was fine. The next day, if you asked if you could have another look at it, he'd say he had broken it up; he'd had another idea now!'
46 J L Baird, 'Television: A Paper', *Experimental Wireless and the Wireless Engineer*, December 1926, p. 734; *Journal of Scientific Instruments*, April 1927, p. 141. See also figure 1.
47 Jack Sanderson, interview with AK, 19 January 2000
48 P Waddell, W V Smith, and J Sanderson, 'John Logie Baird and the Falkirk Transmitter', *Wireless World*, January 1976
49 John Trenouth, Senior Curator of Television, National Museum of Photography, Film and Television, telephone conversation with AK, 20 January 2000; see also McLean, p. 69. A clip of film survives showing an identical piece of apparatus working (in *Here's to the Memory*, Reel 2, 1929 British Pathé Newsreel).
50 James G Lyon, personal letter to AK, 22 October 2000
51 *This is Your Life*, BBC TV, 28 October 1957 (BBC T12/505/1 J L Baird)
52 SS&T, p. 65
53 *Nature*, 5 February 1927, pp. 198-9
54 SS&T, p. 63
55 The term 'invisible smoke' derives from an incident at a demonstration on 30 December 1927, reported by Baird at the First General Meeting of the Television Society, 1 May 1928 (see *Television*, June 1928, p. 13): 'I gave a demonstration of the noctovisor to the Royal Institution, and one of the members at the previous demonstration had seen the office boy smoking. He wanted to see a repetition of this with infra-red rays.' However hard the lad puffed, nothing but a tiny wisp could be seen. The cigarette smoke was transparent to infra-red rays. The reference to a demonstration 'to the Royal Institution' infuriated Campbell Swinton, who complained that the implication that it was official

would be used to fleece the public on the Stock Exchange. Baird, in the July 1928 issue of *Television*, explained that the demonstration at Motograph House was 'attended by some fifty members of the Royal Institution'.

56   Herbert, p. 11

57   'Navigation by Invisible Rays', *Television*, October 1928, p. 45

58   285,738

59   289,104

60   Reproduced in *Journal of Scientific Instruments*, April 1927, pp. 138-43. In that year of 1927 Baird was elected a fellow of the Physical Society, his first scientific honour. He was subsequently made a fellow of the Royal Society of Arts (1929), a member of the International Faculty of Sciences (1936), which awarded him its gold medal in 1936, and an honorary fellow of the Royal Society of Edinburgh (1937).

61   Herbert, p. 11

62   SS&T, p. 63

63   SMDiaries, p. 295

64   See McLean for a full account.

65   292,632

66   324,904, accepted 3 January 1930

67   Quoted in Moseley, p. 168

68   T H Bridgewater, interview with Ray Herbert, 23 November 1989

Chapter 6: Hands across the Sea 1927-1928

1   6 January 1927, reproduced in *Journal of Scientific Instruments*, April 1927, pp. 138-43

2   *Nature*, 15 January 1927, pp. 73-4

3   *Nature*, 29 January 1927, pp. 161-2

4   *Nature*, 29 January 1927, p. 162

5   SS&T, p. 76

6   SS&T, p. 128

7   Ian Anderson, quoted in Moseley, p. 87

8   SS&T, p. 73

9   Company prospectus (Hastings)

10   John Trenouth, Senior Curator of Television, National Museum of Photography, Film and Television, telephone conversation with AK, 20 January 2000; see also McLean, p. 69.

11   Hastings. Of Hutchinson's general hyperbole, there is in Exwood p. 22, the comment, 'On the whole I don't accept that Baird should be absolved of all blame for the method of promotion of his systems, but I do not believe that we should continue to allow this to diminish his status as an inventor.'

12   A Dauvillier, 'La télévision électrique', *Revue Générale de l'Electricité*, 7 January 1928, pp. 5-23

13   Abramson, p. 99

14   SS&T, p. 74

15   Abramson, p. 101

16   SS&T, p. 76

17   W C Fox, interview with Ray Herbert, 30 January 1986

18   Quoted in M Baird, p. 63

19   M Baird, pp. 63-4

20   M Baird, p. 63

21   Moseley, p. 164

22   SS&T, pp. 80-1

23   Allan Gaw, Robert A Cowan, Denis St J O'Reilly, Michael J Stewart, James Shepherd, *Clinical Biochemistry* (1995), p. 82; Robert A Cowan, personal letters to AK, 5 September and 5 October 2000

24   E Taylor Jones, 'Television', *Nature*, 18 June 1927, p. 896

25   SS&T, p. 75

26   Moseley, p. 164

27   SS&T, pp. 78-9

28   Moseley, pp. 164-5

29   Burns (1986), p. 76

30   Ben Clapp, Radio 2

31   Herbert, p. 7

32   SS&T, p. 89

33   'Seen, Across the Atlantic', supplement to *Television*, March 1928. Fox was technically off duty from his job as a sub-editor at the Press Association. According to an article he wrote thirty years later, his face was recognised by Hutchinson. The Reuter's correspondent, watching beside him, released this information through the Press Association, whose chief was much displeased with Fox for not having lodged with the association first a 'full and complete biography of [himself] with dates and other metic-ulous data' ('I Worked with Baird', *The Times House Journal*, January 1958, pp. 63-4, 66)

34   *New York Times*, 11 February 1928

35   *Sun Telegraph*, Pittsburgh, 9 February 1928

36   *New York Herald-Tribune*, 12 February 1928

37   *Virginian-Pilot*, 9 February 1928

38   'Radio Amateurs Here Catch London Picture', *New York Times*, 14 March 1928

39   3 March 1928, quoted in Burns (1986), p. 81

40   Abramson, pp. 108-9

41   Burns (1986), p. 116

42   David Sarnoff, in a filmed interview in 1953, stated that the development of the system based on Zworykin's cathode-ray tube, first tested in 1933, had cost RCA/EMI more than $120 million.

43   *Daily Telegraph*, 10 March 1928

44   SMDiaries, p. xiv

45   SMDiaries, p. 78

46   SMDiaries, p. 89

47   SMDiaries, p. 292. In his biography of Baird, p. 100, Moseley suggests that their first meeting took place earlier in the year, at the time of the *Popular Wireless* challenge. In the absence of any conclusive evidence either way, we have opted for the date in his published diaries.

48   Moseley, p. 102

49   SMDiaries, p. 292

50   SS&T, p. 82

51   Moseley, p. 103

52   SS&T, p. 83

53   M Baird, p. 79

54   Moseley, p. 161. Baird even referred to his friend as a 'dirty dog' in correspondence (see Baird/Moseley, 13 November 1941).

55   W G Mitchell, personal letter to Margaret Baird, 2 January 1960

56   SS&T, pp. 84-5

57   Press handout, quoted by W G Mitchell, personal letter to Margaret Baird, 2 January 1960

58   Television Society, Report of the first general meeting, *Television*, June 1928, p. 9

59   Television Society, Report of the first general meeting, *Television*, June 1928, pp. 13-15

60   *Morning Post*, 21 September 1928

61   In November 1931 Moseley arranged the sale to Alfred Bates of all the shares of Television Press Ltd, becoming managing director at a salary of seven guineas a week, plus twenty-five per cent of the profits. 'I have promised to retain the managing-editorship of the Television Magazine. More money for jam!' (SMDiaries, p. 314)

62   Dr J A Fleming FRS, 'The Inventor of the "Fleming Valve" visits the now World-famous Baird Laboratory', *Television*, July 1928, pp. 5-7

63   *Popular Wireless*, 4 August 1928

64   'Improvements in or relating to apparatus for transmitting views or images to a distance', application 21 December 1926, the *annus mirabilis* of the development of Baird's television techniques.

65   J D Percy, Radio 2

66   J D Percy, interview with Bruce Norman, *circa* 1980

67   Philip Hobson, 'The Story of Noctovision', *Television*, July/August 1988, p. 166

68   'A Diary of Events', introduction (Hobson)

69   Percy, p. 8

70   See p. 68. In the course of a discussion at the Royal Society of Arts following a lecture by J C Wilson on 'Trichromatic Reproduction in Television' in 1934, Baird, who was in the chair, stated that for his original experiments in colour television he used a disc with only fifteen holes (*Journal of the Royal Society of Arts*, 29 June 1934, p. 862).

71 *Morning Post*, 7 July 1928
72 *Nature*, 18 August 1928, p. 284
73 Percy, p. 8
74 Professor Cheshire, CBE ARCS FIP, 'Stereoscopic Television', *Television*, September 1928, pp. 9-11. A further article, 'The Stereoscopic Televisor' by Denison A Verne (which sounds to be another pen name of James Denton), appeared in the same issue, pp. 20-1.
75 Glasgow, 10 September 1928 (Royal Television Society 5/42). Lord Kelvin (1824-1907), who held the chair of natural philosophy at Glasgow University for fifty-three years, succeeded in 1866 in laying the first cable across the Atlantic.
76 McLean, pp. 52-4. Another innovation was the introduction of the phonic wheel synchroniser, developed in the Baird laboratories by G B Banks and incorporated into the 'tin box' televisor (1930), of which Plessey manufactured a thousand models for the company.
77 Hobson, 'A Diary of Events', September to 31 December 1928
78 The illustrated catalogue, of twelve pages including cover, was designed and printed by Hazell, Watson & Viney, 52 Long Acre (courtesy of Michael Bennett-Levy). See also page 140.
79 William J Brittain, 'What I Think *Now* of Baird Television', *Television*, November 1928, pp. 21, 27
80 W MacQueen Pope, *The Footlights Flickered* (1959), p. 43
81 'Baird Television as We Last Saw It', *Amateur Wireless*, 22 December 1928, p. 1082
82 *Television*, January 1929, p. 25
83 See, for example, 'BBC and Television', *Popular Wireless*, 14 July 1928.
84 20 July 1928
85 BBC T16/42/1
86 See p. 85.
87 SS&T, p. 24
88 J C W Reith, *Into the Wind* (1949), p. 11
89 Marista Leishman, personal letter to AK, 5 October 2000
90 SS&T, pp. 83-4
91 Moseley, p. 114
92 *The Reith Diaries*, ed. Charles Stuart (1975), p. 295
93 Reith, 8 August 1934. Ian Hay was the pen name of the Scottish-born novelist and dramatist John Hay Beith, who became in 1938 director of public relations at the War Office, with the rank of major-general. *David and Destiny* was published in 1934.
94 Waddell, pp. 162-3
95 Michael Holroyd, personal letter to AK, 11 January 2001
96 Marista and Murray Leishman, interview with AK, 26 July 2000
97 Quoted in Malcolm Muggeridge, *Muggeridge: Ancient and Modern* (1981), p. 116
98 The authors are indebted to Murray Leishman for this interpretation of

his father-in-law's attitude to television. The Scottish poet and critic Edwin Muir (1887-1959) records a similar religious background to that of Reith, in which Christianity was presented 'chiefly as the Sacred Word' (*Autobiography* (1954), pp. 246-7).

99   15 October 1928, reproduced in Exwood, p. 16

100   Burns (1986), p. 157

101   Marista and Murray Leishman, interview with AK, 26 July 2000

102   Quoted in Malcolm Muggeridge, *Muggeridge: Ancient and Modern* (1981), p. 123

103   *Hansard*, 22 May 1952

104   Marista Leishman, interview with AK, 26 July 2000

105   A S Angwin, 'Baird Television Demonstration', a memorandum 19 September 1928, GPO Minute 4004/33

106   SMDiaries, p. 335

107   SMDiaries, p. 294

108   BBC, T16/42/1. From a series of notes on the birth of television and the origins of the Television Society by Geoffrey Parr, honorary secretary of the society 1947-61, it would appear that Television Press was initially a subsidiary of Baird Television Development Ltd (Royal Television Society Archive 3/12). The authors are grateful to Clare Colvin, Archivist, Royal Television Society, for discovering this document.

109   Probably 'The Inventor of the "Fleming Valve" Visits the Now World-Famous Baird Laboratory', *Television*, July 1928, pp. 5-7

110   Quoted in Andrew Boyle, *Only the Wind will Listen: Reith of the BBC* (1972), pp. 252-3

111   He went to York by train on the afternoon of 9 October (Reith).

112   Quoted in Burns (1986), p. 113

113   *Evening Standard*, 18 October 1929

114   Reported in the *Manchester Guardian*, 1 November 1928

Chapter 7: Sound and Vision 1929-1930

1   A Hartley, 'John Logie Baird: Written about One Year Ago', January 1959;* Margaret Menzies Campbell, personal letter to Peter Waddell, 3 June 1975

2   SS&T, p. 101

3   M Baird, p. 91. His salary from Baird International was £3000 a year, plus £1500 a year from Baird Television Development.

4   Paul Reveley, personal letter to AK, 28 May 2000

5   Moseley, p. 167

6   J D Percy (Radio 2)

7   Moseley, p. 163

8   Quoted in M Baird, p. 71

9   'Sydney A Moseley writes from Berlin', *Television*, June 1929, p. 175-6, suggests that such reports should be treated '*cum grano salis*'.

10 Burns (1986), p. 244

11 The deputation comprised Dr Hans Bredow, Secretary of State for the Post Office, his chief engineer for state broadcasting, Dr Reisser, and Dr Banneitz, of the German post office ('Sydney A Moseley Writes from Berlin', *Television*, June 1929, p. 175).

12 *Manchester Guardian*, 9 January 1929, quoted in Burns (1986), p. 124

13 Quoted in Burns (1986), pp. 125-6

14 Moseley, typically, did not see it quite like that: 'Sir Herbert Samuel, who has been helping me to get broadcast facilities for Baird Television, writes to me that he has heard from the Postmaster General, *and things are going to happen*' (SMDiaries, p. 298).

15 Sydney Moseley, 'At Last', *Television*, March 1929, p. 21

16 Reith, 30 January 1929

17 BBC, T16/42/2

18 7 February 1929 (BBC, T16/42/2)

19 SS&T, p. 96

20 'Engineer', 'Television Proves Itself', *Television*, May 1929, p. 116

21 Moseley, p. 127

22 Burns (1986), pp. 137-8

23 SS&T, p. 98. From Myles Eckersley, *Prospero's Wireless: a biography of P P Eckersley* (1997), Eckersley emerges as a brilliant, rebellious spirit.

24 Quoted in Burns (1986), pp. 141-2

25 SMDiaries, pp. 293-4

26 Hobson, 'A Diary of Events', 1 January to June 1929

27 According to Baird's passport,* he arrived on 26 May 1929.

28 'Sydney A Moseley Writes from Berlin', *Television*, July 1929, p. 244. A group photograph (p. 245) includes Dr Bredow, President Kruckow, Moseley, Dr Banneitz, Hutchinson, and Jacomb, who had presumably taken over the working of the system from Baird.

29 Michael Buckland, 'Zeiss Ikon and Television: Fernseh AG', *Zeiss Historica*, Autumn 1995, pp. 17-19. Goldberg was kidnapped and forced to leave Germany in 1933. The company's principal contribution to television research in the 1930s was the development of the intermediate-film technique. In 1939 Bosch acquired the complete ownership of Fernseh, which carried on after World War II as Fernseh GmbH and then Fernsehanlagen GmbH. Since 1993 it has been a part of Broadcasting Television Systems GmbH, wholly owned by N V Philips.

30 From a note in Reith's diaries (30 January 1929), it would appear that it was Eckersley's public behaviour, rather than his subsequent divorce, that was the reason for his dismissal. It was 'alleged that divorce was inevitably followed by resignation or termination of appointment. Never such a rule. But neither Company nor Corporation could disregard happenings of this sort. They were judged, as in other public bodies, on

the circumstances of the divorce and of the individual's employment' (J C W Reith, *Into the Wind* (1949), p. 140).

31 Burns (1986), pp. 142-6. At this time 2LO did not start broadcasting until midday, and there was a break between 2pm and 3pm (Exwood, p. 21).

32 25 September 1929 (BBC, T16/42/2)

33 Waddell, pp. 164-5

34 Margaret Baird, notes for a broadcast for SABC, October 1958.* From 1929 the property housing the laboratory was known as Kingsbury Manor (Burns (2000), p. 172). It was also known as 'The Studio', Kingsbury, in which name it was granted by the GPO on 12 March 1930 an experimental licence to broadcast on wavelengths of 49.66 metres with a power of 500 watts, and 155.44 metres with a power of 250 watts (Letter from GPO to BBC, 7 May 1932 (BBC, T16/42/6)).

35 SS&T, pp. 86-7

36 'Sydney Moseley on the Future of Television', *Television*, October 1929, p. 407

37 Herbert, p. 10

38 Philip Hobson, 'The Story of Noctovision', *Television*, July/August 1988, pp. 166-7

39 'An "Eye" for Ships' by 'Our Special Correspondent', *Television*, September 1929, pp. 337-8

40 'Eyes for Ship in the Densest Fog', *Daily Chronicle*, 12 August 1929

41 According to Hobson's report, 21 January 1931, to his laboratory manager it was 100 watt, 12 volts, with revolving concave mirrors around it (Hobson MS Gen 606/1f.2).

42 *The Times*, 20 August 1929

43 *Television*, September 1929, p. 353

44 300,592, accepted 13 November 1928

45 'In the Oliver machine the letter is situated on the bottom of a U-shaped bar. The U is inverted and the two ends are pivoted in bearings, which makes an exceedingly strong type bar and gives excellent alignment' (*Everyman's Encyclopaedia* (1913), volume 12, p. 347).

46 It was first brought to notice in Waddell, p. 219. In doubting Heath's veracity one critic stated that the authors of the book were fortunate to have a dead witness who could not be cross-examined (Waddell, p. 304).

47 Defence Records 2b, letter to AK, 2 October 2000

48 Deposition regarding the estate of the late James Guy Heath, 10 March 1978 (National Archives of Scotland). The address given for him, which also appears on his death certificate, is that at the head of Heath's letter of 1 June 1976.

49 T A Stankus, Archivist, Royal Signals Museum, personal communication with AK, 4 January 2001. Short-term, at that time, meant a period of six or nine years.

50 Defence Records 2b, letter to AK, 22 August 2000

51 T A Stankus, personal letter to AK, 3 October 2000

52   Trevor Royle, personal letter to AK, 20 September 2000. Sir John Keegan, Defence Editor, *Daily Telegraph*, has made a similar point: 'I can only think that Baird was commissioned in special circumstances' (personal letter to AK, June 2000).

53   Margaret Scott, Annie Baird's housekeeper in Helensburgh, recalled seeing an army uniform in a wardrobe in the house (Diana Richardson, personal letter to AK, 6 January 2001). A BBC internal memorandum of 7 April 1933 to Commander V H Goldsmith, director of business relations, information and publicity, refers to lunch with Moseley and 'Captain Baird' (BBC, T16/42/5). This may suggest that in the meantime Baird had received a supplementary reserve promotion.

54   PRO, AIR 2/S24132, courtesy of Peter Waddell. This system is also described in a report by F S Barton, a civilian research officer with RAE, 'Television', 18 November 1929, also with the file number AIR 2/S24132 (cited in Burns (2000), p. 109). The Baird connection may be said to be confirmed by a letter (25 October 1929), 'For attention of Mr Barton', Royal Aircraft Establishment, from the Vidal Engineering Co., Croydon, discovered by Adrian Hills in PRO file AVIA 13/294, to which it appears to have strayed. V M Allen, Chief Electrical Engineer, regrets that the Baird Television Development Company will not let Vidal supply RAE with units for 'Baird Television Sets', but will be contacting RAE about 'supplying them themselves'.

55   *Who Was Who 1961-1970*, p. 406

56   299,076, 'Improvements in or relating to Facsimile Telegraphy', application 20 June 1927, acceptance 22 October 1928. A drawing, photograph, or document could also be transmitted, by being cut up into strips joined end to end to form a continuous band. Related files (prefaced AVIA) in PRO are Area System Using Television (1929-32), 23/553, Area System of Message Transmission (1929), 23/458, Facsimile Telegraphy (1929), 23/447, Secret Telegraphy (1928), 23/404. The authors are grateful to Peter Waddell for this information.

57   Report no. 566, December 1932 (PRO, AVIA file 23/553), courtesy of Peter Waddell. There is a plan of the transmitter. A single light source is beamed by a reflector through a chopping disc (light chopper) and then the scanning disc, behind which is the moving message on a piece of film, and beyond that the 'photo cell'. A similar arrangement of lens (to concentrate the light source), light chopper, and scanning disc (in that order) may be observed on the 'Tunbridge Wells transmitter' (see plate 12), which, if the childhood testimony of Helena Walker is correct, was also used to transmit an image from transparent film.

58   Harold Bradly, 'Studio Topics', *Television*, November 1930, p. 378

59   Patents 324,029 (application 10 October 1928) and 324,904 (application 2 November 1928)

60   Abramson, pp. 140, 145; Herbert, p. 10

61   Burns (2000), pp. 206-7 and 245-7

62   Herbert, p. 10

63   Reith

64   Burns (2000), pp. 177-9

65   Moseley, p. 119

66   SMDiaries, pp. 304-5. Commentators on the standards of modern tele-
      vision may care to note that this may well represent the first occasion on
      which the dumbing down of a programme has been resisted.

67   Quoted in Norman, p. 61

68   *The Times*, 1 April 1930

69   Moseley, p. 133

70   SS&T, p. 101

71   Margaret Baird, script for BBC broadcast, *Woman's Hour*, 12 May 1959*

72   19 November 1930, information sheet

73   J D Percy, interview with Bruce Norman, 1980, courtesy of Ray Herbert

74   Holograph reproduced in SS&T, p. 94

75   Hobson, 'Report', 19 June 1930

76   Ian Anderson, formerly of E N Vowler and Co, quoted in Moseley, p. 88

77   SS&T, p. 91

78   5 July 1929 (Royal Television Society Archive, 5/38). If this refers to the
      company's catalogue of television receivers (see page 105), or a further
      edition of it, the bonus was well deserved.

79   6 June 1930 (Royal Television Society Archive, 5/38)

80   23 and 25 June 1930 (Royal Television Society Archive, 5/38)

81   W C Fox, interview with Ray Herbert, 30 January 1986. Fox was then
      ninety-seven. He died on 21 October 1987.

82   Moseley, p. 135

83   Andrew Boyle, *Only the Wind Will Listen: Reith and the BBC* (1972), p. 231

84   *The Dictionary of National Biography 1981-1985*, pp. 161-2

85   Lance Sieveking, *This Is Your Life*, BBC TV, 28 October 1957 (BBC,
      T12/505/1 J L Baird)

86   14 July 1930 (Hobson)

87   *The Times*, 15 July 1930. The article was anonymous, reflecting the policy
      of *The Times* at that time. Moseley, in an internal memorandum on
      publicity (23 July 1930), refers to its author as 'Mr Morgan, [whom] I was
      able to introduce to Mr Baird' (Church). Charles Morgan (1894-1958),
      dramatic critic of *The Times* 1926-39, was a distinguished novelist,
      dramatist, and literary critic.

88   Control board minutes, 22 July 1930 (BBC, T16/42/3)

89   Burns (1986), pp. 154-5

90   Control board minutes, 9 September 1930 (BBC, T16/42/3)

91   Burns (1986), p. 156

92   Quoted in *The Dictionary of National Biography 1971-1980* (1986), p. 774

93   J C W Reith, *Into the Wind* (1949), pp. 188-9

94   Quoted in M Baird, pp. 95-6

95   During the week beginning Monday, 8 December 1931, each morning

transmission included a competition. Five or six objects would be put before the transmitter for viewers to recognise. The winner, who correctly identified all twenty-five objects, received the programmes in Antwerp, Belgium (*Television*, January 1931, p. 442). In February 1932 the normal BBC transmission through Brookmans Park was picked up on a standard televisor in a train travelling at 70mph between Sandy and Huntingdon, 60 miles from London (H J B C, 'Television on an Express Train: A Novel Experiment', *Television*, March 1932, p. 26).

96   SS&T, p. 100

97   Moseley, p. 142

98   Hobson. 'At 20 minutes past the hour Mr Barford will start up and get a simple picture synchronised. During the revolving of the stage, Mr Rees will see that the cable runs free and is not caught up anywhere. As soon as the stage is revolved, Mr Hobson and Mr Rees will run on the Speaker and plug in, and start up the motor generator' (Memorandum to Staff, from W W Jacomb, courtesy of Ray Herbert).

99   *The Times*, 29 July 1930

100   *Daily Express*, 29 July 1930

101   Moseley, p. 148

102   Herbert, p. 16

103   Abramson, pp. 140-1

104   A puffy face is another symptom of hypothyroidism. See page 91.

105   Interview with Jan Leman, March 1994, for the film *TV is King* (1994), directed by Jan Leman

106   SMDiaries, p. 306

107   SMDiaries, p. 307

108   SMDiaries, pp. 307-8

109   See pages 85/6.

110   Engagement diary, 1931.* '[Gregory] was getting younger in outlook with the years and gaily essayed in 1929 a trip to South Africa for the British Association. There he met (and married two years later) Dorothy Mary Page, daughter of Dr Page the historian. He bought the Manor House at Middleton-on-Sea, near Bognor, where he entertained gaily. The Manor House ménage proved both a comfort and a centre of renewal' (W H G Armytage, *Sir Richard Gregory: His Life and Work*, 1957, p. 112).

111   BBC, T16/42/3

Chapter 8: Meeting Difficulties, January to October 1931

1   BBC, T12/505/1, 'This Is Your Life, Baird J L'

2   Burns (2000), pp. 246-7. It has not been possible to establish precisely when Hutchinson left the company. A memorandum about publicity by

Moseley dated 23 July 1930 is addressed to the 'General Manager' for 'submission to the Board, copy to Mr Baird' (Church). Burns (2000), p. 246, has Hutchinson holding talks with representatives of the Gramophone Company (HMV) on 17 November 1930. The letter heading on which Lord Ampthill wrote to Lord Gainford on that same day does not list Hutchinson among the directors (BBC, T16/42/3).

3   SS&T, p.104. As so often in Baird's memoir, events tend to be tele-scoped or their sequence rearranged. Napier, describing himself as general manager, wrote a report for the board on his visit to Fernseh AG (25-31 August 1931), and a further one, dated 2 November 1931, on the possibilities on the French market (Church). He was still employed by the Baird company on 3 December, though in a state of 'temporary absence', to judge from a letter to Church from the assistant general manager (Church). Moseley's name, inserted with a rubber stamp, appears as a director on the firm's notepaper at the head of a letter dated 9 September 1931 (BBC, T16/42/3). By this time, both Manville and Winch had ceased to be directors of the company. See also chapter 15, reference 30.

4   Abramson, pp. 16, 125

5   Quoted in Norman, p. 66.

6   *Today's Cinema*, 2 January 1931

7   Church, who was born in east London in 1886, served in action in World War I and won his DSO in 1919 as a lieutenant (acting major) in northern Russia, fighting for the allied forces against the Bolsheviks. His unit of the Royal Garrison Artillery was attached to 6th Brigade, Royal Field Artillery. His citation reads: 'For conspicuous gallantry and zeal during the operations from Medveja-gora to Unitsa, 8 June to 26 July 1919. When the Russian infantry were driven back near Perguba he pushed his guns up to the front line and restored the situation by his accurate shooting. At Fedotova, on the 22nd June, under heavy shelling, he kept his guns in action, silencing the enemy and causing them to move their guns' (*London Gazette*, 21 January 1920).

8   W H G Armytage, *Sir Richard Gregory: His Life and Work* (1957), pp. 93, 94-5

9   SS&T, p. 120

10   On joining the company as a director, Church relinquished his post with the Association of Scientific Workers (Obituary, *The Times*, 24 August 1954).

11   BBC, T16/42/3

12   *The Dictionary of National Biography 1971-1980* (1986), p. 715.

13   Marista Leishman, 'Always Impossible', *Scottish Review*, Autumn 2000, pp. 55-6

14   Reith, 2 January 1931

15   Murray to Carpendale, 'Baird Television. The Portable Transmitter at No. 10', internal memorandum, 4 September 1931 (BBC, T16/42/3)

16   Burns (1986), pp. 176-80. On 25 March 1931 Baird had a meeting with 'Mr K. E. Shelley (Gramophone Co.)'. Shelley, who will reappear in this narrative, was a barrister of the Middle Temple who specialised in patent law.

17   Hobson

18   Abramson, p. 162

19   Ronald W Clark, *Sir Edward Appleton* (1971), pp. 68-9. The first recorded instance of this particular phenomenon seems to have been at Leamington Spa, which Hobson visited on 1 April 1930 to adjust a recently installed Plessey receiver. He wrote in his report, 'The reception of the midnight transmission was spoilt by a curious effect. A "ghost" image was present, situated about half way between the true picture. This corresponds to a time lag of about 1/720 of a second. It occurred to me that this was probably due to the reception of the signals reflected from the Heaviside layer. From this time lag it is possible to calculate what the height of the layer would be, and comes to about 150 miles. This is, I think, in agreement with calculation by different methods' (Hobson). He calculated the distance by dividing the 'time lag' by 0.0027 seconds, which is the time taken for a single line to be traced out on a screen of thirty lines at 12.5 images a second.

20   Board meeting minutes, 15 February 1932. Appleton was also employed temporarily on company business in December 1931 and January 1932 (Church).

21   SS&T, p. 131

22   Archibald Church, 'Recent Developments in Television', paper read to the British Association, Section A (Mathematical and Physical Sciences), Leicester, 13 September 1933, reprinted in *Nature*, 30 September 1933, pp. 502-5

23   Hobson. The Kerr cell (with a rectifier designed by Jacomb) was a device which Baird developed for his purposes to modulate the light for his three-zone large-screen experiments with a mirror drum as the receiving scanner. It contained a liquid (nitrobenzene), which instantaneously changed its optical characteristics when subjected to a voltage. Thus the cell could act as an interrupter of light without the need for mechanical moving parts.

24   Ray Herbert, 'The Viseotelephone', *British Vintage Wireless Society Bulletin*, volume 22, no. 1, 1997. Includes the quotation from *The Times*.

25   Moseley, p. 169

26   *The Dictionary of National Biography: Missing Persons* (1993), p. 447

27   *The Dictionary of National Biography 1961-1970*, p. 938. Abramson, p. 189, suggests that Shoenberg did not become director of research until 22 August 1932.

28   Burns (1986), pp. 187-8

29   Percy, p. 5

30   *Daily Mail*, 9 May 1931

31   J D Percy, interview with Bruce Norman, 1980; quoted in Norman, pp. 68-9.

32   He had taken up this appointment in December 1930 (SMDiaries, p. 309).

33   *Daily Herald*, 14 May 1931; reprinted in *Television*, June 1931, pp. 147-8.

34   Reith, 18 April 1932 (see chapter 9). On 9 June 1932 he wrote, 'Lunched with WJB[Odhams] and spoke very angrily to him about the miserable Moseley in the "Daily Herald", who has "another BBC surrender" with regard to sponsored programmes. I hope I was not too hard on the old man, but I certainly made him move in the matter, because Elias rang up later and asked if he could come and see me on Monday.' Odhams had been since September 1929 proprietor of the *Daily Herald*. Julius Salter Elias (later Viscount Southwood) was at this time managing director of the Odhams group.

35   Reith, 7 December 1935

36   Moseley, pp. 150-1

37   See, for instance, in 'Sydney A Moseley on Televising the Derby', *Television*, July 1931, pp. 172-3.

38   Abramson, 172

39   Curriculum vitae of A D G West MA BSc, January 1932; courtesy of Richard West

40   Reith, 10 October 1939

41   M Baird, pp. 100-1

42   Malcolm Baird, *The Albus, the Reids and the South African Connection* (1998), unpublished monograph

43   M Baird, pp. 97-8

44   M Baird, p. 99

45   Baird's 1931 engagement diary has three pages of addresses at the end, the first page in Margaret Leslie's handwriting, the others in that of Caffrey, who took over responsibility for the book in May. 'G F Robertson Esq, c/o Richards, 4 Allenbank Way, Hanwell' appears at the top of the third page of addresses, above Holloway the dentist, Appleton, and Church.

46   M Baird, p. 128. Baird's reference in his memoir to the 'usual type of Jewish solicitor, a little withered up man with beady eyes smoking a thin black cigar' (SS&T, p. 124), is not in the general literary and social context of the times an unusually anti-Semitic observation. It is, however, no less venial for that.

47   Moseley, pp. 170-202

48   To judge from a note in SMDiaries (p. 313), Moseley returned briefly to Britain in September: 'SEPT. 21: Still fighting determinedly – and not unsuccessfully – for Baird Television. Sir Herbert Samuel, as Home Secretary [in the national government which Samuel, as acting leader of the Liberal party, had proposed to George V as a means of resolving the country's economic problems], again writes to me hopefully – although he doubts whether it would be practicable "to engage the Prime Minister's

attention, unless you have in mind some definite proposal on which we can obtain Mr [Ramsay] MacDonald's approval if necessary". ... Off to New York again. It is possible to get millionaire dollar help for Baird Television. This is vital to our future.' According to the company secretary's report to the board, 18 December 1931 (Church), Moseley was in New York from 19 August to 11 September, and then not again until 23 November. In the light also of the situation in London at this particular time, it is probable that even if Moseley considered returning to New York in September, he decided not to do so.

49   SMDiaries, p. 139
50   Moseley, pp. 185–6
51   'Here to Push Television', *New York Times*, 20 August 1931
52   W H Knight, report to the board of the Baird company, 14 March 1932 (Church)
53   Moseley, p. 201
54   Newsflash, 27 February 1932 (BBC, T16/42/4)
55   SS&T, p. 128. The sum was probably included in the payment into his deposit account on 29 December 1931 of £3500, by far the largest single amount deposited since the account was opened on 19 October 1928.*
56   SMDiaries, pp. 328–30
57   Baird/Moseley
58   Meeting of Ashbridge and Murray, 24 August 1931 (BBC, T16/42/3)
59   Reith chose similarly not to be involved, to the detriment of the reputation of both the BBC and himself, in the case of the 'talking mongoose' libel suit in 1936, when a prominent figure in London politics made disparaging remarks, overheard by Gladstone Murray, about the editor of the BBC's journal, the *Listener* (Andrew Boyle, *Only the Wind will Listen: Reith of the BBC* (1972), p. 278–9).
60   Ashbridge, internal memorandum, 'Report on Television Demonstration at Electrical & Musical Industries', 6 December 1932, and Carpendale's handwritten comment (BBC, T16/65). See also p. 231.
61   Moseley, p. 112
62   Obituary, *The Times*, 16 May 1959. There are also references to Dalton in JBLD, for instance 27 January, 15 May, 3 June, 7 June 1943, at which time Dalton was regional fuel and power controller for the London and South East England regions.
63   C Day Lewis, *The Buried Day* (1960), p. 190
64   Humphrey Carpenter, *W H Auden: A Biography* (1981), p. 131. Auden befriended the younger Snodgrass son, Arnold ('Nob'), and wrote an epithalamium for the wedding of the Snodgrass daughter, Iris, to Alan Sinkinson, the Larchfield mathematics master.
65   Sydney A Moseley, 'Wireless Notes', *Daily Herald*, 31 September 1931
66   Baird had given notice of such a policy for an independent station three years before (Burns (1986), p. 123).

67 'Television', Ashbridge to Reith (copy to Carpendale), private and confidential memorandum, 14 October 1931 (BBC, T16/42/3)

68 In 'Wireless Notes', *Daily Herald*, 21 October 1931, Moseley wrote of the BBC, 'It is my determination to discover who really was at the back of the prolonged and senseless obstruction that has held up British television for years. I shall expose this some day.' He never did.

Chapter 9: New York, and Marriage 1931-1932

1   Russell W Burns, *Television: An International History of the Formative Years* (1998), p. 284

2   Russell W Burns, *Television: An International History of the Formative Years* (1998), pp. 365-9

3   Moseley, p. 204

4   SS&T, p. 122

5   See, for example, Burns (2000), p. 250.

6   Knickerbocker Broadcasting Co, application to Federal Radio Commission for radio station construction permit, 3 June 1931

7   Donald Flamm, interview with Jan Leman, 1 August 1996

8   Waldemar Kaempffert, 'How Baird Sees through Space by Radio. Scotch inventor holds the secret of television in his sensitive photo-electric cell – he transmits images nine miles and adds "looking in" to "listening in" – predicts development of perfect device', *New York Times*, 6 March 1927

9   *New York Times*, 28 August 1931

10 Church

11 W R Roberts, secretary, Baird Television Ltd, notes for the board, 18 December 1931 (Church)

12 SS&T, p. 122

13 SS&T, p. 123. In Moseley, p. 205, there is a footnote to the effect that the publicity agent later had the temerity to send the Baird company a bill for his services!

14 'Baird Here to Make $25 Television Sets', *New York Times*, 14 October 1931

15 'Baird Discusses His Magic', *New York Times*, 25 October 1931

16 SS&T, p. 123

17 W H Knight, report on American negotiations, New York, 13 March 1932 (Church)

18 W H Knight, letter to the directors of Baird Television Ltd, 10 December 1931 (Church)

19 Milton Winn, Wise & Seligsberg, letter to Baird, 30 October 1931 (Church)

20 SS&T, p. 124

21 Donald Flamm, 'Baird in America: What Was and What Might Have Been', *Television*, March/April, p. 22

22   Baird himself later suggested that Radio Pictures was a nominee of RCA, who did not want competition from the Baird company in the USA (SS&T, p. 125).

23   See p. 174. Presumably this was the apparatus which had been seen and favourably commented upon the previous week by Ashbridge.

24   SS&T, p. 124. The passage in italic type was omitted from the published version.

25   Church. 'Daylight' referred to the mirror-drum camera which had been used on the occasion of the Derby. C L Richards was a technical assistant who had worked in the Baird studios in Berlin in 1929, and was now at the Kingsbury laboratory. He arrived in New York on 18 November.

26   M Baird, p. 109. Margaret, on another occasion, recalled the telephone conversation in more detail. '"Can you hear me?" I said "Yes." "When are you coming over?" Before I could collect my thoughts he had said, "There is a ship leaving on Wednesday, I shall meet that, and don't waste time, as this call is costing £1 a minute"' (Margaret Baird, script for BBC broadcast, *Woman's Hour*, 12 May 1959).*

27   *New York Times*, 14 November 1931

28   Baird/Moseley, 30 November 1945

29   *New York Times*, 14 November 1931. The suggestion in the article that the bride and groom had also known each other for thirteen weeks was not far out; it was fourteen weeks and six days.

30   Margaret Baird, quoted in Burns (2000), p. 279. A wedding photograph in the press has Baird in bedroom slippers, but wearing a suit. See plate 37.

31   M Baird, p. 110

32   SS&T, p. 126

33   Donald Flamm, personal letter to Margaret Baird, 10 June 1976

34   Federal Radio Commission, Washington DC, Examiner's Report no. 322, 23 January 1932

35   SS&T, p. 125

36   Donald Flamm, 'Baird's Proper Place in Television History', an address at the Royal Television Society Council and Fellows Dinner, Arts Club, London, 11 September 1984

37   W R Roberts, secretary, Baird Television Ltd, notes for the board, 18 December 1931 (Church). Baird states in his memoir that he repaid the company half of his expenses (SS&T, p. 126).

38   Ulises A Sanabria demonstrated a television apparatus at a meeting of the Radio Manufacturers Association in Chicago on 13 June 1928, the first time that television equipment was shown at a radio convention (Abramson, pp. 119-20). It is reasonable to assume that de Bosdari was the person of that name who was instrumental in Baird giving his demonstration at Selfridge's in 1925 (see p. 57).

39   One of these demonstrations was at the B S Moss Broadway Theatre in New York on 21 October 1931, which was just after Baird's arrival in

the city. There was a report in the *New York Times* on 23 October (Abramson, p. 176).

40   M Baird, p. 113

41   M Baird, p. 126

Chapter 10: Baird and his Company, October 1931–May 1932

1   BBC, T16/42/3

2   Abramson, p. 177. British patent 391,887, application 19 November 1931, was accepted 11 May 1933.

3   'Television Plans', *The Times*, 29 December 1931

4   Moseley, p. 253

5   E V Appleton, report on cathode-ray television in Germany, 7 January 1932 (Church). Appleton received a fee of £150 for his work on the report, while £70 was remitted to the Department of Scientific and Industrial Research for Watt's time and expertise (Memorandum from company secretary, 8 March 1932 (Church)).

6   Loewe held significant von Ardenne patents (Archibald Church, 'Recent Developments in Television', paper read to the British Association, Section A (Mathematical and Physical Sciences), Leicester, 13 September 1933, reprinted in *Nature*, 30 September 1933, p. 504).

7   These figures would seem to be optimistic. Fernseh claimed, at the Berlin Radio Exhibition in 1932, to have reduced the delay between filming and transmission to 10-15 seconds (Abramson, p. 186). In 1935, film was being 'developed, fixed and washed in a period of less than 30 seconds' (Captain A G D West, Technical Director of Baird Television, 'A Practical Outline of Television', *Television and Short-Wave World*, August 1935, p. 466). In 1937, the total process of filming, developing, and transmitting was taking Fernseh between sixty and ninety seconds, depending on which kind of apparatus was being used (Michael Buckland, 'Zeiss Ikon and Television: Fernseh AG', *Zeiss Historica*, Autumn 1995, pp. 17-19). In the system designed by the Baird company for the French government in 1939, the 'exposed film was processed immediately in sealed developing and fixing tanks ... emerging 16-20 seconds later and then passed still wet to the scanning unit' (R M Herbert, 'Historic Baird TV Transmissions from Aircraft', *Television*, March/April 1987, p. 92).

8   Sir Ambrose Fleming, 'The "Waveband" Theory of Wireless Transmission', *Nature*, 18 January 1930, pp. 92-3. Broadly speaking, Fleming's argument was that the *strength* of the signal, not its complexity, determined the necessary bandwidth.

9   See note 3 above.

10   Appleton to Church, 8 January 1932 (Church)

11   Ampthill to Reith, 21 January 1932 (BBC, T16/42/3)

12   Andrew Boyle, *Only the Wind will Listen: Reith of the BBC* (1972), p. 228

13   Burns (1986), pp. 228-9

14   Bridgewater, p. 8

15   News flash (BBC, T16/42/3). The Gaumont-British subsidiary was International Acoustic Films, also controlled by Isidore Ostrer. Between them, these two companies held over fifty per cent of the nominal capital of LTV Ltd of 800,000 shares, and thus also had control of Baird Television Ltd. Other major shareholders in LTV Ltd at 5 May 1933 were Moseley (149,000) and Alfred Bates (150,000); Baird held 40,000 shares, and his cousins George and James Inglis 20,000 each. None of these owned any shares in July 1937, according to Burns (2000), p. 203. Baird cleared his bank deposit account of £5400 on 18 February 1932, maybe in order to purchase shares in the syndicate. A deposit of £11,600 on 14 September 1935 may include the sum obtained for the sale of these shares; on 12 May 1936 the only securities held on his behalf by his bank were 1822 preferred ordinary shares and 433 deferred ordinary shares in Baird Television Ltd. Moseley records being offered a 'fantastic sum' for his shares in February 1935, but Ostrer refused to release him from the syndicate (SMDiaries, p. 335).

16   Federal Radio Commission, Washington DC, Examiner's Report no. 322, 23 January 1932

17   W H Knight, report on American negotiations, New York, 13 March 1932 (Church)

18   Ampthill to Church, 26 February 1932 (Church)

19   Donald Flamm, 'Baird's Proper Place in Television History', an address at the Council and Fellows Dinner, Arts Club, London, 11 September 1984

20   Michael Stenton and Stephen Lees (eds), *Who's Who of British Members of Parliament 1919-1945* (1979), p. 137

21   'Directorate', memorandum 30 May 1932 (Church)

22   SS&T, p. 128

23   M Baird, p. 127

Chapter 11: Baird and the BBC, March 1932-June 1933

1   See p. 203.

2   Advertising leaflet (1931), courtesy of Richard Dean

3   Maurice Exwood, 'The Birth of Television', *Radio and Electronic Engineer*, December 1976, p. 632. Reith, in an internal memorandum of 2 December 1932, wrote, 'Mr Baird says he thinks there are about 500 sets of their own throughout the country. ... He thinks, however, that for every set of his sold, there are about ten which have been made up privately' (BBC, T16/42/4). At this time, according to a memorandum from Robb to

Reith, a publicity agent of the Radio Manufacturers' Association estimated that there were '5000-10,000 sets in operation' (24 November 1932, BBC, T16/42/4). At the beginning of 1934, the journal *Television* sold 7000 copies a month (Robb, 23 February 1934). Answering a question from Robb on the telephone, Baird estimated that there were between twenty and thirty thousand sets in use, of which his company had sold 'more than 1500 disc machines complete not counting kits, mirror drum machines or home made sets' (Robb, 9 March 1934).

4   *The Reith Diaries*, ed. Charles Stuart (1975), p. 111
5   BBC, T16/42/4
6   According to the *1933 BBC Handbook*, there were 4,523,118 licences issued as at 31 August 1932, one for about every ten of the population. Baird's proposal would therefore at that time represent a government research grant of about £9400 a year to his company.
7   Reith, 18 April 1932
8   BBC control board minutes, 19 April 1932 (BBC, T16/42/4)
9   The meeting was to be on 2 May, but a handwritten note on the BBC's carbon copy of the letter suggests that it was postponed to 4 May.
10   Carpendale, letter to Secretary, GPO, 28 April 1932 (BBC, T16/42/4)
11   Baird company press handout (BBC, T16/42/4)
12   *The Dictionary of National Biography 1981-1985*, p. 281
13   M Baird, p. 117
14   9 June 1933, copy in BBC, T16/42/4
15   DG to DIP [Gladstone Murray], copy to CE [Noel Ashbridge], 15 June 1932 (BBC, T16/42/4)
16   Postmaster General to J L Baird, 20 June 1932, copy to Sir John Reith (BBC, T16/42/4)
17   The first combined sound and vision licence was introduced in 1946.
18   Reveley. Paul Vernon Reveley joined the Baird company on 15 February 1932 (at £3 a week) after graduating in light current engineering at the City and Guilds Engineering College of Imperial College, University of London. Between 1934 and 1937 he had five British patents accepted relating to television: numbers 415,155, 437,340, 437,988, 459,171, 474,776.
19   D R Campbell, *This Is Your Life*, BBC TV, 28 October 1957 (BBC, T12/505/1)
20   'Derby Thrills by Television', *Television*, June 1932, p. 127
21   *News Chronicle*, 2 June 1932
22   *Daily Herald*, 2 June 1932
23   Ben Clapp, quoted in Norman, p. 73
24   The source of this anecdote is J D Percy, interview with Bruce Norman, 1980.
25   Bridgewater, pp. 4, 6. Bridgewater and Campbell were transferred to the staff of the BBC on 1 September 1932 as maintenance engineers (Burns (1986), p. 241).

26   Wilson patented the apparatus in his own right: 404,281, application 13 June 1932, accepted 9 March 1933.

27   Bridgewater, p. 4

28   Robb

29   Bridgewater, p. 10

30   Abramson, p. 186

31   Captain A G D West, 'A Practical Outline of Television', *Television and Short-Wave World*, August 1935, p. 466

32   SS&T, pp. 120-1, where Baird places this incident in 1931. A handwritten note beside this passage in MS A states that it happened in 1932, after Baird's visit to America. This fits better with the historical record: only a few days before Baird was in Berlin, Hitler was using the Kaiserhof as a base (William L Shirer, *The Rise and Fall of the Third Reich* (1959), p. 168).

33   Quoted in Norman, p. 82

34   Bridgewater, p. 12

35   'The BBC "First Night"', *Television*, September 1932, p. 243

36   *Television*, September 1932, p. 246. A further report was received from Crieff, Perthshire, 470 miles from London: 'While signal strength was maintained the image was quite good, and showed considerable detail; and we are looking forward to an interesting season.'

37   Bridgewater, pp. 6, 12

38   Norman, p. 83

39   Reith, 2 December 1932. This is the nearest Reith got in his personal diaries to an outright criticism of either Baird himself or the Baird company, unless it be his attempt to blackball a candidate for election to the Athenaeum Club on the grounds that 'his sole qualification appeared to be that he was a director of Baird Television' (see pp. 274-5).

40   Church

41   His name appears in this capacity as the signatory of a letter to the BBC on 31 May 1933 (BBC, T16/42/5).

42   Ampthill to Church, 13 July 1932, written from the Officers' Mess, Fire Camp, Swanage, where he was camping for two days with members of the National Fire Brigade Association (Church).

43   SMDiaries, p. 316. Clayton is listed as deputy chairman on a letter from Baird to Reith, 6 December 1932 (BBC, T16/42/4).

44   SS&T, p. 128

45   Reveley

46   SMDiaries, pp. 317-18

47   Percy, p. 13

48   Director of Technical Services [Ashbridge], BBC, internal memorandum, 'Moseley's book on Baird', to Director General, 9 June 1952 (BBC, T23/121 TV Publicity. Baird TV)

49   Actually, 130 lines (Abramson, p. 191)

50   Ashbridge, 'Report on Television Demonstration at Electrical & Musical

Industries Ltd', 6 December 1932 (BBC, T16/65, TV Policy EMI 1931-1935)

51　But see p. 201 and note.

52　Abramson, p. 191

53　S A Pandit, *From Making to Music: The History of Thorn EMI* (1996), pp. 55, 60

54　Ashbridge, 'Television', memorandum to Director General, 5 January 1933 (BBC, T16/65, TV Policy EMI 1931-1935)

55　BBC, T16/42/5

56　Ashbridge, letter to Baird, 30 January 1933 (BBC, T16/42/5)

57　In letter from F W Phillips, GPO, to Carpendale, 1 February 1933 (BBC, T16/42/5). Moseley also wrote to Stanley Baldwin, Lord President of the Council: 'I wonder whether, in the welter of cynicism of modern politics, there is any sincerity in the plea of "British first"' (27 January 1933, quoted in Asa Briggs, *The History of Broadcasting in the United Kingdom: volume 2, The Golden Age of Wireless* (1965), p. 573). Moseley wrote again on 9 February. He had a reply to both letters from the Privy Council Office on 1 April: 'Mr Baldwin has asked me to write to you with reference to your letters on the subject of television, and to say that he understands that Mr Baird has since been in touch with the Postmaster General on this matter.' He commented, 'Isn't that typical of Baldwin? The "passed to you" attitude! And how different from the intellectual virility of Sir Herbert Samuel' (SMDiaries, pp. 319-320).

58　Burns (1986), p. 257

59　Baird, letter to Ashbridge, 9 February 1933 (BBC, T16/42/5)

60　Sir Godfrey Thomas, letter to Roger Eckersley, 21 February 1933 (BBC, T16/42/5)

61　M Baird, p. 124

62　SS&T, p. 120

63　William L Shirer, *The Rise and Fall of the Third Reich* (1959), p. 216. Brüning was in London in July 1934, when Ian Anderson gave a lunch for him at the Savoy. Other guests included Moseley and Lord Ampthill (SMDiaries, p. 332). He subsequently went to the USA.

64　Knowlton Nash, *The Microphone Wars: a History of Triumph and Betrayal at the CBC* (1994), pp. 128-9, 133

65　Filson Young, 'The World We Listen In', *Radio Times*, 28 April 1933, p. 204

66　Greer, letter to Reith, 1 June 1933, in which he asked for a meeting to discuss the propriety of holding the demonstration, 'in view of the developments that have been made on the 120 line pictures' (BBC, T16/42/5). At their meeting Reith reminded Greer that the previous February Baird had been informed that the thirty-line system was obsolescent. Greer immediately undertook that no more of the new sets would be manufactured and that all the company's energies 'would be directed to the production of a satisfactory high-definition receiver and the development of a high-definition television transmitter' (Church, letter to the Right Hon. Sir Kingsley Wood MP, Postmaster General, 27 April 1934 (Church)).

67   Assistant Chief Engineer [Bishop], 'Baird Television. Press Demonstration', memorandum to Director General, 30 May 1933

68   Ashbridge to Reith, memorandum, 12 May 1933 (BBC, T16/42/5)

69   Copy in BBC file T16/42/5

70   Postmaster General, letter to Baird, 13 June 1933 (copy in BBC, T16/42/5)

Chapter 12: Crescent Wood Road 1933

1   Alison Edwards and Keith Wyncoll, *"The Crystal Palace Is On Fire!" Memories of the 30th November 1936* (second edition 1992), pp. 10-12

2   Herbert, p. 18

3   M Baird, p. 128

4   M Baird, p. 129

5   M Baird, p. 128

6   Estate agent's leaflet 1933 (Hastings Museum, HASMG 002.1) The house was bought leasehold.

7   Reveley

8   269,658, application 20 January 1926 (spotlight scanning), and either 269,834, application 21 October 1925, or 275,138, application 3 May 1926 (synchronisation of transmission and receiving apparatus)

9   Church, letter to Greer (dictated but not personally signed), 7 April 1933 (Church). By HMV Church of course meant EMI, which had been formed in 1931 as the result of the merger between HMV and Columbia Graphophone.

10   See pp. 248-9.

11   30 May 1933 (BBC, T16/42/5). Moseley's name is crossed out in the list of directors at the head of a letter from Baird to the BBC dated 25 May 1933.

12   SS&T, pp. 128-9

13   Moseley, pp. 214-15

14   4 October 1932, quoted in Burns (2000), p. 259. The alleged breach of patent rights was almost certainly to do with the Marconi 'telewriter', which had elements in common with the machine developed by Baird (pp. 134-5). The initial cause of the dispute was an article, 'News by Television. A Marconi Development', *Television* July 1932, to which Layzell replied on behalf of the Baird company (Burns (1986), p. 202).

15   Moseley, p. 216

16   Quoted in Burns (1986), p. 250. The 'set' referred to would almost certainly have been one of the six 'super home receivers' (see p. 229).

17   Moseley, p. 215

18   A letter from the company to Baird, 17 July 1936,* amending his salary to

£3000 a year after deduction of tax, refers to an agreement dated 9 June 1933. This, then, may be taken as the date on which the new arrangements took effect.

19   Company staff list, 17 November 1936 (Church)

20   Herbert, p. 22

21   Gilbert Tomes, *Jumbo's Diaries* (second edition 2000), p. 29

22   Paul Reveley, personal letter to AK, 28 May 2000

23   Paul Reveley to AK, 28 May 2000

24   Ray Herbert, personal letter to AK, 7 December 2000

25   Paul Reveley, personal letter to AK, 18 March 2001

26   Paul Reveley, telephone conversation with AK, 12 May 2000

27   SS&T, p. 129, where he calls him Gerrard

28   Church

29   M Baird, pp. 128-9. Margaret was wrong about the lawn. The estate agent's leaflet (see note 6 above) shows that it was already in place when Baird bought the house.

30   Diana Richardson, 'Sydenham, Bude and Bexhill', unpublished manuscript, May 2000

31   Paul Reveley, personal letter to T H Bridgewater, 28 September 1958

32   9 May 1943 (Baird/Moseley)

33   Paul Reveley, personal letter to AK, 7 December 2000. Baird was also, with West, a member of the company's technical committee under the chairmanship of Church (Church), and would keep himself abreast of what was going on in the Rotunda by dropping in to see demonstrations, though he would never reveal to the staff there what he himself was doing at 3 Crescent Wood Road (Gilbert Tomes, interview with Jan Leman, 20 February 2002).

34   Murray, letter to Baird, 15 February 1933 (BBC, T16/42/5). See also p. 235.

35   Baird, letter to Greer, 20 October 1933*

36   See pages 234 ff. There is in BBC files no letter from the BBC to Baird dated 31 January; the reference must be to Ashbridge's letter of 30 January.

37   SS&T, p. 121

Chapter 13: The Baird Company 1933-1939

1   *The Dictionary of National Biography 1971-1980* (1986), p. 20

2   Curriculum vitae of A G D West, January 1932, courtesy of Richard West

3   See p. 235.

4   Chief Engineer, 'Record of interview with A G D West, 13 July 1933' (BBC, T16/42/6)

5   'Notes on Discussion between Mr Ashbridge, Chief Engineer of the

British Broadcasting Corporation, and Mr West, representing Baird Television Limited, on Thursday Afternoon, July 13th 1933' (BBC, T16/42/6)

6 Chief Engineer to Controller, 'Letter from A G D West', 17 July 1933 (BBC, T16/42/6)

7 Quoted under 22 June 1933 in SMDiaries, pp. 320-1

8 See p. 240.

9 Quoted in Burns (1986), p. 279

10 Abramson, p. 202

11 'All About the Crystal Palace Tests', *Wireless World*, October 1933

12 See pp. 211-12.

13 BBC, T16/42/6 (July to December 1933), T16/42/8 (October to December 1933)

14 Reith, 30 August 1933

15 Ashbridge, letter to Baird Television Ltd, 4 September 1933 (BBC, T16/42/6)

16 Jarrard, letter to BBC, 6 September 1933 (BBC, T16/42/6)

17 Carpendale, letter to Baird Television Ltd, 8 September 1933 (BBC, T16/42/6)

18 'Scophony Limited',* notes by Joel Sagall, son of Solomon, undated. See also Tom Singleton, *The History of Scophony* (1986).

19 Assistant Chief Engineer [Bishop], 'Television – Future Policy', memorandum to Director of Business Relations [Goldsmith], 12 October 1933 (BBC, T16/42/7). Ashbridge's own ambivalence was revealed in the course of a conversation with Robb. '[Ashbridge] said that he was all against 30-line transmissions being continued because it would encourage independent manufacturers to flood the market with 30-line receivers, thereby putting the Corporation into the position of being unable to terminate 30-line transmissions when we thought fit. On the other hand, he admitted that in his opinion, from a practical point of view, 30-line transmission should be continued in order to sustain interest – say from month to month – if we were free to discontinue when we liked. He also agreed that the present stage of cathode ray was not so satisfying as 30-line' (Robb, 26 October 1933).

20 Burns (1986), pp. 279-80. The estimated number of eight thousand receivers in operation is not inconsistent with the five thousand (see p. 209), if the latter figure is taken to be sets manufactured under the auspices of the Baird company or made from Baird components.

21 Reith, letter to Postmaster General, 31 October 1933 (BBC, T16/42/7)

22 Bridgewater, p. 16

23 West, letter to Ashbridge, 19 October 1933 (BBC, T16/42/7)

24 Bishop, telephone conversation with West, 9 December 1933 (BBC, T16/42/7)

25 Bishop, memorandum to Chief Engineer, 18 December 1933 (BBC, T16/42/7)

26 Burns (1986), pp. 290, 295. Reith was invited to EMI's demonstration, but pleaded pressure of work!

27 Burns (1986), pp. 296-7

28 Abramson, p. 207

29 Burns (1986), p. 296

30 SS&T, p. 130

31 Correspondence between West and C C Patterson (GEC), June 1935 (Church)

32 Reith, letter to Greer, 8 March 1934 (BBC, T16/42/8). According to Reith's personal diary, in the morning of 12 March he had a general discussion with Carpendale, who was to be at the demonstration, and Alan Dawnay, controller (output), about 'leakage, Bolshevist contacts, etc.'. Later he had lunch in the BBC canteen with Mary Agnes Hamilton, whom, as a governor of the BBC, Greer had invited to attend. From his diary entry for that day, there seems no reason why Reith should not have gone to Wardour Street, a few hundred yards away, at midday, had he wished to do so.

33 Chief Engineer, 'Report on Demonstration of Baird Television, at Gaumont British Studios, Wardour Street, on Monday March 12th 1934' (BBC, T16/42/8). Ashbridge was less than fair, however, in other respects. Five months earlier, he claimed to have been 'impressed' by a Baird cathode-ray demonstration of film transmission (Robb, 27 October 1933). Robb himself recorded, 'Impressive demonstration of [Baird] 180-line film; able to read cast sheet with comparative ease' (Robb, 22 November 1933). Yet as early as March 1934, 'Ashbridge said to Shoenberg he was very impressed [by an EMI demonstration], nothing left but financial terms to be discussed' (Robb, 19 March 1934). The programme experts did not share Ashbridge's enthusiasm for the transmission only of film. Robb felt that the EMI demonstration was 'very interesting. Good results by radio. Still feel the appeal of film limited unless confined to topical and short doses of cartoons. ... Gielgud viewed the whole thing with misgiving. The only relief is that the engineers say it will take five years, by which time he will be out of it' (Robb, 28 March 1934). A month later, 'West told me on the phone that 7 metres transmission had been picked up in picture form at Hitchin, 28 miles from Crystal Palace, and in Ashdown Forest. That he had sent a general staff invitation to see Studio High Definition. This never reached us' (Robb, 26 April 1934).

34 Reith, letter to Greer, 27 March 1934 (BBC, T16/42/8)

35 Chief Accountant [Thomas Lochhead], to Director General, BBC, 'Baird Television Ltd', confidential BBC memorandum with copy of balance sheet, 4 September 1934 (BBC, T16/42/8)

36 Reith, 7 February 1934

37 Certificate of candidate for ballot, Archibald George Church, Esq DSO MC BSc London, Director of Baird Television Ltd, formerly MP, 7

February 1934. Details are from editions of *Who's Who* and *The Dictionary of National Biography*.

38   The authors are grateful to the Athenaeum for judging that the 'events of 66 years ago are sufficiently distant for this information now to be revealed'. The club abolished the blackballing system in 1935, as members felt it was too embarrassing; the Church case probably contributed to this decision (Sarah Dodgson, Librarian, the Athenaeum, personal letter to AK, 15 June 2001).

39   See, for instance, p. 153.

40   It was not a good year for Church. On 22 May 1934 he was stopped in his car by the police while driving on the Marylebone Road and subsequently charged with 'driving with undue care and attention'. He was fined £20 plus £2.12s.6d. court charges (PRO, WO 339/36927). The authors are grateful to Adrian Hills for drawing this unhappy incident to their attention.

41   Burns (1986), p. 298

42   Minutes of 'Conference at General Post Office, 5 April' (BBC, T16/42/7)

43   J C W Reith, *Into the Wind* (1949), p. 188

44   *The Reith Diaries*, ed. Charles Stuart (1975), p. 166

45   J C W Reith, *Into the Wind* (1949), p. 219

46   *The Dictionary of National Biography* (compact edition 1975), p. 2548.

47   Reith, 30 November 1934

48   Church, letter to the Right Hon. Sir Kingsley Wood MP, Postmaster General, 27 April 1934 (Church)

49   Herbert, p. 19, and Ray Herbert, 'G2TV: The First Television Transmitting Station', for the Radio Society of Great Britain, 13 May 1996

50   Reith, 31 May 1934

51   Robb

52   *The Television Committee. Report*, Command 4793 (1935), pp. 4, 5, 27

53   *The Television Committee. Report*, Command 4793 (1935), pp. 23, 25-6

54   Reith, 22 January 1935

55   Carpendale, 'Record of telephone conversation with Mr Phillips of the Post Office', 14 June 1935 (BBC, T16/42/8)

56   Bridgewater, p. 18. Robb, having been passed over for the new post of director of television, and offered a subordinate position, left the BBC in 1936 (Robb).

57   Herbert, p. 13

58   McLean, p. 191

59   Ray Herbert, 'G2TV: The First Television Transmitting Station', Radio Society of Great Britain, 13 May 1996

60   Moseley's judgment of people was as shrewd as ever. Tallents was a civil servant who had been secretary of the Empire Marketing Board and then public relations officer of the GPO before joining the BBC in July 1935. Reith, who appointed him, had already confided in his diary on 3 June, 'Lunched with Tallents and had a good talk about the 3rd controller job.

I am not sure that he is the man for it' (*The Reith Diaries*, ed. Charles Stuart (1975), p. 167).

61   SMDiaries, pp. 349-50
62   'Television for Air Defence. German Service under Military Control', *The Times*, 9 August 1935
63   SS&T, p. 121
64   Gilbert Tomes, *Jumbo's Diaries* (second edition 2000)
65   Burns (2000), pp. 310, 317
66   Quoted in Norman, p. 118
67   Paul Reveley, personal letter to AK, 18 March 2001
68   Burns (2000), pp. 316-17; Paul Reveley, personal letter to AK, 18 March 2001. Church, in a report to the Baird company board in September 1936, following the Berlin radio exhibition, stated, 'The intermediate-film method of transmission of outdoor scenes is still much superior in performance to the emitron and still more so than the electron camera. The disc-scanner at present gives better results than the emitron and electron camera in tele-cinema transmission' ('The Television Situation', 17 September 1936 (Church)).
69   Mrs Elma G 'Pem' Farnsworth, *Distant Vision: Romance and Discovery on an Invisible Frontier* (1990), pp. 166-9
70   Andrew Henderson, 'Television Comes to Radiolympia', *405 Alive*, Summer 2000, pp. 6-11
71   Andrew Henderson, 'What the Papers Said', *405 Alive*, Spring 2001, pp. 26-9
72   Burns (1986), p. 420
73   Schedule and shooting script, 2 November 1936 (BBC)
74   SS&T, p. 134. In MS A, Baird has added at the end of this passage, 'Such was the nature of my thoughts as I returned to my abode.'
75   Reith
76   Norman, p. 134
77   Quoted in Norman, p. 131
78   Mrs Elma G 'Pem' Farnsworth, *Distant Vision: Romance and Discovery on an Invisible Frontier* (1990), pp. 181-7
79   Abramson, p. 234
80   Alison Edwards and Keith Wyncoll, *"The Crystal Palace Is On Fire!" Memories of the 30th November 1936* (second edition 1992), p. 58-9
81   Alison Edwards and Keith Wyncoll, *"The Crystal Palace Is On Fire!" Memories of the 30th November 1936* (second edition 1992), p. 17
82   SS&T, p. 138
83   M Baird, p. 133
84   Gilbert Tomes, *Jumbo's Diaries* (second edition 2000), pp. 26, 28
85   Baird company staff list, 17 November 1936 (Church)
86   Nuttall's letter is quoted in Alison Edwards and Keith Wyncoll, *"The Crystal Palace Is On Fire!" Memories of the 30th November 1936* (second edition 1992), pp. 54-5

87 H C Spencer, interview with Ray Herbert, 1 May 1983

88 Baird company staff list, 17 November 1936 (Church). Clapp, who is described as 'Buyer' in the administration department of the research sector of the business, was then earning £700 a year. The salary of T M C Lance, technical supervisor, was £1000 a year, and that of L R Merdler, engineer in charge of radio receivers, £750 a year. Percy, in charge of the intermediate-film process, was earning £550 a year, the same as Dr I C Szegho, head of cathode-ray tube research, who had been taken on in October 1934. Reveley, on Baird's personal staff, but still designated 'technical assistant', was now receiving £520 a year. In the photo-cell research department, Dr K A R Samson, physicist, earned £500 a year, and Dr A K Denisoff, research physicist, and Dr A Sommer, physical chemist, each £350. The wages of H G Flood, glassblower in the same department, were £338 a year. The total number of staff at this juncture was 382.

89 Ben Clapp, interview with Clare Colvin and Ray Herbert, 24 March 1987

90 Joan Woodcock, née Hilton, personal letter to Margaret Baird, 8 February 1960

91 Mrs Elma G 'Pem' Farsnworth, *Distant Vision: Romance and Discovery on an Invisible Frontier* (1990), p. 188

92 BBC, T16/42/8

93 Gilbert Tomes, *Jumbo's Diaries* (second edition 2000), p. 29. Between fifty and sixty of the more skilled of these were subsequently offered their jobs back (Ray Herbert, telephone conversation with AK, 23 July 2001).

94 Quoted in Burns (2000), p. 321

95 Church, letter to Shoenberg, 11 December 1936 (Church)

96 Burns (2000), p. 328

97 Paul Reveley, personal letter to AK, 18 March 2001

98 SS&T, pp. 139-40

99 Major A G Church, memorandum on 'Publicity on Television', 5 August 1936 (Church)

100 'Baird Television Ltd: Future Technical Development', 8 January 1937 (Church). With regard to point 4, according to the staff list (Church), there does not appear at this time to have been a sales department as such. The function seems to have been exercised by the service department, under Desmond Piper, engineer-in-charge. He, his secretary Joan Hilton, her fiancé (who was not connected with the firm, but was interested in her work), and the service engineers attended classes in television, and between them compiled an instruction book for viewers. Piper and others wrote it in technical language, and Hilton translated it into layman's terms. As part of their training on the job, the engineers were required to construct a receiver themselves (Joan Woodcock, personal letter to Margaret Baird, 8 February 1960).

101 Waddell, p. 244. The receiver was a large T5 type.

102   Hills
103   'Baird Television Ltd: Contracts with French Air Ministry and USSR &
      Their Relation to the Technical Development Programme', 12 April 1937
      (Church)
104   R M Herbert, 'Historic Baird transmissions from aircraft', *Television*,
      March/April 1987, pp. 92-4
105   J A Lodge, Thorn EMI Central Research Laboratories, 'EMI Airborne
      Television Equipment', 23 October 1986, courtesy of Peter Waddell
106   5 May 1937 (Church)
107   Clayton appears on the company letter heading in his extended
      capacity on 27 April 1937. It might be wondered why the job of joint
      managing director was not formally given to West. It may be that
      though West 'was an approachable and pleasant boss, [he was] not
      strong on the management side' (Ray Herbert, personal letter to AK,
      31 August 2000).
108   Professor R V Jones, personal letter to Peter Waddell, 6 March 1986,
      and Hills
109   Moseley, letter to Church, 1 November 1937 (Church)
110   SS&T, pp. 140-1
111   Moseley, p. 222
112   SMDiaries, pp. 367-8
113   SS&T, p. 141. This was presumably the figure before tax.
114   M Baird, p. 135
115   Herbert, pp. 19, 20; Ray Herbert, personal letter to AK, 26 July 2001
116   Ray Herbert, telephone conversation with AK, 23 July 2001
117   Ray Herbert, personal letter to AK, 31 August 2000
118   McLean, p. 194
119   J L Baird, 'Television Yesterday, Today and Tomorrow', *News-Letter*, 26
      August 1939, pp. 347-50
120   Norman, p. 212
121   16,000, L Marsland Gander, 'When "the box" was opened 40 years ago',
      Daily Telegraph, 1 November 1976, quoted in Maurice Exwood, 'The
      Births of Television', *Radio and Electronic Engineer*, December 1976, p. 632;
      23,000, M Baird, p. 142, and Abramson, p. 254
122   Burns (2000), pp. 356, 360.
123   SS&T, p. 145. Cinema-Television is thought to have been established
      between the middle of November and 7 December 1937 (Hills).
124   Schedule of securities held by Barclays Bank on a/c of J L Baird, 12 May
      1936*
125   Moseley, p. 229

Chapter 14: Crescent Wood Road 1933–1939

1   SS&T, p. 92
2   M Baird, pp. 127–8
3   Paul Reveley, personal letter to AK, 28 May 2000
4   Reveley
5   SS&T, pp. 91–2
6   Diana Richardson, 'Sydenham, Bude and Bexhill', unpublished manuscript, May 2000; personal letter to AK, 3 August 2001
7   Baird company staff list, 17 November 1936 (Church)
8   Malcolm Baird, 'Television on the West End Stage in 1935', *405 Alive*, Summer 2000, p. 19
9   *The Dictionary of National Biography* (compact edition) 1975, p. 2816
10   M Baird, p. 132
11   SMDiaries, p. 354
12   Paul Reveley, personal letter to AK, 28 May 2000: 'She was a lady of formidable appearance with whom I never had any personal conversational contact. Baird however did not attempt to disguise from me his distaste of her entry upon the scene.'
13   Diana Richardson, interview with AK, 25 August 2000
14   In July 1937, Annie took Malcolm back to Helensburgh, where he was baptised in St Bride's Church.
15   Paul Reveley, personal letter to AK, 28 May 2000
16   Mrs Elma G 'Pem' Farnsworth, *Distant Vision: Romance and Discovery on an Invisible Frontier* (1990), p. 184
17   Joan Woodcock (née Hilton), personal letter to Margaret Baird, 8 February 1960. This reference is to the summer of 1936, before the destruction of the south wing of the Crystal Palace. The autobiographical notes were probably for James Spence, a journalist friend of Baird. They may also have served as a basis for *Sermons, Soap and Television* (see SS&T, p. 147).
18   Abramson, p. 235
19   L Marsland Gander, 'Television in Cinema', *Daily Telegraph*, 8 December 1936
20   Burns (2000), p. 336
21   Burns (2000), p. 337
22   'I Saw the Birth of British TV', *Evening Telegraph* (Dundee), 10 August 1959
23   Abramson, p. 241; 'Scophony Limited', notes by Sagall's son. Church, in a report (17 September 1936) on the Berlin Radio Exhibition, 1936, concluded, 'No matter by what method it is done, if, within the next twelve months any firm in the television field produces a receiver capable of showing a clear picture of 2 feet or more square, our expenditure on plant and materials for the production of large cathode-ray receivers will have to be written off' (Church).
24   Paul Reveley, personal letter to AK, 18 March 2001

25   Abramson, pp. 252-3. The signals were transmitted from the South Tower of the Crystal Palace to 3 Crescent Wood Road, and shown on a small receiver.

26   Herbert, pp. 22, 26

27   'Colour Television Shown on World's Largest Screen', *Sunday Referee*, 12 December 1937. The actual date would probably have been 9 or 10 December.

28   Herbert, p. 22

29   Paul Reveley, personal letter to AK, 6 August 2001

30   SMDiaries, p. 369

31   Moseley, pp. 160-1. In addition to his membership of other learned and scientific societies, Baird was also a member of the British Institute of Philosophy (1935).

32   Moseley, pp. 10-12

33   Moseley, pp. 161-2

34   Burns (2000), p. 341

35   Paul Reveley, personal letter to AK, 20 June 2000

36   SS&T, p. 142

37   *Daily Telegraph*, 25 February 1938. M Baird (p. 138) follows SS&T (p. 142) in stating that they sailed from Marseilles on 22 February. Baird's passport* confirms the evidence of the interview that he passed through Calais on 24 February.

38   M Baird, pp. 138-9

39   M Baird, p. 139. Rabindranath Tagore (1861-1941), prose writer, poet, philosopher, educationist, and artist, had been awarded the Nobel Prize for literature in 1913 for his free English verse translations of his own Bengali poems. He was knighted in 1915, but resigned from the order in 1919 in protest at the British action in Amritsar during the riots in the Punjab.

40   SS&T, p. 142

41   SS&T, p. 143

42   M Baird, p. 140

43   SS&T, p. 143. Baird's reputation in Australia still stands high. Television was introduced there in 1956, and two years later the first Australian television awards were initiated by the Melbourne-based journal, *TV Week*. The first 'star of the year' winner was Graham Kennedy, who christened the awards Logies, after Baird's second name. He thought it sounded like an award, and it was 'short, easy to remember and had a link to the history of television' (*TV Week* handout).

44   Baird/Moseley, 12 April 1938. The toilet paper of that time made an adequate substitute for lightweight airmail writing paper.

45   John L Baird, *Television – A General Survey*, Proceedings of the World Radio Convention, Sydney April 4 to 14, organised by the Institution of Radio Engineers, Australia (Hastings Museum, HASMG 002.1)

46   SS&T, p. 143. Fisk was chairman of Amalgamated Wireless (Australia) Ltd,

which had the exclusive rights in the region to the patents of Marconi and Telefunken.

47   M Baird, p. 141

48   Diana Richardson, personal letter to AK, 3 August 2001. Apparently the accident happened when Cecilia Albu ran to the phone while bathing her granddaughter. Five-year-old Diana got out of the bath, put on her dressing-gown, and went to help. Between them they managed to ring the doctor, who came, and the leg was set and plastered.

49   SMDiaries, p. 370. According to Diana, the 'tinned food' was probably McConachie's stew.

50   SMDiaries, p. 376

51   M Baird, p. 141

52   Burns (2000), pp. 346, 348

53   Herbert, p. 20

54   Burns (2000), p. 352

55   *The Times*, 24 February 1938

56   Paul Reveley, letter to T H Bridgewater 28 September 1958, courtesy of Paul Reveley

57   Moseley, pp. 225-6

58   SMDiaries, 20/25 September 1938, p. 375

59   SMDiaries, 26 January 1939, p. 381

60   Moseley, p. 226

61   SMDiaries, p. 383

62   SMDiaries, p. 389

63   SMDiaries, pp. 389-90

64   M Baird, p. 143

65   £15,000 in 1939 had the purchasing power of about £600,000 in 2001.

Chapter 15: Carrying on: Bude and London 1939-1942

1   Diana Richardson, 'Sydenham, Bude and Bexhill', unpublished manu-script, May 2000

2   SS&T, p. 145

3   A E Sayers, 'To Whom It May Concern', typed note 6 March 1989, courtesy of Ray Herbert. Baird refers to 'total staff three' on 14 February 1941 (Baird/Moseley).

4   Ray Herbert, telephone conversation with AK, 12 August 2001. Bernard went to the Royal Aircraft Establishment in 1941.

5   T M C Lance, interview with Ray Herbert, 26 April 1989. Lance, the company's research manager, records meeting Baird at his home several times during the war to get his signature to patents.

6   Hills

7   'History of Cinema-Television Limited's War Work', a report by Captain

A G D West, 4 June 1945 (PRO, AVIA 12/184), for which the authors are grateful to Adrian Hills. At the foot of the document West describes himself as a director of Cinema-Television. This advancement, well deserved in the light of the company's contribution to the war effort, does not seem to have been implemented at least until after June 1943 (see reference 30 to this chapter).

8   Douglas Brown, 'The Electronic Imaging of Baird Television', unpublished PhD thesis, University of Strathclyde, 2000

9   Gilbert Tomes, *Jumbo's Diaries* (second edition 2000), p. 67. It has also been suggested that, much to the displeasure of West, Sommer supplied Baird with apparatus that he made for him, in or out of the firm's time (Ray Herbert, telephone conversation with AK, 18 August 2001). It would appear that Baird, with Church, was instrumental in getting Samson and Sommer out of Germany (Gilbert Tomes, interview with Jan Leman, 20 February 2002).

10   Baird/Moseley. The letters were in one of thirty-one folders that Moseley bequeathed to the BBC. The others contained mainly press cuttings about himself!

11   SMDiaries, p. 391

12   Carstairs was born on 1 January 1900, probably in Glasgow. He worked for the Arusha Development Oil Exploration Company and, during World War II, for MI5. He met Baird through Moseley.

13   Moseley, p. 236

14   The heading of the letter is Stella Jaye, Bookseller and Librarian, 65 Union Street, Ryde, IW.

15   SS&T, pp. 146-7

16   M Baird, p. 146. Margaret told Malcolm many years later that some of these letters contained references to Baird's affair with 'Alice', which he did not want anyone to see.

17   Richard Smout, County Archivist, Isle of Wight, personal letters to AK, 24 August and 27 September 2000. If Mephy did serve in France during World War I (see page 13), then the bombing of Portsmouth could have triggered off memories which were too ghastly for him to bear.

18   Notice of probate, 12 November 1941, Probate Registry, York

19   William died in the mid-1950s, and Helena on 24 May 1958, shortly after which Helen ceased to live at Barfield Lodge. The authors are grateful to Richard Smout for his research into the Pearce family in the local press and electoral rolls.

20   JBLD

21   Moseley, pp. 224-5

22   Iain Carstairs, grandson of Lindsay Carstairs, telephone conversation with Douglas Brown, 5 February 2001. This is also Diana's recollection.

23   M Baird, p. 144

24   John Logie Baird, 'Improvements in Television Apparatus', Patent 545,078, application 7 September 1940, accepted 11 May 1942

25   'Progress in Colour Television – Mr Baird's Achievement', *The Times*, 21 December 1940

26   14 January 1941*

27   M Baird, pp. 149-50

28   'Television in Colour – J L Baird's New Advance', *Electronics and Television & Short-Wave World*, April 1941, pp. 152-3. The photograph was subsequently reproduced in colour in *Television*, January/February 1990, p. 27.

29   Peter C Goldmark, 'Colour in Television', lecture reported in *Communications*, May 1944. A copy of the report was sent to Baird on 22 July 1944 by John L Young of Cable and Wireless Ltd.

30   Baird/Moseley. For Moseley's staff cuts, see p. 51. Isidore Ostrer had 'gone to New York to look after the Baird Television interests (according to the Daily Film Renter). I have not seen or heard from him, he has been quite unapproachable' (Baird/Moseley, 4 March 1940). In 1941 J Arthur Rank (later Lord Rank) acquired a controlling interest in Gaumont-British and its subsidiary companies (Geoffrey Macnab, *J Arthur Rank and the British Film Industry* (1993), p. 205). Baird refers to the deal in a letter to Moseley, 13 November 1941 (Baird/Moseley). In June 1943, the directors of Cinema-Television Limited (Incorporating Baird Television Limited) were J Arthur Rank (chairman), L W Farrow, Mark Ostrer, and W B Robinson (Company letter heading, courtesy of Ray Herbert). Scott's was, and still is, an exclusive London fish restaurant. In the end, there was no formal winding up of Baird Television Ltd until 1945, owing to the difficulty encountered in assessing the value of certain French holdings (Hills).

31   Baird/Moseley. No other reference is known to the 'cheap colour television set' with a screen of that size. It would have been quite revolutionary for its time also because the cheapest monochrome set in 1939 had cost £47. Sir William Wiseman (1885-1962), 10th baronet, served in military intelligence in World War I, during which he acted as liaison between the British government and President Woodrow Wilson. After the war he joined the banking firm of Kuhn, Loeb and Co in New York.

32   SS&T, p. 147

33   Information taken from a brochure of the time, courtesy of Steve Cooney, Tempsford, June 2000. The hall is now the head office of the Kier group, a French-owned construction company.

34   See p. 304.

35   From time to time Baird jotted down in his diary alternative titles: '(Sermons) Socks Soap and Television', 'Before I Forget' (27 July 1940); 'Unfit for any service', 'Theology Trade Television' (1 September 1940); 'Television and Other Things', 'The Road to Television', 'Television and Myself', 'A Tale of Television' (in the section for 'Accounts' at the end of 1941). The ultimate title *Sermons, Soap and Television*, rather than *Sermons, Socks and Television*, came about through an error during the publication

process (Ray Herbert, telephone conversation with AK, 21 August 2001). See also Postscript, p. 389.

36 SS&T, pp. 145-6

37 See pp. 74-5.

38 S S Swords, *Technical History of the Beginnings of Radar* (1986), p. 43

39 See pp. 199-200.

40 Exwood, p. 29

41 Stanley Radford, a member of a scientific section of military intelligence in World War II, talking to Jeffrey Cohen, in personal letter from Cohen to Peter Waddell, 31 October 1986.

42 Christopher Lee, BBC defence correspondence, talking to Jeffrey Cohen, 14 September 1986, in personal letter from Cohen to Peter Waddell, 31 October 1986; David White, Diplomatic Wireless Service Museum, personal letter to Peter Waddell, 25 January 2000.

43 Ray Herbert, interview with AK, 18 May 2001. Herbert was himself in radar research in World War II, during which he also worked as a volunteer for MI6, attached to Bletchley Park, listening in to radio messages from agents in France, to detect any change in identity on the part of the sender.

44 7 August 1951, quoted in Moseley, p. 245. Wilshaw was secretary of Eastern Telegraph Company from 1922 until it was merged with the Marconi telegraph interests in 1929, to become Imperial and International Communications Ltd, of which Wilshaw was appointed secretary and general manager. This would suggest that the meeting took place during the years 1927-1929, and that Baird's 'manager' was Hutchinson. International Communications was renamed Cable and Wireless in 1934.

45 'Improvements in Television', patent 552,582, applied for 11 July and 6 October 1941, accepted 15 April 1943

46 J L Baird, 'Stereoscopic Television', *Electronic Engineering*, February 1942, pp. 620-1

47 Richard B Head, note to Malcolm Baird, received 9 September 1981

48 A search of back numbers of *Punch* around this time has failed to reveal any reference to television, suggesting that there may after all be such a thing as a free lunch! It may or may not, however, be significant that a younger brother of 'E V', Dillwyn Knox, had his own decoding section at Bletchley Park, which broke the Italian naval code and contributed to breaking the German Engima code.

49 R B Head, 'Baird's Stereoscopic Colour Television in 1941', *British Vintage Wireless Society Bulletin*, Autumn 1997, pp. 38-9; Richard B Head, note to Malcolm Baird, received 9 September 1981. If Head's recollection about the provenance of the press releases is correct, this is the only known occasion on which Baird used a typewriter to produce a document.

50 See pp. 58-9.

51 'Stereoscopic Television Pictures: A Notable British Achievement', *Illustrated London News*, 9 May 1942, p. 557

52 Burns (2000), pp. 371-2

53   *The Dictionary of National Biography 1961-1970* (1981), p. 445

54   Ministry of Supply, reference C.P.R./B.M./45, 19 December 1941.[*]
      Entries in Baird's diary before the 13 December visit refer to 'Director of
      Scientific Research', and suggest that Church would be accompanied
      by Goff [*sic*], almost certainly a phonetic reference to Gough. The letter
      is not signed by Gough, which has led to some confusion in that accord-
      ing to *The Dictionary of National Biography*, note 53 above, and *Who Was
      Who 1961-1970*, p. 443, Gough was director of scientific research at the
      War Office from 1938 to 1942. A study of Gough's personal file (PRO,
      SUPP 20/5), however, undertaken on the authors' behalf by Adrian
      Hills, reveals that he was appointed director of scientific research at the
      Ministry of Supply on 15 December 1937. It therefore seems likely that
      Gough dictated the letter of 19 December 1941, which was a Friday,
      and that it was signed on his behalf after he had left the office, in order
      to catch the post.

55   E Parker and P R Wallis, 'Three-Dimensional Cathode-Ray Tube Displays',
      Journal of the Institution of Electrical Engineers, volume 95, part III, pp. 371-
      89. Wallis was contacted recently, and pointed out that the objectives of
      Baird and those working in the field of radar were different. He admitted,
      however, that there are similarities between the three-dimensional
      imaging techniques employed (P R Wallis, personal letter to Malcolm
      Baird, 31 December 2000).

56   SS&T, p. 78

57   Waddell, p. 164. Keith Wallis, who has written a biography of Plugge,
      believes that Baird first met Plugge in 1925, when he was demonstrating
      his system to the public at Selfridge's. Plugge was at that time negotiating
      with the store to sponsor his first commercial radio station, from the Eiffel
      Tower in 1926 (Keith Wallis, personal letter to Malcolm Baird, 31
      December 2000).

58   Waddell, p. 293

59   *Who Was Who 1981-1990*, p 602. His commercial radio activities were
      recalled in a BBC radio programme, *The First Pirate*, broadcast in January
      2000.

60   *The Dictionary of National Biography 1971-1980* (1986), p. 83.

61   Sir Harry Brittain, personal letter to Malcolm Baird, 23 September, 1959.
      W S Morrison (later Viscount Dunrossil) was called 'Shakes' not just
      because of his initials, but also for his love of Shakespeare. He was
      Postmaster General 1940-1942, Minister of Town and Country Planning
      1943-1945, and Speaker of the House of Commons 1951-1959 (*The
      Dictionary of National Biography 1961-1970* (1981) pp. 773-4). According
      to JBLD, Baird lunched with Brittain on 26 March 1942, and on 11 April
      made a note about arranging a demonstration 'to PMG'.

Chapter 16: The End of the Road:
Bude, London, and Bexhill 1943-1946

1   Diana Richardson, 'Sydenham, Bude and Bexhill', unpublished manu-
        script, August 2000

2   Margaret's own diary records that on 4 July 1943 she played a Saint-Saëns
        piano concerto with the Bournemouth Symphony Orchestra, for which
        she earned a fee of ten guineas. Baird's diary indicates that he went to
        the performance, which started at 3pm. She played at a Red Cross con-
        cert later the same month in London, where she stayed two nights.

3   Margaret Baird, interview with Bruce Norman, *Listener*, 19 February
        1976. In the interview she mistakenly gave the venue as Torquay.

4   M Baird, p. 40

5   See p. 338.

6   M Baird, p. 152. According to Margaret's diary, the tribunal sat on 9
        March. She spent the week in London, returning to Bude with Baird.
        With the reduction of the bombing in 1943, she resumed her occasional
        trips to London, to shop and to meet some of her friends from before
        the war. On these expeditions, she and Baird stayed at the Palace Hotel
        in Lancaster Gate.

7   Manager, Barclays Bank, Cambridge Circus Branch, letter to Baird 24
        December 1942*

8   M Baird, pp. 145-6

9   JLBD

10   Honor Clerk, Curator, 20th Century Collection, National Portrait
        Gallery, letter to Laura Hamilton, Curator, Collins Gallery, University
        of Strathclyde, and AK, 16 March 2001. The authors are grateful to Laura
        Hamilton for explaining the technical processes involved in making a
        bronze casting.

11   Martin Muncaster, letter to B Clive Rawes, Presentation Editor, BBC
        Television, 5 January 1959 (BBC, T23/121 TV Publicity. Baird TV)

12   A M Andrews, Administrative Officer (Television), memorandum to
        Rawes, 20 January 1959 (BBC, T23/121 TV Publicity. Baird TV)

13   Donald Gilbert, personal letter to Margaret Baird, 30 December 1959.*
        Sir Alfred Gilbert RA (1854-1934) sculpted the memorial fountain to
        Lord Shaftesbury surmounted by Eros, which stands in Piccadilly
        Circus. Donald Gilbert's father, Walter Gilbert, was also a sculptor, and
        founded the Bromsgrove Guild. He and his son did a number of
        works together, including the reredos of the Anglican Cathedral in
        Liverpool. Though Sir Alfred and Walter are said to have been very
        close, the precise relationship is a family mystery (Iona Muncaster,
        daughter of Donald Gilbert, telephone conversation with AK, 21
        October 2001).

14   Donald Gilbert, letter to C K Adams, National Portrait Gallery, 8
        December 1959 (National Portrait Gallery, Registered Package 4125)

15   'Baird is commemorated at Strathclyde', *Electronics Weekly*, 25 June 1966

16   John Logie Baird, 'Colour and Stereoscopic Television', 28 October 1943, lecture notes and bibliography*

17   Dennis McMullan, personal letter to AK, 9 August 2001. The lecture was announced in *Nature*, 23 October 1943, p. 482.

18   *Who Was Who in the USSR* (1972), p. 520. Sobolev, after a distinguished career as a statesman, was USSR permanent representative to the United Nations 1955-1960. He died in 1964 at the age of sixty-one. Baird refers to him in his diary first as Sobileff and later as Sobieleoff.

19   JBLD, 27 November 1943

20   Baird/Moseley

21   Moseley, p. 241

22   SMDiaries, p. 430

23   Cable and Wireless minute book, 8 June 1944, quoted in Hills

24   Hills. See also Adrian Hills, 'The Baird Holding and Development Trust', *405 Alive*, Summer 2000, pp. 20-1.

25   In his memorandum to the Hankey television committee 1944 (see p. 351), Baird referred to Sobolev as the 'Russian Minister'.

26   Margaret Baird, 'Chapter Ten'. See Postscript, p. 389.

27   Letters and documents relating to Baird and the Baird Holding and Development Trust were sold at Christie's in London on 19 May 2000 for £2400. That Baird also had had second thoughts about the deal is suggested by a comment in a letter to Moseley: 'There are also a number of millionaires pursuing me with offers of cash but I am still holding them at bay. Seriously speaking I honestly believe I have the possibility of a very big business and think there should be an opening in America. Now is the time to act. If you wait the whole thing may pass out of my control. ... I would like to come out for a visit particularly during the winter months. This climate is appalling and with advancing years I feel the cold more and more' (Baird/Moseley, 31 March 1944).

28   W MacQueen-Pope, *The Footlights Flickered* (1959), p. 170

29   *The Dictionary of National Biography* (compact edition) 1975, p. 2539

30   Michael Marshall, *Top Hat and Tails* (1978), p. 147. *Happidrome* was originally a BBC radio show with Harry Korris, who starred in the film.

31   'Improvements in Television', patent 562,168, application 23 July 1943, accepted 21 June 1944

32   JLBD, 19 July 1944

33   Herbert, p. 26

34   *News Chronicle*, 17 August 1944, quoted in Burns (2000), p. 380

35   *British Government Publications: Index to Chairmen and Authors*, volume III 1941-1978 (1982)

36   *Report of the Television Committee 1943* (1945)

37   Baird, letter to Moseley, 31 March 1944 (Baird/Moseley)

38   The full memorandum is quoted in Burns (2000), pp. 404-7.

39   Handwritten draft letter from Baird to Buchanan, 22 July 1944*

40   *Report of the Television Committee 1943* (1945), p. 7, clause 17

41   *Who Was Who 1961-1970*, p. 1025

42   A S Adams, Honourable Society of the Middle Temple, personal letter to Malcolm Baird, 12 February 2001

43   Rusty MacLean, Archivist, Rugby School, personal letter to Malcolm Baird, 12 April 2001. Shelley may have been a grandson or great-nephew of Womesh Chandra Bonnerjee (1844-1906), a Calcutta barrister who was also called to the Middle Temple (1867), and who later became famous as one of the first leaders of the Indian National Congress.

44   Margaret Baird, who had a waspish sense of humour when she chose to exercise it, in her engagement diary for 7 November 1944, added later, 'Bad day, met K E S[helley]'.

45   A E Sayers, 'To Whom It May Concern', typed note 6 March 1989, courtesy of Ray Herbert

46   *Report of the Television Committee 1943* (1945), clause 34, p. 10

47   JBLD, 23 November 1945

48   E G O Anderson, paper read before the Television Society, 25 January 1948, courtesy of Ray Herbert

49   'Ring Jacob ask to see facsimile' (JBLD, 6 May 1942).

50   'Intermediate film' occurs several times. References to spool boxes and the photographic company Ilford (4 August 1942) also suggest that he was working with film for the transmission of text (Ray Herbert, personal letter to AK, 24 March 2001).

51   Hills

52   In 1942 he applied for a patent on an improved technique for the wet film process: 'Improvements in Film Processing Tanks for Television Apparatus' (559,549, application 18 August 1942, accepted 24 February 1944). See also plate 57.

53   JBLD, notes for 1944

54   JBLD, 25-27 May 1944. Baird had publicly predicted the television transmission of newspapers ten years earlier, in the course of the discussion following the lecture by J C Wilson on colour television at the Royal Society of Arts, at which he took the chair. Harold W Sanderson asked whether there was any possible truth in the prophecy that a whole newspaper could be sent by television from London to Manchester, rather than the present system of word for word transmission. Baird replied that the 'future covered a multitude of sins, but taking a wide view of things, the statement was quite justified' (*Journal of the Royal Society of Arts*, 29 June 1934, p. 863).

55   'Television of Books. John Baird's New Invention', *Glasgow Herald*, 17 August 1944

56   Leon Laden, 'Television in Great Britain', *Radio News*, January 1945, pp. 32-4 and 85

57   Waddell, p. 296

58   Sir Edward Wilshaw, letter to Moseley, 7 August 1951, quoted in Moseley, pp. 245-6

59   Burns (2000) p. 384

60   Waddell, p. 269

61   Andrea Maloney, Directorate of Corporate Communications (Navy), Ministry of Defence, personal letter to AK, 10 April 2001

62   See, for instance, pages 37, 157-8, and 338-9.

63   *Electronic Engineering*, October 1945, p. 742

64   *Wireless World*, December 1945, p. 357

65   JBLD, 24 December 1945. The renewals were never made. He became seriously ill shortly afterwards.

66   Moseley, pp. 241-2

67   Moseley, p. 242

68   Moseley, pp. 242-3

69   Paul Reveley, personal letter to AK, 6 August 2001

70   Edwin Pritchard, Commissioner of Customs, China, 'To whom it may concern', 19 November 1945, courtesy of Paul Reveley

71   Reveley

72   Professor Dr Walter Heimann later founded Heimann Systems, a large German company which manufactures electronic security systems.

73   Andrew Emmerson, 'Pioneers of UHF Television', *Wireless World*, February 1983, pp. 62-3

74   NASA historical website: www.hq.nasa.gov/office/pao/History/Timeline/1940-44.html

75   Susan Scott, Archivist, Savoy Hotel, telephone conversation with AK, 15 March 2001

76   William Cowper, *The Task* (1785), Book II, 'The Time-Piece', lines 206-7: 'England, with all thy faults, I love thee still – / My country!'

77   Hastings tourist website: www.1066.net/Baird/
       This is still the case. A resident in the house, which is now flats (called Baird Court), confirms that a booster is needed to get proper reception (Nina Ball, personal letter to AK, 23 November 2000).

Chapter 17: Epilogue 1946-2002

1   Principal Probate Registry, 24 January 1947

2   Margaret Baird, letters to Malcolm Baird, 5 December 1961 and 19 February 1962. She was one of what she called a 'battalion of creditors', who between them were owed £22,110. She was offered 4s. in the pound of what was due to her, out of which she would have to pay solicitor's fees for eight years, a situation she herself described as 'really a laughable bit of fiddle'. Shelley died in 1964.

3   An excuse which Shelley made for retaining Baird's estate was that Margaret was not in a fit state to handle it.

4   Michael Bennett-Levy, *Historic Televisions and Video Recorders* (1993), pp. 18-19

5   Suzzie Bassett, quoted in Michael Marshall, *Top Hats and Tails* (1978), p. 207. Their marriage, in 1949, 'gilded [Buchanan's] last few years' (W MacQueen-Pope, *The Footlights Flickered* (1959), p. 169). Further information from Suzzie Bassett, now Mrs Susan Dillon, telephone conversation with Malcolm Baird, 11 September 2001.

6   Michael Marshall, *Top Hats and Tails* (1978), p. 207

7   Ray Herbert, personal letter to AK, 3 June 2001, and telephone conversation, 12 September 2001

8   'Ultrafex [sic] and the telerecording system, which has been so useful, were based on the telefilm recording technique' (M Baird, p. 148). Anderson also stated, of Ultrafax, that 'JLB undertook the development of this system of message transmission. Really in its simplest form it was an extension of our intermediate film system used as a receiver instead of a transmitter so that a length of film was exposed to a high definition [TV tube]' (E G O Anderson, personal letter to Peter Waddell, 26 June 1974, quoted in Hills).

9   'Ultrafax', *Electronics*, January 1949, pp. 77-9

10   Alex Magoun, David Sarnoff Memorial Library, email correspondence with Malcolm Baird, 6 July 2001

11   Peter C Goldmark with Lee Edson, *Maverick Inventor* (1973), chapter 7

12   Andrew Emmerson, 'Pioneers of UHF Television', *Wireless World*, February 1983, pp. 62-3. See also p. 363.

13   Douglas Brown, 'The Electronic Imaging of Baird Television', unpublished PhD thesis, University of Strathclyde, 2000

14   *The Times*, 16 December 1947

15   John Swift, *Adventure in Vision*, John Lehmann (1950)

16   Moseley, letter to Annie Baird, 31 July 1951★

17   On the evidence of Moseley's diaries, he had been thinking of writing a biography of Baird at least since the previous April: 'After *God Help America!*, the story of my one-man broadcasting crusade during the war years in America, is out, I must write a biography of dear old John Baird, "the father of television". I have a vast mass of material to draw upon – published articles, letters from all sorts of people, pages from Baird's private papers, my own notes and diaries. ... If only my health holds out. ... Fortunately I have a fine staff – besides Harold Goodwin [SM's nephew], three highly efficient secretaries and a sub-editor, and, as far as the books are concerned, some technical help from old colleagues' (SMDiaries, p. 483).

18   SMDiaries, p. 484. Buchanan surprised him 'by saying that Baird was not really one of his particularly close friends'. Possibly Buchanan, now sixty-one, still liked to think of himself as a matinée idol, which indeed to many

of his fans he was, and was chary about being revealed as a childhood contemporary of Baird, whose age was in the public domain.

19   Sydney Moseley, *John Baird: the Romance and Tragedy of the Pioneer of Television*, Odhams Press (1952)

20   Director General, internal memorandum, 'Moseley's book on Baird', to Director of Technical Services, 27 March 1952 (BBC, T16/86 TV Policy. Baird TV)

21   Director of Technical Services, internal memorandum, 'Moseley's book on Baird', to Director General, 9 June 1952 (BBC, T16/86 TV Policy. Baird TV)

22   Sir Alexander Aikman, letter in the *Sunday Times*, 14 July 1946

23   *Tatler and Bystander*, 6 April 1955

24   Sir Albert Mumford (assistant engineer-in-chief, GPO) and G R M Garratt, 'The History of Television', *Proceedings of the Institution of Electrical Engineers* (1952), 99, part 3A, pp. 25-42

25   *Electronics and Power*, December 1975, p. 1193, February 1976, pp. 113-14, April 1976, pp. 246-7

26   *The Dictionary of National Biography 1986-1990* (1996), p. 40. Winston Churchill referred to Boothby in a parliamentary debate as the 'member for Television'.

27   Harry Traynor, letter to Cecil McGivern, BBC, 13 January 1958 (BBC, T23/121 TV Publicity. Baird TV)

28   Cecil McGivern, letter to Harry Traynor, 27 January 1958 (BBC, T23/121 TV Publicity. Baird TV)

29   Reported at controllers' meeting, 28 January 1958, minute 51 (BBC, T23/121 TV Publicity. Baird TV)

30   Television Programme Board, 5 February 1958 (BBC, T23/121 TV Publicity. Baird TV)

31   Harry Traynor, personal letter to Malcolm Baird, March 2000

32   Harry Traynor, letter to Cecil McGivern, 5 February 1958 (BBC, T23/121 TV Publicity. Baird TV)

33   Margaret was interviewed about her religious philosophy in the Scottish Television programme *Quo Vadis*, December 1966.

34   Introduced by Eamonn Andrews, produced by T Leslie Jackson, 28 October 1957

35   See p. 303

36   Produced by Peter Graham Scott, broadcast 18 December 1957, with Michael Gwynn as Baird, Gwen Watford as Margaret, and Leslie Phillips as Mephy. Under the title of 'Shadows', it had won first prize at the Cheltenham Festival of Contemporary Literature in 1955 for a television play in category C (involving biography), in which Associated Rediffusion had an interest. Moseley was delighted, until he found out that the play was to be broadcast on independent television, since he had hoped that the BBC would take up the drama rights to his book (Correspondence between Scanlan and Moseley, and Moseley and the BBC, 1955-1957 (BBC, T23/121 TV Publicity. Baird TV)).

37   *Daily Herald*, 22 October 1959

38   Board of Management, minutes of 2 November 1959 (BBC, T23/121 TV Publicity. Baird TV)

39   M Baird, p. 159

40   Letter heading, dated 3 May 1950, courtesy of Ray Herbert; Douglas Brown, 'The Electronic Imaging of Baird Television', unpublished PhD thesis, University of Strathclyde, 2000. When television started in Scotland in 1952, Scophony–Baird gave Annie a set for 'The Lodge' on permanent loan. Thus were the Baird family (and many invited neighbours) able to watch the coronation the following year.

41   Brian Swanson, 'Baird, a Man of Invention Who Defied Convention', *Daily Express*, 5 March 1989

42   Tom McArthur and Peter Waddell, *The Secret Life of John Logie Baird*, Century Hutchinson (1986); second revised edition as *Vision Warrior: the Hidden Achievement of John Logie Baird*, Orkney Press (1990). See also P Waddell, 'The Achievement of John Logie Baird and how Secret British–American Technology Changed the World', *Journal of Economic and Social Intelligence*, volume 2 (1992), pp. 115-21.

43   Ray Herbert, *Seeing by Wireless*, PW Publishing, Broadstone, second revised edition 1997. Since 1983 Herbert has issued a regular *Baird Television Newsletter*, which he circulates to an ever dwindling number of former Baird employees and to other interested people.

44   Burns's publications include *British Television: The Formative Years* (1986), *Television: An International History of the Formative Years* (1998), and *John Logie Baird: Television Pioneer* (2000), all published by the Institution of Electrical Engineers.

45   See Donald F McLean, *Restoring Baird's Image*, Institution of Electrical Engineers (2000).

46   *The Mousetrap* opened in London in 1952, and was still running in 2002.

47   Donald Flamm, 'Baird's Proper Place in Television History', an address at the Council and Fellows Dinner, Arts Club, London, 11 September 1984. There was a brief report in *Royal Television Society Bulletin*, October 1984.

48   K Geddes and G Bussey, *The Setmakers* (1991), p. 351

49   Ray Herbert, telephone conversation with AK, 3 September 2001

50   The title reflects Baird's own description (SS&T, p. 29) of his decision to give up his job with the Clyde Valley Electrical Power Company and become his own master. The programme was produced by Dorothy-Grace Elder. The part of Baird was played by Paul Kermack.

51   Royal Television Society (1998, second edition 1990). See also Postscript, p. 389.

52   Baird's example also led to the establishment in 1988 of the annual John Logie Baird Awards, which encourage small businesses and university innovators in Scotland. They were administered by Scottish Innovation until that company closed in 2002; a national award ceremony was held

in Glasgow in November of each year. Margaret presented the awards for the first few years; more recently Malcolm performed the honour.

53 Knowlton Nash, *The Microphone Wars: A History of Triumph and Betrayal at the CBC* (1994), pp. 174-7

54 Curriculum vitae of Paul Vernon Reveley, 6 August 2001

55 Mechanical scanning is used today in the most advanced weather satellites to build up their pictures, and in thermal infra-red television cameras for military use on land, at sea, and in the air (McLean, p. 3).

56 Published by Carrick Media (1999)

57 'Greatest Scots: A Special Issue for the Millennium', *Scottish Review*, Christmas 1999. The first eight for the twentieth century, in ascending order, were Lord Reith, 32 votes; Alexander Graham Bell, inventor of the telephone, 35 votes; Eric Liddell, athlete and missionary, 36 votes; Keir Hardie, co-founder of the Labour Party, 38 votes; Andrew Carnegie, industrialist and philanthropist, 52 votes; Hugh MacDiarmid, poet, 63 votes; John Logie Baird, 194 votes; Sir Alexander Fleming, 414 votes.

58 Ethereal Technologies Inc, Ann Arbor, Michigan

59 The system uses a large (1.2m diameter) lightweight flexible mirror, developed about fifteen years ago by Waddell. It provides a full-colour volumetric image up to 80cm wide, 60cm high, and 30cm deep.

60 Annie died in Helensburgh in 1971, three days after Reith. She was eighty-eight. Her younger sister Jeannie died in 1955 at the age of sixty-nine, having been a widow for twenty-five years.

61 SS&T, p. 139

62 L Marsland Gander, 'Father of Television', *Daily Telegraph*, 31 March 1986. Marsland Gander's judgment that Baird was not given to making extravagant claims is consistent with that of one of Baird's obituarists: 'To some extent Baird's early work suffered some discredit and lack of recognition as a result of the exaggerated publicity and premature claims given to it by his supporters, but Baird himself was a shy and modest man, and there is no doubt that his pioneer achievements were a great incentive to other workers, and contributed materially towards the success attained by radio engineers and physicists, placing Britain in the forefront in this fascinating application of electromagnetic waves' (R L Smith-Rose, *Proceedings of the Physical Society*, vol. 58 (1946), p. 780).

Appendix: John Logie Baird and the Supernatural

1 SS&T, p. 9

2 Lord Reith, interview with Malcolm Muggeridge, 23 November 1967, in *Muggeridge Ancient and Modern* (1981), pp. 107-8

3 For instance, 'The Story of the Inexperienced Ghost' (1902) and 'A Dream of Armageddon' (1903)

4   SS&T, p. 11
5   'The Soul of Dominic McSharkey', *Technical College Magazine*, March 1910, p. 179
6   SS&T, p. 69
7   SMDiaries, p. 281
8   See, for instance, Joe Cooper, *The Case of the Cottingley Fairies* (1990).
9   SMDiaries, pp. 217–18, 253–4
10   'NOV. 3 [1928]: The Spiritualist organ, *Light*, reports that in an address given at St Luke's Church, Forest Hill, Sir Arthur Conan Doyle told the congregation that among the "well-known public people who had recently declared their conviction of the truth of Spiritualism were Sir Edward Marshall Hall, KC, the Duchess of Hamilton, Mr Robert Blatchford, and Mr Sydney Moseley". I am not too happy about his including me among the converts. My innumerable articles on the séances I have attended are purely objective reporting. I want to get at the truth. But I am *not* convinced, and, therefore, cannot allow Sir Arthur's public statement to go unchallenged' (SMDiaries, p. 296). Robert Blatchford (1851-1943) was a journalist, critic, and committed Socialist, who took to spiritualism after his wife's death in 1921.
11   Website: www.castleofspirits.com/ghostclub.html

Postscript: The Manuscripts of Sermons, Soap and Television: A Brief Account

1   See p. 438 for Baird's ideas on titles.
2   M Baird, p. 147
3   See p. 35.
4   See pp. 330-1.
5   SS&T, p. 129, quoted on p. 257 above
6   SS&T, pp. 146-7, quoted on p. 323 above
7   For example, 'Take MSS 4.30 Spence' (JLBD, 10 December 1942), 'Ring Spence biography' (JLBD, 30 January 1943), 'Spence return book and photos' (JLBD, 17 May 1943).

Index

Plates are shown as 'P' and drawn figures 'F' (with page number in parentheses):
eg 'P5' denotes plate 5; 'F5(123)' denotes Figure 5 on page 123.
Endnotes are referred to by page number followed by n. Complex entries are listed with bold headings.
Subentries and sub-subentries are listed in chronological order according to their first appearance in the narrative.